THE BIG BOOK OF HOUSEHOLD TIPS

EASY, ECONOMICAL WAYS TO MAKE YOUR HOME LIFE SMARTER, HEALTHIER AND HAPPIER

FROM THE EDITORS OF BOTTOM LINE PERSONAL

BottomLineBooks

BottomLineInc.com

Contents

Contents

Contents

15. PERSONAL CARE

16. PEST CONTROL

17. PET CARE

18. PROBLEM SOLVERS

Contents

CHAPTER 1

Automotive Care

6 Things Car Dealers Don't Want You to Know

Karl Brauer, former executive publisher of *Kelley Blue Book*, which provides information about new and used cars. He has more than 15 years of experience as an automotive journalist and was the first web-based journalist to be named to the jury of the prestigious North American Car and Truck of the Year award. KBB.com

Today's car shoppers are harder to trick. Many know to refuse overpriced add-ons such as rust-proofing and fabric protection. They even may know they can get price quotes from multiple dealerships online and detailed information on dealer costs, rebates and financing.

But that doesn't mean customers—even those who think they have learned many of the standard tricks—can withstand all the tactics that a car salesperson can throw at them. That's especially true when they face some new twists on the classic sales techniques.

Of course, not all salespeople are out to trick you, but here are the things that a car salesperson might say that could signal he/she intends to try to get you to pay more than you should...

•**"I'm selling it to you for just $300 over cost. Look up the invoice price yourself—you'll see I can't go any lower."** Salespeople know shoppers have become used to looking up the so-called "invoice price" of a new vehicle online. So rather than try to hide this information, they sometimes encourage buyers to look up invoice prices...and encourage them to believe that these prices are what dealers actually pay for cars. They aren't. Invoice prices are sometimes referred to as "dealer cost," but in fact, automakers typically use "dealer holdbacks" and "dealer incentives" that reduce the amount dealerships pay to hundreds of dollars below invoice price—sometimes thousands.

What to do: Do not let a salesperson convince you that you are getting an incredible deal just because the price you are paying is fairly close to the invoice price. A better sign you're getting a good deal is if you are paying less than the typical buyer in your area paid for the same vehicle. Several major car-shopping websites provide this information, including my company's site, KBB.com.

•**"You have to decide today."** Car buyers can easily get quotes online from multiple dealerships, even dealerships hundreds of miles away. That gives salespeople more incentive to convince shoppers to buy the first time they set foot on a dealership lot—if they walk away, there's a strong chance they'll buy somewhere else. To encourage a quick purchase, a salesperson might claim a price is available only today...that supplies of a model are very limited...or that the dealership has only one vehicle with the desired colors and options and that another buyer is interested in it, too.

What to do: Ignore these classic high-pressure tactics. Buyers who move slowly and shop around

1

almost always get better deals than those who rush. Any "today only" price you are offered is likely to be offered in the future, too.

Exception: It is possible that a "today only" price is available only today if it is the last day of a month and the dealership needs to make some final, quick sales to meet its quota and earn a bonus from the manufacturer. Even so, do not rush to buy unless you have researched the prices other buyers have paid for this vehicle and you are confident you are being offered a competitive price.

•**"We're a different kind of dealership—we offer no-haggle pricing."** No-haggle pricing, also called "guaranteed pricing," has been tried on and off for decades and is becoming increasingly common as dealerships try to attract buyers who dread the difficult, protracted negotiation process. It sounds sensible—almost everything we buy has a fixed price, so why not cars?

Trouble is, at many dealerships, the no-haggle guaranteed price is guaranteed to not be a very good deal. In fact, it often is not much different from the opening price the salesperson would have offered to a buyer who did negotiate. Choosing the no-haggle option just might mean you don't get to make a counteroffer.

What to do: Use a car-shopping website to check how the no-haggle price that you are offered compares with the price the typical buyer in your area is paying for the car. (You even can do this right at the dealership using your smartphone, tablet or laptop.) While some no-haggle prices are fair, in many cases you can save perhaps up to $500—potentially much more on a high-end vehicle—by haggling just a little at a no-haggle dealership.

Exception: If you buy a car from Tesla, the luxury electric-car maker, there is a fixed price and no haggling.

•**"Bad news—you didn't qualify for that interest rate."** Unscrupulous salespeople sometimes offer an attractive deal…then make up an excuse for changing the terms when the deal is nearly finalized. Even smart buyers often fall for this—the buyer has invested so much time and mental energy in the purchase by this point that it would be psychologically difficult to walk away.

Better Than an Air Freshener

Deodorize your car by placing several paper or plastic grocery bags or cardboard boxes filled with wadded up newspapers in the car overnight. Shut all the doors and windows. The carbon used in the black newsprint acts like the activated carbon used in odor-removing filters.

Alternatives: Place a shallow bowl filled with white vinegar or baking soda or used or fresh coffee grounds in the car. Be sure to air out the vehicle before driving.

The late David Solomon, former certified master auto technician and founder of MotorWatch, an automotive safety watchdog organization.

Increasing the interest rate charged for an auto loan is perhaps the most common way to do this. The dealership claims the buyer did not qualify for the low interest rate originally quoted. This lets the dealership pretend it's the buyer's fault that the original deal fell through—he/she didn't have a good enough credit rating.

What to do: Have a financing offer in place from a credit union, bank or some other third-party lender before you shop for a car. If the dealership tries to charge a steeper interest rate, use this financing instead.

Variation: The salesman offers a very appealing price for a buyer's trade-in in addition to a competitive price on a new car. When the deal is nearly done, the salesperson apologetically says he cannot offer nearly as much for the trade-in as promised because the dealership's service department discovered the vehicle had a hidden mechanical problem. Either walk away from the deal or pull the trade-in out of the deal and sell this used car through the classifieds or Craigslist.com.

•**"But everyone pays the vehicle-prep fee."** If a savvy car buyer won't pay a steep purchase price, the salesperson might move to plan B—agree to a fair price, then tack on hundreds of dollars in extra fees at the last minute when you are about to sign the papers. If the buyer protests, the salesperson

A Fair Estimate

Get unbiased estimates of car-repair costs at RepairPal.com. Enter information about your car, location and what service you need, and the site will give you an estimate of how much the service will cost. You also can find local shops and read reviews of their services. Lists more than 270,000 individual shops.

will act surprised and claim that these fees are standard and unavoidable.

What to do: Well before you are about to sign the final papers, ask the dealership to quote you an "out-the-door price" that includes absolutely all charges. Some fees, including destination charges and tax, title and licensing fees, are truly unavoidable. Many dealerships also refuse to budge on a "documentation" fee, which covers processing the paperwork for the title and registration, although it is worth at least trying to negotiate this fee if it is significantly above $50. Many other fees, however, are negotiable, especially if you threaten to walk away. This includes dealer prep fees…delivery fees in excess of factory destination charges…and charges for add-ons you did not request and that are not necessary, such as vehicle identification number (VIN) etching on the windshield. Any fees that are charged should have been included in the out-the-door price you were quoted.

• **"If you buy a car, we'll pay off your loan on your trade-in."** The dealership might try to roll your current loan into your new one. Or it might delay paying off your loan, sticking you with late-payment penalties while it enjoys what amounts to an interest-free loan.

What to do: Check the total amount being financed in the new loan contract to confirm that the balance on your existing loan has not been rolled into it. Confirm that the contract stipulates that the dealership will pay off your loan by your next payment deadline.

Used-Car Sales Tactic

In a tactic that applies only to used cars, the car salesperson says…

"This used car is in great shape—I'll even show you the Carfax." Salespeople know that sophisticated used-car buyers are likely to check a vehicle's Carfax report before buying. This report lists the vehicle's accident records and certain other aspects of its history. So salespeople steer sophisticated buyers to vehicles that have clean Carfax reports, then offer to provide these reports for free. This creates the impression that the salesperson is honest and that the car is problem-free. In reality, the salesperson might be using the buyer's faith in the Carfax report to trick him/her into failing to take prudent steps to uncover other significant issues. Automotive problems that do not result in insurance claims often do not find their way onto Carfax reports.

What to do: Pay an independent mechanic $200 to $400 to give a used car a prepurchase inspection before buying even if it has a clean Carfax report.

Buying vs. Leasing

James Bragg, founder, FightingChance.com, Long Beach, California.

Buying a car costs less than leasing if you keep the car long enough. Leasing is less expensive on a monthly basis, but you are left with nothing when you turn in the car. Buyers who hold on to the car for enough years make out better because of the car's residual trade-in or resale value. Calculations can be complex—they depend on loan interest rates and lease agreements. In general, cars that depreciate slowly and are not expensive to maintain, such as the Honda s1770 and the Mini Cooper, can be much less costly to buy than lease. Cars that depreciate quickly, such as the Ford Crown Victoria and the Suzuki Forenza, may be better lease deals, because the manufacturer may artificially inflate the assumed value at the end of the lease. Check depreciation ratings at Edmunds.com. Plan to keep a car for at least five years to have the best chance of spending less in the long run by buying than by leasing.

How to Be Sure Your Car Is Safe for Ice, Snow and Cold

Paul Brand, retired motoring columnist for the Star Tribune in Minneapolis. He is author of *How to Repair Your Car* and *How to Repair Your Pickup or SUV*. He also is a driving instructor with the Skip Barber Racing School and teaches law-enforcement pursuit driving. He is based in Lake Placid, Florida. StarTribune.com

Winter weather brings slippery roads and reduced visibility. Is your car up to the challenge? *Simple things to do to keep your car running safely this winter…*

Tires

•**Check tire condition—but not the old-fashioned way.** Car owners often are advised to use a quarter to gauge tire tread. According to this advice, if the top of Washington's head disappears into the groove between treads, the tire still has at least 5/32 of an inch of tread and remains viable. That's fine for summer, but when you drive in snow, anything less than 5/32 of an inch of tread increases the risk for skids.

Put away the quarter, and buy a tire-tread gauge, available in auto-parts stores for around $5. If the reading is less than 5/32 of an inch, replace your tires with a new set of all-weather tires or, even better, set them aside until spring in favor of a set of winter/snow tires.

Helpful: Make sure that any tire you use carries the rating "M+S" (sometimes written MS, M/S or M&S) on its sidewall. This means that the tire meets the Rubber Manufacturer Association's standards for use in mud and snow.

•**Increase tire pressure to the upper limit of the vehicle's acceptable tire pressure range.** Tires lose around one pound of pressure for every 10°F that the outside temperature drops. If you fail to add air in late autumn, your tires are likely to be badly under-inflated by the dead of winter. Driving on underinflated tires not only reduces gas mileage and tire life, it reduces traction, making winter skids more likely.

Maintain the tire pressure that is recommended on the sticker inside your car's driver-side doorpost, gas cap or glove compartment door—not the one on the sidewall of the tires. The inflation figures on sidewalls are the recommended air pressure when the tires are carrying their maximum load, not the recommended pressure for your particular vehicle.

Windows

•**Top off the windshield washer reservoir, and store an extra bottle of washer fluid in the trunk.** Drivers use up washer fluid very quickly during winter storms. Driving without washer fluid in the winter is unsafe.

•**Replace wiper blades with special winter blades. Your current blades still might be up to the job of clearing away rain,** but fresh blades will be stronger, sharper-edged and better able to cope with ice and snow.

Select a "winter blade" that has a rubber covering around the blade's structural elements. This covering prevents the parts of the blade that need to flex from freezing, increasing the odds that the blade will work in the cold.

Do not pay extra for winter blades that claim to be crafted from special high-tech materials or that are heated. These features are just marketing gimmicks that do little or nothing to improve performance.

Helpful: When you use a gas station squeegee to clean the exterior of car windows, also run the squeegee's sponge along the surface of your wiper blades that comes in contact with your windshield. The cleaner your wiper blades, the better they will clean your windshield.

•**Give windows and the windshield a thorough cleaning on the inside.** Even drivers who diligently clean the exteriors of their cars' windows and windshield often neglect interior glass surfaces. These interior surfaces can collect fingerprints and dog-nose prints, which are not particularly visible in warm weather. When temperatures drop in winter, however, moisture adheres to the prints, increasing window fogging and decreasing visibility.

Use a "foaming" automotive glass cleaner to remove smudges from interior glass. Foaming cleaners won't run down the glass and into defrosters or doors. Use wadded newspaper to wipe the glass cleaner away. Newspaper doesn't leave lint and does a wonderful job of grabbing hold of stubborn window debris.

Winter-Proofing Maintenance

•**If you change your own oil, do so now.** Don't wait for the scheduled 3,000- or 5,000-mile service interval if temperatures are likely to plummet soon—it's no fun to crawl under a car in a frozen garage or driveway. Check the levels of coolant, brake fluid and power steering fluid before the cold arrives as well.

If you miss the comfortable-weather window, don't put off a required oil change until the next warm period—that might not come until April.

Best: Pay $20 or $30 to have a pro do it now.

•**Clean battery terminals—or buy a new battery.** Batteries are most likely to fail in winter when engine oil thickens in the cold, making it more difficult to get the engine to turn over. Cleaning the corrosion and grime from battery terminals makes it easier for the battery to do its job. You can have a mechanic do this or do it yourself.

To do it yourself: Don safety goggles and gardening gloves, then disconnect the battery cables, negative cable first.

If the battery terminals are white and powdery, pour a cup of diet cola onto them, then wash the cola away with water. Cola neutralizes the corrosive acids. Use a wire brush or steel wool to remove any remaining residue and grime. Wire brushes specifically designed for battery terminal cleaning are available at auto-parts stores for $3 to $6. Apply a thin coat of petroleum jelly or battery terminal anticorrosion coating, available in auto-parts stores for $5 to $10, to the cleaned terminals, then reattach the positive cable first. Make sure that these cable connections are very tight.

Alternative: If you don't want to bother with battery maintenance, you can replace the battery every three years. The typical cost of a new battery is $50 to $120. Premium batteries can be as much as $200. You might want to write the purchase date with permanent marker on the battery, so you don't forget when you bought it.

Cool Cars Quickly

To draw out hot air, open one window. Then open and close the door on the opposite side about five times.

Variation: Open all windows. Then go around the car twice, opening each door on the first circuit and closing each door on the second.

Bottom Line Personal

•**Replace the cabin air filter.** If you live in a cold region, you likely drive with your windows rolled up all winter. The quality of the air in your car until spring depends on the condition of the cabin air filter. An old, clogged cabin air filter also can reduce the effectiveness of your windshield defroster.

Cabin air filters typically are located in plastic compartments found near the base of the windshield. Replacing these filters is an easy do-it-yourself job in some vehicles but requires removing several parts in others. If your vehicle's manual does not provide directions, ask an auto-parts store employee if this is an easy do-it-yourself task with your vehicle. A replacement air filter costs about $10 to $15.

Note: Some cars more than 20 years old do not have cabin air filters at all.

•**Apply a silicon spray to the car's rubber door gaskets.** This reduces the odds that the gaskets will freeze to the frame and prevent entry or exit. Respray every month or so until spring. Spray a small amount of aerosol lubricant into your car's door locks, too. This makes it less likely that the locks will freeze shut.

5 Colors That Boost Your Car's Resale Value

Analysis by iSeeCars.com.

On average, cars depreciate 33.1% in the first three years of ownership. But yellow ones depreciate

Best Times to Buy a Car

•**Mondays,** when discounts average 8.1%, because few people take the time to test-drive and negotiate at the start of the workweek.

•**December,** when SUVs, including luxury models, get price drops as dealers try to earn year-end sales incentives and bonuses.

•**New Year's Eve,** when monthly, quarterly and annual sales goals all merge—December 29 and 30 are almost as good for buyers.

•**May,** if you are looking for a midsize SUV, since new models start coming out in June.

•**October** for big pickups—the biggest discounts are on October 30.

•**November** for compact and midsize sedans—the biggest discounts are on mainstream cars often used for commuting.

Analysis by TrueCar, reported at Cars.USNews.com.

only 27%...orange, 30.6%...green, 30.9%...white, 32.6%...red, 32.7%. Yellow, orange and green are not common car colors—they make up only 1.2% of all three-year-old cars. This may increase the demand for them as used cars.

Car colors with lower-than-average resale value: Gold, which depreciates 37.1% over three years... purple, 36.7%...beige, 36.6%...silver, 34%...black, 33.6%...gray, 33.5%...brown, 33.5%.

Check This Before You Buy

Roundup of experts on car values, reported at Kiplinger. com.

Always check a new car's resale value before buying it. Even if you plan to keep it for many years, this is important because if the car is totaled in an accident, the resale value will affect how much the insurer pays you. Midsize pickup trucks and midsize and large SUVs hold their value best...followed by performance vehicles such as the Volkswagen Golf R and Subaru WRX. Brands that hold their value best are Toyota, averaging 36.2% of original

value after five years...Chevrolet, 36%...Subaru, 33.9%...Ford, 32.1%...Porsche, 31.6%.

To make depreciation work in your favor: Buy a used car instead of a new one.

The New Car-Safety Features That Could Save Your Life

Carroll Lachnit, consumer advice editor for Edmunds. com, a leading automotive information and vehicle review website.

Just because a new car boasts a top safety rating and lots of impressive-sounding safety features doesn't necessarily make it very safe. Effectiveness and availability vary widely. Some very effective features, including backup cameras, now are common in new cars. Electronic stability control (ESC), which helps prevent rollovers, is standard equipment on all new vehicles. Other features, such as the Tesla Model X's air-filtration "bioweapon defense mode," seem excessive. But with many of the other safety features that are available, it's not clear yet how effective they are. *Here's a rundown of today's safety features and verdicts on their effectiveness...*

•**Automatic emergency braking.** Studies have found that automatic braking can reduce the odds of getting in an accident by more than 25%. Sometimes called "autobrake," this feature uses cameras, radar or lasers to sense the danger of a forward collision and then automatically slows or stops the vehicle. This technology, available on some high-end vehicles for some time, is becoming available on more affordable cars, often as part of an options package. (The technology should not be confused with the similarly named "antilock braking system," or ABS, which prevents brakes from locking up.)

Examples: Automatic braking is included or optional on certain versions of the Honda CR-V... Subaru Impreza, Legacy and Forester...Volvo S60, S80, V60 and XC60...Chevrolet Impala...and Chrysler 200.

Warning: Not all emergency braking systems are equally effective. The Insurance Institute for Highway Safety (IIHS), a nonprofit funded by auto insurers, gives the Subaru EyeSight system top scores among nonluxury brands, with the Chrysler 200 and Honda CR-V systems close behind. These systems slowed or stopped vehicles in both slow- and high-speed tests, while some other systems were effective mainly in low-speed situations.

Verdict: This is worth having.

•**Headlights that turn from side to side with your car.** "Adaptive headlights" that turn to the left or to the right when the steering wheel is turned do a better job lighting the road ahead than standard headlights and significantly reduce the risk for accidents. They're available mainly on luxury cars but are offered as an option on a few mainstream vehicles as well.

Examples: Adaptive headlights are included or optional in some versions of the Mazda3 and CX-5...and Volkswagen Golf and Jetta.

Verdict: Worth getting if you do lots of nighttime driving on curvy roads.

•**Systems that warn drivers of potential dangers.** It's impressive to hear about "lane departure" alarms that sound when drivers start to drift out of a lane...and "blind spot" alarms that inform drivers when obstacles lurk where they cannot easily be seen, but an IIHS study has found that vehicles equipped with these do not get into significantly fewer accidents.

Verdict: Choose these only if they don't add a lot to the price.

Potential exception: A blind spot warning system could make sense for a driver who has limited physical flexibility and difficulty turning to fully check blind spots in the usual manner...or for a vehicle that has very large blind spots or limited rear visibility.

•**Less powerful engine that can serve as a safety feature for a teen driver.** Many of today's vehicles, even some moderately priced ones, have breathtaking amounts of power compared with vehicles from even 10 years ago. For example, the Honda Civic Si has 205 horsepower (hp), the Ford

---

5 Ways to Increase Your Car's Trade-In Value

For a higher trade-in value on your vehicle...

•**Keep some of your personal belongings inside the vehicle.** If your car is empty, the dealer may lowball you because he believes that you are in a rush to sell.

•**Focus on the tires.** If your tires are in good shape, don't worry about buying a new set. However, if they are not, purchase an inexpensive set. Heavily worn tires can decrease the trade-in value by more than the cost of cheap new tires.

•**Make minor repairs.** Fixing small problems such as a burned-out headlight or buffing out a scratch can increase the price you will get by more than the cost of the repair.

•**Present documentation.** Bring oil-change records and other maintenance-related paperwork to show that your car was well-kept.

•**Play one dealer against another.** Get purchase offers from multiple dealerships to maximize your bargaining leverage.

GoBankingRates.com

Focus ST has 252 hp and the Ford Mustang V-6 has 300 hp—and each of these cars starts below $25,000. Less powerful engines tend to be associated in our minds with low price and good fuel economy, not safety—but buying a modestly powered car can be a low-tech, low-cost way to reduce the odds that a teen will travel at dangerously high speeds.

Verdict: Choose a midsize sedan with a four-cylinder engine and moderate power.

•**"Head-up" display.** A growing number of cars now can project information such as speed and navigation system directions up onto the windshield, where drivers can see it without moving their line of sight from the direction of the road. That sounds like a great safety feature—accidents can occur when drivers glance down at the dash. But concerns have been raised that projecting information into a driver's field of view actually could increase the danger by distracting the driver and shifting the focus of the eyes even though the eyes remain pointed forward. And because the information is right in front of the driver, it actually might distract him/her more often. On the other hand, many test drivers who regularly drive with head-up systems swear by them.

Verdict: These systems remain uncommon enough that there is not yet sufficient data to reach a conclusion.

Evaluating Safety Scores

There are two major organizations that evaluate vehicle safety in the US—IIHS and the National Highway Traffic Safety Administration (NHTSA), run by the US Department of Transportation. Both produce valuable safety ratings—but not every vehicle that earns a seemingly stellar score from these organizations is as safe as car buyers might imagine…

•**"Top safety pick" doesn't really mean "top."** A car that is advertised as an IIHS "top safety pick" hasn't actually achieved top safety status. There's a rating above top—the very safest vehicles get "top safety pick-plus" status. These vehicles not only do a great job protecting occupants in crashes—they also have advanced collision-avoidance technology to reduce the odds of getting into an accident in the first place. Pricey luxury cars dominate the top safety pick-plus list, but some affordable vehicles do make the cut.

Examples: The 2021 Kia Forte, K5, Seltos, Stinger, Sorento, Soul and Telluride…2021 Subaru Impreza, Legacy, Outback, Crosstrek (Hybrid and Wagon), Forester and Ascent…2021 Hyundai Tucson, Kona, Sonata, Palisade, Veloster and Venue…2021 Toyota Camry, Corolla, C-HR, Venza, Highlander and RAV4…2021 Honda Insight, Civic, Accord and CR-V…2021 Mazda 3, 6, CX-3, CX-30, CX-5 and CX-9…2021 Volvo XC40, XC60 and XC90…and 2021 Lexus UX. Most of these vehicles achieve this status only when optional safety or technology packages featuring emergency braking systems are purchased. (Visit IIHS.org for annual updates.)

•**Performing well on crash tests does not guarantee that a car will perform well in all real-world crashes.** Automakers know exactly how NHTSA and IIHS test-crash cars—and they design

their cars to do well on these specific tests. Trouble is, doing well on these tests does not guarantee that vehicles will do a good job protecting occupants in other types of accidents.

Because IIHS is not a government agency, it says it has greater freedom to modify its tests as it feels necessary. In 2012, it added a "small overlap front" test to find out how well vehicles protect their occupants when the vehicle's front corner experiences an impact. Many vehicles fared poorly—including some that did very well in the more common head-on collision tests.

Example: The 2015 Kia Forte car received the top five-star safety rating from NHTSA but a score of "marginal" on the IIHS small-overlap-front test. The 2015 Dodge Grand Caravan and Chrysler Town & Country minivans received a respectable four-star score from NHTSA, but the lowest score—poor—on the small-overlap-front test.

What to do: Shop for a car that performs well in IIHS and NHTSA tests.

•**A high safety score for a small vehicle does not necessarily mean that it's safe.** If you want a safe vehicle, other things being equal, bigger is definitely better. Don't be fooled into thinking a small car will do a great job protecting your family because it earned five stars from NHTSA or "top safety pick-plus" from IIHS. Both of those organizations rate vehicle safety within that vehicle's category. In other words, a small car that earns top safety marks likely is safe compared with other small cars—but it likely isn't as safe as a large sedan or SUV. When you're in a big vehicle, there's simply more metal around you to absorb an impact.

Examples: Most of the vehicles with the highest rates of driver fatalities are small cars such as the Kia Rio…Scion tC…Nissan Versa…Chevrolet Spark…and Hyundai Accent. The list of vehicles with the lowest death rates is dominated by SUVs such as the Volkswagen Tiguan (2WD)…Lexus RX 350 (4WD)…Mercedes GL and M class (4WD)…Toyota 4Runner (2WD) and Venza (4WD)…Nissan Murano (4WD)…Jeep Cherokee (4WD) and Grand Cherokee (2WD)…Ford Explorer (4WD)…Nissan Pathfinder (4WD)…and Mazda CX-9 (4WD). The difference in fatalities between these two groups is massive. While the small cars listed above each experienced at least 86 driver deaths per million registered vehicle years in a recent study, the SUVs each had death rates of ten or fewer per million registered vehicle years. (Death rates are based on research by IIHS featuring the 2014–2017 model years and equivalent earlier models. The latest models have not yet been driven long enough to compile sufficient data.)

●A used car from 2010 or earlier might not be as safe as its NHTSA rating makes it appear. The government agency made it significantly more difficult to earn high scores starting with the 2011 model year—but it did not go back and adjust pre-2011 scores downward when it did so.

How to Choose a Roadside-Assistance Plan—AAA May Not Be Right for You

Philip Reed, senior consumer-advice editor at Edmunds. com, an automotive information website that does extensive research on vehicles and trends. He is author of *Strategies for Smart Car Buyers*.

A Missouri woman had a minor auto accident on her way to church. She was billed $913 for a five-mile tow. Most but not all roadside-assistance plans would have covered the towing and prevented the extreme overcharge.

Years ago, roadside-assistance plans, which tend to provide several other kinds of assistance as well, such as jump-starting a battery and changing a tire, used to be available only from auto clubs such as AAA (AAA.com) and the Better World Club (Better WorldClub.com). But now these plans are offered by many types of companies, including auto dealers, insurers, credit card issuers, cell-phone service providers and warehouse clubs.

Although all the plans tend to cover some basics, the full roster of what you get from each plan, how well it delivers services and how much it costs var-

ies widely. Choose unwisely, and you will end up paying a lot more than you need to and/or getting much less than you expect.

How to choose…

●If your vehicle is still under warranty, there's a good chance that you already are covered. Most auto manufacturers now include roadside assistance when you buy a new or certified used car. This typically lasts as long as the basic warranty—perhaps three or four years—but not always.

Examples: Mercedes roadside assistance lasts for the life of the vehicle, including all future owners. But Toyota's ToyotaCare plan lasts just two years or 25,000 miles, whichever comes first. That is less than the length of the warranty. (*Exception*: The Toyota Prius Plug-In Hybrid comes with three years of roadside assistance. Manufacturers sometimes provide additional roadside assistance with hybrid and electric vehicles to reassure car buyers that these cars will not leave them stranded.)

Most of these auto manufacturer plans provide fairly comprehensive coverage, including towing, lockout service, jump-starting, tire changing and fuel delivery. Roadside service often is provided through a company called Agero (formerly Cross Country Automotive Services), which provides coverage for 90% of new passenger autos sold in the US and works with a wide network of independent towing companies all across the country.

Downside: Many manufacturer plans provide tows only to the nearest dealership, which might charge higher repair rates for nonwarranty service than an independent garage. This is the case with Ford and GM's roadside-assistance plans.

●AAA Plus memberships generally offer the most comprehensive coverage other than manufacturer-provided roadside assistance. Other auto clubs and membership organizations such as AARP (AARPRoadside.com) might offer what looks on paper like comparable services for a slightly lower cost, but they generally can't match AAA's extensive roadside-assistance provider network. A smaller network can mean longer waits when you are stranded.

Downside: AAA roadside assistance is pricier than most other options, although AAA membership provides various types of discounts ranging from hotels to clothing retailers that help defray the cost of membership. The cost for AAA Plus membership varies widely, from $66 to $163 per year, depending on where you live. AAA Basic membership costs less but provides very limited towing—often just five miles or less—so you still could get stuck with a big towing bill if you break down in the middle of nowhere. Also, AAA membership covers just one motorist. Adding family members to a Plus plan can cost between $34 and $117 per additional person.

•**Explore the add-on plans offered by your auto insurance providers, credit card issuers and/ or cellular service providers.** These add-on plans tend to be very inexpensive—sometimes they're offered at no additional cost with an insurance policy or a credit card. But be very cautious about relying on them. While some are legitimate roadside-assistance programs, others are little more than sales gimmicks that do not truly remove the financial risk of calling a tow truck, which is supposed to be the point of any roadside-assistance plan.

Example: Insurer MetLife's roadside-assistance plan provides a maximum benefit of $50 per breakdown in most states—much less than what you might be charged for a tow.

Some of these programs also might have relatively limited service-provider networks. And taking frequent advantage of an insurance company's towing program could increase your insurance rates, though occasional calls to such a program are unlikely to have any significant effect. Still, there are some fine add-on plans out there if you take the time to check the program rules and understand what you're truly getting.

Example: American Express Premium Roadside Assistance, offered at no additional cost with certain American Express gold and platinum cards, has fairly extensive benefits.

Check These Features

Don't automatically assume your credit card offers roadside assistance. (Discover recently discontinued this benefit.) *When you investigate the add-on*

roadside-assistance plans available to you, weigh the following factors…

•**Towing-distance allowance.** Plans might cover only five miles of towing or less. Others might cap the amount they will pay for a tow at $100 or less, with any overage coming out of your pocket.

•**Number of roadside-assistance calls allowed per year.** Three or four assistance calls per year are typical.

•**Out-of-pocket costs.** Most credit cards that offer roadside assistance charge an annual fee. Some plans require members to pay a fee each time they request roadside assistance.

Examples: Chase Sapphire Preferred card requires a $95 annual fee. Its roadside assistance services are covered up to $50 per event. Visa Roadside Dispatch, available with select Visa cards, costs $69.95 per service call. On the plus side, cards that charge annual fees offer multiple benefits, such as airfare-cancellation and rental-car insurances.

•**Who's covered?** Some plans cover an entire household with a basic membership, while others cover just one vehicle or driver unless you pay extra—or they place other restrictions on coverage.

Example: Some plans offered by cell-phone companies provide coverage only when an enrolled cell phone is with the vehicle.

•**Average response time.** Call the plan's 800 number to ask if it tracks average response time to roadside-assistance requests. If not, enter the plan's name and keywords such as "reviews" or "opinions" into a search engine to see what other members have to say about response times.

Never Buy a Lemon: Tricks to Check Out Any Used Car

Corey Sandler, author and journalist who has written more than 200 books about consumer topics over the past 30 years including *Econoguide Buying or Leasing a Car*. His latest book, *Bottom Line's Secrets of the Savvy Consumer*, is available at BottomLineInc.com/consumer.

Hundreds of vehicles are engulfed by floodwater each year (such as when hurricanes hit both Texas and Florida in 2017). Some of these now-ruined cars and trucks—that can be shined up today but will without question rot, lose their electrical systems and fall apart over time—will be snuck onto the used-car market by disreputable sellers and go on to bedevil their owners. (For more on the signs of flood damage, see page 12.)

In general, buying a used vehicle can save you big bucks—but only if you manage to dodge basket-case cars and trucks that will require endless or expensive repairs.

You might know the standard advice to pay a mechanic you trust $100 to $200 to examine a used vehicle before you buy…and purchase a vehicle history report from a company such as Carfax (Carfax.com, $39.99 for a single report). That can be money well-spent—but you don't want to spend it more often than necessary.

You can be the first to spot trouble in a used vehicle offered by a dealer or an individual—even if you are in no way a car expert. Here are six savvy things anyone can do to weed out bad used vehicles before consulting a mechanic or buying a Carfax report, potentially saving hundreds of dollars in the process…

•**Look where there shouldn't be paint.** If the vehicle was in a significant accident, it probably was repainted by a body shop. If you know where to look, you might be able to find "overspray" from this second paint job—that is, paint where there is not supposed to be paint. This might include tiny spots of paint inside wheel wells…on the rubber trim around windows…or under the hood on stickers or on parts that would not have been present when the bare body panels were originally painted in the factory.

Next, step back from the vehicle and compare its body panels. If the paint on some panels seems subtly different from the paint on others, it might mean that certain panels were repainted following an accident. This will be much easier to spot on a bright, sunny day. (Make sure you're comparing metal parts. It's perfectly normal for the color of plastic body panels, such as bumpers, to not quite match the color of painted metal.)

•**Check the gaps between body panels.** If a gap is visibly wider than the same gap on the other side

of the vehicle…or the same gap is wider at one end than the other…it might mean that the car was in a serious accident that bent its frame. If any of the doors appears slightly out of line with the rest of the vehicle when shut, that, too, could point to a major accident.

•**Look for areas under the hood that appear much cleaner than the rest of the engine compartment.** These areas might have been cleaned to hide the fact that the vehicle has been leaking fluids, or a particular component might be clean because it was only recently replaced. If you see an oddly clean area, ask the seller whether the vehicle has needed any work or experienced any problems lately. If he/she says that a part needed to be replaced, ask to see the paperwork from the mechanic and confirm that it was something straightforward, such as a new starter or alternator. If the seller denies that anything has gone wrong, ask why this one area looks so much cleaner than the rest of the engine compartment. Walk away if he cannot offer a reasonable-sounding explanation.

•**Check the wear on the accelerator pedal, the driver's seat upholstery and driver's seat springs.** The pedal and upholstery typically should not show significant wear if there is less than 50,000 miles or so on the odometer, and the seat springs should not sound or feel old and squeaky. If any of these things are true, there might be more miles on the vehicle than its odometer suggests.

Also: If the brake pedal shows significant wear, the vehicle might have endured lots of tough stop-and-go driving.

•**Put your hand on the hood before starting the vehicle.** Certainly, you should take the vehicle for a test-drive to make sure that there are no obvious issues with how it handles or sounds and to make sure there are no liquids dripping from it afterward. But before this test-drive, feel the hood. If it feels warmer than other body panels, the seller might have started and run the vehicle just before you arrived. This might have been perfectly innocent—maybe he backed the car out of the garage for you—or it might have been to hide the fact that this vehicle does not start reliably when its engine is cold. Let the engine cool for perhaps 20 to 30 minutes before starting it up again for the test-drive. Use this time to examine it inside and out.

•**Do not be lulled by the existence of a warranty.** A warranty might guarantee that any problems with the car can be fixed without paying out of pocket—but not necessarily. Ask who is providing this warranty and who will do the repairs. If the protection is being offered by a dealership that sells this make of car and has its own service department, the warranty could well be reliable. If it is offered by an independent used-car lot, it could have little or no real value. Either way, ask for a printed copy of the terms of the warranty and read it before buying.

If you are assured that a used vehicle is covered by its original manufacturer warranty—the most reliable type of vehicle warranty—jot down the vehicle identification number (VIN) found on the driver's doorjamb or visible through the windshield on the driver's side above the dash. Contact the service department of a dealership that sells that make of car, give the VIN and ask about the vehicle's warranty status. In some cases, the full manufacturer's warranty does not carry over if the car is resold by the original owner. *Example:* Hyundai and Kia vehicles come new with a 10-year/100,000-mile power train warranty—but this is reduced to a five-year/60,000-mile warranty for subsequent owners.

If you are told by a car's seller that the vehicle still is covered by an extended warranty purchased by an earlier owner, ask to see the warranty contract covering this specific vehicle and read this carefully to confirm that it will transfer to a subsequent owner. Also, look up reviews of the company providing this extended warranty to get a sense of whether it can be trusted.

•**Three additional things worth doing when buying a used car from an individual, not a dealership or lot...**

•Ask, "Has it been garaged?" If the answer is yes, ask to see its garage space and examine the floor. Stains where the car was parked could mean that the vehicle has had oil or other fluid leaks.

•Ask to see the vehicle's maintenance records. It's a bad sign if the owner cannot produce a well-organized file showing that maintenance has been handled on schedule.

•If the vehicle has a trailer hitch and/or you see a travel trailer or boat in the driveway, ask, "Oh, is it powerful enough to tow?" If the seller brags that it is, make polite conversation about what the owner has towed, where and how often. If you give the impression that you are impressed by the vehicle's towing capacity, you're likely to get honest answers. But in fact, towing is tough on many parts of a vehicle, including its engine, transmission and brakes. If the vehicle has done lots of towing, that could be a reason to walk away.

Spot a Flood-Damaged Car

Vehicles that have been in floods are prone to a wide range of problems, some of which might not appear until years later when corrosion has taken its toll. *To avoid getting stuck with one of these...*

•**See if a vehicle has a known history of flood damage.** You can search this for free through Carfax (Carfax.com/press/resources/flooded-cars). This database includes a vehicle only if its flood damage was reported to an insurance company, however. To be even safer, pay for the full Carfax Vehicle History Report ($39.99 for one report...$59.99 for three or $99.99 for six) and check where the vehicle previously was owned—if it was owned in Florida or in or near Houston, sites of recent hurricanes, stay away.

Car Dealer Trick

It's easier for a car dealer to trick you with an electronic contract. The dealer instructs the customer to use a finger to sign a computer screen rather than printing a copy for signing. Consumers are less likely to examine on-screen contracts, upping the odds that the dealer could sneak in extra costs.

Best: Insist on a printed contract, and review it before signing.

Rosemary Shahan, founder and president of Consumers for Auto Reliability and Safety, Sacramento, California. Car Consumers.org

A Sign Can Help

A sign in your garage may save your life if you have a car with a modern keyless ignition. It's easy to forget to push the button to turn the car off. The risk is even greater with hybrid cars, which are silent on battery power. Dozens of people have died from carbon monoxide fumes when cars were left on in a garage. And while some keyless cars shut off automatically, putting up a big sign may be the best reminder.

Robert Sinclair, Jr., is senior manager of public affairs for AAA Northeast, Garden City, New York.

•**Examine the carpeting.** Look for mud on and under the vehicle's carpeting. Also be suspicious of any used car that has carpeting that looks brand-new and/or does not fit the floor of the car perfectly. This replacement carpeting might have been installed because original carpeting was ruined in a flood.

•**Look for mud under the hood.** Pay particular attention to the tight spots where it would be hard to fit a hand. These spots are tricky to clean, so they might still show signs of mud.

•**Take a good whiff.** Get inside the vehicle, shut its doors and windows and see whether your nose picks up a musty odor. The smell of mold and mildew can be harder to hide than the visual signs of flood damage.

Hidden Danger in Your Car's Infotainment System

Nathan Wenzler, former chief security strategist at AsTech (now Moss Adams), an information-security consulting firm that helps Fortune 1,000 companies and their employees protect digital data. MossAdams.com

There's a hidden danger when you sell your vehicle…take it to a repair shop…reach the end of a lease…or return a rental car. The danger is in leaving detailed personal information in the auto's onboard computer, making you vulnerable to cybertheft.

For several years, infotainment systems in many vehicles have let you connect, or "pair," your smartphone wirelessly via Bluetooth or through a USB cable.

Problem: As drivers increasingly use car infotainment systems to send texts and e-mail, browse the Internet, log into mobile apps, get directions and even open garage doors, a vehicle's computer might store much of the data, which can be accessed easily by a tech-savvy thief.

What to do: When you sell a vehicle or return a leased one, wipe personal data from the computer. Many vehicles have a factory-reset option that returns the settings and data to their original state. Check the owner's manual or contact a dealer. Otherwise, delete information manually. Go to the infotainment system's main menu. Navigate to the list of paired devices, and follow the instructions to delete yours. If you used the vehicle's navigation system, clear your location history…and clear any garage-door codes.

For rental cars, doing a factory reset might violate a rental agreement requirement to not modify the vehicle's functionality. Instead, manually delete paired devices and location history. Ask rental-car personnel to walk you through the steps if you need help. If you visit a mechanic you don't trust not to snoop, delete your paired devices temporarily and reload your data when you get the vehicle back.

Long-Term Parking

Dan Neil, automotive columnist writing for The Wall Street Journal.

Leaving a car parked drains the battery, sometimes in as little as one week. Modern cars use electricity constantly for features such as GPS, antitheft systems and proximity sensors. Larger and newer batteries last longer when a car sits unused, but even they can be drained in two to three weeks—a major issue for people using long-term airport parking or otherwise not driving regularly.

Self-defense: Keep jumper cables in the car at all times…buy a portable jump starter or battery booster...to maintain optimal charge while the car is parked at home or anywhere the charger can be used, use a plug-in trickle charger, such as CTEK MUS 4.3, $152 at SmarterCharger.com...disconnect the negative battery terminal when leaving the car parked—but this may be very difficult depending on where the battery is located.

Don't Let Potholes Destroy Your Car

Michael Calkins, technical services manager for AAA, the not-for-profit federation of motor clubs that serves more than 53 million members in the US and Canada. Based in Heathrow, Florida, he is certified by the National Institute for Automotive Service Excellence as a Master Automobile Technician. AAA.com

Pothole.info

Running over a big pothole can be a bone-rattling, car-crushing and money-draining experience. And potholes are not limited to the snowbelt. Los Angeles and San Francisco have some of the worst-ranked roads in the country.

Hard-to-miss potholes often mean punctured tires, damaged suspensions, broken shock absorbers and/or misaligned wheels, possibly costing hundreds of dollars—or even more—to fix.

The US spends about $68 billion per year to repair road surfaces (according to Pothole.info).

But you can take actions to avoid potholes...reduce the possible damage if you hit one...and lower the cost of repairing damage.

Avoiding/Reducing Damage

What to do to lessen the chances of pothole damage...

•**Increase your car's trailing distance behind the car in front of you to at least two car lengths at slower speeds and four car lengths at faster speeds on pothole-prone roads**—the heavily trafficked asphalt ones with signs of previous patch repairs. This allows you more time to react and avoid a pothole or at least brake and decrease your speed before you hit it, which can greatly minimize damage.

Wet-weather alert: Brake before you hit puddles because they can conceal deep, sharp-edged potholes that are filled with water.

•**Don't keep braking as you roll over a pothole that you can't avoid**—instead, release the brakes the moment before your tires reach the pothole, and let your car roll freely through it.

Reason: Braking, especially braking heavily, tilts the vehicle forward and places added stress on the front suspension. This increases the chance that your suspension will be damaged when you hit the hole.

Repairing the Damage

It's pretty obvious very quickly if a pothole has punctured your tire, but it might cause more serious damage that is harder to detect and more costly to fix. *What to do...*

•**Have your vehicle inspected if you notice the following signs...**

•The car pulls to one direction instead of maintaining a straight path. *Likely problem:* The pothole knocked your wheels out of alignment. *Cost:* $75 to $150 for a realignment.

•You feel a light-to-moderate vibration in the steering wheel. *Likely problem:* A wheel balance weight has been knocked off. *Cost:* $15 to rebalance.

•You feel a moderate-to-heavy vibration from the tire area. *Likely problem:* Your wheel is bent. *Cost:* $75 to $500 to replace the wheel.

•The car sways or rocks during turns and bounces more than normal on rough roads. *Likely problem:* Broken shock absorber or strut. *Cost:* $200 to $400 to replace it, plus the cost of an alignment.

•The steering wheel is no longer centered, and/or there is noise from under the car. *Likely problem:* Damage to the suspension system on the underside of your vehicle. *Cost:* $100 and up, plus the cost of an alignment.

Cutting Your Costs

You might be able to lessen the cost of recent and/or future pothole damage in various ways...

•**Purchase a road-hazard warranty from a tire store or repair shop when you buy new tires and wheels.** It is not always available, but the warranty typically lasts for at least a year and costs $10 to $20 per tire, although sometimes it's free. The warranty typically covers the cost to repair the tire/wheel or replace it with a new one for a prorated charge, depending upon how many miles you have driven on the old one.

●**Contact your insurer to determine what it covers.** Most insurers treat pothole damage as an "at-fault" accident. That means you are covered for repair costs above your collision deductible. You generally do not need to file a police report to submit a claim, but the accident likely will remain on your insurance company's records for three years and could affect your premium rates. Tire damage is generally excluded in insurance policies, but wheels may be covered.

●**See whether the state, city or county government will reimburse you for damages.** It depends on which government body is responsible for the upkeep of the road that you were driving on.

Example: In 2013, Chicago paid $181,217 on 754 claims, or about $240 per claim. You typically need to submit substantial evidence, including photos of the pothole, the exact location, witness statements and a police report.

Note: Some government bodies accept responsibility only if they had prior notice of a dangerous roadway condition and had sufficient time to repair the problem.

Example: To win a claim against the state of Michigan, there must be a previous record of complaint that is at least 30 days old about the specific pothole you hit.

Does Your Car Smell Like Rotten Eggs?

Eric Peters, a Washington, DC–based automotive columnist and author of *Automotive Atrocities! The Cars We Love to Hate.* EricPetersAutos.com

Especially if it's very strong and constant, a rotten egg/sulfur smell could be a sign that your car's catalytic converter isn't properly processing the by-products of combustion. There could be a problem with the converter itself or with the engine.

What to do: Get a constant sulfur smell checked out quickly to avoid ruining the catalytic converter.

Cost: A car manufacturer's factory replacement unit can cost $300 or more.

Helpful: Avoid buying gas at lightly trafficked gas stations. The fuel may be old and possibly contaminated, which can trigger problems with your car's emissions control system and possibly damage the catalytic converter.

How Auto Insurers Trick You with Their Language

J. Robert Hunter, director of insurance for the Consumer Federation of America, Washington, DC, and former commissioner of the Texas Department of Insurance. ConsumerFed.org

When buying auto insurance, do you really know what you are getting and why? The language used in auto insurance ads and policies often is misleading or confusing—and can lead you to be underprotected or overcharged.

Solution: Do what the insurance industry hopes you won't do—understand the tricky auto insurance terms explained below. Then you will be able to ask the right questions when buying auto insurance…reject the options you don't need…avoid hidden auto insurance traps…and get the best price for the protections you do need…*

Terms you may think you understand but don't…

●**"New-car replacement."** If your car is totaled in an accident, you typically get only its depreciated value, which may be less than what you still owe on your car loan. New-car-replacement coverage is an option that pays the full cost (minus your deductible) for the latest make and model of your vehicle, up to 110% of the manufacturer's suggested retail price.

*Availability and details of various types of coverage in this article may vary by state.

What's tricky: New-car replacement can increase your premiums by 15% or more. Plus, the coverage is available for only a limited time for any given car.

Example: Ameriprise and Liberty Mutual offer new-car replacement until cars are one-year old or have been driven 15,000 miles (whichever comes first).

What to do: From a financial standpoint, most drivers should skip this coverage. It's unlikely to pay off, considering that there is less than a 1% chance in any given year of having an accident in which one's vehicle is totaled.

• **"Gap coverage."** This option often is pushed on people who have made small down payments on their vehicles. It pays the difference between the balance of a loan due on your totaled vehicle and what your insurer pays you if the car is totaled.

What's tricky: What this covers can vary. *Example*: Most gap coverage does not include your out-of-pocket deductible. However, Allstate's gap coverage pays deductibles up to $1,000. And although gap coverage typically pays off your car loan regardless of your car's value, Progressive's version pays a maximum of just 25% of the car's actual cash value at the time of the accident.

What to do: This might be a cost-effective add-on for some drivers who still owe a lot on their cars because it typically costs just $30 a year and the premium decreases as the vehicle ages (but see pages 18–19 for why it might be unneccessary). And you can drop it after a few years as you pay off the loan. Before you buy it, be sure to clarify with the insurer the extent of the coverage.

• **"Decreasing deductible."** This feature, also known as "vanishing deductible," reduces the deductible on your collision insurance without increasing the premium if you remain accident-free.

Example: At Travelers, the Premier Responsible Driver Plan will reduce your deductible by $50 every six months that you go without an accident, up to a total reduction of $500.

What's tricky: To qualify, all drivers covered by the policy must remain accident-free. That includes accidents that aren't your fault, such as another car

hitting yours. If you have an accident, your original deductible is reinstated and you must reestablish a clean record to qualify for future reductions. This feature typically is available only as part of an upper-tier insurance package that adds 5% or more to your premiums.

What to do: It's not worth that extra cost on its own, so be sure you think it's worth paying for the package, which can include new-car replacement and/or accident forgiveness.

• **"Accident forgiveness."** This feature helps you avoid a rate increase following your first at-fault accident. Without this benefit, some insurers push up base premiums by 10%, 20% or more after just one accident, and the higher rates can last as long as five years.

What's tricky: The coverage may exclude teenage drivers. If you do have an accident, it may take three to five years to requalify for this feature.

What to do: This essentially is asking you to pay up front for accidents you might have in the future. Avoid this coverage unless you are a very bad driver.

• **"Appraisal clause."** If you and the insurer can't agree on how much will be paid to repair or replace your vehicle after an accident, this clause allows for the appointment of an appraiser by each side. If the two appraisers can't agree, they can jointly choose a third appraiser as umpire.

What's tricky: Under an appraisal clause, the insurer might be able to force you to accept arbitration rather than take the matter to court. Also, the appraisers may have a conscious or unconscious bias in favor of the insurer.

What to do: You always want to retain the option to get a lawyer and go to court. Twenty-six states prohibit or restrict insurance companies from imposing this type of arbitration on drivers. Check with your state's department of insurance. If your state allows forced arbitration, this is an important consideration in choosing insurers. Check whether a potential insurer includes an appraisal clause in its policy.

• **"As defined by us."** This phrase can refer to a variety of different terms or concepts in a policy.

What Not to Say to Your Auto Insurer After an Accident

Be careful when talking to your auto insurer after an accident…

•**Don't say you're fine**—soft-tissue injuries may not show up immediately.

•**Don't mention whiplash**—it is a red flag that you might be trying to scam the insurer.

• **Avoid saying "sorry" or accepting blame for the accident.**

•**Before letting the insurer tape-record the conversation, make sure you know exactly what you want to say.**

•**Stick to the facts as you remember them.**

•**Don't volunteer information beyond what is requested.**

•**If you are injured,** see a doctor to get documentation—insurers will not pay without it.

•**For damage to your car,** most states let you have repairs done where you choose—if your insurer refuses, contact your state insurance department.

Amy Bach, executive director, United Policyholders, a consumer-advocacy group, quoted in *USA Today*.

Watch out when it's used to give the insurer the right to make its own determination about the proper cost for a repair even if that is a below-market rate. Look for this phrase in the limits of liability section of your policy.

What's tricky: You might be stuck paying the difference if you want to use a repair shop that's more expensive than the insurer deems necessary.

What to do: If you have a favorite auto-repair shop, ask the insurer whether it has approved and paid for work at that shop in the past. If not, find out which shops the insurer knows in your area that will accept its rates and make sure that you are OK with using them…or seek another insurer.

•**"Collision" and "comprehensive."** You probably already know the basic meaning of these auto-insurance terms—but it's not their meaning that often trips up drivers. Collision includes damage to your car when you hit another car or an inanimate object such as a tree or fence or you drive over a hazard such as a deep pothole. Comprehensive (really not comprehensive in its extent of coverage) covers loss or damage caused by an event other than what collision covers, such as fire, theft, vandalism or hitting an animal.

What's tricky: Despite what many people think, no state requires either of these two types of coverage. What's required by most states is liability coverage, which protects you if you're at fault for an accident and the other car is damaged or if the driver and any passengers in either vehicle are hurt. However, if you have a loan on your car, the lender probably requires that you carry both collision and comprehensive.

What to do: In general, drop collision coverage, which can be about three times as expensive as comprehensive, when the value of your car is less than 10 times the annual cost of the collision coverage. Set aside what you save on your premiums for buying your next vehicle.

•**"Uninsured/underinsured motorist."** This coverage protects you if you're in an accident involving an at-fault motorist who has no insurance (or not enough) to pay for your damages and/or medical care for injuries. Or if the other driver cannot be located (a hit-and-run). If you live in one of the dozen states with no-fault insurance, insurers typically don't offer this option. (In no-fault states, if you are injured in an accident, your auto insurance covers both your vehicle damage, regardless of who was at fault, and your medical expenses through a personal-injury-protection policy that you are required to buy.)

What's tricky: Of the states that do assign fault in accidents, 23 do not require drivers to have uninsured/underinsured motorist coverage. Insurers in those states generally offer this coverage as two separate policy options—one for uninsured/underinsured motorist property damage (UMPD), the other for uninsured/underinsured motorist bodily injury (UMBI).

What to do: Everyone should consider having UMBI, even in a no-fault state, if the option is offered.

Reason: About 15% of cars are uninsured, and many insured cars are covered by low-tier policies with low coverage limits. If you are hit by an uninsured or underinsured driver and incur medical expenses, your UMBI coverage kicks in before your health-care insurance coverage does. That means you typically won't face out-of-pocket deductibles and co-payments. UMBI also will cover some lost wages, depending on the policy, if your injuries prevent you from working and may compensate you for your pain and suffering, which your health-care insurance may not. How much UMBI coverage you need will depend on what other insurance you already carry, including any short-term disability insurance, and the out-of-pocket requirements of your health insurance. Consider getting at least "100/300" coverage (a maximum of $100,000 for your injuries and up to $300,000 total for injuries to everyone in your car).

• **"Credit-based insurance score."** Yes, there is a score related to your credit that can affect your auto insurance rates.

What's tricky: This special credit score, used by almost all auto insurers, comes from the same company that issues the FICO credit score used by mortgage lenders and other lenders, but it's not the same score. Government studies have shown a correlation between credit scores and the likelihood of filing auto insurance claims. The lower a customer's credit score, the greater the likelihood he/she will make a claim. Car insurers believe that this is because people who manage their money responsibly also are more careful in how they drive. (*Note:* Three states—California, Hawaii and Massachusetts—prohibit auto insurers from using consumer credit information to determine premiums.)

What to do: You cannot get access to your credit-based insurance score. However, you should monitor your regular credit reports to make sure that they are accurate, and ask to be reevaluated by your insurer if you have found and corrected errors in your reports.

• **"Multipolicy discount."** Some insurers reduce your auto-coverage premiums as much as 10% to 15% if you buy one or more other types of insurance from them such as a homeowner's policy.

What's tricky: You don't necessarily save money bundling policies. An insurer that specializes in insuring cars may have its homeowner's business handled by a third party and offer uncompetitive rates or less comprehensive coverage.

What to do: Shop for the best rates on comparable policies, including discounts and bundles at various insurers.

Auto Insurance You Don't Need

J. Robert Hunter, director of insurance for the Consumer Federation of America, Washington, DC, and former commissioner of the Texas Department of Insurance. Consumer Fed.org

A recent disclosure involving scandal-plagued Wells Fargo bank underlines how important it is to pay close attention to the fine print of auto insurance coverage.

The disclosure involves "guaranteed asset protection" (GAP) insurance, which Wells Fargo and other lenders sell aggressively through dealerships when consumers take out car loans. Because the vehicle quickly loses much of its value, GAP insurance is meant to compensate lenders for that diminished value if the vehicle is totaled, stolen or repossessed. Wells Fargo charges a onetime fee of $500 to $700. In nine states—Alabama, Colorado, Indiana, Iowa, Maryland, Massachusetts, Oklahoma, Oregon and South Carolina—when borrowers pay off the loan early, lenders are required by law to refund part of the fee.

Wells Fargo has reportedly come under regulatory scrutiny for failing to refund GAP insurance fees to many consumers whose auto loans were paid off early.

If you are paying off a vehicle loan early in one of those nine states and are having trouble getting a GAP refund, contact your state insurance commissioner (content.naic.org/state-insurance-departments).

If you don't have GAP insurance coverage, which is not required by law in any state and can't be forced on you by a lender, you don't need it. *Here's why…*

In the unlikely event that you suffer a total loss of your vehicle during the life of your loan, your insurer will always pay the current value of the vehicle at that time. If you can't afford to buy a new vehicle for the original price of the lost vehicle and pay off the remaining loan balance, you could buy a less expensive new or used vehicle and take out a new loan.

Example: Your new $20,000 car is totaled in an accident…your insurer covers $18,000, reflecting the current value…you buy a used car with a similar number of miles for no more than $18,000 and you still owe the same total of $20,000.

Also, if you shop around, you can get a variation on GAP coverage without an extra fee.

Example: Car loans from State Farm Bank automatically come with a Payoff Protector provision.

12 Hidden Discounts on Car Insurance Save $200 a Year or More

Amy Danise, editorial director at Insure.com, an independent website that provides articles and tools to aid consumers in making insurance decisions. It recently conducted a study of nearly 25,000 auto insurance discounts nationwide.

These discounts* sometimes subtract 15% to 20% or more from collision, liability, comprehensive and/or overall premiums. Policyholders usually are allowed to combine discounts to increase their savings, though total discounts often are capped, sometimes at around 25%. The average auto insurance policy costs around $800 a year, so that 25% off represents an annual savings of

*Availability and details of various types of coverage in this article may vary by state. All discounts are subject to change.

$200—possibly more if your coverage is especially expensive.

Don't assume that your insurer will automatically apply all of the available discounts. It's often up to the policyholder to inform the insurer that he/she qualifies. That's especially likely if you didn't qualify for a discount when you initially signed up for the coverage but do now.

The discounts vary dramatically in type and size from insurer to insurer, and even from state to state with the same insurer.

If any of the discounts listed here fit your situation, call your insurer to find out whether it's available and, if so, whether you currently are receiving it. When you shop around for your next auto insurance policy, ask insurers which discounts are available to you and make sure that their price reflects the discounts.

Among the discounts…

1. Good-student discount. If there's a high school or college student in your family, your auto insurance probably is pretty pricey—young drivers are charged steep rates. But if one or more of the students on your insurance policy does well in school, there might be a way to trim your bill. More than 75% of insurers offer discounts to students under age 25 who get good grades. Good students tend to be safer drivers than their less academic-minded classmates.

Rules vary, but a 3.0 GPA (or B average) often is required. In some cases, the student must maintain this GPA…in others, he need only achieve it in the most recent semester to qualify for the discount in the following policy period.

Average savings: 16%.

2. Marriage discount. Tying the knot makes you eligible for a discount with about 40% of all auto insurers. Insurers have found that married people tend to be safer drivers than unmarried ones. In some cases, even civil unions qualify.

Average savings: 14%.

3. Low annual mileage discount. The fewer miles you drive, the lower your odds of getting into an accident. Your insurer likely asked you to estimate the length of your daily commute and/or the number of miles you drive each year when you applied for coverage. But perhaps you overestimated these distances or perhaps you're driving less now than you were then. Calculate your commute and annual mileage. If you drive substantially less than the national average of 15,000 miles a year, call your insurer to confirm that you're receiving any discounts you're due.

Average savings: 11% for car owners who drive less than 5,000 to 8,000 miles per year. Smaller discounts may be available to car owners who drive more than this but less than 15,000 miles per year.

4. Farm-vehicle discount. Around 40% of all auto insurers offer discounts based on "use" of the vehicle, such as farm use. The odds of getting into an accident with another vehicle are much lower when a vehicle is driven primarily on a farm.

Average savings: 10%.

5. Facebook "like" discount. Allstate's Esurance website offers a discount to residents of Texas and Arizona who "like" Esurance on Facebook.

Savings: 10%.

6. Membership discounts. Insurers often offer discounts to members of clubs and associations with which they have partnered. These could include professional associations, workers' unions, large employers or membership organizations such as AARP or AAA. You even could qualify for savings based on the college you attended or the fraternity or sorority you belonged to decades ago.

Examples: Geico offers a discount of up to 8% to members of Mensa, the high-IQ organization, and up to 8% to active and retired federal employees. Country Financial offers up to 10% off for full-time teachers of kindergarten through 12th grade and up to 5% for emergency first responders. Allstate's Esurance offers up to 15% to students and alumni of the Pacific-12 collegiate athletic conference schools who reside in Arizona, Colorado, Oregon and Utah.

7. Up-front payment discount. About half of all insurers offer a discount for paying premiums in full at the start of the policy period rather than in monthly installments. The savings can be significant, so if you can afford to pay in advance, it's often worth doing so.

Average savings: 9%.

8. Bundled-policy discount. Insurers often offer discounts to customers who purchase both auto and homeowner's insurance from the same company. But many people don't realize that this bundling discount also might be available if you combine auto insurance with renter's insurance, life insurance or some other type of insurance.

Average savings: 9%.

9. Advance-purchase discount. More than 25% of auto insurers offer a discount to existing customers who renew their coverage seven to 10 days before the old policy expires, though this varies.

Examples: In Florida, Travelers, Allstate, Progressive, Safeco and Infinity are among the insurers offering this discount. Some insurers extend this discount to new customers who sign up for coverage well before their current policy with a different insurer expires.

Average savings: 8%.

10. Owning a home. Insurers have found that home owners are less risky as customers because they tend to act more responsibly and are less likely to file claims.

Average savings: 6%.

11. Automatic-payment discount. Around one-third of insurers offer discounts to customers who agree to have their premiums automatically withdrawn from their bank accounts.

Average savings: 4%.

12. Advanced-degree discount. A small number of insurers offer discounts to customers who have earned master's degrees or PhDs.

Average savings: 4%.

Never Overpay for Car Repairs Again

Jill Trotta, ASE Certified Technician/Adviser with more than 25 years of experience. She is president/GM, RepairPal Express, which offers auto-repair information including repair-cost estimates and evaluations of more than 4,200 independent repair facilities. RepairPal.com

When it comes to repair costs, many car owners are driving blind. Cars have become increasingly complex, making it increasingly hard to know how much repairs should cost…or to know about money-saving alternatives. To make car-repair cost decisions…

When You Take Your Car for Repair

These tips apply to independent garages and service departments at dealerships…

•**Some "aftermarket" replacement parts are as good as original parts**—but you should know which to accept. A garage might make its repair prices lower by always using "aftermarket" replacement parts—parts not made by the same companies that made the parts originally installed on the car—and might tell you that costlier "original equipment manufacturer" (OEM) parts never are worth the extra money. Meanwhile, a new-car dealership might always recommend OEM parts despite their high cost and tell you that aftermarket parts are inferior—even though the automakers themselves sometimes buy parts from these aftermarket companies.

The truth lies in between—it's fine to save money by buying certain aftermarket parts and from certain parts makers…but there are times when it's better to pay up for OEM.

What to do: Ask what company makes the aftermarket part. If it's ACDelco, Bosch, Denso or NTK, the part likely is every bit as reliable as the OEM part. These companies are highly respected in the industry—the automakers themselves often buy parts from them. If the aftermarket part is made by a different company, ask someone at your repair shop (or your dealership's parts department) if he/she would trust this part in his own car. You'll probably get a straight answer because the shop could easily sell you the OEM part instead.

Exception: If you need to replace a component that performs a significant amount of computer processing, pay extra for the OEM part if it is available. Opting for an aftermarket computer component is a false savings—it might cause problems with other systems in your car that could be very expensive for your mechanic to chase down.

•**High-end brake pads are one upgrade that truly is worth the price.** When you take your car for a brake job, you might be offered several brake pad options including "organic" brake pads for as little as $10 per set…"low metallic organic" pads for perhaps $20…or ceramic brake pads that could cost $80 to $120. Is a garage that recommends high-end brake pads just trying to up-sell you for little or no benefit?

What to do: Ante up for ceramic brake pads— they likely will stop your vehicle faster than other pads and therefore keep you safer. They also last longer than organic pads and don't cause as much wear to brake rotors as metallic pads, so in the long run they won't add as much to your car-ownership costs as their up-front cost suggests.

•**Female drivers are more likely to be overcharged in major metro areas.** It's not news that female car owners sometimes get charged more than men for the same repairs—studies show that they pay around 8% more, on average. But while these overcharges are common in big cities, it turns out that they are much less likely in small cities and rural regions. Repair shops and service departments in small communities cannot risk ruining their reputations with the locals—if word got out that they were overcharging, everyone in the area would soon know it.

What to do: Anyone—woman or man—would be wise to use an online auto-repair price estimator, such as the "Get an Estimate" tool at my employer's site RepairPal.com, to judge whether an offered price is fair. And unfortunately, this is especially true for women who live in large cities or other densely populated areas.

•**Bills for "scheduled maintenance" might be inflated by fluid flushes that you don't need.** If a shop recommends replacing your car's coolant, brake fluid, power-steering fluid and/or transmission fluid when you take it in for scheduled maintenance, beware—the shop might be trying to sell you a service that your car does not need. These fluid changes once were routine, but they are needed far less often with modern cars.

What to do: Check the scheduled maintenance section of your vehicle's owner's manual—not a maintenance schedule created by the shop!—to see whether this fluid replacement is recommended at your current mileage. If it isn't, ask the shop to justify the fluid change. There might be a valid reason—perhaps the mechanic did a test that revealed the presence of excess water in your brake fluid, for example…or perhaps the fluid change is a potential solution to a problem that you have been experiencing with the car. If the shop's only explanation is some form of "It's better to do it more often than the owner's manual says," decline the service and, if the shop persists in pushing the service, find a different shop.

Before You Buy Your Next Car

High-end cars don't just cost more to maintain than economy cars, they cost a lot more. Thinking about treating yourself to a $50,000 or $60,000 luxury car this year…or something even more expensive? Get ready to treat your mechanic as well. As a rule of thumb, a vehicle's cost of repairs will be roughly proportional to its original sticker price—for example, it costs about four times as much to keep an $80,000 luxury sedan on the road as a $20,000 economy car.

Expensive vehicles have more systems and features than economy cars, so there's more that can break. When their parts do break, they often are very expensive to replace—and less expensive aftermarket parts might not even be available. And the complexity and relative rarity of high-end cars means that mechanics may take longer to diagnose and fix problems or that the vehicle must be taken to a specialized mechanic who charges a steep hourly rate.

What to do: Don't stretch your budget to buy an expensive car unless there's also room in your budget for four-figure annual repair bills once the warranty ends. RepairPal's Cost Index Score can give you an idea about the repair bills you might be in for with a particular model (RepairPal.com/reliability).

If you want a luxury car that won't inflate your maintenance and repair bills any more than necessary, buy from one of the Japanese luxury brands—Lexus, Infiniti or Acura. Lexus is a division of Toyota…Acura is a division of Honda…and Infiniti is a division of Nissan, so these generally can be worked on by mechanics familiar with mainstream Japanese cars. They even use some of the same parts as those brands. If you don't want to pay thousands per year, on average, in repair bills after warranty,

avoid European luxury brands such as Audi, BMW, Mercedes and Porsche, which tend to be among the most expensive cars to maintain and repair.

•**One make of car known for reliability can be more expensive to repair than buyers expect—Subaru.** Subaru has a reputation as a reliable brand (although in the latest reliability rankings by Consumer Reports and JD Power, the brand didn't do as well as you'd expect). But while Subarus often are reliable, they can be surprisingly expensive to repair when something does go wrong. In many ways, they are built a bit differently from other makes, so they can be tricky—and time-consuming—for mechanics who do not work on them regularly.

Example: Many Subarus have "boxer" engines mounted in an unusual position in the engine compartment and with pistons that move horizontally rather than up and down.

What to do: If your Subaru is out of warranty, take it to a dealership or independent mechanic specializing in Subarus even if that means traveling a bit farther. If there is no such shop in your area, that's a reason to lean toward a different make of car instead.

•**One type of car is less expensive to maintain than car buyers fear—electric vehicles.** Despite car-buyer concerns about the high cost of replacing worn-out lithium ion batteries, electric cars (and some hybrids, such as the Toyota Prius) actually have proved very affordable to keep on the road. The current generation of batteries generally will last at least 150,000 miles if not longer. And overall, electric cars break far less often than gasoline or diesel cars because they have many fewer moving parts and because the parts they do have tend to be less stressed.

Example: An electric vehicle has no gas engine, so you never have to replace a timing belt or a head gasket—or even change the oil.

A recent study by AAA found that average annual maintenance and repair costs for electric cars were nearly 20% less than those for the average gas-powered vehicle. The savings can be even greater if you opt for an economy-oriented electric car, such as the Chevy Bolt or Volt, rather than a performance-oriented one such as a Tesla.

What to do: If you're looking for an economical car for short-to-medium trips—say, up to around 200 miles—strongly consider buying electric. Not only will you save money on fuel, you'll probably save on repairs and maintenance as well.

Car Maintenance You Don't Need—Including Most Every Kind of "Flush"

The late Tom Torbjornsen, former host of *America's Car Show with Tom Torbjornsen* on the SSI Radio Network. He spent nearly two decades as an automotive technician, service manager and auto service center manager. He was maintenance editor for *AOL Autos* and author of *How to Make Your Car Last Forever*.

Even the smartest people sometimes feel foolish when speaking with car mechanics. We often say yes to maintenance services because we figure that the auto mechanic knows what is best for our cars. However, car owners sometimes overspend because less-than-honest auto repair shops talk them into services that their cars don't really need. They also may not understand that today's vehicles have different needs than those of decades past.

Among the most common money-wasting mistakes car owners make...

Fluid Flushes

Some quick-lube shops, independent mechanics and car dealerships pressure car owners into replacing automotive fluids that still are perfectly fine. In some cases, this will mean draining the fluids... in others, they might recommend actually flushing the system out completely, cleaning out virtually every drop of the old fluid. In either case, these services can cost $70 to $150 or more apiece.

•**Brake fluid flushes.** Don't trust a shop that recommends you flush your brake fluid regularly. Brake fluid can last as long as your vehicle. There are exceptions, however. Your brake fluid might legitimately need to be flushed if moisture gets into the system or the brake fluid has overheated.

What to do: Visually inspect your brake fluid once or twice a year, or ask a mechanic you trust to do so when you stop by for some other service. Brake fluid should be clear or translucent. If the fluid is rust-colored, moisture might have gotten in and a flush might be warranted. If your brake fluid is black or has a burnt smell, your braking system likely has a problem that requires a mechanic's attention, not just a flush. If it is below the recommended level, it might have a leak.

If the brake fluid is clear or translucent, does not smell burnt and is at the correct level, agree to a flush only if your vehicle's maintenance schedule calls for it, which is rare.

•**Power steering fluid flushes.** Power steering fluid can last the life of a vehicle, too, unless otherwise noted in the vehicle's maintenance schedule.

What to do: Inspect the fluid once or twice a year, or ask a trusted mechanic to do so for you. It should be flushed and replaced if it smells burnt or you see black grime or metal flakes in the fluid—shining a light into the reservoir can help you spot these flakes. There could be an underlying problem that requires a mechanic's attention as well. Otherwise there's no need for the flush.

•**Transmission fluid flushes.** Automatic transmission fluid should be flushed occasionally—but some disreputable quick-lube shops recommend these flushes to seemingly every customer who comes in for an oil change. Most of those flushes are completely unnecessary and in some cases, might even hurt the transmission.

What to do: Have your transmission fluid flushed every 35,000 miles or so. Make sure that the shop replaces the filter when it changes the fluid. Some automakers say a transmission fluid flush isn't necessary until perhaps 100,000 miles, but transmission fluid is an oil and oil can break down over time, so this is one situation where it makes sense to err on the side of caution.

•**Engine oil flushes.** Ask some quick-lube shops and mechanics for a $25 oil change, and they will try to sell you a $100 to $200 engine oil flush. They'll claim this is the only way to clear years of sludge out of the engine. Trouble is, any sludge that an oil flush does dislodge could clog the oil pump pickup screen, causing more problems than it solves.

What to do: Have your oil changed, not flushed. Get oil changes according to your vehicle's maintenance schedule—that's likely every 5,000 miles or 7,500 miles, not every 3,000 miles, the old rule of thumb. Lean toward a high-quality synthetic oil, such as AMSOIL or Mobil 1, assuming that synthetic oils are recommended as an option in your vehicle's owner's manual. These cost a few dollars more but do a far superior job protecting your engine.

Unneeded Cleanings

Keeping a car clean might seem like a wise investment, but in some cases it's money misspent.

•**Brake system cleanings.** This typically involves taking the brakes apart and washing or even sandblasting the components, usually at a cost upward of $100. It's probably unnecessary. Modern braking systems are designed to pretty much take care of themselves without this treatment.

What to do: Don't agree to this unless it is recommended by a mechanic you trust and your vehicle has experienced a braking problem, such as a high-pitched squealing even though the brake pads are not yet worn out, which could be a sign that glazing has developed on the brake parts.

•**Fuel system cleanings.** Quick-lube shops sometimes recommend these every 5,000 or 10,000 miles. They inevitably claim that this $100-to-$150 service will pay for itself in improved gas mileage. That's true only if the fuel injectors were badly clogged. Fuel injectors can become clogged and require cleaning, but this generally happens slowly.

What to do: Get a fuel system cleaning every 35,000 miles or so. Anything more is overkill. Have this work done by a mechanic in a fully equipped shop that appears very well-stocked with modern-looking computerized equipment. Doing fuel system cleanings properly requires specialized equipment, tools and know-how that many shops lack.

•**Any service offered by a car wash beyond the wash itself.** The paint sealants, protectants, under-car sealant and color waxes that car washes offer tend to be virtually worthless. They're likely to wash away the first time the car is out in the rain.

What to do: The only service worth paying for at a car wash is a car wash.

But Don't Cut Corners

Sometimes not spending enough on vehicle maintenance ends up costing car owners. *Examples…*

•**Buying generic brake pads or delaying brake pad replacement.** Low-quality brake pads will wear out faster than higher-quality pads. That means you'll have to return to the shop sooner to replace them, more than offsetting any money saved by buying the cheaper part.

Delaying brake pad replacement or using low-quality brake pads also can increase the wear on the brake rotors. That could force you to replace both the pads and rotors, which could easily double or triple the cost of the brake job. Using worn-out or low-quality brake pads also could reduce your ability to bring your vehicle to a stop in an emergency.

What to do: Replace your brake pads as soon as they have worn down to less than one-quarter inch in depth. It might be time to replace the pads if your brakes consistently screech, too—perfectly good brake pads might screech on wet days, but if the brake pads are still good, that screeching likely will not persist throughout a long trip or once the weather dries up. Opt for high-quality brake pads, such as those made by Wagner or Bendix. These typically cost $15 to $20 more per pad than the generics, but that's a small price to pay for longer pad life, longer rotor life and greater safety. The original-equipment brake pads sold by dealerships likely are fine, too, but might be expensive.

•**Not replacing the air filter regularly.** There's no good excuse for not replacing your vehicle's air filter every 10,000 to 12,000 miles. Air filters are inexpensive—usually $15 to $20—and putting in a new one is a simple do-it-yourself job in most vehicles. If you don't want to do this yourself, a mechanic should be able to do this for you for the cost of the filter and a half-hour's labor or less. Continue to use a dirty air filter, and you cost yourself money by reducing your car's fuel efficiency.

What to do: If you want to minimize the long-term cost and hassle of replacing air filters, buy a K&N air filter (800-858-3333, KNFilters.com). These typically cost $60 to $110, but unlike conventional paper air filters, they can provide excellent fuel efficiency and filtration for the life of your vehicle. Just clean them every 50,000 miles using a K&N cleaning kit designed for the purpose. The kits cost around $15 and last for many cleanings.

•**Washing your car with household soap.** Common household soaps, such as dishwashing soap, might remove the wax coating from a vehicle or otherwise damage its finish.

What to do: Wash your car only with pH-neutral wash solutions specifically designed for use on vehicles. These are available in auto-parts stores and in the auto sections of discount stores. Or take the car to a car wash.

Questions to Ask When You Buy a Used Car from a Private Seller

Greg Macke, a car-buying specialist based in Ventura, California. CarBuyingSupport.com and YourCarAngel.com.

Nine questions to ask when you make the initial call to someone who is selling a used car...

Are you the original owner? It's a great sign if the answer is yes—it means that this owner should be able to make the car's entire history of service records available to you (more on service records below). If you get the sense that you are speaking with an honest, responsible person, it also suggests that the car has been in good hands for its entire life.

Follow-up question: If the seller is not the original owner, ask, "How long have you owned the car?" Having multiple owners does not necessarily mean that you should not buy this car, but do walk away if the seller has owned it for six months or less. This person might be reselling so soon because after buying, he learned that the vehicle has

a major problem...or he might be a flipper (also known as a "curbstoner") who regularly buys cars at auction and resells them by posing as a private seller. A high percentage of cars that pass through the auction system have serious problems. Asking about length of ownership also can help sniff out dishonest sellers because you can check the veracity of the seller's responses by getting a CarFAX report (see below).

•**Do you have the title? Is your name on that title?** Lack of a title—or a title in someone's name other than the seller's or perhaps the seller's spouse—might mean the seller is a flipper, scammer or thief. Flippers often do not re-title vehicles in their own names after obtaining them, so the title still might have a prior owner's name. Scammers have been known to sell cars they do not own, perhaps selling someone's car right out of his driveway while he is out of town if they can get their hands on the key. And of course, a car thief might sell stolen cars. Lack of a title also could mean that a lender still is owed payments on the car or that the title simply has been lost. The safe move is to walk away—at best, this is a complication you don't want to deal with...and at worst, someone is trying to sell you a car he doesn't own.

•**Has it ever been in an accident or repainted?** If the answer is yes to either, the safe move is to move on to other cars. Cars that have been in accidents are much more likely to have problems than cars that are accident free. Asking about repainting increases the odds that you will be told the truth here. A seller might be tempted to rationalize that a minor incident doesn't really count as an accident, but if repainting was required—as it usually is following accidents—this seller must either answer yes or tell an outright lie. (The Carfax report, which may include mention of accidents and other damage, often can help you spot lies here, too.)

•**How many miles are on it?** This probably was noted in the used-car listing, but ask anyway—it's a way to sniff out scammers. The actual owner/driver of a car usually knows its approximate mileage off the top of his head...while a flipper or scammer sometimes must check—these people might not recall the mileage they cited in the posting if it's not really a car they drive, they sell many cars and/or the car they are selling does not exist at all.

●**Where was it mostly driven—highways or around town?** A used car with 100,000 miles on its odometer still might be in great shape if 90,000 of those miles were on highways—and it might be a great deal, too, because the book value of high-mileage cars tends to be low regardless of how those miles were accrued. Highway miles are far easier on a car than city or town miles because they are smooth sailing with little of the stop and go that puts extra wear on brakes, suspension and transmission.

Insider tip: When you examine a high-mileage car that you were told was driven mostly on highways, check the bottom-right-hand corner of the brake pedal. If this looks heavily worn, the car probably has endured lots of hard stop-and-go driving… but if it looks relatively new, most of the miles likely were indeed highway miles. Also, look through the front grill at the radiator's thin metal fins. Ironically, the more dented these radiator fins are, the better. Dents in these radiator fins generally are caused by gravel and debris kicked up by cars ahead on the highway—such dents are less common and less substantial at sub-highway speeds—so lots of dents generally mean lots of highway use.

●**Do you have the service records? Can I see them?** A vehicle's service records let you confirm that it has received its scheduled maintenance. They provide key information about the seller, too. If the records show that maintenance was done by a new-car dealership, that's a great sign—this owner paid more than he had to in order to make sure that the work was done right. If the service records are all from the same independent garage, consider this a good sign as well—it generally shows that the seller has a good working relationship with a mechanic. It's extremely troubling if the seller does not have any service records or has only one or two recent receipts—the car might not have been properly main-

tained…or the seller might be a flipper who only recently acquired the car. It's somewhat troubling if the service records are available but disorganized or incomplete—people who do not take proper care of their records sometimes do not take proper care of their cars, either.

●**Why are you selling?** Be wary of responses along the lines of "I just have too many cars." That's an evasion that raises the question "Well, why did you end up with too many cars?" Maybe the seller had to buy an additional car because he could no longer rely on the car he's selling. Maybe he is a flipper who has too many cars because he buys lots of cars to resell. Better answers point to life changes and/or personal tendencies such as "We had another child and need something bigger"…"We're moving to the city and don't need two cars anymore"…or "I treat myself to a new car every few years."

●**What's the earliest I can see it?** It's crucial that you see used cars offered by private sellers as soon as possible—the best tend to be snapped up by the first buyer who sees them.

Tip: If your call to a seller goes to voice mail, leave a message and then immediately send a text asking if the seller has a minute to talk about the car. Your text will go through if the number is for a smartphone—and many people check and return texts more frequently than voice mails.

●**What's the VIN?** A car's vehicle identification number will help you obtain its report from Carfax, a company that provides vehicle owner histories and accident histories. Carfax reports don't necessarily contain every bit of pertinent data, but you generally can use one to confirm that the seller told the truth about ownership history and accident history. Also, a Carfax report can provide information about whether the original warranty still is in effect. (A single report costs $39.99, three cost $59.99, a package of six reports, $99.99, Carfax.com.)

CHAPTER 2

Cleaning and Laundry Tips

Housecleaning Shortcuts: Do Your Bathroom in Seven Minutes...Your Kitchen in 12...

The late Jeff Bredenberg, who wrote extensively about consumer issues and home management. He was based in Oreland, Pennsylvania, and wrote three cleaning books, including *How to Cheat at Cleaning*.

Keeping your house clean doesn't have to take hours. By learning a few tricks and shortcuts, you can have an orderly home in minutes.

The Right Supplies

Keep cleaning supplies in a plastic caddy with handles so that you can easily move items around the house as you work. If you live in a multistory home, keep a caddy and cleaning supplies on each floor.

Supplies that you should never be without (all available at supermarkets, discount stores and online)...

•**Microfiber cloths.** Microfiber pulls dirt into the fabric better than standard cotton fiber cloths or paper towels, requiring fewer swipes—often just one—to clean a surface. Between launderings, microfiber is easy to clean—just rinse under warm water and squeeze.

•**Electrostatic cloths.** Treated with chemicals to make them negatively charged, electrostatic cloths pick up dust particularly well. You can buy washable or disposable cloths.

•**Scrubber sponges.** Buy sponges that have a white, abrasive surface on one side. The white scrubber pad is abrasive enough to scour tough grime but less likely than other types of sponges to scratch surfaces.

•**Plastic toilet brush.** Unlike wire brushes, plastic won't scratch porcelain. Look for the type that comes with its own stand to catch drips.

•**Duster with extension wand.** Lamb's wool dusters and disposable dusting heads work well. (With feather dusters, sometimes the feathers break and the sharp ends can scratch furniture.)

•**Flat mop.** The flat style reaches under furniture easily. The removable pad can be washed in the washing machine. Or you can use a Swiffer mop with disposable moist pads.

•**Cleaning solutions and sprays.** You'll need a disinfecting cleaner. Look for both words—"disinfecting" and "cleaner"—on the label. (See page 30 for a homemade disinfectant that's safer than bleach.) A cleaner without disinfectant may not kill germs, while a disinfectant without cleaner won't loosen as much dirt from surfaces. You also will need glass cleaner and toilet bowl cleaner.

Bathroom: 7 Minutes

•**Clear counters** by putting toothbrushes, deodorant and other toiletries into drawers and cabinets.

•**Squirt toilet bowl cleaner** around the inner rim of the toilet.

• **Spray disinfecting cleaner on the toilet seat and exterior,** as well as on the sink, faucet, counter and tub.

• **Using a toilet brush, scrub the toilet bowl for 10 seconds.** Flush.

• **Spray glass cleaner on the mirror, and wipe with a microfiber cloth.**

• **Use a damp sponge to wipe (in order) sink and faucets, counter, tub, toilet seat, toilet exterior.** Use a microfiber cloth to wipe chrome so that it doesn't spot.

• **Tear off a six-inch length of toilet paper,** and use it to sweep up loose hair and other debris from floor and corners.

If you have an extra five minutes, add these steps: Toss the bath mat, tub mat and towels into the washing machine. Hang fresh towels. Mop the floor. Empty the trash can. Spray cleaner onto a microfiber cloth, and wipe off the doorknobs and any smudges on the door, light switches and cabinets.

Living Room: 12 Minutes

• **De-clutter all surfaces by putting magazines in racks,** DVDs in the TV cabinet and books on shelves.

• **Move all lightweight furniture**—such as chairs, end tables and magazine racks—into the center of the room (to make vacuuming and dusting easier).

• **Dust from the top down.** Walk around the room in a circle, using your duster's extension wand and a stepstool if needed to reach high moldings, shelves and lighting fixtures.

• **Walk around in a circle again, using an electrostatic cloth to dust any surfaces between your head and knees.** Switch to a clean cloth when necessary.

• **Run your dusting wand along the baseboards.**

• **Vacuum the perimeter of the room.**

• **Put furniture back in place, and vacuum the center of the room.** Vacuum sofa and chairs with

the upholstery attachment. If you have an extra few minutes, mop hard-surface floors.

Kitchen: 12 Minutes

• **Clear all counters**—put food away in the refrigerator and cupboards, place utensils in drawers and sweep papers into a basket to sort later. Put dirty dishes in the dishwasher.

• **Wipe counters with a sponge sprayed with disinfecting cleaner.**

• **Spray the sink with disinfecting cleaner, and wipe with a damp sponge.** Dry handles and faucet with a dish towel or microfiber cloth to prevent spots.

• **Pick up stray items from the floor, and put them away.**

• **Take throw rugs outside, and shake for 10 seconds.** Vacuum the floor. If it looks like it needs it, give the floor a quick mopping. Put throw rugs back.

• **Spray disinfecting cleaner onto a sponge and wipe the refrigerator, stove, microwave and other appliances.**

• **If you have a window over the sink,** spray it with window cleaner and wipe with a microfiber cloth.

Small Appliances

Cleaning tricks for small appliances…

• **Food processor.** Rinse the bowl to remove most food, then fill it halfway with water. Add a squirt of dishwashing liquid. Close, and turn the food processor on for 30 seconds. Rinse. Let the blades spin for a few seconds to dry.

• **Microwave oven.** Pour two cups of water into a microwave-safe bowl. Place the bowl in the middle of the microwave, and cook on high for five minutes to create steam. Using oven mitts, remove and empty the bowl—the water will be scalding hot. Wipe the inside of the oven with a damp sponge.

• **Garbage disposal.** Put a few lemon, lime or orange rinds in the disposal. Run cold water, and turn on the disposal. Grind until rinds are gone. The disposal will smell clean and fresh.

MORE FROM JEFF BREDENBERG...

Five Things to Stop Cleaning

1. Grill grate. Instead of scrubbing the grate after using it, leave the grill on high with the cover on for 15 minutes. Residue will cook away.

2. Shower curtain liner. Liners are so cheap that laundering them to remove mildew is a waste of time. Just replace your liner every six months.

3. Pillow. After washing and drying a pillow, it's never quite the same. Instead, throw it out, and buy a new one every six months.

4. Making the bed. Microscopic dust mites—a leading cause of allergies—thrive on moisture in your mattress and bedcovers. Leaving the bed unmade allows moisture to escape.

If you really can't stand an unmade bed, then use a duvet instead of a top sheet and bedspread. Just shake out the duvet, and you're done.

5. Waxing the car. Newer cars have tough finishes that don't need wax for protection.

Try a "Fresh Air" Cleaning

Jamison Starbuck, ND, a naturopathic physician in family practice in Missoula, Montana.

Increasingly, researchers are finding health risks associated with scented everyday household items, including cleaning products, laundry detergent, shampoo, bath gel, cat litter, air fresheners, incense, dryer sheets and body lotion. Research links air contaminants in these products to nervous system disorders (such as tremors), certain types of cancer, asthma, hormone imbalance, irritability, headache and fatigue. In one study conducted at the University of Washington in Seattle, air coming from laundry machines using top-selling liquid laundry detergent and scented dryer sheets was found to contain seven hazardous air contaminants, including two chemicals—benzene and acetaldehyde—that the Environmental Protection Agency classifies as carcinogens.

10 Ways to Clean with Baking Soda

Teapots and coffeepots come clean with one-quarter cup of baking soda in one quart of water—for tough stains, also add a little detergent and let soak overnight. **Fruits and vegetables** clean up safely with a little baking soda on a clean sponge. **For oil and grease stains,** sprinkle on some baking soda and scrub with a brush. **Car parts** come clean with one-quarter cup of baking soda in one quart of water—or make a paste for stubborn spots, such as tar or tree sap. **Tubs, sinks and tile** can be cleaned with baking soda and water. **For hands with onion or garlic smell,** rub on a baking-soda-and-water mixture. **To keep sneakers fresh,** shake some baking soda into them when not in use and shake them out before wearing them. **Washing machines** that have odors can be cleaned by running them empty with one-half cup of baking soda.

SavingFreak.com

Important: You may be surprised to learn that manufacturers of cleaning and laundry supplies as well as air fresheners are not required to inform consumers of the potentially harmful compounds found in their products. It's worth noting that the University of Washington study found that all of the scented products contained pollutants—even so-called "green" products.

To avoid these potentially harmful products, here's my advice...

•**Choose unscented household products.** This will not eliminate all risky compounds from these products, but it will improve your indoor air quality and reduce the related health risks. If you must use more noxious cleaning compounds, such as ammonia, do so sparingly and avoid nonessential products, including dryer sheets and air fresheners.

•**Use natural cleaning substances.** The granddaddy is vinegar (you can use equal parts of white

29

distilled vinegar and warm water for such chores as cleaning your windows...and straight vinegar will remove soap residue from shower doors). But there are other good natural options if you use a little old-fashioned elbow grease with such products as baking soda (good for cleaning sinks and deodorizing carpets) and steel wool pads (for scouring ovens).

•**Freshen your air naturally.** Rather than the toxic air fresheners that you buy at the supermarket, add a natural scent to the air.

What to do: Put a pint of water in a saucepan on your stove, and heat until it's almost boiling. Add one-quarter teaspoon of a spice, such as cinnamon, ginger or clove. Turn down the heat, and let the water simmer for about 10 minutes. The gentle scent will diffuse through your home without leaving any toxins behind.

Try all these quick and easy remedies for a home that's naturally clean.

The 8 Best Homemade Cleaners: Much Safer Than Store-Bought

Mandy O'Brien, Wisconsin-based biologist and coauthor of *Homemade Cleaners: Quick-and-Easy, Toxic-Free Recipes.* LivingPeacefullywithChildren.com

---

There's no way to know all the chemicals you are bringing into your home when you use commercial cleaning products. Thanks to loopholes in ingredient-disclosure laws, cleaning-product makers are not required to supply a complete list. But independent testing shows that many cleaners contain harsh or even toxic chemicals that have been linked to cancer, asthma, and skin and lung irritation. That includes some cleaners labeled with reassuring words such as "green," "nontoxic" and "biodegradable."

Example: The product Simple Green Concentrated All-Purpose Cleaner says "nontoxic" and "biodegradable" on its label, but testing by the Environmental Working Group, an organization of independent scientists, found that it contains a solvent known to damage red blood cells.

If you make your own cleaning products, you can better control what comes into your home. *The following eight do-it-yourself cleaners are safe, effective, inexpensive and easy to make...*

•**Two-step disinfectant that kills germs better than chlorine bleach**

1. Combine white distilled vinegar and water in a spray bottle in a 1:1 ratio. Spray this on surfaces as you would bleach.

2. Thoroughly wipe away the vinegar with a cloth or sponge.

3. In a separate bottle, add hydrogen peroxide and spray on the surface. Wipe off.

A researcher at Virginia Polytechnic Institute found that this system kills germs better than chlorine-based bleach. It's safer, too. Chlorine-based bleach (and commercial cleaners that contain it) can cause skin irritation and respiratory problems including asthma attacks, among other health concerns. Hydrogen peroxide is a type of bleach but is safer.

Important: Do not skip the wipe-down step. When vinegar and hydrogen peroxide combine, they produce peracetic acid, which has respiratory health risks similar to those of chlorine bleach.

•**Sweet-smelling sink scrub**

1. Mix one cup of baking soda...one tablespoon of ground cinnamon...and five drops of sweet orange essential oil in an airtight container. (Essential oils are available online and in pharmacies, health-food stores and at big-box retailers such as Target and Walmart. Prices vary but start at about $3 per ounce.)

2. Sprinkle a small amount of this mixture on a wet sink, and scrub with a cloth.

3. Rinse.

Baking soda is a wonderful mild abrasive—it removes grease, grime and soap scum without scratching surfaces.

•**Safe liquid hand soap**

1. Combine three tablespoons of liquid castile soap with one cup of water. (Liquid castile soap can be purchased online and in pharmacies, health-food stores and at big-box retailers such as Target and Walmart, typically for 50 cents to $1 an ounce.)

2. Add up to 10 drops of your favorite essential oil. (This step is optional. Essential oil makes the soap slightly more antibacterial, but mainly it adds scent.)

3. Stir until the soap dissolves.

4. Pour the mixture into a liquid soap dispenser.

Traditional detergent soaps contain harsh chemicals derived from petroleum. Castile soaps are instead made from plant oils and are extremely safe to use in our homes and on our skin.

Helpful: Unlike some all-natural hand soaps, this one foams. Foaming does not improve soap's cleaning power, but it could save you money—when soap does not foam, people tend to use more than necessary.

●**Floor cleaner with that familiar lemony scent**

1. Fill a bucket with hot water.

2. Mix in two tablespoons (or two large squirts) of liquid castile soap and 20 drops of lemon essential oil.

3. Allow your mop to soak in this mixture until it's saturated, then mop as normal.

This simple mixture cleans hard-surface floors including wood, tile and linoleum without harsh chemicals. It leaves behind a lemon smell that those of us raised in the era of Lemon Pledge associate with cleanliness.

Tip: If you're bored with lemon-scented cleaners, feel free to substitute another essential oil, such as lime, orange or grapefruit.

●**Glass cleaner that won't streak**

1. Combine one-half cup of white distilled vinegar with three-quarters cup of water in a spray bottle, and shake until mixed.

2. Spray on windows and mirrors.

3. Dry with a lint-free cloth or crumpled newspaper. (Newspaper is slightly more abrasive than paper towels, so it does a better job of removing dirt and debris...and newspaper does not leave behind bits of lint.)

Commercial glass cleaners often contain detergents that can leave streaks of residue. This simple vinegar-based detergent-free cleaner will not streak. (You might see streaks the first time or two you use it—that's the lingering residue from a previously used commercial cleaner.)

Tip: If you dislike the smell of vinegar, soak lemon peels, lime peels and/or orange peels in one-half cup of vinegar for at least one week. Strain out the peels, then use the now citrus-scented vinegar in place of the standard vinegar in the recipe above.

●**Effective, all-natural dish soap**

This soap is meant for washing dishes by hand...

1. Add one-quarter cup of tightly packed, grated bar soap (castile soap is available in bar form) to one-and-a-quarter cups of boiling water, and stir until dissolved.

2. Add one tablespoon of washing soda (washing soda can cause skin irritation, so be careful handling it) and one-quarter cup of liquid castile soap, stir again, then remove the mixture from the heat. (Washing soda can be found in the laundry aisle of many supermarkets.)

3. Allow the mixture to cool, then add 20 to 30 drops of the essential oil of your choice.

4. Store in a glass jar or a soap dispenser.

●**Effective natural dishwasher soap**

To make a natural dishwasher soap, combine one cup of borax...one cup of washing soda...one-half cup of kosher salt...and one-half cup of citric acid. Store in an airtight container. Use one tablespoon per dishwasher load.

●**Safe air freshener**

1. Mix one cup of baking soda with 20 to 30 drops of your favorite essential oil. (Citrus oils, such as grapefruit, lemon, lime or orange, are good options.)

2. Sprinkle the mixture on surfaces that require deodorization, such as carpets or upholstery. Leave on for 20 minutes or more, then vacuum up. Or place an open container of the mixture near the source of the odor.

Some commercial air fresheners actually spread neurotoxins throughout the home. Rather than remove or cover the odor, many work by deadening your sense of smell.

(For more ways to keep your home free from dangerous chemicals, see chapter "Healthy Home" on page 129.)

Homemade Hand Cleaner

If your hands are grimy from working on a grill or a car, mix one tablespoon of sugar with enough water to make a paste. Scrub your hands with it, then wash as usual.

TheManual.com, a website offering lifestyle advice for men.

Little-Known Uses for Plain White Toothpaste

Roundup of experts on uses of toothpaste, reported at FamilyHandyman.com.

Little-known uses for plain white toothpaste. *Shine jewelry:* Brush diamonds and other jewelry instead of using jewelry cleaner. *Get rid of car-interior smells:* Smear toothpaste on a paper towel, fold the towel and place it underneath car seats while the vehicle is parked in sunlight—as the car heats up, the paste will give it a fresh, minty odor. *Scrub nail stains caused by dark polishes:* Use a nailbrush or unused toothbrush. *Deodorize hands and containers:* Scrub hands with toothpaste. If a container has a residual smell, put some toothpaste in it before scrubbing it. *Remove table rings caused by placing glasses on wood:* Rub out the stain using toothpaste on a soft cloth, then finish the job using furniture polish or oil.

How to Clean Where It's Hard to Clean

Julie Edelman, known as "The Accidental Housewife," is a rich source of everyday tips to maintain your home, family, health and sanity. She is author of *The New York Times* bestseller *The Accidental Housewife: How to Overcome Housekeeping Hysteria One Task at a Time*. JuliesTips.com

Clever tricks to make your home clean and fresh…

•**Freshen your mattress.** Mix three to five drops of an essential oil (such as lavender, peppermint, citrus or eucalyptus) with one cup of baking soda. Sprinkle it on your mattress, and work it in with a stiff brush. Leave for one hour so that the baking soda can absorb odors and the oils can infuse the mattress. Vacuum, using an upholstery attachment for best results.

•**Remove toilet rings with cola.** Pour a can of cola into the bowl, and let it sit overnight to get rid of rings and rust. Or use a wet, used dryer sheet.

•**Keep air vents debris-free with car wax.** If you can, remove the vent grilles for a more thorough cleaning. (If not, take the hose of your vacuum and set it on the grille to remove as much dust and other debris as possible.) If the grilles are very dirty, wash them with dishwashing soap and water. Then vacuum inside the vent as far as you can reach, and wash with soap and water as you did the grilles. Wipe away any remaining dirt with a damp cloth. Before replacing the grilles, coat them with a thin layer of car wax and buff to prevent dust from building up and to maintain better air flow.

•**Use your hair dryer to clean radiators.** Place damp newspapers or cloths between the rungs and behind the radiator. Blow with your hair dryer to dislodge debris and dust. The papers or cloths will catch the dirt.

•**Put glass light fixtures in the dishwasher on the top rack.** Make sure to leave enough space to avoid potential breakage. Run on the gentle cycle.

•**Remove dust on cloth lamp shades with a lint roller.** Roll on the inside and outside of the shade until the dust is gone.

•**Prevent mold on houseplant soil with cinnamon.** Remove any visible mold growth on the surface of the soil, and discard it in a sealed plastic bag. Replace with a layer of fresh potting soil. Sprinkle on cinnamon or an essential oil such as tea tree oil or lavender to repel future mold growth.

• **Use a "Post-it" to clean your laptop keyboard.** Slide the sticky side of a Post-it note between the keys to remove dirt, dust and crumbs.

• **Wash makeup brushes in shampoo.** Most makeup brushes are made of hair, so clean them with a little shampoo and warm water. Use baby shampoo or another gentle shampoo that does not have conditioner in it. Rinse with cool water. Then reshape and lay the tips over the edge of the sink to dry.

• **Revive potpourri with vodka.** Revitalize your potpourri by spraying it lightly with vodka.

Easy Computer Clean

Dave Boyer, associate editor, *Bottom Line Personal.*

Easy way to clean a computer screen. Use a foam paint-brush to gently wipe away dust. They are available at most hardware stores for $1 or less. For cleaning more stubborn spots on your monitor, try a lightly dampened microfiber cloth.

The Queen of Clean's Amazing Stain-Removing Tricks for Counters, Carpets, Furniture, More

Linda Cobb, known as the Queen of Clean, author of *Talking Dirty with the Queen of Clean* and six other books on cleaning. Based in Glendale, Arizona, she has appeared as a cleaning expert on local and national radio and television talk shows and offers her tips at guest speaking engagements. QueenOfClean.com

No matter what household miracles a cleanser promises, certain stains appear destined to become permanent fixtures in our décor. These unsightly spots resist our best efforts to scrub or spray them away, whether we're using a popular product or great-grandma's homegrown concoction. Before throwing in the paper towel, you might do well to try these effective ways to remove seemingly immovable spots on counters, carpets, furniture, walls and appliances.*

The Kitchen

• **Countertops.** On porous granite or marble countertops, tough spills, such as wine and tomato-based stains, require quick action for the best results. Immediately blot up and spray water on the spot, then cover the area with a paste of baking soda and water that is the consistency of thick pancake batter. Cover this poultice with plastic wrap for 24 hours, then remove and wash with mild dish soap and water. Reapply if the stain isn't gone.

For especially difficult stains that are resistant to the baking soda poultice, especially stains that you have not dealt with immediately, try 3% hydrogen peroxide, first testing a small, discreet area for possible discoloration of the stone. Fold a piece of cotton gauze so that it is roughly the size of the stain, and saturate it with the hydrogen peroxide. Place the pad on the stain, then cover with plastic wrap and secure the edges with painter's tape. Leave a plate or other heavy object on top for 24 hours. Reapply if necessary. Wash off well when done.

On laminate countertops, which are especially prone to coffee, tea and wine stains, try a mixture of cream of tartar and lemon juice as thick as pancake batter. Rub gently in a circular motion, letting the mixture sit for an hour if necessary. Again, test in an inconspicuous spot first. For especially tough stains, nail polish remover or paint thinner may work, but if either one touches the counter seams, it can damage the glue. To avoid scratches, never use steel wool or abrasives on the counter.

On a wood counter, for a heat mark (a white mark where a hot object drew moisture from wood), massage petroleum jelly into the mark with your fingers, let it sit overnight and then wipe it off in the morning. If the mark is lighter but not gone, repeat

*With any cleaning method that you are trying on a particular surface for the first time, always test an inconspicuous area to make sure there are no adverse effects that outweigh the benefits.

the treatment. If this doesn't work, consider the following, but use extreme care.

Lay a folded towel over the spot, and press with an iron on the medium-hot setting for about a minute. If the mark isn't disappearing, turn to the steam setting on your iron and go over the towel again, alternating between steam and no steam.

Caution: Keep the iron moving, and keep it on the towel.

•**Stainless steel appliances may look impressive, but they pose a huge cleaning problem—** their finishes easily becoming smeared. Trying to clean them with soap and water can build up residue. After much trial and error, I found two methods that work.

CLR Stainless Steel Cleaner, a quick spray-and-wipe product, leaves a streak-free shine and removes fingerprints. CLRBrands.com

For mix-it-yourselfers, wring out a microfiber cloth in a solution of 50% warm water and 50% white vinegar. Wipe down the stainless steel surface, and quickly buff with a clean, dry microfiber cloth.

The Bathroom

•**Shower.** Soap scum on glass shower doors can pose a tough problem. To clean, rub on some undiluted liquid fabric softener, let it sit for about an hour, apply more softener, then rub with a gentle scrubbing sponge. Wash with liquid dish soap and water, then rinse and buff.

To remove soap scum, mold and mildew from plastic shower curtains and liners, put them in the washing machine with regular detergent and two cups of white vinegar. Add several old towels, and run them through the regular wash cycle. When the wash is done, gather the curtain in a towel to avoid dripping water and rehang in the bathroom, stretching it fully to dry.

•**Toilet.** Waterline ring can be a stubborn, nasty eyesore. To clean, shut off the water at the toilet tank and flush. Then spray on white vinegar, and sprinkle on borax. Rub the line with a piece of very fine drywall sandpaper. Turn the water back on, and flush.

•**Tile and grout.** Try one cup of borax, two cups of baking soda and one-to-two cups of hot water. Mix to pancake-batter consistency, then scrub on tiles and grout with a brush, and rinse well when done. Make sure that the brush is soft enough to avoid scratching the tile.

Carpets and Beds

•**Rugs and wall-to-wall carpeting attract all manner of stains.** Spray-on carpet spot-and-stain removers are an affordable solution for most stains, but effectiveness varies greatly from product to product. I've found Carpet CPR ($16.95 for a 32-ounce bottle, LeatherCPR.com)...Folex Instant Carpet Spot Remover (around $16 for a 32-ounce bottle, FolexCompany.com)...and Spot Shot ($10 for a 32-ounce bottle, SpotShot.com) to be effective. All are available on Amazon.com.

Warning: Never use laundry spot remover, laundry detergent, shampoo or dish soap on carpet stains. These contain detergents and other cleaners that you will never completely get out of your carpet. Dirt and grime are likely to stick to this detergent residue, making the carpet appear even dingier.

Pet urine is probably the number-one carpet stain problem. Pet urine stains are best treated as soon as possible. First blot up all that you can with paper towels. Once you have done that, spray on a solution of one-third white vinegar and two-thirds cool water. Again blot, blot, blot. Allow to dry, and then treat with carpet spot remover if there is a stain.

For odor, try Pee Whiz. It is an enzyme-based solution that eliminates odor by breaking it down rather than covering it up (available at Peewhiz.com). Use according to directions.

If you own a carpet-cleaning machine, now is the time to use it. Blot up all the urine you can, then treat with the vinegar/water mixture and extract it using cool water.

Some pet "messes," including vomit and feces, sit on top of the carpet. These require a special cleaning strategy.

Don't rush to scrape up the mess as most people tend to do. That smears the material deeper into the carpet fibers. Instead, pour a significant amount of baking soda onto the mess—cover it completely. Use a whole box if necessary.

The baking soda should draw the moisture out of the mess until the material is dry enough—you probably want to leave it overnight—to be gently lifted up with a paper towel, plastic bag or a plastic putty knife. Next, vacuum up the remaining baking-soda-and-mess residue using your vacuum's hose with no attachment—a hose alone provides the strongest suction on a vacuum cleaner. If there's discoloration, use one of the carpet spot-and-stain removers listed in the section about small stains.

●**Food.** For food on carpets, keep a bottle of club soda handy. When you have a liquid spill, pour on club soda and blot with a paper towel or cloth. The carbonation will lift the spill to the surface, and the salts will reduce staining. Keep applying and blotting until you see only clear water on your towel. Place a large pad of paper towels on the spot, and stand on it until the area is mostly dry, then gently brush the carpet.

●**Red wine.** White wine not only pairs well with fish, it also works on red-wine carpet spills. Pour white wine on the spill to neutralize the red wine and blot well. Follow by pouring on club soda and, again, blotting thoroughly.

Carpet Fixes with Household Items

To brighten heavily used carpeted areas, sprinkle the carpet with cornstarch, which absorbs dirt. Wait an hour, then vacuum.

To spot-clean carpeting, rub in white shaving cream, then blot with a damp white cloth. If the stain remains, pour a small amount of hydrogen peroxide on it, then cover with a damp white towel and steam with an iron.

Caution: Before trying any of these remedies, first test for colorfastness in an inconspicuous area.

Barbara Weltman, Esq., author/publisher, *Big Ideas for Small Business*, a free online newsletter, Millwood, New York. BigIdeasForSmallBusiness.com

●**For any sort of set-in carpet stain, try one cup of 3% hydrogen peroxide and one teaspoon of ammonia.** Saturate the stain, let it sit for a few hours, then blot. If the solution releases some of the stain, continue to treat until the spot is gone.

Caution: Never mix ammonia and chlorine bleach.

Walls and Furniture

●**Walls.** Young children often leave their creative marks in unexpected places. For felt-tip marker on hard surfaces such as furniture and plastic, rub firmly with a clean dollar bill. This often will remove the spot entirely.

Using washable crayons can prevent problems. For regular crayon on walls, spray a paper towel with WD-40 lubricant and wipe off the marks. Wash with warm water and liquid dish soap, then rinse.

To remove kids' stickers from walls or other hard surfaces, heat the sticker with a blow dryer, pointing it at an angle to the sticker. Use a dull edge—a credit card or putty knife—to gently peel up the sticker.

If you have soot on the wall near a fireplace, don't touch it with water. Instead, use a dry dirt-and-soot-removal sponge to erase the soot. You can find these at most hardware stores.

●**Furniture.** Have water rings on wood furniture? Add a little salt to a glob of regular mayonnaise, work it into the ring in a circular motion for a few minutes and leave overnight. Wipe it off in the morning. If there's improvement, keep at it until the mark is gone.

Easy Silver Cleaner

Graham and Rosemary Haley, household task experts, Toronto, and authors of *Haley's Cleaning Hints: A Compilation.*

Fill the kitchen sink with one quart of hot water. Add one tablespoon of water softener, such as borax, and one tablespoon of salt. Place a sheet of aluminum foil at the bottom of the sink and place silver on it. Silver should come clean within seconds.

Fast Paint Cleanup

Popular Mechanics, 300 W. 57th St., New York City 10019.

Put the paint tray inside a plastic bag so that the bag acts as a sleeve. Then pour the paint on top of the bag. When you're finished painting, just throw away the bag.

Many Wood Floor Cleaners Are Bad for Wood Floors

Debbie Gartner, founder of TheFlooringGirl.com, which provides flooring and home décor advice. She previously owned a flooring store in the New York City area.

Many of the best-known, most heavily advertised wood cleaners, including Murphy Oil Soap, Mop & Glo and Orange Glo, actually are poor choices for your wood floors. They contain oils or waxes that can temporarily make floors look shinier…but that also build up a residue on the floor and degrade the polyurethane finish. Instead, select a cleaner that specifically says it is formulated for hardwood floors and leaves no residue. One good choice is Bona Hardwood Floor Cleaner. It's effective, widely available, inexpensive and easy to use (US.Bona.com).

Clever Cleaners for Odd Spots (and Situations!) in Your Home

Julie Edelman, aka "The Accidental Housewife." Julie appears regularly on the *Today* show, *Rachael Ray* and *The Doctors*. She is author of *The New York Times* best-seller *The Accidental Housewife: How to Overcome Housekeeping Hysteria One Task at a Time*. JuliesTips.com

Sure you can buy cleaners with special chemicals. But often you don't need to! *Here are clever ways to clean and fix things using items that you probably have at home…*

Use an Onion to Clean Your Grill

All you need to clean a grill is half an onion and a fork (the longer, the better). While the grill is very, very hot, spear the top of the onion (cut horizontally) with the fork and scrub the grill with the cut side to remove the grime.

The Food Republic blog explores the "culture of food" for people who want to eat, drink and live better. FoodRepublic.com

Clean & Simple

• **Polish faucets and more with newspaper.** Newspaper ink is a terrific polishing agent that requires no water or liquid, so just crumple a piece of newspaper and rub.

• **Shine shoes and plants with bananas.** Banana peels contain oil and potassium, key ingredients in store-bought shoe polish. Wipe shoes with the inside of the peel (discard the stringy parts of the peel first). Then buff with a clean cloth. You also can use the peels to clean the dust and debris from leafy houseplants.

• **Clean car tires with mayonnaise.** To rid your tires of tree sap and road tar, dab a bit of mayonnaise onto the marks. Leave on for 10 minutes. Wipe away residue with a clean cloth. The vinegar in the mayo acts as a natural cleaner, and the oil and eggs add shine.

• **Remove mold in a refrigerator drip pan with white vinegar.** Vinegar is a natural sanitizer and bacteria killer. Put some in a spray bottle, and apply directly to the area. Let it sit for 20 minutes before wiping with a clean cloth.

• **Get rid of dishwasher gunk and odors with Kool-Aid.** Fill the dishwasher dispenser with a packet of lemonade Kool-Aid or any powdery drink mix that contains citric acid. Run the empty dishwasher for a full normal cycle to remove gunk, lime and rust stains as well as odors.

• **Remove scuff marks on floors and shower curtain scum with tennis balls.** *Scuff marks*: Cut an X in a yellow tennis ball (pink could leave color on your floor). Place the ball on the top part of a broomstick. Rub the ball back and forth on the floor to erase scuffs. *Shower curtain scum:* Throw one or two tennis balls into your washing machine with your shower curtain along with one cup of white vinegar and your usual amount of laundry detergent. Run on the regular cycle. The ball acts as a scrub to remove scum and mildew…vinegar kills mold.

• **Clean latex paint from your skin with baby oil.** Gently rub baby oil anywhere on your skin that has paint. Then wash with soap and hot water.

• **Remove deodorant marks on clothing with the foam from dry-cleaner hangers.** Remove the foam from a hanger, and rub it back and forth forcefully on deodorant marks. Panty hose works too.

• **Clean silver jewelry with toothpaste.** Squirt a small amount of regular nongel toothpaste onto your jewelry (gel toothpaste is too slippery to scrub away dirt and tarnish). Brush with a toothbrush, then rinse with warm water and blot dry with a soft towel. This works great and is easier and cheaper than silver polish.

• **Wash inside vases and Thermoses with eggshells.** For hard-to-clean objects such as vases and Thermoses, rinse with warm water, then add two crushed eggshells. Fill with warm water and a squirt of dishwashing soap. Shake thoroughly, and rinse with hot water.

Prior to cleaning vases and Thermoses, wash the eggshells with hot water to remove any remaining egg or residual membrane. You can store cleaned, air-dried shells in a cool, dry place.

• **Remove dust and debris from artificial plants and silk flowers with salt.** Dust can adhere and be hard to remove. Pour one cup of salt into a paper shopping bag. Place the plant in the bag, and shake vigorously for 30 seconds to remove dust and dirt. Use a pastry brush to remove remaining debris.

• **Clean tarnished copper pots and silver with ketchup.** Apply a thin coat of ketchup to the item. (First test on a small inconspicuous area to be sure that it doesn't cause any discoloration.) Leave for 15 minutes. For nooks and crannies, work the ketchup in with a toothbrush. Rinse off with warm water, and dry. Due to its high acidic composition (vinegar and tomato paste), ketchup is a nontoxic alternative to store-bought cleaners and less expensive.

• **Clean with lemon and baking soda.** If you don't like to use chemical cleaners, sprinkle baking soda on a nonporous surface, such as stainless steel, quartz or laminate, and buff with half a lemon. Then wipe with a damp cloth. For tougher messes or burnt-on gunk, coat the halved lemon in salt—this makes it a more abrasive scrubber. Make sure not to use lemon on porous surfaces such as marble and limestone because the citric acid can cause damage. And to be ultra-safe, test on an inconspicuous area before using to ensure that this won't harm the surface you're cleaning.

• **Remove bubble gum from hair with creamy peanut butter.** Before you snip those locks, reach for peanut butter—the oilier, the better! Put a dab on a toothbrush, and brush the gummy area. Use a little at a time. Repeat if necessary, and then shampoo. Plain oil works, too, but kids tend to get a kick out of peanut butter.

Soap-Scum Removal Trick

RD.com

You know how hard it is to wipe off the soap buildup on shower stalls, unless you use a harsh chemical solvent that's rough on the lungs. Use this handy pantry item instead…

Spray the shower-door glass with cooking spray and leave for 30 minutes. The oil "slides" between

Neater Way to Clean Grout

Use a bleach pen, such as the one sold by Clorox, to trace light or white grout lines without getting bleach all over your tiles. Wait 10 minutes and rinse. You may need two tries to get really mildewed grout clean. Be sure to run the bathroom fan, and avoid contact with skin.

The Family Handyman. FamilyHandyman.com

Fizzy Toilet Cleaner

Clean a toilet bowl with Alka-Seltzer. Drop two Alka-Seltzer or Polident effervescent tablets into the bowl. Let them fizz and remain for 15 to 20 minutes. Clean with a toilet brush scrubber and flush.

Julie Edelman, aka "The Accidental Housewife," is a rich source of everyday tips to maintain your home, family, health and sanity. She is author of *The New York Times* best-seller *The Accidental Housewife: How to Overcome Housekeeping Hysteria One Task at a Time*. JuliesTips.com

the scum and the glass, making it easy to wipe away. Clean off the oil with a vinegar-water spray solution (mix one-half cup hot water with one-half cup white vinegar in a spray bottle) and a damp sponge or rag. Your shower doors will sparkle!

Note: Be sure to wipe off any residual oil off your shower floor or bathtub with a clean, dry towel so you (or other showerers) don't slip.

Keep Dark Clothes Dark

Heloise, internationally syndicated newspaper and magazine columnist, San Antonio, and author of many best-selling books, including *All-New Hints from Heloise*. Heloise.com

Turn dark clothes inside out before putting them in the washer to limit abrasion, slowing the fading process. Air-drying further limits fading.

•**Eliminate ring around the collar.** Squirt a small amount of inexpensive hair shampoo onto the ring, and rub it together before putting the shirt in the wash. Shampoo is designed to clean body oil and sweat from hair, and it does this just as well on shirt collars.

Helpful: To avoid future rings, wipe your neck with rubbing alcohol or a baby wipe in the morning after you shower. Those with chronically sweaty necks also can apply antiperspirant on their necks before dressing.

•**Remove ballpoint-ink stains.** Place the washable garment on a towel, stain-side down. Lightly dampen

a cloth with rubbing alcohol (test an inconspicuous area of the garment first to make sure the fabric is alcohol-safe), and use this to dab the stain from the opposite side of the fabric—just dab, don't rub. Don't dab from the stain side, which can push ink further into the fabric. Continue dabbing until no more ink comes off onto the dabbing cloth or towel beneath. (Move the towel frequently so that there is always a clean area under the stain to absorb the ink.)

Apply stain pretreater or liquid laundry detergent directly to the remaining ink stain, let it set for a few minutes, then wash according to the garment's care instructions. Air-dry.

Never put any stained item into a dryer. The dryer's heat makes any stain that remains more difficult to remove.

Keep Front-Loader Free of Mold

Derek Laquerre, former appliance repairman for Sears.

Front-loading washing machines are particularly prone to a buildup of mold, which can cause foul odors and stains on light-colored clothing, but it's easy to get rid of. Once a week, give the rubber door seal a wipe with a cloth moistened with white vinegar. And once a month, run a tub-sanitizing wash cycle (check your washer's manual because the names for this cycle vary). When the machine fills, add one gallon of white vinegar through the detergent drawer. If you don't have a sanitizing feature, set the machine to a heavy-duty wash setting and the hottest water temperature and add the vinegar when the machine is finished filling. Do this once a month, and your machine should stay mold-free.

Also: Using glass cleaner on the inner door can help maintain a good seal. And leave the door ajar when the machine is not in use to help discourage mold from growing.

Tricks to Save on Dry Cleaning

Mary Marlowe Leverette, who has taught fabric care at Clemson University. Based in Columbia, South Carolina, she has a degree in home economics with a specialty in textiles and is the Guide to Laundry expert for the website TheSpruce.com

Having a garment dry-cleaned can cost any-where from a few dollars to $20 or more, depending on the garment and your region. *Here's how to greatly reduce dry-cleaning costs…*

Is It Really "Dry Clean Only" ?

Dry cleaning is truly required only if…

•**The garment is "structured," meaning that it's designed to hold its shape.** This includes most suits, jackets and some heavily tailored blouses.

•**The garment is made from acetate, rayon, leather or suede, fabrics that can be damaged by washing in water.** Dry cleaning also is pru-dent with silk and wool garments that have "dry clean only" tags. But nonstructured wool gar-ments with "dry clean only" tags usually can be gently hand-washed using a delicate detergent designed for wool, such as Woolite.

•**The garment isn't colorfast.** Place a few drops of water on an interior seam, and rub it with a cotton swab. If color comes off on the swab, the garment should be dry-cleaned.

If a garment does not fall into any of the above categories, it probably can be safely washed using a gentle, natural soap that contains no enzymes, such as Castile soap. Hand-wash if you have the time. If not, set your washer to cold water and gentle cycle. Hang to dry, or lay the garment flat on a towel or a mesh rack.

Do-It-Yourself Dry Cleaning

If clothes do require dry cleaning…

•**Use home dry-cleaning kits.** These kits are effective at removing odors, light wrinkles and minor stains, but they are not for major stains, oil-based stains or heavy creases.

Basically, you treat the stains using the solu-tion in the kit…put the garments into a sealable dryer bag with a towelette moistened with dry-cleaning solvent…then put the bag in the dryer for 30 minutes. Remove, and hang garments (or lay them flat) immediately after the dryer cycle ends.

Example: Dryel home dry-cleaning kits do an excellent job (Dryel.com).

•**Keep a stain stick or stain removal wipes handy.** These prevent many types of stains from setting. They're safe for most "dry clean only" fab-rics, but not silk or wool.

•**Buy a laundry steamer.** These can remove light wrinkles and freshen up "dry clean only" clothes.

Example: Steamfast SF-452 ($39.99, Steam fast.com).

•**Let "dry clean only" garments air out for at least several hours after wearing.** Wrinkles some-times fall away when fabrics are allowed to hang freely.

Smart idea: Keep a 12-inch section of hanger space open in your closet for the clothes you wore the prior day.

•**Search for coupons on cleaners' websites and in local papers.** Also some cleaners offer dis-counts when garments are brought in midweek.

Trick to Protect Clothes In the Wash

Jeff Yeager, author of *The Cheapskate Next Door* and *Don't Throw That Away!*

Zip up your jeans and other garments that have metal zippers before laundering. The little teeth are like miniature chain saws that can damage oth-er clothing in the washer and dryer.

Best Months to Dry-Clean Drapes and Bed Linens

Nora Nealis, executive director, National Cleaners Association, New York City.

January, July and August. These are slow months for most dry cleaners. Many offer discounts of about 15%. If a discount is not advertised, ask for one.

Laundry Error to Blame for Persistent Athlete's Foot

Study titled "The effect of domestic laundry processes on fungal contamination of socks," published in *International Journal of Dermatology*.

Why is it so tough to make athele's foot go away and not come back? A recent study suggests a surprising reason—you may be inadvertently reinfecting yourself by doing your laundry wrong! Worse, you're putting more than just the skin of your feet at risk—because the same fungi responsible for athlete's foot also can spread, bringing on toenail infections (tinea unguium) and jock itch (tinea cruris). *Here's what your laundry has to do with the unsightly scaling and unbearable itching...*

Laundry lesson: Yes, we all want to save energy—but skimping on the hot-water wash isn't the way to go to fight athlete's foot, toenail fungus and jock itch. According to a recent study publish in the *International Journal of Dermatology*, warm water just doesn't cut it because it's barely above body temperature. Problem is, in the US, household water heaters typically are set to 120°F to minimize the risk of scalding.

Solutions: If you are prone to recurrent fungal infections, you could set your water heater to 140°F (and then take care not to scald yourself while using a sink, shower or tub). Or if you have a top-loading washing machine, you could (carefully!) pour in a kettleful of boiling water once the machine has filled.

What about the dryer? The study mentioned above did not look at the effects of drying fungi-contaminated socks in a clothes dryer, so we can't say. However, many clothes dryers may not get hot enough to kill off fungi (for instance, according to GE, its high heat setting is 135°F)...and researchers didn't examine how long a drying cycle might be needed to destroy fungi. One thing we do know, though, is that no matter whether you line-dry or use a clothes dryer, dark and moist environments are fungi-friendly—so make sure that your socks and underwear get thoroughly dried before you put them away in a drawer.

CHAPTER 3

Declutter and Make Money

Quick Cures for Clutter— All You Need Is 10 Minutes or Less

Julie Morgenstern, organizing and time-management expert, consultant and speaker based in New York City. Her books include *Organizing from the Inside Out and Time to Parent.* JulieMorgenstern.com

You may be putting off clearing out clutter because the task seems daunting and tedious— but it doesn't have to be. Simply by breaking clutter-clearing into smaller projects, you can make progress in as little as five to 10 minutes at a time.

And you'll be glad you did. Your living or working space will become much more pleasant and efficient almost before you know it.

Important: Be sure that each "mini-project" you do can be completed in the allotted time. The satisfaction and sense of control you gain will keep you motivated for the next mini-project and the next one.

Here, quick clutter-clearing steps for common clutter problems. *You can do each step in 10 minutes or less...*

KITCHEN: Organize Your Storage Containers

10 minutes: **Cull and sort.** Pull everything out of the container cupboard. Sort through what you have. Keep only the containers that you use most often and that have lids. Put the rest in discard/giveaway bags.

Put the keepers back in the cupboard. To save space, nest containers that are the same shape.

10 minutes: **Organize the lids.** Double-check that every lid in your collection has a container that it fits. Toss any stray lids. If you have more than one lid for a container you love, you can keep the extra, but don't keep more than two lids for any container.

Stack lids of similar shape underneath their nested containers, or place all lids together on their sides in a single storage container so that they stand up vertically and are easy to pull out.

KITCHEN: Clean the Refrigerator

10 minutes: **Clean just one shelf or drawer.** By working in 10-minute chunks, you soon will get through the whole refrigerator.

Pull all items out of the section you've chosen, and place them on the kitchen table or counter. Throw out all food that is past its printed expiration date... any produce that is going limp...leftovers whose age you are unsure about...and anything that causes you to ask, Is this still good?

Wipe the shelf or drawer with a clean, damp sponge sprinkled with baking soda, then dry with a dish towel. Replace the fresh items.

BATHROOM: Organize the Cabinet Under the Sink

5 minutes: **Measure and order.** The inside of the typical under-sink cabinet is just a big, inefficient space.

Solution: Fit your cabinet with stacking drawers. First, measure the inside of the cabinet. Then order stacking drawers online in plastic or metal mesh. Each stack should be at least two drawers high and narrow enough to fit on either side of the sink's drainpipe. If you keep tall cleaning supplies such as glass or toilet bowl cleaners under the cabinet, allow space for those.

Recommended source: The Container Store, ContainerStore.com.

10 minutes: **Assemble and assign.** Unpack and assemble the drawers, and decide what category of object will go in which drawer.

Example: One drawer could hold cleaning supplies such as sponges, scouring powder and rubber gloves…one drawer could hold extra toilet paper and facial tissues…another could hold a hair dryer and accessories.

10 minutes: **Toss and install.** Pull everything out of the cabinet. Discard any used sponges, old razors and toiletries you no longer use. Place the drawers inside the cabinet, and put all objects into their new locations.

HOME OFFICE: Tidy Papers

10 minutes: **Sort.** The papers cluttering the surface of your desk represent to-dos. Quickly divide the papers into stacks, with one stack for each type of to-do.

Examples: Call…write…pay…return…order…check with family member…brainstorm…file.

Label each stack by writing the category name on a sticky note and putting the note on top of the stack.

Remind yourself to do nothing else but sort in this session. Do not stop to read any of the papers or do any of the tasks. Otherwise you will never get through the clutter.

5 minutes: **Set up a simple action system.** Put each stack into its own manila folder. If you are a highly visual person, use colored folders. Write the task category on the front of the folder in large bold letters and on the side tab.

Keep the folders handy and visible. Either stack them on the corner of your desk, put them in stacking trays or place them in a vertical rack.

Whenever you have five or 10 minutes between other activities, you can go through one of the folders and take action. Often you can get through an entire folder in 10 minutes when you are focused.

BEDROOM: Clear Your Night Table

5 minutes: **Choose what will stay.** Decide what few objects you want/need on your bedside table.

Examples: Reading lamp…alarm clock or mobile phone…book…small basket that holds reading glasses, bookmarks, highlighter, pen, small notepad.

10 minutes: **Cull.** Remove everything else from the table—many items will be objects that have found their way in from other rooms. Discard trash, and put items that belong elsewhere into a basket with handles, a small plastic tub or other portable container.

10 minutes: **Carry the container around the house,** and deliver anything that belongs elsewhere to its appropriate spot.

FAMILY ROOM: Organize CDs and DVDs

10 minutes: **Choose categories.** On a piece of paper, list the broad categories of your video and music collections. Use terms that you and your family would be most likely to think of when looking for a CD or DVD.

Examples: Your movie categories might include action…comedy…kids…drama. Your music might be sorted by genre such as jazz or classical, or by mood, task or time of day you would be likely to listen to it, such as relaxing on Sunday afternoon…cleaning the house…working out…entertaining guests.

10 minutes: **Sort and retrieve.** Quickly go through all the cases—whether or not they contain their CDs or DVDs—and sort them by category. Then gather all loose CDs and DVDs, and put them back in their cases. Return the cases to their storage shelves, separated by category. If you like, label the categories.

If your collection is large, you can spend five to 10 minutes at a time alphabetizing each section to make titles or artists easier to find. However, don't bother alphabetizing unless the rest of your family values the convenience and will commit to replacing recordings in alphabetical order every time.

Best Places to Turn Your Clutter into Cash

Lauren Greutman, author of *The Recovering Spender: How to Live a Happy, Fulfilled, Debt-Free Life.* LaurenGreutman.com

Craigslist and eBay are not the only online ways to sell your unwanted possessions—and not necessarily the best, either.

Alternatives for selling locally: Facebook marketplace. There are several easy-to-use apps to sell locally, such as 5miles, OfferUp and Mercari, but their customer base can be limited. Facebook marketplace, launched in 2016, has a messaging feature that allows you to remain private to Facebook's enormous audience until you have a committed buyer. You can list anything, including cars and real estate (you must be 18 or older to use this platform). The caveat is that you might receive multiple messages and questions from individuals who are "just looking." Facebook also has a link to report problems and a Purchase Protection feature on shipped items. Facebook.com/marketplace

Similar to 5Miles: If 5miles (or other apps like it) has few or no listings in your area, suggesting that it is not yet widely used there, see whether VaragesSale has a larger number of listings. Like 5miles, this app offers a safety-first way to sell things locally, with no cost for buying or selling. You can post the items you have for sale from VarageSale's website rather than its app if you prefer. Buyers and sellers initially connect via Facebook so that they can see who they are dealing with before they agree to meet. Local administrators review all the prospective buyers and sellers before they can engage in transactions. 5Miles also features a "5 Miles Dash" for on-the-spot bidding. 5milesapp.com, VarageSale.com

Also consider the following websites and free Android/iOS apps that can help you reach precisely the type of buyers who will pay you the most for what you have to sell…

Best for selling women's fashion: Poshmark. Women's clothes, shoes and accessories sold through this app tend to fetch higher prices than they would on eBay or Craigslist. Poshmark shoppers generally are style-conscious and willing to pay a bit more for pieces they love. The app is ideal for items made by desirable designers such as Michael Kors, Louis Vuitton and Alexander Wang. (You can sell men's and kid's clothes through Poshmark as well, but those categories typically attract fewer buyers.) The app makes selling simple—use your phone to take photos of an item and fill in a few details such as size and price. Poshmark takes a 20% commission on most sales or a flat $2.95 commission on sales under $15. Poshmark.com

Best for selling books: Amazon Seller app. Internet retailing behemoth Amazon.com lets you sell things through its very popular site. The Amazon Seller app makes this sales process especially easy—use your smartphone to scan the book's barcode, and most of its details will be automatically entered into Amazon. (You also can type in book titles if there is no barcode. Or items can be listed directly through Amazon's website if you'd rather not use your phone.) You can use this app to sell virtually anything Amazon sells, but the app is especially useful for selling books, given the huge number of book shoppers on Amazon. If your item sells, Amazon typically takes a 15% commission plus a 99-cent per-item fee, although the commission varies by the type of product. (If you're selling a lot of items, you can avoid that 99-cent per-item fee by paying a $39.99 monthly fee to become an Amazon Professional Seller.) Amazon.com

Best for selling consumer technology: Gazelle. If you are trying to sell a smartphone, tablet, laptop computer or some other piece of relatively modern consumer technology, Gazelle is the simplest option. With Gazelle you don't have to take photographs, write up a listing, figure out packaging or deal with buyers. Just identify your product on Gazelle.com (Gazelle is a website, not an app), and if the product is something that the site thinks it can sell, the company will send you appropriate prepaid packaging so that you can easily ship the device to it. Gazelle sends you a payment either via PayPal or check. With the plethora of electronic items on the market, including all models of cell phones, tablets and laptops, Gazelle can be quite selective and the payout is usually significantly less than you might get from a private sale (see local apps above). Gazelle.com

Best for selling antiques: Tias.com has been the Internet Antique Shop since 1995. It has a huge amount of listings, and gives you a broad audience because it's used by many antiques shoppers. (You can sell antiques through eBay and Etsy as well, but large items will do better on 5miles, Craigslist or VarageSale.) You can also open an online antique store at Tias for $39.95 a month. Call 800-OLD-STUFF for more information. If the item sells, Tias claims a 10% commission. You can create a Tias account at their website. Tias.com

Get the Most Money for Your Collectibles

Harry L. Rinker, owner of Rinker Consulting, an antiques-and-collectibles appraisal service based in Kentwood, Michigan. HarryRinker.com

Surprise! Your kids don't want Grandma's china. And neither do anyone else's kids. Their reluctance reflects the fact that today's young adults and even middle-agers are not collectors. They've taken decluttering to heart and have little interest in filling their shelves with figurines (or anything else) or their living rooms with uncomfortable 100-year-old furniture. At the same time, generations that did collect now are seeking to downsize.

Result of this double whammy: Sellers of most kinds of antiques and collectibles dramatically outnumber buyers these days. If you try to sell yours, you might discover that they're worth a lot less than you thought. Some once-sought-after items are selling for prices no higher than they fetched in the 1970s and 1980s.

Antique wood furniture and anything associated with fancy dining room meals—china services and antique flatware, for example—have fared especially poorly, but values have dropped sharply virtually across the board.

Exceptions: Values have been strong among items sporting labels from a small number of famous high-end luxury brands that young adults know and respect such as Gucci handbags or Rolex or Patek Philippe watches…and among 1980s and 1990s toys, games, fashions and music and movie memorabilia. When today's younger generations do collect, it tends to be things that they are nostalgic for from their youths.

If you're thinking, I'll wait for prices to rebound to sell, think again. The antiques-and-collectibles market is unlikely to rebound in the foreseeable future. With prices in steep decline, even people who do enjoy collecting are cutting back on buying—they don't want to invest in objects that seem likely to continue to lose value.

So what's the best way to sell antiques and collectibles in this market?

STEP 1: **Determine the true current value of the item.** If your goal is to sell, it doesn't matter how much you paid for an item…how old it is…or how much sentimental value it has for you. It doesn't matter that there are similar items for sale for big bucks online—some sellers continue to ask steep prices, but those sellers are not finding buyers. It might not even matter that the item has an impressive value in a price guide, because many prices in guides are out of date in this fast-moving market. If you're selling, the only thing that matters is what buyers will pay today. *To determine that…*

•**Check online sale prices on WorthPoint.com and/or eBay.** WorthPoint tracks actual sale prices —not asking prices—in auctions on eBay and elsewhere. Pay most attention to the most recent sales. (WorthPoint costs $26.99 to $42.99/month following a seven-day/seven-item lookup free trial.)

You also can look up recent auction results on eBay. Only the past 90 days of completed auctions are accessible for free, but these recent results are the most meaningful anyway. Enter a description of your item, then click "Sold Items" in the left menu to see the prices that similar items brought.

•**Pay an appraiser to do a "walk-through appraisal."** Expect to pay $125 to $400 per hour for an appraisal that might take one to three hours depending on how many antiques or collectibles you have, where you live and the appraiser's level of expertise. Choose an appraiser who is certified by the American Society of Appraisers (Appraisers.org) and/or the International Society of Appraisers (ISA-Appraisers.org). Extensive training is required to receive these certifications. Ignore other appraisal certifications, many of which can be obtained simply by paying a fee. Seek an appraiser who specializes in the types of antiques and collectibles you own…or a generalist if you have a wide-ranging collection. A local museum might be able to recommend appropriate appraisers.

Tell the appraiser that he/she will not be allowed to purchase anything from your collection. That reduces the odds that a disreputable appraiser will provide intentionally low estimates of certain items in your collection in hopes of buying them from you at unfair prices. And ask the appraiser whether he operates according to Uniform Standards of Professional Appraisal Practice (USPAP) guidelines, the profession's code of ethics.

STEP 2: **Sell smart.** Where and how to sell depends on what you have, how much time you are willing to invest and your goals…

•**eBay is the best place to sell an item if you discover that comparable items tended to attract multiple competitive bids there recently.** To improve the odds that your item attracts bids, list it for a starting price perhaps 20% below the starting price of other, similar listings. In a declining market, it's better to sell an item for a little less than you might have than risk not selling it at all.

•**Using an estate-sale company is the best option for items that are not in demand on eBay.** Despite what they're called, these companies don't sell only estates of the recently deceased. This selling route is a better bet than garage sales, which require lots of work and don't always draw big crowds or big spenders. And estate-sale companies are much more likely than auction houses to be interested in selling your possessions these days—auction houses are struggling to find bidders and tend to want only very high-end items.

•**Find estate-sale companies in your area through EstateSales.net**—click the "Hire a Company" tab. Most estate-sale companies work for a percentage of the sale's revenues, generally between 25% and 50%. Before hiring one of these companies, ask how much it charges…whether it has a professional appraiser on its staff (request that appraiser's qualifications, as described earlier)…and how it will advertise your sale. Speak with at least two companies before making a choice. If the commissions you're quoted are close to 50%, double-check whether local auction houses are interested in any high-value items before including them in the estate sale.

•**See whether your china, crystal and flatware have any value to pattern-matching services.** Websites such as Replacements.com and IADM.com buy these items to sell to people who need replacement pieces for their own sets. Unfortunately, these companies rarely pay very much—sometimes as little as 50 cents to $1 per piece. The seller is responsible for shipping costs, so this often is not worth doing.

•**If you want to keep certain items in the family for emotional reasons, take one last stab at convincing your heirs to accept them.** Don't just hector your children, grandchildren, nieces or nephews to take your stuff—even if this succeeds, they'll get rid of it later if they don't really want it. Instead, try to build happy memories for them around the items by using them at family events.

•**Donate items to charities,** such as your town's or religious organization's furniture bank, Goodwill or the Salvation Army, if all else fails. You'll get a tax deduction if you itemize your deductions (though fewer people will itemize under the new tax law).

The Yard Sale Queen's Guide to Making Money from Your Stuff

Chris Heiska, who edits the Yard Sale Queen website (YardSaleQueen.com). She lives in Lusby, Maryland, and attends 10 to 15 yard sales most Saturdays from spring through autumn, and she holds three or four sales each year. She has been quoted about yard sales everywhere from *The Wall Street Journal* to CNN.

Holding a garage or yard sale can be a great way to clear out clutter and earn some cash. *Here's how to increase the odds that your sale will be a success…*

Scheduling

The best time to hold your sale is on a weekend when a local church or civic group is staging a large rummage sale. These big sales draw bargain hunters from surrounding towns, and many of those shoppers will visit nearby garage sales as well. Post signs with arrows leading from the exit of the big sale to your own sale.

Otherwise, choose a weekend when a large number of garage sales are scheduled in your neighborhood…or ask your neighbors to join you in a multi-family or block-wide sale. The more sellers in the area, the more buyers who will visit.

Saturday morning usually is the best time of week for a garage sale because that is when the most garage sale shoppers are on the prowl. Other times are acceptable only if sales are commonly held at those times in your region. *Also…*

●**Start your sale 30 minutes earlier than other sales.** This will encourage shoppers to begin their garage sale day with you.

●**Avoid scheduling your sale for a holiday weekend when people are away**—unless your home is in a resort community or located on a heavily used route to, say, a local beach.

●**If there's one big employer in your region, schedule your sale for a weekend that closely follows its payday.** That's when people are most likely to be in a spending mood. To find out when payday is, ask someone who works there or try calling the company.

●**If it rains on sale day, take down your signs and postpone your sale.** You can proceed with your sale if your merchandise is protected by a garage roof, but expect business to be slow. Many garage sale shoppers make other plans when it rains.

Merchandise and Pricing

Small, inexpensive items, including housewares… tools…costume jewelry…DVDs and CDs…books… and child-related products, sell well at garage sales. Large items, such as furniture, typically do not sell well, because most shoppers cannot fit them into their cars. Items priced above $10 or $20 tend not to sell well either and are better sold through eBay, Craigslist or a Facebook marketplace ad.

Before holding your sale, visit a few garage sales in your area to determine appropriate prices. Relatively new, clean items can bring as much as one-third of their original prices, but most goods sell for much less.

Examples: Used hardcover books rarely sell for more than $1 or $2 apiece …used adult clothing rarely brings more than $2 or $3 per item. Used designer clothing is likely to fetch a better price in a consignment shop.

Shoppers do not like to have to ask the prices of merchandise. Attach a price sticker to each item… or post price signs when multiple items all cost the same amount.

Example: "Paperbacks 50 cents each."

Goods bring better prices when they have been cleaned, but consider the value of your time before you start scrubbing. Cleaning a child's toy might increase its sale price from $1 to $3—but the 10 minutes you spend cleaning might be worth more to you than $2.

Other smart sales strategies…

●**Scan newspaper circulars for store ads offering the products that you are selling**—particularly if you're selling things that are relatively new or priced above $10. Clip out these ads, and attach them to your items so that shoppers can see what good deals you're offering.

•**If you sell electrical items,** have an outlet and extension cord handy so you can show that they work.

•**Put in cheap batteries.** Items powered by batteries bring much higher prices when they contain working batteries. If an item requires many batteries or large batteries, however, the cost of these batteries could eat up much or all of your profit. Buy cheap generic batteries at a dollar store…or pull used batteries near the end of their lives from electronics that you are not selling and buy new batteries for these.

•**Place all of your merchandise (except large items) on tables,** even if this means borrowing folding tables from neighbors…or improvising tables from upturned boxes or boards placed across cinder blocks. Goods are less appealing when displayed on the ground, and many shoppers won't bend down to examine merchandise.

•**Be sure to have a variety of items.** Have at least one table of merchandise that's likely to interest the stereotypical man, such as tools, DVDs, electronics and sports gear. If possible, also position a lawn mower, barbecue grill or large tools near the front of your sale, where they can be seen from the road. Many garage sale shoppers are married couples, and these couples are more likely to stop at your sale—and remain longer—if there is something for everybody to want to look at.

Advertising

Spread the word about your sale through ads in your local newspaper classifieds…on the free classified ads website Craigslist.org…and on community bulletin boards in local stores. Emphasize the size of your sale in these ads. Use words such as "huge" or "multifamily" if appropriate.

On the morning of your sale, post signs on the roads around your home. Provide large, easy-to-follow arrows pointing toward your sale, along with the words "Garage Sale" (or "Yard Sale") and your address in big, thick print so that it can be read from a moving vehicle.

Caution: Do not post your signs any earlier than the morning of your sale…and don't leave them up after your sale ends. Many towns and neighborhood associations prohibit private signs along roadsides. Garage sale signs often are ignored by the authorities and accepted by neighbors, but the longer you leave your signs up, the greater the odds that you will face a fine. Ask your homeowners association or town about garage sale sign rules in your area.

Sale Day

Greet those who visit your sale, then give them space to shop undisturbed. Chat with customers only if they initiate conversations. Background music can make shoppers feel more comfortable. Garage sale cash boxes can get stolen, so carry the cash generated by your sale (along with plenty of $1 and $5 bills for change) in a carpenter's apron or pouch worn around your waist. Be wary of accepting checks, which might bounce. Do not let strangers into your house to use your bathroom or make phone calls—they could be thieves.

Odd "Junk" That You Can Actually Sell

Terry Kovel, author of more than 100 books about collecting including *Kovel's Antiques & Collectibles Price Guide 2022.* Her nationally syndicated newspaper column appears in more than 150 newspapers. Kovels.com

You knew vintage toys could be valuable…but empty toy boxes? And you can probably guess that rare posters of famous rock bands can be valuable…but posters of unknown bands?

Take care the next time you clean out your attic or scan the dollar table at a flea market—some objects that seem like junk actually can be worth hundreds of dollars.

If you find one of the following items, enter its description into eBay.com or a search engine to see whether other people have sold similar things online and how much they fetched. It might be worth posting yours on eBay, too, or perhaps selling it to a local antiques store or through a consignment shop…

•**Empty boxes from collectible items.** Collectibles often are worth more if they're in their original boxes. That's good news if all you have is a box—someone who has only the collectible might buy your box to put the two together. Boxes from collectible toys tend to be especially desirable.

Also: Empty Tiffany jewelry boxes can be worth anywhere from a few dollars to $50 or more depending on age and size. Any vintage box can have value if its graphics are very attractive—even if the item itself is not tremendously valuable. The box can be displayed as art.

Warning: If you sell the empty box from a particular product on eBay, include the phrase "empty box" or "box only" very prominently in the item description. Otherwise a buyer might think that the product is in the box and feel scammed when only an empty box arrives.

•**Posters from unknown psychedelic rock bands.** It's no secret that rare posters from famous rock acts of the 1950s and 1960s can sell for thousands of dollars. But vintage posters from virtually forgotten bands can be valuable, too—if these posters have attractive psychedelic graphics. Buyers are drawn to these as artwork and mementos of the 1960s, not necessarily for the bands. Prices can range from less than $50 to $1,000 depending on the condition and quality of the artwork. Any psychedelic poster, especially glow-in-the-dark designs, sell in the hundreds.

Note: Obscure bands didn't usually sell posters in the 1960s, but they often stapled advertising posters to walls to promote upcoming performances. Some music fans took these promotional posters home.

•**Old electric fans—even rusty, broken ones.** Electric fans from before World War II often are worth $100 or more if they're in good working order. Perhaps more surprisingly, even vintage fans that are broken and beaten up still have some value—often $25 to $50. Fans of fans buy these because they enjoy restoring them. Electric fans that have brass blades are especially desirable.

•**Old fountain pens.** It's not news that high-end vintage pens, such as those made by famed pen-

maker Montblanc, can sell for hundreds or thousands of dollars. But most people do not realize that relatively common fountain pens can be worth decent money, too—often $40 to $100. Even badly damaged fountain pens can have significant value if they feature solid gold or silver components.

Example: The Parker 51 was sold in huge numbers for many decades. It's among the most common fountain pens—the sort of pen high school students often received as graduation presents in the 1950s and 1960s. Yet Parker 51s can be worth anywhere from $40 to more than $500 depending on the specific model. Models from the 1940s featuring solid 14-karat gold caps can bring $750 or more.

•**Tiny tins.** Very small consumer products such as phonograph needles, pills and condoms were sometimes sold in miniature tin boxes in the late-19th and early-20th centuries. Some of these tiny tins were barely big enough to hold a quarter. These undersized tin boxes have become very collectible—particularly those that have attractive graphics.

Example: A tiny phonograph needle tin from the Berliner Gram-O-Phone Company featuring a picture of a dog listening to an old-fashioned record player recently brought $177.50 on eBay.

•**Colorful graniteware kitchen items.** Graniteware is a type of enameled tin or iron that has been on the market since the 1870s without attracting a lot of attention. Most graniteware is an unexciting white or gray in color. It is most closely associated with bedpans—an item with very little appeal to collectors. Yet in the past few years, the collecting market for certain graniteware kitchen items has gone through the roof. Graniteware in rare colors and patterns is desired by collectors—red, green, turquoise or patterns such as "checkerboard" or "chicken wire."

Example: A coffee boiler with a chicken-wire pattern was priced at $900 at a graniteware convention.

•**Griswold cast iron cookware.** Old cast iron toys and doorstops aren't the only cast iron collectibles. Old cast iron cookware can be valuable, too. The cookware made by Griswold Manufacturing of Erie, Pennsylvania, is particularly desirable. Even a standard-sized Griswold pan from the 1940s can be worth $100 to $200 in good condition, and older and more obscure Griswold cast iron products can be worth even more.

Example: A Griswold Erie Spider 8 Skillet with a spider logo that dates the piece to the 19th century recently sold for $872 on eBay.

Helpful: Enter the words "Griswold" and "cast iron" into a search engine to find websites that can help you date Griswold items based on their markings. Some Griswold items are marked "Erie," rather than "Griswold."

However, the Griswold name was sold to a different cookware maker after Griswold went out of business in the late 1950s, and "Griswold" items that were not actually made by Griswold might not be especially valuable. Fakes can be hard to spot, so don't pay a lot for a Griswold item unless you are confident that you can trust the person selling it.

•**Men's vintage high-end suits and jackets.** There has long been a resale market for used women's clothing. Recently, a robust market has developed for certain used men's clothing as well—though generally only garments of extremely high quality. Used suits and jackets from prestigious Italian designers such as Brioni or Zegna…and used suits custom-made by Savile Row tailors can bring $500 to $1,000 or more. Vintage clothing generally will fetch the best price not online but at a high-end clothing consignment shop in a fashion-conscious city such as New York.

•**Pyrex kitchen bowls and dishes.** Pyrex pieces are collected by pattern, and some rare patterns sell for hundreds of dollars. Old milk bottles from the 1940s with patriotic slogans (watch out for fakes) are also growing in popularity.

•**Old video games and vinyl records.** In 2018, the first video games made news. An unopened 1985 Super Mario Brothers video game for a Nintendo system sold for a record price of $100,150. Now collectors are looking for other video games, and prices are unpredictable. Vinyl records with the right music in excellent condition including the sleeve also are attracting buyers. Of course, that means record players also are going up in price.

•**"Brown furniture."** Reproductions of past styles by top makers in the 1950s now sell for an almost-new price, since 18th-century examples are scarce and new furniture is often made of plywood and plastic, not wood and metal. The one-drawer Sheraton bedside table that only a few decades ago was not worth taking to a flea market is now on display for $150 to $200 or more and sells out early in the day. There's also a demand for bookcases and chests of drawers in old styles.

Your Coffee Mug Could Be Worth $1,000

Terry Kovel, author of more than 100 books about collecting including *Kovel's Antiques & Collectibles Price Guide 2022.* Her nationally syndicated newspaper column appears in more than 150 newspapers. Kovels.com

Coffee mugs don't attract much attention from very many collectors. There are no published mug price guides or large collectors' clubs for mug aficionados. That lack of attention creates an opportunity—old mugs often can be found for just $1 or so at thrift stores, flea markets and yard sales…but some of these mugs can be worth quite a bit of money when sold on eBay.

Valuable coffee mugs include…

•**Rare Starbucks mugs.** The well-known coffee chain sometimes sells mugs linked to particular cities or regions. These local Starbucks mugs have become collectible, and the rarest examples can fetch $100s.

Examples: A 2009 Puerto Vallarta mug featuring a picture of a seahorse recently sold for $1,350 on eBay.* A 2009 Sacramento mug featuring California's state capitol recently sold for $405. A 2008 Seattle mug with a picture of Mount Rainier recently sold for $400.

2009 Starbucks Sacremento mug

*All prices listed reflect results of recent eBay auctions. But mug values can be very volatile, in part because this is not yet a well-established collecting field. *Caution:* Hand wash old and potentially valuable mugs—some can be damaged by dishwashers.

●**Out-of-production Disney mugs.** Anything Disney is likely to be collectible, though, of course, old and rare items tend to be worth the most.

Examples: A set of six black mugs, each featuring a Disney villain, recently sold for $175. A mug from Disney's Epcot Center in the shape of a purple dragon head sold for $139.50. A mug textured

Disney Dragon mug

to suggest a woven basket, featuring silhouettes of *Lion King* characters, brought $49.95. A mug picturing a flying *Mary Poppins* in silhouette brought $32. A mug from Starbucks' "You Are Here" collection picturing Disney's Epcot Center recently sold for $152.50, even though it is not at all old. This Epcot mug was discontinued not long after its release because it shows a monorail with a purple stripe, and the actual purple-stripe monorail was involved in a fatal crash in 2009.

●**Non-Disney cartoon mugs.** Out-of-production Looney Toons and Peanuts/Snoopy mugs often have value, as do some mugs from less well-known cartoons.

Examples: A set of four glass mugs from the 1980s featuring Snoopy in election-themed drawings sold for between $50 and $90. An orange-on-white mug featuring Snoopy and the phrase "Curse You, Red Baron!" on the back sold for $295. A mug shaped

1980's Snoopy election mug

like the Looney Tunes cartoon character the Tasmanian Devil sells for anywhere from $60 to $130.

●**Superhero mugs.** Anything featuring a comic book superhero has a decent chance of being collectible. Famous superheroes such as Superman and Batman are always good bets, but mugs featuring less popular characters sometimes are rarer and even more valuable.

Examples: A pair of Warner Bros. Studio Store mugs featuring Harley Quinn and Poison Ivy—two of Batman's comic book adversaries—recently sold for $140.

●**Mugs featuring TV shows or movies from the 1980s or earlier.** There are many Hollywood

memorabilia collectors, so mugs tied to popular actors and productions can have value.

Examples: A cast mug from the John Wayne movie *The Hellfighters* recently sold for $1,580. A mug from the 1950s promoting the show *I Love Lucy* and featuring a drawing of Lucille Ball

1974 John Wayne film *McQ* mug

sold for $350. A mug given to the cast and crew of the 1974 John Wayne film *McQ* recently sold for $100.99. A mug promoting the 1978–1982 sitcom *WKRP in Cincinnati* sold for $158.60. A white glass mug promoting the 1984 film *Ghostbusters* sold for $134.50.

Warning: Some popular TV show and movie mugs were produced in such large quantities that they are not very rare or valuable. A 1981 M*A*S*H "Officers Mess" mug rarely brings more than $10, for example.

●**World's Fair mugs.** There are collectors who buy items from old World's Fairs.

Examples: A mug from the 1933 Chicago World's Fair picturing that fair's Electrical Building recently sold for $108.25 on eBay. A red-on-white mug from the 1964 New York World's Fair featuring an image of the iconic

1964 New York World's Fair mug

"Unisphere" on one side and the words "A 'Fair' Size Mug" on the reverse brought $29.99.

●**Tiki mugs.** These mugs were made to serve tropical drinks such as mai tais, not coffee. Vintage examples sold decades ago by Pacific Island–themed restaurants such as Trader Vic's now can have value.

Examples: Trader Vic's 1963 "Honi Honi" tiki mug, which features swimmers diving into the sea, sells for anywhere from $25 to $149.95 on eBay. A tiki mug marked "Tiki Bob's San Francisco" recently sold for $405.

1933 Trader Vic's tiki mug

●**Moscow Mule mugs.** The "Moscow Mule," a vodka-based drink that enjoyed brief popularity in the 1950s, traditionally is served in a copper mug. The drink currently is experiencing something of a resurgence, creating demand for vintage Moscow Mule mugs in good condition.

1950s Moscow Mule copper mug

Example: A set of four Moscow Mule mugs stamped "A Cock 'N Bull Product" on the bottom dating to the 1950s recently sold for $89.

• **Fiestaware mugs.** Fiestaware, a line of ceramic dishes typically glazed in bold solid colors, is very collectible, and Fiestaware mugs are no exception. The value of Fiestaware varies greatly depending on the rarity of the glaze color—lilac is rare and quite valuable, for example. A small percentage of Fiestaware features images, and some of this atypical Fiestaware is valuable.

Examples: A sunflower-yellow Fiestaware mug with images of Fiestaware plates in multiple colors sold for $54.75. A set of four white Fiestaware mugs featuring an image of Tweety Bird and the words "Seasons Greetings" sold for $69.99. An 18-ounce jumbo mug and saucer in the rare lilac color recently brought $44.50.

• **Russel Wright mugs.** Wright, an acclaimed industrial designer, created some very popular dinnerware sets in the 1940s and 1950s. These sets are in great demand today among collectors of "mid-century modern" housewares—a single mug from one of his sets can bring more than $100 in some cases. Look for Wright's name printed on the underside.

Russell Wright "Casual" line mug

Examples: A mug from Wright's "Casual" line in a rare cantaloupe color recently sold for $244.50. Another from that same line in pastel yellow brought $129.57…and one in white sold for $107.50. Less desirable colors such as avocado, pink and nutmeg often bring between $25 and $65.

• **Mugs from highly regarded art potteries.** Mugs made by respected 20th-century art potteries such as Bauer and Hull are sought after by collectors. For information on distinctive trademarks, put the name of the pottery in an online search engine.

Examples: A blue Bauer Pottery "Ringware" mug dating to the middle of the 20th century recent-

ly sold for $153.50. (Ringware features a series of ridges circling the pottery.) A Hull Pottery mug made between 1943 and 1957 featuring an image of Little Red Riding Hood recently sold for $361.25.

Hull Little Red Riding Hood mug

How to Convert Your Loose Change into a Silver Treasure Chest

Scott A. Travers, president of Scott Travers Rare Coin Galleries, LLC, and the author of seven best-selling books on coins, including *The Insider's Guide to U.S. Coin Values* and *The Coin Collector's Survival Manual.*

It's time to reach for the piggy bank, cookie jar, shoe box or any other place where you might have an assemblage of old coins stored. Empty the contents onto a well-lighted table covered with a soft cloth, and look for U.S. coins dated 1964 and before. Any pre-1965 U.S. dime, quarter, half dollar or dollar coin you pluck from the pile will contain 90% silver, with 10% copper added to harden the metal. Any combination of these pre-1965 coins that has an equivalent face value (legal tender value that is indicated on the coin) of one dollar will be worth at least 70% of the silver troy ounce price. ("Troy ounce" is the unit of measure for precious metals. One troy ounce is 31.1 grams; a regular ounce is 28.35 grams.)

The silver price fluctuates, sometimes considerably. With silver valued at $17.29 per troy ounce on the Chicago Mercantile Exchange, four quarters or ten dimes or two half dollars, for example, would be worth $12.10 or more, with silver dollars commanding a bit more value apiece.

Using that $17.29 per troy ounce value, a silver dime would be worth $1.21; a silver quarter would have a value of $3.02; and a silver half dollar would command $6.04. A silver dollar is also made from 90% silver, but contains about 10% more silver for its face value than the other coins, so it would be valued at $13.37.

And it gets better. Although each and every dime, quarter, half dollar and dollar coin dated before 1965 is valuable for its silver content, nickel five-cent coins dated 1943 through 1945 contain 35% silver, as do some "nickels" dated 1942—those that display a large letter "P" (for the Philadelphia Mint) or "S" (for the San Francisco Mint) above Monticello, the building pictured on the coin's reverse. Those silver nickels, produced during World War II, are worth about 80 cents each, with silver valued at $17.29 per troy ounce. Kennedy half dollars dated from 1965 through 1970 contain 40% silver. These have a value of $2.25 each when silver is at $17.29 per troy ounce.

The coins I refer to here are common-date silver coins that are in average circulated condition. In the coin trade, the term for these coins is "junk numismatic silver." Numismatic refers to the study of coins, paper money and medallic art. Coins that have no wear and are Mint State often bring higher prices, as do coins that have scarce or rare dates. Listings of scarce or rare date coins can be found in my book, *The Insider's Guide to U.S. Coin Values* or online from the Professional Coin Grading Service.

If silver is in great demand, U.S. coins that fall into the category of junk numismatic silver might trade at a premium of 10% or more. However, when demand for silver is lagging, sometimes Mint State coins bring junk (or "melt value") prices.

Junk numismatic silver coins fluidly trade in $1,000 face-value bags that contain about 715 ounces, taking the wear of the coins and the silver worn away into consideration. These coins, when originally minted, contained 723 ounces of silver. Investors like to buy these silver coin bags by their denomination. Some investors are holding bags of silver coins as an insurance policy against economic calamity, as these silver coins can be used for barter purposes in the event of an economic collapse. A bag of silver dimes, quarters or halves would be worth about $12,000, with silver at that $17.29 per troy ounce level.

Back in 1965, the U.S. Treasury was granted Congressional approval to change the composition of the dimes and quarters that it was manufacturing to contain copper and nickel and not be made from any silver, as silver was rising in value. Treasury lowered, but did not eliminate, the amount of silver contained in the half dollar. Beginning in 1971, that coin saw production for circulation without silver.

After Treasury removed all silver from the dimes and quarters it was producing in 1965, there was a mad rush by the American public to remove these silver coins from circulation. Many of those silver coins were ultimately melted for their precious metal value by refineries. But a large number remain scattered around the nation in attics, dresser drawers, home safes and even in secret hiding places within walls.

Since 1970, no U.S. coins manufactured for people to spend have contained precious metals. The Eisenhower and Susan B. Anthony dollar coins made for circulation contain no silver and are made from copper and nickel. However, the U.S. Mint has become the world's largest coin dealer by selling special issue coins made from gold, silver and platinum at premium prices to collectors.

As long as we are on the topic of searching your coin stash for silver coins, it might be helpful to know which Canadian coins have silver content. Canadian dimes, quarters, half dollars and dollar coins dated 1967 and earlier are usually made from 80% or more silver. In 1967 and 1968 (a transition year), some of the dimes and quarters manufactured by Canada for people to spend were made from 50% silver. Canadian silver coins with their approximate 80% silver content are valued at $9 per one dollar face value, with silver at $17.29 per ounce.

Whether your silver coins are American or Canadian, you can visit a reputable coin and precious metals dealer or check for the next American Numismatic Association convention, where you can go to the proverbial cash window and celebrate.

CHAPTER 4

Decorate and Design Right

You're Decorating Wrong

Maxwell Ryan, an interior designer in the New York metropolitan area and founder of ApartmentTherapy.com, a popular interior design website. His books include *Apartment Therapy: The Eight-Step Home Cure*.

Minor decorating decisions can have a major impact on how your home looks and feels. For example, it isn't just the quality of the art on your walls that matters, but also how that art is hung. And it isn't just how bright a room is, but also the number of lamps that are providing the light.

Seven seemingly small decorating mistakes that can greatly diminish a room's visual appeal...

MISTAKE: **Hanging art too high.** When people hang art on their walls, they tend to position it at their eye height when standing. But at that height, the art looms uncomfortably above them when they're seated. It also feels disconnected from the furniture below, and it makes rooms feel top heavy and unbalanced, as if they might tip over.

Professional decorators have discovered that the ideal height to hang art is 57 inches from the floor to the center of the artwork (the hook will be positioned higher). This might seem too low when you're hanging the art—because you're standing when you hang it and you're probably used to hanging art higher—but once you live with it a while, the whole room will feel more cohesive.

Hanging all the art in a room so that the center points are at the same height allows the eye to move comfortably around the room. When the center points of hanging art are at different heights, the eye bounces around as it scans the room, creating a sensation of clutter and disorder.

Keep in mind that this is a guideline. Ceiling height, size of furniture, intensity of color and amount of pattern all will affect the height and position of where your art looks best.

MISTAKE: **An insufficient number of light sources.** The secret to a well-lit room isn't just having a sufficient amount of light. Having a sufficient number of different light sources is crucial, too—every room should have at least three. A room with fewer than three light sources tends to have shadows. The eye does not venture easily into shadowy areas, so shadowy rooms usually feel small, tight and depressing. Well-lit rooms with few shadows, on the other hand, feel happy and stimulating.

Tip: Arrange the three lights in a room to form a triangle, with two on or near one wall (such as on either side of a bed or sofa) and a third on or near the opposite wall.

Table and floor lamps tend to be preferable to overhead lighting, which can cast harsh, unflattering shadows. The light produced by incandescent and LED bulbs tends to have a more appealing tone than that from fluorescents such as compact fluorescent lamps (CFLs). Cree LED bulbs, available at The Home Depot, are excellent and less expensive than most other brands. Use lamps with lamp shades whenever possible—indirect light is less harsh than direct light.

MISTAKE: **Distributed collections.** If you have lots of one type of thing—hundreds of books or dozens of collectible plates, for example—bring them all together into a single location. Cover an entire wall with shelves to display this collection if necessary—but do not let the collection trickle out into other rooms in the house. A collection housed in a single space feels special. That same collection spread throughout a home feels like clutter.

MISTAKE: **Fearing bright colors.** Most people lean heavily on tans, beiges and whites when painting and decorating. They fear that they lack the decorating savvy to make aggressive colors work well and think that they're playing it safe by using neutral tones. Trouble is, decorating entirely with tans, beiges and whites guarantees their homes will look dull.

If you fear bright colors when decorating and still want to decorate mainly with tans, beiges and whites, make around 20% of each room's paint and/or decor bright and bold.

Add a colorful rug…paint one wall in a room a bright color to create a unique design element (often called an accent wall)…place a colorful throw on a bed or over a sofa. Because only 20% of the room is decorated in a bright color, there's little reason to fear—the splash of color will be visually interesting, not overwhelming.

Tip: Choose "warm" colors including reds, yellows or oranges as your bright colors in most rooms in the house, including any room where the main color is tan or beige. "Cool" colors such as blues or greens tend to feel less inviting but are an option as a pop of color or in private spaces such as bedrooms and bathrooms. Choose different accent colors for different rooms in your home—our eyes appreciate variety.

MISTAKE: **Skipping the rug.** Rugs are worth having even if you love the beauty of your hardwood or tile floors. Not only will a rug add color and texture, it will dampen sound. Much of how we perceive a space depends on its "aural feel"— how our minds interpret the way the space sounds. Rooms with rugs or carpets tend to have a cozy,

comfortable aural feel—while those without them often seem harsh and unpleasant.

Tip: Rugs should be nearly as big as the rooms they are in. Smaller rugs are acceptable if large rugs are cost prohibitive. A rug in a living room won't seem badly undersized as long as the front legs of the room's seating are on it, even if the back legs of those seats are not.

MISTAKE: **Skipping the window treatments.** Some home owners don't bother with curtains or shades these days—they don't want anything to block their home's natural light. But a room without any window coverings feels unfinished, and uncovered rectangular window frames look hard and harsh.

If you don't want window coverings that block your natural light, install sheer curtains or shades. Sheer fabric can filter incoming sunlight rather than blocking it, giving sunlight an appealingly soft, varied feel.

MISTAKE: **Putting all the furniture against the wall.** Not every sofa and chair needs to be pushed back against a wall. In fact, if all the seating in a large room is up against a wall, that seating is likely to be too far apart—someone seated on a sofa against one wall will be too far from someone seated against the opposite wall to have a comfortable conversation. The seats in a seating group should be no more than eight feet apart, even if that means that all or some of them are not against a wall.

Tricks to Make a Small House Feel Bigger (No Renovations Required)

Maxwell Ryan, an interior designer in the New York metropolitan area and founder of ApartmentTherapy.com, a popular interior design website. His books include *Apartment Therapy: The Eight-Step Home Cure.*

In a recent survey, 80% of home owners had at least one major regret about their home. Among the most common regrets—nearly 16% said their

Decorate and Design Right

home was too small. But you can make a small home look and feel bigger. *Here's how....*

Go for Light

It's not the size of a room that gives a sense of space but how your eyes travel through it. The eye is drawn to light and open space, so use both to make your small space feel bigger.

•**Use curtain rods that are wider than your window.** Install rods that extend a few inches beyond the window so that, when the curtains are open, the entire window is exposed. You'll have more light, and your windows will seem larger.

•**Use at least three light sources, of varying heights, in every room.** One light source should be low and indirect (such as a table lamp). A second could be a standing floor lamp, which is space-efficient and great for reading. Your third source could be a pendant, which both illuminates and adds visual depth to a space.

•**Put dimmers on all the lights.** Being able to adjust light intensity to suit the time of day and occasion can make a small room more inviting. Dimmers make your home feel cozy.

•**Clean windows twice a year so you'll have more natural light.** Few people do this, but it makes a huge difference. It is one of the easiest, most powerful things you can do. Shiny, clean windows bring in tons of natural, beautiful sunlight while inviting the eye to travel beyond the boundaries of your home to the outdoors.

•**Place light outside your windows.** With nice clean windows, adding some lighting outside your windows (in the yard, on the deck or on the windowsill) will draw the eye out the window and provide the visual feeling of more space. Simply being able to see something outside will feel very expansive. I like to put votives in lanterns outside my windows at night when giving dinner parties. This is particularly stunning in the snow!

•**Install lighting in closets.** Closets can be one of the darkest and most cluttered areas of the home, but they are improved dramatically when there is light inside of them. You can find things more easily and organize the space much more effectively. In the old days, all closets had light fixtures, but

today you often have to add them. It's not expensive to do and even a battery-operated light makes a difference.

Consider Walls and Floors

To keep the walls from feeling like they are closing in, try these tricks...

•**Use mirrors.** Mirrors enlarge a space by making walls melt as your eye travels through them while also brightening up a room by multiplying light. Hanging a big mirror on a wall facing a window doubles its light, brightens the entire space and allows you to enjoy the view from more than one place. A mirror also can be fabulous in a dining room at night, with candlelight.

•**Paint walls bright, light colors—but choose whites with care.** Painting walls with light, bright colors expands your space. Avoid pure white or "photographer's" white (cold!). Instead, choose whites that have a hint of color. My favorites are China White in flat for the wall and White Dove in semigloss for the trim—both by Benjamin Moore. For the ceiling, use a pure "ceiling white" to draw the eye upward by providing contrast.

•**Use paint as camouflage.** Paint things that you'd rather not accentuate, such as radiators and shelves, the same color as the wall. They'll disappear into the wall.

•**Opt for dark floors.** With light walls, a dark floor makes your walls feel brighter by contrast and gives a warm, grounded feeling to a room (dark-stained floors are very warm in their effect...blond floors are colder). Dark floors also have a more earthy feeling underfoot and seem to disappear beneath you as you enter a room. This will make your walls seem taller.

•**Get rid of interior doors that you don't need.** Removing unnecessary doors—such as a door between the dining room and living room—lets the eye travel without interruption. Leave doors for bedrooms and bathrooms. Remove all the other doors.

Clear Out Clutter

Most people can easily get rid of a quarter to half of their stuff. Keep necessities and things that enhance your life—lose the rest. *Also...*

•**Create a "welcome home" landing strip.** Every home benefits from a hospitable entry that conveys calm and order while also keeping unwanted and unnecessary stuff from creating disarray in your home. *Your "foyer" should include the following…*

•Doormat for wiping shoes (and I suggest taking them off).

•Coat hook or tree to hang outerwear, bag, umbrellas, dog leash, etc.

•A flat surface (I call it a "landing strip") where you can lay down your wallet and keys and sort the mail. This can be a small table or bookshelf. If space is very limited, look for a shelf or photo ledge to mount directly on the wall.

•Basket for recycling. This makes it easy to dump unwanted mail at the door.

•**Plan your empty space, too.** This may sound counterintuitive, but don't use every nook and cranny for storage—you'll just keep more stuff! Allow open space for the eye to rest by keeping at least 10% of your space (walls, doors, tabletops, shelves) empty. Visual breathing room makes rooms feel spacious.

•**Try long, lean shelving.** A bookshelf (but just one!) that goes all the way up the wall draws the eye to the ceiling and creates an illusion of a bigger space. Or go long and low with console-style shelves for a smart use of otherwise wasted space, such as underneath windows.

•**Use shelving inside your closet.** To maximize your closet space and keep it more organized, install hanging shelving (such as Elfa, available at The Container Store) in at least one section of your closet. Instead of trying to get a dresser in your closet or simply giving it all over to hanging clothing, a number of solid shelves that run from the floor up to the top of the closet will give you a great new useful space with easy access for clothes, shoes or accessories.

Choose Furniture Carefully

Get rid of furniture that you rarely use. For example, if there is a chair that no one sits in because it is uncomfortable, give it away. *Then…*

•**Go big.** It's a common misconception that small spaces can't handle large furnishings. A great sectional that accommodates all seating in one swoop actually can make a small room feel more gracious. It multitasks by defining space, providing space to stretch out for a nap and accommodating guests with plenty of seating for everyone. To keep the space open, choose small nesting tables instead of a big coffee table.

•**Embrace multifunctionality.** Try to use pieces that serve two or three purposes. The more multifunctional a piece is, the less you'll have to buy or bring in to your home.

Examples: Storage bed…dining table/office desk…sleeper sofa…trunk/coffee table…ottoman/storage unit.

•**Look for legs.** When choosing furniture, it will help to keep the room visually light if your sofa, chair or even bed is lifted up off the floor on legs that you can see. This idea works particularly well in small spaces because air (or "negative space") provides the visual illusion of spaciousness.

•**Be crystal clear.** Create a feeling of spaciousness by choosing glass or acrylic tables instead of wood, which blocks your view of the space.

Design on a Dime

Kelly Edwards, cohost and design coordinator for HGTV's *Design on a Dime* and for the makeover show *Tacky House* on the STYLE Network. She lives in Santa Monica, California, KellyEdwardsinc.com

You don't have to have a big decorating budget to dress up your home. Here, ways to give your place a welcoming, stylish look without spending a lot of money…

•**Layer one rug over another.** Large area rugs with a lot of detail can be expensive. If you have a small, patterned carpet in an area that could use a larger one, place a larger, inexpensive jute rug (TheCompanyStore.com has several styles) underneath it to give the feeling of a large, elegant area rug.

•**Frame black-and-white pictures.** They make a sophisticated wall display. At a thrift store or used-book store, buy books illustrated with black-and-white photographs or drawings. Cut out the pictures that appeal to you, place them in simple inexpensive frames—Ikea has nice ones—and group them on a wall. For bigger prints, I like to do three on a wall…for smaller prints, five or six.

•**Shop hotel liquidator outlets.** These stores buy furniture from hotels that are redecorating, and the pieces often are in great condition and surprisingly stylish and affordable.

Example: I paid $25 each for two marble end tables and $40 for a marble console from a high-end hotel in Los Angeles. New, these would have cost hundreds of dollars.

Search the Internet under hotel liquidators and the name of your city. I also shop at salvage yards (for architectural artifacts from old buildings), estate sales and CraigsList.org.

•**Declutter your bookcases.** Instead of covering every inch of space with books, give the eye places to rest—leave some shelves empty except for a single, treasured object. You also can group books by size or color.

To create the look of custom built-ins, stand two freestanding bookcases side by side and attach molding between them and around the edges.

•**Wallpaper the powder room.** Wallpapering a small room gives you a lot of impact for little money. Prepasted wallpaper makes the job easy. Bold, graphic prints are trendy now. If you prefer a classic look that won't go out of style, grass cloth is a sophisticated choice. Even if you want to have a professional put up the wallpaper for you, it shouldn't cost more than $30 to $60 for the labor per roll of wallpaper.

•**Add glass to kitchen cabinet doors.** You can change the look of your kitchen without going to the trouble of replacing the cabinets. Remove just two or three cabinet fronts, and have a handyman use a jigsaw to cut a big rectangle in each one. (You can do this yourself if you are skilled with a jigsaw.) Smooth the edge of the cutout…stain or paint it if necessary…and have a glass cutter cut a piece of glass to fit each door. The glass costs about $4 to $8 per square foot. Behind the glass doors, display your collection of vases, a stack of colorful dishes or your good china.

•**Spray paint older appliances.** White kitchen appliances look dated now. To get the look of an expensive new refrigerator, I painted my old one using Rust-Oleum Universal Spray Paint in glossy black. Unplug the empty fridge, remove the doors and roll it outside. Sand it lightly, give it two coats of paint and let dry overnight.

Important: Protect the inside of the fridge by sealing it off with sheets of plastic and painter's tape from the hardware store.

•**Add a mirror to any room.** Mirrors add ambient light, and their frames draw the eye. Place a mirror behind a lamp or underneath a sconce to reflect light.

•**Cover light-switch plates with wallpaper.** The color and pattern add visual interest to a wall. Ask your local wallpaper store if it has any leftover pieces you can buy cheaply. Take the switch plate off, and trim the wallpaper to fit the plate. If the paper is not prepasted, use a little spray adhesive. You also can wallpaper the inside of bookcases.

•**Give new life to old curtains.** Instead of replacing the whole curtain, buy fabric, cut it into wide strips and add a contrasting border to curtain panels. Or you can use wide ribbon. If you don't sew, use iron-on fabric adhesive to attach the border.

•**Freshen up bedroom furniture.** Change the knobs on a dresser or a nightstand—my favorite now is brushed bronze ring pulls. For an updated look, combine stain and paint. I like to stain the outside of the piece dark walnut and paint the drawer fronts white.

•**Display collections on old silver trays.** Sterling silver trays are easy to find in thrift stores. I clean them up with half a lemon. Use them to organize shells, jewelry, old bottles or demitasse cups. A tray makes any group of objects look intentional and artistic.

•**Make your entryway welcoming.** If your entryway is small, use a table or dresser that fits comfortably to one side without limiting your walkway. Top it with fresh flowers in a vase. Have a brightly painted chair or bench for guests to sit on as they remove or put on their boots and wraps.

Arrange Furniture for a Great New Look

• **Find the room's natural focal point.** Most rooms have an architectural feature that draws the eye—often a window or fireplace. Arrange furniture around that feature. If you add an additional focal point, such as a TV, position it near the architectural focal point.

• **Separate "heavy" furniture.** If a room contains a dark armoire and a dark-colored couch, place them on opposite sides of the room. Left together, they can make a space feel unbalanced.

Joanne Hans, owner, A Perfect Placement, an interior-arrangement firm in Mechanicville, New York, APerfect Placement.com.

• **Pull the sofa away from the wall.** Then put a table behind it to create depth and interest. The table should be just a bit shorter than the couch and 12 inches deep. Because the table will be hidden behind the sofa—and perhaps covered with a cloth—even a cheap table will do (check Goodwill, Salvation Army, Craigslist, Facebook). Top them with plants, books and framed photos. If the table is not hidden, put a basket with a fern underneath.

Gina March, owner of the St. Louis–based interior rearrangement firm Huegah Home.

Where to Place Your TV

Houzz.com

The center of a TV screen should be at eye level. Calculate the placement based on the size of your TV. A 60-inch television is about 32 inches high, so the screen's center is 16 inches from the bottom of the TV. Most sofa seating is 18 inches above the floor, and adult eye level is about 24 inches above the seat. So the center of the TV should be 18 + 24 = 42 inches high. The TV should be installed with the bottom of the screen 26 inches above the floor—because 26 + 16 = 42.

Brighten the View of a Wall-Facing Window

Roundup of experts on city decorating, reported in The New York Times.

Stick a decorative decal on the window—choose a design that lets light through and provides a pleasant view such as bamboo shoots. Replace the windowpane with etched glass—or simply hang a pane of etched or stained glass in front of it for the light to pass through. Decorate to distract your vision and that of others from the wall-facing window—for example, add a decorative mirror or wall of mirrors elsewhere in the room to bring light in and draw the eye away from the window that faces a wall.

Smart Shades

Mark Westlake, founder and CEO of GearBrain, a website that provides reviews and news about smart-home technology and other "Internet of Things" devices. GearBrain.com

Does sunlight fade your furniture and your carpeting or hardwood floor? Do you want cool summer breezes when you sleep but hate to wake with the first rays of dawn? Do you have high-up windows that are a pain to access?

There are clever solutions for all these problems. "Smart" window shades and blinds can be opened and shut wirelessly via remote control...a smartphone app...or, in some cases, with voice commands when paired with a digital assistant such as Amazon's Alexa or Apple's Siri. They can be programmed to operate on a schedule, too, so that you don't have to remember to shut blinds to block décor-damaging rays every day...and you could go to sleep with blinds one way and wake up with them another way, according to your preference.

Here are the best wireless window blinds and shades for different price points and purposes...

• **Soma Smart Shades are very affordable because they are not actually shades.** They are devices that motorize your existing shades, assuming that your shades have ball-chain pull strings. They are easy to install—you feed the bottom of a ball chain into the Soma device, stick the device to your window trim using an adhesive backing and program the device with an app on your phone. Then you can control your shades with an Android or iOS phone app or Amazon's Alexa, among other options. (A $79 "Soma Connect" device is needed to control up to 10 shades with Alexa.)

Soma Smart Shades can be programmed to open or close at particular times of day. Their rechargeable batteries can provide 50 up/down cycles per charge, and a small solar panel (included) can recharge those batteries automatically.

Downside: Once you install the device on a shade, anyone without access to a connected phone or other remote controller would need to take the ball chain out of the motor housing to operate the shade.

Price: $149 for a single-window system. Soma SmartHome.com

•**Lutron Serena** includes both the automation system and the shade itself, ensuring that everything works well together. A wide range of shade styles is available. Do-it-yourself (DIY) installation is possible for handy home owners, or a Lutron dealer can install. You can control Serena shades with the included remote…a smartphone app…or voice commands through Apple's Siri and Amazon's Alexa. Shades can be programmed to open and shut on a preset schedule. Serena shade systems can be powered by six to eight hidden D-cell batteries—the batteries should last from three to five years depending on type of shade, size and usage—or you can opt for units that plug into wall power if there are outlets positioned where this won't be obtrusive.

Downside: The abundance of options can make Serena difficult to order online. DIY installation is tricky.

Price: Varies by shade type and size, but expect to pay perhaps $500 per window plus $79.95 for the Lutron "Smart Bridge" that is required for Caséta Wireless technology that links the shades with a smartphone or Siri. (This bridge also lets you control home lighting, overhead fans and other devices if you install additional Lutron home-automation modules.) SerenaShades.com

•**Pella Insynctive Designer Series Between-the-Glass Blinds/Shades** are smart blinds or shades enclosed between the panes of multipane windows. They could be a good option if you are installing new windows. The enclosed look is very tidy…greatly reduces the need to dust…and prevents blinds or shades from being damaged by strong winds or rambunctious children or pets. And Pella windows themselves are of high quality. This system is especially useful for patio doors, since the blinds/shades slide out of your way right along with the doors. Power comes from hidden rechargeable batteries that are recharged continually by a small solar panel that is included. (The batteries can be plugged into a wall charger to recharge periodically if the solar panel does not get sufficient light.) These systems, including the "Pella Insynctive Bridge," needed to operate the system via a smartphone or other home-automation system, are available where Pella windows are sold, including Lowe's home centers.

Downside: Since you'll be replacing not just your shades but also your windows, these are pricey and professional installation is required.

Price: Expect to pay $1,000 or more per typical double-hung window—with prices varying widely based on window size, type (casement, fixed, etc.) and other details. Pella.com

Why Colors Always Fool You When Decorating

Ron Reed, an interior designer based in Dallas who has served as program coordinator for interior design programs at Texas State University and University of North Texas. He is author of *Color + Design: Transforming Interior Space.*

You may already know that the color of paint you see in a paint store or on a sample card at home can seem different when you put it on your walls. But do you know why—or how to prevent it? There are many tricks that colors can play on you—not just when choosing paint but also in selecting flooring, drapery, tiles, countertops and even furniture. That's because you often shouldn't believe what your eyes are telling you!

Your perception of color can be influenced by factors including the amount and "temperature" of light in the room…the amount of surface area that is covered by the color…other nearby colors…the texture of the surface beneath the color…and more.

Many people end up spending hundreds of dollars extra to repaint—or they just keep colors that they never really intended and don't really love. *To prevent that, here are five things you need to know to keep color-perception problems from undermining your home's interior design…*

•**The brightness and tone of the lighting profoundly affect the way you see colors.** Your home's lighting likely is very different from the lighting used by the store where you shop for paint, flooring, tiles, drapery, etc. Most stores have little or no natural light and are lit by fluorescent bulbs…while most rooms in homes get at least some sunlight and are lit by incandescent, LED or compact fluorescent bulbs that have a different "color temperature" than retailers' bulbs.

What to do: Whatever design element you are shopping for, whether paint, flooring, tiles, fabrics or other elements, ask to take home a sample of what you have selected plus samples of any colors that are very similar to this color, including those that are slightly lighter or darker. Because of lighting differences, there's a very good chance that one of your "close" color samples will actually end up being your favorite, once you view everything at home. Also ask at the store whether there is a "light box" that you can use to view colors under lighting conditions that are closer to those of your home. Many paint stores and even some home centers now have these devices.

•**The size of a color sample greatly influences how you see that color.** Those little paint store color cards and other small samples are tremendously deceptive—colors look different when they are covering a wall, door, countertop, fireplace trim or any other large surface from when they are contained in a little square. This is not just because an intense color can seem appealing in small doses but overwhelming when it's all around us, though that

can be true—it's also because small areas of a color appear darker to the eye than do large areas of the very same color.

What to do: If you're choosing paint, don't settle for small printed color-sample cards—you want actual samples of the paint. If the paint store won't provide samples of the paint for free, it's worth paying for small cans of paint, especially if this paint is a color you intend to use prominently in your home. Then, at an art-supply store or online, buy artist foam core boards that are at least 20" x 30"—get one board for each paint sample—and cover the entire surface of each board with a paint color you are considering. That 20"-x-30" size is large enough to perceive the color as it will look in your home. And the surface of foam board is similar enough to that of drywall that it accurately re-creates how the paint will look on a wall. The boards cost $3 to $6 each.

If you are choosing drapery, flooring, a countertop or tile, obtain enough of the sample material so that you can view an area measuring 20" x 30" or larger at home.

•**A color that works well in one part of a room might not work well in another part of the same room.**

Examples: The color that seems perfect on the wall directly across from a window might not look right at all in a shadowy corner of the room. The color that you love under artificial lighting at night might seem off when the same room is bathed in sunlight in the morning. Or the color that's perfect in the middle of a wall might not work well where the room meets an adjacent room that's painted a different color.

What to do: Don't place the artist foam core boards or other large color samples in just one location in the room you're decorating. If the color will be used throughout the room, move these samples around to confirm that the color appeals throughout. Also, view them at different times of day.

Helpful: If a color you love does not work well in the darkest parts of a room and/or at night, you might not have to choose a different color. Instead, consider adding lighting to the shadowy area…or experiment with lightbulbs that have different color temperatures. (The color temperature of a bulb should be listed on its packaging in "degrees Kelvin." A bulb below 3,000 will have a warm yellow or orange tone…between 3,000 and 4,500, a neutral white tone…and above 4,500, a crisper blue-white tone.)

•**The sheen of a paint, flooring, tile, fabric, etc.,** affects how you will perceive its color. The very same color of paint, for example, will appear brighter if you opt for a gloss or semigloss finish rather than a less shiny eggshell or satin finish…and it will seem much brighter than the same color with a flat or matte finish. Shiny finishes reflect more light back to the eye, creating the illusion that the colors themselves are brighter.

What to do: Decide which paint sheen or type of flooring, tile or fabric is appropriate for a room before you select its color. Be sure any color sample has the same sheen that you selected.

The texture of a surface will affect your perception of the surface's color. The same paint will appear darker when applied to a textured wall or textured wood paneling than it would on a smooth surface. The tiny bumps and ridges of the textured surface cast shadows that make the surface color appear darker to the eye, even if each individual shadow is so small that you can hardly see it. The same is true with textured tiles and fabrics.

What to do: If a color will be applied to a textured surface but you can sample it only on a flat surface, such as a piece of foam board, select a color that is one shade lighter than the color you prefer on the flat surface.

Better Front-Door Painting

Roundup of experts on front-door painting, reported at BHG.com.

Stick with neutral or traditional colors such as brown, black, gray, deep red or navy blue. Use only latex exterior paint—if the door is metal, get paint with built-in rust protection. If the front door has a screen or storm door, consider painting that door a contrasting color for more visual appeal. If unsure about colors, look at foliage nearby—colors that look good in nature will work well on a home, and they make the house blend in better with its surroundings. Choose a paint color outdoors—tape swatches to the door and look at them throughout the day to see how they will appear in different light. Consider using a contrasting color for the door trim.

Beautiful Houseplants That Clean Indoor Air

B.C. Wolverton, PhD, founder and past president of Wolverton Environmental Services, Inc., an environmental consulting firm in Picayune, Mississippi. He previously spent more than 30 years working for the US military and the National Aeronautics and Space Administration (NASA) as a civilian scientist developing systems to protect against toxic chemicals and pathogenic microbes. He is author of *Plants: Why You Can't Live Without Them* and *How to Grow Fresh Air*. WolvertonEnvironmental.com.

Homes and office buildings are being built and remodeled tighter than ever today to save energy. But sealing out drafts can mean sealing in dangerous chemicals such as benzene and formaldehyde, which are off-gassed by many things, from carpet to pressed-wood furniture. Cleaning products used at home and the office also may release chemicals, including ammonia and chlorinated solvents.

Prolonged breathing of chemicals such as these can cause headaches, throat irritation, congestion, even cancer. The Environmental Protection Agency (EPA) now ranks indoor-air quality among the five top threats to human health. The problem is worse in winter, when we spend the most time sealed in our homes and offices.

Expensive air-filtration systems are not the only solution. When I worked at NASA, we discovered that simple houseplants can filter many dangerous chemicals out of indoor air. The plants' leaves absorb and destroy certain volatile organic compounds, while the microbes that live around the plants' roots convert chemicals into a source of food and energy for themselves and their host plant.

Some houseplants are much more effective at air filtration than others. *Ten that do a great job cleaning the air and are easy to grow…*

The Top Four

The following four plants are exceptionally effective at cleaning the air.

• **Areca Palm** (*Chrysalidocarpus lutescens*) also is known as yellow palm or butterfly palm.

Care: Keep its root-ball damp, and mist the leaves with water often. Feed monthly with liquid fertilizer except in winter. Remove dead branches promptly.

• **Lady palm** (*Rhapis excelsa*) is one of the most effective houseplants for improving indoor-air quality, and it is highly resistant to most insects. It has fans, six to 12 inches wide, made up of shiny green leaves.

Care: Water generously, especially during spring and summer. Feed monthly with liquid fertilizer per label instructions. Leaf tips can be trimmed with pinking shears if they turn brown.

• **Rubber plant** (*Ficus robusta*) is a hearty plant with thick, leathery, dark green leaves. It will tolerate limited light and cool temperatures and is very effective at removing chemical toxins from indoor air—the best of the ficus genus yet tested.

Care: Water regularly from mid-summer through autumn, but let the soil dry slightly between waterings. Water sparingly during the rest of the year—rubber trees struggle when overwatered. Feed monthly with liquid fertilizer during the summer only.

• **Peace Lily** (*Spathiphyllum sp*) produces beautiful white flowers, making it one of a relatively small number of plants that bloom reliably indoors.

Care: Keep the soil evenly moist, and feed monthly with liquid fertilizer from spring through autumn. Discontinue feedings, and keep the soil slightly drier in winter. Wash the leaves occasionally with a damp cloth to reduce the odds of infestation by insects such as spider mites.

The Runners-Up

These plants work well, too, but not quite as well as the first four…

• **Dracaena "Janet Craig"** (*Dracaena deremensis* "Janet Craig") is a pest-resistant leafy plant that can live for decades. It will tolerate poorly lit areas, though its growth will be slowed. Favor the "Compacta" variety, which grows to one to three feet in height, not the regular variety, which requires more care and can reach 10 feet if not pruned.

Care: In spring and summer, keep soil evenly moist so the root-ball does not dry, but never water so much that the soil becomes soggy. Feed with liquid fertilizer twice a month. In autumn and winter, water less often and do not feed. Spray with a water mist.

• **English Ivy** (*Hedera helix*) is best known as a ground cover, but it also grows very well in indoor hanging baskets. And it adapts well to a wide range of indoor conditions—though it does benefit from some time outdoors in spring or summer. English Ivy does not like high temperatures.

Care: Water well, and feed once a month with liquid fertilizer in spring and summer. Discontinue feedings, and allow to dry slightly between waterings in fall and winter. Mist regularly in winter.

Warning: English Ivy contains chemicals that can irritate the skin or cause illness if consumed. Wear gloves when handling, and keep out of reach of pets and young children.

• **Golden Pothos** (*Epipremnum aureum*) tolerates neglect and low light and is extremely resistant to insects. Golden Pothos's name refers to the splashes of gold or cream color on its green, heart-shaped leaves. It usually is grown in hanging baskets, but it also can climb.

Care: Allow the soil to dry slightly between waterings. Feed with diluted liquid fertilizer weekly in spring and summer. Clean the leaves occasionally with a damp cloth.

• **Corn Plant** (*Dracaena fragrans* "Massangeana") is so named because its leaves look like those of corn stalks, not because it actually produces corn. It tolerates low light, though it prefers bright light.

Care: Keep soil moist but not soggy from spring through autumn, then drier in winter. Feed monthly in spring and summer with liquid fertilizer. Mist often. Brown leaf tips can be trimmed.

•**Syngonium** (*Syngonium podophyllum*) produces visually appealing, arrow-shaped, green-and-white or green-and-silver leaves.

Care: Keep soil evenly moist but not soggy from spring through autumn. Allow the soil to dry between waterings in winter. Feed monthly with a liquid fertilizer except in winter. Syngonium appreciates frequent mistings. Pinch back shoots if you want a thicker, bushier plant.

•**Snake Plant** (*Sansevieria trifasciata*) is about 50% less effective at cleaning indoor air than the other plants on this list, but it is so hard to kill that it's worth including as an option for those who struggle to keep other houseplants alive. The snake plant has visually appealing, spearlike leaves that stand upright, typically two to four feet in height. It occasionally produces small greenish-white flowers.

Care: Water sparingly, allowing the soil to dry between waterings. Overwatering is one of the few ways to kill a snake plant. Feed with diluted liquid fertilizer once a month. Remove flowers if they appear, or they might release a sticky, hard-to-clean substance.

How Many Plants?

As a rule of thumb, one to two good-sized plants from the list above per 100 square feet of interior space tend to be sufficient. There's no health downside to having more plants than this as long as mold doesn't develop in the potting soil.

Helpful: Our latest research suggests that growing plants in hydroculture significantly increases their ability to clean the air. With hydroculture, plants are grown in watertight containers and rooted not in potting soil, but in expanded clay pebbles sold for this purpose at some garden stores.

All of the plants listed above will grow in hydroculture, and the Peace Lily, in particular, thrives when grown this way. Hydroculture also reduces the risk that fungal spores, mold and soil-borne pests will develop on houseplants. Plants grown in hydroculture need a complete fertilizer that contains micronutrients. Ask your garden store for details.

Grow These Three Decorative Houseplants... From Food

Janet Loughrey is a horticulture photographer, writer and master gardener based in Portland, Oregon. Her work has been featured in *Garden Design, Sunset* and *Better Homes & Gardens* as well as in numerous books. LoughreyPhoto.com

Remember third grade, when your teacher suspended an avocado pit with toothpicks in a jar and put it on a windowsill? It's still a great way to create a beautiful houseplant. But that's just the beginning. *Here are three even more beautiful houseplants you can grow from parts of fruits and vegetables that you would otherwise throw out...*

•**Pineapples.** Pineapples are easy to grow and, with patience, produce fruit.

Here's how: Twist off the leafy crown and peel off a few rows of leaves at the base to expose about one inch of stem. Let the crown dry for a day or two, then plant in an eight-inch-diameter pot filled with potting soil and place in a sunny location.

Pineapple plants like hot temps (65°F to 85°F) and moist soil. As the plant grows, repot it to roomier pots.

To encourage fruiting: After about a year, cover the pot and plant and an apple with a large plastic bag (the apple gives off ethylene gas, which hastens blossoming). Move the bagged plant out of the sun for about a week, then remove the bag and apple and put the pot back in a sunny spot. With luck, you'll see a baby pineapple in a few months.

•**Gingerroot.** Gingerroot creates an exotic-looking houseplant with tall, grassy stems and plenty of new roots (technically, rhizomes).

Tip: Some supermarket ginger may be treated to prevent sprouting, so use organic ginger.

Here's how: Snap a piece of ginger, using the normal joint lines, into several pieces about two-inches square each, and push each piece about an inch deep into an eight-inch-diameter or larger pot filled loosely with potting soil. Water and place in a warm, sunny location. Keep moist. Sprouts will emerge in two to four weeks and will grow two feet or more in a few months. Cuttings are great to flavor soups! Harvest gingerroot in eight months to a year by pulling up the stalks.

●**Citrus fruits.** Lemons, limes, oranges and other citrus seeds all will produce lovely houseplants, although they may not fruit.

Here's how: Harvest seeds from fresh fruit. Carefully snip the pointy tip of the seed casing with a sharp knife or small sewing scissors, and peel back to remove the seed within. Place seeds on a dampened paper towel, fold that in half, seal in a zipper bag and place in a dark, warm corner. If the towel starts to look dry, spritz it with water to keep it damp. Roots should emerge in about a week. Plant rooted seeds in damp potting soil, and move to a bright windowsill. Leaves will start to grow in a week or two.

Looking for an Interior Designer?

Metropolitan Home.

To find the one who best meets your needs, ask these questions during a phone interview before your first meeting: Do you have a signature style? Is my budget enough for what I want to do in my home? What should I bring when we meet? Are you willing to start with a smaller project...or do you always decorate the entire house? Are you willing to use my furnishings?

Bedroom Makeover for More Restful Sleep

Lawrence J. Epstein, MD, assistant professor of medicine at Harvard Medical School in Boston and regional medical director of the Harvard–affiliated Sleep HealthCenters, a Brighton, Massachusetts–based network of specialized sleep medicine centers. He is the author of *The Harvard Medical School Guide to a Good Night's Sleep.*

Follow the eight simple guidelines below to create a space conducive to restful, restorative slumber...

1. Clear out clutter. Ideally, a bedroom should be simply furnished and decorated so that there isn't a lot to distract you from the primary purpose of sleep. Keeping the bedroom neat and well organized helps minimize anxiety.

Reason: A messy room often is an oppressive reminder of other things that need to be done, making it harder to fall asleep.

2. Don't work—or play—in the bedroom. Keep your computer, checkbook, to-do list, briefcase and other paraphernalia related to your chores, job or responsibilities in your home office, where they are less likely to intrude on your thoughts during the night. If you must have a phone in the bedroom, use that extension only for emergencies, not for potentially exciting or disturbing conversations.

Recreational activities (other than sex, of course) also should be done elsewhere—so remove the TV, DVD player, stereo and anything else that shifts the bedroom's focus to entertainment. If you play music in your room every night before bed, for instance, and then wake up in the middle of the night, you may be unable to fall back to sleep unless you turn on the music again.

3. Banish dust bunnies. Dust mites are microscopic creatures that provoke nasal congestion and/or asthma attacks in allergy-prone people. Because airways naturally constrict at night, allergy flare-ups are likely to interfere with sleep.

Best: Regularly wash bedding in hot water, vacuum under furniture, and dust all surfaces.

4. Block the light. Light sends a strong message to the brain to wake up. Of all the external cues that keep the body clock operating on a 24-hour cycle, light striking the eyes—even when they are closed—is the most influential. Though you may not become fully conscious, light can move you out of deep-stage sleep and into lighter, less restful stages.

Solution: Hang shades, blinds or curtains made from "blackout" material over windows. Remove or cover any electronics that light up, including your alarm clock. If you cannot block ambient light, wear a sleep mask.

For safety's sake: It is fine to use a low-level night-light—for instance, to see your way to the bathroom.

5. Hide the clock. When you have insomnia, repeatedly checking the clock only makes the problem worse by providing an unwelcome reminder of just how much rest you are missing. Turn the face of the clock away so it won't taunt you as you toss and turn.

6. Muffle or mask sounds. Noise is extremely disruptive.

Recent findings: People whose partners suffer from sleep apnea (which causes loud snoring and gasping) lose about the same amount of sleep each night as the apnea patients themselves do. Also, people who live near airports often experience blood pressure elevations and disturbances in the heart's normal resting rhythm when planes fly by.

Self-defense: Use heavy draperies, double-paned windows and rugs to muffle outside sounds. Earplugs are very effective—try an inexpensive foam or silicone drugstore product. If you find earplugs uncomfortable, turn on a fan or white-noise machine (sold at household-goods stores) to create a low, steady background sound that masks more disruptive noises.

7. Make the bed comfortable. The older the mattress, the less support it generally provides (and the more dust mites it may harbor), so if you have had yours for more than 10 years, consider getting a new one. Take your time testing mattresses to see which brand and level of firmness feel best to you, and lie on your favorite one for as long as you need to before you buy to make sure it is comfortable.

Helpful: Replace pillows when they no longer feel comfortable. Avoid products filled with natural down if you are prone to allergies. Keep extra blankets at the foot of the bed—body temperature drops a few degrees during sleep, so you may wake up chilled during the night.

8. Keep a pen and paper on your bedside table. If you are fretting over impending tasks or feeling excited about a new idea as you're trying to fall asleep, jot down some notes about the situation. This way you won't worry about not remembering your thoughts in the morning—clearing your mind for a good night's sleep.

Safe Romance

Jon Jesse, former vice president for industry development at the International Housewares Association (IHA), Rosemont, Illinois. He is a former senior vice president of Kohl's and, prior to that, was a housewares buyer for Marshall Field's in Chicago. Housewares.org

Make romance hot and live to tell about it: Candle Impressions flameless candle. Candles in your bedroom (or living room) set a romantic mood—but so do these easy-to-use and surprisingly realistic battery-powered LED "candles." They're made of wax and feature a "burnt" wick at the top to support a flickering "flame." (And all with no fire risk.) A timer lets you program the candle. Two AA batteries provide up to 1,000 hours of romantic light. About $30 for a set of three. BatteryOperatedCandles.net

Forget What You Know About Mattress-Buying: How to Shop Now

Nick Robinson, founder and editor of SleepLikeTheDead. com, which has been offering unbiased mattress reviews and research for 10 years.

For decades consumers have lost sleep over the frustrating intricacies of mattress selection. But there's been a revolution in the once-sleepy mattress industry. New brands have been pouring into the market...foam and memory foam mattresses have been gaining ground on the venerable innerspring...and consumers now can easily buy high-quality mattresses online and in big-box stores such as warehouse clubs, not just in mattress and department stores.

These new options offer the potential for big savings and a more comfortable night's sleep—but you still need to understand the choices and distinguish fact from hype.

Here's what you really need to know now to get a good deal on a mattress you'll love...

• **The "tried-and-true" test is often unreliable.** The standard advice for mattress shoppers has long been to lie on a mattress in a store for at least 15 minutes to determine whether it feels comfortable. But I've studied thousands of consumer mattress reviews and complaints, and when you dig into this data, you discover that people are nearly as likely to be happy with mattresses bought online—mattresses they never tested—as they are with those bought in stores. That tells us that 15 minutes of lying fully clothed on a brand-new mattress in a showroom is not an effective way to judge whether it will be a comfortable place to spend eight hours every night.

Better ways to increase the odds that you will end up with a comfortable mattress...

•**Buy a medium or medium-firm mattress.** Mattresses are sold in "supportiveness" levels ranging from soft to extra firm—but it turns out that almost everyone is happiest with a medium or medium-firm model. And despite the conventional wisdom, a firm mattress usually is not best for reducing back pain.

Rule of thumb: Back sleepers, stomach sleepers and people who weigh more than 230 pounds usually prefer medium-firm...while side sleepers and people who weigh less than 120 pounds usually prefer medium, though this can vary. (You might reasonably opt for firm if you intend to put a "mattress topper" on your mattress—see below.)

•**Buy from a seller that has a liberal return policy.** The truth is, no matter how much you pay for a mattress and no matter which brand and type you select, there is a chance that you won't like sleeping on it. The best solution is to buy from a company that will give you a hassle-free full refund if necessary. The best return policies these days are from direct-to-consumer online foam and hybrid foam/memory foam mattress sellers such as Casper (Casper.com, now also sold through Target)...Leesa (Leesa.com)...Purple (Purple.com) ...and Tuft & Needle (TuftAndNeedle.com). Each offers 100-day, no-hassle, no-cost returns in the continental US. Usually you just contact the company, which will send a courier to pick up the mattress and donate it to a charity or recycle it if no charity is available.

Warehouse clubs generally have liberal return policies. However, a buyer usually must transport the mattress back to the store.

If you shop elsewhere, confirm that you can return your mattress at low or no cost if necessary after at least a month or two. Get this return policy in writing.

•**The most popular type of mattress is the least likely to satisfy.** The classic innerspring mattress is far from the only option these days. New types of foam mattresses, in particular, have been gaining ground. But most people still end up buying an old-fashioned innerspring mattress—it's what they've always slept on, so they assume it's the safest choice. In fact, it's the riskiest.

My research has found that only 64% of innerspring mattress buyers are satisfied with their mattresses—compared with 77% to 80% of buyers of other types of mattresses. One reason—innerspring mattresses are about twice as likely as other types to develop permanent sags, dips or body impressions within three years of use, which is the leading cause of dissatisfaction with mattresses.

Also, some people who opt for innerspring fear that a foam mattress will "sleep hot" (make them feel too warm). But although about 10% of memory foam mattress users complain that their mattresses are uncomfortably hot—because memory foam conforms closely around the sleeper's body—foam mattresses that are mostly or entirely a type of regular foam rather than memory foam actually are even less likely than innerspring mattresses to generate heat complaints.

This doesn't mean that every foam mattress is a good mattress. Foam and memory foam mattresses often fall short on "edge support"—sitting or sleeping near their perimeters can be a problem. And thin foam mattresses can flatten out under sleepers who weigh a lot. As with any type of product, quality varies from brand to brand and model to model.

But what if you've been happy with an innerspring mattress and really want to stick with that type? In that case, buy one—but perhaps not one with a "pillow top," a thick extra layer of cushy padding on top. The pillow top often is the part of an innerspring mattress that develops a problematic dip or body impression. If you want the soft pillow-top feel, consider instead adding a "mattress topper" to a nonpillow-top mattress. Mattress toppers serve the same function as pillow tops but can be removed and replaced if they degrade. This strategy is likely to be a money saver, too—nonpillow-top mattresses tend to be at least 25% less expensive than comparable pillow tops, and highly rated mattress toppers are available online for just $30 to $100.

• **The best-known brands often are not the best.** Mattress maker King Koil and the so-called "S" brands—Sealy, Serta, Simmons and Stearns & Foster—are among the best-known mattress brands, mainly because of their long histories and wide availability in stores. But these well-known brands tend to have some of the lowest customer satisfaction scores in the mattress industry—only 62% to 65% of buyers of these brands are satisfied with their mattresses.

The highest consumer satisfaction scores, ranging from 78% to 80% satisfied buyers, are earned by the new breed of Internet-sold foam and hybrid foam/memory foam mattress makers mentioned earlier—notably Casper...Purple...Tuft & Needle... and Leesa. Among innerspring mattress brands, relatively unknown web-sold Saatva registers the highest satisfaction score—81%—partly because of very strong customer service.

Other innerspring mattress brands that score relatively well in satisfaction include the upscale but little-known Hästens (77% satisfaction) and Aireloom/Kluft (75%)...and economical Ikea (70%).

In two other mattress categories, the most famous brands score well for satisfaction—but not for value—and there are great alternatives...

• **Tempur-Pedic,** the biggest name in memory foam mattresses, has an 81% customer satisfaction score. But a company called Zinus (Zinus.com) makes memory foam mattresses that have a 78% satisfaction score and cost just $250 to $300 versus $2,000 or more for most Tempur-Pedic mattresses. Zinus mattresses are sold on Amazon.com under the brand names "Sleep Master" and "Best Price"... and on Walmart.com under the brand name "Spa Sensations."

• **Sleep Number** is the biggest name in adjustable-firmness mattresses and has a 77% owner-satisfaction score—but lesser known adjustable brands Boyd (BoydSleep.com), Innomax (Innomax.com, sold at Sam's Club as "Dual Digital" mattresses) and Personal Comfort (PersonalComfortBed.com) all earn satisfaction scores of 78% to 82% and typically cost at least 15% less than comparable Sleep Number mattresses.

Best Memory Foam

Consumer Reports.

Top-scoring memory foam mattresses, based on sleeping-position preferences, durability, stabilization and firmness: The Casper, available at Casper.com...Novaform 14-inch Serafina Pearl Gel from Costco... Tuft & Needle T&N Mattress...Serta iComfort Savant EverFeel...Spring Air Back Supporter Natalie from Costco.

Top-scoring innerspring mattresses: Charles P. Rogers Powercore Estate 5000...Sealy Posturepedic Hybrid Elite Kelburn...Sealy Posturepedic Hybrid Trust Cushion...Denver Mattress Doctor's Choice... Charles P. Rogers St. Regis Pillowtop.

Luxury Hotel Pillows Anyone Can Own

Craig Clark, cofounder and CEO of Pillows.com, an online pillow retailer specializing in pillows found in luxury hotels and resorts. Pillows.com

Hotels spend a lot of time trying to find ways to give you a great night's sleep.

Good news: Often, you can buy the same pillow that you take a liking to at a hotel for your bed at home.

Among the hotels that feature excellent pillows*...

• **St. Julien Hotel and Spa (made by Down Etc.) has a Down 75% White Goose Feather/25%**

*All prices are typical for standard-size 20-inch-by-25-inch pillows. Prices and availablity are subject to change.

White Goose Down Pillow that may be the best down/feather pillow on the market for side sleepers. It offers the softness of white goose down, but it is overfilled for extra neck support. The double stitching ensures the overfill won't burst out. *Price:* $95. Pillows.com

•**Marriott usually provides the Pacific Coast Down Surround Pillow from Pacific Coast Feather Company.** These medium-firmness down-and-feather pillows feature a two-compartment system—an inner compartment contains mostly feathers for structure and support, while a surrounding outer compartment contains mostly goose down for fluffy softness. It's a great choice for back and stomach sleepers, but it provides insufficient neck support for most side sleepers unless combined with a second pillow. The Down Surround is sometimes marketed as DownAround or Touch of Down. *Price:* $63. 888-297-1778, PacificCoast.com.

•**The MGM Grand in Las Vegas provides the Down Etc Diamond Support Feather Pillow.** It contains 95% Grey Duck feathers and 5% Grey Duck down. Pillows with such a high ratio of feathers to down provide lots of support, but they generally lack softness, and the quills create a slightly bumpy feel against the skin that some find annoying. Down Etc solved these problems by enclosing the Diamond Support Feather Pillow in a double layer of quilted fabric, which supplies a soft barrier between feathers and skin. It's an excellent choice for side sleepers. *Price:* $65. 866-369-6382, DownEtc.com.

•**Ritz-Carlton provides the Pacific Coast Double DownAround Pillow.** These are similar to the Pacific Coast Down Surround pillows at Marriott Hotels, mentioned earlier, only with more depth and loft, which makes them appropriate for side sleepers. This pillow sometimes is sold as Double Down Surround. *Price:* $63. 888-297-1778, PacificCoast.com.

•**Westin usually provides the DownLite Hotel 50/50 Down & Feather Pillow.** Few hotel pillows can match its softness because few contain this much down (50%)—25% is more common. And white goose down produces wonderful loft and recovery even compared with other down. This is an excellent pillow for back sleepers and acceptable for side sleepers. It has too much fill for stomach sleepers. *Price:* $70. 866-931-3696, ShopDownLite.com (click on "Feather Pillows").

Do-It-Yourself Fix-Its

5 Home-Repair Tips from the Pros

Greg Chick has been a licensed plumbing contractor for 40 years based in Ramona, California. He offers plumbing how-to videos on his website, DIYPlumbingAdvice.com.

Danny Lipford has been a remodeling contractor for 40 years. He is based in Mobile, Alabama, and is host of *Today's Homeowner with Danny Lipford*, a nationally syndicated program. TodaysHomeowner.com

Eric Kleinert has more than 40 years of experience in major appliance and heating, ventilation and air-conditioning (HVAC) service and installation. He has served as program director for Fortis Colleges and Institutes in Palm Springs, Florida, and is author of *Troubleshooting and Repairing Major Appliances*.

Handling common home repairs on your own rather than bringing in expensive repair people could save you hundreds of dollars—or cost you thousands of dollars if you make a big mistake. Because of the possible pitfalls, home owners often are too scared to attempt repairs that are surprisingly doable. Before you attempt to tackle any of these, you need to know the secrets that experts rely on to avoid catastrophe.

We asked three experts to identify some low-risk home repairs that truly are worth tackling as DIY projects and to reveal the twists and turns that will help guide you to success.

Plumbing—GREG CHICK

Bungled plumbing repairs can cause costly water damage or other problems—but certain repairs are relatively simple and have limited downside...

•**Clear a clogged bathroom-sink drain.** A plunger isn't always enough. And chemical drain cleaners such as Drano and Liquid-Plumr can damage plastic pipes and other plumbing components... corrode metal pipes...and/or alter the chemistry of a septic system if used frequently.

Instead, tackle the problem without chemicals. Start by removing the stopper. If it doesn't simply lift out, remove the nut located on the back of the drain pipe just below the sink. The lever that passes through this nut is holding the stopper in place. (Some sinks have slightly different stopper systems.) You might be able to use a thin grabbing tool, such as hemostat forceps (available at medical-supply stores or online for less than $5), to remove the obstruction. If not, reattach the nut you removed when freeing the stopper (to prevent leaking and loss of suction)...then run the water...cover the sink's overflow opening with your hand...and place the nozzle of a running wet/dry vac over the clogged drain. (If you don't own a wet/dry vac, buy one—at around $60, they cost less than most plumbers charge for a single service call.) After a few seconds, move the vac nozzle to the overflow opening for a few seconds...then back to the drain (again covering the overflow). Continue moving the nozzle back and forth until the changes in pressure dislodge the clog—pulling it up to the vac or sending it down the drain—and the water flows freely down the drain.

Helpful: Dislodging the detritus from your sink drain in this manner might result in noticeable drain odor. If so, use a bottle brush to scrub the drain line. If the odor persists, put the stopper back in, close the drain, then run the hot water for three to five minutes with the water flowing down the overflow opening. This washes away the detritus that was causing the smell. Monitor the sink to make sure that water doesn't spill onto the floor.

●**Fix a running toilet the right way.** First, make sure that nothing simple has gone wrong—remove the tank lid and look inside. Is the chain that is connected to the flush handle caught under the flapper (the part lifted by the chain when you flush)? If so, shortening this chain slightly should solve the problem.

Flush the toilet. Is some part of the mechanism snagging on another part? If so, making a small adjustment to one of these parts—adding a slight bend to a float ball arm, for example—could be the solution.

If neither of these things is happening, the problem probably is a warped flapper. These fail faster than ever these days due to the chemicals put in the water by local water districts and the cleaning chemicals that some home owners put in their toilets. It isn't always easy to select the proper replacement. Shut off the water to the toilet…flush to empty the tank…disconnect the chain connecting the flapper to the flush arm…then lift out the flapper—flappers vary, but removing them usually is simple and intuitive.

The most challenging part of replacing a flapper is buying the right replacement. You could bring the old flapper to a home center or plumbing-supply store and ask for a match—but if the last person to replace this flapper chose the wrong part, this would get you the wrong part, too. A safer solution is to jot down your toilet make and model and see if one of the flappers at the parts store lists this model. Also, look under your toilet's tank lid—some provide a list of replacement-part numbers.

●**Unclog a showerhead.** Clogged spray holes in a showerhead often can be cleared without even removing the showerhead from the wall. Soak a washcloth in white vinegar, then use a rubber band to secure it around the showerhead with the cloth tight against the nozzle. The vinegar can clear

clogs in as little as 20 minutes, though longer soak times improve your odds. This technique works on clogged faucet aerators, too.

If the washcloth doesn't work, fill a gallon-size plastic bag halfway with vinegar and secure it over the showerhead (rubber bands work) so that the head is immersed.

Driveways—DANNY LIPFORD

This is relatively easy for home owners but relatively costly if you hire a pro…

●**Seal an asphalt driveway.** Sealing an asphalt driveway can prevent cracks from becoming large holes. Pros charge $300 to $600 or more—depending on the size of the driveway—and you might not get your money's worth. There are many shady operators that do low-quality work.

Clear away encroaching grass and weeds from the edges, then clean your driveway with hot water or use a pressure washer if you have one. Next use a driveway caulk to fill small cracks…asphalt patching paste to fill large cracks…and a "tamp and set" product such as Latex-ite Super Patch (about $12.50 for one gallon or $22 for 3.5 gallons) to fill potholes. (Remove loose materials before filling these cracks and holes.)

Buy a good-quality sealant from a home-improvement store. Then follow the instructions on the container. Pay attention to temperature recommendations—applying sealants when it is too hot or cold can cause them to fail. If your driveway is sloped, start at the uphill end.

Caution: Sealant quality varies. It's worth it to pay extra for a product intended to be applied with a squeegee, not a paint roller. (Pulling the squeegee toward you will work better than pushing it away from you.) The best I've found is Latex-ite Optimum Driveway Filler Sealer (about $35 for a 4.75-gallon bucket sufficient for 400 to 500 square feet of driveway, Latexite.com).

Appliances —ERIC KLEINERT

Modern appliances are computerized, which makes them very difficult for home owners to fix. *But here's a repair that's still fairly easy…*

• **Fix a washing machine that is no longer spinning or agitating.** The problem could be a snapped or dislodged drive belt—that's the rubber belt that connects the unit's motor to its drum or transmission. Unplug the washing machine, and remove its access panel. With a top loader, it typically is the front panel that detaches. You might have to remove a few screws near the base…and/or slide a putty knife along the top of this panel, releasing several clips. With a front loader, access is typically from the rear. If you cannot figure out how to get inside your washer, enter its make and model online and search for videos on gaining access.

Once you get the washer open, look for a rubber belt lying near the bottom of the unit or hanging loose from the motor or drum pulley. If it is intact but dislodged, the repair might simply require putting it back in place. If it's snapped, take it to an appliance parts store and ask for a replacement.

Helpful: Tipping the washer back and resting it against a wall can provide easier access—just make sure it is stable. If it is difficult to stretch the belt into place, first position it on the motor, then hold it in place along one side of the drum pulley. Ask someone to slowly rotate the drum, which should ease the belt the rest of the way around the pulley—be careful not to catch your fingers between the belt and pulley.

Note that some washers don't have drive belts at all—they use a "direct drive" connection between the motor and the drum. When they stop spinning, it's generally time to call a repair person or replace the washer.

Don't Call a Plumber for a Clogged Sink Until You Try This First

Men's Health. MensHealth.com

Fill an empty milk jug or a two-liter soda bottle with water. Cover the overflow drain of the sink with duct tape (to stop air from escaping). In one quick motion, jam the top of the bottle into the drain and squeeze the bottle hard to send a jet of water into the drain. Remove the duct tape, and run the water to see if the clog is gone. If not, you can repeat these steps up to three times. If that doesn't work, it's time to call a plumber.

What Most Plumbers Won't Tell You, But This One Will

Terry Love, owner of Love Plumbing & Remodel in Bellevue and Bothell, Washington. He has been a plumber since 1974 and runs a popular Internet forum on plumbing issues at TerryLove.com.

We don't think much about our plumbing until something goes wrong—but when it does go wrong, it can turn our lives upside down. Leaks can cause thousands of dollars' worth of water damage and/or mold problems that are not covered by insurance.

Many costly plumbing problems can be prevented if home owners take some simple preventive steps. And some plumbing problems are well within the abilities of the average home owner to repair on his/her own.

How to keep your plumbing running right and your money in your pocket…

Preventing Problems

Preventive maintenance moves that are worth making…

• **Replace the hoses connecting your washing machine to your home's water supply.** These hoses endure significant stress each time your washer starts or stops. They sometimes burst, flooding laundry rooms, even though they showed no prior outward signs of damage.

Best: Replace the hoses every 10 years, even if they still look fine. Braided stainless steel replacement hoses are somewhat more dependable than rubber ones. Expect to spend $10 to $20 per hose.

Cost: $50 for a set of two.

Helpful: Shut off the water to the washing machine before removing the old hoses, and drain any water remaining in those hoses into a bucket. Once you've attached the new hoses, turn the water back on, and watch for leaks at both ends of the hose to make sure that the connections are tight before pushing the machine back against the wall.

•**Check for small puddles under your water heater.** Even tiny leaks from water heaters can signal that full-blown failure is just days or weeks away. If you spot leaking water and the water heater is at least 10 years old, buy a new water heater as soon as possible, and clear everything of value from the area so that it won't be damaged if the current water heater gives out before it's replaced. If yours is less than 10 years old, consider calling a plumber for a repair. Be aware, though, that a repair might cost $250 to $500 and a replacement water heater may not cost much more than that.

•**Watch for leaks when you turn on external faucets for the first time each spring.** Ice might have caused cracks in the pipes leading to these faucets during the winter. Such leaks can occur inside the home, so head down to your basement or crawl space, and check the pipes leading to your external faucets where they exit the home.

To reduce the odds of this ice damage in future years, shut off the water to external faucets before the first freeze, then open these faucets and disconnect any hoses. If your home does not have shut-off valves for its external faucets, buy Styrofoam faucet covers (available in home centers for around $5 apiece). These provide some insulation for faucets exposed to winter weather.

•**Watch for unexplained water use.** If you have access to your water meter, periodically turn off all taps and water-using appliances, and then see if your meter continues turning. Monitor water bills for sudden increases, too.

The most common problem is a running toilet. It doesn't just inflate water bills—it could flood your home if the toilet clogs. (See the next page for strategies for fixing running toilets.) Do not assume you will hear it running. Running toilets sometimes are virtually inaudible.

Do-It-Yourself Solutions

Home owners don't need to pay a plumber to solve these problems...

•**Dripping faucets.** Most modern kitchen and bathroom faucets are what's known as "cartridge faucets." To stop a drip, simply replace the cartridge, which regulates water flow.

You might not even have to purchase this replacement. Many major brands now offer lifetime guarantees and supply new cartridges for free to home owners who call their customer service phone numbers. If your faucets don't have this coverage, expect to pay $10 to $25 or more.

To replace a cartridge, shut the valves below the sink to turn off the water to the faucet, then turn the faucet on to relieve any remaining water pressure. If there's a decorative cap on top of the faucet handle (or handles, if this is a two-handle faucet), unscrew it or (depending on the faucet model) gently pry it off. Remove the screw holding the handle in place, then remove the handle. This should provide access to the top of the cartridge, a cylindrical part usually made of brass or plastic. There's likely a locking nut or retaining clip holding the cartridge in place. Remove this, then remove the old cartridge. Insert the replacement, and put the faucet back together. If your faucet does not conform to the steps described above, search the manufacturer's website for specific directions.

Some bathrooms and kitchens have older faucet styles, which fall into a few categories. You have a "Delta-style" faucet if the handle feels like it's rotating backward slightly—not moving straight up—when the water is turned on. You have a compression two-handle faucet if it feels like additional force must be applied to turn the water flow off completely. Drips in these styles of faucets often are simple to fix, too, but the parts and processes are different. Check the manufacturer's site for repair directions, or use Google.com or YouTube.com to search for directions.

Virtually all compression faucets and most Delta-style faucets now are decades old. Drips and leaks start to become common in faucets of this age, so replacing these might make the most sense.

•**Running toilets.** When a toilet won't stop running, it usually means that the flapper—that plastic or rubber piece in the tank that's lifted up by a chain when the toilet is flushed—is no longer sealing properly. Remove the tank's lid, and use a stick to gently push down on the flapper. If the toilet stops running, you've identified the problem. Turn off the water to the toilet, flush to drain the tank, remove the flapper and take it to a home center to find a new one of the same size and shape. Chlorine is the culprit in most flapper failure, so it's worth a few dollars extra for a flapper made from advanced materials designed to stand up to the chlorine in tap water. Chlorine-resistant models often are red, not black.

If the flapper isn't the problem, the toilet's fill valve likely is. New fill valves cost less than $20 and are easy to install. Select a reliable fill valve brand, such as Fluidmaster or Korky, and follow the installation directions that come with it. Don't worry if the new fill valve looks different from the one that it's replacing—"float ball" fill valves have been replaced by "float cup" fill valves in recent years, but they serve the same purpose. Standard fill valves, available in any home center or hardware store, will fit most modern toilets, though some replacement fill valves are specifically designed for certain one-piece toilets.

•**Clogged toilets and drains.** Most home owners buy the wrong plunger, use it incorrectly, then wonder why they have trouble clearing clogs. Instead of the traditional red dome plunger, select one with a fold-out black rubber flange that, when extended, reduces the diameter of the plunger's mouth to approximately two inches so that it forms a tighter seal with the toilet bowl opening. The insert can be left tucked in when dealing with a clogged sink or tub drains.

Home owners often use too much force with a plunger. Strenuous plunging is likely to break the plunger's seal with the toilet or drain, reducing suction. Instead, position the plunger in the toilet or over the drain, and help it create a seal by vibrating it in and out a few times by just a half inch or so. Then gently pull the plunger up to remove the clog.

Helpful: A closet auger (also called a toilet auger), which has a flexible cable and a crank handle to maneuver the cable, is another good tool for clearing clogs, but augers sold in home centers often have ⅞-inch-wide heads—so small that they pass right through clogs without moving them. Select an auger with a head approximately 1⅜ inches in width at a plumbing-supply store.

•**Low flow from a faucet or showerhead.** This often is caused by sediment buildup. Remove the showerhead or faucet's aerator—the aerator is the small screen screwed into the end of the faucet. If this requires the use of a wrench, apply a few layers of masking tape or duct tape to the faucet or showerhead to reduce the odds that you'll scratch the finish. Clean the aerator or showerhead with an old toothbrush, and soak it in white vinegar if necessary. If the aerator won't come clean, buy a replacement.

Smart: Shut the sink's drain before removing the aerator so that small parts won't be lost.

4 Terrific Home Improvements

Katie and Gene Hamilton are authors of 20 home-improvement books including *Fix It and Flip It* and creators of DIYorNot.com, an award-winning website about the cost of home improvements.

You can tap the hidden potential in your home with products and materials that make the most of the space…solve problems…and make your home more attractive and comfortable.

Here are four projects that do just that—along with what it would cost if you do them yourself or if you hire someone.*

•**Conceal ugly support columns in a basement.** You can turn an unfinished basement into a playroom, home office, family room or whatever kind of space you need. But what to do about those ugly steel support columns?

You can't remove the basement columns, often called Lally posts, because they are structural supports. But you can make them more attractive by covering up the supports with a product called Pole-

Wrap. The material is a half-inch hardwood veneer that comes in cherry, light maple or red oak and has a flexible backing. It is sold in eight-foot lengths with three different widths so that it fits most support columns. The material is installed with construction adhesive, and the top and bottom of the pole are finished with a matching cap and base. Pole-Wrap is presanded and requires staining or a polyurethane finish. To cover two four-inch-diameter support columns with Pole-Wrap and add caps and bases, a contractor will charge $460, which includes labor and materials. You can buy the materials and wood stain or polyurethane for $320 and do it yourself and pocket a 30% savings. For more information, go to PoleWrap.com.

●**Change a seldom-used bathtub into a shower with an easy replacement.** If, like many home owners, you use a tub primarily for showering, you can make it easier and safer by replacing the tub with a shower stall that has a low step-over threshold.

After the tub is removed, a preformed fiberglass shower receptor pan forms the base for the shower stall. You can get one from Sterling Ensemble that fits into a standard five-foot bathtub alcove space. The 60-by-30-inch receptor fits directly between the walls that enclosed the tub and comes in both left- and right-drain configurations. To prevent pooling water, it is molded with a slight draft toward the drain. Complete the project with a matching fiberglass wall surround kit, tile or a solid surface on the three surrounding walls, and add new faucet fixtures.

If you have a contractor do this project, expect to pay $2,900, which includes labor and materials, to remove the old bathtub and fixtures and install a new shower pan receptor, fiberglass wall surround kit and fixtures. The cost can easily double if you decide on ceramic tile or a solid surface wall covering such as marble. Add about $100 for a shower rod and curtain. A glass shower door can add any-

*The DIY cost of projects is based on national average cost data from major retailers and e-commerce websites with home-improvement products. The cost of hiring a professional is determined by averaging cost and data information in several construction books that are updated annually and used by contractors to prepare job bids.

where from $200 for an inexpensive sliding door to more than $1,000 for a frameless glass door.

If you have experience with carpentry and plumbing projects, you can buy the receptor and wall surround kit at bath and home centers for $1,200 and do the job yourself. For more information, go to SterlingPlumbing.com.

●**Install a floor area in an unfinished attic for light storage.** An accessible attic with exposed floor joists has untapped potential—all it needs is flooring to create a usable destination for all your lightweight stuff.

Georgia-Pacific makes a tongue-and-groove particleboard flooring in four-by-eight-foot panels called Sturd-I-Floor (available at lumberyards and home centers) that is suitable for this purpose.

Most attic floors with at least two-by-six-floor joists will support light loads such as boxes of clothing and decorations, but consult a professional contractor if you want to store heavy objects such as furniture. Your local building department can be of help, too.

Nailing the flooring to the joists is a straightforward project. But getting the new flooring into the attic can be a challenge. In most attics, it's impossible to get full four-by-eight panels up there. If that's the case for you, cut the panels in half to make two-by-eight-foot panels. You may even have to cut these in half again to fit through a trapdoor.

Place the first panel on the joists, and nail it in place. Then use this panel as a base from which you can install the others. Be careful if you walk on the joists because putting your foot through the ceiling will cancel any potential saving that comes from doing it yourself and you could get hurt.

A contractor will charge you $473, which includes labor and materials, to lay an area of approximately 120 feet square. A handy home owner with carpentry tools and experience can do the job for $180 and pocket $293, a 62% savings. For more information, you can go to Buildgp.com and search "Sturd-I-Floor."

●**Expand outdoor storage under a raised deck with an under-deck ceiling.** The space under a second-floor deck can become useful storage space when it's protected from dripping rain and snow coming through the deck boards above. You can catch any runoff with an under-deck ceiling. The vinyl material is designed as a drainage system that attaches to the underside of a second-level deck and directs the water to a gutter system. This creates a ground-level outdoor room or useful space for storing bicycles and gardening equipment and other items.

A contractor will charge $2,430, which includes labor and materials, to install an under-deck ceiling below a 14-by-20-foot deck. A DIY home owner can purchase the materials for $1,900 and pocket a 22% savings. For more information, go to UnderDeck.com.

Kitchen Spruce-Ups You'll Love

Kelly Morisseau, certified master kitchen and bath designer and lead designer for the San Francisco–area remodeling firm MSK Design Build. She has more than 25 years of experience in kitchen and bath design and is founder of the Kitchen Sync blog and author of the book *Kelly's Kitchen Savvy: Solutions for Partial Kitchen Remodels.* KellyMorisseau.com/blog

A full kitchen renovation is likely to cost more than $20,000, according to HomeAdvisor.com—and potentially much more if you select high-end appliances and materials. But there are ways to make a drab, dated or worn-out kitchen look significantly better for a whole lot less money. Of course, a new coat of paint and new cabinet hardware can get you started—but there are other low-cost ways to spruce up your kitchen that can have surprisingly dramatic results. *Here are seven great kitchen spruce-ups, ranging from $35.99 to $1,000…*

●**Replace underpowered bulbs and "flush mount" ceiling lights.** Insufficient lighting is a big reason why many older kitchens look dated and dingy. Hiring an electrician to install additional fixtures can cost thousands, but for a few hundred dollars you could replace the "flush mount" overhead lighting fixtures often found in older kitchens with "semi flush" fixtures. Unlike flush-mount fixtures, which position bulbs at or very near ceiling level, semi-flush fixtures extend down perhaps a foot

from the ceiling. They're generally more attractive and almost always do a better job of distributing light throughout the room.

Example: Feiss Prospect Park Semi-Flush Mount light in satin nickel can be found for around $315 (LampsPlus.com).

●**Install laminate countertops and backsplashes that look like high-end stone.** Laminates lack the prestige of high-end quartz or stone countertops, but today the best of these man-made products really do resemble stone countertops for a fraction of the price.

Example: Formica 180fx laminate effectively mimics marble, granite and travertine, yet it can be found for $100 to $200 per 48-inch-x-96-inch sheet.

If you have a small kitchen, you might be able to have new laminate countertops installed for about $1,000. Granite would likely cost at least twice that. If new countertops aren't in your budget, you still could use these laminates as an eye-catching backsplash.

Additional backsplash options: If you have a traditional-style kitchen, consider installing a painted bead-board backsplash—bead board costs around $20 per 48-inch-x-8-inch panel. Tile is a fine choice for traditional or modern kitchens—choose large-scale 18-x-18-inch tiles, which are in style and easy to install. Larger tiles mean fewer tiles and less grout work. You'll find plenty of tile options for less than $3 a square foot.

●**Replace the countertop microwave.** If your budget is tight, you almost certainly can't replace a kitchen full of older appliances. But for $200 or less, you can replace an old or a low-end microwave with a new one that looks modern and stylish. Microwaves generally are positioned prominently on countertops or hung at eye level, so updating this one seemingly minor appliance can make a kitchen feel more modern. Today's microwaves tend to be smaller than the microwaves of decades past, too, so updating a countertop microwave could free up counter space, making a small kitchen seem a bit less cramped.

•**Update the inside of your cabinets with roll-outs, stacked shelving and cutlery holders.** Painting kitchen cabinets is an inexpensive and oft-mentioned way to pep up their appearance...but a coat of paint won't make old cabinets any more functional on the inside, and that's important, too. Today's cabinets often feature roll-out racks, rotating trays and other amenities that help home owners get the most out of kitchen storage space. Efficient cabinets don't just make kitchens more convenient—they make them more attractive, too, because clutter will more likely be stowed out of sight.

Fortunately, you do not need to install new cabinets to accomplish this. There is a wide range of after-market kitchen roll-out racks and other organization products on the market that can transform old, basic cabinets into modern, functional storage spaces. The Container Store has perhaps the best selection, but you also can find kitchen-cabinet organizing items at places ranging from Amazon.com to a home-improvement center or a hardware store.

Example: The Container Store's Chrome Roll-Out Cabinet Drawers recently were available for $54.99 to $69.99 apiece (ContainerStore.com).

•**Add a rolling or freestanding island.** Installing a permanent kitchen island costs thousands, but attractive rolling and freestanding islands are available at home centers for $500 or less. These islands can provide additional counter space and serve as an attractive addition to the kitchen. (They're not right for every kitchen, however. If there isn't enough room to position the island at least 36 inches from the main kitchen counters, it will make the kitchen feel cramped.)

If you decide on a rolling island, make sure its wheels lock and—if you have vinyl or softwood kitchen floors—the island should be relatively lightweight so that it won't damage your flooring.

•**Install or expand moldings.** Crown moldings, which run along the top edge of walls...decorative baseboards, which run along the bottom edge... and decorative door and window casings can make a plain kitchen seem much more upscale. Add these moldings if your kitchen lacks them.

•**Hang colorful window coverings.** Brightly colored kitchen curtains or shades can instantly make a dull kitchen seem more stylish and interesting. In fact, this is among the cheapest, easiest ways to significantly update the look of a kitchen, particularly a kitchen that currently features mostly whites and neutral tones.

Caution: If a kitchen window is near a sink, make sure that the curtain or shade is made from stain-resistant material.

Best Do-It-Yourself Home Security Systems

Mike Prospero, US editor-in-chief (specializing in smart-home devices) for *Tom's Guide*, an online news resource that reviews new technology products. TomsGuide.com

People want to feel secure in their homes. But the lofty price of home security systems is a big reason why only one-quarter of US homes have any home security setup. Now the latest generation of do-it-yourself systems provide many features of professionally installed setups at a more attractive price.

A starter kit that you install and monitor starts at $200 to $300, although adding features or outfitting a larger home could add a few hundred dollars. In comparison, a basic professional system could cost about $1,300 for equipment and installation...and a monitoring contract for two years will add about $35 a month.

DIY kits include a wireless base station that connects to your home Internet and a built-in alarm...a battery-powered door/window and interior-motion sensor...a wall-mounted keypad or key fob and smartphone app that controls everything...and cellular and battery backup in case your electricity or Wi-Fi fails. Some DIY systems offer professional monitoring with flexible contracts ranging from $10 to $25 per month if you'd rather have the security company alert the police and/or fire department when your alarm is triggered.

Best DIY systems, all of which feature cellular and battery backup if you purchase a monitoring plan...

Best overall: Abode Smart Security. This is the easiest to set up and use. It integrates with Amazon Alexa, Apple HomeKit and Google Assistant, so you can control the system with voice commands.

Professional monitoring: $22 per month. Or order three- or seven-day monitoring for when you are away for $8 or $15, respectively.

Included: One entry sensor for a door or window, one motion detector. $245. GoAbode.com

For low-cost professional monitoring: Ring Alarm Security costs $10 a month for the service of alerting the police if your alarm sounds. Ring's Neighbors app lets you get crime and safety alerts from neighbors if they have Ring installed. Includes one entry sensor and one motion detector.

Smart-home capabilities: Works with Alexa but only a limited amount of third-party smart-home devices. $199. Ring.com

For extra security features: SimpliSafe Essentials has a wider range of add-ons than many competitors, including smart locks...panic buttons to activate your alarm silently...a 105-decibel alarm, about 15% louder than typical alarms...and sensors that detect water, smoke, low temperatures and breaking glass. The advanced motion sensor can distinguish between people and pets.

Professional monitoring: $28 monthly. Includes three entry sensors, one motion detector.

Smart-home capability: Works with Alexa and Google Assistant, but only a limited amount of third-party smart-home devices. $275. SimpliSafe.com

12 Tips That Will Help You Paint Walls Like a Pro

Chris Berry, a Boise, Idaho–based painter and contractor with three decades of experience. He is founder of The Idaho Painter, a website and YouTube channel that provides painting advice. TheIdahoPainter.com

Painting walls with latex paint is one of the most common do-it-yourself projects, but home owners often make mistakes that look bad or even force them to paint all over again. Some of those mistakes occur before the DIYers even apply paint—when they buy equipment and prep the walls. *Here are 12 tips from an experienced painter that will give you prolike results when you paint your walls...*

Selecting Supplies

Home owners often spend hours picking out the perfect paint color...then just grab any nearby rollers, brushes and other supplies at the home center. That's a mistake. Using the wrong tools makes painting harder and makes the result worse, too. *The painting supplies you should buy...*

•**Brand-name ⅜-inch-nap, nine-inch-long roller covers.** Home centers and painting stores offer a wide range of roller-cover options, but a nine-inch length with a ⅜-inch nap (the depth of the roller's pile) is almost always a home owner's best choice. A nine-inch length is large enough that you can paint quickly but small enough to be manageable. A ⅜-inch nap holds lots of paint yet still produces a smooth finish.

Exceptions: A slightly shorter nap could be appropriate if you want a very smooth finish and are willing to take more time (it holds less paint)...a slightly longer nap could be appropriate if you are painting a rough surface such as concrete block and don't mind that textured finish.

•**Brand-name roller covers are worth their higher price**—they hold paint better than off-brand covers and are less likely to shed lint into painted surfaces, which looks terrible. Good roller-cover choices include Purdy White Dove and Sherwin-Williams's Contractor Series Soft Woven.

Also buy a roller handle (what pros call a "frame") with an extension pole long enough that you can use the roller on your walls and/or ceilings while standing on the floor, not on a ladder. This will cut painting time in half.

•**Paintbrush with Chinex bristles.** Chinex is a DuPont nylon that holds its shape and stiffness very well and cleans up easily. A two-to-three-inch-wide Chinex-bristled brush might cost $15 to $20— they're not cheap—but it will last a long time if you prevent paint from drying on it. To do this, clean the brush with warm water every two to three hours even if you intend to go right back to painting.

Recommended: Corona Performance-series Chinex-bristle brush. An angle-cut brush is a good choice for painting walls near trim or ceilings.

•**Canvas drop cloth.** DIY painters tend to put little thought into drop cloths—many just use old sheets or shower curtains. Only later do they learn that paint can soak right through bedsheets and can roll right off the edges of plastic shower curtains. It's worth buying a thick canvas drop cloth—a nine-foot-by-12-foot one can cost as little as $20. Or pay a bit more for a canvas drop cloth that has a slip-resistant coating on one side to reduce the risk that the cloth will slide when someone walks on it, causing a fall or shifting a ladder.

•**Deep-well roller tray…or a paint bucket and grid.** The deeper your paint tray, the less time you must spend refilling it. Buy disposable paint tray liners, too—they save you from having to clean your tray. Or do what many pros do, and skip the tray entirely. Instead, dip your roller directly into a bucket of paint. To do this, buy a five-gallon bucket large enough to fit a roller, and buy a "paint roller grid." Hang this grid inside the bucket, and roll your roller along the grid to remove excess paint as you would on the incline section of a paint tray.

Prepping to Paint

Use a degreaser before painting surfaces within five feet or so of a cooktop. Paint will not stick properly to kitchen walls, ceilings or cabinets if these are coated with the oil that typically comes from cooking. Use a product specifically designed to prepare greasy surfaces for paint. Do this even if the surface to be painted is not visibly greasy—applying a degreaser once is a lot easier than painting twice.

Example: Krud Kutter Prepaint Cleaner, typically $10 or less for a 32-ounce spray bottle.

Press down on your painter's tape…and then press again. When DIYers peel away painter's tape after painting, they may discover that paint has gotten underneath.

The fix: After you position tape, run the pad of a finger firmly along its length to improve the seal. If the paint job takes more than an hour or so, run your finger along the tape in that section once again.

Combine cans of store-mixed paint if you expect to use more than one. If you are going to use multiple cans of the same color paint, mix them all together in a five-gallon bucket before painting. Pros call this "boxing" the paint. Paint stores don't always mix paint exactly the same for each can, so if you don't do this, some sections could end up being a slightly different color from others.

Add latex extender to latex paint before applying it with a brush. When DIYers brush on latex paint, their brushstrokes often remain visible. Pros use an additive that causes latex paint to dry more slowly and smoothly. (This additive isn't necessary when latex paint is applied with a roller.)

Recommended: X-I-M Latex X-tender, $13 per quart—enough to treat five to 16 gallons of paint.

Tips for Applying Paint

Paint edges first. Use a brush to "cut in" paint on the wall around moldings, ceilings and other edges before you use your roller on the rest of the wall. DIYers sometimes do this in the reverse order because they want to delay doing the tricky edge bits as long as possible—but doing the edges last often results in a visible "halo" effect around fixtures, windows, doors and other edges because the brushed area overlaps the rollered area rather than getting hidden beneath it.

Load up your roller with lots of paint. Painting with too little paint on a roller, known as "dry napping," results in tiny gaps in the paint. A too-dry roller even could pick up paint already applied, rather than lay more paint down.

Not sure whether you have enough paint on the roller? Listen. A dry roller makes a hissing sound as it rolls along the surface. A roller with sufficient paint sounds moist. (Once you hear these sounds, the difference should be clear.)

Tip: Some DIYers use too little paint on their rollers because they want to avoid the drips that can occur when a roller heavily loaded with paint is lifted to the wall or ceiling. These drips can be minimized by rotating the handle of the roller

180 degrees once or twice to reverse the drippy paint as you lift it.

Load up a section of wall with paint, then even out that paint. Don't try to make paint look perfectly even from the moment you apply it to a surface. Instead, first get enough paint onto every part of a section of wall roughly two to three feet wide. Apply enough pressure to the roller to get the paint down into the texture of the surface, use enough paint so that there are no tiny gaps, and overlap your previously painted section by around half of your roller's width. Then position your roller at the top of the section, and gently and smoothly roll from top to bottom in successive swaths, taking the roller off the wall each time you reach the bottom, to even out the previously applied paint in the section.

How to Paint Trim

If you are painting both walls and trim, paint the trim first. Apply multiple coats of paint to trim, if necessary, and wait for these to dry completely before taping off trim and painting walls. (If you're painting the ceiling, too, paint it after the trim but before the walls.)

Use an airless sprayer—a sprayer can't leave brushstrokes. Such sprayers can be rented at many home centers and paint stores. Be sure to follow the directions that come with the sprayer and to carefully cover surrounding areas with tape and plastic sheeting.

If you don't want to bother with a sprayer, use a brush that's made for trim and that has 100% polyester bristles such as the Purdy XL Glide angle sash brush. The soft bristles make such a brush less likely than others to leave brushstrokes. And use a latex extender, such as the X-I-M Latex X-tender described on page 78, when applying latex paint to trim—without this, latex paint is more likely to dry too quickly and leave brush marks.

As with walls, the best strategy for painting trim is to first get sufficient paint onto every part of the trim...and then "lay out" that paint using long, smooth, single-direction strokes.

New Paints for Easy Work

George Susca, former owner of the Bayside Paint Place, Bayside, New York, and partner of the five-outlet Paint Place chain, one of the largest volume paint retailers on Long Island. Susca has more than 20 years in the paint business, first as a housepainter and now as a retailer.

Painting is one of the most daunting tasks for home owners, especially for those who try to tackle the job themselves. Several new types of paint have made the job much easier and often more satisfying.

No Need for Primer

The following paints use new technologies to make paint molecules link together so that the colors last longer and cover better. No separate coat of primer is needed before putting these paints on your walls or other surfaces. Only one or two coats of paint are needed to cover a surface, even if there is a darker color already on the wall, thus saving time and money.

Benjamin Moore Aura interior and exterior paints offer great depth of color and exceptional durability. Approximately $90 per gallon.

Valspar Duramax, an exterior paint that is sold only at Lowe's home-improvement stores, includes ingredients that provide extra resistance to mold, mildew and algae. $49 per gallon and up.

Behr Premium Plus Ultra exterior paint is available only at The Home Depot stores. Between $28 and $39 per gallon.

Metallic Colors

A metallic paint (such as silver patina, gold leaf and copper) can be a very strong look, so use it more as an accent—in a bathroom, on one wall of a larger room or as a striped effect, combining a wide strip of metallic with a similar or slightly contrasting color in a flat or eggshell paint.

These colors are pricey and may require several coats for even coverage. They can be used alone or over a nonmetallic base color to create a faux finish.

Examples: The Valspar Signature Colors Brilliant Metals line, about $56 per gallon, provides a dramatic metallic sheen.

Stop a Screen Snag

BobVila.com

Nail polish stops window-screen tears. Just apply clear polish directly over snags and slits on fiberglass screens to prevent damage from getting worse.

Save $3,000 and Improve Your Home's Value

Katie and Gene Hamilton are creators of DIYorNot. com. Based in St. Michaels, Maryland, they are authors of 20 home-improvement books, including *Home Improvement for Dummies* and *Fix It and Flip It*. They are founders of HouseNet.com, which they sold to R.R. Donnelley & Sons.

If you're a home owner who likes working outside, consider doing these home-improvement projects yourself. You'll save at least 50% of what hiring a professional would cost.* These projects require more grunt work than talent and only a small investment in materials and tools. Each of them will improve the value of your property.

Power washing: To keep your house looking its best, consider an annual cleanup with a power washer. You can hire a building cleaning service for $377 to power wash a typical 1,200-square-foot house. Or you can rent a gas-powered washer rated at least at 1,200 psi (which means that it delivers 1,200 pounds per square inch of water) with detergent for $160 and pocket a nice 58% savings. Figure that you'll spend a solid two days on the job. *Savings:* $217.

Gutter cleaning: An important seasonal maintenance chore for every home owner is cleaning and repairing gutters. A handyman will charge $102 to clean and make minor repairs to 200 linear feet of gutters on a one-story house. If you have a sturdy ladder, garden hose, bucket and rubber gloves, you can do the job in two hours for $40 (the cost

*In this article, the costs to hire a professional are based on several of the estimating publications that contractors use to bid on their jobs. The material costs are based on information from major national retailers and manufacturers.

of some caulk and roofing cement) and save 61%. *Warning:* If you have a very high home or uneven terrain, it may be safer to hire a pro. *Savings:* $62.

Painting the garage: You'll pay a painting contractor $307 to spray paint the exterior of a typical one story, two-car garage. You can do the job in a weekend for $100, for the cost of the paint and renting an airless sprayer for a day. That's a 67% savings. Figure that you'll spend the better part of the first day prepping the area before you paint. *Savings:* $207.

Pruning: A landscape service will prune and groom a small tree and some bushes for $80, but for an investment of $36 (for pruning shears and a lopper), you can do it and save 55% in three hours. You'll save the full $80 the next time you prune. *Initial savings:* $44.

Mulching: You can pay a yard service $324 to lay a four-inch-deep spread of organic mulch in a 300-foot area or buy mulch (30 to 35 bags) yourself for $75. In a day, you can complete the job and save 77%. If you have a vehicle that can haul it, you won't have to pay extra to have the mulch delivered. *Savings:* $249.

Lawn seeding: You can seed a lawn and create a luscious green landscape, but whether or not to do it yourself depends on the condition of your soil. Assuming it is level and free of grass, weeds and rocks, a landscaper will charge $201 to prepare the soil and seed 2,000 square feet. You can buy seed for $50, do it yourself and save 75%. But if rocks, weeds and grass need to be removed, leave it to the pros. In most areas, the best time to seed is late August or early September. *Savings:* $151.

Laying a gravel path: Consider laying a gravel path as a walkway or winding path through your garden. The work involves digging and hauling material, but you'll save 57% by doing it yourself. For a three-foot-wide, 100-foot-long gravel path, a landscape contractor will charge $349 including gravel. It'll cost you a long day's work and $150 for the material. *Savings:* $199.

Building a patio: This is strenuous labor and time-consuming—it takes about a week to do— but every time you use your new patio, you'll appreciate your sweat equity. A contractor will charge $2,275 to build a 15-foot-by-20-foot brick patio. You can do it for about half that ($1,100 for the material). *Savings:* $1,175.

Building a split-rail fence: A split-rail fence is one of the most attractive ways to enhance your yard and define your property. The most difficult thing is digging the post holes. You can rent a post hole digger for about $80/day, buy a manual digger for $30 to $100 or use a shovel. A fence contractor will charge $1,091 to build a 100-foot-long rail fence. You can do it for $500 (the cost of the material) and save 54%. But fence building is not for the faint of heart—it's a good three-day project and hard work. *Savings:* $591.

You'll find step-by-step directions for the projects in this article at DIYorNot.com, along with cost analyses of hundreds more home-improvement projects.

Common Home Fix-It Mistakes That Can Be Very Costly

The late Sonny Lykos, who was a contractor in Illinois, Michigan and Florida for 35 years. His firm, Construction Solution Systems, Inc., focused on small projects around Naples, Florida.

Seemingly small oversights and errors in do-it-yourself projects and home maintenance can have costly consequences. A single misstep might mean that a job must be completely redone—or that hundreds, even thousands, of dollars must be spent to solve the resulting problems.

Among the most common mistakes that can easily be avoided…

MISTAKE: **Failing to apply grout sealer after laying tile.** Grout stains easily and is extremely difficult to clean. After you grout your tile, whether on a floor, wall or countertop, wait three to five days for the grout to cure, then apply a solvent-based grout sealer. (Latex-based sealers are less effective.) Apply with a small brush or spray bottle,

and wipe off the excess. Add a new coat of grout sealer every year—do it twice a year if the grout is in or near the shower. Expect to pay around $12 for a quart of sealant.

Helpful: Environmental restrictions are making solvent-based grout sealer more difficult to find. If it's not sold at your local home center or hardware store, try a specialty tile store. Latex-based grout sealers are better than nothing, but you'll have to apply three or four coats to get effective protection.

To clean grout that is already dirty: Use a cleaner specifically made for grout, such as ZEP Grout Cleaner & Whitener, available at tile and hardware stores.

MISTAKE: **Applying a latex paint directly on top of an oil-based paint.** Latex paint, the most popular paint these days, won't stick to a surface painted with oil-based paint, which used to dominate the market. Within weeks, the new coat of latex will begin to peel, and you'll have to strip it off and start again.

To determine whether existing paint is oil- or latex-based, wash a section with soap and water, let it dry, then swab it with rubbing alcohol. If some paint lifts off, it's latex—if not, it's oil.

If you must apply latex paint on top of oil paint, first apply a coat of deglosser (also known as "liquid sandpaper"). Check the instructions on the deglosser—some are effective only if you paint within hours of deglossing. Expect to pay $12 to $15 per gallon.

MISTAKE: **Using the wrong caulk or not preparing properly to caulk.** Caulking is one of the cheapest, easiest do-it-yourself tasks, but it's still possible to make mistakes that lead to serious problems. Some home owners fail to thoroughly clean the surface that's about to be caulked. Then caulk bonds to the dirt and dust, not to the wood, metal or ceramic underneath, allowing moisture to get into the home's structure.

Others use the wrong caulk. Cheap caulks can fail in just a few years, and simple latex caulks won't take paint. (Wall trim often needs to be caulked before being painted.) The best choice is a high-quality siliconized latex caulk or a latex-elastomeric caulk. Either should last 20 years. Expect to pay $3 to $4 for a 10-ounce tube.

MISTAKE: **Painting metal without properly treating rust.** Most metal that is exposed to the elements will rust. Painting over your home's rusted metal doors, railings, fences, patio furniture or steel gutters only cloaks the problem—the rust will continue to consume the metal.

Before painting any rusty surface, sand down the rusted area, then apply Ospho—a phosphoric acid product that retards rust. Let sit overnight. The rusted areas should appear black by the next day, a sign that the rust has been chemically altered, so it won't continue to spread. Apply a coat of Rust-Oleum metal primer over the entire surface of the metal to prevent the spread of any rust that isn't yet visible—where there was visible rust, there's additional rust that can't yet be seen. Once the primer dries, you're ready to paint. Expect to spend about $25 for a quart of Ospho and about $17 for a quart of Rust-Oleum.

MISTAKE: **Not "exercising" water shut-off valves.** When the shut-off valves beneath sinks and toilets go untouched for years, mineral deposits can cause them to seize up, and the valves can't be opened or closed. Often the only recourse is to hire a plumber to cut the valves out and replace them, at a cost of hundreds of dollars. This won't happen if you shut and reopen water valves every six months.

MISTAKE: **Neglecting exterior door hinges.** The hinges on an exterior door can rust and seize up, causing significant damage to the door when it is used. This typically happens to little-used doors, but it can even happen to a front door while you are on a vacation. If you lubricate exterior door hinges once a year with a silicone spray, they'll give you a lifetime of trouble-free service. (Don't use an oil-based lubricant—it can trap dirt in the hinge.) Open the door before applying the silicone to ensure that the lubricant gets inside the hinge barrel.

MISTAKE: **Allowing a garbage disposal to rust.** Rust can develop in a garbage disposal when it goes unused for as little as a week. Pour a shot glass of vegetable oil into the disposal before leaving on vacation and it should stay rust-free. When you return, pour a small amount of dishwasher detergent down the disposal to clean out the oil.

Tear Out an Old Carpet Yourself

The Family Handyman, 2915 Commers Dr., Eagan, Minnesota 55121, FamilyHandyman.com

Tear out old carpet yourself to save money when replacing it. Carpet installation should be left to a professional—but removal of old carpet is not difficult. An installer will charge $3 to $5 per square yard to pull out the old carpet—so taking it out of a 12-by-15-foot room yourself, which takes about an hour, will save you $60 to $100. Grab the edge of the carpet with pliers, and pull to remove.

Read This Before You Finish Your Basement

Dave Schrock, a licensed contractor who is founder and owner of Basement Spaces, Inc. He has been designing and finishing basements in the greater Chicago area for more than 20 years. He is producer of the DVD *Create a Beautiful Basement.*

Finishing a basement often is the most cost-effective way to increase a home's living space—one of several reasons that the appeal of a finished basement has been on the rise in recent years. Expenses tend to be around 30% to 50% lower than the cost of putting a similarly sized addition on the home. And you can expect to recoup more than three-quarters of the cost when you sell, according to *Remodeling* magazine, a better payback rate than most home-renovation projects.

Also, limited exposure to natural light makes basements the perfect place for today's big-screen high-definition home theaters and media rooms... and the privacy of basements makes them an attractive place to add bedrooms for adult children and aging parents—an increasingly common concern with multi-generational households on the rise.

But whether you're finishing your basement yourself or paying a contractor, there are issues that must be considered before work begins...

Repair Things Yourself... and Other DIY Websites

Do-it-yourself home repair not only will save you money, it's also quite easy. *Websites to help you get started...*

• **Enter a question starting with "How to" at the free website FindHow.com.** You will get a targeted response with step-by-step instructions, often including photos or a video.

• **Also try Fixya.com,** which offers technical support, instructions and repair service.

• **For appliances, go to RepairClinic.com,** which provides free diagnostic help and offers live chats with experienced repair people. You can order needed parts directly through the site.

• **Smarter home spruce-ups.** Easy bathroom fixes, driveway and window repair, interior/ exterior painting, deck care and other topics. Includes videos and a Q&A section. DoItYourself.com

• **Help with home fix-ups.** How to silence squeaky floors...replace broken tile...repair shower doors...replace faucets...get rid of carpenter ants, mice and other pests...etc. Natural Handyman.com

• **Grow your own food.** Blueberries, cherries and other fruits—Gardening.Cals.Cornell.edu. Herbs—PlanetNatural.com/herb-gardening-guru. Vegetables—BackyardGardener.com.

Mary Hunt, founder and editor, Debt-Proof Living, Cypress, California, DebtProofLiving.com

Bottom Line Personal Research.

Ceiling Height

In most towns, building codes require that finished basement ceilings be at least seven feet high. But don't be fooled—a seven-foot ceiling will not make for an enjoyable space. Anything below seven feet, nine inches may feel cramped—and that figure refers to the height of the finished space. Finishing the ceiling and floor will subtract at least a few inches of headroom. So to achieve a seven-foot, nine-inch finished height, the unfinished space would need to be at least eight feet high.

What to do: Install a drywall ceiling rather than a drop ceiling. Drywall ceilings use up less headroom and look better. Costs are comparable. Drop ceilings often are selected because they provide easier access to valves in the pipes above. Instead, insert plastic access panels into a drywall ceiling as needed.

Example: Access panels from Oatey start at less than $20 (Oatey.com).

Paint basement ceilings and walls white. Light colors make tight spaces feel larger. Adding abundant artificial lighting can help, too. Install at least one recessed canister light in the basement ceiling for every 36 square feet of floor space, then add accent lights to eliminate any remaining dim areas. Use high-wattage LED bulbs.

Two options if ducts (or pipes) along the basement ceiling result in low headroom...

• **Have ducts rerouted.** Perhaps they can be moved to sections of the basement that you are not finishing or at least to the edges of finished spaces where a strip of lower ceiling will be less obtrusive. Rerouting ducts typically costs $1,000 to $3,000, depending on the amount of work required.

• **Leave the ducts where they are and vary the level of the drywall ceiling.** The finished ceiling can be high where there are no ducts and lower only where necessary. A multilevel ceiling might add a few thousand dollars to drywall installation costs. Install track lighting along the sides of the lower ceiling sections—that makes them seem like intentional design features.

If there is no way to avoid having a finished ceiling height of less than seven feet, nine inches, finishing the attic or adding an addition to the house might be better.

Water and Moisture Problems

Water is enemy number one of finished basements. Even a small amount of moisture seeping in can lead to major mold or mildew problems.

What to do: If water leaks into your basement through cracks in your foundation—or through another route—have this remedied months before your basement-finishing project begins. That way you can be fairly confident that the problem is solved before wallboards and/or flooring block the area from view.

This is not a good time to try to save a few dollars by tackling a home-repair project yourself—a recurrence of the water problem could lead to thousands of dollars in damage to your newly finished basement. Hire a company that specializes in correcting basement water issues, not a general contractor. Choose one that has been in business for at least five years. These pros have many water-beating techniques, including injecting foundation cracks with advanced epoxies capable of stopping most minor leaks.

Additional waterproofing steps might include adding or improving roof gutters…modifying landscaping or excavating a "French drain" around the perimeter of the home to encourage water to flow away from the foundation…and/or installing a sump pump (with battery or generator backup).

Warning: Modern moisture-resistant wallboards are less susceptible to moisture problems than traditional drywall, but they are not a solution on their own. If water is consistently finding its way into the space between your foundation and your finished basement walls, it eventually will cause problems no matter what wallboards are used.

If you are installing a bathroom—or any other plumbing—in your finished basement, insist that your contractor include an "ejector pump" in the plans. This greatly reduces the odds that a backed-up sewer line or septic system will flood the basement.

Attractive and Functional Flooring

Wood flooring is a poor choice for basements—flooding could ruin the floor, and wood floors typically are installed above a subfloor, further reducing headroom. Roll-out laminate floors tend to show the imperfections of the concrete floor below and might be damaged by flooding as well.

What to do: Two basement-flooring options are worth considering…

•**Laminate or vinyl interlocking tile or plank flooring systems will not be ruined if the basement floods.** These tiles typically are not attached to the floor below, only to each other—a system referred to as "floating" tile—and can be removed, dried, then put back in place if necessary. Some effectively mimic the look of wood floors or stone tiles.

Expect to pay perhaps $5 to $7 per square foot. Laminate tiles are constructed from layers of mate-

rials, with the core layer typically of high-density fiberboard, while vinyl floors are entirely vinyl. Either should handle moisture relatively well, though the typically more rigid laminate tiles might do a better job of hiding imperfections in a concrete basement floor.

Example: Fusion Hybrid MAX and SUMMIT vinyl flooring (visit FusionFloorCovering.com).

•**Carpeting makes finished basements feel warm and homey.** It is susceptible to mold and mildew, however. Having mildew-resistant padding installed underneath can minimize—though not eliminate—this risk.

Potential compromise: Install interlocking vinyl tiles, then place area rugs on top. This offers some of the warmth of carpeting, and area rugs can be easily replaced (or done away with) if they develop mildew.

The Best Layout

An unfinished basement might seem like a blank canvas, but some layouts work better than others.

What to do: Favor an open layout as much as possible. Unless it is unusually large, chopping a basement up into smaller rooms will make the spaces feel uncomfortably small—especially if you have relatively low ceilings and limited natural light.

Exception: Consider sectioning off part of the basement as a storage room. A lack of storage space is a common complaint of home owners who finish their entire basements. Leaving part of the basement unfinished also will reduce renovation costs.

If you must carve up your basement into separate rooms such as a bedroom, home office, media room or other specific spaces, consider these often-overlooked factors…

•**Flow.** Avoid layouts featuring long, windowless hallways…or that require you to pass through one basement room to get to another.

•**Zoning laws.** Basement bedrooms might need windows, and they might have to be a specified size.

•**What's above.** A basement room that requires quiet, such as a home office or a bedroom, should not be directly below a loud upstairs space, such as a living room with a TV. A home theater should not be below an upstairs bedroom. Adding insulation above the basement ceiling won't block all the noise.

•**Basement components.** Furnaces and water pumps can be loud and annoying when they're adjacent to a basement bedroom or home theater.

•**Existing plumbing.** If you're having a bathroom, laundry room or sink installed in the basement, position this below an upstairs room that has water pipes to control costs. It is worth paying extra to put the basement bathroom in a convenient spot, however.

Clever Fix-Its...

Julie Edelman, aka "The Accidental Housewife," appears regularly on the *Today* show, *Rachael Ray* and *The Doctors.* She is author of *The New York Times* best-seller *The Accidental Housewife: How to Overcome Housekeeping Hysteria One Task at a Time.* JuliesTips.com

•**Replace lost earring backs with pencil erasers.** Snip the tip of a pencil eraser, and use it to temporarily replace a lost back so that you can wear the earring until you replace the back.

•**Quiet squeaky doors with cucumber.** Take a slice of cucumber, and rub it up and down several times all around the hinge. Have a clean cloth handy to wipe away any excess. I am not sure why it works—it just does!

•**Fix holes in screens with dental floss.** Use dental floss to mend small holes in a window or door screen. Weave in and out by hand or with a sewing needle. Then tie the ends.

•**Mend minor cracks in fine china with milk.** Milk contains casein, a protein that, when heated, turns into a natural plasticlike glue. Place your cracked dish in a pan or pot large enough to cover it completely in milk. Bring the milk to a boil, and then reduce to a simmer. Let it simmer for 45 to 60 minutes, then let the milk cool. Rinse the plate. The crack should be sealed!

DIY Secrets to Fix Car Dings, Dents and Scratches

Russ Evans, an ASE Master Certified Automotive Technician and cohost of the syndicated automotive radio show *Under the Hood.* UnderTheHoodShow.com

A small scratch or dent can be all it takes to make a car look old and worn—and make it harder to sell at a good price if you are looking to do so. Even seemingly minor cosmetic flaws can be expensive to repair if you bring the car to a body shop—repairing a small scratch typically costs $350 to $700, and dent repairs usually climb into four figures.

If you're not willing to pay such steep prices, there are do-it-yourself solutions that can make some flaws much less apparent for far more palatable prices. *DIY options for two common car cosmetic issues…*

Scratched Paint

There's a layer of protective clear coat over your car's paint. If a scratch has penetrated only this clear coat, not the paint below, then a product called rubbing compound, available in auto-parts stores, could make the scratch much less apparent.

Rule of thumb: If you can see primer or metal, the scratch is too deep for this strategy. But if you don't and your fingernail doesn't catch when you gently run it across the scratch, the scratch likely is shallow enough to try this.

Rubbing compound gently smooths out these sharp edges. It also can remove paint left behind by a vehicle that made contact with yours. Choose a highly regarded brand, because a bad rubbing compound could make the car look worse.

Examples: Meguiar's Ultimate Compound (about $14 for 16 ounces) is made by the most respected name in this field. Turtle Wax Premium Grade Rubbing Compound (about $11 for 18 ounces) also is well-respected.

After applying a rubbing compound according to directions on the package, apply polish and then wax to restore the shine and protect the paint.

Examples: Meguiar's Ultimate Polish ($12 for 16 ounces) and Meguiar's Ultimate Liquid Wax ($22.99 for 16 ounces).

If the scratch removed some of the paint below the clear coat, you'll have to add new paint to make it less apparent. Small bottles of touch-up paint are available in auto-parts stores, from dealership parts departments or on Amazon.com and elsewhere online, typically costing $15 to $30. Use the touch-up paint sold by the automaker itself... or a highly regarded paint company's brand, such as Sherwin-Williams Dupli-Color, which offers a wide range of colors. A lesser paint might not match your car's color as well. The "paint code" identifying the proper paint for your car typically is listed on a sticker inside the driver's-side door or doorjamb (sometimes it's under the hood or under the trunk lid). If you can't find it, give your vehicle identification number (VIN) to one of the make's dealers and ask what your color code is. If your paint is badly faded, it might no longer match perfectly.

Expert tip: Don't use the nail polish–like paintbrush that often is included in the paint bottle—this tends to spread paint over too wide an area. Instead use the tip of a toothpick to slowly and cautiously apply a very thin coat of paint into the scratch...or ask at an art-supply store for a paintbrush appropriate for painting extremely narrow lines. Apply the paint only inside the scratch, not over the surrounding area. Too much touch-up paint can look almost as bad as missing paint.

Dents

Shallow dents in metal body panels sometimes can be pulled out using a suction-cup dent-puller, available at auto-parts stores for $10 to $20. Most brands of suction tools are pretty much the same. They are most effective when there's a relatively flat section inside the dented area large enough for a four-to-five-inch suction cup to stick to. If the metal inside the dent has a sharp crease, the odds of success are far lower.

Clean the dented area well before using the suction cup—dirt makes it harder to form a seal. Spraying a light water mist on the cleaned dented area can help improve suction, too. It might take several tries and a bit of arm strength to pull out a dent. These tools don't work every time, and even when they do, the result might not be perfect—some waviness could be visible in the metal surrounding the spot where the dent used to be. Still, it's an inexpensive option worth trying.

If the dent is in a plastic body part, such as the caved-in corner of a bumper cover, it's often possible to push the dent out from behind. The secret is heat—use a heat gun or even a hair dryer on its maximum setting to heat up the dented area, rendering the plastic more pliable, then use your hand to push out the dent from the inside. Wear work gloves to shield your hand from the heated plastic.

Try to maneuver the plastic back into place every few minutes, and heat it some more if it still won't budge. If there's no obvious way to get your hand behind the dent, you still might be able to reach thin tools such as metal pry bars into the area and use them to push from behind...you can sometimes remove a part or two to improve your access to the area behind the dent....and/or you could try using a suction tool to pull out the dent, as above.

If you cannot repair a metal or plastic dent on your own, seek out a "paintless dent removal" specialist. These body-repair pros tend to be much more affordable than traditional body shops because they use dent-removal techniques that don't require repainting the dented area—they typically charge only $100 to $200 per body panel repaired. This isn't a viable option with every dent, however, particularly if the paint in the dented area has cracked. Search for someone who has been doing paintless dent removal in your area for years, not someone who suddenly pops up offering these services after a hailstorm rolls through.

Helpful: Call the service departments at local auto dealerships, and ask if someone can recommend an independent paintless dent-removal pro. Some dealerships do this work in house, but others hire outside pros and know which ones can be trusted.

CHAPTER 6

Family Time

The Secrets of Happy Families

Bruce Feiler, a *New York Times* columnist and six-time best-selling author based in Brooklyn, New York. His books include *The Council of Dads: A Story of Family, Friendship & Learning How to Live* and, most recently, *The Secrets of Happy Families.* BruceFeiler.com

It's hard for stressed-out modern families to feel like effective, close-knit teams these days. *New York Times* columnist Bruce Feiler—himself part of a two-career couple with twin eight-year-old daughters, aging parents and a large extended family—wanted to find ways to make his family life richer and reduce tensions.

He looked to unexpected sources, gathering and adapting innovative ideas about team-building and problem-solving from corporate boardrooms, university campuses and even the US military.

We asked Feiler for the strategies he found most helpful. *He says incorporating just one or two of these ideas can make a significant difference in family closeness…*

Rethink the Family Dinner

Eating dinner together has long been shown to unify families and reduce behavioral problems in children. But fewer and fewer families are actually eating dinner together. And nearly everything in my life conspired against regular nighttime meals—

from longer working hours for my wife and me to more extracurricular activities for the kids.

The Columbia University Center for Addiction and Substance Abuse has studied the role of family dinners in uniting families. It found that most of the benefits are derived from just 10 minutes of connection time during the meal—and you could get the same results at any meal. It's really about coming together as a family.

What my family does: We have a family-bonding experience over food every day. Sometimes, we opt for a family breakfast or a family dessert in the evening depending on our schedules.

Important: Adults tend to take up around two-thirds of the conversation. Family meals are most effective in building cohesion if you let your kids speak for at least half the time.

Tell Family Stories

Researchers at Emory University who studied myth and ritual in American families created the "Do You Know (DYK) Scale," widely regarded as one of the best single predictors of children's emotional health and happiness. It asks 20 questions about family history, such as "Do you know where your parents met?" and "Do you know of an illness or something really terrible that happened in your family?" Children who provided the most comprehensive answers to the test had a stronger sense that they controlled their lives and a deeper belief that their families functioned well. You can find the full list of questions at TheMustardSeedHouse.com.

What my family does: We tell stories of our family history that convey our values and emotional toughness. Kids need to know that they are part of something bigger and more important than just the ups and downs of their own daily needs and behavior. We don't try to shield our children from struggles or failures that have occurred in our family's past.

For example, one of our family's most memorable stories was my diagnosis with a rare and potentially deadly form of cancer at 43. Wracked with worry that my daughters would grow up without a father figure, I wrote a letter to six of my closest friends, asking them to be there for my daughters if I died. Each man represented a different era of my life and had different characteristics and values that I hoped to pass on to my girls. My "council of dads" are not just my friends now but also my daughters' friends, and they enrich all of our lives.

Strike the Word "You" from Family Squabbles

William Ury, a senior fellow at the Harvard Negotiation Project, gets called in to handle some of the toughest disputes in the world, including nuclear-test-ban treaties and major labor strikes. He and other conflict experts sometimes make headway over deadlocked issues by simply changing up their language. For example, using the pronoun "you" throws the blame for a dispute on the other party. Rephrasing issues with the pronoun "we" can force both sides to acknowledge that there's a joint problem and to seek joint solutions.

What my family does: Instead of telling my wife, "I waited for an hour, and you never called," I say, "I waited for an hour. We need to improve our scheduling and communication during the day." *Other big-league negotiating ideas we adapted...*

• **Keep your facial expressions neutral and especially avoid rolling your eyes.** Eye rolling conveys not just impatience or annoyance but contempt.

• **Walk away from fights after three minutes.** Beyond that, family members just repeat themselves at higher and higher decibels. Instead, I separate my

bickering daughters until both cool down. Then I ask each girl to come up with a few alternative solutions to the conflict before she speaks again. This way they move from rigid positions in an argument to starting with new options that they can shape together.

Rearrange Your Family Room Furniture

Sally Augustin, PhD, founder of Design with Science, is well-known in the corporate world as a "place coach." One of the country's leading environmental psychologists, she redesigns workplaces so that employees can relate better. I realized that many of her ideas were applicable to home life.

What my family does: We circled the furniture so that it resembled an O shape (seating in a circular pattern) rather than the more alienating L-shape (two sofas at a right angle) or V-shape (a sofa flanked by two chairs). If O-shaped layouts aren't possible or offend your decorating tastes, use ottomans or other portable seating that can be easily repositioned during family gatherings. We also use plush surfaces for tense conversations. Sitting on chairs with soft cushions makes people more flexible and conciliatory than hard-backed surfaces.

Keep Everyone Very Busy During Family Get-togethers

Many extended families dread these gatherings because the focus is too often on sitting around, watching TV, drinking or gossiping. I was having trouble finding good advice about how to create camaraderie among disparate individuals until I ran across groundbreaking research done by the US military's special forces unit, the Green Berets. They use a constant cycle of games and exercises to promote cooperation and team-building among recruits.

What my family does: We never rest when the extended family gets together each July 4th on Cape Cod and then again on Labor Day off the coast of Georgia. At "Camp Feiler," as it is known, we have a watermelon seed–spitting contest, make homemade ice cream and play touch football or Frisbee, complete with team colors, cheers and flags. While these activities may seem hokey, friendly competition is very effective at uniting different generations and personalities in our families and allowing moments of genuine connection.

Important: Conclude family gatherings with an emotional ritual. What happens last is often what's most deeply remembered. Camp Feiler ends with an elaborate family play. The children take the lead roles...aunts and uncles wear silly costumes...and my mother paints the backdrop on the stage.

Happy Homes, Happy People

Dan Buettner, founder of Blue Zones, an organization that studies the regions of the world where people commonly live active lives past the age of 100. Based in Minneapolis, he is a writer for *National Geographic* and author of *Thrive: Finding Happiness the Blue Zones Way*. BlueZones.com

National Geographic author and explorer Dan Buettner spent five years talking to people in areas identified by researchers as the world leaders in happiness—Denmark's Jutland Peninsula...Singapore...Nuevo León, Mexico...and the town of San Luis Obispo in California.

In his new book, *Thrive*, he identified the main characteristics of what he calls thrivers, people who consistently report the highest levels of well-being. Here, secrets from the world's happiest people specifically connected to family life...

●**Own one TV, no more.** Americans spend more than four hours a day, on average, in front of the television. This is time that they're not spending with other people, including their families. (Family time in front of the television is not the same as real interaction.)

In the places where happiness is highest, people spend the least time watching television. It's not that they never watch—they just watch less than most people.

I advise people to own no more than one television—and to keep it in an out-of-the-way place, such as the basement. You still can watch your favorite programs, but watching will become a deliberate activity, not something you just do automatically.

●**Create a "flow room."** In Danish society, most families have an area in the house where everyone naturally congregates. I call these rooms "flow rooms" because they're places where time seems to flow away when people are engaged and enjoying one another's company. Flow rooms have no screens (TVs or computers) and no clocks. They are quiet environments where it's easy to engage in meaningful activities with family.

In our house, I chose a room with good lighting and the best views—it's comfortable, and everyone in the family wants to be there. I keep it stocked with good books, musical instruments and the best family games.

There's nothing formal about our gatherings. People wander in and out. Because it's so pleasant, we spend a lot more time there than in front of the TV or separated in different parts of the house.

●**Stop shopping.** The satisfaction that we get from buying things—an expensive watch, a new suit, a fancy car—wears off within 14 months. Yet in the US, we're pressured by the media and social expectations to always want more. In order to get it, we have to work longer hours and take fewer vacations, which generally reduces happiness.

In Denmark, regulations limit the number of hours that shops can be open. In Mexico, most of the inhabitants are not running a status race with their neighbors.

For more happiness, take the money that you could spend on nonessential items and spend it on something that lasts. For example, take a vacation with your family or sign up for a painting class together. The experiences and good memories will continue to give satisfaction for the rest of your life.

Chores Matter More Than Homework

Charles Fay, PhD, author, consultant and therapist, Love and Logic Institute, Golden, Colorado, writing in *Love & Logic Journal*. LoveAndLogic.com

Chores matter more than homework for making good students. Kids who do real, meaningful work around the house—without reminders and without pay—learn self-control...the benefits of structure and limits…and the importance of being needed. Kids who regularly do chores feel proud of themselves and their accomplishments, and homework and schoolwork seem easier to them.

Make Your Family Reunion a Success…By Avoiding These Common Mistakes

George G. Morgan, genealogist and author of 10 books, including *Your Family Reunion: How to Plan It, Organize It, and Enjoy It*. He is cohost of "The Genealogy Guys Podcast," the longest-running genealogy podcast on the Internet (GenealogyGuys.com). His company, Aha! Seminars, Inc., trains genealogists and librarians, organizes genealogical research tours and consults on reunion planning. AhaSeminars.com

A big family reunion is a wonderful opportunity to create and renew deep connections, learn about your roots and foster a sense of belonging. And big reunions have been growing in popularity over the past 20 years. It is not uncommon to see reunions of 100 to 200 or more people. But if you're planning a big reunion, it's easy to make these very common mistakes. *Here's what to do instead…*

MISTAKE: trying to do it all yourself. If you organize an event single-handedly, you will be too busy and overwhelmed to enjoy and interact with people at the reunion itself, missing out on the whole purpose of the event.

Also, the more people involved in the planning, the more people will spread the word and encourage others to attend. *What to do…*

•**Get input.** Send a simple questionnaire to family members via e-mail, supplemented by snail mail and/or phone calls for those who don't use e-mail. Ask about people's level of interest in a reunion… how many from their families might attend and their ages…preferred time of year…preferred locations…and willingness to volunteer.

•**Form a planning committee.** Start with three to five people who expressed interest in volunteering. (Others who volunteered can later be recruited for subcommittees.) Have one or two initial meetings—in person or by telephone conference call—to

review the questionnaire results and narrow down the location, potential dates, duration, size and areas of responsibility.

Once date and location have been determined, have committee members contact other family members and invite them to help. Depending on how large a reunion you are planning, you will need a chairperson or two co-chairs and people in charge of areas such as communication and contact list, finances, meeting space and lodging, food, activities and entertainment, and on-site coordination.

MISTAKE: underestimating costs. In an effort to make the reunion a success, costs easily can get out of control. *What to do…*

•**Create a budget.** List the estimated costs for every potential component of the reunion. You will need to do research and contact vendors in order to make the budget realistic. In addition to major costs such as banquet rooms, lodging, meals and organized activities, remember to include incidentals such as photocopying, postage, phone calls and gas mileage for errands. Use this information to calculate the cost per person.

•**Negotiate with vendors.** Get several bids for each major expense, such as meeting rooms and catering. Always ask what discounts are available.

Examples: Many hotels will give a discount on meeting rooms if a minimum number of sleeping rooms are booked. Caterers may offer a lower rate on meals for children and seniors.

•**Give options.** Before committing to expensive activities such as a guided tour, lake cruise or catered banquet, send potential attendees a list of possibilities and their estimated cost per person.

MISTAKE: skipping the name tags. Name tags may seem unnecessary among family. However, forgetting someone's name can be embarrassing and sets the festivities off on the wrong foot. Name tags also can serve as conversation starters. *What to do…*

•**Provide plenty of tags.** If you opt for sticky-backed name tags and felt-tip markers, make sure that you have enough on hand for each day of the event because sticky tags are impractical to reuse. This type of tag is fine for casual gatherings, but keep in mind that the sticky backs may not adhere to all clothing and can even damage dressy clothing.

If you choose more expensive, durable name tags with plastic sleeves—either clip-on or with strings around the neck—keep extra sleeves and tags on hand in case people forget to bring theirs each day.

•**Use large type.** Whether you preprint the tags on a computer or have people write their own names, make sure that the first name is large enough to read from a distance.

•**Provide interesting information.** In addition to first and last name, consider including the person's city and state, maiden name, age (ask permission first) and family line of descent.

MISTAKE: **lack of structure.** Although some family members may jump into conversations immediately, more introverted people—or those who don't know many people at the event—will need help getting acquainted. *What to do…*

•**Start with a multigenerational icebreaker.** A good icebreaker is the Family Information Scavenger Hunt, where individuals or teams look for answers to preprinted questions.

Example: Find a family member who traveled more than 1,000 miles to attend…whose parents hail from Ireland…who has a specific maiden name …who has more than four siblings. For more icebreaker ideas, see FamilyReunionHelper.com.

Include age-specific activities—such as pizza-and-movie/DVD night for teenagers…storytime for young children…softball for grown-ups…canasta or poker for seniors.

•**Allow some downtime.** Don't go to the opposite extreme and structure every minute. Spontaneous interactions create some of the best memories.

MISTAKE: **assuming that someone is taking photos.** Even when everyone seems to be snapping pictures with smartphones, it doesn't guarantee that all attendees will be included in photos or that the pictures will be distributed. *What to do…*

•**Assign the job.** Either hire a professional photographer or ask, in advance, two or three family members to be responsible for photo-taking. (This can be a good task for teenagers.) Tell whoever does the photography to make sure that everyone at the

reunion is in at least one shot. Give each photographer a list of everyone at the reunion so that he/she can check off names. Also, make sure that someone keeps track of the names of people in the photos to ensure that the photos are labeled for posterity.

•**Arrange for distribution.** After the reunion, have a volunteer burn photos to CDs and send to all attendees…or upload the photos to a shared folder website such as Dropbox.com. Ask another volunteer to make prints for people who don't have online access.

MISTAKE: **neglecting storytelling.** Sharing stories about the family, present and past, is one of the great joys of multigenerational gatherings and one of the best ways to strengthen family ties. But storytelling doesn't come naturally to all families, and the opportunity may be lost. *What to do…*

•**Prime the pump.** Before the reunion, ask attendees to come up with three fun facts about their own childhoods…and/or think about which family members have influenced them the most. At the reunion, pair up older people with younger ones, and have them share their answers to these questions. Or invite each person to come up in front of the group.

•**Facilitate table discussion.** During a meal, assign someone at each table to encourage each person to answer questions such as, What's something you remember about your grandmother or grandfather?…What was your first job?…What did/do you like/dislike most about school?…What's the most amazing thing that happened in your life?

•**Get young people involved.** One family came up with an activity they called "I'm My Own Grandparent," in which each of the children under 12 dressed up in costume and acted out a story about his/her grandparents—either a story that the child had heard directly from the grandparent or a story that had been told to him. (An adult monitored the rehearsal and program.) All the kids who took part got a gift card, and special prizes were awarded for the most enthusiastic portrayal.

How to Throw a Great Potluck Party (Hint: Don't Rely on Luck!)

Linda Gassenheimer is an award-winning author of several cookbooks, most recently *The 12-Week Diabetes Cookbook, Delicious One-Pot Dishes, Quick & Easy Chicken* and *The Flavors of the Florida Keys.* She writes the syndicated newspaper column "Dinner in Minutes." DinnerInMinutes.com

So you've decided to throw a "Bring Your Own Dish" party, aka a potluck party, where everyone brings food and then you all share it. Fun! And kind of easy for you. But don't make it too easy for you, or you'll end up where a lot of potluck parties end up—too much of one kind of food, such as salads, and not enough of another, such as entrées or desserts…no food for guests with special dietary needs…a really bland spread of boring dishes that are your guests' go-too potluck dishes because they're so easy (or cheap) to make.

That's not nearly as fun as you envisioned.

Here are the easy steps to take to make your potluck party rise above most others…

•**Make a list of types of foods you'd like guests to bring such as dips…salads…main courses… side dishes…desserts.** Share it with everyone who's invited, and ask each invitee to let you know what he/she would like to bring…whether he has any dietary restrictions…or if he has no preference. Do this in writing, whether by e-mail, e-invite or however you let people know about the party. There's something about seeing a host's intentions in writing that says, "This is something I should actually pay attention to."

•**Your list of guests who say they have no preference of what to bring is very valuable**—keep it in your back pocket for now.

•**Keep track of what the other guests say they'd like to bring,** and note whether this collection of food, taken together, seems more like a party…or a macaroni salad contest. If the latter (or if your guests are veering toward too much of any type of food), gently guide guests to bring what's needed based on how you envision a reasonably varied menu.

•**Remember that part of the fun of going to a potluck party for guests is making and bringing a dish that reflects their own cooking,** so when you guide guests on what to bring, don't be too specific. For example, instead of saying, "We could really use some teriyaki chicken," you might say, "We have a lot of salads coming—would you be able to bring a warm chicken entrée?" Most guests will be happy to oblige and to show off their signature dish of the type you ask for.

•**Ask how many servings each guest's dish will provide.** Each dish doesn't need to serve everyone, but knowing what's coming will help you plan well.

•**Make sure that if you have any guests with special dietary needs,** the dishes they bring are not the only ones they will be able to eat. You are the host, after all, even if it's a potluck party—if your other guests aren't going to bring at least one or two appetizers, entrées and desserts that fit this bill, you should provide this food yourself.

•**Remember that list of guests who said they have no preference of what sort of food to bring?** Use them to fill in any gaps that remain after sorting out what all the others will bring.

•**Ask guests whether they will bring their dishes ready-to-serve on platters or in bowls.** It's great if you can encourage them to do so. But you don't need to insist. If it's not practical for them, you'll know how many platters, bowls and serving forks and spoons to have on hand.

•**At the party, provide guests bringing food with blank labels and pens** so that they can display the names of their dishes and any allergens (nuts, eggs) they contain or special information such as "vegetarian" or "gluten free."

•**Once food arrives,** keep food safety in mind. If the party is outside on a warm day or in a warm room, put food out just before it is to be served. Do not leave it out for more than two hours.

Big Fun in Your Yard!
6 Unusual Lawn Games Anyone Can Play

Paul Tukey, coauthor of *Tag, Toss & Run: 40 Classic Lawn Games*. Based in Potomac, Maryland, he previously ran Lawn Games for Life, a company that staged outdoor games for corporate events and parties, and he was director of the SafeLawns Foundation, an organization that promotes pesticide-free lawns.

They are games with unusual names such as Kubb and Mölkky, and they originated in various parts of the world. And you can have fun playing them on your lawn as an alternative to the more familiar games of badminton, croquet, horseshoes and boccie.

These games also can serve as unusual gifts. And for people handy with woodworking, some of the game pieces can be crafted at home. (Do-it-yourself instructions for many of the games listed below can be found by typing the name of the game and the phrase "make your own" into a search engine.)

Six wonderful lawn games that you may not have heard of…

•**Kubb** (pronounced "koob") is an ancient Swedish game sometimes called "Viking chess." Unlike actual chess, it's played on a lawn or a beach, not on a small board.

Ten rectangular wooden blocks, known as kubb, are placed upright, five on each opposing side of a rectangular playing area measuring approximately 16 feet wide by 26 feet long. A slightly larger wooden kung, or king, is placed upright in the center.

On each side, two players position themselves behind a row of kubb and take turns trying to knock over the blocks on the other side by tossing six wooden casting pins, or kastpinnar (pronounced "cast-pin-yor"), at them. When a kubb is knocked down, a player closest to the fallen kubb tosses it onto the other side of the field, where it's placed upright in its landing spot. This player must then knock down that kubb before attempting to knock down more of the regular kubb targets.

When one team has knocked over all the kubb on the opponents' side of the field, they can try to win the game by knocking over the king. Knocking over the king too soon is an automatic loss.

Kubb is somewhat known in Wisconsin and Minnesota but is only now starting to appear elsewhere in the US. Visit USAKubb.org/rules for additional details. Amazon.com sells hardwood Kubb sets made to world championship standards starting at $35. Sets can also be found at outdoor-supply stores, such as REI.

•**Mölkky** (pronounced "Mole-kuh") is a Finnish game in which bowling meets billiards. A dozen skittles—numbered one to 12—are placed upright in a cluster. Skittles are wooden dowels six-to-eight-inches long and two-to-three-inches wide with angled tops. Players take turns tossing a foot-long dowel at these skittles from about 12 feet away. They earn one point per skittle knocked down—unless only one skittle is knocked down on a toss, in which case they earn the number that is printed on that skittle.

Knocked-over skittles are righted after each throw in the spot where they fell, not in their original location, so the cluster soon spreads out. Three consecutive nonscoring throws knock a player out of the game. You need to score exactly 50 points to win—go over 50, and your score resets back to 25. Visit Molkky.com for additional details.

Amazon.com sell a Mölkky set for $47.29. YardGames (YardGames.com) offers a "Scatter Number Block Tossing Game" for $39.99. It's the same equipment but without the official Mölkky name.

•**Quoits** (pronouned "koits" or "kwoits") is an ancient ring-toss game similar to horseshoes, except players throw metal O's instead of U's. That difference in shape changes the strategy significantly. Ringers—getting the ring around the target stake—are rare in quoits, so there's greater emphasis on playing defense by blocking or knocking away opponents' quoits. Originally used as weapons of war, quoits showed up in the form of a discus throw at the Olympic Games in ancient Greece around 200 BC.

Quoits is a better choice than horseshoes for small lawns because the three-to-four-pound rings generally are thrown from just 21 feet away in the traditional American version of the game, versus 40 feet for horseshoes.

Players typically earn three points for a ringer, two for a quoit that's touching the stake and one for having the closest quoit. The first to reach 21 points wins. (You might encounter slightly different quoits rules and equipment in parts of New Jersey, Pennsylvania, England and Scotland.) Visit Quoits. info for more information.

You can purchase a quoit set that comes with four quoits and two stakes at QuoitOutlet.com. The sets range from $50 to $200. The site offers sets of regulation four-pound quoits, three-pound quoits or rubber quoits.

•**Ladder golf,** sometimes called ladder toss or ladder ball, actually isn't much like golf. Players take turns tossing bolas—pairs of golf balls connected by a short rope—at a ladder (three horizontal poles positioned above one another like rungs) from five paces away. Points are earned for getting bolas to hang from this ladder—three points for the top rung, two for the middle and one for the lowest. The first player to reach exactly 21 wins.

Well-made sets are available from Ladder Golf, Inc. (LadderGolf.com) for $79.95. Shipping rates vary by location.

•**Cornhole,** a beanbag toss game, is becoming popular among parking lot tailgaters because it can be played safely in relatively crowded areas.

Two wood boards measuring 24 x 48 inches are positioned 27 feet apart. There's a six-inch-diameter hole cut into each of these boards nine inches from the top. Legs elevate the back of each board one foot off the ground. The front of each board is elevated just three to four inches so that the board is angled at around 20 degrees.

Players (or teams) stand next to one board and try to toss beanbags through the hole of the other. They earn one point for each beanbag that ends up on the wood surface, three for any that go through the hole.

"Cancellation" scoring is sometimes used, meaning that after each round, the player or team with the most points subtracts the opponent's score and earns the resulting number of points. The first to

reach 21 wins. Visit the site of the American Cornhole Organization to learn more (AmericanCorn hole.com).

Well-made sets are available through the American Cornhole Organization, but prices tend to be $349 or more per board, including eight beanbags, and shipping can be expensive. Local toy stores and sporting-goods stores are increasingly likely to offer cornhole sets at more reasonable prices, or make your own using instructions at CornholeHowTo.com.

•**Cherokee marbles,** an ancient Native American game originating in what is now Oklahoma, is somewhat comparable to golf or croquet, only without most of the equipment.

A five-hole "course" that is similar to a golf course is laid out on a lawn or gravel road. Traditionally, this course forms an L shape, so it might start in a side yard, then cross a front yard.

The holes need not be as deep as those on a golf course and can be dug with a bulb planter. Set the plug of turf aside so that it can be reinserted without damage to the lawn when the game is over.

Each player tries to roll a ball the approximate size of a billiard ball into each hole of the course in order, alternating turns with his opponents as in croquet.

Also like croquet, players then turn around and roll the ball into the holes in the reverse order. Whoever gets back to the first hole wins. After the second hole, players can earn an additional roll by hitting an opponent's ball with theirs—with the added advantage of sending the opponent's ball off into the distance. (No more than two opponent-ball hits per player per hole.)

Polished stone balls are what the Cherokees traditionally used, but these typically are found only in Oklahoma museums these days. I don't know of any merchants selling these balls. Billiard, lacrosse or field hockey balls, available in any sporting-goods store, work well in their place.

The Marriage Fix

Harville Hendrix, PhD, a clinical pastoral counselor, therapist and clinical trainer with more than 40 years of experience, and his wife, Helen LaKelly Hunt, PhD. Together they founded Imago Relationship Therapy, which offers couples' workshops, and have authored several books on relationships, including *Making Marriage Simple: Ten Truths for Changing the Relationship You Have into the One You Want.* HarvilleandHelen.com.

Negativity between spouses is the toxin that triggers most marriage problems. We might argue with our spouse about money or sex or something else, but the underlying reason for the argument usually is that our spouse has said or done something that we considered negative—something that made us feel devalued, a put-down of some sort. Feeling "one down" stirs the fear center in the brain and is so painful that we instinctively try to reverse positions and become "one up," so we put our partner down. In the end, neither partner feels completely safe with the other and trust and intimacy erode.

Here's how to overcome negativity and reinvent your marriage…

Eliminate Negativity Patterns

Negativity is our brain's default state. When early humans heard a twig snap behind them, they didn't assume that it was someone they loved coming to hug them. They assumed that it was something scary coming to eat them, and they reacted accordingly.

Our brains still are predisposed to sense attack when none really exists—particularly when we're under stress—which makes negativity difficult to expunge from a marriage. But it is possible.

Couples can change their patterns and turn their relationships into safe places where negativity is replaced by pleasure and lighthearted enjoyment of life—and they can do this surprisingly quickly. *A four-step plan to make it happen…*

1. Resolve with your partner to go 30 days without negativity in the relationship. If your spouse is unwilling to attempt this with you, you might be able to do it on your own. When one spouse removes all negativity from his/her side of a relationship that previously was very negative, it throws that relationship into crisis. When the couple's normal patterns are broken, the second spouse becomes uncertain how to respond. This second spouse might try to maintain the old, negative patterns, but if you can manage to remain negativity free, our research suggests that 98% of the time the previous pattern will break down within 30 days and a new negativity-free pattern will take its place.

2. Replace negativity with affirmation. Each night, share at least three things you like about each other or express an appreciation for three things you did for each other that day. Don't repeat what you said the night before—come up with three different things each night. Not only does this help both spouses feel appreciated, it also retrains our brains to notice things we appreciate about each other on a daily basis so that we have something to mention that night. This trains you to catch your partner doing something right. We don't need any training in how to catch him/her doing something wrong. What we attend to is what gets our attention.

Example: You might notice that your partner makes you a cup of tea every morning without asking, something he has been doing for so long that you were taking it for granted.

3. Replace judgment with curiosity. Rather than become negative when your partner says or does something that you disagree with, become curious—why did he say or do this thing? Why does he feel this way? Usually your partner is not intending to frustrate you. He is just being himself. Being curious rather than judgmental about his behavior offers you the opportunity to know your partner better. And you may discover something new about yourself and your own vulnerabilities. But it has to be a sincere and loving inquiry, not an interrogation. If it's the latter, it's just negativity in disguise.

Ultimately, we learn to see our partners for themselves, with their own private world of personal meaning, their own ideas and dreams, and not merely as extensions of ourselves or as we wish they were. We no longer say, "You liked that awful movie?" but rather, "Tell me why you liked that movie. I want to know how you think." Genuine curiosity is sexy—it leads to vulnerable sharing and deepens connection.

4. Strive to create a zone of safety for your partner. Your partner wants to be a wonderful partner to you—but first he must feel completely safe around you. When you're not sure what to do or say, ask your partner, "How can I be a safe person for you?" Also, try to have fun together. Short moments of pleasure, on a daily basis, lay down new pathways in the brain and regulate the fear center of the brain. You become predictable as a source of pleasure rather than pain.

Hidden Negativity

Negativity is not only insults and criticisms that are meant to cause pain. It's anything that makes our partners feel unsafe or devalued, even things we never intended to be negative.

Example: You might consider a jibe that you make to be playful and witty, but if your partner considers it hurtful, then you have brought negativity into the marriage regardless of what you intended.

Sometimes even things that are useful and productive in other phases of life can create negativity when applied to a spouse, including…

•**Critical thinking.** The ability to examine evidence rationally is a very useful skill. But when we aim our critical thinking at our partner's words or deeds, it can make our partner feel that we're devaluing his/her way of seeing things.

Example: Your spouse is trying and failing to explain why something made him upset. Your critical-thinking skills tell you that to solve this problem, you need your spouse to calm down and explain the situation more clearly. But if you tell your spouse that he needs to calm down and be rational, it could make him feel even smaller at a moment when he already is hurt.

•**Competition.** Competition is a normal part of life and sometimes necessary to get ahead. But in a marriage, we must take care that our desire to establish that we were right doesn't diminish our spouse by calling attention to the fact that he was wrong.

Example: You disagree with your spouse on the best route to take when driving. If you follow the route you suggest and successfully avoid a major traffic jam, mentioning this to your spouse could be taken as negativity, because it implies that your spouse's route was wrong.

•**Constructive criticism.** This is intended to assist, as the word "constructive" implies. But your partner likely already has plenty of people providing criticism. Your role as spouse is to be an advocate, not a critic, so that your partner feels safe with you. Provide constructive criticism only when it's specifically requested by your partner. And even then, make sure that you state that it is your opinion or best judgment and does not represent divine intervention.

Helpful: When your spouse says that he feels devalued by something you said or did, accept this and apologize, even if no negativity was intended. You should not argue that your partner is misinterpreting the situation—that devalues your partner's viewpoint, only adding to his sense that you are making him feel diminished. You should ask to backtrack and restart the conversation, then you should restate things in a way that's less likely to be taken negatively. Both partners should agree to allow these do-overs. Take note of what made your partner feel devalued so that you can avoid this in the future.

Living Together?

Frederick C. Hertz, an attorney with an office in Oakland whose practice frequently deals with cohabitation agreements, property co-ownership agreements and other matters related to unmarried partners. He is coauthor of *Living Together: A Legal Guide for Unmarried Couples.* FrederickHertz.com

---

Millions of Americans are no longer wed to the institution of marriage. As of 2016, about 18 million US adults were in cohabiting relationships, up 29% since 2007. That includes 4 million age 50 or older, a sharp 75% increase.

Not getting married might seem like a way to avoid financial and legal complications, but in some ways, it actually creates new problems. The legal system, financial accounts, insurance policies and more tend to be designed with married couples in mind. Unmarried couples often need to take extra steps to gain the same advantages—if they can access these advantages at all. And it is crucial for any unmarried couple to have certain specific money conversations before these challenges threaten the relationship or the well-being of each partner.

Here's what unmarried couples who decide to live together need to do…

1. Know what your insurance won't cover. If one partner owns the home that both share, the homeowner's insurance is unlikely to cover the other partner's possessions. This partner should obtain a renter's policy to cover these.

If you drive a car owned by a partner to whom you are not married, that partner's insurance policy likely will cover you (the policyholder should contact the insurer to confirm this and to list the partner on the policy if necessary), but it might not cover the non–car owner's possessions if they are stolen from the car. And the non–car owner will not be covered when driving a rental car even if the policy features rental-car coverage.

Also, unmarried couples generally must obtain separate health insurance coverage, though there are exceptions. Ask your insurer or your employer's benefits coordinator if your policy can cover your domestic partner.

2. Decide whether you want your partner to make financial and/or health-care decisions for you if you cannot make them for yourself. This decision-making right is not automatically conferred on your unmarried partner as it often is on a spouse. If this partner is the person you want making these crucial decisions for you, name him/her as your proxy on a financial power of attorney and/or a health-care directive. Speak with an estate-planning attorney, or look for the forms online by entering the names of the forms into a search engine.

3. Understand the tax consequences of remaining unmarried. Married couples typically choose between "married filing jointly" and "married filing separately" status when they file their income tax returns. Unmarried people file separate returns, typically with the tax filing status "single." This is one area where the system is not slanted in favor of the married—tax bills tend to be lower with "single" status, though this can vary.

While a married person can share money with his partner without any tax consequences, an unmarried person must file IRS Form 709, United States Gift (and Generation-Skipping Transfer) Tax Return, if he/she gives the other partner gifts with a value totaling more than $16,000 during a year—and that includes not only cash but also gifts of almost any sort with the potential exception of help with medi-

cal or tuition expenses if these are made directly to the medical provider or educational institution. Gifts to a nonspouse partner will count against the giver's lifetime gift tax exemption and estate tax exclusion. This exclusion is currently $12.06 million, however, so the gifts will result in federal estate tax only for very large estates. (They could lead to state estate taxes for more modest estates, however.)

In some states, an unmarried partner can face real estate transfer taxes if he inherits a home from his partner (or inherits his partner's share of a home that the couple co-owned).

4. Decide whether any assets will change hands if you eventually split up or one partner dies. If you're married, there are laws that ensure a surviving spouse will inherit much or all of the estate…and divorce settlements tend to ensure that assets will be divided. But if you're not married, your partner will not automatically inherit anything at all if you die… and the situation is not as clear-cut as you might expect if you split up. Unmarried people often assume that each will automatically keep his own assets in a split, but in most states, it is possible for an unmarried person to take a former partner to court and make a financial claim, perhaps arguing that there were verbal promises of financial support.

To avoid this uncertainty, both partners should sign a document waiving any claim on each other's assets…or a document spelling out exactly what each partner will receive from the other if the relationship ends. This not only protects the assets of the partner with greater assets but also gives the other partner a way to ensure that he is not left destitute. Rather than depend on a lawsuit that could very possibly fail, this partner could secure an agreement that the wealthier partner will provide a specific amount of financial assistance if the relationship ends after many years.

There's no need to pay a lawyer to draft this document unless the agreement you have in mind is complex. Use the forms in my book or search online for "living together agreement" or "cohabitation agreement."

Each partner should have a will drafted and fill out beneficiary designation forms for various financial accounts to detail precisely what assets go to the other partner. Unlike surviving spouses, a surviving unmarried partner will not necessarily receive anything at all if the other partner dies without having these documents in place.

5. Decide how you will divide expenses. Will you and your partner share all expenses or share only expenses that are clearly joint living expenses that benefit both of you—things such as groceries, utilities and vacations? And how will these expenses be divided? The obvious 50/50 split might not be appropriate if one partner has much higher earnings or savings.

One common sticking point is how to handle expenses that are legally specific to one partner but that benefit both, such as the mortgage bill, property taxes, home maintenance and home repairs when the home is not jointly owned. The home-owning partner might think that these expenses should be shared because both partners are benefiting from the home…while the non–home owner might not agree because only the home owner will later benefit from the sale of the property.

Example: A man moves into his retired girlfriend's home. The pair have roughly similar savings, so the commonsense division of expenses would be for them to split expenses 50/50. But the boyfriend's arrival means that the girlfriend can no longer rent out a room to a boarder, so the boyfriend agrees to pay rent equal to what the boarder had been paying in addition to splitting other living expenses.

What's crucial is not necessarily the decisions a couple makes but that the topic is discussed at all. Problems arise when couples make assumptions about expenses rather than talk this through.

6. Decide how to own jointly owned property. If you and your unmarried partner purchase real estate (or certain other valuable assets such as a car, boat or RV) together, you will have to decide whether to title your ownership as "joint tenancy" or "tenancy in common." Joint tenancy, which means two or more people co-own property, is the best option if you and your partner will own an equal share of the property and you want the surviving partner to receive the property outright when the other one dies. (Note that in the case of an unmarried couple, inheriting this property could generate a tax bill.) Tenancy in common, which means two or more people each own separate and distinct shares

of property, is the better choice if you will not each own a 50% share and/or you want each partner to be able to leave his share to whomever he likes.

7. Agree to save separately. Unmarried couples should maintain separate investment and savings accounts even if they expect to spend the rest of their lives together. There is little upside to combining these accounts, and doing so would put both partners' savings at risk if either partner were sued, pursued by creditors or required an extended stay in a long-term-care facility.

Exception: It is reasonable to maintain a joint checking account of modest size to pay the couple's joint expenses.

8. Sign an agreement stating that you don't intend to create a "common-law marriage" if you live in a state that recognizes these. In certain states, if you live with a partner for years and "present yourselves as a married couple" during that time—a phrase that's open to interpretation—you could be considered to have a common-law marriage and be legally wed even if you never got a marriage license or had a marriage ceremony.

Common-law marriage rules create ambiguity that isn't beneficial for anyone—even the partner who has less income and assets. Are you married or not? If you split up, are you entitled to a share of your partner's assets and income or not? Can you leave your entire estate to your children from a prior marriage or not? State laws do not even spell out how many years you must be together for common-law marriage to be a possibility.

If you live in one of the states that recognizes common-law marriage, the sensible move is to eliminate this possibility so that you and your partner can be sure about your legal status. If you want to be married, get a marriage license and get married…and if you don't, sign an agreement stating that you do not intend to form a common-law marriage.

Where: Common-law marriage is recognized in Colorado, the District of Columbia, Iowa, Kansas, Montana, Oklahoma, Rhode Island, South Carolina, Texas and Utah. It is also recognized in several other states if it began earlier than a specified date.

Traditional Gender Roles Around the House Lead to More Sex

Study of data led by researchers at Juan March Institute, Madrid, Spain, and University of Washington, Seattle.

In marriages where chores were divided based on traditional stereotypes—women did the housework and men handled car care and lawn mowing, for example—couples had sex an average of 4.8 times a month. When both partners helped with everyday chores, the frequency dropped to 3.9 times a month.

How to Get Grown Kids to Move Out

Kevin Leman, PhD, a psychologist based in Tucson, Arizona, who specializes in parenting, family and marriage issues. He is author of numerous books including *Making Children Mind Without Losing Yours* and *Planet Middle School: Helping Your Child Through the Peer Pressure, Awkward Moments & Emotional Drama.* DrLeman.com

There's nothing wrong with letting an adult child live at home temporarily during times of turmoil. A child who has lost his/her job or his partner might need a safe place to lick his wounds. But it is in no one's interest for a parent's home to become a place where this adult child can hide from life. So when a child asks if he can return, say yes—but that you're concerned that he might not be happy if he does, because of the rules he would have to live by. *These rules might include…*

• **You must get a job.** If the child protests that he can't find anything better than flipping burgers, tell him he'll have to flip burgers. It's not enough for the child to promise to "look for work." This could mean nothing more than sending out a résumé every now and then. He must understand that living in your house will not help him escape or delay joining the work force. Besides, working in an unpleasant or low-paying job could be the motivation he needs to go out and find something better.

You must contribute 25% of your take-home pay as rent. This reinforces the message that living at home is not a free ride. The adult child also should be responsible for paying his personal expenses.

Helpful: If you do not need this rent money, set it aside in an interest-bearing account. If the adult child works hard to get his life on track, present the money to him when he moves out. This return of rent must come as a surprise, however—if the child expects it, that could undermine the message that he must pay his own way.

• **You will have to do housework.** List specific chores that he will have to do such as his laundry, clean his room, take out the garbage, etc.

Also: If this adult child has young children who will be moving in, too, and you have offered to help with child care, set limits. Perhaps you will provide child care one or two days a week or you will help when the adult child is working, but he should not expect you to babysit every evening while he goes out with friends.

You will have to abide by the house schedule. This might mean guests must be out by 10 pm… the TV volume must be turned way down (or off) by 11 pm…or that there's a midnight curfew.

• **You must deal with your own debts.** Do not get sucked into your adult child's financial problems. Not only could this cripple your retirement, it could cripple the adult child's sense of financial responsibility. It's fine to offer guidance, but don't bail him out.

• **You must move out by a specific departure date.** This could be one month, three months or six months down the road—the timetable is up to you. The important part is that there is a deadline so the adult child doesn't start to see living at home as a permanent solution.

If these rules sound severe, they're meant to be. If living in your house is unrestrictive, the adult child will have less reason to move out and get on with his own life.

When you pitch all of this to your child, explain that you understand that it probably doesn't sound very appealing and that you won't be offended if he opts to get together with some friends and split a cheap apartment—no harm in floating this idea.

If the child still wants to move in, get a handshake agreement that he will abide by the terms you laid out. If he does, treat him with respect—don't joke about the bad job he has been forced to take or tell him he's made a mess of his life. Instead, commiserate by sharing stories about your struggles as a young adult—the child might not realize that you faced challenges early on, too. Offer advice when it is requested, but do not try to run his life—that will not foster the sense of responsibility you are trying to help him develop.

If an Adult Child Already Is Living in Your Home

If you failed to establish strict rules and a departure date before your adult child moved in, this child might now be showing little interest in moving out. If so, tell the child these five words—"I owe you an apology." This is more likely to get the child's attention than yet another admonition to get a job or an apartment.

When the child asks the reason for the apology, reply, "When we let you return home, we had the best of intentions, but in retrospect, it wasn't what was best for you. We should have had an agreement in place for how this would work, because without that, it clearly isn't working for anyone. We realize that you're not going to like this, but if you're going to continue staying here, this is what will be required..." then list rules and deadlines such as those described earlier.

How to Raise Kids Who Return Only for Visits

Four ways to increase the odds that young children and teens will move out when they grow up...

●**Encourage without overpraising.** By all means tell your child "good job" when he works hard and accomplishes something—but do not consistently tell your child that he is the greatest thing in the world. Overpraised children can turn into adults with an inflated sense of self-worth. They might consider entry-level jobs beneath them and end up living at home when no one offers them a six-figure salary and corner office right out of school.

●**Assign children chores.** Kids raised in households where everyone pulls his weight tend to become adults who understand that they must work hard and take responsibility to achieve anything.

●**Remind laggard teens that your home has a check-out time.** If a teen lacks drive and responsibility and doesn't want to adhere to your rules, remove a strip of 18 squares of toilet paper from a roll, then sit the child down for a talk. Count off one sheet of the toilet paper for each year this teen already has lived—16 for a 16-year-old, for example—then hold up the small number of remaining squares and say, "You have just two more years living under my roof." This is likely to earn you some teenage eye rolling, but it truly can be an effective wake-up call.

●**Let the child take the lead on college money matters.** College is supposed to prepare kids for adult life. Taking charge of college finances is a crucial part of that. Help your kids pay their tuition (or even pay for college outright) if you are in a financial position to do so—but insist that college kids take part-time or summer jobs to cover some costs. If college loans are needed, the child—not the parent—should take these out. Your role is to help the child understand loan terms and the dangers of going deeply into debt.

Best Chores for Kids of All Ages

Roundup of experts on tasks that children can do, reported in *The Wall Street Journal.*

Five and under: Pick up toys...brush teeth...comb his/her hair.

Six to nine: Take care of pets...operate appliances, such as a vacuum cleaner or dishwasher... make his/her own bed.

10 to 12: Take out trash...make his/her lunch... clean the bathroom.

13 to 15: Mow the lawn...wash windows... clean the garage.

16 to 18: Wash clothes...do grocery shopping... handle car maintenance, such as getting an oil change or emissions testing.

How to Stay Close to Your Grandchildren When You Live Far Away

Nancy Samalin, MS, founder and director of Parent Guidance Workshops, a New York City–based organization that has been working with parents and grandparents for more than three decades. She is author of four best-sellers, including *Loving Without Spoiling: And 100 Other Timeless Tips for Raising Terrific Kids.* Samalin.com

The bond between grandparents and grandchildren is unique. Ideally, grandparents enjoy the company of a grandchild free of the stresses and responsibilities of a parent, and the grandchild basks in the grandparents' undemanding attention and love.

If you live far away from your grandchildren, you may worry that this bond will be harder to maintain. When you don't spend time with grandchildren, will they grow up barely knowing you? You worry that they may feel closer to the "other" grandparents because they see them more often.

You can be an integral part of your grandchild's life even if you aren't geographically close. *Here's how…*

Maximize Video Calls

You don't have to be a technical wiz to use video-call services such as FaceTime (for iPhones), Google Hangouts (for both Android and Apple devices) or Skype (for computers, tablets and smartphones). Being able to see each other on a call creates a greater feeling of closeness and involvement. Video also lets you see how your grandchildren are changing over time so that you feel part of their development.

To get the most out of video calls…

•**Favor frequent, short calls over less frequent ones.** Grandparents often think that the key to a close relationship is long, in-depth conversations. Not true! Calls can be short, but they should be frequent. A video chat allows you to stay in touch without being intrusive. Schedule a recurring day and time so that the call is an expected routine that the child looks forward to.

•**Enlist the child's parents as allies.** Tell your children—your grandchild's parents—that you want to build the most positive relationship possible for the grandchild's sake as well as yours, and find a regular time that is convenient for the family. Get the parents' input on the activities, projects and interests that are central to their kids' lives so that you can bring these up during chats.

•**When a new grandchild arrives, start your video chats soon after.** As the baby grows and begins to respond to your voice and face, you will be establishing a connection and a ritual that are special to the child.

•**Ask questions that are easy to answer.** Children—even teenagers—generally are not good at small talk. They tend to clam up at questions such as, "How are you? What did you do in school today? What's new?" Make your questions specific instead of open-ended—"What was something funny or weird that happened in school today? Do you like your teacher?"

Just as you do with your friends, ask your grandchild about the things he/she enjoys.

Example: If the child is interested in dinosaurs, you could ask, "What's the biggest dinosaur? The scariest? Wow, that's such a long name—can you show me a picture? What else can you tell me about Tyrannosaurus rex?"

Ask an older child about sports, crafts, shopping, movies, theater, video games or other interests.

•**Don't just talk.** Read the child a story or have him read to you. Based on your grandchild's interests, ask him to teach you the words to a song… share a favorite poem…play the piano for you… demonstrate a new toy. Ask an older child to show you a model car, craft project or scrapbook. Find out her favorite food, and offer to cook it together the next time you visit.

Send Surprises by Mail

As people rely more heavily on electronic communication, receiving packages in the mailbox every few weeks is a very special treat. Don't make these gifts elaborate or expensive. Depending on what your grandchild enjoys, you might alternate among books, puzzles, craft kits, games the family can play together, notebooks, key chains, costume jewelry or homemade delights such as a cartoon or other picture you drew just for the child. Search the Internet for "inexpensive gifts for kids" or "inexpensive gifts for teens" for more ideas.

Learn Your Grandchild's Communication Tools

Find out what methods your grandchild uses to communicate with his friends, and try using one or two of those tools. Expect these methods to change as the child grows—and be sure to embrace those changes.

Example: Older children often prefer text messaging or Instagram to Facebook, e-mail or talking by phone.

Have fun exchanging jokes, funny videos, cute animal pictures and photos you take of interesting sights in your neighborhood. On smartphones, you can play games together, in real time, from a distance, such as Scrabble, Words with Friends or the trivia game QuizUp.

Make the Most of Visits

Whether you visit the family on their turf or they visit you, arrange to spend at least some time alone with your grandchild or grandchildren without their parents. If possible, spend time with each sibling individually as well. You will interact differently with each other one-on-one. Children feel special when you spend time alone with them.

•**Consider a family vacation destination.** If budgets allow, a vacation for the whole family away from home—whether at a cabin or a family-friendly resort—can be a wonderful way for all generations to reconnect away from the tensions of school and work.

•**Make kid time convenient for the parents.** During a visit, offer to take the children for an excursion so that the parents can have some uninterrupted time together...or, if possible, watch them for the weekend so that the parents can have a child-free getaway.

•**Keep outings simple.** When spending time with your grandkids, don't get caught up in planning elaborate outings that put everyone under pressure to have a good time. Often, the most enjoyable and memorable excursions involve low-key activities that will be fun for all and that give you something to talk about together.

Examples: Miniature golf, a movie, the zoo, a library or children's bookstore or just a walk in nature searching for signs of the season.

•**At home, enter your grandchild's world.** When at your grandchild's home for a visit, do what the child loves to do. Draw pictures together...play dress-up or make-believe...read to each other...find nursery rhymes on YouTube and sing them together. Play a card game, and let the child make up the rules. Ask an older child to teach you the finer points of using your smartphone, walk you through a dance routine or play you a song or video he downloaded.

In addition to playing, take part in the activities of daily life. Help your grandchild wash up at bedtime...look after the family pet...make lunch for each other. Some of the closest feelings and fondest memories are created during relaxed, everyday time together.

When Other Grandparents Live Nearby

Living far from your grandchildren can be especially painful if other grandparents live close to them. You may feel left out or at a disadvantage.

This doesn't have to be the case! If you shift your thinking so that you do not view the situation as a competition, everyone will benefit. And if you don't, your anxiety and resentment may negatively affect how you act around your grandchildren—and around the other grandparents. Remember that the more people who love a child, the better, and children have a limitless capacity to receive affection.

Focus on enjoying your interactions with your grandchild, and you will be able to build a unique and rich relationship no matter where you live.

CHAPTER 7

Food Smarts

12 Tricks to Keep Food Longer

Joan Wilen and Lydia Wilen are health investigators based in New York City who have spent decades collecting "cures from the cupboard." Their most recent book is *Bottom Line's Treasury of Home Remedies and Natural Cures* (Bottom Line Books).

Americans typically throw out 21% of their food, mostly uneaten leftovers and food that has gone bad. That waste costs the average American family of four between $1,350 and $2,275 a year. To help prevent and reduce the amount of wasted food in your kitchen, here are ways to perform CPR (Culinary Preservation and Resuscitation) on some popular grocery items. These tips work well for us. We will share the best of them with readers.

Avocado

Never put an unripe avocado in the refrigerator, because it may never ripen. But once it is ripe, put it in the refrigerator drawer or vegetable bin and it should stay fresh for about two weeks.

To save half an avocado and prevent it from turning brown, put lemon juice or a thin layer of mayonnaise on the exposed avocado meat and then cover it with plastic wrap. Another option is to put it in an airtight container with a piece of cut-up onion and refrigerate. The sulfur that makes you cry when you chop onions also works as a preservative. Incidentally, it's a myth that leaving in the pit will help prevent browning—it will prevent browning only on the area directly under the pit.

Bagels

Bagels last about two months in the freezer. Cut them in half, and wrap each half in plastic wrap before freezing. But don't microwave a bagel when it's time to defrost. Microwaving will dehydrate a bagel and make it hard to bite. Instead, warm a bagel in a toaster.

Bananas

By the time little brown spots appear on the peel, a banana is getting close to being overripe. Put a ripe banana in a plastic bag (with the peel on), and keep it in the refrigerator's fruit bin. The peel will turn black, but the flesh of the fruit will be fine for several more days. If a banana is too ripe for your taste, wrap it—peel and all—in plastic wrap and freeze. When you're ready, defrost it and add the flesh to smoothies or pancake or muffin batter or make banana bread.

Beer

Keep beer flavorful by placing cans or bottles upright in or out of the refrigerator. When beer is on its side, more of its contents are exposed to the oxygen in the container. Oxygen depletes the beer of flavor.

Coconut

To revive shredded coconut that has dried out, let it soak in whole milk for about a half hour. Drain, then spread it out on paper towels and pat dry. You may want to use the leftover coconut-flavored milk when baking or in a smoothie.

Corn

If you buy too many ears of corn, you can freeze them with the husks on. Break off the handle of the corn from the bottom end. From the other end, the top, cut off the flopping-over silk tassels. Place the corn in a freezer bag—about six full-sized ears fit into a gallon-size freezer bag. Once you've squeezed out as much air as possible, seal the bag securely. The corn will stay good for up to six months. When you're ready to have corn, put the frozen ear of corn, husks on, into the microwave and zap it for about four minutes before serving.

Cottage Cheese

Once you have opened a container of cottage cheese, the oxygen layer where bacteria grow is exposed to the air. After you take a portion of cottage cheese, close the container and store it in the refrigerator upside down. That way, you create a vaccuum, eliminating most of the oxygen layer and preventing bacteria from proliferating. This upside-down trick will allow the cottage cheese to last an extra week or more. This also works for sour cream.

Cream

When you have cream left in its container, you can prolong freshness for several days by adding about one-eighth of a teaspoon of baking soda to the container (this small amount will not affect the taste). The baking soda is safe and will neutralize the lactic acid that builds up and causes the cream to sour.

Or you can freeze cream in an ice-cube tray (and use one cube in your morning coffee each day). Once the cubes are thoroughly frozen, you can transfer them to a freezer bag to save space.

Eggs

Keep eggs in their original container. Eggshells are porous, and if they are not in a closed container, they will absorb refrigerator odors. If you go on vacation and want the eggs in the fridge to be edible when you get home, seal the eggs' pores by coating the shells with a thin layer of vegetable or mineral oil.

Flour

If you keep white flour in an airtight container and in a cool, dry place, it will last about 15 months. Whole-grain flours will keep for one to three months. If you want to keep any flour longer, put it in the freezer. When you're ready to use it, let the flour thaw to room temperature.

Lettuce, Carrots, Celery

Place the limp veggies in very cold water with a few slices of raw potato—it shouldn't take long for them to crisp up. We are not sure why the potato works, but it does!

Potatoes

When you bring potatoes home from the store, keep them in a paper bag and put a small chunk of gingerroot in the bag with them. It will prevent the potatoes from sprouting.

A Chef's Strategy for Buying Seafood at the Supermarket

Aliza Green, a Philadelphia-based chef and author of more than a dozen books about food including *The Fishmonger's Apprentice* and *Field Guide to Seafood*. AlizaGreen.com

---

The key to preparing delicious seafood occurs before you set foot in your kitchen—you must buy a great piece of fish. Unfortunately, many areas do not have top-notch seafood stores. That means most Americans must buy their seafood at supermarkets. This is not necessarily a bad option—some supermarkets have excellent seafood departments—but quality can vary dramatically.

How to decide where to buy seafood and how to pick the best seafood...

Ways to Evaluate a Market or Seafood Department

Before buying from a supermarket seafood department or stand-alone fish market...

Longer-Lasting Fruits and Vegetables

Double, triple, even quadruple the life of your spinach, berries and other produce by laying down a sheet of FreshPaper in your refrigerator's produce bin. It contains organic spices that inhibit bacterial and fungal growth. Each sheet lasts about a month (until its maple syrup–like scent, from fenugreek, fades). An eight-sheet pack costs about $10—and saves up to $50 a month on produce that didn't spoil. Freshglow. co/freshpaper

Jon Jesse, former vice president for industry development at the International Housewares Association (IHA), Rosemont, Illinois. Housewares.org.

●**Take a whiff as you approach the counter.** You should smell ocean brine or nothing at all. If instead you get a low-tide–like fishy odor, walk away—the store does not pay sufficient attention to freshness or cleanliness.

●**Examine whole fish on display—even if you intend to buy a fillet.** The fishes' eyes should be bright and clear, not cloudy...scales should be shiny and metallic-looking, not dull. If you can touch the fish, gently press its flesh—if it is fresh, the depression you create will quickly disappear. It speaks poorly of the store if there are past-their-prime whole fish on display.

●**Look for liquid in packaged fish fillets.** Tip a few packaged fish fillets to one side. If you see liquid sloshing around, the fillet has been sitting around too long—those are juices that have escaped the fish as it aged and dried out. You could simply select a different fillet, but the smarter move is to not buy seafood there at all—liquid in fillet packages is a red flag that a store is not sufficiently focused on freshness.

●**Eye the ice in fish display cases.** This ice should look clear. If it is cloudy or yellowed, it likely is not changed very often—another sign of inattention.

●**At a supermarket, ask to speak to the fish-department manager.** I always consider it a warning sign if this manager is summoned from the meat department—supermarkets that take seafood seriously tend to have specialists running their seafood sections. The main point of asking for the manager is to see who he/she is. To that end, you can ask about his background with seafood...and you might also ask, "What's the freshest fish you have today?"

●**Notice fish-department traffic.** The more customers a seafood department or seafood store has, the faster it will turn over its inventory and the fresher its seafood is likely to be. Be wary if you've been to a store several times and rarely see anyone buying fish.

●**Seek out markets that cater to immigrant groups from coastal, seafood-loving nations.** I have found that if there's a market in the area that has a large clientele of people from Portugal, Korea, Vietnam or Italy, for example, it likely is a great place to buy excellent seafood for reasonable prices. Members of these communities tend to be savvy seafood shoppers. And because these groups tend to eat lots of seafood, inventory turnover often is high.

Ways to Select Seafood

Even at a well-run seafood store or supermarket seafood department, some pieces of fish inevitably will be fresher and better than others...

●**Look for a slight blue tint in white-flesh fish.** A white, flaky fish such as cod, flounder or haddock should be translucent or such a brilliant white that it seems to have a slight bluish tint. If there's a slight yellowish tint instead, the fish has begun to oxidize and won't taste very good.

●**Seek a distant sell-by date.** Prepackaged fish should include a sell-by date on the label. But it's not sufficient that a packaged piece of fish hasn't passed its sell-by date—you want to find fish that is at least two days away from this date.

Warning: If seafood has a far-off sell-by date but seems past its prime, don't buy it—disreputable stores occasionally repackage fish as it nears its original sell-by date.

●**Don't be afraid of the word "frozen."** When it comes to seafood, fresh is best only if you live very near where that fish was caught. Otherwise you may be better off buying frozen, particularly when the frozen fish is vacuum-sealed and the packaging says it was "flash frozen"—that is, frozen almost immediately after coming out of the water.

Warning: When you choose frozen fish, avoid packages that have frost on the fish inside the packaging…and/or where sections of the frozen fish's flesh appear discolored. These are signs that frozen fish has been sitting around too long.

●**Lean toward seafood that is sold in thick steaks.** The higher a piece of seafood's ratio of volume to surface area, the better it likely will hold up over time, whether fresh or frozen. All else being equal, that means the best bet for freshness often is large fish that's cut into thick steaks, which might include tuna, swordfish, salmon or Chilean sea bass. (Be aware that swordfish—and to a lesser extent tuna and Chilean sea bass—sometimes have high mercury levels, so they should not be eaten very frequently, especially by children and pregnant women.)

●**Avoid seafood imported from Southeast Asia.** Fishing industry standards and quality controls are not as reliable in Southeast Asia as they are in North, South and Central America. Among other issues, fish imported from Southeast Asia—including from large exporters such as Vietnam, Thailand, Indonesia and China—might not have been frozen promptly and properly, increasing the odds of flavor and safety problems.

Warning: Virtually all the tilapia sold in the US is imported from Southeast Asia. Much of the shrimp sold in the US comes from Southeast Asia, too, but it is possible to find shrimp from Mexico, Venezuela or the US Gulf Coast instead.

●**Don't automatically skip the fish that's on sale.** Buying bargain fish might sound like a bad idea—because fish sometimes is marked down because it is about to go bad. But sometimes the fish that's on sale is the freshest fish in the store because there have been big recent catches of a certain type of fish and distributors must temporarily slash prices to move this inventory.

●**Avoid exotic or obscure fish unless you have great trust in the store.** Some people find it fun to try new foods—but most don't, which means unusual types of fish tend to sit around in stores longer than well-known types of fish. It's fine to buy unusual fish if a store you trust assures you that it's fresh, it's a fish that is popular in the community that frequents the store (such as whiting in an Italian market or monkfish in an Asian market) and/or you have faith in your fish-selection skills.

●**Buy shellfish that grew in northern waters, especially if you're planning to enjoy it raw.** These are less likely than warm-water shellfish to harbor dangerous parasites, and they often have more flavor, too.

Examples: Oysters and mussels from Atlantic Canada or New England are excellent options.

After You Buy Your Fish…

It might not be the store's fault when a piece of seafood tastes less than fresh. *How you transport and store seafood after you buy it matters, too…*

●**Ask for ice for the trip home.** Seafood can significantly degrade in the time it takes to get it home from the store, especially on hot days. Most seafood stores and departments will provide a bag of ice upon request.

●**Store seafood on ice in your fridge.** Unless you're cooking seafood as soon as you get home, fill a container with ice and put the seafood on this bowl in your fridge. (Wrap the seafood in plastic wrap first if it is not already sealed well.) This ice provides additional cooling—I find that seafood is best stored at around 28°F, which is colder than a fridge on its own.

●**Defrost frozen seafood in the fridge.** This takes longer than defrosting it at room temperature, but it's safer—there's increased risk for contamination when you defrost seafood at room temperature. Defrosting in the fridge leads to tastier seafood—too much liquid often drips out when seafood is defrosted at room temperature, taking a lot of the flavor with it.

Helpful: The ideal time to cook a piece of seafood that has been frozen is when it is no longer rigid but you can still feel tiny ice crystals in its flesh. If you wait until these ice crystals melt, some flavor will be lost even if you do defrost in the fridge.

●**Don't let seafood languish, even frozen.** Even frozen, most fish should be kept tightly wrapped and positioned in the back of the freezer where it's coldest and used within one month for the best flavor.

Cook Meat Like a Master: 5 Myths Busted

Meathead Goldwyn, who shares the science of cooking meat at his popular website, AmazingRibs.com. He is author of *The New York Times* best-seller *Meathead: The Science of Great Barbecue and Grilling*.

Myths about the best way to prepare and cook meat are plentiful—and many cookbooks still promote this misinformation. At AmazingRibs.com, meat fanatic Meathead Goldwyn and his scientific advisers debunk myths about all kinds of cuts of meat with methodical testing.

Result: The truth about the tastiest ways to prepare meat.

Here are five myths you shouldn't believe...

MYTH: Let meat come to room temperature before cooking.

Reality: Many recipes, especially those for thick steaks or large roasts, direct you to take the meat out of the refrigerator an hour or two before cooking to allow it "to come to room temperature."

Theory: Room-temperature meat will cook more quickly than cold meat.

That may be true, but when we tested this theory, a one-and-a-half-inch steak took more than two hours for the center to come to room temperature. A three-and-a-half-inch-thick, four-and-a-half-pound pork roast took a whopping 10 hours! The meat's temperature had risen from 38°F (refrigerator temperature) to only 49°F after two hours. And after five hours, it began to smell funny.

Important: At room temperature, dangerous microbes can reproduce quickly.

Also, cold meat attracts more smoke than warm meat, a process called thermophoresis. It's the same phenomenon that causes your mirror to fog up after a shower. And a smoky flavor is something we like in our meat, right?

MYTH: Boil ribs to make them tender.

Reality: Many people boil ribs before grilling them to save time and to achieve the desired "fall off the bone" results. This is a mistake. When you boil meat and bones, the flavor—and many nutrients—are pulled from the meat and left behind in the water. That's why the water is cloudy...and why soup is so tasty.

Ribs are most flavorful when roasted. If you need to speed up the cooking process, you are better off steaming or microwaving them and then finishing them on the grill or under the broiler.

Properly roasted ribs are tender but still have some chew to them, similar to a tender steak. The meat should not fall off the bone—if it does, chances are the ribs have been boiled and won't be as flavorful.

MYTH: Marinating meat makes it more tender.

Reality: Marinades do not penetrate meats very far, rarely more than an eighth of an inch, even after many hours of soaking. Meat is about 75% water, and there is not much room for more liquid. Think of a kitchen sponge that is loaded after wiping up a spill—once full, it cannot absorb any more liquid. A marinade can soften the proteins in muscle fibers and connective tissues, but because the marinade does not penetrate very far, it does not tenderize much beyond the meat's surface.

Spices and herbs on the surface of meat can add a wonderful aroma, and a touch of sugar can help with browning and add flavor—but marinades can tenderize only very thin cuts of meat such as skirt steak.

MYTH: Chicken is done once the juices run clear, and pink meat means that it is undercooked.

Reality: The meat and juices in chicken, turkey and pork are colored pink by the protein myoglobin. When cooked, myoglobin absorbs light differently and no longer appears pink. However, there is no fixed temperature at which myoglobin changes color.

In addition, red or purple bones, or pink meat next to bones, do not indicate that chicken is undercooked. Bones can be red because marrow is where the blood is made. As birds age, more calcium is deposited on the bones, so the marrow becomes less visible and less porous. Red or purple bones are more common now because chickens grow faster (they have been bred to grow faster, and they are fed foods that make them grow fast), so most are only seven to eight weeks old when they are butchered.

Purple bones can discolor adjacent meat, making it appear pink even when safely cooked. The pink color also can come from nitric oxide or carbon monoxide, by-products of smoke or combustion gases in gas ovens and grills and charcoal grills.

Bottom line: Chicken meat, including any that remains pink, is safe to eat when a food thermometer indicates that the meat is at 165°F.

MYTH: Pop-up turkey thermometers are fine to let you know when your bird is done.

Reality: You cannot rely on the pop-up thermometer that comes with your turkey or pop-up thermometers that you buy yourself.

How they work: The thermometer tip melts at a specific temperature and releases a spring that pops the stem up. Although these thermometers can be accurate in some cases, they also can stick. And they read only one small part of the turkey. Plus, they often are set to pop up at 175°F or higher, which is too high—and which is why so many turkeys are overcooked and taste like cardboard.

What to do: Pop out the thermometer that comes in your turkey. Then, when you think the cooking might be done, check the temperature with a digital meat thermometer, which is more accurate and faster than a dial thermometer. A whole turkey is safe when cooked to a minimum of 165°F. Check the temperature in several places—especially the innermost part of the thigh and the thickest part of the breast—and make sure that all parts of the turkey have reached that level.

Safe, Tasty Grilling…

Kim O'Donnel, a chef and journalist. She is the author of *The Meat Lover's Meatless Cookbook.* KimODonnel.com

Outdoor grilling is hands-down one of the best things about summer. But with all the warnings about artery-clogging fat in hamburgers and the potential dangers of grilled meat in general (veggies are OK), should you just let your grill sit

idle? Absolutely not! The good news is that you don't have to give up meat altogether. If you crave a burger, have one (see below for safer grilling tips). Make it as fatty and juicy as you want and enjoy it—now and then.

When you grill beef, lamb or the increasingly popular bison, free radicals and potentially harmful chemicals are produced when dripping fat hits the coals and produces a smoky flare-up. (Pork, poultry and fish also produce the chemicals but generally less so than red meat.) *To minimize these dangers…*

•**Add dried oregano and/or dried cherries to ground meat.** These potent antioxidants reduce the production of harmful compounds during high-heat cooking of meat.

Tasty option: For one pound of ground meat, add about two teaspoons of dried oregano, one-quarter cup of dried cherries, three-quarters teaspoon fine sea salt and three-quarters teaspoon paprika. Mix well, and use one tablespoon of olive oil to brush the patty before grilling.

The National Cancer Institute also advises grilling precautions such as…

•**Don't put the meat directly over an open flame.** That way, the meat won't reach the ultrahigh cooking temperature that causes charring and promotes the formation of harmful compounds.

•**Turn the meat often.**

•**Remove any charred portions of the meat before eating.**

The Best Grilled Veggie Recipes

Linda Gassenheimer, an award-winning author of several cookbooks, including *The 12-Week Diabetes Cookbook* and *Delicious One-Pot Dishes* and the *Food, News and Views* podcast on 880thebiz.com. She also writes the syndicated column "Dinner in Minutes." DinnerInMinutes.com

Vegetables don't have to be boring, especially during grilling season! *Here are six recipes that are so good, they give steak a run for its money…*

Grilled Asparagus, Chickpea and Orzo Salad

This easy salad can be served warm or at room temperature. You can substitute quinoa for the orzo if you prefer.

You can place asparagus directly on the grate and turn it with tongs. Or you can skewer several together crosswise—this keeps asparagus from falling through the grate. Place four spears together. Push a wooden skewer through all four near the top of the asparagus. Push a second skewer through near the bottom of the asparagus.

- 2 pounds fresh asparagus
- ¼ cup olive oil
- 1 cup canned chickpeas, rinsed and drained
- Salt and freshly ground black pepper
- 1 cup orzo or quinoa
- ½ cup oil-and-vinegar dressing
- ¼ cup chopped fresh basil or parsley
- 1 package short wooden skewers
- Small disposable aluminum baking pan

Snap off the stems of the asparagus at the point where they break easily, about one inch from the bottom. Pour olive oil onto the disposable baking pan, and roll the asparagus in the oil. Remove the asparagus. Add the chickpeas, and toss them in the oil. Add salt and pepper to taste. Heat the grill to medium.

Place the pan with the chickpeas on the grill grates. Skewer four asparagus at a time crosswise. Place the asparagus on the grates. Grill, covered, five minutes. Turn the asparagus, and stir the chickpeas. Grill, covered, three minutes. If using thin asparagus, reduce grilling time to two minutes per side and remove from grill, leaving the chickpeas to grill about five to 10 minutes or until golden. Cut the asparagus into one-inch pieces.

While the vegetables are cooking, bring a large pot with about four quarts of water to a boil. Add the orzo, and boil 10 minutes, or until the orzo is cooked through but still firm. (If using quinoa, cook it in boiling water for 15 to 20 minutes or until soft.) Drain.

Pour the dressing into a large bowl. Add the orzo, asparagus and chickpeas. Sprinkle on the fresh herbs and salt and pepper to taste. Toss again. Serves four.

Teriyaki Mushroom Kabobs

Any type of mushroom can be used. The trick is to make sure that they are all about the same size so that they grill evenly.

Helpful: I like to use skewers that have two prongs to keep the food from swiveling.

- ¼ pound cremini mushrooms
- ¼ pound shiitake mushrooms
- ¼ pound oyster mushrooms
- ¼ pound button mushrooms
- 1½ cups low-sodium teriyaki sauce (about one 12-ounce bottle)
- 6 skewers

Clean the mushrooms by wiping them with a damp paper towel. Trim the stem ends a bit. Thread the mushrooms onto six skewers, alternating the different types. Brush the mushrooms with some of the teriyaki sauce. Reserve the remaining sauce. Heat the grill to medium.

Place the skewers on the grate over direct heat. Grill, covered, three minutes. Turn and grill, covered, three minutes more. While mushrooms grill, warm the remaining reserved sauce in a saucepan or in a microwave oven for 30 seconds. Remove the mushrooms from the grill, and slide them off the skewers. Place the mushrooms over cooked brown rice if desired. Spoon the sauce over the mushrooms. Serves four.

Grilled Parmesan Corn

A tasty twist on a classic favorite.

- 1 Tablespoon butter
- 4 medium ears corn, shucked
- 4 Tablespoons grated Parmesan cheese
- Salt and freshly ground black pepper

Spread the butter over the corn. Place each ear on a piece of foil. Sprinkle Parmesan cheese and salt and pepper to taste over the corn. Wrap the foil around the corn, and place it on the grill for 10 minutes. Turn and grill for five minutes more. Serves four.

Grilled Pesto Cauliflower Steaks

Cutting cauliflower into steaks is an unusual way to serve it. You also can break the cauliflower into florets and grill them in a grill basket and then toss with pesto.

1   medium head cauliflower
Olive oil spray
¼   cup prepared pesto
Salt and freshly ground black pepper

Cut half-inch slices from the top of the head to the bottom stalk of the cauliflower. This will give you four good steak slices. Save any florets that fall off or are not part of the slices for another meal or to use as crudité. Spray both sides of the steaks with olive oil spray. Heat the grill to medium, and place the steaks on the grill. Cook, covered, for five minutes, turn and grill five minutes more. The steaks will be cooked through but a little firm. Remove the steaks to a platter, and brush or spoon the pesto over the steaks. Add salt and pepper to taste. Serves four.

Grilled Eggplant Parmesan

Grilling the sliced eggplant instead of frying it lightens this Italian favorite.

1½   pounds eggplant
2   Tablespoons olive oil
6   cups no-sugar-added pasta sauce
½   cup fresh basil leaves
½   pound mozzarella cheese, sliced
1   cup freshly grated Parmesan cheese
Salt and freshly ground black pepper

To grill the eggplant, heat the grill to medium. Wash the eggplant, but don't peel it. Cut eggplant into half-inch slices. Brush with olive oil, and place the slices on the grill. Grill for four minutes, covered, turn and grill four minutes more, covered. Remove the eggplant, and sprinkle with salt and pepper to taste.

Spoon a layer of pasta sauce in a 9-by-13-inch metal baking pan. Place a layer of eggplant slices over the sauce, place basil leaves over the eggplant (tearing any large leaves into small pieces), place a layer of mozzarella slices over the basil. Sprinkle Parmesan cheese over the mozzarella cheese. Repeat with the sauce, eggplant, basil and mozzarella. End with a layer of sauce and Parmesan.

Place the pan on the grill grates, and grill, covered, 10 minutes, or until the sauce is bubbly and the cheese is melted (or place the pan in a 400°F oven for about 15 minutes). Serves four.

My Favorite Grill Tools

These make grilling easier and more fun…

●**Long-handled, spring-loaded tongs** are a big help in placing food on the grill, moving it around, turning and removing it.

My favorite: OXO Good Grips 16-inch locking tongs, $15.99.

●**A good basting brush** with a long handle and preferably silicone bristles.

My favorite: OXO Good Grips large silicone basting brush, $11.99.

●**A flat vegetable grate** or basket grill with small holes.

My favorite: Weber style 6434 professional-grade vegetable basket, $30.99, and Weber professional-grade grill pan, $30.99.

●**Two-prong skewers** to keep food from swiveling when turning over.

My favorite: Elizabeth Karmel's Grill Friends 15-inch double kabob skewers, set of four, $15.

Lots of Uses for Those Single-Use Kitchen Appliances

Linda Gassenheimer, an award-winning author of several cookbooks, including *The 12-Week Diabetes Cookbook* and *Delicious One-Pot Dishes* and the *Food, News and Views* podcast on 880thebiz.com. She also writes the syndicated column "Dinner in Minutes." DinnerInMinutes.com

Many kitchen appliances appear to have one use. Not true! You can use your bread machine, waffle iron, ice cream maker and fondue pot for other easy and delicious recipes.

Bread Machine

You can make your favorite meat loaf in your bread machine or use the recipe below. You can walk away and let it cook on its own, using little electricity. Use the bake setting on your bread machine.

Maple Syrup–Glazed Meat Loaf

Vegetable oil spray

- 1 cup chopped fresh or frozen onion
- 1 cup chopped fresh or frozen green bell pepper
- 1½ pounds extra-lean ground beef
- 4 teaspoons ground sage
- 1 cup plain bread crumbs
- 2 Tablespoons Dijon mustard
- 6 Tablespoons maple syrup
- 2 large eggs
- 1 teaspoon salt
- ½ teaspoon ground black pepper

Spray the bread machine pan with vegetable oil spray. Place frozen onion and green bell pepper in a microwave-safe bowl, and microwave one minute on high to defrost. If using fresh onion and green bell pepper, microwave on high for two to three minutes. Add the beef to the bowl, and mix well. Mix in the sage and bread crumbs. In a small bowl, combine the Dijon mustard and maple syrup. To the meat, add four tablespoons of the maple-syrup mixture (reserving the rest) plus the eggs and salt and pepper. Mix well. Spoon into the prepared bread pan. Smooth out to evenly fill the pan. Close the lid, and cook on the bake setting for one hour and 15 minutes.

Ten minutes before the time is up, open the lid and spoon the remaining maple-syrup mixture over the meat loaf. Close the lid. Continue to cook the last 10 minutes. A meat thermometer should read 160°F. Remove the pan from the machine, and pour off any liquid. Let the meat loaf sit in the pan five to 10 minutes. Using a spatula, remove the meat loaf from the bread pan. Makes four servings.

Waffle Iron

Use your waffle iron for more than just breakfast! You can make any grilled sandwich, for example. *Also…*

Waffle Iron Chicken Quesadillas

- ¼ cup shredded Monterey jack or Mexican-style cheese
- 1 cup shredded cooked chicken or turkey
- 2 10-inch flour tortillas

Vegetable oil spray

Salt and ground black pepper

Place the cheese, chicken or turkey and salt and pepper to taste on one flour tortilla. Cover with a second tortilla. Heat the waffle iron on high, and spray with vegetable oil spray. Add the quesadilla, and close the lid. Cook three minutes or until the cheese melts. Remove and cut in half and then in half again to make four segments.

Waffle Iron Caramelized Apple Slices

- 1 apple
- 1 Tablespoon brown sugar

Vegetable oil spray

Cut the apple in half and then in quarters. Remove the core, and cut each quarter into three slices. Place the brown sugar in a bowl, and add the apple slices. Toss to make sure all sides are coated with the sugar. Heat the waffle iron on high, and spray with vegetable oil spray. Add the apple slices in a single layer, close the lid and cook three to four minutes. Makes one serving.

Ice Cream Maker Slushies

Slushies are very quick and easy using an ice cream maker with a core that stores in the freezer. Put in 12 ounces of fruit juice or any flavor soda, and if it's a manual machine, turn the machine's paddle until a thick slush forms. Scoop into two glasses, and serve immediately. Makes two six-ounce slushies.

Frozen Cocktails

You can make frozen margaritas and daiquiris in your ice cream machine. Add all of the ingredients for the drink except the alcohol to the ice cream maker. Turn the paddle until the liquid is frozen. Add the alcohol, and process for a minute. Spoon into cocktail glasses.

Fondue Pot

You can serve hot dips or hors d'oeuvres in your fondue pot at your next party. It's an attractive way to keep food warm.

Cheese Crab Dip

Canned tuna or salmon can be used instead of crab.
Serve the dip with crackers, small pieces of French
bread or celery and carrot sticks.

- ½ cup mayonnaise
- ½ cup shredded sharp Cheddar cheese
- 6 ounces lump crabmeat
- ½ cup fresh or frozen chopped onion
- Salt and ground black pepper

Mix together all the ingredients except the salt
and pepper in a fondue pot. Place the pot on a stove
top, and cook over medium heat, stirring constantly
until the cheese melts. Taste for seasoning, and add
salt and pepper to taste. Place the pot on the fondue
stand with a small serving spoon on the side so that
your guests can spoon the dip onto either bread or
crackers. Makes four to six servings. If you are using an electric fondue pot, heat the ingredients on
the stand on medium-high heat. Once the cheese
melts, reduce the heat to low.

Good-for-You Comfort Food

Laura Cipullo, RD, CDE, a registered dietitian and certified
diabetes educator in private practice in New York City. Cipullo
is author of *The Diabetes Comfort Food Diet* and is president of
the New York chapter of the International Association of Eating
Disorders Professionals. LauraCipullo.com

With a few smart tweaks and swaps, you can
enjoy even the most decadent-sounding
comfort foods without sabotaging your
health.

Creamy Mashed Potatoes

Instead of mashed potatoes loaded with saturated
fat from butter, enjoy these mashed potatoes made
with yogurt and a surprise ingredient…

What to do: In a large pot, combine 1 pound of
peeled (I like to leave the peels on for extra fiber
and nutrients) and halved russet (baking) potatoes
and 1 small head of cauliflower, cut into florets.
Cover with water, bring to a boil, then reduce heat
to medium and simmer for 20 minutes, or until the
potatoes and cauliflower are easily pierced with a

fork. Drain and place in a large bowl with ⅓ cup of
vegetable broth and 2 tablespoons of olive oil. Using an electric mixer on medium speed, beat until
creamy. Add ½ cup of plain nonfat Greek yogurt
and beat until just blended. Try adding garlic or
rosemary if you desire. Makes six servings.

Traditional recipe: 250 calories per serving, 5 g
saturated fat, 2 g fiber, 39 g carbs.

New recipe above: 132 calories, 1 g saturated
fat, 3 g fiber, 19 g carbs.

Why it's good for you: The addition of cauliflower is a sneaky-but-healthy nutrition hack—cauliflower delivers more fiber than potatoes, while
cutting the carb content of this dish in half! Plus, a
2014 study in *BMJ* offered further proof that diets
high in produce are associated with lower risk for
death, particularly cardiovascular mortality. Olive
oil is a great source of monounsaturated fatty acids (MUFAs), and the yogurt adds creaminess and
even a little protein while curbing carbs.

Broccoli Penne

Instead of white, blood sugar–spiking pasta with
high-fat alfredo sauce, have this healthful broccoli
pasta dish with mozzarella…

What to do: Cook 6 ounces of multigrain penne
pasta in boiling water. Add 2 cups of fresh broccoli florets to the pot during the last two minutes
of cooking. Drain the pasta and broccoli, reserving
½ cup of the water. In a large bowl, place the pasta,
broccoli, 1 cup of halved grape tomatoes, 6 ounces of fresh, part-skim mozzarella cheese cubed,
¼ cup of pesto sauce and 1 tablespoon of lemon
juice. Add the reserved pasta water to the bowl,
one tablespoon at a time, stirring gently until the
ingredients are combined. Makes four servings.

Tip: Cook the pasta al dente (just until firm).
Longer cooking times break down starches, which
causes more carbohydrates to be absorbed into your
blood, resulting in a faster rise in blood sugar.

Traditional recipe: 800 calories per serving, 30
g saturated fat, 4 g fiber, 69 g carbs.

New recipe above: 341 calories, 5 g saturated fat, 5 g fiber, 34 g carbs.

Why it's good for you: A 2015 study confirmed what we already knew—diets rich in whole grains protect against diabetes, while diets rich in refined carbohydrates like conventional white pasta increase risk. High-fiber broccoli and tomatoes fill you up, which enables you to halve the amount of pasta in this recipe. Flavorful olive oil–based pesto means you can pass on the alfredo sauce—full of artery-clogging saturated fat—and get a dose of MUFAs instead. (*Surprising*: Multigrain pasta contains MUFAs, too.) Ideally, make your own pesto using fresh basil, Parmesan cheese, olive oil, crushed garlic and pine nuts. If you're using store-bought pesto, choose a local brand, which is more likely to have high-quality ingredients and fewer preservatives than a big-box brand. Grilled chicken or trout goes well with this pasta dish.

Way Beyond Apple Pie

Linda Gassenheimer, an award-winning author of several cookbooks, including *The 12-Week Diabetes Cookbook* and *Delicious One-Pot Dishes* and the *Food, News and Views* podcast on 880thebiz.com. She also writes the syndicated column "Dinner in Minutes." DinnerInMinutes.com

Here are some new ways to enjoy apples beyond eating them or using them in salads or baked in a pie. The apples in the recipes below are commonly available in the autumn and winter in most markets. But before we get to the delicious recipes, here's a quick guide to how best to use some popular apples…

Apples that hold their shape when cooked: Fuji add an intriguing zing to quiche…Granny Smith are very tart with a high acid content that makes them good for baking.

Apples for snacking and salads: Cortland is good for salads or instead of crackers with dips…Gala can be used in salads, fruit salsas, relishes and chutneys…McIntosh's tender white flesh cooks down quickly.

Apples for snacking but not for salads: Red Delicious are best eaten fresh—they don't hold their shape when cooked, and the flesh turns brown quickly.

Each recipe makes two servings, but it is easy to multiply if you want to serve more…

Curried Soup with Crunchy Apples

Curry powder, ginger and coconut milk flavor this warm and inviting soup. The Cortland apples used are crisp, blending with sautéed onion, lentils, almonds and cilantro and adding a pleasant contrast in texture and flavor.

2 teaspoons canola oil
1 cup sliced onion
½ cup sliced carrot
½ cup sliced celery
2 teaspoons curry powder
1 Tablespoon flour
1 teaspoon ground ginger
2½ cups low-sodium chicken broth
¾ cup light coconut milk
½ cup dried lentils
  Salt and freshly ground black pepper
1 Cortland apple, cored, unpeeled, cut into small cubes (about one cup)
¼ cup slivered almonds, toasted
2 Tablespoons chopped fresh cilantro
2 lemon wedges

Heat the canola oil in a large saucepan over medium-high heat. Add the onion, carrot and celery. Sauté for five minutes, stirring occasionally. Add the curry powder, flour and ginger, and sauté for about 30 seconds. Stir in the chicken broth and coconut milk. Bring to a boil, and add the lentils. Reduce the heat to a simmer and cover. Cook for 20 minutes. Add salt and pepper to taste. To serve, divide the apple cubes and almonds between two bowls, and ladle the soup over them. Sprinkle with cilantro, and place lemon wedges on the side.

Fall Harvest Sausage Stew

This tasty autumn stew that also works well any time of the year. There are several types of turkey sausage available at most supermarkets. I prefer the mild ones for this dinner, but if you like your stews with a kick, buy the ones marked hot.

- 2 teaspoons canola oil
- 2 low-fat turkey sausages, cut into two-inch pieces
- ½ pound sweet potato, peeled and cubed (about 1⅓ cups)
- 1 medium onion, sliced
- 1 green bell pepper, sliced
- 1 Golden Delicious apple, unpeeled, seeded and sliced
- 2 cups (approximately one 14.5-ounce can) canned low-sodium, no-sugar-added diced tomatoes, undrained
- 1 bottle (12 ounces) beer (any type)
- 2 teaspoons fennel seeds
  Salt and freshly ground black pepper
- ¼ cup broken walnuts

Heat the canola oil in a large saucepan over medium-high heat. Add the sausages, sweet potato, onion and green pepper, and sauté for five minutes, stirring occasionally. Add the apple, tomatoes, beer and fennel seeds. Bring to a simmer, lower the heat, cover with a lid, and simmer gently for 15 minutes. Add salt and pepper to taste. Divide the stew between two large soup bowls, and sprinkle with walnuts.

Apple Fluff

This light, fresh dessert is like biting into an apple-cinnamon cloud. It calls for McIntosh apples, which are sweet and tangy with tender white flesh and cook down easily to make a purée.

- 1 large McIntosh apple, peeled and cored, cut into one-inch pieces (about 2 cups)
- 1 cup water
- 2 Tablespoons honey
- 4 teaspoons sugar
- 2 teaspoons vanilla extract
- 1 teaspoon ground cinnamon
- 4 egg whites, separated from whole pasteurized eggs
- 2 Tablespoons unsalted walnut pieces

Add the apple pieces to a saucepan with the water, honey and sugar. Stir to combine ingredients. Place over medium heat, bring to a simmer, lower the heat and cover. The apples should be soft after about five minutes. Simmer for one or two minutes longer if needed. Strain and purée the apples in a food processor or sieve. Mix in the vanilla extract and cinnamon, and set aside to cool. Beat the egg whites to stiff peaks, and gently fold in the apple purée. Spoon into two small bowls. Sprinkle walnuts on top. Serve immediately.

Guilt-Free Chocolates

Ellie Krieger, RD, host of *Healthy Appetite*, which ran on the *Food Network*. She is a winner of the James Beard Foundation Award for "Best Cookbook with a Healthy Focus." Her most recent cookbook is *Weeknight Wonders: Delicious Healthy Dinners in 30 Minutes or Less*. EllieKrieger.com

D o-it-yourself candy-making is surprisingly easy. You can whip up decadent-tasting treats that actually are good for you by using just three key ingredients…

•**Top-quality dark chocolate.** Chocolate is derived from the cacao bean, which is high in heart-healthy flavonoids (antioxidant-containing plant pigments), as well as iron, magnesium, phosphorus, potassium, zinc, copper and manganese. The higher the cocoa percentage in the chocolate, the more antioxidants it has—but also the more bitter the taste. To reap the health benefits with optimal taste, choose dark chocolate containing 60% to 70% cacao. I generally use Scharffen Berger…Ghirardelli…or Green and Black's. You can get it in bar form or as chips—60%-to-70% dark is comparable to "bittersweet" chocolate.

•**Dried fruits.** Yes, dried fruits are high in sugar—but it is naturally occurring sugar, not the refined type. And the drying process concentrates the minerals and the antioxidants. Look for dried fruits with no sugar added.

•**Nuts.** Nuts provide healthful monounsaturated fats and omega-3 fatty acids that help reduce LDL cholesterol and triglycerides and also modulate the blood sugar spike that you otherwise would get from the candy. What's more, nuts fight inflammation, thanks to the antioxidant vitamin E and the soluble fiber that increases production of anti-inflammatory proteins.

Easiest Chocolate Candy Recipes

For these simple treats, start by melting chocolate. Place chopped chocolate in a microwave-safe bowl, and heat on high for 30 seconds, then stir. Repeat the 30-second heating-then-stir process until the chocolate is mostly melted but you still can see a lump or two—at that point, some stirring and the residual heat will finish the melting job for you.

For a flavor boost, sprinkle flaky salt, such as fleur de sel, over any of the following while the chocolate is still liquid.

Chocolate-dipped fruit: Dip dried apricots, figs and other fruits in melted dark chocolate, covering one-quarter to one-half of each piece of fruit. Place on waxed paper to cool.

Super-nutty bark: Melt dark chocolate, spread it about one-quarter-inch thick with a spatula on a parchment-lined baking sheet, and top with three or more different types of chopped nuts. Let set, then break into bite-size pieces.

Chunky chocolate squares: Melt dark chocolate. Stir in a combination of chopped nuts and chopped dried fruits—for instance, pistachios plus apricots…peanuts plus raisins…walnuts plus blueberries…hazelnuts plus figs. Pour the mixture into a square baking dish lined with waxed paper. Refrigerate until firm, then cut into squares.

Creative, Delicious Way to Eat Tea Leaves

Robert Wemischner, a pastry chef and culinary educator based in Los Angeles. He is coauthor of *Cooking with Tea* and author of *The Dessert Architect.*

Chances are you've heard quite a bit about the health benefits of drinking tea—the polyphenols, the flavonoids, the antioxidants, the tannins…and so on.

Well, you may not realize that you can get health benefits from eating tea, too—or more precisely, by using tea leaves in your cooking. In fact, there are simple and tasty ways to incorporate tea leaves into meals.

Tea Time!

Your first question might be, "Do you mean that I should actually eat tea leaves?" Yes! Though that might seem out of the ordinary, it's perfectly safe and also quite healthy.

No matter which kind of tea leaves you use, you'll get the zest and the nutrients—without any added calories, sodium, sugar or fat. You can choose the leaf based on the type of dish and taste you're going for—and experiment until you find just the right combination. Ready to get started?

Tea-licious Recipe Ideas

Buy dried tea leaves (fresh are rare) online (I recommend UptonTea.com) or at a health-food store, Asian market or large grocery store. If you shop for tea leaves in person, whenever possible, check their aroma. If it's weak, the flavor will be weak, too—so buy only tea leaves that smell robust. If you have tea bags, you also can just cut the bags open and use those tea leaves.

Here are a few easy, yummy ways to use tea in your cooking…

1. Use tea leaves in a rub. Grind one tablespoon of tea leaves in an electric coffee grinder or spice mill until they become a fine powder. (Make sure it's not a grinder that has been used to grind coffee.) Add the powder to one tablespoon of another type of flavoring, and then rub it onto one serving of raw fish, poultry or meat with your hands. Let stand for 10 minutes before cooking. For example, try lapsang souchong tea with freshly grated orange peel on turkey or salmon…green tea with roasted sesame seeds on shrimp or scallops…black tea with brown sugar on beef brisket…or Earl Grey tea with salt and pepper on duck.

2. Use tea leaves in a marinade. Add one tablespoon of tea leaves, ground as above, to eight ounces of a marinade. Marinate one serving of fish, poultry or meat in the mixture for 30 minutes before grilling or sautéing. Try oolong tea with either a soy-based marinade or an herbal-lemon-pepper marinade on shrimp or scallops…or Earl Grey tea with an orange juice-based marinade on chicken…or green tea with chive-honey-ginger-garlic blend on pork.

Avoid Mistakes When Storing Wines

Jeff Siegel, the Wine Curmudgeon, is a wine writer, wine critic and wine judge who specializes in inexpensive wine—the wine, he says, that most of us drink. He is author of *The Wine Curmudgeon's Guide to Cheap Wine*. WineCurmudgeon. com

There are two big myths about wine—that any good wine will benefit from aging...and that it costs a bundle to store it so that it ages properly. Neither is true. Most wine today—about 90%—won't benefit from aging. It is best when drunk within a year or two of bottling.

But even if you're just storing wine for a few weeks or months, you can ruin it. *To avoid that...*

•**Don't store it in the kitchen.** Countertop wine racks are convenient, but heat ruins wine—and the room you cook in usually is the warmest in the house. Wine can bake...and taste stewed.

Telltale sign: A little wine has seeped out of a corked bottle. That's heat pushing the cork up.

•**Keep it still.** Skip that wine rack on top of your refrigerator, too—when the motor kicks on, the bottle vibrates, and over time that movement can spoil the wine.

•**Keep it away from windows.** Sunlight is wine's enemy because it brings heat. You've probably seen expensive wine-storage furniture in someone's living or dining room next to a sunny window—not good!

Storing Wine Well

Wine refrigerators have a place, but if you're storing wines for up to a year or two, you can do it quite well for free.

How? In a closet! Most closets work fine as long as they don't get hotter than the mid-70s (so no bathroom closets or those near heat pipes). Ask your wine store for a shipping box, stack it on its side and slide wines into the slots. Plastic or wooden crates work well, too. A wine rack is fine, of course, either in a closet or in another dark, relatively cool spot.

Wines Worth Aging

Certain wines do get better with age, especially expensive reds (those that cost more than $30) and some chardonnays. The fruit becomes less intense and the wine deeper and richer. Unless it's a "great wine," though, don't store it more than seven or eight years—after that, the wine will start to fade.

For keeping wines more than two years, a wine fridge is worth it, and you can get one that holds 24 bottles for about $200 to $300.

CHAPTER 8

Garden and Plants

8 Big Gardening Mistakes to Avoid in the Spring

Teri Dunn Chace, author of *The Anxious Gardener's Book of Answers* and more than 35 other gardening titles. She has gardened in a variety of climate zones and soil types and was the winner of the prestigious American Horticultural Society Book Award in 2016 for her book *Seeing Seeds*. TeriChaceWriter.com

Late winter is hard on a gardener. Your green thumb is twitching, but the days still are short and the garden is far from ready for planting.

My advice: Get started! "Stage-setting" late winter/early spring tasks will make all the difference when it comes time to plant (and beyond). *But it's important not to act too soon or improperly—you could damage your plants, the soil or your yard's good appearance…*

First Task: Spruce Up Your Tools

Why it matters: Dirty blades, loose bolts and dull edges make garden tools less useful and make chores more difficult—even dangerous.

Mistake: **If tools are dirty, don't force off or chip off caked-on crud.** That can gouge a tool surface—and might strain your hand, wrist or arm in the process.

What to do instead: Wipe down each tool with a damp rag. Still dirty? Immerse it in a bucket of lukewarm water for an hour or more. This may reveal still-persistent crud or rust spots—sand these off or scrub with steel wool. Then wipe blades with a soft, oil-soaked rag. Some people swear by linseed oil, but vegetable oil from the kitchen will do just fine, honestly. Burnish wooden handles with the oily cloth, too. Check bolts on loppers and clippers, and tighten loose ones with a wrench.

Make sure all edges are sharp. A dull pruner, for example, will mash stems rather than slicing them. Not pretty or healthy. Clamp a dull tool in a vise so it won't wiggle while you work. Then use a 10-inch single-cut file—the kind with a single set of parallel diagonal lines—to patiently, neatly restore the original factory bevel. Or ask at your local garden or hardware store about professional sharpening—usually about $10 a tool.

Repair Winter-Damaged Shrubs and Trees

Why it matters: Snow and ice can snap off branches, and extreme cold can kill branches, too. To improve your garden's looks and health, prune branches with damaged or dead parts in early spring (once daytime temps are above freezing).

Tip: Cutting on a warmer, sunny day is more pleasant for you and better for the tree.

Mistake #1: **Cutting only at the point of damage.** That can leave the plant looking awkward. Also, stubs left behind eventually rot and may spread rot to the rest of the tree.

What to do instead: Clip or saw off a branch or stem all the way back to the trunk or a main stem. Make it flush.

Exception: If there is a substantial branch collar—that thick area where a branch attaches to the trunk—don't cut into it. It forms a protection zone, helping to keep infection out of the trunk. Also, removing the collar can cause unwanted sprouts to grow in the wound area.

Mistake #2: **Cutting too liberally.** For example, taking out an entire limb when only a branch or two coming off it is damaged. That can set a plant back years in looks and health.

Not sure a branch is dead? Leave it! A dormant limb can look dead but still have life in it. Check back in a few weeks to see if it is showing signs of life.

Tip: Truly dead branches will snap, not bend, and they feel lighter and hollower and may be shedding bark.

Mistake #3: **Cleaning up a shrub or tree too late.** If you wait until such plants leaf out, it's harder to get a good overview, and it's harder to see the shoots that sprout from the roots, which divert energy from the rest of the plant.

What to do instead: Get busy before the leaves emerge to take care of problems that are damaging the plant. Take out shoots at the base of the plant, and thin out branches that are rubbing or crossing one another so densely that healthful air can't easily circulate.

Prune (Some) Flowering Shrubs

Why it matters: Cutting back flowering shrubs improves looks and helps the plants focus energy on blooming.

Mistake: **Doing major aesthetic pruning on stems that could have bloomed, diminishing a shrub's flower show.**

What to do instead: Plants that bloom on "old wood"—last year's growth—should not be pruned for appearance until the year's flowering is over. But do it right after the blooms fade or drop their petals.

Some common plants to prune right after they bloom: Beautybush, daphne, forsythia, honeysuckle, kerria, jasmine, lilac, mock orange, smoke tree, weigela. (*Note:* It's fine to cut back dead/damaged branches any time.)

If, however, a shrub blooms on "new wood"—the current season's growth—it's safe to cut it back in early spring while the plant is still dormant, before the buds show green. The surge of spring energy will lead to fresh new branches ready to bloom.

Some common plants to prune early: Abelia, beautyberry, broom, butterfly bush, caryopteris, crape myrtle, nandina, Pee Gee hydrangea, potentilla, rose-of-Sharon, roses and viburnum.

Prepare Your Flower Beds

Why it matters: Spring, not fall, is decidedly the best time to prep your garden perennials. Research has shown that it's better for hardiness if perennials aren't trimmed back until after winter.

Mistake: **Jumping the gun on removing mulch from your flower beds.** If you laid down compost, straw, chopped leaves or some other organic mulch last fall, don't remove this protective covering too early. Spring's temperature swings can cause harm to treasured plants.

What to do instead: Wait until the daytime temperatures are reliably above freezing. That's true even if the plants below have started to show growth. Better safe than sorry! When you do remove mulch, use your hands, a light rake or a leaf blower rather than a shovel, hoe or heavy-duty rake. Work rather gently so that you don't inadvertently break or uproot plants.

Once you remove the mulch, cut all dead perennial stalks right down to the ground or at least to the crown of the plant (the spot where the plant stems meet the roots). Fresh new growth will soon follow.

Prepare the Soil

Why it matters: Healthy, aerated, well-drained soil is the garden ideal, and fooling with it too early can compromise this.

Mistake #1: **Inadvertently compacting your soil.** If you get to work outside too early in the year, when the ground is still semifrozen or muddy, your footsteps or the wheelbarrow can over compact the soil. (Semifrozen soil goes through freeze-thaw cycles and is easy to compact.) That denies the reawakening plants the oxygen in the soil that they need.

What to do instead: Hold off until the ground dries out a bit more, or try placing a plank where you walk or kneel to distribute your weight more evenly.

Mistake #2: **Leaving open ground.** A cleared garden area (flower bed or vegetable garden patch) may look tidy, but not for long—it's an open invitation to weeds. And exposed ground is vulnerable to compaction or erosion when drenching spring rains pound your soil.

What to do instead: Sprinkle nourishing compost (homemade or store-bought) over the beds to a depth of one to three inches. Take care not to bury the crowns of emerging perennials or spring-flowering bulbs. Do this on a pleasant day when there is no rain or wind in the forecast. Unlike some mulches, compost is rich in organic matter, contributing nutrition and texture to soil. As it breaks down, it generates heat—a hedge against springtime's temperature swings.

Spring Lawn Dos and Don'ts

Did you know that winter's cold toughens grass and strengthens its roots? That's the good news. But the freezing season can leave your lawn looking ragged. *Here's what to do—and what not to do—to get your lawn off to a good start this spring…*

DO: **Thoroughly remove all debris (sticks, twigs, last year's leaves).** Use a rake or even a good outdoor broom, which is gentler.

DON'T: **Be rough, lest you uproot shoots or dislodge chunks of sod.**

DO: **Patch bare spots.** If you use seed, water frequently with a gentle spray until the grass is up and growing strongly. If you use sod, be sure to remove enough soil in the area so that it is level with surrounding grass.

DON'T: **Use sod in shade.** It will struggle. And don't use a weighted roller over any freshly sown lawn areas—sod or not. Once standard practice, it's now discredited because it compacts soil.

DO: **Spread ground limestone to nourish the emerging grass (follow label directions).**

DON'T: **Fertilize yet.** Instead, wait until spring is well under way and you've mowed a few times. At that point, a dose of lawn fertilizer will be beneficial (follow label directions).

Growing the Right Vegetables Saves $$$$

Niki Jabbour, a food gardener and garden writer based outside Halifax, Nova Scotia. She is author of *The Year-Round Vegetable Gardener: How to Grow Your Own Food 365 Days a Year, No Matter Where You Live* and host of *The Weekend Gardener*, a call-in radio show that can be heard online at News957.com Sundays 10 to noon, eastern time.

Having a green thumb can save you some green. Growing your own vegetables will lower your grocery bills—potentially by hundreds of dollars a year—and put fresher, tastier produce on your table.

Choose your veggies carefully if saving money is your goal. Some, such as artichokes and cauliflower, are tricky to grow or susceptible to pests and diseases that can reduce yields and quash savings. Others, such as onions and potatoes, are so inexpensive in stores that growing your own won't save you much money.

Easy-to-grow garden vegetables that offer big savings…

• **Salad greens such as arugula, Swiss chard and spinach can cost $4 to $5 for a bag sufficient for perhaps two salads when bought in a market.** Or for $2 to $2.50, you can buy a packet of seeds that can produce enough greens for daily salads starting 40 to 50 days after the initial planting and continuing until the first frost.

Sample savings: If your garden produces five months' worth of daily salads and you previously had been spending $2 per day on greens for those salads, your savings would be approximately $300.*

To ensure an extended supply of fresh greens, plant a small number of seeds each week throughout the growing season rather than all the seeds at once. When you require only a small quantity of greens, harvest just the outer leaves so that the plant can continue growing.

Arugula, Swiss chard, spinach and most other greens are easy to grow. They need only four to six hours of sun each day. They do best in soil at least

*The sample savings in this article are estimates. Your actual savings will vary significantly depending on the size of your garden, the amount of sunlight your plants receive, the quality of your soil and other factors.

six inches deep with good drainage. Keep the soil moist until the seeds germinate.

• **Heirloom cherry tomatoes can cost $4 to $5 per pint in a farmers' market.** Or you can grow them yourself from a packet of seeds costing $2 to $2.50 (or from starter plants costing perhaps $2 to $3 for four). Under favorable conditions, each plant could yield 20 pints or more of heirloom (nonhybrid) cherry tomatoes.

Sample savings: If you have four plants that produce 20 pints of heirloom cherry tomatoes apiece, that's the equivalent of $320 worth of produce if you had been paying $4 a pint.

Heirloom cherry tomatoes are a better money saver than larger heirloom tomato varieties because they tend to have a longer growing season and larger overall crop. They're easy to grow but require at least six hours a day of sunlight to thrive.

• **Heirloom green beans (also called string beans or snap beans) can cost $6 or $7 per pound in farmers' markets.** Or grow them yourself from a packet of seeds costing $2 to $2.50. Each plant could produce several pounds of beans.

Sample savings: If you grow 20 plants and each produces three pounds of beans, that's around $350 in savings if you would have paid $6 a pound at a farmers' market.

Green beans are very easy to grow but prefer full sunlight. Favor green beans that grow on a vine rather than on a bush—they will yield two to three times as many beans per square foot of garden space. You will need to provide poles or trellises for the vines to climb, which will add a few dollars to your costs if you don't own these things already.

• **Herbs including basil, parsley, chives, thyme and rosemary can cost $2 to $3 for a few sprigs if you buy them fresh.** Or for that same $2 to $3, you could buy a four-pack of starter herb plants at a nursery. Each of those plants could produce 50 times as much as that supermarket package, for savings in the hundreds if you use fresh herbs frequently.

Sample savings: If you grow four herb plants and each provides 50 times as much as that $2

container of fresh herb sprigs in the market, that's nearly $400 in potential savings—though realistically few people buy that many herbs.

Herbs generally require at least four to six hours of sunlight per day. Clip flower buds when they appear—your herbs won't be as flavorful if the plants flower, and flowering stops growth. If your plants produce more herbs than you can use, freeze the excess for winter use.

To freeze: Place a spoonful or two of chopped herbs in each compartment of an ice-cube tray. Top with water to cover the herbs. Freeze.

Revitalize Your Perennials

Teri Dunn Chace is a gardening expert who has written more than 30 books, including *The Anxious Gardener's Book of Answers*. She lives in a small village in upstate New York. TeriChaceWriter.com

Sure, you planted perennials for a carefree, flowering garden, but you may have noticed that they're not as attractive as they once were. *Here's how to divide them in the fall to revitalize them for the spring…*

Why do it: Plant clumps take up more real estate with each passing year. Often the interior dies back, and sometimes a plant stops producing flowers altogether. Simply put, your plants are aging. It's time to discard the inner, depleted portion and rescue the younger, outer parts.

Best candidates: This project is most successful with spring and early-summer bloomers such as peonies, irises, daylilies and coral bells.

Why fall? It's always best to intervene during a "shoulder season" to lessen transplant trauma. Fall is better than spring because not only are the plants heading into their winter sleep (dormancy), but the periodic soaking rains that most areas get at this time of year encourage root growth.

How to divide: Don't divide at midday when it's hot. A cool, drizzly autumn morning or late afternoon is ideal.

With clippers or a scythe, shorten the target plants to within about six inches of the ground so they're easier to work with. Then dig up each large clump, getting as much of the root-ball as you can (this may require digging down eight inches or even more—this is the depth of the majority of the roots). Divide the root systems into three or more smaller plants. You may need to use a sharp-edged implement such as a trowel or shovel to do this or something even bigger. I've used two big garden forks, back to back, to pry apart a big daylily clump—and even then, the roots separated reluctantly. If the roots are dry, hosing them down helps.

Each section you save for replanting should include a strong clump of healthy-looking roots, ones that are white and crisp. Cut off any black, wiry, damaged or rotten roots, and throw them away.

If you aren't able to replant sections immediately, don't let the roots dry out. Plunk the divisions in pots, and cover the roots with water...or wrap the roots in damp towels or burlap for a few hours or overnight.

How to replant: Create ample holes for each plant—how big depends on the size of the divisions, but eight inches or more, deep and wide, is a safe rule of thumb. You've seen how big the plants eventually get, so space them well apart so that they can fill in over time.

Also, take this opportunity to improve the soil. Dig in organic material such as equal parts of loam, dehydrated cow manure and compost. Water generously, and repeat every other day unless fall rains do the job for you.

Best Ways to Attract Birds to Your Yard

Stephen Kress, retired vice president of bird conservation, National Audubon Society, Ithaca, New York. He is author of *The Audubon Society Guide to Attracting Birds.*

It isn't hard to attract birds to your yard in the winter—just fill a bird feeder with seed. Unfortunately, some bird feeders can be dangerous to our feathered friends...

Common Dangers

•**Windows.** Most bird feeders are placed near a window to facilitate bird-watching, but this makes it likely that some birds will fly into the windows when they leave the bird feeder. To reduce this risk, move the feeder even closer to your window. When a feeder is three feet or less from the glass, departing birds can't build up enough momentum to seriously harm themselves.

•**Cats.** Position your feeder six feet or more from the nearest shrub or other ground cover so that cats can't hide and pounce on birds.

•**Squirrels.** If squirrels are an issue in your yard, place your feeder on a pole at least five feet high and isolated from trees and buildings so that squirrels can't leap onto the feeder. A metal cone-shaped baffle at least 20 inches in diameter (available at garden shops) installed under the feeder should prevent squirrels from climbing up. Or purchase a "squirrel-proof" feeder. However, squirrels are very clever, so you might have to experiment.

•**Diseases.** Salmonella can be transferred among birds when droppings mix with feed in the feeder, and other bird health problems can result from birdseed that has begun to mold. Clean your feeder at least twice a year—in early fall and early spring. Hose the feeder down before bringing it inside, then scrub with a stiff bottle brush using a mixture of hot water and 10% nonchlorine bleach. Rinse well.

Helpful: Birds are not likely to become dependent on bird feeders, so don't worry that local birds will suffer if you stop providing feed.

Feed and Feeders

The best way to attract interesting birds to your yard is to have more than one bird feeder. Tube-shaped seed feeders are popular with the widest variety of birds, but flat-platform feeders appeal to ground-feeding birds, such as sparrows.

Mixed birdseed often contains low-quality fillers that birds might discard onto the ground, where they could mold or attract rodents. Black oil seed, a type of sunflower seed, is the single most popular choice among most birds. Small-beaked birds, including sparrows, juncos and doves, prefer white millet. Offer these two feeds, and you'll keep most feeder birds happy.

Grow Beautiful Roses

Teri Dunn Chace, a gardening expert who has written more than 30 books. Her latest book is *Seeing Flowers: Discover the Hidden Life of Flowers*. She lives in a small village in upstate New York. TeriChaceWriter.com

Roses are the divas of the gardening world—or so it seems. But growing these beauties actually is a lot less work than most people think. *You just need to avoid these common mistakes…*

MISTAKE: Devoting entire beds to roses alone. Break away from the old garden style of devoting entire beds to roses. Rose foliage is vulnerable to bugs, mildew and black or rust spots on the leaves. Tucking rosebushes into your overall garden plan tends to thwart such problems, especially when the companion plants aren't prone. Some practical and pretty companions include lavender, Russian sage, foxglove, irises, lamb's ears and clematis vines.

Take care, though, not to crowd your plants—good air circulation goes a long way toward preventing common rose problems. Maintain six or more inches around the projected full-grown size (noted on the tag or vendor description).

MISTAKE: Not giving them a smart start. A spot in full-day sun is key. Other flowers might forgive half-day shade but not most roses. Dig an ample hole (a few feet wide and at least one foot deep) and fill it with rich garden loam, compost, rotted cow manure or a combination of these.

Before you put a bare-root plant in the ground, soak the roots in a bucket of lukewarm water overnight to rehydrate them. (If you bought a potted rose, just give it a thorough watering beforehand.) Clip off damaged roots and foliage. Finally, remove any flowers and most of the buds. Why? Flowers take a lot of energy. Let a new plant concentrate on establishing its roots for a few weeks first.

After planting, make a shallow basin around the base so that water won't run off. Mulch to keep weeds at bay and hold in soil moisture.

MISTAKE: Using a sprinkler to water. Sprinklers are inefficient, and wet foliage can lead to plant diseases. Use a hose to water slowly and steadily with a nozzle, or use "soaker hoses" threaded around your plants. This encourages roots to grow deeper. In the first season, it's wise to water every four or five days, more often if conditions are dry. In ensuing years, a rosebush may need to be soaked only once a week unless the weather is hot and dry.

MISTAKE: Overfeeding. I consider feeding my roses optional. Roses respond to plant food with extra growth and flowers, but healthy roses in a mixed garden don't need extra growth to look beautiful. If you choose to fertilize, follow rose fertilizer directions about amounts and frequency—more is not better. Also, don't just sprinkle granules around the plants and walk away—water in plant food well so that it reaches the roots.

MISTAKE: Not battling problems early and often. Should you spot insects, marred leaves or damaged buds, intervene immediately. Take a

Lower-Cost Home Gardening

Use empty soup cans with tops and bottoms removed to protect seedlings—bury the cans partway in planting holes so that the above ground portion protects plants. Place glass jars upside down over starter plants that need protection—they act as natural greenhouses. Kitty litter buckets can be used to cover plants in case a storm is expected to bring hail. Keep coffee grounds for garden compost—collect them from work if you do not have enough at home. Make fertilizer "tea" using old panty hose by filling the legs with garden compost and dunking them up and down in a bucket of water. This budget drink is great for plants.

Examiner.com

sample of the afflicted parts to your nursery for the right remedies. Or you can make your own. For example, I use a baking soda/water mixture (two tablespoons to one gallon of water) sprayed for powdery mildew. (Instructions for homemade rose remedies can be found on YouTube and at WenkeGardenCenter.com/home-remedies-plant-disease.)

MISTAKE: **Not buying the right kind of roses.** Some roses do poorly in hot, humid summers. Others struggle through cold and snowy winters. Check what's prospering in local gardens, or get advice from the nearest rose club. Consider shopping at a nursery that specializes in roses (check the websites of Roses Unlimited, Heirloom Roses and High Country Roses, to name a few).

How to Grow Delicious Tomatoes...Problem-Free

Teri Dunn Chace, a gardening expert who has written more than 30 books, including *The Anxious Gardener's Book of Answers*. She lives in a small village in upstate New York. TeriChaceWriter.com

Homegrown tomatoes are typically better than store-bought. But sometimes things go awry just when you're looking forward to that wonderful flavor. *How to diagnose and address four common tomato woes...*

●**Splitting fruit.** The cause? Inconsistent watering. Soak your plant roots thoroughly every few days (more often in hot, dry spells). Either run the hose at a trickle for a while or use soaker hoses. Apply an inch or two of mulch (straw is ideal) around your plants.

Small cherry tomatoes often split despite your best efforts. This is a case of the flesh outgrowing the thin skin. If it bothers you, pick them early.

●**Yellow or whitish blotches.** This is most likely due to sunscald. Insufficient coverage from the leaves often is to blame. Not only does it mar the look of the fruit, it spoils the flavor.

Tomato leaves dry and drop off when weather is hot and you've neglected watering. To prevent this, follow the watering recommendations above.

Pests and disease also cause leaf loss, which can lead to sunscald. Tomato hornworms—green caterpillars with a hornlike tail—can strip a plant. Keep a lookout, and the moment they appear, handpick them, then drop the worms into a bucket of soapy water. Soil nematodes (root-infesting worms), tiny flea beetles and various fungal diseases can damage leaves. In the future, look for resistant plants labeled VFNT (for verticillium wilt, fusarium wilt, nematodes, tobacco mosaic virus).

When tomato leaves become dried or tattered, remove them. They aren't going to recover. Dispose of them in the trash, not the compost pile, which won't get hot enough to kill pathogens or pests. You can then try to rescue tomatoes on already partially defoliated plants by providing shade, such as a strategically placed board, tarp or lawn chair.

●**Puckering at the blossom end.** This is called catfacing, and the tomato may go on to develop crevices, holes and scars. This malady usually is caused by cold weather. High nitrogen levels in the soil also can cause it.

Avoid it by waiting to plant your seedlings until danger of frost is past. If an unseasonable cold spell is predicted, protect plants with cloches (bell-shaped clear glass or plastic covers) or row covers—available wherever gardening supplies are sold.

If you suspect high nitrogen, don't grow tomatoes near grass if you use high-nitrogen lawn fertilizer, or you can withhold plant food in the vegetable garden until fruit starts to form.

●**Disappointingly small crop.** The most and best tomatoes are produced when daytime temperatures are in the 80s and drop to the 50s or 60s at night. If your summer is hotter or cooler, quality can suffer and the plants may produce less. Dry soil, too, discourages fruit set. See watering instructions above. Insufficient sunshine is a problem as well—tomato plants produce plentiful crops when they receive eight hours of sun a day.

How to Choose the Best Garden Hose

Monica Hemingway, PhD, former owner of Hemingway Horticulture, a garden design service in Stamford, Connecticut. She is a Licensed Arborist, Accredited Organic Land Care Professional and graduate of the School of Professional Horticulture at the New York Botanical Garden. She edits the website GardeningProductsReview.com.

One garden hose might look as good as the next on the store shelf, but unseen differences can have a substantial impact on how long the hose lasts and how frustrating it is to use. *To buy the right hose…*

•**Measure the maximum hose length you'll need.** Hoses are sold in 25-, 50-, 75- and 100-foot lengths. Don't buy a longer one than necessary. Not only will it cost more, it will be heavier to haul around and more difficult to drain before storing, and it will provide lower water pressure.

Helpful: A hose width of five-eighths inch (based on the inside diameter) usually is best. A half-inch hose is acceptable only when the hose is no longer than 50 feet and the rate of water flow is not a major concern, such as when you water delicate plants at close range.

•**Rely on rubber.** A hose made of either rubber or a combination of rubber and vinyl generally will be more durable and less prone to kinks and splits than a vinyl-only hose. Although additional layers (or "plies") tend to suggest a stronger hose, don't put too much stock in this figure—the number of layers doesn't matter as much as what those layers are made from. A strengthening "mesh" layer is a good sign, other things being equal.

If you will be using a nozzle or a pulsating sprinkler, consider a hose that lists a "burst pressure" above 350 psi to keep it from rupturing.

•**Bend the hose into a U.** If it kinks, pick another. Kinking can lead to splitting.

Warning: Avoid expandable hoses—the scrunchielike hoses that expand when filled with water. They soon stop contracting properly after use and usually have crack-prone plastic couplings.

•**Check for cast-brass couplings.** Hose couplings are the end pieces that attach to spigots,

sprinklers and nozzles. Those made from cast brass are the most durable and leak-resistant. You can identify cast brass because it's thicker than sheet metal and usually has an octagonal shape so that the coupling can be turned with a wrench. Thin stamped-metal couplings and plastic couplings are more prone to leaks and breaks.

•**Look for a collar.** Quality hoses often have a plastic or rubber "collar" extending perhaps four to six inches up the hose from one coupling. This reduces the odds of a kink or split near the spigot, where they are particularly common.

Consider the following high-quality hoses, available online and in stores…

Craftsman Premium Rubber Garden Hose. Available in 50-foot length for about $80.

Dramm ColorStorm Premium Rubber Garden Hose. Available in 50-foot length, typically for $66 to $75. ColorStorm hoses come in bright colors, reducing the odds of tripping over—or mowing—the hose.

Gilmour Flexogen Super Duty Hose. Prices range from $24 for the 25-footer to $73 for the 100-footer.

Teknor Apex 8650 Industrial Duty All-Rubber Hose. Available in 50-foot length for $37 to $57.

Best Ways to Store Your Garden Hose

Monica Hemingway, PhD, licensed arborist, Stamford, Connecticut, and editor of GardeningProductsReview.com.

Best ways to store a garden hose for the winter: Drain the hose completely by disconnecting it from the spigot and stretching it down any gentle incline. Otherwise, water left inside the hose will expand as it freezes, stretching and weakening the inner tube. Connect the ends of the hose together to keep out ants, spiders and other pests. Use a wall rack that supports the coiled hose at two or more points. Throwing the hose over a hook, or worse a nail, concentrates all the weight on one spot and compresses the hose lining.

Better: Drape it over two L-shaped brackets, or create a simple hose hanger by nailing a coffee can to the wall.

How to Keep Your Garden Colorful All Summer Long

Teri Dunn Chace is author of more than 35 gardening titles, including *Seeing Flowers: Discover the Hidden Life of Flowers.* She lives in upstate New York. TeriChaceWriter.com

It happens every year. Spring arrives in a rainbow burst of tulips, daffodils and other fall-planted bulbs, but it fades away after a few short weeks. Meanwhile, trees and shrubs burst into colorful but brief bloom, then leaf out, and all that remains is green. It's an awkward color gap.

You can have lots of color during this time, though. Here are some tricks to get your garden and yard through the color gap in style. The punch these plants provide improves the look of your yard for the in-between weeks of early to midsummer and often beyond...

•**Install plants with colorful leaves.** Flowers don't have to be the only burst of color in your garden or yard. Splashy and patterned leaves of red, maroon, pink, white and cream can enliven any space. Coleus and caladium are good, affordable choices and widely available. (If you want these plants to liven up your garden in future years, bring them inside when summer is over. They don't like the cold and will otherwise die off.) Mix a few of these into your flower beds, and they'll distract as your spring flowers start to drop off and their leaves turn yellow, and still be around to highlight your midsummer blooms when those finally appear. You also can use perennials such as hosta, ivy and brunnera, which all come in variegated selections that help them stand out if your garden is going through a mostly green phase.

•**Choose double-duty flowers.** Look for ones that add a bit of interest even when they're not flowering. Try irises with yellow-striped foliage, gaura with white-edged leaves or an array of pretty purple, rose or even chartreuse heucheras. These selections look terrific even when not flowering. Any red-colored flower, such as impatiens, salvia or geranium, that you add will look amazing when paired with these leaves.

•**Don't play it too safe.** A blend of various complementary hues—created when you, say, plunk an entire flat of assorted marigolds or pansies into a bed—can get visually boring. With temporarily less competition for attention from other flowers, this is the time for annuals to shine. Aim for contrast. Pair strongly contrasting colors—yellow marigolds with purple scaevola, red impatiens with white impatiens, blue salvia with orange zinnia.

•**Avoid planting "singletons."** A single, bold flowering plant doesn't give the eye a good chance to enjoy the rest of the garden because your gaze almost can't help but be drawn to it. And a color tends to make more of an impression if there's more of it. So plant the same or similarly colored flowers in groups of at least three.

In the "gap time," annuals are great for this purpose. A ribbon of white impatiens threaded through a perennial garden, for instance, or a section of purple-flowered salvia can be really dramatic without being overpowering.

•**Get maximum impact from potted plants.** Potted plants can be a beautiful and useful addition to your garden. Since they easily can be moved from spot to spot, just plop them down in whatever area needs a color boost. When choosing pots, don't settle for ordinary clay pots or plain window boxes. Use vibrant solid-color containers or patterned and painted ones. If you find a pot that you really like but it lacks necessary drainage holes, just "nest" a practical pot inside this decorative one.

Move those containers around! You can tuck a pot of, say, cheery geraniums into a flower bed that needs some color, then simply move it to another spot as the garden's other flowers come and go. A "scene-stealer" is another good trick. Site a large pot, urn or other container in a prominent spot. Make it impressive, filling it to overflowing with your favorite colorful flowers and foliage plants. Nobody will notice that its surroundings aren't as exciting.

•**Don't forget garden décor.** It's not cheating to add nonplant items to take up the slack—it's practical and fun! The early-summer lull is actually an opportunity to take a good look at your yard and go shopping. Add a colorful gazing ball, a garden statue, pretty tiles or stepping stones, a bird house, a birdbath, a pretty flag, a bench or other garden furniture. Such items create a welcome distraction when your garden is not at peak color.

•**Look at the bigger picture.** The gap time also is a chance to look at what colors your home adds to the overall garden scene. What color is the trim, the front door, the garage door, the porch? Work with these colors, matching or contrasting them with flowers and containers. If you don't work with your house's color (and style, for that matter), your landscaping may end up looking out of place or like a hodgepodge.

Gardening Is Good for Your Health!

Marianne Thorsen Gonzalez, PhD, professor, Norwegian University of Science and Technology, Trondheim, Norway.

Learn to love your garden and yard work. Why? Outdoor chores are good for your mental and physical health. In a recent study, clinically depressed adults who spent six hours a week gardening reported a significant decline in depression and improved attention span after 12 weeks. Outdoor exercise, which is believed to reduce stress hormones, also improves sleep quality and burns calories.

Make Cut Garden Flowers Last

Teri Dunn Chace, a garden writer based in upstate New York, is author of *Seeing Flowers: Discover the Hidden Life of Flowers* and other gardening books. TeriChaceWriter.com

A bouquet of homegrown flowers is one of the great joys of gardening—whether you proudly display it in your house or give it as a gift.

But if you want to make your homegrown cut flowers last as long as florist flowers often do, forget that romantic image of laying flower stems gently in a pretty basket slung over your arm as you gather them.

Here's why: When a plant stem is severed from a plant, not only is its source of moisture cut off but air bubbles can form in the stem's base, slowing or preventing water uptake later. By the time you get the plant inside and plunk your flowers inside a vase, it may be too late. The result? Limp flowers mighty soon.

Here's a better way…

In Your Garden

Fill a bucket with a few inches of lukewarm water.

Use a sharp, clean cutting tool such as a knife or garden shears—sharp so that the stems don't get mashed…and clean so that harmful bacteria don't invade the plant tissue.

For flower stems, cut on a slant, allowing maximum surface area for water uptake.

For slender flowering shrub or tree branches, make a square (perpendicular to the branch) cut.

Immediately after cutting, place stems in the bucket with water.

In Your Home

Relax if you can't or don't want to arrange your flowers in a vase immediately after cutting them. They'll be soaking up water from the bucket and getting plump. Just put the bucket in a cool, dark place. Overnight is fine.

When it's time to put the flowers in a vase, work on a table or counter close to a sink. Fill a clean vase about halfway—you can always add more water later.

Next, recut each flower stem under water (while still in the bucket) with a sharp, clean knife—a half inch or more above the garden cut. This may feel awkward at first, but you'll master it after a few stems. For the woody stems that you cut square, recut them and then slit them up the middle about one inch up.

That's it! Now you've done what good florists do to make their flowers look great and last long. If you want flowers to last even longer, recut them and refill the vase with fresh water every day.

I don't know if DIY cut-flower preservatives such as an aspirin or a few drops of lemon juice help, but here's one final tip that really will make a difference. At night, or when you're not home, move the flowers, vase and all, to the fridge or just some cool, dark spot—and then return it to the display spot the next day.

Love to Garden, But Suffer from Allergies?

Boyan Hadjiev, MD, adult and pediatric allergy, asthma and sinusitis specialist in private practice in New York City. DrSneeze.com

Garden after 10 am, when pollen counts are not at their highest, and take frequent breaks to avoid lengthy exposure to allergens. Also, be sure to cover up—wear gloves and long sleeves and tuck long pants into socks…a mask and goggles or wraparound sunglasses…and a wide-brimmed hat. Take a shower as soon as you come inside, and put a cold compress on your eyes. Store gardening clothes separately or wash them immediately.

Kill Garden Weeds Naturally

Teri Dunn Chace, author of more than 35 gardening titles, including *How to Eradicate Invasive Plants*. She lives in upstate New York. TeriChaceWriter.com

Yes, weeds in your garden are tough to deal with, but you don't need to use toxic commercial weed killers in flower beds, vegetable gardens or other gardens to get rid of them. *Here, an expert gardener's weed-beating strategies…*

•**Start early.** You can save yourself a lot of trouble if you intervene promptly. In early spring, yank weeds out by the roots (right after a rain, when the ground is soft and damp). Or drag a sharp hoe across them, which dislodges them, roots and all.

•**Kill top growth.** For larger weeds that are deeply rooted, try an aboveground attack. If you persist, the root systems will struggle and eventually die. *There are several ways you can do this…*

•Cut. Use a weed whacker or lawn mower set low to scalp them.

•Smother. Lay cardboard, one-half inch of old newspapers, a plastic or heavy cloth tarp or a combination of these, over a weed patch. Anchor with rocks or bricks. For a badly infested or very weedy area, leave the covering in place for an entire growing season. It won't look beautiful, but neither would the weeds, and it's only temporary. To inhibit an invasion among desired plants, lay down at least one inch of bagged bark mulch or straw.

•Scald. It is possible to kill weeds by dousing them with boiling water. This works best for spot-treating small patches. Use a tea kettle filled with just-boiled water. Use oven mitts, and pour with care so that you don't splash the water on your legs or shoes.

•**Use homemade weed killer.** In a large, clean plastic jug, mix one gallon of white vinegar, one cup of table salt and one tablespoon of liquid dishwashing soap. Shake well. Vinegar and salt dry out plant cell membranes, causing death by dehydration—soap helps the mixture adhere to the plants. Fill a spray bottle with the mixture, and direct it at all aboveground growth on a sunny day—sunlight boosts the vinegar's effectiveness. Repeated applications often are necessary. Protect nearby valued plants by covering them with an old towel or with an empty carton.

If the above options fail, use one or more of the following products, available at garden stores or online. Follow the label directions on your product, and be prepared to repeat treatments on larger plants and stubborn targets.

•Citrus oils. Organic herbicides, such as Avenger, have citrus oil as their active ingredient—this strips leaves of their protective waxy covering, drying them out past the point of no return. These work best on broadleaf weeds including dandelion, pigweed and bindweed.

•Garden torches. You can zap pesky weeds with a propane-fueled flame tool called the Mini Dragon. This works brilliantly on nonflammable surfaces such as stone terraces, walkways and sidewalks where weeds have encroached or reared up between cracks and in rock gardens. For safety, follow the instructions that come with this product to the letter.

Easy Way to Grow a Berry Patch

Teri Dunn Chace, author of more than 35 gardening titles, including *The Anxious Gardener's Book of Answers*. She lives in upstate New York. TeriChaceWriter.com

You may know that blueberries, cranberries and lingonberries are packed with disease-fighting antioxidants, but did you know that you can easily grow them yourself in containers on decks, patios and balconies?

What to look for: You'll want to plant plants, not seeds. Seek out smaller plants specifically touted as "dwarf" or "for containers" that are right for your climate. If there are none for sale in your area, turn to a reputable online mail-order source such as Backyard Berry Plants...Indiana Berry & Plant Co...Nourse Farms...Raintree Nursery...or Stark Bro's. They ship the plants directly to your door, along with planting instructions. *Also...*

●**Blueberries.** If you get only one plant, pick a variety labeled as "self-pollinating."

●**Cranberries.** Unlike what many people think, these do not require a bog. But they can be slow starters, so buy a three- or four-year-old plant (the age typically is stated on the label).

●**Lingonberries.** This cranberry relative has sweet-tart fruits the size of large peas. As with cranberries, you'll get fruit sooner if you buy a larger, more mature plant.

Container savvy: The pots should be at least two feet deep and wide to house the eventual root system. Exceptions are for the smallest cranberry plants, which can grow in a one-foot-wide-and-deep hanging basket or deck planter.

Fill your containers with "acidic mix" potting soil (often labeled for use with rhododendrons and azaleas). Select a spot that gets at least six to eight hours of direct sunlight per day.

Care: Keep the soil mix consistently moist but not soggy. Fertilizing in spring as new growth begins boosts productivity. Use a plant food specifically labeled for acid-loving plants. Your first-season harvest may be modest, but there will be more berries every year as the plants establish themselves.

When winter comes: These plants can live for many years if well cared for. If your area gets freezing weather, cover the soil surface with insulating mulch such as several inches of chopped dried leaves or bagged pine-bark mulch. If your containers are small enough, you can dig temporary holes in your yard, sink the containers into the ground and then mulch. You also can put them in the garage.

Pest control: Berry patches sometimes experience pests and diseases.

Good news: These rarely appear when you grow just a plant or two, especially in containers. The only trouble you may encounter is birds stealing your ripening berries—thwart them by covering the plants with special bird netting (available at home and garden outlets). Deer and rabbits tend not to raid containers, because they're higher off the ground and/or near the house. But if these animals do become a problem, netting is a deterrent for these critters, too.

Grow Vegetables Without a Garden

Thomas J. Fox, author of *Urban Farming: Sustainable City Living in Your Backyard, in Your Community, and in the World.*

Self-watering containers grow produce in small spaces. Each container holds from 1.5 to 2.5 cubic feet of soil above an integrated reservoir system that lets the plants take in moisture by the roots. The containers are big enough to grow lettuce, carrots, cucumbers, peppers or tomato plants. Reliable models include the EarthBox ($38, 800-442-7336, EarthBox.com)...City Pickers Patio Garden Kit ($37.47, available at The Home Depot)...and The Garden Patch's GrowBox ($39.95, 800-519-1955, AGardenPatch.com).

CHAPTER 9

Healthy Home

Beware: New Dangers from the Chemicals All Around Us

David O. Carpenter, MD, professor of environmental health in the School of Public Health, and director of the Institute for Health and the Environment at the University at Albany, State University of New York. He is the editor of the book *Effects of Persistent and Bioactive Organic Pollutants on Human Health*.

Until recently, the health risks associated with exposure to toxic chemicals were thought to be limited to serious ills such as lung disease and cancer.

Now: The dangers, which few people (including most doctors) are aware of, are even more far-reaching than previously thought. Certain synthetic chemicals—such as those that pervade our food, water, air and many of the products and items we use and live with at home and at work—are now being linked to a much wider array of health problems, including diabetes, stroke, heart disease and other chronic conditions.

A surprising finding: Even though diabetes has traditionally been linked to poor lifestyle habits, such as an unhealthy diet and lack of physical activity, epidemiological studies conducted in Sweden recently found that reducing exposure to certain synthetic chemicals, including polychlorinated biphenyls (PCBs) and phthalates, by 25% lowered the rate of diabetes by 13%.

Here are synthetic chemicals you should know about...*

•**PCBs.** Before these 200 or so man-made chemicals were banned in the US in 1979, hundreds of millions of pounds of PCBs were produced—and used as flame retardants in electrical devices such as transformers...as solvents in paint and caulking...in carbonless copy paper...and in plastics.

Those PCBs accumulated in the soil, in the water and sediment of lakes and rivers, and in the ocean. They continue to "volatilize" into the air, forming harmful gases. In short, we eat, drink and breathe PCBs.

PCBs have long been associated with increased risks for cancer, suppression of the immune system, damage to bones and joints, lower testosterone levels and negative effects on the brain, such as reduced cognitive function and focus.

However, an increasing body of recent evidence in both animals and humans shows that these chemicals also increase risk for diabetes, heart disease and stroke.

In fact, my research has shown that high levels of PCBs in the blood are a stronger risk factor for the development of high blood pressure—itself a risk factor for heart attack and stroke—than any other factor, except for age.

*Because researchers have not yet determined the level of exposure tied to health risks, it's wise to avoid these chemicals whenever possible.

To minimize exposure: PCBs are stored in animal fat—such as red meat, poultry, fish and dairy products. To reduce PCB exposure, minimize fatty cuts of red meat and emphasize lean cuts, such as round roast and top sirloin steak. For poultry, remove the skin and opt for white meat. For dairy, minimize full-fat products such as cream.

For fish, minimize fatty fish high on the food chain, such as tuna. Atlantic and farmed salmon are also typically loaded with PCBs, as are farmed carp and catfish. Fish low in PCBs and other contaminants include wild-caught Alaskan salmon and Pacific sardines.

For a reliable guide to other low-PCB fish and seafood: Visit the website of the Monterey Bay Aquarium Seafood Watch (SeafoodWatch.org).

Note: Fish oil supplements typically have fewer PCBs than fish because the manufacturing process used to minimize the fishy taste and smell helps remove some of the PCBs.

•**Phthalates and bisphenol A (BPA).** Phthalates (also called plasticizers) are used to make plastic more flexible, transparent and durable. Phthalate-containing products include adhesives, scented products, printed store receipts, plastic clothes

Avoid Scents

Avoid scented cleaning and laundry products. Even products that claim to be "green," organic or natural may emit hazardous chemicals.

Recent finding: Nearly one-quarter of chemicals emitted by scented household products, such as air fresheners, detergents, fabric softeners and disinfectants, are classified as toxic or hazardous…and more than one-third of products tested emitted at least one chemical identified as a probable carcinogen.

To avoid potentially dangerous chemicals: Clean with baking soda and/or vinegar…open windows for ventilation instead of using air fresheners…and buy products without any fragrance.

Anne Steinemann, PhD, former professor of civil and environmental engineering and public affairs, University of Washington, Seattle, and lead author of study of 25 fragranced consumer products, published in *Environmental Impact Assessment Review.*

such as raincoats (vinyl is loaded with phthalates), synthetic leather used in clothing and furniture, sunglasses and eyeglasses with plastic lenses and contact lenses, dental fillings and sealants, DVDs and CDs, and personal-care products such as soaps, shampoos, moisturizers, hair sprays and nail polish. Phthalates are also prevalent in plastic food containers and plastic kitchen utensils.

Phthalates are endocrine-disrupting chemicals (EDCs). They mimic or interfere with the endocrine system, which manufactures hormones—chemical messengers that regulate every system, organ, tissue and cell in your body. That's why EDCs increase the risk for almost every chronic disease, ranging from diabetes and cardiovascular disorders to learning disabilities and attention deficit hyperactivity disorder. Phthalates also mimic the female sex hormone estrogen, increasing risk for breast cancer.

Another endocrine-disrupting chemical: BPA, which is found in the linings of many canned food products and beverages. In adults, BPA has been linked to diabetes, heart disease, breast cancer, infertility and erectile dysfunction.

Important: Because of consumer demand, many manufacturers have switched from BPA to BPS (bisphenol S), but there's no proof that it's less toxic. It is just less studied.

To minimize exposure to phthalates and BPA: Don't believe that there are "safe" plastics. Never microwave food in plastic—not even plastic that is labeled "microwave safe." Avoid drinking water or any beverage that is bottled in disposable plastic—even if the bottle is labeled "BPA-free." Don't store food in plastic—use glass, ceramic or stainless steel containers. In a study in the journal *Environmental Health Perspectives,* scientists tested more than 455 plastic products and found that almost all of them leached EDCs.

Minimize canned food and beverages—many linings contain BPA.

Don't use scented candles or air fresheners. (Beeswax candles do not contain phthalates.) Don't use scented detergents and dryer sheets.

Avoid personal-care products that list "parfum" or "fragrance" as an ingredient—a sure sign of the presence of phthalates.

Don't use vinyl, which is loaded with phthalates.

Example: Trade in your vinyl shower curtain for fabric. Also, avoid clothes and accessories made with polyvinyl chloride (PVC), such as coats, shoes and bags.

Note: It's helpful to check product labels for phthalates, but phthalates can be present even when not listed on the label.

To find phthalate-free personal-care products: Consult the Environmental Working Group (at EWG.org, under "Consumer Guides," click on "Skin Deep").

•**PFCs (perfluorinated compounds).** PFCs are found in food packaging, in Teflon and other nonstick cookware, in waterproof or rainproof jackets, in stain-resistant brands and treatments and in many furniture fabrics and carpets. They are also widely used in pesticides, and in the automobile, electronics and aerospace industries.

According to human and animal studies, PFCs are not only linked to increased risk for diabetes but also contribute to a host of other health issues, such as cardiovascular disease, cancer, a weakened immune system, thyroid disease, obesity and problems with fertility in both women and men.

To minimize exposure: Don't buy or use Teflon and other nonstick pans. If you already own nonstick cookware, do your best to avoid scratching or chipping it, which releases PFCs, and cook on low heat to minimize release of PFCs into food and as vapors. When you're ready to buy new cookware, choose stainless steel, cast iron or glass.

Nonstick chemicals are also used in some personal-care products—don't buy anything that has an ingredient starting with "perfluoro-."

Avoid microwave popcorn or pizza—the coating of the interior packaging may contain PFCs. For other microwavable frozen foods, be sure to remove the food from the packaging before microwaving.

PFCs are also found in many fish—follow the same guidelines as those listed for PCBs.

Don't use clothing or furniture labeled stain resistant, or clothing labeled water resistant—most of these items contain PFCs.

Use a carbon filter to reduce exposure to PFCs and other synthetic chemicals in your drinking water.

PFCs, phthalates and other disease-causing synthetic chemicals can also end up in household dust—and in your lungs. Vacuum regularly, using a vacuum with a chemical-catching HEPA filter—they're available from brands such as Hoover, Eureka, Bissell and Dyson.

Cleaning Your House Can Harm Your Lungs

Philip J. Landrigan, MD, dean for global health and professor in the departments of pediatrics and environmental medicine and public health, Icahn School of Medicine at Mount Sinai in New York City.

You might expect people who clean houses or offices for a living to develop lung problems from harsh cleaning products. But it happens even to people who regularly clean just their own homes.

So finds a new study published in *American Journal of Respiratory and Critical Care Medicine* that followed more than 6,200 adults for 20 years. Compared with people who didn't clean their own homes, those who did so at least weekly scored significantly lower on a measure of overall lung function. In this one measure, the decline was similar to that found in people who have been smoking cigarettes for years.

To learn more, we spoke with environmental expert Philip J. Landrigan, MD, of the Icahn School of Medicine at Mount Sinai in New York City. *His advice to keep your lungs from being harmed…*

•**Use your nose.** Ammonia and bleach are known irritants that can, over time, impair lung function even when inhaled in low concentrations. You can tell just by opening a product and giving it a sniff that it is irritating—avoid those products.

•**Buy safe.** Choose gentler products. While labels are no guarantee—they're not regulated—look for products that use terms such as "gentle," "nontoxic" and "ecofriendly."

•**Make your own.** For total control over what you breathe in when you clean your house, use in-

131

gredients such as distilled white vinegar or borax to make your own safe cleaning products.

Example: Mix three-quarters cup of vinegar with three-quarters cup of water in a spray bottle to clean windows and mirrors.

No matter how long a person has been using irritant chemicals, there are health benefits that come from stopping their use. Some will be immediate… others take months or years…but all the results are positive.

How Cleaners Harm Children

Study of 757 infants by researchers at University of Alberta, Canada, published in *CMAJ*.

Everyday cleaners may make kids overweight. In homes where parents frequently used household disinfectants such as multisurface cleaners, babies three to four months old had lower levels of certain gut bacteria, compared with babies in households using ecofriendly cleaners. Scientists theorize that this altered gut bacteria may be a factor in obesity. Babies from homes using antibacterial products had higher body mass indexes at age three than babies from homes that did not use disinfectants frequently.

Areas in Your Home That Can Make You Sick

DumbLittleMan.com, a self-improvement website.

Vacuum cleaners can harbor bacteria that can cause breathing problems—clean the filter often, open windows when vacuuming and wear a mask while cleaning. *Refrigerator shelves and drawers* can harbor bacteria—clean shelves and fruit and vegetable drawers regularly with warm water and baking soda, and wash fruits and vegetables before refrigerating them. *Bath mats* may contain mold, dust mites and bacteria—wash them several times a

month. *Blenders* can collect microorganisms at the bottom—take a blender apart and wash it after each use, before putting it away.

Easy Ways to Steer Clear of the Nasty Bugs That Spread Colds, Flu and Even More Serious Infections

Philip M. Tierno, Jr., PhD, director of clinical microbiology and immunology at New York University Langone Medical Center and a member of the faculty at New York University School of Medicine, both in New York City. He is the author of *The Secret Lives of Germs*.

During the fall and winter, we're all on high alert to avoid germs that cause colds and flu. But there are other microbes—some quite dangerous—that we should also protect ourselves from all year long.

The majority of people know that methicillin-resistant Staphylococcus aureus (MRSA), an antibiotic-resistant organism that often affects hospital patients, is now infecting more and more people in community settings, such as health clubs, assisted-living facilities and other public places.

What you may not know: There's been a significant increase in the prevalence of MRSA in the noses of healthy adults and children, according to research published in *The New England Journal of Medicine*. Since anyone can harbor MRSA without getting sick, this means that an infected person could unknowingly spread the dangerous bacterium by sneezing into his/her hand before touching a doorknob, for example, or other surface.

Know Where the Germs Hide

Most people know that hand-washing with warm water and plain soap for at least 20 seconds is a highly effective germ-control strategy. However, there are some little-known secrets that you also should be aware of to help protect yourself—and your family—from germs that cause colds or the flu or infection with MRSA or other dangerous bacteria...

SECRET 1: Opt for sanitizer wipes instead of gel. Alcohol-based gels are effective, but sanitizer wipes (with 62% ethyl alcohol) are better because the friction caused by wipes helps remove bacteria and skin debris containing dead skin cells that can harbor infectious agents.

My advice: Keep sanitizer wipes in your bag or a shirt pocket, and use them whenever you've been out in public and can't get to a bathroom to wash your hands.

If you do use gel: Apply a dollop about the size of a quarter. Whether you're using a gel or wipe, use the product for at least 20 seconds. It takes this long to completely cover the hands, rub between fingers, etc. Let the sanitizing agent dry, do not wipe it off, and be sure to apply it under the fingernails, too.

SECRET 2: Bring your own reading material to the doctor's office. Cold and flu viruses can survive up to 48 hours on the pages of magazines— longer if the reader has left behind smudges of hand cream or makeup, which can help some organisms survive. Avoid pens at the sign-in desk too.

My advice: Bring your own magazine or book to read. If you do read one of the doctor's magazines, do not moisten your finger in your mouth when turning the pages—and keep your hands away from your eyes, nose and mouth until you've had a chance to wash your hands.

SECRET 3: Air-dry bath towels. Most people, after using a bath or hand towel, fold it over and hang it neatly on a towel rod. This is the worst thing you can do because it traps moisture and makes it possible for germs to thrive.

A few staph bacteria deposited on a damp towel will increase to about 100,000 in four hours. Some organisms can live for several hours to days on a damp towel.

Danger: Suppose you have a cut on your skin, then wipe yourself with a staph-infected towel. Because of the bacterial "bloom," you'll be exposing the cut to very high concentrations of staph bacteria.

My advice: To avoid doing multiple loads of laundry, completely air-dry towels between uses by hanging them in such a way that air can reach every part of the surface. If you follow this practice, it's fine to wash towels just once or twice a week. If someone in your home has a communicable illness, he/she should use a personal towel and keep it separate from other towels.

SECRET 4: Keep your toothbrush upright. Like bathroom towels, a toothbrush that stays moist can accumulate enormous quantities of bacteria and cold and flu viruses in just a few hours.

My advice: Don't lay your brush down to store it—stand it up with the bristles at the top so that it will dry completely between uses. Also close the toilet lid before you flush. The flushing action in some toilets can spray invisible water droplets— which contain fecal and other disease-causing organisms—up to 20 feet. An exposed toothbrush is an easy target.

Also helpful: Sanitize your toothbrush by submerging the bristles in a germ-killing mouthwash for about five minutes. Do this several times a week or with each use if you are ill.

SECRET 5: Use hotter water. Everyone wants to save money on utility bills, but some people do this by turning down the thermostat on the water heater.

The risk: Undergarments and bath towels can harbor enormous amounts of dangerous organisms, including the hepatitis A virus (transmitted primarily via human stool) and bacteria such as staph and Escherichia coli. Washing clothes in cool or warm water will remove some of these germs, but it won't kill them. Hot water is needed to kill these organisms as well as cold and flu viruses.

My advice: Make sure the water temperature in your washing machine is at least 150° F by checking it with a candy thermometer. This is hot enough to kill microbes. If your washer doesn't have a heating cycle that uses water this hot, raise the hot-water setting on your water tank—just be careful of scalding from tap water.

Helpful: Wash underwear separately so that any surviving organisms won't be transferred to other clothes.

Also: Use bleach on whites—it kills microbes.

Beware CO Poisoning

The late Richard O'Brien, MD, associate professor of emergency medicine at The Commonwealth Medical College of Pennsylvania in Scranton.

Unintentional carbon monoxide (CO) exposure accounts for about 400 deaths in the US each year. CO gas from a poorly maintained oil, natural gas, propane or wood burner or other household source is odorless, colorless and tasteless. As CO levels rise in the home, nausea, headache, vomiting, dizziness and eventually death can result. Children, pets and those with compromised immune systems (the elderly) are usually the first to get sick.

What to do: Have your home heating system professionally inspected annually. And be sure to place a CO detector on every floor of your home. To learn more about CO, go to EPA.gov (search "Carbon Monoxide poisoning").

Top 10 Germy Spots in Your Kitchen

Cheryl Luptowski, home-safety expert and public information officer, NSF International (a global public health and safety organization), Ann Arbor, Michigan. NSF.org

You don't want germs in your food, so, of course, you keep your kitchen clean...right? Maybe not! All of the cleaning in the world does little good if you miss the dirtiest spots because you don't know where germs are most likely to lurk.

For example, when was the last time you gave much thought to your blender gasket? Or to the wooden block you use to store your knives? Probably ages ago, if ever. *Well, you should—and here's why...*

Seeking Out the Icky Spots

Recently, microbiologists at NSF International, a global public health and safety organization, analyzed a wide variety of common kitchen tools and appliances for the presence of various microorganisms that can cause foodborne illness, including the bacteria Salmonella, Listeria and E. coli, as well as yeasts and molds.

In addition, the NSF team wanted to gauge public awareness of where such germs typically are found in kitchens. So they asked a panel of volunteers to say which kitchen items they thought were likely to be the most contaminated—and boy, were the volunteers off! For instance, they thought that the microwave keypad would be #1 and that the flatware storage tray would be #5...but neither of these items even made it onto the actual top 10 list of germiest items. What's more, the true #1 germiest item—the refrigerator water dispenser—didn't even appear in the volunteers' top 10. *Here, the top 10 most contaminated areas, starting with the highest germ count...*

1. Refrigerator water dispensers.
2. Rubber spatulas.
3. Blenders.
4. Refrigerator vegetable compartments.
5. Refrigerator ice dispensers.
6. Refrigerator meat compartments.
7. Knife blocks.
8. Rubber seals of food storage containers.
9. Can openers.
10. Refrigerator insulating seals.

What makes these particular spots so germ-prone? *There are several reasons...*

•**Dark, damp environments are perfect breeding grounds for germs.** When asked where germs thrive, people generally think of warm environments—but fully half of the top 10 contaminated areas were in the refrigerator. That's because fridges offer moisture and darkness, which help germs take hold. Refrigerators also have lots of nooks and crannies where germs can hide. The panel of volunteers guessed that the microwave keypad would harbor the most germs because people are always touching it. However, that keypad is exposed to the air, and it has a smooth surface where germs can't take hold, and people tend to wipe it down a lot. In contrast, people tend not to clean the fridge that often...and when they do, they might just swipe at it with a damp cloth rather than really sanitizing it.

•**Germs build up on items that aren't often disassembled and cleaned.** When is the last time you removed the head of your plastic spatula from its handle? Or scrubbed your can opener? Or took your blender apart? Do so now and you're likely to find a disconcerting accumulation of crud (and the same probably goes for your food processor).

•Utensils and small appliances often get put away before they are thoroughly dry. The moisture on the items plus the darkness inside the drawer or cabinet can encourage bacteria to breed. The same goes for the slots of a knife block—if the knives aren't completely dry when they're put away, bacteria can thrive in those damp, dark slots.

Get the Yuck Out

Kitchen pathogens aren't just disgusting, they also can lead to serious health problems. Though anyone can fall prey, some people are at particular risk—for instance, those with compromised immune systems, including many of the elderly...pregnant women, for whom foodborne pathogens such as Listeria can increase the risk for miscarriage, preterm labor or stillbirth...and people allergic to yeasts or molds. That's why it is so important to clean all your kitchen tools and appliances properly. *Here's how...*

•Refrigerator water dispenser. Check your owner's manual. Many manufacturers recommend that you clean the dispenser's waterspout weekly by dipping a small brush in distilled white vinegar and brushing the inside of the spout...then open the spout and allow it to run to clear away dirt and excess vinegar. Close the lever once there are no more traces of vinegar. Does this seem like overkill, given that we have all sorts of similar spouts in the house (i.e., every single faucet) that are never cleaned this way? It's actually a good idea to clean all your drinking water faucets regularly to prevent the buildup of germs and bacteria. The kitchen sink area tends to harbor a lot of bacteria, and thus both the sink and the kitchen faucet surface should be cleaned at least weekly with a sanitizing cleaner.

Also, at least once a year, you should clean the refrigerator's whole water dispensing system. To do that, turn off the water supply to the refrigerator and loosen the screw connecting the water line to the fridge. Once disconnected, pour four cups of distilled white vinegar into the tube (use a funnel). Wait 10 minutes, then reconnect the water line. Turn the

dispenser on, allowing the vinegar to flow through the system and come out the dispenser's waterspout. Continue until all the vinegar is gone and the water comes out clean. Don't assume that having an inline water filter would solve the water dispenser germ problem. Although filters can help reduce many different contaminants as well as water-treatment chemicals like chlorine, they don't protect against bacteria or most other types of microorganisms.

•Refrigerator ice dispenser. Turn off the ice maker. Empty the ice bin, and wash it with hot soapy water, then rinse and dry with a clean towel. Clean monthly. If you have just done your annual whole-system cleaning of the water dispenser, discard the first batch of ice to make sure there's no vinegar in those first cubes.

•Refrigerator meat and vegetable drawers, Once a month, remove drawers from the fridge, wash with hot soapy water and a clean cloth, rinse well and dry thoroughly with a clean towel. If your drawers are on top of each other, store the meats in the bottom drawer in case they leak. (Double-wrapping meats in plastic wrap or bags helps reduce that risk.) If meats do leak, clean the drawer immediately. With produce, to avoid cross-contamination, separate ready-to-eat produce from unwashed items.

•Refrigerator insulating seal. At least monthly, wipe thoroughly with a damp, soapy dishcloth. Rinse the cloth well, wipe again, then dry with a clean towel. Be sure the seal is dry!

•Blender. After each use, unplug the blender and remove the jar from the base. Completely disassemble the jar, separating the blade and gasket at the bottom from the main container and separating the lid handle from the rest of the lid. If components are dishwasher-safe (check your user's guide), wash all pieces in the dishwasher (except the motor unit, of course). If hand-washing, use hot soapy water, rinse and dry before reassembling. Do the same for your food processor.

•Can opener. After each use, wash handheld can openers in the dishwasher or hand-wash with hot, soapy water, then rinse well and dry. For electric openers, thoroughly wipe with a clean, damp, soapy dishcloth, paying special attention to the area around the cutting blades to be sure all food residue is removed...then rinse the cloth and wipe the can opener again. Dry with a clean dishtowel.

●**Rubber or plastic spatula.** What many people fail to do when washing spatulas is to separate the handles from the heads when the spatulas are made of two pieces—and bits of food (and germs) can accumulate in that joint. So for a two-piece spatula, separate the handle from the head and place both sections in the dishwasher. If hand-washing, separate the pieces and use hot soapy water, then rinse and dry thoroughly. With one-piece spatulas, if washing by hand, pay special attention to the area where the handle joins the head—there are sometimes crevices there.

●**Food storage container with rubber seal.** This is likely to get clean enough when washed in the dishwasher—but sometimes people wash a container by hand (doing a less than thorough job) or even just rinse it and then reuse it. In that case, any food that has gotten trapped in the seal becomes a bacteria haven. So if you are hand-washing, use hot soapy water, giving extra attention to the seal and to the area where the cover attaches to the container. Rinse well, and allow to air dry completely.

●**Knife block.** Thoroughly clean your knife block monthly. First, turn the block upside down and shake...or use a can of compressed air to remove debris from slots. For nonwood blocks, hand-wash in hot soapy water, using a small brush (like a baby bottle nipple brush) to scour inside each knife slot, then rinse. To sanitize, mix one gallon of warm water with one tablespoon of bleach...then immerse the block in the bleach mixture or pour the mixture into each slot and wait one minute. Rinse thoroughly. Place the block upside down to dry, allowing air to get into the slots.

Note: If you have a wooden block, this method could damage the wood—so check with the manufacturer for cleaning and sanitizing instructions.

Easy alternative: Consider getting a magnetic knife rack, which doesn't have any tough-to-clean slots. And however you store your knives, wash them in hot soapy water after each use, then dry completely before putting them away.

Cleaning Sponges Does Not Destroy Germs

Markus Egert, PhD, is professor for microbiology and hygiene, faculty of medical and life sciences, Institute for Precision Medicine, Furtwangen University, Schwenningen, Germany.

Cleaning kitchen sponges does not work, reports Markus Egert, PhD. Sponge-cleaning techniques—such as boiling in hot water or cleaning in a washing machine with hot water and bleach—do reduce germ count temporarily. But germ densities can range from 25 billion to 54 billion per cubic centimeter, so any reduction is modest. And the germs that survive are the resistant ones—they reproduce rapidly and create a community with an even higher share of potential pathogens.

Best: Replace sponges weekly.

Don't Rinse the Chicken... and Other Secrets to Avoiding Food Poisoning

Richard Besser, MD, former chief health and medical editor of *ABC News*. He is also the author of *Tell Me the Truth, Doctor: Easy-to-Understand Answers to Your Most Confusing and Critical Health Questions*.

Here's the dilemma: Kale, spinach and other leafy greens are some of the most healthful foods you can eat...but they also are among the most likely sources of food poisoning.

A very real threat: Every year, one in six Americans gets sick after eating contaminated foods. While the symptoms, including upset stomach, abdominal cramps, diarrhea and/or vomiting, usually are not life-threatening, about 3,000 people will die from the illness, according to the Centers for Disease Control and Prevention (CDC).

So how do you get the health benefits of vegetables, fruits and other common foods without running the risk of getting sick? *Here's how you can minimize your risk...*

Fresh Produce

Vegetables account for about one-third of all cases of food poisoning in the US, and leafy greens, such as spinach, lettuce and kale, are the highest-risk produce. That's because leafy greens grow close to the ground and are easily contaminated from irrigation water and livestock runoff. Leafy greens also have shapes and textures that make them harder to clean than other types of produce.

Important: Bagged and prewashed lettuce mixes may be somewhat riskier than "whole" produce because multiple heads of lettuce are used and mixes are handled more during processing. *To minimize risk…*

•**Get a package from the back of the store's refrigerator when buying precut lettuce.** The colder temperature in this location inhibits bacterial growth.

•**Check the expiration date.** While most people are careful to check the expiration date on dairy, that's not always the case for produce. Packaged fresh produce that's eaten at least five days before the "sell by" date is less likely to cause food poisoning than older produce.

Rinsing produce, including prewashed lettuces, will remove some harmful organisms, but not all of them. In addition to rinsing, buy the freshest produce possible, keep it refrigerated and, if possible, cook it thoroughly to kill any bacteria.

Poultry

Most Americans wouldn't think of preparing a chicken or turkey without rinsing the bird first. The common belief is that rinsing washes away Salmonella or other disease-causing microbes. In fact, rinsing poultry is the worst thing you can do. It isn't very effective at removing bacteria—and it sprays potentially contaminated water droplets around the kitchen.

Some harmful organisms can survive for days or even weeks on faucets, countertops, the refrigerator handle, etc. They cause cross-contamination when other foods (or your fingers) touch the invisible hot spots. *To minimize risk…*

•**Always cook poultry (whether in your kitchen or on the grill) to an internal temperature of 165°F.** High temperature—not rinsing—will ensure that the bird is safe.

•**Wash your hands after handling poultry.** Most people remember to wash their hands before handling foods, but it's actually more important to do so afterward to prevent the spread of bacteria.

The Cutting Board

It's one of the most contaminated surfaces in your kitchen, particularly if you use the same one for all of your food preparation. The bacteria from poultry and other meats are easily transferred to other foods. Wiping a cutting board with a sponge isn't an effective way to remove microbes. Unless it's new or sanitized (put it in the dishwasher or microwave on "high" for one minute), it might actually introduce new organisms.

To minimize risk: Every home should have two cutting boards—one that's used only for poultry/other meats and one that's used only for produce.

Common mistake: Not washing a knife you've used to cut poultry before cutting other foods. Wash it with hot, soapy water or use a clean one.

Plastic or wood? Plastic cutting boards are less porous and easier to clean. Wood boards have natural bacteria-inhibiting properties. Either is acceptable—just keep it clean by using hot, soapy water or sanitize it in the dishwasher.

Unpasteurized Dairy

According to a CDC study, dairy products (mostly unpasteurized) accounted for 14% of all cases of food poisoning in the US—and the organisms in contaminated dairy are more likely than those in other foods to cause illness that leads to hospitalization.

Some states require all dairy foods to be pasteurized, while others allow the sale of unpasteurized (raw) milk, cheese and other dairy products. *To minimize risk…*

•**Buy only pasteurized milk, cream, cheese and other dairy products.** One study found that unpasteurized dairy was 150 times more likely to cause a food-borne illness than pasteurized versions.

Left-Out Leftovers

Bacteria need just two things—enough time and a high enough temperature—to multiply.

To minimize risk…

•**Never eat food that was left out overnight.** This guideline applies even if the food was originally cooked at a high temperature or reheated the next day. The risk for contamination is just too high if food was unrefrigerated for that long.

•**Throw out food that you dipped into after the cooking was completed but didn't refrigerate within two hours.** Let's say you prepared a pot of stew or soup, then had seconds or thirds after it was cooked. If this food wasn't refrigerated within two hours, throw it out. By introducing the spoon multiple times into the pot, you could have introduced harmful organisms that may have multiplied. Some bacteria do grow at cold temperatures but at slower rates. For this reason, you should reuse leftovers within a few days.

Don't Forget the Sink

Multiple studies have shown that kitchen sinks, including the faucet handles, have extremely high bacterial loads. *To minimize risk…*

•**Thoroughly wash the sink—and faucet handles.** Use hot, soapy water or a bleach solution—mix one tablespoon of unscented, liquid bleach per one gallon of water, and let stand for five minutes. Rinse well and air dry.

The Danger Growing in Your Fridge: Answers to Common Questions About Mold and Food

C. Leigh Broadhurst, PhD, research scientist at a government agriculture research lab and research associate in the department of environmental and civil engineering at University of Maryland, College Park. She is author of *Natural Relief from Asthma: Breathe Freely, Naturally.*

When you see greenish spots on the surface of cottage cheese or a patch of fuzzy nastiness on a tomato, you know that you're dealing with mold. But a lot of people don't know about mold in food—including hidden mold. *Here are answers to the common questions…*

•**If I eat something moldy by mistake, how dangerous is it?**

Some food molds can trigger sinusitis, asthma and allergies. Mold also can cause, in susceptible people, a host of less serious but uncomfortable symptoms, including cramps, headaches and nausea. The people who are most at risk are those with compromised immunity due to chronic illnesses (especially of the lungs), organ transplants, treatment with chemotherapy, etc.

•**What about the moldy yogurt products recalled in the past? Is yogurt more likely to have mold?**

In September 2013, there was a recall of a popular brand of yogurt after the FDA received reports that the yogurt had mold that might have been causing cramps, diarrhea and other symptoms.

In general, if you or someone in your family has an illness that suppresses the immune system or you take medications that have a similar effect, be particularly careful with yogurt that contains fruit. Some fruits contain naturally occurring yeasts (a type of mold) that thrive in yogurt. Even if the fruit doesn't contain these yeasts, the combination of "sugaryness" and yogurt's soft texture creates an environment for other mold spores. It can grow overnight. Signs of mold include a swelled container…off colors or flavors…fermented or mildewy smell…and/or black or green spots.

•**Are any food molds deadly?**

Some mold species produce poisonous substances called mycotoxins. The most dangerous of these is aflatoxin. It's typically found in grains and peanuts, mainly in developing parts of the world. With repeated exposure, it can cause liver cancer as well as a severe form of fungal hepatitis. It's rare in the US because manufacturers test for it constantly.

Important: If you buy a bag of peanuts and notice a moldy smell…blackened areas on any of the nuts…or a very foul taste, throw it away. You don't want to take chances with aflatoxin.

•**If I cut off the moldy part, can I still eat a food?**

No one likes to throw away food that has a few spots. It's tempting to just skim or trim off small areas of mold. In general, I don't recommend that.

Molds are filamentous organisms. They have long, threadlike structures beneath the part that you can see on the surface. The threads grow rapidly, particularly in soft foods with a high liquid content. That's why it is much better to assume that the mold has spread throughout a container even if you can't see it. The same goes for bread. If a slice of bread has mold, throw out the entire loaf.

Exception: It's safe to trim the mold from hard foods, such as cheddar cheese. Cut off at least one inch around (and below) the mold spot. Be sure to keep the knife out of the mold so that it doesn't contaminate the rest of the food.

●**But some cheeses are supposed to be moldy. Can these cheeses grow harmful molds on them?**

Some molds taste delicious. The white coating on Brie cheese, for example, is a surface mold. Other cheeses, particularly the blue-veined varieties, such as Roquefort and Gorgonzola, are laced all the way through with mold. These cheeses are highly protected by their specific culture, and as long as they are refrigerated and sealed, they will keep without growing anything harmful for many months. But the cheese may develop a sharp, almost alcoholic, taste.

●**I have had honey in my cabinet for years. Why doesn't that get moldy?**

Foods such as honey that have a 50% or higher sugar content do not have enough water to grow most molds. Very salty foods, such as some preserved meats, also are unlikely to grow mold.

●**What's the best way to keep mold from growing on food?**

Many people think refrigeration is the best way to deter mold, but that's actually the opposite of what you should do in many cases. Instead, store fresh foods in the same environment that they were in when you bought them. If you bought berries from the refrigerator case at the supermarket, keep them in the refrigerator at home. If you bought tomatoes at room temperature, keep them on the counter.

Exposing foods to different temperatures—and changing levels of humidity—can encourage mold growth.

Also important: Buy whole, fresh produce whenever possible. The risk for mold is much higher in precut foods.

●**Is it true that one bad apple can spoil the bunch?**

When you buy produce by the box or in large bags, you often will find at least one moldy item, usually somewhere in the middle. If you don't get rid of it quickly, the mold will spread.

What to do: When you come home with a bulk container such as a bag of oranges, dump it out. Spread out the produce, and inspect each piece. Look for discolored or mushy areas. Throw out the bad ones.

Important: Berries are particularly susceptible to mold because they have a soft skin, plenty of moisture and contain sugar. Homegrown berries are less likely to get moldy than supermarket varieties because they're fresher. You might want to buy berries from a farmers' market—and buy only as much as you'll use in the next few days.

●**Sometimes I see mold on the door seal of my refrigerator. Could that spread to the food inside?**

Yes. Mold that grows inside the grooves of the refrigerator door seal could eventually migrate to the inside of the refrigerator. Wash the seal and the inside of the fridge with a mild bleach solution.

Also, wash the inside of crisper drawers if any moldy produce has been in them. (If gaskets on food-storage containers have mold, wash those, too.)

If food in your fridge seems to get moldy quickly, check the internal temperature of the refrigerator with a thermometer. The ideal temperature is between 35°F and 38°F.

If adjusting the temperature setting doesn't help, you might need to repair or replace your refrigerator. If the door seal has gone bad, or if the air inside isn't circulating the way that it's supposed to, you might notice that your refrigerator is "sweating." The increased moisture is ideal for mold growth.

Hidden Horror in Your Food

C. Leigh Broadhurst, PhD, a research geochemist in the USDA's Beltsville Agricultural Research Services, Beltsville, Maryland.

We humans aren't the only ones who relish lush, juicy summertime produce—mold, too, thrives happily on the sugar and moisture so readily available in ripe fruits and vegetables. It even can grow deep into these foods where you can't see it!

●**Citrus fruits.** When you get home from the market, do an immediate and thorough check of citrus fruits in bags and boxes—if you find one or two with even a bit of visible mold, there are likely to be more—return them all to the store or toss them all into the trash. Mold spreads easily and fast with these fruits, and eating citrus with mold can make you quite ill. Since it's sometimes hard to see, if a fruit tastes moldy when you bite into it, spit it out.

●**Soft fruits and vegetables.** This category includes peaches, nectarines, plums, grapes, melons, cucumbers, zucchini and the like, all of which are prone to announce mold by developing soft spots. For these, it's OK to cut small moldy spots away (meaning those that are less than a quarter of the total piece), taking one-half inch around the spot. To avoid cross-contamination, don't let the knife touch the mold. Larger soft areas, though, mean mold has invaded the whole fruit or vegetable even though you don't see it...throw the food away.

●**Firm vegetables.** Hard vegetables, like cabbage, cauliflower, carrots, peppers and others, have little moisture, making them less vulnerable to mold. It is fine to cut off any small patches of mold you see, in this case at least one inch around the mold.

●**Tomatoes.** Brown spots on the outside and dark seeds inside mean you should throw the entire tomato away.

●**Berries.** The ones with hollow centers (like raspberries) may grow mold from the inside out, so cut these in half and look before eating.

Block That Mold!

The safest produce, of course, is that which hasn't had a chance to grow mold.

●**Shop at local farmer's markets, where produce is more likely to be just picked.**

●**Wash produce only when you are ready to eat, cook or freeze it.** Fruits and vegetables naturally have protective microorganisms on their surfaces that are harmless—washing strips these off and opens the way for mold to settle in.

●**Use "freshness preserving" containers and/ or bags.** These are designed to release the ethylene gas produced as fruits and vegetables mature, which if allowed to accumulate increases the speed of ripening and thus spoilage.

●**Use the freezer, in particular for fresh berries you want to save.** Place the entire package (washed first) into a sealed plastic bag and put it in the freezer, then use the fruit as you need it. (It won't have the same consistency as fresh fruit, but it's delicious...nutritious, too.)

Also a good choice: Frozen berries from the supermarket—they do not mold and are good year-round.

6 Surprising Places Where Mold Lurks

Jeffrey C. May, a certified indoor air-quality professional (CIAQP) and founder and principal scientist of May Indoor Air Investigations, LLC, an air-quality-assessment company located in Tyngsborough, Massachusetts. He is also the author of several books, including *The Mold Survival Guide.* MayIndoorAir.com

We all know that mold thrives in obvious places such as damp basements, steamy bathrooms and storage areas with piles of old books and/or clothing. But there are plenty of other spots you'd never suspect that also can harbor these nasty fungal spores.

For the 10% to 15% of Americans who are allergic to mold, inhaling (or ingesting) the spores can trigger symptoms such as sneezing, runny nose, swollen eyelids, an itchy throat and wheezing.

Six surprising mold hot spots…

HOT SPOT #1: **Your coffeemaker.** In one study, mold was found in the water reservoirs of about half of the tested drip-type coffeemakers.

What to do: Once a month, fill your coffeemaker's reservoir with a 50/50 mixture of water and white vinegar. Turn the coffeemaker on, just as you would if you were brewing a pot of coffee. When the reservoir is half emptied, turn off the coffeemaker. Wait 30 minutes and then finish the brewing cycle. Rinse the machine by running plain, cool water through the cycle twice (or check manufacturer's instructions). When you finish your coffee each day, allow the reservoir to dry completely by leaving the lid open.

HOT SPOT #2: **Your washing machine.** Mold has no problem growing inside the rubber gaskets on the doors of front-loading machines. Those gaskets prevent water from pouring through the door, but water is often trapped inside the rubber folds. In all kinds of machines, detergent trays can stay damp between cycles, and the agitators of top-loading machines can be an area for mold growth, too.

What to do: Keep the door and detergent tray open when you're not using the washing machine. For front-loaders, wipe the inside of the gasket bottom with a rag or paper towel to dry it if no more loads will be done that day.

If you think you have mold, run an empty cycle with the machine on its hottest setting, using a mixture of one cup of baking soda, one cup of bleach and one-half cup of powdered dishwasher detergent. Some front-loading washers have a separate cycle for washing the inside of the machine. If a top-loading washer smells musty, the agitator may have to be removed and the shaft and agitator cleaned.

HOT SPOT #3: **Under your refrigerator.** Keep an eye on frost-free refrigerators and freezers.

Here's why: Your freezer section isn't actually frost-free. Frost is automatically melted during a heating cycle, and then the water accumulates in a pan at the bottom. The heat released from the condenser coils is supposed to speed up this evapora-tion, but often there is standing water in the pan. This water allows bacteria, yeast and mold to grow in the dust in the pan, and air movement can disperse these organisms into your kitchen.

What to do: Keep the condenser coils on your refrigerator clean by removing the grille at the bottom or back of the appliance and vacuuming the dust from the coils. A 25-inch Flexible Crevice Tool is available at Amazon.com for $11.99. Cleaning the coils once a year improves the efficiency of the refrigerator and can eliminate dust-containing pollen, mold spores and pet dander.

Cleaning the drip pan might not be as easy—with some refrigerator models, the pan is accessible only from the back of the fridge and/or may be attached to the condenser. Check the refrigerator manufacturer's instructions for proper cleaning of the condenser coils and drip pan.

HOT SPOT #4: **The underside of the toilet tank.** You probably don't look, but moisture often lingers here—and so does mold.

What to do: If it's easy enough, get on the floor (otherwise, use a mirror and flashlight) and take a look at the underside of each toilet tank in your home. If there's mold, mix one cup of bleach with one gallon of water, open a window or door for ventilation and scrub the moldy areas with gloved hands. Clean these areas with a nonabrasive bathroom cleanser once a month during times of high outdoor humidity.

Also helpful: Use a squeegee (found at home-supply stores) to remove moisture from the shower walls. A ceiling fan or oscillating fan that directs air at the shower walls will also help dry surfaces and reduce the threat of mold. Generally, small exhaust fans commonly used in bathrooms do not effectively remove moisture—but they do help, so if you have one, use it when showering and for about an hour afterward.

HOT SPOT #5: **Your Waterpik and toothbrush.** The water reservoir of your Waterpik or other water-jet appliance may not dry out between uses, and mold may grow on rubber gaskets and/or the water reservoir. Toothbrushes generally dry too fast for mold to grow, but it can grow inside the hollow heads of electric toothbrushes.

What to do: After each use of your Waterpik, remove the water reservoir, invert it and let it dry. To drain the pump, lower the sprayer in the sink so that it is below the level of the pump. Gravity will allow the water to drain. To clean electric toothbrush heads, soak in diluted bleach, 3% hydrogen peroxide or vinegar for a few minutes once a month.

HOT SPOT #6: **Your dehumidifier.** Dehumidifiers are designed to remove moisture and help prevent mold. But condensed water accumulates on cooling coils and can lead to mold growth in any dust trapped on the cooling-coil fins.

What to do: Empty the water basin at least weekly. During hot, humid weather, empty it daily. A few times a year, wash the plastic filter in a sink, scrub the inside of the bucket with nonabrasive cleanser (use diluted bleach if it is moldy) and spray any dust off the fins with water. Before storing the dehumidifier when it's not in use, wash and dry all of the parts carefully. Follow the manufacturer's instructions for cleaning the machine.

Nasty Germs Are Lurking in Your "Clean" Home: 7 Hot Spots Most People Miss

Lisa Yakas, MS, a microbiologist and senior certification project manager, food equipment, for NSF International (formerly National Sanitation Foundation), based in Ann Arbor, Michigan. The nonprofit group has a professional staff of engineers, microbiologists, toxicologists and other health experts who provide testing, certification and technical services, along with human health-risk assessments. NSF.org

A clean house feels great! But germs are wily and can thrive even in sparkling "clean" homes—particularly in areas that people don't realize are microbial hot spots. Research shows that about 12% of foodborne diseases in the US actually start in the home.

Shocking statistics: Coliform bacteria (a family of organisms that includes Salmonella and E. coli) were present in 81% of tested households...nearly one-third of the homes tested positive for yeast and molds...and more than 5% harbored Staph, a bacterium that can cause serious—sometimes antibiotic-resistant—diseases and infections, such as abscesses, pneumonia and food poisoning, according to the NSF International Household Germ Study. These germs can make anyone sick—especially people who are immunocompromised, young children and the elderly.

Where Germs Hide Out

Most people know that doorknobs are often teeming with germs, and the kitchen sink, even a shiny one, can harbor more bacteria than the average toilet seat.

Smart ideas: Use disinfectant wipes to clean high-touch areas, such as doorknobs and kitchen door handles. The kitchen sink should be washed and disinfected on the sides and bottom once or twice each week with a disinfecting cleanser.

Even worse: The kitchen sponge. It can harbor more than 321 million germs, so put wet sponges in the microwave for two minutes once a day, and replace them often—every two weeks or so.

But in every home, there are other areas that people simply don't think to disinfect. *Where you're vulnerable...**

•**Toothbrush holders.** You probably know to store toothbrushes upright to air-dry between uses—it helps prevent the growth of microorganisms that could cause oral or systemic infection. This is good advice, but it doesn't address the holders themselves.

What most people ignore is the significant amount of "drippage" from multihole toothbrush holders. This provides a perfect germ environment. We found that 64% were contaminated with yeast or molds...27% had coliform bacteria...and 14% tested positive for Staph.

What to do: Clean the holders at least once a week with warm, soapy water. (If you can't reach inside, fill the holder with soapy water and give a vigorous shake...rinse...and repeat until the water

---

*Use dishwashing liquid whenever soapy water is mentioned.

runs clean.) If the holder is dishwasher-safe, run it through a hot cycle.

Also: There are no regulations that brand-new toothbrushes must be sterile, so give yours an overnight soak in antimicrobial mouth rinse before the first use.

●**Can openers.** How often do you clean yours? Once a week? Never? Can openers are actually among the most germ-laden objects in the entire house. E. coli and/or Salmonella were found on can openers in 36% of the households we studied.

What to do: Wash the can opener every time you use it. If it's dishwasher safe, place it in the dishwasher after every use. If you are hand-washing it, wash the can opener in hot, soapy water and rinse thoroughly before air-drying. Be sure all food residue is removed from the area around cutting blades. Use an old toothbrush to scrub hard-to-reach crannies.

●**Refrigerator door seals.** Research we conducted has found that refrigerator door seals (along with refrigerator vegetable compartments) often are contaminated with Listeria, a bacterium that can cause serious illness such as sepsis or meningitis.

What to do: Run a damp, soapy cloth across the surface of the door seal and through the inner channel once a week. Pay particular attention to areas where crumbs or drippings are most likely to accumulate.

●**Blenders.** They're among the "dirtiest" items in the kitchen. Many people, inspired by the smoothie craze, use their blenders daily. To save time, they just give the blender a quick rinse. Not good enough.

The rubber gasket at the base of the pitcher is often contaminated with mold, yeast, E. coli and/or Salmonella. Washing the pitcher will clean only the outer edge of the gasket and won't touch the "sealed" part that can come in contact with the food.

What to do: You have to disassemble the blender to get it really clean. After every use, remove the screw-on bottom, the gasket and the top components. Clean each item separately in warm, soapy water, then let everything dry completely before putting it back together.

●**Pet bowls.** Not surprisingly, the food/water bowls used by your dogs and/or cats are often contaminated with Staph, E. coli and other germs.

What you may not realize: When you pick up your pet's bowl, bacteria from the rim/sides can be transferred to your hands—and from there to counters, kitchen knives, cutting boards, etc.

What to do: Pet bowls should be washed daily either in a sanitizing dishwasher (with the family's dishes if you like)...or scrubbed by hand in hot, soapy water, then rinsed. Once a week, soak pet bowls in a bleach rinse (one tablespoon of bleach per one gallon of water) for 10 minutes. Rinse well and allow to dry.

●**Remote controls.** In general, objects with hard, smooth, cool surfaces—remote controls, cell phones, computer keyboards, etc.—tend to harbor fewer germs than other objects/places in the home. But "fewer" doesn't mean "none." For example, in tests, 55% of remote controls were found to be contaminated with yeasts/molds, and 5% had coliform bacteria. Nearly one-quarter of cell phones had yeast and mold, and 5% had Staph or coliform bacteria.

What to do: Use a disinfectant wipe (or an alcohol cleaning pad) to wipe the surfaces and keys at least weekly. Be sure to check the manufacturer's cleaning instructions first.

●**Dirty laundry.** It's not surprising that germs love dirty laundry. Clothes that you've worn have skin cells, bodily secretions and plenty of moisture—all the things that germs need to survive. And the fecal material that's always present on used underwear is a common cause of infections.

What to do: Use the "hot" setting when washing underwear. The water should be 140°F to 150°F. If you're buying a new washer/dryer, look for one that's NSF certified. To earn certification, the machine must be able to reduce microbe populations by 99.9%.

Danger in Your Hair— Deadly Dyes, Straighteners, Sprays and More

Sonya Lunder, MPH, former senior analyst with the Environmental Working Group, a nonprofit environmental health research and advocacy organization in Washington, DC. The Environmental Working Group's Skin Deep website offers safety profiles for more than 80,000 cosmetics, hair-care products and related items. EWG.org/skindeep

Hair-care products generally are not required to pass government safety tests before being sold in stores or used in salons. Some contain ingredients known to be toxic or to trigger potentially severe allergic reactions. This can be true even of hair-care products labeled "natural" or "hypoallergenic" or that salons insist are perfectly safe.

Sonya Lunder, senior analyst with the Environmental Working Group, a nonprofit organization that provides safety ratings for thousands of hair-care products on its Skin Deep website (EWG.org/skindeep) shares her important warnings for men and women…

•Chemical hair straighteners usually contain formaldehyde, which can cause skin irritation, allergic reactions and even cancer. This is true even of the hair straighteners used at high-end salons.

Example: The makers of the popular hair straightener Brazilian Blowout claimed that this product did not contain formaldehyde, but tests revealed that it did.

Even if a hair straightener truly does not contain formaldehyde, it likely contains chemicals closely related to formaldehyde that have similar health effects…or chemicals that are not technically formaldehyde but that release formaldehyde when heated by a hair dryer. Some hair straighteners also contain lye and other highly caustic chemicals.

What to do: There is no chemical hair straightener that's safe enough to recommend. Chemical-free heat straightening—that is, straightening blown-dry hair with a flat iron—is safer but, of course, not long-lasting.

•"Gradual-change" hair dyes often contain lead acetate. Some men's hair dyes are designed to alter hair color slowly over a period of weeks to make the change less jarring. But gradual-change hair dyes often contain lead acetate, which is extremely toxic and can lead to serious health issues including cancer. These hair dyes actually can cause elevated lead levels throughout the homes of people who use them, triggering health issues for other family members, too.

Examples: Grecian Formula for Men and some Youthair hair dyes have been found to contain lead acetate.

What to do: Avoid hair dyes that list lead or lead acetate as an ingredient. Check the safety rating on the Skin Deep website of any hair dye that claims to change hair color gradually.

•Permanent dark hair dyes frequently contain coal-tar ingredients linked to cancer, such as aminophenols and/or pheylenediamines. (Other hair dyes sometimes contain potential carcinogens and allergens, too.) The European Union recently banned 181 hair-dye ingredients for health reasons, yet many of these remain in use in the US because the FDA does not have to approve the majority of products used in hair salons.

What to do: Consider using temporary or semi-permanent hair dyes rather than permanent dyes, particularly with dark-color dyes. These tend to be safer. If you use a permanent dark dye, do full dye jobs as infrequently as possible—just touch up your roots in between.

Wear plastic gloves when applying hair dyes to limit exposure to your skin. Before using any hair dye, enter its name into the Skin Deep site to find out about any potential health risks.

•Aerosol hair sprays often are inhaled, because aerosol cans typically distribute a mist of hair spray throughout the area around your head. Inhalation increases the risk for internal exposure and any associated health consequences. Even natural fragrances could trigger allergic reactions when inhaled.

What to do: Choose a hair spray that comes in a pump bottle rather than one that comes in an aerosol can. The spray from pump bottles tends to be less widely dispersed than that from aerosol cans, decreasing the odds of significant inhalation.

●**Shampoos and conditioners can cause allergies.** Shampoos and conditioners tend to be rinsed off relatively quickly, reducing exposure to any problematic ingredients relative to leave-on products. However, some people are allergic to the ingredients in these products, including the chemicals that add fragrance…preservatives and antibacterials that increase a shampoo's shelf life…and surfactants that, for example, work as an antistatic agent in conditioners.

What to do: If your scalp or neck gets itchy or red, look up your shampoo and conditioner on the Skin Deep site. If you discover that one or both contain ingredients known to cause allergic reactions, try a different shampoo or conditioner that doesn't contain these ingredients and see if the condition improves.

Your Cash Could Make You Sick

Philip M. Tierno, Jr., PhD, a microbiologist and director of clinical microbiology and diagnostic immunology at New York University Langone Medical Center, New York City. He is author of *The Secret Life of Germs*.

Your cold hard cash could give you a cold—or worse. Recent research conducted by New York University's Center for Genomics & System Biology identified roughly 3,000 types of bacteria on paper money, including germs that cause food poisoning, staph infections and pneumonia.

Touching a germy bill will not necessarily make you sick. Typically, a relatively large number of germs must enter the body to cause infection, and that usually does not occur when you handle money in normal ways—but there are exceptions.

Example: A single norovirus virion (the infectious form of a virus) can cause infection.

The health risks from germ-covered money increase greatly when money is handled by someone who also handles food, such as a sandwich-shop

How Often Should You Change Your Sheets?

Change your sheets and pillowcases at least once a week. Dust mites, lint, mold spores, pet dander and chemicals from cosmetics and lotions can accumulate on bed linens.

This can lead to allergic reactions such as coughing and sneezing even in people who don't normally have allergies. Washing and drying bed linens at hot temperatures gets rid of potential allergens.

Philip M. Tierno, Jr., PhD, director of clinical microbiology and immunology, New York University Langone Medical Center, and professor of microbiology and pathology, New York University School of Medicine, both in New York City. He is author of *The Secret Life of Germs: What They Are, Why We Need Them, and How We Can Protect Ourselves Against Them*.

worker or street-food vendor. This opens the door for germs to be transferred from money to the food we eat, allowing many more of the germs to enter the body.

Coins tend to harbor fewer germs than paper money because certain metals used in coins, including copper, nickel and zinc, naturally inhibit germ growth. Crisp, new bills tend to harbor fewer germs than old, worn ones because US paper money has antimicrobial properties that seem to diminish with time and usage.

What to do: Wash your hands or use a hand sanitizer as soon as possible after handling money. Choose a hand sanitizer with an alcohol percentage of 85% or higher—unlike most germs, the norovirus can survive 60% to 65% alcohol hand sanitizers.

iPad Radiation

David O. Carpenter, MD, director, Institute for Health and the Environment, University at Albany-SUNY, Rensselaer, New York.

I would like to buy an iPad or some other e-tablet to use when relaxing on the sofa. Should I be concerned about radiation?

Yes, but only if you hold it on your lap. No one has studied cancers of the abdomen from iPads or laptops. But an iPad is a wireless device, and there is some evidence, though not definitive, that holding a cell phone to your head may increase risk for brain cancer on the side of the head where it is used intensely for many years. But if the iPad or the cell phone is held away from your body, it will not give significant exposure. Holding an e-tablet on your lap will expose your pelvis, and research shows that men who wear cell phones on their belts in the "on" mode have lowered sperm counts and reduced bone density in the hip bone where the phone is placed. Until we have more information, it is best not to hold an e-tablet or a laptop on your lap for long periods.

Radiation from Your Washing Machine? Hair Dryer? These Secrets Will Help Keep You Safe

David O. Carpenter, MD, director of the Institute for Health and the Environment and a professor of environmental health and toxicology at the University at Albany, New York. He is a member of the editorial board of *Environmental Health Perspectives*, published by the National Institute of Environmental Health Sciences, and an editorial adviser for *Cellular and Molecular Neurobiology*.

You've probably heard about the scientific studies linking cell phones to a variety of tumors, including brain cancer. The World Health Organization has now classified cell phones as a "possible carcinogen."*

What's being largely overlooked: Electromagnetic radiation—from electrical appliances, such as hair dryers, microwave ovens and washing machines...as well as that from wireless signals for

*A team of 31 scientists from 14 countries analyzed peer-reviewed studies before classifying radiofrequency electromagnetic fields from wireless cell phones as "possibly carcinogenic to humans" based on an increased risk for glioma, a type of brain cancer.

Mold Can Grow in Your Washing Machine

Inhaling spores can cause respiratory distress and disease.

To prevent mold: Leave the machine's door open when not using it so that air can circulate. Find out if the manufacturer offers a product to stop mold or prevent it from forming.

David O. Carpenter, MD, is director of the Institute for Health and the Environment, University of Albany, SUNY, Rensselaer, New York.

computers—also may contribute to cancer risk independent of cell-phone use.

What you need to know...

Invisible Pollution

Every electrical appliance in your home emits electric and magnetic fields (EMFs) of energy. An appliance that is plugged in has an electric field even when it is turned off. The appliance produces a magnetic field when it is turned on and the electrical current is flowing. However, the EMFs from appliances are considered extremely low frequency (ELF), meaning that the radiation flows at very low levels.

Still, some studies show that regular exposure to even low levels of ELF electromagnetic radiation, such as 3 milligauss (mG), may increase the risk for leukemia in children—and possibly, to a lesser degree, in adults. Preliminary research has also linked this form of energy to Alzheimer's disease and Lou Gehrig's disease, but this association is still being debated.

Some experts maintain that the electromagnetic radiation from cell phones and electrical appliances is too weak to cause the types of cell damage that can lead to cancer. But evidence is emerging that even weak forms of energy may interfere with normal cell functions, perhaps contributing to the development of cancer and other diseases.

Safer Power

Appliances that use the most electrical current, such as handheld hair dryers, emit the highest levels of

ELF radiation. But even small appliances, such as coffeemakers, produce some.

Important: ELF fields are strongest at the point where the electrical wires enter the device. The fields diminish to almost nothing within a foot or two.

To test electromagnetic radiation around your appliances: Use a gauss meter—available online for about $90 to $500.

Important: ELF fields are directional—if you hold the meter to the right of a washing machine, for example, the reading might be zero, but it may be much higher a foot to the left. For accurate readings, test in different locations around the electrical appliance within a radius of a few feet.

Electrical wiring in the walls also can be an issue.

What I've found: In my son's bedroom, most of the wiring that carries electricity to lights and electrical outlets is in one of the walls. When we tested with a gauss meter, the EMFs were highest near his bed, so we moved his bed to the other side of the room.

In general, electrical wiring in walls generates high ELF only when the current is flowing or there is a ground current created by faulty wiring. However, the ELF exposure from wiring adds to the total exposure from appliances.

To reduce exposure…

•**Don't linger near appliances when they're running.** Even though the ELF levels are typically highest at the back of an appliance where the electrical cord plugs in, the magnetic field directly in front of a typical washing machine can reach 20 mG. You'll be exposed to only normal background levels by moving a foot or two away.

Important: Even the best microwave ovens leak some of the radiation they use to heat the food, so stand at least four feet away from the front of the oven when it's running. Microwave ovens also produce high levels of ELF electromagnetic radiation from the electricity used to power the oven, so there's a double risk.

•**Towel-dry your hair.** Hair dryers are among the most dangerous sources of magnetic fields because they use a lot of power and the motor/heater is held close to the head. Although using a low-fan

and/or low-heat setting helps some, it's better to avoid hair dryers altogether.

If towel-drying is not convenient, consider using a low-EMF hair dryer such as the Chi Pro Low EMF Hair Dryer available for about $117 at Chi.com.

•**Use the electric blanket before you get into bed.** Electric blankets don't draw a lot of electrical current, but they expose your entire body to ELF radiation for the entire night if you leave them on. If you want a warm bed, turn on the blanket half an hour before bedtime, then turn it off when you get into bed.

•**Get a new bedside clock.** Old-style alarm clocks—analog clocks with lighted dials—produce surprisingly high levels of electromagnetic radiation.

My advice: Get a digital bedside clock, which emits almost no ELF.

•**Throw out your cordless phones.** Cordless phones emit electromagnetic radiation whether or not they are being used. If you still own a landline, I recommend replacing cordless phones with corded phones.

Safer Computer Use

Most computers give off electromagnetic radiation. If you use a desktop model, position it toward the back of your desk. Most monitors, which produce lower levels of electromagnetic radiation than computers, have conductive screens to block the ELF exposure. But it's still wise to position your monitor as far away from you as possible.

What I've found: I once measured the fields near my secretary's desk. The reading was about 10 mG, which is extremely high. I realized that the high-powered electrical wiring used by the computer was behind the wall closest to her. We had to move her desk 10 feet to get out of range.

Also, virtually every modern computer (including laptops) is designed to receive wireless signals. If you have a wireless router, which connects to a cable and wirelessly "routes" this connection to one or more computers in your home, your exposure to electromagnetic radiation is constant.

To be safer…

• **Turn off the router when it's not in use.** If you do use a router, turn it on only when you need the signal for using the Internet, streaming video to the TV, etc.

• **Disable Wi-Fi settings on your computer if you don't use a router.** Otherwise, the computer—or any device that operates wirelessly, such as some printers—will constantly emit electromagnetic radiation as it tries to find the nearest wireless source. Shut down your computer when it's not in use to reduce ELF radiation in your home.

Hidden Poisons in Your Clothes…and in Your Mattress, Mouthwash, More

Myron W. Wentz, PhD, a microbiologist based in Salt Lake City, who founded Gull Laboratories and developed the first commercially available diagnostic test for the Epstein-Barr virus. He is coauthor of *The Healthy Home: Simple Truths to Protect Your Family from Hidden Household Dangers.* His website is MyHealthyHome.com.

Dangerous chemicals are all around us—even in everyday items that we think of as safe. Some of the most common dangers—and what to do…

Wrinkle-Free Fabrics

Perfluorochemicals (PFCs) are added to fabrics for durability, stain resistance and wrinkle resistance. Clothing labeled "no iron," "permanent press" and "wrinkle-free" often contain PFCs. PFCs are extremely long-lasting in the body because they cannot be broken down and eliminated. They accumulate in the body's cells and have been linked to reproductive and developmental toxicity, as well as cancers of the liver and bladder.

The chemicals in clothing may be absorbed through the skin or inhaled when they outgas from the fabrics. Numerous cycles through the washer may release some, but not all, of the PFC coating from the fabrics.

In addition, synthetic fibers, including polyester and nylon, may contain substances such as polyvinyl chloride, a known carcinogen, and phthalates, a group of chemicals that disrupts hormones.

What to use instead: Clothes made from 100% natural fibers, such as cotton, linen, wool and cashmere and that are not labeled "wrinkle-free," "stain resistant," "static resistant," etc.

Dry Cleaning

A chemical cleaning solution, usually perchloroethylene (perc), is used to saturate clothing and remove dirt and stains. Unfortunately, plenty of the solution remains in clothing fibers after the cleaning is done.

Exposure to perc has been linked to kidney and liver damage. It causes cancer in laboratory animals. Even short-term exposure can result in dizziness, headaches and a rapid heart rate. One study that looked at air samples found elevated levels of perc for up to 48 hours after dry-cleaned fabrics were brought into the home.

California and other states have mandated that dry cleaners stop using perc by the year 2023. *In the meantime, you can…*

• **Air it out.** Remove the plastic from dry-cleaned fabrics and hang them outdoors or in a garage or other well-ventilated area for one to two days. If they still have a chemical smell, air them out for another day or two.

• **Use a barrier layer.** Wear a T-shirt or tank top underneath a jacket or other clothing that has been dry-cleaned.

• **Find a "green" dry cleaner.** Look for one that uses liquid carbon dioxide. To find a green cleaner, go to GreenCleanersCouncil.com.

Mattresses

Most innerspring and foam mattresses are made with polyurethane, a product so flammable that it is known as "solid gasoline." To counteract that, manufacturers are required to add chemicals with flame-retardant properties. Before 2005, these included highly toxic polybrominated diphenyl ethers. Since then, to combat flammability, manufacturers have added the dangerous heavy metal antimony…and brominated fire retardants, which can disrupt hormone activity and may interfere with normal brain functions.

If you're sleeping on a mattress made prior to 2005, consider replacing it. A good choice is an organic mattress. These usually use natural latex (from rubber trees) and/or naturally flame-resistant wool.

If you do buy a synthetic mattress, remove it from the packaging and let it outgas in the garage or outdoors for several days before sleeping on it.

Also helpful: A natural latex mattress topper or an organic cotton or wool mattress protector can provide a barrier between you and the flame-retardant materials.

Light at Night

Most people don't think of light as a "toxin," but when it comes at the wrong time, it can have toxic effects. Humans evolved to be exposed to light during the day, not at night, but since the invention of electric lights, we rarely experience a completely dark night.

The risk: Even a blink of light at night signals the body's pineal gland to curtail the production of melatonin, frequently known as the "hormone of darkness." Low levels of melatonin can reduce immunity…increase the oxidation that can lead to degenerative diseases such as heart disease…and impair our natural sleep-wake cycles.

●**Keep your bedroom dark.** Make sure that drapes and blinds fit snugly to block out all external light at night.

●**Opt for red light.** Use electronic devices, including night-lights, that are illuminated with red light. Melatonin appears to be more sensitive to blue lights, such as those commonly used on alarm clocks, DVD players, etc.

Mouthwashes and Antiperspirants

Antiperspirants contain aluminum compounds, which in high doses can increase the risk for cancer and neurological conditions such as Parkinson's and Alzheimer's diseases.

Most mouthwashes contain the germ killers phenol, cresol and ethanol that are used in bathroom disinfectants, though in lower concentrations.

These ingredients and others such as formaldehyde can be harmful when absorbed by soft tissue and/or swallowed. *Instead…*

●**Freshen your breath by using a tongue scraper** (available at drugstores) rather than a chemical-filled mouthwash…brush your teeth with baking soda.

●**Avoid using antiperspirants,** especially during the cooler months or on weekends when it may not matter so much if you sweat a little. Deodorant (without an antiperspirant) is an option for people concerned about odor.

Dryer Sheets, Detergents and Fabric Softeners

If a product smells "clean," it's probably bad for your health. The National Academy of Sciences reports that up to 95% of the substances used to make fragrances in detergents, dryer sheets and fabric softeners are petroleum-based synthetic chemicals that can trigger asthma, damage the lungs and nervous system and cause cancer.

Luckily, your laundry is one everyday part of life in which you can easily eliminate unnecessary chemicals…

●**Opt for nontoxic natural detergents.** These are readily available in many supermarkets. Good brands include Seventh Generation, Method and Nellie's.

Ask yourself if you really need dryer sheets or fabric softeners. If you feel that you must use such products, you can find reusable cloth dryer sheets online. These dryer sheets are not coated with chemicals, unlike disposable dryer sheets, and they contain carbon fiber that helps eliminate static electricity in the dryer.

Or you can try one-half cup of white vinegar in place of fabric softener in the washer to reduce static cling and soften clothing.

Warning: Never combine vinegar and bleach in the same load—toxic fumes could result.

Toss Those Products with Dyes

Jamison Starbuck, ND, is a naturopathic physician in family practice and a guest lecturer at the University of Montana, both in Missoula. She is past president of the American Association of Naturopathic Physicians and a contributing editor to *The Alternative Advisor: The Complete Guide to Natural Therapies and Alternative Treatments.*

Peek inside the typical American's medicine cabinet, and you're likely to see a virtual rainbow of brightly colored products that contain potentially harmful dyes. Among the most popular are intensely colored cold and flu formulas and cough syrups.

Scientists have long suspected that dyes can be dangerous for human consumption. In the early 20th century, metals used for coloring, such as arsenic, lead and mercury, were banned from use in foods and medicines. Coal-tar derivatives then became the new dye source—bright, almost fluorescent colors with numbers for names—Blue 1 and 2...Yellow 5 and 6...Red 3 and 40. Over the years, some coal-tar dyes (but not all) have been banned due to health concerns. Now, scientists have become increasingly concerned about research linking food dyes to allergies and attention deficit hyperactivity disorder. In animal studies, dyes have been linked to tumors. Some manufacturers now produce dye-free products. Interestingly, however, the European Union requires warning labels on products that contain many dyes that the US Food and Drug Administration (FDA) still allows. Armed with the right information, you can be smarter than the FDA by stocking your home medicine chest with dye-free natural remedies for the following conditions...*

- **Cold and flu.**

What to skip: Theraflu, which contains such dyes as Blue 1 and Red 40.

*Check with your doctor before trying these remedies—especially if you take any medication or have a chronic medical condition.

Better choices: Botanical antivirals (in tincture or capsule form), such as echinacea, Oregon graperoot, osha and elderberry.

- **Cough.**

What to skip: Delsym, which contains Yellow 6 or other dyes.

Better choices: Effective herbs for cough include ivy leaf, wild cherry bark, olive leaf and elecampane—all of which are available in syrups made with honey or stevia.

- **Gas and indigestion.**

What to skip: Pepto Bismol, which contains Red 22 and Red 28.

Better choice: Gas, bloating and acute diarrhea respond well to activated charcoal, which binds toxins from the gastrointestinal tract. It's inert and will pass through the gastrointestinal tract without being absorbed into the blood. Activated charcoal can be found in drugstores. Follow label instructions.

- **Sleep.**

What to skip: NyQuil PM, which contains Green 3, Blue 1 and other dyes.

Better choices: For occasional insomnia, take 50 mg of 5-HTP, an amino acid that plays a role in the production of sleep-promoting serotonin, at bedtime. (Do not try this remedy if you take an antidepressant.) When you use 5-HTP, it also helps to take Rescue Remedy, a Bach flower remedy that relaxes the nervous system.

What to do: Add two drops of Rescue Remedy to the water you use to take the supplement, and keep some of this water next to your bed to sip on if you awaken during the night.

Caution: To make their products appear more visually appealing, some manufacturers have begun adding dyes to herbal medicines. If a packaged natural product is overly bright—check labels on all medicines, and avoid dyes whenever you can.

Is Your Drinking Water Safe?

Robert D. Morris, MD, PhD, physician, environmental epidemiologist, researcher in the field of drinking water and health, scientific director of Eco Logic Consulting and author of *The Blue Death: The Intriguing Past and Present Danger of the Water You Drink.* MorrisEcologic.com

Each year, millions of Americans suffer the effects of illnesses related to contaminated drinking water. Here's how to keep yourself from becoming one of them.

Contaminated drinking water is a public health risk, and lead is just one threat. Drinking water can be contaminated with microbes, minerals, metals, radon, chemicals from treated sewage, industrial chemicals, and agricultural chemicals including nitrates, atrazine and other pesticides. But ironically, the most common contaminants are by-products of adding chlorine to disinfect water. According to the CDC, there are at least 600 "disinfection by-products," including chloroform and bromodichloromethane, both possible carcinogens.

So why are we still using chlorine in our drinking water? Chlorine is the most common method used in the US to disinfect water for a number of reasons. It has been in use for a long time…it's good at killing most pathogens in water…and if you add enough chlorine for there to be residual chlorine in the water, it continues to work as the water flows through pipes. But here's the problem—that chlorine also continues to form those by-products.

There are alternatives for treating water including ozone, ultraviolet light and membrane filtration, but none of those methods allows for residual treatment, and each alternative has its own challenges. So at least for the time being, chlorine is still considered the best option for large-scale water disinfection.

Safety Concerns Beyond Chlorine

Many of the problems in our drinking water originate from fundamental problems that are complicated and expensive to address…

•**Aging infrastructure.** Water pipes in many areas of the US are 50 to 100 years old—sometimes even older—corroded and filled with bacteria. They contain lead, too (see below). Treatment plants may be just as old, and most rely on technologies from the early 1900s.

•**Regional issues.** Your drinking water is affected by many variables, from the source of the water to how it's treated and distributed where you live, all of which will determine what contaminants are most likely to be found in your local supply.

•**Chemical contaminants that aren't regulated.** Water utilities and the Environmental Protection Agency (EPA) are tasked with addressing the issues that affect drinking water, but regulating chemicals is a very complicated process. The way regulation works is that the EPA doesn't list what can be in drinking water—it has to say what specifically cannot. The problem is that the list of chemicals that it would be better not to have in drinking water is potentially in the many thousands. Deciding what actually gets on the EPA list takes a lot of time and money, so most chemicals will not be added, at least not anytime soon.

•**Volume of water that must be treated.** The EPA states that all the water going into your house must meet the health standard for drinking water even though 99% of that water goes for other uses such as bathing, washing your car, flushing down the toilet and doing laundry. The sheer volume of water that has to be treated makes it too expensive to meet a higher standard of quality for our drinking water.

•**Lead pipes.** The recent problem of widespread lead contamination that occurred in Flint, Michigan, is not limited to Flint. Houses built before 1986 (the year the EPA banned lead pipes and fixtures made with lead) may still have lead pipes, brass fixtures that contain lead and lead solder. Because the EPA can't force people in older homes with lead pipes to change them, it tries to control how corrosive our drinking water is—the more corrosive, the more it causes lead from pipes to leach into water. A change in the Flint water supply caused a significant change in the corrosiveness of the water—lead that had been slowly leaching into the water suddenly started leaching quickly, leading to lead exposure for many people, including children. This can happen in any area that has older homes and, even if you don't have a lead pipe to your water main, the pipes and fixtures may still contain lead.

•**Climate change.** Climate change leads to more droughts and more extreme "water events" such as floods and torrential hurricanes, all of which have significant effects on water quality that can be short-lived or long-lived. This will likely only get worse over time.

What to Do for Safer Drinking Water

Most water utilities have some violations of the safety standards during the course of a year, so the number-one recommendation is to add a point-of-use filter to the faucet that provides your water for drinking—for most people, this means at their kitchen sink. A filter gives you that next level of quality that everyone should have in drinking water. Also, keep in mind that water is regulated as it's coming out of a treatment plant…it then gets sent through potentially miles of pipes before it reaches your faucet.

If you have lead pipes, replacing them could mean ripping up a lot of your house. Most people can't afford to do that unless it's part of a major home renovation that's being done anyway. A properly selected filter can remove most if not all of the lead that leaches into your water from pipes.

There are two general types of filters…

•**A cartridge filter is usually "activated carbon"**—the carbon, or charcoal, in the filter attracts and captures impurities as water passes through it—that your water filters through. It significantly reduces most contaminants including, for selected filters, lead.

•**A reverse osmosis filter is a membrane that takes virtually everything out.** It is more expensive than a cartridge filter—from over $100 for a single-sink system to over $1,000 for a whole house system plus $100 to $200 a year for replacement filters, and you may need a plumber to install it. However, if you're a woman who's pregnant or could become pregnant or have young children in the house, it's worth investing in this kind of filter because contaminants have a much greater effect on developing embryos and small children.

One more step before buying a filter: Read the water report your water company sends out every year and look specifically for any violations it had. Choose a filter that lists that contaminant among all the ones it filters out (this information will be listed on the box).

You might be wondering whether, with all these possible contaminants in your drinking water, you should just buy flats of bottled water or a dispenser that uses large, multiple-gallon jugs. The same regulations that apply to water utilities apply to bottled water manufacturers. Most of these manufacturers either find a very pure source or use reverse osmosis filtration to purify the water, so it does tend to be more pure than tap water. However, it is an expensive alternative to a filter and it has a significant environmental impact related to all the plastic used for the bottles and jugs and the inefficient transport of heavy bottles of water by trucks.

Do You Need to Test Your Water?

If you get your water from a large municipality, the water utility is testing it constantly. Unless you'd be testing it for something specific, it's hard to know where to begin since there are thousands of possible contaminants. Also, you would be testing just one sample at one particular point in time, so it is unlikely you would find anything at that moment. However, if you know of a problem in your area regarding a specific contaminant (remember, that's why you're reading through those annual water reports), you could test your water for that.

If you get your water from a small municipality, you have even more reason to check your utility's water reports for violations and install a point-of-use filter in your home. A February 2018 study published in *Proceedings of the National Academy of Sciences* found that water utilities in smaller, more rural and lower-income communities had more violations than utilities in larger, more urban areas with more money. Consider testing your water on your own, especially if there's been an outbreak to see if it was resolved.

If you have a private well, your water likely won't be tested nearly as frequently as with any municipal system. Testing varies by community

Turn Up Your Thermostat

For every one-degree decrease in indoor temperature reading, there was a 0.48 point rise in systolic (top number) blood pressure readings and a 0.45 point rise in diastolic (bottom number). This study, based on nearly 5,000 people in their homes, may help explain the spike in hypertension rates in the winter.

To help prevent winter increases in blood pressure: Keep the inside of your home at a minimum temperature of 69.8°F, particularly if you have hypertension or a family history of heart disease.

Stephen Jivraj, PhD, associate professor in quantitative science, epidemiology and public health, University College London, UK.

and in some areas it is never done by the government, making it your responsibility to check for yourself. Contact the local agency responsible for the safety of private wells in your area (possibly the state department of natural resources or the health department) and ask whether they're aware of any contaminants being found in local wells and what they are. If there are any farms or big industries around you that result in coliform bacteria, nitrates or other chemicals contaminating the ground water, he recommends hiring a company to test your well water for you. Ask your local agency for a recommendation of a water testing company, when to test, and how often to test.

One more thing…to ensure safe drinking water, elect public officials who you know understand the importance of protecting our water supplies.

Clean Swimming Pool?

Jonathan Vapnek, MD, associate clinical professor of urology, Icahn School of Medicine at Mount Sinai Hospital, New York City.

Can urinating in a pool cause health problems for other swimmers?

Probably not, as disgusting as that may sound. Healthy urine does not contain bacteria or anything else that could make someone sick. The water will dilute the urine, and chlorine removes most germs. Surprisingly, one in five adults admitted in a survey to urinating in swimming pools, so chances are your son isn't the only one secretly doing this.

A bigger problem is fecal contamination, which can lead to diarrhea, respiratory illness and skin, ear and eye infections if someone swallows or comes into contact with even a tiny amount of pool water. Anyone who has had diarrhea in the past two weeks should avoid swimming pools, according to the Centers for Disease Control and Prevention. Tiny amounts of fecal matter contain germs such as *Cryptosporidium* that could take days for chlorine to kill.

To avoid spreading germs, make sure everyone showers before using the pool.

Do This When You Clean Your Aquarium

University of California, Berkeley Wellness Letter.

Wear rubber gloves when cleaning an aquarium. The nonchlorinated water in a fish tank can harbor bacteria that cause the skin infection fish tank granuloma. Symptoms include a reddish tender lump or a string of lumps under the skin on the exposed body area, fever and swollen lymph nodes. Symptoms don't appear for about two to four weeks or longer after exposure, so people often don't realize the source of the infection. People who have compromised immune systems or are in poor health are more prone to the infection. Once identified, it can be treated with antibiotics.

Paint Strippers Can Kill You in Minutes

Katy Wolf, PhD, former director of the Institute for Research and Technical Assistance, a nonprofit organization that identifies safer alternatives for industrial and consumer solvents and other products, Los Angeles. IRTA.us

A 21-year-old Tennessee man died in 2017 while refinishing a tub in an unventilated bathroom. Fumes from methylene chloride, a chemical in the paint stripper he was using, caused carbon monoxide to build up in his blood, and within minutes his heart stopped beating.

Most paint strippers sold in hardware stores and home centers contain methylene chloride, yet few people who use these products understand the danger. These products are known to be responsible for at least 56 accidental-exposure deaths in the US since 1980, and the true death toll is no doubt higher—some methylene chloride fatalities are likely recorded as heart attacks, with no one realizing that this chemical is to blame.

Methylene chloride also is known to cause cancer, though that's a risk mainly for people who have prolonged exposure to it because they use paint strippers in their professions, not for consumers who use them only occasionally.

What to do: Choose a benzyl alcohol–based paint stripper rather than one that contains methylene chloride. It's safer and does a good job stripping paint, though it does not work as quickly as methylene chloride.

If you do use a methylene chloride paint stripper, do so outdoors or in a large, well-ventilated area, never in a small and/or enclosed space. Do not use methylene chloride to strip the inside of bathtubs, storage tanks or similar objects even if they are not fully enclosed—its fumes are heavier than air, so they can quickly build up to lethal levels inside these, even outdoors.

CHAPTER 10

Home Remedies and Cures from Your Kitchen

These 4 "Super Spices" Have Hidden Benefits

Joshua Levitt, ND, a naturopathic physician and medical director at Whole Health Natural Family Medicine in Hamden, Connecticut. Dr. Levitt is a clinical preceptor for Yale School of Medicine and collaborates with the Integrative Medicine Center at Yale New Haven Hospital. He is author of *The Honey Phenomenon* and numerous other books and articles. WholeHealthCT.com

When it comes to "superfoods," fruits and veggies aren't the only heavy hitters. A handful of popular spices also have gained a rightful place on this list because of their own research-supported therapeutic effects.

Examples of the best known: Cinnamon for diabetes. Garlic for high cholesterol. Ginger for nausea. Cayenne for pain relief.

What you may not realize: Those same spices have even more benefits—little-known but powerful—that are also backed by scientific evidence. *How to use these spices for even greater preventive and curative effect…*

Cinnamon

A small daily dose of cinnamon has been proven in many studies to lower and help regulate blood sugar—crucial for those trying to prevent or manage type 2 diabetes.

Little-known benefit: Cinnamon also can lower high blood pressure.

Scientific evidence: In a recent study published in *Lipids in Health and Disease*, people who ingested 3 g (about two-thirds of a teaspoon) of cinnamon daily had a significant drop in blood pressure after four months—from averages of 136/88 to 122/80.

How to get more: Because cinnamon is so tasty, it's easy to include more in your diet. As a heavy cinnamon user, I buy organic Ceylon cinnamon (the highest quality) by the pound.

Note: Supermarket cinnamon is usually cassia (or Vietnamese), which contains a compound called coumarin that may damage the liver at high doses in susceptible individuals.

Cinnamon is great on roasted sweet potatoes and squash and adds delightful sweetness to pancakes and waffles. Plus, because it's such a powerful antioxidant, a sprinkle of cinnamon stops apple slices from turning brown—making the treat more delicious and more appetizing.

Ginger

Dozens of studies have proven ginger's usefulness in easing nausea and vomiting due to everything from chemotherapy to motion sickness to morning sickness.

Little-known benefit: Ginger also inhibits the COX-1 and COX-2 enzymes that play a role in the production of inflammation-causing compounds in the body. This means it works the same way as pain-relieving drugs such as *ibuprofen* (Motrin) and aspirin.

Scientific evidence: A study published in *Phytotherapy Research* found that ginger supplements are comparable to aspirin, ibuprofen, *naproxen* (Aleve) and other over-the-counter painkillers in easing muscle pain caused by exercise and other types of strenuous activity.

Research also has shown that ginger is just as effective as the migraine drug *sumatriptan* (Imitrex).

How to get more: For a therapeutic, pain-relieving dose of ginger, take a 1,000-mg supplement, twice daily. For migraine, I recommend up to 1,000 mg at the onset of a migraine. If you want to use ginger to help prevent migraine, add fresh ginger to your daily diet or take a ginger supplement (250 mg to 500 mg daily).*

In the kitchen, add fresh ginger—finely diced or crushed—to sauces and marinades. Used three or more times a week, ginger in doses commonly consumed in the diet can have a mild pain-relieving and anti-inflammatory effect. Ginger is also great in smoothies.

Cayenne

Cayenne is a powder made from dried, red chili peppers, and it's very hot when used to spice food. But the natural intensity of cayenne and its active ingredient capsaicin affect more than your taste buds.

It's the only natural compound that—when applied topically—can degrade substance P, a neurotransmitter that tells the brain to transmit pain signals. With less substance P, there's less pain—which is why capsaicin is a common ingredient in many creams, ointments and salves for pain problems such as arthritis, nerve pain, foot pain and back pain.

Little-known benefit: Cayenne can also help you lose weight. Capsaicin and other compounds in cayenne work because they have several effects that help you shed pounds—they suppress appetite...increase calorie-burning ("basal metabolic rate")...and burn up ("oxidize") body fat.

*If you take blood thinners such as *warfarin* (Coumadin) or if you have gallstone disease, talk to your doctor before using ginger supplements.

In a recent meta-analysis of nine studies on capsaicin and weight loss, published in *Critical Reviews in Food Science and Nutrition*, researchers concluded that the spice "could be a new therapeutic approach in obesity."

How to get more: For patients who want to lose weight, I usually recommend adding cayenne to the diet or using low-dose (2 mg) capsaicin supplements daily. (High-dose supplements can irritate the gastrointestinal tract.)

As a weight-loss aid, I recommend drinking one or more cups a day of warm water with a pinch of cayenne, juice from half a lemon, a teaspoon of honey and ground ginger (using a chunk of fresh ginger the size of half your thumb, from knuckle to tip). Cayenne is also excellent in marinades for fish and poultry and sprinkled on eggs. Plus, it adds a kick to salad dressings.

Baking Soda Is Good Medicine

ScienceDaily.com

Baking soda can work as a handy remedy for a number of minor conditions. It reduces the stinging and itching of insect bites and other skin irritations...relieves heartburn and indigestion... and even may reduce whole-body inflammation, which has been linked to numerous autoimmune diseases, including rheumatoid arthritis. In a recent study, people who drank baking soda in water daily for two weeks had higher levels of inflammation-fighting cells called macrophages than people who did not drink the mixture. Further research is needed—but anyone who wants to try out the baking-soda drink can do so by just adding one-quarter to one-half teaspoon of baking soda to a glass of water and drinking the mixture once or twice a day. (*Note*: Baking soda can slow the absorption of medications, according to Bottom Line's medical expert Andrew Rubman, ND, so it is best taken about an hour before any medication.)

Foods That Fight Pain— Some Work Even Better Than Drugs

David Grotto, RD, founder and president of Nutrition Housecall, LLC, a consulting firm based in Chicago that provides nutrition communications, lecturing and consulting services as well as personalized, at-home dietary services. He is author of *The Best Things You Can Eat: For Everything from Aches to Zzzz.* DavidGrotto.wordpress.com

Many of us turn to medications to relieve pain. But research has shown that you can help reduce specific types of pain—and avoid the side effects of drugs—just by choosing the right foods. Here, the common causes of pain and the foods that can help. *Unless otherwise noted, aim to eat the recommended foods daily…*

Osteoarthritis

Osteoarthritis causes pain and inflammation in the joints.

Best foods: Bing cherries, ginger, avocado oil and soybean oil.

A study in *The Journal of Nutrition* found that men and women who supplemented their diets with Bing cherries (about two cups of cherries throughout the day) had an 18% to 25% drop in C-reactive protein, a sign of inflammation. Bing cherries contain flavonoids, plant-based compounds with antioxidant properties that lower inflammation.

Ginger also contains potent anti-inflammatory agents that can reduce joint pain. A double-blind, placebo-controlled study found that 63% of people who consumed ginger daily had less knee pain when walking or standing. I recommend one to two teaspoons of ground fresh ginger every day.

Avocado oil and soybean oil contain avocado soybean unsaponifiables (ASUs), which reduce inflammation and cartilage damage in arthritis patients.

Rheumatoid Arthritis

This autoimmune disease causes systemic inflammation—your joints, your heart and even your lungs may be affected.

Best foods: Fish and vitamin C–rich foods.

The omega-3 fatty acids in fish increase the body's production of inhibitory prostaglandins, substances with anti-inflammatory effects. A recent study found that some patients who consumed fish oil supplements improved so much that they were able to discontinue their use of aspirin, ibuprofen and similar medications.

Ideally, it's best to eat two to three servings of fish a week. Or take a daily fish oil supplement. The usual dose is 1,000 milligrams (mg) to 3,000 mg. Be sure to work with a qualified health professional to determine what supplement regimen is right for you.

Foods rich in vitamin C (citrus fruits, berries, red bell peppers) are effective analgesics because they help decrease joint inflammation. These foods also help protect and repair joint cartilage. A study in *American Journal of Nutrition* found that patients who ate the most vitamin C–rich fruits had 25% lower risk for inflammation.

Gout

Gout is a form of arthritis that causes severe joint pain that can last for days—and that "flares" at unpredictable intervals.

Weight loss—and avoiding refined carbohydrates, such as white bread, commercially prepared baked goods and other processed foods—can help minimize flare-ups. You also should eat foods that reduce uric acid, a metabolic by-product that causes gout.

Best foods: Celery and cherries.

Celery contains the chemical compound 3-n-butylphthalide, which reduces the body's production of uric acid. Celery also reduces inflammation.

Both sweet (Bing) and tart (Montmorency) pie cherries contain flavonoids, although the bulk of science supporting the anti-inflammatory and pain-relieving properties of cherries has been done using tart cherries. (An exception is the study that found that Bing cherries relieve osteoarthritis.) It is hard to find fresh tart cherries, so I recommend dried tart cherries or tart cherry juice.

Migraines

These debilitating headaches are believed to be caused by the contraction and dilation of blood vessels in the brain.

157

Best foods: Oats, coffee and tea.

Oats are high in magnesium, a mineral that helps reduce painful muscle spasms—including those in the muscles that line the arteries. In one study, researchers found that people who took 600 mg of magnesium daily had a 41.6% reduction in the number of migraines over a 12-week period, compared with only a 15.8% reduction in those who took a placebo.

You can get plenty of magnesium by eating high-magnesium foods. A small bowl of cooked oat bran (about one cup), for example, provides more than 20% of the daily value. Other high-magnesium foods include oatmeal, almonds, broccoli and pumpkin seeds.

The caffeine in coffee and tea helps relieve migraine pain. The antioxidants in both beverages also are helpful.

Caution: Consuming too much caffeine—or abruptly giving it up if you are a regular coffee or tea drinker—can increase the frequency and severity of headaches. Limit yourself to a few cups daily.

Muscle Pain

It usually is caused by tension, overuse or an actual injury, such as a strain or sprain. Because tendons and ligaments (the tissues that attach your muscles to your bones) have little circulation, muscle-related pain can be very slow to heal.

Best foods: Tart cherries and rose hip tea.

Eating as few as 20 dried tart cherries can help reduce pain. So can tart cherry juice.

Example: At the Sports and Exercise Science Research Centre at London South Bank University, researchers gave one-ounce servings of tart cherry juice twice daily to athletes who did intense workouts. These athletes regained more of their muscle function more quickly than those who didn't drink the juice. Studies also have shown that the juice can reduce muscle pain after exercise.

Rose hip tea is high in vitamin C, as well as anthcyanins and a substance called galactolipid—all of which have been shown to combat inflammation and may help ease muscle and joint pain. Have several cups daily.

Nerve Pain

Inflammation or injury to a nerve can cause a burning, stabbing pain that is difficult to control with medications. Examples of conditions that cause nerve pain include sciatica (pain along the sciatic nerve from the lower spine down the back of the leg) and neuropathy (nerve damage), a painful complication of diabetes.

Best foods: Turmeric, figs and beans.

Turmeric, a yellow-orange spice that commonly is used in Indian and Asian cooking, is a very effective analgesic. Like ginger, it is an anti-inflammatory that has been shown to reduce pain about as well as ibuprofen—and with none of the side effects.

Both figs and beans—along with whole grains and green leafy vegetables—are rich in B-complex vitamins, which are essential for nerve health. One study, which looked at a form of vitamin B-1, found that patients who took as little as 25 mg four times daily had an improvement in neuropathy. Other B vitamins may have similar effects.

5 Foods That Fight High Blood Pressure

Janet Bond Brill, PhD, RD, a nationally recognized nutrition, health and fitness expert who specializes in cardiovascular disease prevention. She has authored several books on the topic, including *Blood Pressure DOWN, Prevent a Second Heart Attack* and *Cholesterol DOWN*. DrJanet.com

Is your blood pressure on the high side? Your doctor might write a prescription when it creeps above 140/90—but you may be able to forgo medication. Lifestyle changes still are considered the best starting treatment for mild hypertension. These include not smoking, regular exercise and a healthy diet. *In addition to eating less salt, you want to include potent pressure-lowering foods, including…*

Raisins

Raisins are basically dehydrated grapes, but they provide a much more concentrated dose of nutrients and fiber. They are high in potassium, with 220 milligrams (mg) in a small box (1.5 ounces). Potassium helps counteract the blood pressure–raising effects of salt. The more potassium we consume, the more sodium our bodies excrete. Researchers also speculate that the fiber and antioxidants in raisins change the biochemistry of blood vessels, making them more pliable—important for healthy blood pressure. Opt for dark raisins over light-colored ones because dark raisins have more catechins, a powerful type of antioxidant that can increase blood flow.

Researchers at Louisville Metabolic and Atherosclerosis Research Center compared people who snacked on raisins with those who ate other packaged snacks. Those in the raisin group had drops in systolic pressure (the top number) ranging from 4.8 points (after four weeks) to 10.2 points (after 12 weeks). Blood pressure barely budged in the no-raisin group. Some people worry about the sugar in raisins, but it is natural sugar (not added sugar) and will not adversely affect your health (though people with diabetes need to be cautious with portion sizes).

My advice: Aim to consume a few ounces of raisins every day. Prunes are an alternative.

Beets

Beets, too, are high in potassium, with about 519 mg per cup. They're delicious, easy to cook (see the tasty recipe below) and very effective for lowering blood pressure.

A study at The London Medical School found that people who drank about eight ounces of beet juice averaged a 10-point drop in blood pressure during the next 24 hours. The blood pressure–lowering effect was most pronounced at three to six hours past drinking but remained lower for the entire 24 hours. Eating whole beets might be even better because you will get extra fiber.

Along with fiber and potassium, beets also are high in nitrate. The nitrate is converted first to nitrite in the blood, then to nitric oxide. Nitric oxide is a gas that relaxes blood vessel walls and lowers blood pressure.

My advice: Eat beets several times a week. Look for beets that are dark red. They contain more

protective phytochemicals than the gold or white beets. Cooked spinach and kale are alternatives.

Dairy

In research involving nearly 45,000 people, researchers found that those who consumed low-fat "fluid" dairy foods, such as yogurt and low-fat milk, were 16% less likely to develop high blood pressure. Higher-fat forms of dairy, such as cheese and ice cream, had no blood pressure benefits. The study was published in *Journal of Human Hypertension*.

In another study, published in *The New England Journal of Medicine*, researchers found that people who included low-fat or fat-free dairy in a diet high in fruits and vegetables had double the blood pressure–lowering benefits of those who just ate the fruits and veggies.

Low-fat dairy is high in calcium, another blood pressure–lowering mineral that should be included in your diet. When you don't have enough calcium in your diet, a "calcium leak" occurs in your kidneys. This means that the kidneys excrete more calcium in the urine, disturbing the balance of mineral metabolism involved in blood pressure regulation.

My advice: Aim for at least one serving of low-fat or nonfat milk or yogurt every day. If you don't care for cow's milk or can't drink it, switch to fortified soy milk. It has just as much calcium and protein and also contains phytoestrogens, compounds that are good for the heart.

Flaxseed

Flaxseed contains alpha-linolenic acid (ALA), an omega-3 fatty acid that helps prevent heart and vascular disease. Flaxseed also contains magnesium. A shortage of magnesium in our diet throws off the balance of sodium, potassium and calcium, which causes the blood vessels to constrict.

Flaxseed also is high in flavonoids, the same antioxidants that have boosted the popularity of dark chocolate, kale and red wine. Flavonoids are bioactive chemicals that reduce inflammation throughout the body, including in the arteries. Arterial inflammation is thought to be the "trigger" that leads to high blood pressure, blood clots and heart attacks.

In a large-scale observational study linking dietary magnesium intake with better heart health and longevity, nearly 59,000 healthy Japanese people were followed for 15 years. The scientists found that the people with the highest dietary intake of magnesium had a 50% reduced risk for death from heart disease (heart attack and stroke). According to the researchers, magnesium's heart-healthy benefit is linked to its ability to improve blood pressure, suppress irregular heartbeats and inhibit inflammation.

My advice: Add one or two tablespoons of ground flaxseed to breakfast cereals. You also can sprinkle flaxseed on yogurt or whip it into a breakfast smoothie. Or try chia seeds.

Walnuts

Yale researchers found that people who ate two ounces of walnuts a day had improved blood flow and drops in blood pressure (a 3.5-point drop in systolic blood pressure and a 2.8-point drop in diastolic blood pressure). The mechanisms through which walnuts elicit a blood pressure–lowering response are believed to involve their high content of monounsaturated fatty acids, omega-3 ALA, magnesium and fiber, and their low levels of sodium and saturated fatty acids.

Bonus: Despite the reputation of nuts as a "fat snack," the people who ate them didn't gain weight.

The magnesium in walnuts is particularly important. It limits the amount of calcium that enters muscle cells inside artery walls. Ingesting the right amount of calcium (not too much and not too little) on a daily basis is essential for optimal blood pressure regulation. Magnesium regulates calcium's movement across the membranes of the smooth muscle cells, deep within the artery walls.

If your body doesn't have enough magnesium, too much calcium will enter the smooth muscle cells, which causes the arterial muscles to tighten, putting a squeeze on the arteries and raising blood pressure. Magnesium works like the popular calcium channel blockers, drugs that block entry of calcium into arterial walls, lowering blood pressure.

My advice: Eat two ounces of walnuts every day. Or choose other nuts such as almonds and pecans.

Delicious Foods That Prevent Stroke

Roger Bonomo, MD, neurologist in private practice, stroke specialist and former director, Stroke Center, Lenox Hill Hospital, New York City.

Eating foods that are rich in magnesium may save you from having a stroke. *That includes the foods I mentioned above—and others that you might like even more…*

A Mighty Mineral

The researchers found seven published studies over the past 13 years that analyzed the link between magnesium and stroke risk in a total of 241,000 men and women from the US, Europe and Asia. All studies focused on magnesium intake from food. Researchers determined how many milligrams (mg) of magnesium participants consumed from their self-reports of foods they ate each day.

The results: Magnesium was clearly associated with reduced stroke risk. For every 100 mg of magnesium that study participants consumed each day, their risk for an ischemic (blood clot) stroke went down by about 9%. That's a big drop in risk! And the studies' risk estimates were adjusted for other factors that might affect stroke incidence—including diabetes, body mass index, physical activity levels, high blood pressure, alcohol consumption, age and smoking—so it really does seem to be the magnesium that does the trick.

Their study at the Karolinska Institute in Sweden was published in *The American Journal of Clinical Nutrition.*

Prior research has indicated that magnesium reduces blood pressure and the risk for diabetes—two prominent risk factors for stroke.

What's interesting is that among Americans studied, the average daily intake of magnesium from food was only 242 mg—that's less than the 320 mg and 420 mg recommended for women and men, respectively, by the USDA. So even though magnesium appears to be a powerful way to fight off stroke, most Americans aren't getting enough.

Taking a multivitamin might provide some magnesium, but it might not be enough. Check the bottle to see how much you're getting in your multi... but you'll want to eat magnesium-rich foods as well.

More Magnesium, Please!

Consuming an additional 100 mg of magnesium a day may reduce your risk for stroke by 9%. And magnesium isn't an expensive drug with side effects—it's a natural mineral that's already in many of the foods we eat. So what are you waiting for? Most of us, especially those of us at high risk for stroke, high blood pressure or diabetes—would benefit from eating more magnesium-rich foods, such as...

Pumpkin seeds (191 mg per ¼ cup)
Almonds (160 mg per 2 oz.)
Spinach (156 mg per cup)
Cashews (148 mg per 2 oz.)
White beans (134 mg per cup)
Artichokes (97 mg per one large artichoke)
Brown rice (84 mg per cup)
Shrimp (39 mg per 4 oz.)

You can also supercharge your cooking with magnesium if you use oat bran (221 mg per cup) and buckwheat flour (301 mg per cup).

If we do, our kidneys excrete the extra through urine, so only those with kidney failure need to make sure they don't consume too much.

The 10 Very Best Foods to Prevent Depression (and Build a Healthier Brain)

Drew Ramsey, MD, psychiatrist, Columbia University Medical Center, and assistant clinical professor, Columbia University College of Physicians and Surgeons, both in New York City. His latest book is *Eat Complete*. DrewRamseyMD.com

Here's a startling statistic—studies show that people who consume a healthy diet are 40% to 50% less likely to develop depression.

What are the absolutely best nutrients—and most nutrient-packed foods—to protect your brain from depression and other ailments?

What protects mood also protects against dementia and other brain-related conditions. The brain is the biggest asset we have, so we should be selecting foods that specifically nourish the brain.

Here's how to build the healthiest brain possible—starting in your kitchen.

Nutrients Brains Need Most

These key nutrients as the most important...

•**Long-chain omega-3 fatty acids.** There are two major ones. Docosahexaenoic acid (DHA) creates hormones called "neuroprotectins and resolvins" that combat brain inflammation, which is implicated in the development of depression (as well as dementia). Eicosapentaenoic acid (EPA) protects the cardiovascular system, important for a healthy brain.

•**Zinc.** This mineral plays a major role in the development of new brain cells and can boost the efficacy of antidepressant medications.

•**Folate.** Also known as vitamin B-9, folate is needed for good moods and a healthy brain. It helps produce defensin-1, a molecule that protects the brain and increases the concentration of acetylcholine, a neurotransmitter that's crucial to memory and cognition.

•**Iron.** This essential element is a crucial cofactor in the synthesis of mood-regulating neurotransmitters including dopamine and serotonin.

•**Magnesium.** This mineral is required to keep myelin—the insulation of brain cells—healthy. It also increases brain-derived neurotrophic factor (BDNF), which promotes the growth of new neurons and healthy connections among brain cells. A deficiency in magnesium can lead to depression, anxiety, symptoms of ADHD, insomnia and fatigue.

•**Vitamin B-12.** This vitamin, which often is deficient as we age, helps makes neurotransmitters that are key to mood and memory.

•**Vitamin E.** This potent antioxidant vitamin protects polyunsaturated fatty acids in the brain—including DHA. Vitamin E–rich foods, but not supplements, are linked to the prevention of clinical depression as well as slower progression of Alzheimer's disease. One reason may be that most supplements contain only alpha-tocopherol, while other vitamin E compounds, particularly tocotrienols, play important roles in brain function.

•**Dietary fiber.** A high-fiber diet supports healthy gut bacteria (the gut "microbiome"), which growing evidence suggests is key for mental health.

Boosting Your Mood at the Supermarket

The best brain foods are mostly plant-based, but seafood, wild game and even some organ meats make the top of the list, too...

•**Leafy greens** such as kale, mustard greens and collard greens

•**Bell peppers** such as red, green and orange

•**Cruciferous vegetables** such as cauliflower, broccoli and cabbage

•**Berries** such as strawberries, raspberries and blueberries

•**Nuts** such as pecans, walnuts, almonds and cashews

•**Bivalves** such as oysters, clams and mussels

•**Crustaceans** such as crab, lobster and shrimp

•**Fish** such as sardines, salmon and fish roe

•**Organ meats** such as liver, poultry giblets and heart

•**Game and wild meat** such as bison, elk and duck

Eating these nutrient-dense foods is likely to help prevent and treat mental illness. When someone with depression is treated, the real goal is to prevent that person from ever getting depressed again.

Everyday Brain Foods

Not into eating beef heart? Having a little trouble stocking up on elk? When it comes to meat, wild game may not be widely available, but grass-fed beef, which is higher in omega-3 fatty acids than conventionally raised beef, is stocked in most supermarkets—and may be independently associated with protection from depression.

Other foods that didn't make it to the top of the Brain Food Scale but that still are very good for the

brain include eggs (iron, zinc), beans (fiber, magnesium, iron) and fruits and vegetables of all colors (fiber, antioxidants). Plus, small quantities of dark chocolate, which gives you a little dopamine rush. Dopamine, he explains, is a neurotransmitter that provides a feeling of reward.

The Superfoods That Relieve Allergies to Pollen, Dust, Mold...

Leo Galland, MD, founder of Foundation for Integrated Medicine in New York City. An internist, he treats many patients with chronic allergies and specializes in integrating nutrition and herbs with conventional medicine. He is the author of *The Fat Resistance Diet.* DrGalland.com

The right foods can help relieve allergies to dust, pollen, mold and other spores in the air—easing symptoms that include sneezing, stuffy nose and wheezing.

Allergy symptoms occur when an overactive immune system responds to harmless substances as if they could cause disease. Inflammation is an early step in the immune response. Most of the foods that relieve allergies are anti-inflammatory, modulating the immune system response.

Foods That Fight Allergies

The following foods help battle airborne allergies...

•**Fruits high in vitamin C, an antioxidant, may help reduce inflammation.** Year-round, eat two pieces of fruit daily. When you're especially congested, choose from these twice a day—an orange, one cup of strawberries, an apple, one cup of grapes or a medium-sized wedge of watermelon.

Bonus: The skins of red grapes are loaded with the antioxidant resveratrol and were found to relieve wheezing in the Crete study.

•**Nuts, especially almonds, hazelnuts and peanuts, are a good source of vitamin E, which helps minimize inflammation.** Eat a single one-ounce serving of any of these nuts daily year-round to help prevent symptoms. If you do have symptoms, increase the servings—try two tablespoons of peanut butter and one ounce each of hazelnuts and almonds a day.

●**Cold-water fish (wild salmon, mackerel, trout, herring and sardines), as well as walnuts and flaxseed, contain omega-3 fatty acids, which help fight inflammation.** Eat at least two servings of cold-water fish each week year-round and three servings during the seasons when you experience airborne allergies. Also have 12 walnuts and one tablespoon of ground flaxseed a day.

●**Oysters, shrimp and crab, as well as legumes, whole grains and tofu, are all high in zinc,** which has antibacterial and antiviral effects that provide relief for immune systems overtaxed by fighting allergies. Have six oysters, six shrimp or a few crabs every week, and twice that when your allergies bother you. Also have one serving of whole grains and one of beans or tofu a day.

●**Tea, whether green, white or black, is full of flavonoids, plant compounds that reduce inflammation.** Tea also increases proteins in the body that fight infection, again relieving an overtaxed immune system. Enjoy one cup daily, and increase to two when your allergies are a problem.

Helpful: Drink your tea first thing in the morning with lemon and honey to stimulate the cilia—the tiny hairs in the nose that sweep pollen and dust out of the way.

●**Horseradish, hot mustard, fennel, anise and sage also stimulate the cilia and act as natural decongestants.** Add a dash to food whenever possible.

Foods to Avoid All Year

If you experience congestion or other symptoms year-round, ask an allergist to conduct a skin test to identify allergies to dust, mold and foods. Then consider cutting out the following…

●**Mold and yeast in food.** If you're allergic to mold, avoid foods that contain yeast, such as bread and baked goods (unless they are labeled "yeast free")…wine, beer and spirits…fermented foods, such as sauerkraut and cider…foods that tend to get moldy, such as cheese and mushrooms…vinegar

and sauces that contain vinegar, such as mayonnaise, barbecue sauce, mustard and salad dressing.

Helpful: Use lemon juice and spices in dressings instead.

●**Milk and dairy products.** Although there isn't strong science showing that milk aggravates congestion, it's worth experimenting by cutting dairy from your diet for at least two weeks. If your allergies improve when you avoid dairy products, eliminate dairy year-round. You will then need to take a calcium supplement, usually 1,000 milligrams (mg) a day, to compensate for the decreased calcium intake that accompanies a dairy-free diet (but talk to your doctor).

●**Corn, wheat and soy, including soy milk, tofu, soybean oil, edamame and soy sauce.** Even if you don't appear allergic to soy on a skin-prick test, experiment by eliminating soy from your diet for at least two weeks.

The same is true of corn (including cornflakes, corn chips and corn oil) and wheat (including all breads and baked goods unless they are marked "wheat-free" or "gluten-free"). If you find that your symptoms are alleviated when you stop eating any of these foods, eliminate them year-round.

6 Best Foods for Your Skin

Torey Armul, MS, RD, CSSD, LD, a registered dietitian, nutritionist and national media spokesperson for the Academy of Nutrition and Dietetics. She is author of *Bun Appétit: A Simple Guide to Eating Right During Pregnancy.* Armul provides private counseling and consulting services in Columbus, Ohio. EatRightPRO.org

Want healthier skin and fewer wrinkles? Men and women can look younger and lower their risk for skin cancer, psoriasis, eczema and more by eating certain foods. *The following foods have been scientifically proven to boost the health, strength and appearance of your skin…*

Yellow Bell Peppers

Yellow bell peppers are one of the most abundant sources of vitamin C. The body depends on vitamin

C to form collagen, a protein that provides strength, support and elasticity to skin, hair, muscles and other tissues. Collagen also assists with cell regrowth and repair. As we age, our bodies produce less collagen, which can lead to reduced elasticity of the skin and more wrinkles.

The relationship between vitamin C and skin appearance was studied in more than 4,000 women in a report published in *The American Journal of Clinical Nutrition*. Researchers found that higher dietary intake of vitamin C was associated with lower likelihood of skin dryness and fewer wrinkles, as assessed by dermatologists. These results were independent of age, race, sun exposure, body mass index and physical activity.

Why not eat oranges, famous for their vitamin C, instead? A typical large orange contains 163% of the recommended daily value (DV) of vitamin C. That's good—but just half a yellow bell pepper contains nearly 300% of the DV of vitamin C. (Red and green peppers have less vitamin C than yellow ones but still are excellent sources.)

Eat yellow peppers raw to maximize the nutrient content. Vitamin C is sensitive to cooking and, as a water-soluble vitamin, leaches into cooking water. If you prefer to cook yellow peppers, keep the heat as low as possible for your recipe. Use the cooking juices, too (whenever possible), so that the vitamin C in the water is not wasted.

Sweet Potatoes

Sweet potatoes are an excellent source of carotenoids, the antioxidant pigments that give many foods their bright red, orange, yellow and green colors—and help keep skin cells healthy.

In a study published in *British Journal of Nutrition*, participants who ate more carotenoid-rich vegetables had significantly fewer facial wrinkles.

Eating carotenoids also can make you look healthier overall and more attractive to others. Carotenoid levels in skin contribute to healthy skin coloration. In fact, researchers from University of St. Andrews, Scotland, found that people whose faces were rated as healthy by others had consumed an average of 2.9 fruit and vegetable portions each

day...and whose faces were rated separately as attractive had consumed 3.3 daily portions.

Carotenoids are fat-soluble, which means that they're better absorbed when paired with a fat-containing food—so sprinkle nuts or drizzle olive oil over your sweet potatoes for a delicious skin boost.

Salmon

Although protein in your food does not directly affect protein in your body's collagen, some research shows that amino acids (the building blocks of protein) are related to collagen synthesis in the skin.

Some amino acids are "essential," meaning that they're necessary for life but are not made in the body. They must be provided by food or supplements. Salmon contains all the essential amino acids—and essential amino acids play a unique role in skin health. In a study published in *Amino Acids*, researchers found that consuming a combination of essential amino acids significantly increased the rate of collagen synthesis in mice with UV-damaged skin.

Salmon also is a good source of monounsaturated fat, which was found to be positively associated with skin elasticity in older women in a study published in *British Journal of Nutrition*.

Don't love fish? Essential amino acids also are found in poultry, eggs, beans and whole grains.

Walnuts

Walnuts are rich in omega-3 polyunsaturated fatty acids, which help the body make the collagen needed for healthy skin. Omega-3s help reduce inflammation and have been shown to reduce symptoms in inflammatory skin diseases such as psoriasis and acne.

The European Journal of Cancer published research comparing omega-3 fat intake to the development of malignant melanoma in more than 20,000 women. Data showed that higher intakes of omega-3s were associated with an 80% lower risk for skin cancer, leading researchers to conclude that these fats "have a substantial protective association" against melanoma.

Like essential amino acids, omega-3 fats are vitally important but are not made in the body. You must get them from your diet or supplements. Aside from walnuts (and salmon, discussed above), other excellent sources of omega-3s include flaxseed oil, ground flaxseed, chia seeds, canola oil and tofu.

Raspberries and Pomegranates

There is exciting research on collagen and how it is affected by ellagic acid, an antioxidant found in certain fruits and vegetables.

A study published in *Experimental Dermatology* found that mice who received ellagic acid had significantly reduced collagen breakdown from UV light, compared with mice who did not receive ellagic acid. The treatment group also developed fewer wrinkles. While most research focuses on the treatment of skin damage, this study was unique in its ability to show the role of nutrition in the prevention of collagen breakdown, wrinkles and skin damage.

Foods that are high in ellagic acid include raspberries and pomegranates (as well as blackberries, strawberries and cranberries).

Chickpeas

Zinc is an important ingredient for skin health because it supports the regeneration of new skin cells. The benefits are most apparent with skin repair and wound healing, but zinc also may be able to help with other skin problems such as rashes, eczema and acne.

A study published in *BioMed Research International* found a correlation between participants' zinc levels and the severity of their acne symptoms. Researchers believe that this is partly due to zinc's ability to inhibit the overgrowth of Propionibacterium acnes, a bacterium that contributes to acne.

Legumes were the focus of another study in *The Journal of the American College of Nutrition*. Researchers found that higher intakes of legumes, such as chickpeas, appeared to protect against sun-induced wrinkles in people with a variety of ethnic and geographic backgrounds.

Chickpeas are a good source of zinc, as are other beans, oysters, poultry, tofu, oatmeal and zinc-fortified cereals.

Eat Chicken Soup for Healthier Skin

Andrew L. Rubman, ND, founder and medical director, Southbury Clinic for Traditional Medicines, Southbury, Connecticut. He is medical advisor to the nationally syndicated radio show *Bottom Line on Your Health*.

Simmer a quartered chicken (skin, bones and all) with some onion, celery, carrots and a bay leaf for two hours in enough water to cover the contents—leave the pot uncovered for the full two hours, which will allow for evaporation and concentrate the liquid. The poultry and vegetables will give up their flavor and nutrients to the remaining water, and after you remove the solids, you'll be left with a broth rich in hyaluronic acid (HA)—the same substance that we make in our own bodies that provides skin with fullness, volume and plumpness.

As we grow older, our bodies produce less HA, which causes our skin to wrinkle and sag, so consuming extra HA may help. Organic and free-range chickens tend to produce more HA than traditionally-raised chickens because their diets are healthier and they're allowed to exercise more.

Make a big pot of this concentrated chicken broth, and then freeze half and refrigerate half upon cooling. Have a warmed cup every evening before dinner spiced with a pinch of sea salt and fresh ground pepper for extra flavor. Feel free to adjust the recipe with your own choice of herbs and spices, and you'll still get the benefit.

Chicken broth that you buy in a supermarket is just not the same, because valuable compounds in the chicken skin and bones don't make their way into store-bought broths and bouillon cubes.

Figs for Undereye Circles

Joan Wilen and Lydia Wilen are folk-remedy experts based in New York City who have spent decades collecting "cures from the cupboard." They are authors of *Bottom Line's Treasury of Home Remedies & Natural Cures*.

If you have access to fresh figs, try cutting one in half and placing the halves under your eyes. Lie down and relax for 15 to 30 minutes. Then get up and gently rinse the sticky stuff off with tepid water. Dab on some peanut oil.

When figs are not in season, grate an unwaxed cucumber or a small scrubbed (preferably red) potato. Put the gratings on two gauze pads, lie down and put them under your eyes. Rinse thoroughly and dab on some peanut oil.

Yummy Cholesterol Fighters

Allan Magaziner, DO, an osteopathic physician and the founder and director of the Magaziner Center for Wellness in Cherry Hill, New Jersey. One of the country's top specialists in nutritional and preventive medicine, Dr. Magaziner is coauthor of *The All-Natural Cardio Cure: A Drug-Free Cholesterol and Cardiac Inflammation Reduction Program.* DrMagaziner.com

---

For years, oat bran and oatmeal were touted as the best foods for high cholesterol. Rich in soluble fiber, these foods help prevent cholesterol from getting into the bloodstream. A daily serving of oats, for example, can lower LDL by 20%. Other good foods rich in soluble fiber include barley, beans, pears and prunes. But research has now gone beyond these old standby food choices. *Here are some other fiber-rich foods that have been found to give cholesterol the heave-ho…*

•**All nuts.** Walnuts and almonds are great cholesterol fighters, but so are pistachios, peanuts, pecans, hazelnuts and other nuts, according to recent research. Eat a handful (1.5 ounces) of nuts daily.

•**Popcorn actually contains more fiber per ounce than whole-wheat bread.** Just go easy on the salt and butter, and stay away from store-bought microwave popcorn (it can contain harmful chemicals).

Smart idea: Put one-quarter cup of organic plain popcorn in a lunch-size brown paper bag, and pop in the microwave. It's delicious—and there's no cleanup.

Sunburn Soothers from Your Kitchen

Andrew Rubman, ND, founder and medical director of the Southbury Clinic for Traditional Medicines, Southbury, Connecticut. SouthburyClinic.com

---

You could have covered up, but you didn't. You could have used more sunscreen, but that didn't happen either. So now you're coming home from a lovely day of swimming, boating, playing golf or otherwise frolicking in the sun—and your skin is feeling hot…and is turning red.

You've got a sunburn…and maybe a windburn, too. Pain is coming. *Here's what to do…*

A Naturopath's Favorite Sunburn Home Remedies

Most of the time when you have a sunburn, you'll feel better faster—and heal faster—by using certain proven-to-work home remedies.

The exception: If you have a blistering burn or one that is covering a large part of your body, or if the burn is accompanied by fever, chills, headache or severe pain, don't treat it at home—see or call your health-care provider. (If you do have blisters, do not break them—it slows healing and increases risk for infection.)

For everyday sunburn and windburn, you can treat your skin with easy-to-find products that you might not have considered. Your first order of business is something most people don't think about—keeping skin moist. With sunburn or wind exposure, the skin's normal ability to retain moisture is disturbed. If the skin starts drying out, it can become inflamed, and then it can become scaly and more vulnerable to infection.

Cooling the skin and keeping it moist can relieve your discomfort and protect the skin from becoming dehydrated. The way to start is not with a lotion, although that's what most people do. Instead, as soon as possible after realizing you have a burn, apply a cool compress to the sunburned or windburned area—a towel or wash cloth soaked in cool water will work for your arms, legs, shoulders or face—and if it's your torso that's sunburned, wear a cotton T shirt that's been soaked in cool water. As the compresses cool, apply fresh ones until the pain is substantially diminished.

Of course, it's not always convenient to walk around garbed in wet clothes and bath linens, so here are some other top remedies. Any and all of these remedies can be combined and used as often as you like, so try different combinations until you find the right one for you. *Since they all start working immediately, your skin should start to feel better quickly…*

1. Apply witch hazel to the burned area. Using witch hazel, a solution made with an extract from the leaves, twig and bark of the Hamamelis plant, may seem counterintuitive because of its astringent properties. But it is a strong antioxidant with anti-inflammatory effects that are skin soothing and cooling.

2. Coconut oil rubbed into the skin provides a medium-chain fatty acid (lauric acid), which helps keep skin moist. Although the oil is solid at room temperature, it will melt at body temperature and absorb into the skin so you will not leave the house coated in white pasty oil.

3. A soaking bath containing oatmeal powder and a little white vinegar (two or three tablespoons) is soothing, relieves itching and helps the skin regain its normal moisture barrier. The vinegar helps remove inflammatory compounds released by sun-damaged skin and soothes sunburn pain. For the oatmeal powder, try Aveeno, but you can also make your own by grinding uncooked oat cereal in a blender until it becomes a fine powder.

4. Fresh aloe gel is very soothing on damaged skin. If you don't already have an aloe plant, you can purchase one from a home center or nursery for a few dollars. Snip off one of the fronds, squeeze out the gel and apply to your skin. Applying fresh aloe gel feels instantly cooling and soothing. Fresh aloe from a leaf is much better than any store-bought aloe product because the gel's ability to soothe decreases rapidly after it's extracted. Reapply when the soothing effect wears off.

Sleep Better with Honey

Stephen Sinatra, MD, cardiologist and founder of Heart MD Institute, an educational platform that promotes complementary treatments for heart disease, Manchester, Connecticut. He writes the monthly newsletter *Heart, Health & Nutrition* and lectures worldwide about natural and nutritional remedies. He is coauthor of *The Healing Kitchen* (Bottom Line Books). HealthyDirections.com

This natural sweetener can help you get more of the sleep you need.

What research shows: Recent research at the Massachusetts Institute of Technology shows that honey increases the activity of serotonin, a "calming" neurotransmitter in the brain. It also sends a signal to the brain to curtail the release of orexin, a substance that promotes alertness during the day and can interfere with falling asleep at night.

How much: One-half teaspoon to one teaspoon 45 minutes to one hour before bed. I like to add it to a sliced banana and one-quarter cup of plain yogurt.

Cooling Foods That Soothe Hot Flashes

Laurie Steelsmith, ND, is the author of *Natural Choices for Women's Health*. Her private practice in naturopathic and Chinese medicine is in Honolulu. DrSteelsmith.com

When in the throes of a menopausal hot flash, we should rightly be given permission to strip naked and jump into a snowbank. For relief, conventional doctors often recommend hormone therapy for relief, but it has been linked to an increased risk for breast cancer, heart disease and stroke—and a recent study found that users had a 29% greater risk for ovarian cancer than nonusers.

But you can minimize hot flashes by avoiding foods that are "warming"—a classification that, surprisingly, has nothing to do with the temperature at which a food is served and often is not based on its level of spiciness. Rather, warming foods are those with a lot of yang or "hot energy."

According to traditional Chinese medicine, yin and yang are opposites or counterparts that exist everywhere in the universe. Yin is associated with cold, quiet, passivity, water and nighttime...yang is associated with heat, noise, activity, fire and day-time. Women tend to have more yin, while men tend to have more yang. At menopause, yin gets de-pleted—in fact, estrogen and progesterone are both cooling yin hormones—leaving an excess of yang. Stress exacerbates hot flashes because stress hor-mones such as cortisol are yang. Warming foods, which have more yang than yin, promote hot flash-es because they create more of a yin/yang disparity than you already have.

A food is deemed yin or yang based on centu-ries of tradition, the food's innate traits and how it makes the body feel—not necessarily on whether it is hot or cold. You don't want to avoid all yang foods since many are nutritious, but with trial and error you'll see which ones trigger your hot flashes and which are OK for you.

Yang foods to limit...

Fruits: Cherries...coconuts...guavas...kumquats ...lemons...lychees...peaches...raspberries.

Vegetables: Cauliflower...mustard greens...on-ions...pumpkins...scallions.

Grains/nuts/seeds: Chestnuts...pine nuts... pumpkin seeds...sticky (glutinous) rice...walnuts.

Dairy: Butter...goat's milk...yogurt.

Meat/poultry/seafood: Anchovies...chicken... crayfish...lamb...lobster...mussels...shrimp... trout...venison.

Herbs/spices: Anise...basil...caraway...cardamom ...chives...cinnamon...cloves...coriander...dill... fennel...garlic...ginger...nutmeg...pepper...rose-mary...saffron...thyme...turmeric.

Miscellaneous: Alcohol...brown sugar...coffee ...molasses...soybean oil...vinegar.

Regular consumption of cooling foods that are more yin can reduce the number and severity of hot flashes (though eating them during a hot flash won't have a quick enough effect to halt your heat wave). When you do eat a yang food, counterbal-ance its effects by having a cooling yin food at the same time.

Yin foods to keep you cool...

Fruits: Bananas...grapefruit...kiwifruit...loquats ...melon...mulberries...oranges...papayas...pears

...persimmons...plums...pomegranates...straw-berries...tangerines.

Vegetables: Alfalfa sprouts...asparagus...bam-boo shoots...broccoli...burdock root...cabbage... celery...cucumbers...eggplant...lettuce...lotus root ...kelp...mung beans...mushrooms...nori...radish-es...spinach...summer squash...sweet potatoes... tomatoes...turnips...watercress.

Grains/nuts/seeds: Barley...buckwheat...millet ...wheat...wheat bran.

Seafood: Clams...crab...octopus.

Herbs/spices: Green tea...marjoram...pepper-mint...salt.

Miscellaneous: Sesame oil...soy sauce...tofu... water.

Many other foods are fairly equally balanced in yin and yang. These are unlikely to affect hot flash-es one way or the other.

Neutral foods include...

Fruits: Apricots...figs...grapes...pineapple...red dates.

Vegetables: Beets...carrots...olives...peas...po-tatoes...string beans...yams.

Grains/nuts/seeds: Almonds...corn...hazelnuts ...oats...peanuts...rice...rye...sesame seeds... sunflower seeds.

Dairy: Cheese...cow's milk.

Meat/poultry/seafood: Beef...duck...ham...oys-ters...pork...sardines...white fish.

Miscellaneous: Eggs...honey...white sugar.

Foods for a Bright White Smile

Mark A. Breiner, DDS, has a private practice in Fairfield, Connecticut, and is author of *Whole-Body Dentistry: A Complete Guide to Understanding the Impact of Dentistry on Total Health.*

Quite a few foods will actually help maintain your pearly white color.

•**Apples, pears, celery, carrots, cauliflow-er and cucumbers.** These fruits and vegetables have enough fiber to act as natural scrubbing agents.

•**Lettuce, spinach and broccoli.** These veg-etables contain a compound that produces a light film that helps protect your teeth from stains...yet another reason to start dinner with a salad!

•**Cheese.** All cheeses (especially cheddar) contain fats and proteins that counter the acids contained in many foods. Cheese stimulates saliva production and also contains calcium and phosphorous, both of which help to protect teeth by remineralizing enamel.

Easy (and Cheap!) Home Remedies for Whitening

Here are two whitening tricks that you can use as often as you like...

•**Rub orange peel on your teeth.** The white inside of an orange peel—called the pith—contains chemicals that help whiten your teeth. Rub it onto your teeth for a few minutes and then brush a half-hour later.

•**Apply a paste of strawberries and baking soda.** Strawberries contain a compound that acts as a natural bleaching agent, which is especially effective when mixed with baking soda. Mash a just-ripe strawberry, and mix it with some baking soda until it has the consistency of paste. (The strawberries are acidic, but the baking soda neutralizes the acid.) Apply it to your teeth, leave it on for 20 minutes and then rinse. Wait a half-hour and then brush your teeth well to rid your mouth of the natural sugar that strawberries contain.

6 Hot and Healthy Spices to Eat, Inhale, Even Rub

The late James Duke, PhD, botanist and former USDA researcher, author of numerous books, including *The Green Pharmacy Guide to Healing Foods* (Bottom Line Books).

No doubt you've heard about the current "it" spice, turmeric which shows promise at protecting against cancer, inflammation and Alzheimer's disease. But your spice rack can do so much more for you if you also boost your use of six particular hot and healthy spices.

Naturally, adding these six spices to your food is key—but you also can get some surprising health benefits from inhaling a certain spice-infused steam...and even by rubbing a particular spiced-up sauce on your skin!

According to James A. Duke, PhD, author of *The Green Pharmacy Guide to Healing Food*, each of the following spices helps improve cholesterol levels, and each has additional benefits as well. *Today's hottest health-boosting spices include...*

•**Black pepper.** Dr. Duke calls piperine, a compound in black pepper, a "potentiator" because it helps our bodies to better absorb and make use of other beneficial herbs and spices. For example, when used together with turmeric, black pepper increases turmeric's protective effects against cancer, inflammation and Alzheimer's disease, Dr. Duke said. Piperine also blocks the formation of new fat cells and aids digestion by increasing the flow of digestive juices.

To up your intake: Add black pepper to just about any savory dish—eggs, soups, sauces, legumes, salads, etc. Note that there is a huge difference in taste between most preground pepper, which is rather bland, and the black pepper that you grind right onto your food from peppercorns. So get yourself a pepper mill...and also, for maximum potency, chose the most pungent peppercorns you can find.

•**Cardamom.** Used as an aphrodisiac in Middle Eastern countries, both the pods and the seeds within help stimulate the central nervous system. "Cardamom is the richest source I know of the compound cineole, which helps improve memory by preventing the breakdown of the neurotransmitter acetylcholine," Dr. Duke said. Cardamom also contains chemicals that ease stomach and intestinal spasms, reduce gas and speed the movement of food through the digestive tract.

Breathe it in: We absorb cineole best by inhaling it, Dr. Duke noted, so add one or two cardamom pods or a bit of ground cardamom to a cup of hot water, then inhale the steam for several minutes. (Do not inhale ground cardamom directly, as this could irritate the lungs.)

Add to food: Try ground cardamom seeds in rice pilaf and meat dishes.

Caution: If you have gallstones, do not go overboard on cardamom—excessive amounts (beyond what is typically used in food) could exacerbate gallstone-related pain.

●**Fennel seeds.** If you've eaten in an Indian restaurant, you've probably seen a bowl of small seeds (some candied, some not) where you'd normally find after-dinner mints. Those are fennel seeds, and they're there for good reason—with an aroma reminiscent of licorice, the seeds are an effective breath freshener. Fennel seeds also are a digestive aid, relaxing the smooth muscles that line the digestive tract and relieving flatulence, bloating and gas. They soothe the tough-to-relieve symptoms of inflammatory bowel disease.

Try it: Chew whole fennel seeds to freshen your breath...use ground fennel seeds to add flavor to spice rubs for meat or fish, or sprinkle it into vegetable dishes. For best flavor, grind your own seeds using a small coffee grinder or a pestle and mortar, or place the seeds in a sealed bag and crush them with a rolling pin.

●**Fenugreek seeds.** Many women first learn about fenugreek while nursing their infants because the spice stimulates the production of breast milk. It also is an anti-inflammatory...and it helps stabilize blood glucose in people with diabetes by slowing absorption of sugars. Fenugreek's flavor is a cross between maple sugar and celery, though it can be bitter if used in excess. If you can't find it in your supermarket, look instead in Indian or Middle Eastern groceries (where it may be called methi) or purchase it online.

Cooking tip: Fenugreek adds a distinctive flavor to soups, stews and sauces. The seeds are hard, though, so you may want to buy them preground or use a small coffee grinder...or dry-fry the whole seeds in a skillet over medium heat for several minutes before adding them to whatever you're cooking.

●**Horseradish.** This pungent root—which lends a distinctive sharp flavor to cocktail sauce (or Bloody Mary cocktails)—is loaded with isothiocyanates. These compounds have antiseptic properties and also may help protect against the development of certain cancers by promoting elimination of carcinogens from the body.

Healthful flavor boost: Add ground horseradish to dips, hummus, mustard and other condiments, or spread it on a sandwich.

Aromatherapy for colds: Next time you have a cold, try grating some fresh horseradish and inhaling the aroma to open your sinuses and kill germs. Start by inhaling gently—fresh horseradish can be strong, and you don't want to give yourself an uncomfortable blast.

●**Red pepper.** Chile peppers—from which paprika, cayenne pepper, red pepper flakes, and Tabasco sauce and similar hot sauces derive—contain the super-spicy compound capsaicin. This is a potent antioxidant that helps neutralize cell-damaging free radicals. Capsaicin also curbs the appetite...raises body temperature...and may help kill off cancer cells. In addition, capsaicin is used as a topical pain reliever, neutralizing the nerves so they are less sensitive.

Topical treatment: To ease his own knee pain, Dr. Duke has been rubbing on a few drops of hot sauce from the grocery store, as often as needed. He has been using this remedy for several years and it's working for him, but he noted that, for some people, the treatment seems to stop helping after awhile. (If you try this, use your palm rather than fingertips, then wash hands thoroughly so you won't inadvertently get any of the stinging sauce into a cut or your eyes or onto any mucous membrane.) Another option is to use a nonprescription capsaicin cream, such as Zostrix.

Add zip to foods: Add a dash of any red pepper product to pasta sauces, casseroles and veggie dishes...or even sprinkle a bit on ice cream!

How much to use? With any of these spices, the effective (and palate-pleasing) dosage can vary greatly from one person to the next. Dr. Duke recommends starting conservatively, with just a small amount. He said, "If you don't enjoy the flavor, you're using too much. If you like the way you feel, you're probably getting a good dose."

Spices with Surprising Health Benefits

The late James Duke, PhD, a botanist and former USDA researcher, author of numerous books, including *The Green Pharmacy Guide to Healing Foods* (Bottom Line Books).

Common medical conditions that you can help prevent—or improve—with the use of spices*...

Oregano for Arthritis

Oregano helps alleviate osteoarthritis and other inflammatory conditions, such as rheumatoid arthritis. You might be surprised to learn that this favorite spice of Italian cooking contains natural compounds that have many of the same effects as the powerful anti-inflammatory COX-2 inhibitor drug *celecoxib* (Celebrex).

In addition, oregano contains dozens of other anti-inflammatory compounds that act as muscle relaxants and pain relievers. Unlike celecoxib, which may increase heart attack risk in some people, oregano actually protects the heart by helping to prevent blood clots and irregular heart rhythms.

Best uses: Use oregano liberally on salads or on pizzas. Oregano also can be mixed with peppermint and/or spearmint for a hot or iced mixed-herb tea. If you prefer to take an anti-inflammatory supplement, oregano is one of the half dozen spices in a product called Zyflamend (its ingredients also include rosemary and turmeric). The herbs in Zyflamend act synergistically to provide a more powerful effect than each would when used individually. Zyflamend can be purchased in health-food stores and online. Follow label instructions.

*Check with your doctor before using any of the spices mentioned in this article for medicinal purposes. The natural compounds found in spices may interact with some prescription drugs. Pregnant and nursing women should avoid using spices medicinally.

Fennel Seed for Indigestion

Fennel seed is surprisingly effective at relieving indigestion. If I get indigestion, I pick some fennel seeds from the fennel plant in my garden. Fennel is easy to grow, and it keeps coming back year after year. In my experience, it can settle the stomach as well as many over-the-counter products.

Fennel seed relaxes the smooth muscles that line the digestive tract, relieving flatulence, bloating and gas, as well as nausea and vomiting, motion sickness and abdominal pain. If you don't want to grow your own, store-bought fennel seed also works well.

Best uses: Fennel seed can be eaten whole (it tastes and smells similar to anise) or made into a tea by pouring boiling water over it (use one gram to three grams of fennel seed—about one-half to one and one-half teaspoons—per cup). To sweeten the tea, molasses or honey is the best choice.

Caution: Because fennel seed can increase estrogen levels, it should be avoided by women who are pregnant or breast-feeding or who have an estrogen-sensitive medical condition, such as estrogen-responsive breast cancer.

Garlic for the Common Cold

While the research on garlic's positive effect on cardiovascular health is perhaps most widely known, this popular allium also boosts immunity, helping to prevent and treat the common cold.

In one study of nearly 150 people who took a garlic supplement or placebo for 12 weeks during cold season, those taking the garlic had significantly fewer colds (or symptoms that eased more quickly in cold sufferers) than those taking a placebo.

Best uses: To help cure or prevent a cold, add a clove or two of garlic to all soups...sprinkle garlic powder on toast...and/or mix diced raw garlic with olive oil and vinegar.

Natural Remedies for Thinning Hair

David Hoffmann, BSc, founding member and past president of the American Herbalists Guil and a fellow of Great Britain's National Institute of Medical Herbalists. He teaches at the California School of Herbal Studies in Forestville, and is author of 17 books, including *Herbal Prescriptions after 50*.

If you are concerned about thinning hair, first see your doctor to find out whether there's an underlying medical problem, such as a thyroid disorder, that needs treating.

But if no medical problem is found, for many people, the key to reversing hair loss is to increase blood flow in the scalp. Try any or all of the following for six weeks. Continue indefinitely if your hair improves.

•**Rinse hair with nettle tea.** Nettle promotes hair growth not only by improving circulation, but also by reducing inflammation.

To prepare: Mix one-half tablespoon of dried nettle with one cup of water. Bring to a boil, reduce heat, cover and simmer for 30 minutes. Remove from heat. Let sit, covered, for 15 minutes. Strain through cheesecloth. Cool before using. Apply to hair, massaging into scalp for several minutes. Leave on for 15 minutes, then shampoo.

Easier: Steep two nettle tea bags in very hot water for 10 minutes. Cool, then apply as described above.

Good brand: Traditional Medicinals Organic Nettle Leaf tea bags (800-543-4372, Traditional Medicinals.com/products/nettle-leaf).

•**Drink herbal tea.** Consuming certain herbal teas can improve sluggish circulation from the inside out, which can stimulate hair growth. Choose either or both of the following teas and drink a total of three cups per day. *Options…*

•**Hawthorn.** Steep a heaping teaspoon of dried hawthorn berries in one cup of very hot water for five to 10 minutes, then strain. If you prefer, take hawthorn in supplement form as an extract of either dried berries or flowers and leaves at a dosage of 300 mg twice daily.

•**Ginger.** Add several slices of fresh ginger to one cup of water and boil for five minutes, then remove the ginger.

Got a Hangover? Try Honey

Reid B. Blackwelder, MD, family physician, Kingsport, Tennessee, quoted in *Redbook*.

The fructose in honey helps the body metabolize alcohol more quickly. Try a spoonful—or consider other fructose-rich substances, such as 100% fruit juice if you're are suffering from a hangover.

Lemonade for Kidney Stones

Roger L. Sur, MD, is a urologist, professor of urology and director of the University of California, San Diego (UCSD), Comprehensive Kidney Stone Center.

More than half a million Americans go to emergency rooms each year due to kidney stones, and about one in 10 Americans will suffer a kidney stone at some time in his/her life.

Simple home remedy: Drink lemonade. A study I published in *The Journal of Urology* found that patients who drank a little more than two quarts of lemonade (made with about four ounces of lemonade concentrate) daily for an average of 44 months had an increase in urinary citrate that was comparable to the increase in a group taking oral potassium citrate, which is commonly prescribed for kidney stones. More urinary citrate means a lower risk for calcium kidney stones, the most common form. Drinking water alone has not been found to raise urinary citrate levels.

If you've had kidney stones in the past, you have a 50% chance of getting one or more additional stones within five to 10 years. Drinking two quarts of lemonade daily could reduce this risk by 90%—without the expense or side effects of medication. I advise using an artificial sweetener or honey instead of refined sugar.

Other citrus juices, including orange and grapefruit juice, also contain citrate, but not as much as juice made from lemons.

CHAPTER 11

Home Selling and Buying

8 Clever Ways to Boost Your Home's Value Before Selling

Will Johnson, a Nashville, Tennessee–based real estate agent who leads the Will Johnson Group, a team that includes both home-selling and home-staging professionals. He previously led The Sell and Stage Team with RE/MAX International. WillJohnsonGroup.com

Make the right changes and you might boost your home's price by 3% to 7%—maybe more if you invest wisely in some bigger-ticket modifications.

Eight new and little-used strategies for prepping a home for sale in today's real estate market…

•**Install some basic home-automation tech.** In the past, home owners who invested in technology that let them control elements of their homes via remote control or a smartphone tended to get little or none of this investment back when they sold.

Today, however, this kind of home tech might return its cost many times over. In part, that's because the cost of these devices has dropped…but it's also because installing these items can subtly shift buyers' perceptions of your entire home.

Homes that have this tech are more likely to be viewed as up to date…while those that lack it are more likely to seem out of date. And it's more important than ever for homes to seem up to date when they go on the market because an increasing percentage of home buyers belong to younger generations who put great value on technology and modernity.

Examples of home-automation tech: The Nest Learning Thermostat ($249) and "smart" door locks such as Schlage Sense (available for $229) and Kwikset Kevo (available for $215).

•**Paint every interior wall that can be seen from your home's main entrance the same color.** Decorators often recommend using different paint in different rooms or even on different walls in the same room. That can make a home more visually compelling…but more difficult to sell. When every wall within eyeshot of the home's entryway is painted the same color, it creates visual "flow"—each room seems to draw visitors into the next. It creates a warm, welcoming first impression for buyers entering the house for the first time. When each room feels connected to the next, it makes the entire space feel larger, too.

Use off-white or beige paint for these entryway-visible rooms. Certainly, other paint options are more stylish and compelling, but they can be divisive and alienating. If you plan to sell soon, it is best to make the safe paint choice. Create visual interest in these rooms with brightly colored area rugs…throw pillows…furniture…and/or lamp shades.

•**Display positive words as wall art.** You know you should take down your family photos before potential buyers see your home—pictures of your family make it psychologically challenging for buyers to imagine their families living there. But what should you hang instead? Artsy signs or sculptures that feature upbeat words or phrases are an effective option.

Examples: "Happiness"..."Family"...or "Welcome Home."

You can find these signs for $10 to $15 apiece in home stores, hobby stores and online.

Tip: Search online for "positive word art" to find a multitude of inexpensive options. It might sound silly, but putting positive words on display does seem to make some buyers feel more positive about a property. Word signs are so inexpensive that there's no reason not to give this a try.

•**Remove window screens.** You probably know to open blinds and curtains to let as much light as possible into your home when it's shown to buyers. But there's another way to increase the amount of natural light in your home that many home sellers and even real estate pros miss—take out window screens. Mesh screens block about one-third of sunlight. They also obscure the view through the windows...and many screens have frayed wires or small holes that can subtly create a sense that the entire property is old and worn. Store the screens neatly in a closet, basement or garage where potential buyers will see them—that way, they won't worry that they would have to buy new screens for the house if they happen to notice that the screens are not in the windows.

•**Provide a virtual-reality tour online.** Just a year or two ago, it would have been fair to dismiss interactive video "tours" of homes in real estate listings (in which viewers can "move around" inside and outside a home on their computer screens) as gimmicky. But these "3-D" tours have been catching on with buyers rapidly, in part because the technology is improving. The cost of having these video tours made is dropping, too. Some real estate photographers now offer packages for home sellers that include virtual-reality tours for only around $100 more than they charge for still-photography packages.

Tip: Choose a photographer who uses Matterport 3-D scanning technology if possible. It's the state of the art for virtual-reality video tours.

Pricier Upgrades

The following home upgrades usually have price tags in the thousands of dollars—but they often more than pay for themselves when a home is sold. They're particularly worth considering if they're in a part of the home that needs to be renovated anyway.

•**Add showerheads in the master bathroom.** When home buyers see showers with multiple showerheads—two or more directional showerheads plus a "rainfall" showerhead that drops water from directly above—they imagine themselves surrounded by warm, soothing water every morning. A shower with three or more showerheads conveys a sense of peace and relaxation, and buyers are drawn to homes that make them feel these things. Expect to pay at least $1,000 to have a plumber install extra showerheads.

Affordable Ways to Create an Outdoor "Room"

Home buyers increasingly want homes that connect them with the outdoors. A good way to do this is to transform a simple patio or deck into an outdoor "room"—not with actual walls, but with many of the comforts and amenities of a room. *This room might feature...*

•**Fireplace or cooking area**
•**Comfortable-looking outdoor furniture**
•**Patio heaters**
•**Stone wall or some other attractive border to define the edge of the space**
•**Awning or some other covering.**

Include an attractive sink and countertop in your outdoor room, too, if possible—outdoor sinks are an uncommon but attractive amenity, so this can help your outdoor room stand out from those that buyers have seen at other homes.

An outdoor room can make your home feel larger, too—it adds additional living space beyond the home's footprint.

Similar: If your home is in a tight, urban space, it might be possible to transform a roof deck into an outdoor room. Include plants in planters...and walls or screens for privacy from neighboring buildings.

Note: An oversized master-bath bathtub can be a selling point...but if budget or bathroom-size limitations force you to choose between an upgraded shower or tub, opt for the shower. A relatively small percentage of home buyers take frequent baths, so even a very impressive tub will have fairly narrow appeal.

•**Install a big, rectangular sink.** If you're re-doing your kitchen or master bath anyway and space permits, spend a little extra and install a trough sink—an oversized sink that's several feet in length. It's an element that catches the eye of many buyers these days, especially when it's made of concrete or stone. You'll probably pay $1,000 or more for the sink and installation, but this amount might be more than recouped in buyers' additional perceived value of the kitchen or bathroom. Choose a trough sink with a bottom that slopes toward the drain because trough sinks with level basins don't drain well.

How to Sell Your Home in a Changing Market

Jim Remley, based in Oregon, is a REAL Trends Top 500 Broker who leads one of the largest real estate firms in the nation. He is also a speaker and coach, providing training to agents worldwide through his seminars, writings and online coaching programs. He is author of several books, including *Sell Your Home in Any Market.*

Real estate values are stabilizing across the US, with home prices moving away from double-digit appreciation to more healthy levels. With more inventory hitting the pipeline in many markets, buyers have a lot more options, but sellers have it tougher.

Here are strategies that can help home owners appeal to more potential buyers...and make more when they sell...

House-Wise

Fix it up first. "Fixer-uppers" tend to receive less attention in a real estate market that is seeing an increase in inventory because buyers can find good deals without breaking out their tools. If your home is in need of substantial repairs, it is best to get the work done before placing it on the market.

•**Pay attention to curb appeal.** Home buyers have so many options that if a property doesn't look attractive from the street, they will drive past it without even stopping for a look inside.

What to do: Spend a weekend beautifying the front of your home. Replace damaged window screens... tidy up the lawn and landscaping...pressure-wash the sidewalk...add mulch around trees and in flower beds. If necessary, have the home's exterior repainted, particularly the front door and trim...and upgrade outdoor lighting fixtures, doorknobs and your doorbell switch or knocker. These small details can evoke an emotional reaction in a home shopper that can lead to a sale.

•**Freshen up inside.** A fresh coat of paint and new carpet or refinished wood floors can make a big difference. It also pays to hire a professional cleaning service to remove years of grime from your kitchen and bathrooms.

Smell matters, too. It is extremely difficult to sell a home that reeks of cigarette smoke, pets or cooking odors. Perfuming the house with scented candles or potpourri doesn't fool anyone.

What to do: Hire a building restoration company to remove odors if scrubbing does not do it. Services range from a few hundred to a few thousand dollars. (Look online for "Building Maintenance" or "Building Restoration.") You will recoup this expense if your home is worth $300,000 or more.

Money-Wise

Don't start with a high price. Asking price is the single most important reason that a property does not sell. You might have to be a bit more competitive with your price, especially if your local real estate market has more than a six-month supply of homes for sale. In any market, it is a mistake to set a high price and assume that you can lower it later, if necessary, in negotiations.

Most listings that do sell receive offers in the first two to three weeks. This is due to the "backlog of buyers" waiting for new listings to hit the market. If you start out too high, by the time you do lower your price, real estate agents will have newer listings to show buyers. The buyers who do see your home will view your price cut as a sign of desperation and bid low.

Pricing your home as a slight bargain ensures that as many potential buyers as possible will walk through your door and can often result in a bidding war.

Recheck the asking price of comparable listings every two to four weeks if your home has not sold. You might have to lower your price to remain competitive. When you do a price reduction, make it large enough so that the new price is very competitive with comparable homes or is even a "best buy." A 1% or 2% price reduction will probably not motivate buyers to take a second look, just like a 1% sale won't motivate you to walk into a clothing store.

Important: The amounts your neighbors sold their homes for a year or two ago should not even enter your thinking when you set your asking price. It was a very different market then, and those prices are irrelevant today.

Helpful: If your home is not attracting many showings, the price is probably the problem. If it is attracting showings but not offers, the home itself is most likely to blame.

•**Mention special features and construction details in your Multiple Listing Service (MLS) listing.** French doors, mosaic tile or a gated entry sets your home apart from others in the area. Be descriptive. Rather than writing "inground pool," you or the agent should write "inground pool with waterfall and hot tub."

•**Offer incentives to buyers and brokers.** Many home sellers are "bribing" buyers with cash, cars and flat-screen TVs. *But the most effective incentives can be more simple such as…*

•Help with closing costs. Cash-poor buyers might have trouble paying up-front mortgage expenses. Offer to pay a portion of these costs, and buyers have another reason to choose your home.

•Pay for buy-downs. Many lenders will lower interest rates by one-eighth to one-quarter percentage point in exchange for an up-front payment. The payment usually is 1% or 2% of the loan amount.

Include details of your incentives in your MLS listing, social-media boost, flyers, on your website and anywhere else you advertise the property.

You also can offer real estate agents a bonus, which often is an extra 1% to 3% of the purchase price, on top of their usual commission at closing if they find you the buyer. Mention the bonus only in the MLS listing.

Important: If you offer a sales incentive, disclose this in your sales contract with the buyer. If the incentive is not mentioned in the contract and the buyer later defaults on the loan, the lender could claim that you and the buyer engaged in fraud by manipulating the sale price of the home to include an asset that the lender could not foreclose upon.

•**Don't overnegotiate.** If a potential buyer's first offer is reasonable, consider accepting it rather than making a higher counteroffer. Buyers have more homes to choose from today, so they sometimes move on to other properties rather than make second offers when sellers don't accept their initial bids. If you do not need to sell quickly or your home is garnering lots of showings, counter—but if you need to sell fast and the initial offer is reasonable, do not risk losing the sale over a relatively small amount of money.

Ways to Get More When You Sell Your Home

Stan Humphries, chief analytics officer at Zillow, the real estate information service based in Seattle, which has a database of more than 110 million US homes. He is coauthor of *Zillow Talk: The New Rules of Real Estate*. Zillow.com

Real estate economist Stan Humphries says that some of the conventional wisdom about buying and selling a home has changed drastically. That's partly because people have become much more wary about the future of real estate prices in the wake of the 2007–2009 housing-price meltdown… and partly because of the growing role of technology, especially the Internet, in real estate shopping. Humphries has analyzed millions of home listings, as well as data gathered from millions of monthly visitors to the Zillow real estate website. He has developed insights that can earn you thousands of dollars more on the sale of your home.

Conventional wisdom says that as a seller, you should overprice your home by 5% to 10% to leave yourself some wiggle room in negotiations…renovate your kitchen to add the most value to your house…and list early in the year to catch the spring and early-summer home-buying rush.

But here's what national and local housing data say are the rules that work better now…

Rule 1: **Price a home as close as possible to fair market value.** About half of all sellers still price their homes too high and have to make cuts to attract potential buyers. Zillow studied more than a million homes listed for sale and tracked price changes until they sold. Homes that required a 10% price cut spent an average of 220 days on the market and sold for 2% less than their estimated value. That's because buyers bargain more aggressively when a listing sits on the market a long time. Homes that were correctly priced to begin with needed no price cut to sell, spent an average of 107 days on the market and, best of all, sold for 2% more than their estimated value.

Best way to determine fair market value: Have a real estate agent prepare a market analysis of the recent selling prices of comparable homes in your area to help establish fair market value.

Rule 2: **Make sure the last non-zero digit in your original asking price is a nine.** This is the same kind of psychological pricing that works in retail stores, and it leads to faster, more lucrative sales for homes at every price level.

For example, the average US home that was listed initially for $449,000 wound up selling for about $4,000 more than a home listed at $450,000. What's more, comparable homes priced $1,000 lower than their counterparts sold four days faster on average.

Why it works: Consumers are conditioned to see prices ending in nine as signifying an attractive discount. That kind of pricing attracts more attention to your home's listing, which often translates into higher offers.

Rule 3: **Make modest upgrades to your home that restore the basic functioning of the house.** Modest upgrades have a much bigger relative impact on your home's value than renovations that add fashionable but frivolous luxuries. For example, upgrading a bathroom from poor to decent shape completely changes the livability of the property and appeals to just about everyone. But taking a fully functional bathroom and adding high-end elements, such as fancy jet-massage showerheads or dramatic tiling, actually may turn off many prospective buyers. Based on Zillow's analysis, a $3,000, mid-range bathroom remodel—with such steps as replacing the toilet…updating lighting fixtures…adding a double sink…and painting or putting up wallpaper—resulted in a $1.71 increase in home value for every $1 spent on renovation. But plunking down $12,000 for a complete bathroom overhaul, including replacing the floor and moving plumbing, resulted in only an 87-cent increase in value per dollar spent.

Note: In contrast to conventional wisdom, kitchen renovations have a lower return than many other home-improvement investments, with a cost recovery of just 50 cents per $1 spent regardless of the scope of the remodeling.

Reason: Prospective buyers are very particular about what constitutes a dream kitchen. They won't be excited about a kitchen renovation if it doesn't happen to match their needs and tastes.

Rule 4: **List your home for sale in late March or later.** Many home sellers choose to list early in the year, starting in late January or in February. They do this in order to have plenty of time to catch the spring and early-summer home-buying rush. But Zillow's data indicates that listing very early in the year has become so popular that you're better off waiting until after the first few weeks of March or even the second week in April in some markets, such as Boston. The average US home put on the market in late March, for example, sold for over 2% more than the average home listed earlier in the year.

Reason: Your house doesn't get lost in a sea of new listings. That leads to more attention and potentially more offers.

How to Buy a Home That Soars in Value

People choose to buy particular homes for a variety of reasons that have little to do with money. But if one of your primary goals in choosing a home is price appreciation, the data is clear—look at properties in up-and-coming neighborhoods.

If you can get to one of these neighborhoods within the first five years of it becoming hot, you have a chance of snatching a property at a much lower price point than in areas that are already well-regarded.

How to spot these soon-to-be hot neighborhoods…

• **Use the Halo Effect.** Look for less developed areas adjacent to premier neighborhoods that already have taken off and have ample restaurants, cafés, parks and nightlife.

• **Look for a Starbucks.** Believe it or not, having a location of the popular coffee shop within a quarter mile of a house has proved to be one of the strongest, most reliable indicators of neighborhood gentrification and rapidly appreciating home prices. Between 1997 and 2014, US homes appreciated 65%, on average. But properties near a Starbucks appreciated 96%, on average, and they recovered much more quickly from the housing bust.

Reason: Starbucks has an army of analysts and geographic information specialists dedicated to finding the next hot neighborhood, assessing everything from traffic patterns to the kinds of new businesses opening in the area. In addition, the iconic coffee shop is seen as a proxy for gentrification by other potential upscale businesses.

Rule 5: **Write long, carefully worded listings.** Although the Internet allows home sellers to upload videos and lots of photographs of their homes, the data shows that homes with written descriptions longer than the median length of 50-to-70 words routinely sell for more than their asking prices, while homes with shorter written descriptions don't. Prospective buyers want details, and those extra words give them additional information that makes a home worth seeing in person.

Note: After a listing reaches 250 words, additional length did not seem to help the sale price.

What to write: Avoid words in your listing that connote "small," "nothing special" or "needs work." These words include cute…charming…potential…quaint…needs TLC…and unique. Such words turn off buyers and can reduce the selling price by as much as 2% to 7% of the asking price.

On the positive side, lower-priced homes described in listings as luxurious beat their original asking prices by 8%, on average…and using impeccable beat their original asking prices by 6%. In more expensive homes, listings with the word captivating boosted the sale price by 6.5%, on average, and the word gentle (typically referring to the property description such as gentle rolling hills) was worth an additional 2.3%, on average. Words such as remodeled pushed up the selling prices of homes in every price range by an average of 1.7% to 2.9% and landscaped by 1.5% to 4.2%.

The 9 Things That Turn Off Home Buyers: Fix Them Fast!

Will Johnson, a Nashville, Tennessee–based real estate agent who leads the Will Johnson Group, a team that includes both home-selling and home-staging professionals. He previously led The Sell and Stage Team with RE/MAX International. WillJohnsonGroup.com

As a home seller, you can't always guess the things about your home that might turn off potential buyers—but you should try. In many cases, you could add thousands of dollars to the selling price by resolving potential problems—without spending much—before putting your home on the market. *Here are common "home buyer hates" that can be remedied for a very reasonable cost—in some cases for free…*

• **Popcorn ceilings.** These rough-surfaced ceilings, also known as stucco or acoustic ceilings, were popular from the 1950s through the 1970s, but now they make homes look old and outdated.

What to do: Instead of scraping off popcorn ceiling finishes, which is time-consuming and potentially expensive—or even dangerous if asbestos or lead was used—you can have a new layer of ceiling-grade gypsum board installed onto the popcorn ceiling. (Ceiling-grade gypsum board is lighter than regular gypsum board.) This costs about $2 to $2.50 per square foot installed and eliminates concerns about lead and asbestos. It lowers your ceiling height by about one-half inch—not enough to be concerned about.

● **Insufficient storage.** Small closets and cupboards are a major turnoff for home shoppers and a difficult problem to correct, but the effect can be minimized.

What to do: Remove at least half of the things you currently have stored in cramped closets and cupboards. Small storage areas seem roomier when they are half empty.

Example: Create enough room between garments hanging in a closet so that you can run your hand between them and barely brush the fabric on each side. Store excess items in a rental storage unit…or in matching, stackable plastic bins in the garage or basement (available in home centers for as little as $10 to $20 apiece).

● **Messy laundry rooms, garages, basements.** Most home sellers know that they should clean and declutter before their homes are shown. But some don't realize that cleaning for buyers is different from cleaning for houseguests. Unlike guests, buyers look everywhere and make judgments accordingly. If any part of the home is messy, cluttered or dirty, the whole home will seem less appealing.

What to do: If there is a pile of laundry in the laundry room when your real estate agent calls to arrange a quick showing, toss the laundry into the washer or dryer before heading out. If the washer and dryer are full, toss it in your car and take it with you.

If your garage or basement is cluttered, pack the clutter into matching, stackable plastic storage bins or rent a storage locker and stash the clutter there.

If your cupboards or closets are cluttered, buy matching baskets or bins and stow the mess in these inside the cupboards or closets—attractive small baskets or bins can be found for less than $10. They make storage spaces seem organized even when they aren't.

● **Insufficient light.** Dark, shadowy areas can create a sense of foreboding and ill ease. Shadows can make a room or hallway appear dirty, too.

What to do: Open all window blinds, curtains and shades and turn on all lights before showings. If there still are dim areas or dark corners, increase bulb wattage and/or add lamps. Reasonably attractive freestanding lamps are available at stores such as Target, Home Depot and Lowe's for less than $100 apiece—and you can take these with you when you move. Confirm that every bulb in the house is working before showings. Burned-out bulbs don't just make the house darker, they send a message that the home is flawed.

● **Dark or boldly colored paint on interior walls.** Even though distinctive or dark wall colors have become trendy, they turn off many buyers. Any brash colors inevitably are not the ones many potential buyers would have picked, making it hard for them to imagine themselves living in your home. Your colors also might not work with buyers' furniture…and dark walls can make rooms feel smaller and less inviting.

What to do: Apply a coat of primer/sealer over dark or boldly colored paint and then repaint in a neutral color such as beige or off-white. Primer/sealer is especially important—you even might need more than one coat of primer and perhaps two coats of paint, too. There's no need to buy expensive primer or paint, however. A primer that costs about $15 per gallon and a paint that costs $25 per gallon or less should do. If you don't want to do the job yourself, professional painters might charge $400 to $800 or so for an average 10-foot-by-12-foot room, not including the cost of the paint. Four to eight gallons of primer and two to four gallons of paint should do.

● **Wallpaper.** Many types of wallpaper have been falling out of fashion and can make a home seem out of date. There are exceptions—interior designers sometimes hang stylish new wallpaper prints in bathrooms and dining rooms, for example…or a period-correct wallpaper might be appropriate for a historic home. But as a rule of thumb, wallpaper will be a turnoff to most buyers.

What to do: Unless your wallpaper was selected by an interior designer within the past decade—or was selected to match the home's history—strip it away and paint the walls instead. If you don't want to remove the wallpaper yourself—it can be tricky—expect to pay a professional around $1 per square foot for paper removal.

•**Dated or dingy bathrooms.** It's no secret that an unappealing bathroom can greatly detract from a property's appeal. What many sellers do not realize is that they can downplay this problem without renovating the bathroom.

What to do: Buy a set of big, fluffy, bright white towels. Do not use them—just hang them on bathroom towel racks before showings. Roll some smaller white hand towels and stack these rolls in the bathroom, too. Also hang a new, bright-white shower curtain. These items make the whole bathroom feel cleaner, fresher and more welcoming, all for less than $100—and you can bring your new towels and shower curtain with you when you move.

It also can be helpful to bleach stained grout…repaint peeling trim…replace failing caulk…and update dated faucets (see below).

•**Gold faucets and fixtures and crystal faucet handles.** These glitzy fixtures have gone out of style and now make kitchens and bathrooms seem dated.

What to do: Replace these with brushed-nickel faucets—it's a classic, timeless finish. You can find very nice-looking kitchen faucets at home centers

Make Your Home Irresistible

Fresh-baked cookies is not the most inviting scent.

Best: Individual natural aromas, such as fresh lemon, green tea, lavender, cedar, pine and basil. Recent research reveals that these scents help sell a home—and thus can make any home more inviting to guests. Try displaying a bouquet of fresh lavender or decorate a table with cut pine branches.

Study of the effects of aromas by researchers at Washington State University, Pullman, reported in *The Wall Street Journal.*

for $100 to $200…and bathroom faucets for $50 to $100. Professional installation typically costs $100 to $200 per faucet, though this can vary.

•**Pets in the house.** It creates problems when dogs or cats are in a house when it is shown. Some buyers do not like (or are allergic to) animals…and some animals do not like strangers in their homes.

What to do: If your home is going to be shown many times during a short period, board the pet with a kennel, pet day-care service or a friend. Alternately, you could take the pet with you when you go out…or arrange for a neighbor or local pet walker/pet boarder to pick up the pet when necessary.

When to Unconvert a Room

That bedroom you turned into a workshop or den—or that garage you turned into a bedroom—might suit your needs, but it probably doesn't suit the needs of most potential home buyers. Converted rooms often feel out of place, and unless they were converted by a skilled remodeler, they may feel unprofessionally done.

What to do: The prudent option usually is to convert these rooms back to their original purposes before putting the home on the market. The cost of this varies dramatically depending on what needs to be done.

Exception: If you converted a garage into living space, don't undo this if the finished space was (or appears to be) professionally done—the value of this added living space might outweigh the value of the garage for some buyers, particularly when the cost of converting the space back into a garage is taken into account.

Great Photos Matter

Roundup of experts on real estate, reported at Market Watch.com.

Better photos sell your home faster: 98% of buyers who search for homes online say that photographs are among the most useful features in a listing. And listings that have photographs taken by professionals have 61% more views than others.

What to do: Select an agent or broker based in part on the quality of the photos in his/her current listings…judge whether the photos of your home would make you want to visit the home…be sure that the first few photos shown—the ones that will be seen first—are outstanding…ask the agent or broker whether a professional photographer will shoot the photos of your home—that should be the case.

Trying to Sell Your Home? Spruce Up Your Bathroom

Donna Dazzo, president of the home staging company Designed to Appeal, with locations in New York City and the Hamptons, New York, quoted in *The New York Times*.

There are several easy, low-cost things you can do to make your bath more appealing without spending a lot. Regrout the tiles around the tub, and recaulk where the tub meets the tiles and where it meets the floor. Revitalize a wooden vanity with a coat of dark semigloss paint. Replace a worn toilet seat. Install new light fixtures, faucets and cabinet pulls. Add a new shower curtain, bath mat and fluffy towels. Make sure that the bathroom is sparkling clean and that all toiletries have been put away.

Better Time to Buy a Home?

A roundup of experts on mortgages, reported at GoBankingRates.com.

Buy a new home at the end of the month to improve your short-term cash flow. Mortgage interest is paid in arrears—after the month has ended. At closing, buyers pay accrued interest from the time they close through the last day of the month. So the later in the month you close, the less accrued interest you pay at closing.

Best Day to Buy a Home

The best day to buy a home is February 7. Statistically, that is the day when prices are lowest—12% below average. The two next-best days to buy are February 4 and 5—in fact, eight of the top 10 days to close on a home are in February. In all, the median price per square foot is 6.1% lower than average in February, 5.6% lower in January, 3.6% lower in March and 1.8% lower in April. In all other months, median sale price is above average.

It is highest, at 3% above average, in July and August, which makes those the best months for sellers but the worst for buyers.

Analysis by real estate research firm Attom Data, Irvine, California.

Example: If you have a $240,000 loan at an annual rate of 4.5%, daily interest is $29.60. Closing on the first day of a 30-day month would mean paying $888 in prepaid interest at closing. Closing on the last day would mean paying $29.60—a savings of $858.40 at closing. In the long run, the total you pay comes out the same, and prepaid interest may be unimportant if, for example, you need to move early in the month. But if you have a flexible moving date and tight cash flow approaching closing, a late-in-month closing date may be better.

What Real Estate Websites Don't Want You to Know

Robert Irwin, who has more than 40 years of experience as a real estate broker and investor, Westlake Village, California. He is author of several books about real estate, including *Tips & Traps When Buying a Home*.

Nowadays, many home buyers and sellers depend on websites such as Trulia.com, Zillow.com and Realtor.com for real estate listings…information about prices and local market conditions…and real estate trends. But much of the information may be inaccurate and/or out of date.

Ways these sites may mislead you…

1. Their home-value estimates can be way off. Zillow and Trulia estimate the values of most homes across the country—but those estimates are less accurate than people imagine. Placing too much faith in them could lead sellers to set their asking prices too high or too low…or encourage buyers to offer too much or too little.

The sites don't send out home appraisers. They just gather data about the property and nearby properties and run this through a formula to come up with an educated guess.

Example: If the home next door to yours is about the same size as yours and sold for $250,000 last year, these sites probably will guess that yours is worth around $250,000, too. They won't know and so won't factor in that your home was recently renovated while the one next door is decades out of date.

The value estimates tend to be particularly questionable in states where home sale prices are not in the public record—Alaska, Idaho, Indiana, Kansas, Louisiana, Maine, Mississippi, Missouri, Montana, New Mexico, North Dakota, Texas, Utah and Wyoming.

To fix false information about your home: If you are selling your home or expect to do so soon, check the "Zillow Zestimate" and "Trulia Estimate" for the home to make sure that the information is accurate. Review the sales price history, tax assessment history and home description, then report any missing or inaccurate details to the website—though various home owners have complained that these websites can be slow to respond to complaints, sometimes even taking months. There are varying options to try to address a discrepancy. On Zillow, click "Report problem with listing" under the "More" button. On Trulia, you must first claim your home on Zillow, Trulia's sister site, then click "Correct" under the "More" button. Or ask your broker to try to fix the problem.

Home buyers, in particular, also should check how accurate the website claims its estimates are for the area in question. Only if you dig deep into these websites will you discover that even they admit that their estimates can be fairly inaccurate in some parts of the country. Knowing what level of accuracy they claim for the area at least provides a clue as to how reliable the data might be.

On Zillow, click the "Zestimates" tab near the bottom of the home page, then click "States." On Trulia, select "Trulia Estimates" from the "Explore Trulia" menu near the bottom of the home page.

2. Many of their listings are no longer on the market. According to a 2012 study conducted by consulting firm WAV Group, more than 35% of the homes listed for sale on Zillow and Trulia at any given time already have been sold or pulled from the market. Outdated listings linger in part because it isn't in the websites' interest to pull them—the more listings a real estate site has, the bigger and more useful it appears.

3. Their asking prices can be outdated. Third-party real estate sites such as Trulia and Zillow sometimes fail to promptly update listings to reflect asking price reductions. That means that buyers who use the search tools on these sites to view only properties in their price range might never see the listings of properties that weren't originally in their price range but now are because of price cuts.

What to do: Expand your search parameters to include homes 10% above the high end of your price range when you search for properties on Zillow or Trulia. Their current prices might now be in your price range. Even those that aren't may be close enough that the sellers might accept offers in your price range. Also search the listings on Realtor.com, where asking prices tend to be more up to date.

4. Their "days on the market" figures could be way off the mark. Homes new to the market often attract interest from multiple buyers, while those that have sat for 90 days or more tend to be ignored. Buyers often are wise to be aggressive with their offers on new listings, while low-ball offers might be accepted on older listings.

But the days-on-the-market data provided by real estate websites can be misleading. The figure could reflect the number of days since the property was added to the website, which might not have occurred until weeks after it actually went on the market with third-party sites such as Zillow and Trulia. And listing agents sometimes reset the days-on-the-market clock by taking the property off the market briefly, then relisting it.

Open House Advice

Two key questions to ask during a real estate open house…

• **What are the average utility costs?** Older homes tend to be less energy-efficient, but the previous owners may have installed energy-saving upgrades such as a new heating/cooling system or double-paned windows.

• **Has the price changed?** A lower listing price may save you money now, but it could be a sign of issues with a home.

WiseBread.com

What to do: Buyers should dig deeper to see if a listing's "days on the market" is telling the whole story before making an offer. Zillow and Trulia include a "price history" section that lists other recent times the home was on the market. Also, ask your buyer's agent—the real estate agent representing the home buyer—for details about the property's recent sales history. A buyer's agent can tell you if a home was pulled from the market and then quickly returned.

5. Some of the most desirable properties don't appear on sites until after they've sold. It can take a week for a new listing to appear on Realtor.com and longer still to appear on third-party websites such as Trulia and Zillow—and that's if the seller's agent submits the listing promptly to the Multiple Listing Service. Agents have been known to keep a few choice listings to themselves for a week or two when they think they can find a buyer on their own, in hopes of earning the full commission rather than splitting it with a buyer's agent.

Buyers who wait for listings to appear on Trulia and Zillow could miss out, particularly if they're in the market for a rare and desirable property, such as a waterfront home or a home in the area's most prestigious neighborhood.

What to do: If your local real estate market has heated up and your goal is to buy a property that's likely to be in great demand, choose one of the area's busiest, best-known agents as your buyer's agent. That increases the odds that you'll be one of the lucky few who gets to see desirable properties before they reach the sites. Also, visit open houses to meet other area agents, and let them know what you're looking for.

6. Listings on "for-sale-by-owner" sites often have inflated or inaccurate property descriptions. The property descriptions provided in home listings inevitably are written to put the property in the best possible light. In most cases, those descriptions are at least written by real estate agents who understand the difference between portraying a property in a good light and fabricating information. On for-sale-by-owner sites, however, the property descriptions usually are written by home owners themselves, who are more likely to distort descriptions.

Buying a New Home? Take Note of These Red Flags

Kathleen Kuhn, president, HouseMaster, home-inspection company, Somerville, New Jersey. HouseMaster.com

Poor water pressure could indicate plumbing problems…doors that are hard to close, swing open by themselves or don't open fully could point to structural problems…multiple extension cords could mean that the electrical system is inadequate…a porch, patio or driveway that slopes toward the house could lead to water in the basement.

What to do: When having a home professionally inspected before you buy it, go with the inspector to make observations and ask questions.

Moving? Save Money and Make It Easier, Too

Jeff Yeager is AARP's official "Savings Expert" and host of the weekly AARP show *The Cheap Life* on YouTube. He is author of four popular books about frugal living, including his most recent, *How to Retire the Cheapskate Way.*

When my wife and I recently moved from our beloved home of 30-plus years, a friend sent us a greeting card. On the front it read, "Home is where the heart is…" And on the inside, "even if you can't remember what box you packed it in." I think if you've ever moved, you can relate to that! Moving can be expensive and trying, but there have been a lot of changes since you last moved that can make your move easier and save you money, too. *Here's how…*

●**Make your move easier with apps.** Before you even think about packing your first box, arm yourself with these apps to save time and money…

●Unpakt lets you get quotes from multiple moving companies by filling out one form, and you can book and pay for the move on the app or website. You also can read customer reviews of the moving companies. The app lets you add and remove items from your packing list to see how that affects the cost of your move.

●MagicPlan turns pictures of rooms in your new home into detailed floor plans to help you figure out in advance where everything can go…and what stuff you're better off leaving behind.

●Sortly, an inventory organizer, helps you avoid the common problem that my friend pointed out in his bon voyage card. It lets you keep track of the contents of each box you pack by snapping photos and storing them in digital "boxes" in the app… and with an advanced version (starting at $29/month), you can create a label for each actual moving box and later scan the label with your phone to learn exactly what's inside.

●**Downsize and donate.** Selling spare stuff at a garage sale, consignment store or online takes time, which usually is at a premium during the moving process. Instead, consider donating items to a qualified charity before you move and taking a charitable tax deduction. It's true that under the new federal tax law, a much higher standard deduction means far fewer people can benefit tax-wise from itemizing deductions, charitable or otherwise. But depending on the value of what you choose to leave behind when you move, you might save not only on moving costs but also increase your itemized deductions for a tax benefit as well.

You know that Goodwill and the Salvation Army are good choices for donating furniture, clothing and household items, but also consider the following specialized charities to help your unneeded items get to the people who need them the most—for baby toys and supplies, Baby2Baby…leftover building supplies, appliances, large furniture and other household items that many other charities won't accept, Habitat for Humanity ReStores…nonperishable food items, MoveForHunger or your local food bank…last-minute donations, Pickup Please, a program of the Vietnam Veterans of America that will come pick up clothing, many appliances and other household items at your home often within 24 hours.

●**You pack and load it, they move it.** One of the innovations in the moving industry since you may have last moved are services that bring a large (walk-in size) portable storage container to your current home and leave it there—so you can pack and load the container yourself at your own pace and to your own standards of care. Then the company picks up your loaded container and delivers it to your new home, where you can move in at your own pace. It saves do-it-yourselfers the nail-biting exercise of learning to drive a 26-foot rental truck, and it's likely to save you some serious money compared with hiring a moving company. The financial information site MagnifyMoney.com found that a sample move via a portable storage unit ranged from $1,892 to $2,815 while the same move with a full-service mover cost $4,739—a savings of about $2,000 or more. Fees vary greatly depending on the company, where you are moving, and how much storage you need, so comparison-shop carefully. Portable On Demand Storage (PODS) is the company that claims to have invented the concept of portable, noncommercial storage units, although now there are a number of companies offering similar services, including ZippyShell, 1-800-PACK-RAT and U-Box, which is a service of U-Haul.

●**Buy boxes for less.** The cost of boxes can add up fast. When we moved, we found free boxes offered on Craigslist, and between that and our library and trusty liquor store, we managed to come up with the requisite boxes. If you're not so lucky or would rather not bother, you still can save money compared with just buying boxes at a store—check out BoxCycle.com. This website connects people and businesses that have lightly used boxes and want to sell them with folks who need boxes and want to save money buying them. It's good for the environment and good for your bank account, and if you have boxes you want to sell after your move, you can list them for sale on BoxCycle for free. (The service keeps a commission when your boxes sell.)

Tip: If you have a lot of boxes of books to ship, compare the cost of shipping them via US Postal Service Media Mail with what your moving company will charge you—you might be in for some hefty savings.

•**Timing saves you cash.** Last but not least, timing can save you a lot when you move, provided that you're flexible. According to the website Moving. com, if you're looking to save money when hiring a professional mover, plan your move for late September through April, when demand for moving services is lowest. Even if you can't move within that period, try to schedule your move midweek, when moving companies tend to be less busy.

When Moving to a New Home…

Experts on moving, reported at Bankrate.com.

Change the locks—it is impossible to know how many people have copies of the previous locks' keys. Replace all filters—the aeration filters in bathroom and kitchen faucets…the air filter above the stove…and the filter in the heating/air-conditioning unit. Clean the house completely—when it is empty, you can clean more efficiently. Buff and seal wood floors before placing furniture on them. Get a list of contacts and service people from the prior owner—and if you have a good relationship, ask if you can get in touch with the previous owner in case some unforeseen problem arises.

Choose the Right Mortgage Lender to Avoid Big Problems

Craig Martin, managing director of wealth and lending at JD Power, which conducted a "US Primary Mortgage Origination Satisfaction Study." He is based in Costa Mesa, California.

More than one in five home buyers regret their choice of mortgage lender. Many borrow from the first lender that offers them a competitive interest rate and reasonable fees, which might be the bank where they happen to have a checking account…or the lender that their real estate agent recommends. Some lenders turn out to be especially frustrating.

Among the common complaints: They fail to return calls promptly…miss deadlines…and/or demand a lot of unnecessary information and documentation. Many borrowers complain that they were pressured to choose a particular mortgage product. And new regulations have resulted in many lenders increasing the stringency of their underwriting processes in the wake of the 2007–2009 real estate market meltdown. *What to do…*

•**Contact multiple lenders to get quotes** or to ask questions about the quotes you received from their websites, and after you do so, do not just compare their rates and fees—also gauge which ones were most responsive and answered questions to your satisfaction.

•**Get "preapproved" or "prequalified" by a lender before shopping for a house.** Borrowers who do this are significantly more likely to end up satisfied with their lenders because they do not feel as much pressure to arrange financing quickly.

•**Consider how much hand-holding and face time you need as well.** An online-only lender might be a good choice for someone who is comfortable handling financial matters on a computer, but a local bank or credit union might be the more appropriate option if you like to look someone in the eye when you discuss complex topics.

Mortgage lenders that ranked high in a recent survey include Quicken Loans and CitiMortgage.

Those that ranked low in the survey include Nationstar Mortgage, SunTrust Mortgage, Caliber Home Loans, US Bank Home Mortgage, Freedom Mortgage and Flagstar Bank. The full list and details are available for a fee at JDPower.com (click "Business," then "United States," then "All Industries," then "Financial Services," then "Lending Intelligence," then "Mortgage Origination Satisfaction Study").

Rejected Despite Great Credit?

John Ulzheimer, president of The Ulzheimer Group, Atlanta, which offers consulting services related to the Fair Credit Reporting Act. JohnUlzheimer.com

People who have excellent credit scores—750 or above—might assume that they can land any credit card or reasonable loan they apply for. But sometimes a stellar score is not enough. *These problems still could derail your application...*

•**Insufficient income.** You might be rejected for a mortgage or loan (or not be offered the best rates) if your "debt to income" ratio (monthly debt obligations divided by gross monthly income) exceeds 30%. Or a lack of verifiable income could cause a credit card application rejection.

•**Low appraisal.** Issuers of "secured" loans, including mortgages and auto loans, often reject an application if the value of the asset used to secure the loan does not comfortably exceed the amount of the loan.

•**You churn through credit cards.**

Examples: You repeatedly move debt from one card to the next to take advantage of 0% introductory balance-transfer interest rates. Or you repeatedly sign up for cards to snare up-front rewards—but soon stop using those cards.

•**You have discharged a debt to the lender through bankruptcy.** All mention of a bankruptcy

Buying a Condo? What You Need to Do...

Before buying an association-governed home or condominium, get a copy of the group's most recent reserve study to check its financial soundness. Ask how many members are more than 60 days delinquent on fees—that percentage affects the association's cash flow. An estimated 70% of association-governed communities are underfunded. That leaves residents liable for large special assessments for emergency repairs—those who cannot pay the assessments could face property liens or possible foreclosure. Ask your financial adviser for details.

Roundup of experts on the fiscal health of homeowner associations, reported in Kiplinger's Personal Finance.

should disappear from your credit reports within 10 years—but if a lender lost money because of your bankruptcy, it might never lend money to you again.

•**You have a very limited credit history.** It's possible to achieve a credit score in the mid-to-high 700s after just a year or two of using credit, but some lenders and card issuers insist on a longer history of responsible credit use.

•**One of your credit scores isn't as high as the others.** There could be a problem lurking in your file with the credit-reporting agency that the lender uses even when the other agencies assign you excellent scores.

What to do if your loan application is rejected: You always can apply to other lenders or card issuers, of course, and with your excellent credit score, there's a good chance that one of them will approve your application. But to avoid rejections in the future, obtain a free copy of your credit report from all three major credit bureaus through AnnualCredit Report.com, and check each for errors that could be dragging down one score but not the others.

CHAPTER 12

Kitchen Tips

6 Mistakes Even Good Cooks Make

Chef Todd Mohr, founder of WebCookingClasses.com, an online video cooking school. Based in Baltimore, Chef Mohr previously served as executive chef for corporate and government dining rooms, responsible for planning and executing meals for up to 15,000 people. WebCooking Classes.com

Even experienced home cooks sometimes make mistakes that prevent their food from tasting as delicious as it could. *Here, the most common mistakes made by home cooks…*

•**Buying vegetables that look fresh rather than those that feel fresh.** It's no secret that the freshness of the ingredients affects the quality of the meal. Unfortunately, most home cooks rely on visual clues to determine which vegetables are fresh. Produce suppliers and supermarkets know this and use waxes, preservatives and other tricks to keep produce looking fresh as long as possible, but underneath, that produce is losing taste and texture.

Best: Pick produce by feel. Touch the stem, stalk or roots of a vegetable—whatever part would have drawn water from the ground or from the plant. The drier this feels, the older the vegetable likely is.

Examples: The root end of an onion should feel pliable, not dry…the stem of a green pepper or the bottom of a head of lettuce should feel moist.

•**Using water as an ingredient.** Water has essentially no flavor. Most recipes that call for water would be more flavorful and interesting if another liquid, perhaps chicken or vegetable broth, were used in its place.

Example: Cook white rice in broth rather than water for a far more flavorful side dish.

•**Adding seasonings without first testing them.** There's no going back when you toss spices into a dish that you've prepared, especially when it comes to salt. Instead, spoon a small amount of whatever you're cooking into a tiny dish, then add a small amount of the seasonings and taste the result before seasoning the rest of the meal.

If you're adding spices to a dish and not following a tested recipe, use no more than two or three spices. More than three spices in one dish starts to confuse the palate.

•**Trusting the clock when cooking meat or fish.** Just because a recipe says, "Cook for 10 minutes," it doesn't mean that's what you should do. Your stove, your pan or the size of the cut of meat or fish you selected could be significantly different from the one used to test the recipe, which means that your meal could end up substantially over- or undercooked even if you follow the recipe perfectly.

Some recipes attempt to account for this problem by offering a range of cooking times—such as "Cook for eight to 12 minutes," for example, but that doesn't really solve the problem. Many home cooks arbitrarily select the midpoint when a range of cooking times is supplied, while many others choose the longest time mentioned to make sure that meats are cooked through and safe to eat—resulting in overcooked, rubbery meals. Instead, use a meat thermometer to determine when the protein you're cooking has reached its proper temperature.

Poultry, pork and fish typically are cooked properly when the thickest part of the meat reaches 165°F at its center. The proper temperature for steak depends on how you like your steak cooked. Rare is 125°F...medium is 140°F...and well-done is 160°F at the center of the cut of meat.

•**Slicing into meat to see if it is cooked through.** Cutting into meat as it's cooking or shortly after it is done cooking allows the juice inside to flow out, taking much of the flavor with it. Instead, use a meat thermometer to see whether meat is cooked sufficiently, as described above.

Meats generally should not be sliced or served immediately after they have finished cooking, either, to avoid similar juice and flavor loss. Steaks should be allowed to rest for five to 10 minutes. Larger pieces of meat, including whole roasted turkeys, pork shoulder or leg of lamb, should be allowed to rest for 15 to 20 minutes.

•**Deglazing exclusively with wine.** Fat and tiny caramelized pieces of protein typically remain in the pan after meat, poultry or seafood has been cooked. Most home cooks know that this residue, called "fond," has wonderful flavor and can form the basis of a sauce. But many also assume, incorrectly, that wine is the only liquid they can add to the pan to make this sauce, a process called deglazing.

In fact, pans can be deglazed with just about any cool liquid. Spirits, broth, fruit juice or coconut milk are all valid choices. The best liquid to select usually is one closely associated with the ethnicity of the meal you are trying to prepare.

Examples: Deglaze with pineapple juice for a Hawaiian dish...deglaze with tequila for a Mexican dish.

Even if you don't have a specific ethnicity of food in mind, deglazing with something other than wine is a great way to make a recipe that you've prepared many times taste different and new.

14 Little Kitchen Miracles: Quick Fixes for Common Annoyances

Joan Wilen and Lydia Wilen, writers and researchers based in New York City who have spent decades collecting household tips and "cures from the cupboard." Their most recent book is *Bottom Line's Treasury of Home Remedies and Natural Cures*. They are authors of the free e-letter *Household Magic Daily Tips*—sign up at BottomLineInc.com.

Talk about annoying! How about buying a pineapple that never seems to fully ripen? Or having a wrestling match with a piece of Saran wrap? *Here are fixes for these and other common kitchen annoyances...*

•**Unclinging cling wrap.** Keep your roll of cling wrap in the refrigerator. It will keep it from sticking to itself, making it much easier to use. But it still will stick to whatever you put it on.

•**Prolonging the life of uncut lemons and limes.** Lemons will stay fresh for weeks if you place them in a glass jar, fill it with water and cover tightly.

Limes just need to be placed in a jar, covered and kept in the refrigerator.

•**Corn-shucking magic.** Microwave an ear of corn, with the leaves and silk still on, for three to four minutes. It will be hot, so use gloves or a potholder when you remove the corn from the microwave. Cut off about an inch from the stem end. Next, hold onto the silk and top leaves, and shake out the corn. It should come out easily and completely clean. If it doesn't, help it along by squeezing the top and forcing it out. Even if you have to help the corn along, when you remove it from the husk, it will be free of silk.

•**Preventing leftover cake and cookies from getting stale.** Place a slice of bread up against each already-cut-and-exposed side of the cake. Keep the slices in place with toothpicks. The bread will probably get stale, but the cake will be moist and taste fine.

A slice or two of bread in a container of cookies will soften stale cookies.

•**A place for plastic bags.** Plastic bags—the kind you get from the supermarket—can be stuffed into an empty tissue box and kept in your kitchen.

A cube Kleenex box will hold about 15. A rectangular—160-tissue size—box will hold about 25 plastic bags.

●**Unwilting vegetables.** When vegetables' cell walls lose moisture, they wilt. Rehydrate them by soaking them in a big bowl of cold water and ice for about 15 minutes. They'll be crisp again.

●**Cutting fresh bread.** The softer the bread, the more difficult it is to cut. Using a warm knife will make it much easier. Warm the knife by dipping it in just-boiled water. Dry the knife, and while it's still warm, slice the bread.

●**Reviving stale rolls.** Place stale rolls in a paper bag, moisten the bag and twist the bag closed. Place the bag in a 300°F oven for a few minutes until the bag is dry. The rolls will seem like just baked.

●**Making better pancakes or waffles.** Fill a ketchup bottle with the batter, and use it for better batter distribution.

●**Softening hard brown sugar.** Put the hardened brown sugar in a microwavable dish, put a moist paper towel on top, and cover the dish with plastic wrap or a microwavable plate. Zap the sugar in the microwave for 20 seconds. If that doesn't do the job, give it another one or two 20-second zappings to have ready-to-use brown sugar.

●**Preventing brown sugar from hardening in the first place.** When you open a new supply of brown sugar, keep two or three marshmallows in the container to prevent the sugar from hardening. When the marshmallows dry up, it's time to use the sugar or replace the marshmallows.

●**Life extension for berries.** What good is buying strawberries on sale if they wind up in the garbage before you've had a chance to finish them? The bacteria on all kinds of berries cause them to rot rather quickly. As soon as you get berries home, bathe them in a bowl of three parts water to one part distilled white vinegar. After about 30 seconds, rinse them in cold water, dry them thoroughly and refrigerate them. The vinegar mixture will kill off the bacteria and give you a few more days to enjoy them. No need to rinse them again before eating—there is no hint of vinegar taste whatsoever.

●**The best pineapple ever.** Twist off the leaves, being careful not to expose the flesh. Then stand

---

Use Your Kitchen Helpers Efficiently

Microwave: Use round containers to heat food more uniformly—in rectangular ones, the corners usually attract more energy, overcooking some of the food.

Oven broiler: Keep the oven door slightly open to vent steam and help food develop crustiness.

Slow cooker: Avoid opening it until there is less than an hour to go to be sure that your dish cooks properly.

Dishwasher: Put dishes with starchy stains in the middle of the racks, where the strongest spray of water goes.

Blender: To prevent stalling, first put in the liquid or yogurt base of whatever you are blending, then layer ingredients from smallest to largest, keeping ice and other tough-to-blend items at the top.

Roundup of experts on kitchen appliances, quoted in *Reader's Digest.*

---

the pineapple on a plate upside down, resting it on the surface where the leaves used to be. The idea is to allow the sweetness to be distributed throughout the fruit and not just stay in its lower half. When the entire pineapple turns a light-toasty golden brown, the pineapple is ripe.

●**Natural oven cleaner.** The self-cleaning option on ovens can take its toll—the high temperatures have been known to cause fuses to pop and control panels to burn out. And popular commercial oven cleaners warn of inhaling fumes and possible eye and skin irritation. And then there's the unpleasant residual smell next time you use the oven. Here is a nontoxic do-it-yourself formula from a woman with asthma who refuses to risk using a cleaner that may be detrimental to her health. Blend two cups of baking soda, one cup of distilled white vinegar and one-half cup of liquid dish detergent (Dawn is her choice). Pat a thick coat of the mixture on the entire inside of the oven, including the door. Let it sit for at least 15 minutes, then with a damp rag, microfiber cloth or sponge, wipe the oven clean. If the oven has been neglected for some time, it may take some elbow grease to make it spotless and/or you may have to repeat the process a second time.

Great Gifts for Cooks

Linda Gassenheimer is an award-winning author of several cookbooks, including *The 12-Week Diabetes Cookbook* and *Delicious One-Pot Dishes*. She writes the syndicated newspaper column "Dinner in Minutes." DinnerInMinutes.com

These fun, practical kitchen gadgets make great holiday gifts.

•**Butter Blade (Microplane).** This small knife has rows of small holes at the bottom of the blade that, when pulled across the top of a stick of butter, create soft strands that can be used for spreading. These strands won't tear bread when you try to butter it with hard butter. The rounded tip has a hollow semicircle to create attractive curled butter garnishes. Dishwasher-safe, but hand-wash and dry the cover. $9.95.

•**Ginger Peeler (Küchenprofi).** When I use fresh ginger, I find that I cut away a lot of the flesh trying to remove the peel. This little gadget solves that problem, easily removing peel from corners and crevices. Dishwasher-safe. $14.95.

•**Forged Stainless Steel Chef Knife with Edge Keeper Self-Sharpening Sheath, eight inch (Sabatier).** A knife should be drawn across a sharpening steel before each use to keep it sharp. I really like the fact that this step is done for me by the knife sheath, which not only protects the knife when it's stored but has a built-in mechanism that hones the blade before and after each use. I found it's a very good small knife, especially at this very reasonable price. Hand-wash and dry. $19.99.

•**Black Cube Hybrid Skillet (Frieling).** This stainless steel "hybrid" nonstick skillet has a stainless steel grid that sits above a nonstick surface. The food cooks on these raised stainless steel "pixels." The pan lets you sear food at high temperatures, make sauces and still has nonstick properties. I love that I can use metal utensils with it and that it is so easy to clean. I've been using it for months, and it's my go-to pan. The nonstick coating is PFOA-free. Dishwasher-safe. 11-inch skillet, $90.

Weak or Painful Hands? Try These Helpful Kitchen Hacks

Deborah Quilter, ergonomic design consultant and certified Feldenkrais® practitioner based in New York City. She is author of *Repetitive Strain Injury: A Computer User's Guide* and *The Repetitive Strain Injury Recovery Book*.

You may love cooking, or at least not mind it. But what happens if you have a hand injury or a chronic health condition, such as arthritis… or even just weak hands—so it is painful or even impossible for you to cook?

There are solutions! If you are frustrated with packaging that won't open easily, vegetable peelers that don't work for you, kitchenware that puts your hands in awkward positions, and so on, here are some of the special tools and techniques that can get you cooking again—and enjoying it…

Kitchenware That Works for You

If you've ever injured yourself trying to open hard plastic packaging with the wrong tool (e.g., a knife rather than scissors), you know that safe practices are important to protect your hands. But you may not realize that safety factors include the balance, weight and ergonomic design of your kitchen tools. Choosing well, especially if you have a chronic hand or arm issue, can protect you from cuts, scalds and serious kitchen accidents that could require months of rehab. *Use the following as a checklist for evaluating kitchenware…*

•**Weight.** When shopping for items ranging from knives and other utensils to casserole dishes, griddles, pots and pans and even storage containers, the absolute best thing you can do is pick up the item and notice its weight. If it feels heavy to you—especially if it's a vessel that's going to hold food—it weighs too much for your physical ability. Don't buy it.

•**Balance.** When you hold a skillet, pot, or other kitchen item by the handle, how balanced does it feel? Is the length of the handle appropriate for the size of the pot? Is it easy for you to manipulate? This can often be the deciding factor between two equally attractive items.

Example: If you are buying a tea kettle, lift it and pretend to pour water from it. This will tell you how well-balanced it is and how well it works with your physiology or level of ability.

● **Handle design.** How easy and comfortable are an item's handles to grasp? How easy does it feel as you lift the item? When choosing between a lid with a knob and a lid with handle, the handle will most often feel more comfortable because it's a better match for the natural flexion of fingers. A knob is typically (though not always) small and harder to grasp because of the different type of grip you need to use.

● **Versatility.** Unless you're a gadget maven, choose products that can do more than one job well… rather than a lot of separate, very specialized tools.

Why: Having to rummage for the right item in a crowded drawer or cabinet can be just another stressor on your hands and arms, especially if you have to move other items out of the way to find them.

Useful Tools

Give your hands a break by upgrading the tools you use every day—look for specific features will make it easier for you to accomplish a variety of tasks.

● **Spring-loaded scissors.** This tops the list of must-have kitchen tools for opening tough packaging, cutting off wire and plastic twist ties and other jobs that you might not even realize impact your hands, such as snipping grape stems, which requires a surprising amount of hand energy. When using traditional scissors, it's typically the movement needed to open them that exerts undue pressures on your hand, not the movement of closing them to cut. Spring-loaded scissors eliminate this pressure. You might find that having kitchen scissors in a variety of blade lengths is helpful—shorter ones for, say, snipping herbs, longer ones for cutting rounds of parchment paper for baking, etc.

● **Ergonomic knives.** These knives are better-shaped than most knives for the job you need to do with them—the blades are set lower than the handles to allow a more natural alignment of the hand as you cut. This is especially helpful when you need to use significant force to cut hard vegetables or thick or bony meat or when a food processor's blades won't do.

Caution: A sharp knife is easier to use and safer than a dull knife because you don't have to exert as much force with it. But if you buy new ergonomic knives, they're likely to be much sharper than the old knives you're used to—so be extra careful about not casually touching the blades, and store them with protective sheaths on (if they come with sheaths) or in a knife holder, not loose in a drawer.

● **Jar opener.** While there are electric jar openers available, an easier and essentially free trick is to use an ordinary bottle opener inserted under the lid of a new jar to break the vacuum seal…and to then twist off the lid with the grip-assistance of a dishwashing glove. As long as you don't bend the lid very much with the bottle opener, you'll be able to screw it back on easily. If this method doesn't work for you, you might find that it's worth buying an electric jar opener.

● **Plastic or silicone mesh sink mat.** Weak hands, nerve injuries and age-related loss of sensation can lead to poor grip and things slipping out of your hands. As insurance, buy a sink liner—the kind primarily made to prevent scratches to your sink's surface from utensils and dishes—for you, it will help prevent glasses and plates from breaking if you drop them over the sink.

A special shopping note: "Ergonomic" kitchen items are big business these days, and you'll see lots of products labeled that way. But it's important to trust your assessment of a product and your instincts over the labeling. A product might be described as ergonomic or hand-friendly but might not be right for your unique situation. In fact, you might find that a run-of-the-mill item performs just as you need it to. For example, an "ergonomic" salad spinner with a top button you push down on might be great if you have arthritis, whereas someone with repetitive strain injury might find that same arm/hand movement painful. Remember, you know your own body best. Try out numerous models of every tool to find the ones that answer your needs.

Better Biomechanics

How you use your tools is as important as the tools that you choose…

• **Slide rather than lift.** It might sound obvious, but it's not intuitive for many people: If you have, say, a heavy pot on the stove and need to move it to a different burner, slide it and use both hands. This enables your core muscles to do most of the work.

• **Store heavy objects between chest and waist level.** You might have gotten used to storing some of your heavy kitchen items up on a high shelf or down in a low cabinet earlier in life, when lifting things was easier, and just never thought to change that arrangement. Change it now! This way, you'll engage your core muscles to reach for them and not have to bend low or support weight on raised arms.

• **Transfer ingredients to smaller, easier-to-lift containers for storage.** This is especially helpful if you buy food in bulk to save money and time.

• **Keep your elbows near your torso when you're chopping.** You'll use the power muscles of your core and avoid straining your shoulders, which is more likely to happen when you work with your arms outstretched.

• **Get kitchen-prep help.** Instead of slicing and dicing yourself, see if your market will do it for you. Besides offering the services of a meat butcher and fishmonger, more and more markets now have a "produce butcher" who will take fresh, whole produce that you choose and slice or chop it for you (usually for a fee). Let this person know if you want your produce washed first—they don't always do that. This is a more nutritious alternative to buying pre-chopped produce that could be losing nutritional value over the hours, if not days, that it's been sitting already-cut in the market.

Six Ways to Reuse Aluminum Foil

Scour a barbecue grill or remove stuck-on food from pots, pans and oven racks. Scrub rust off chrome and steel. To sharpen dull garden shears and scissors, cut through folded layers of foil a few times. For heavy-duty garden shears, fold the foil even thicker. To reduce static cling, put a crumpled piece in the clothes dryer. Keep cats and dogs away from certain areas by putting foil down—most of them dislike walking on it. To keep birds and deer away, hang strips of foil on strings in the garden.

What else to do with used foil: Wrap leftovers in used foil, but if the foil has come in contact with raw meat, do not reuse it for other food purposes.

Jeff Yeager, Accokeek, Maryland–based author of The Ultimate Cheapskate's Road Map to True Riches *and* The Cheapskate Next Door.

The Smart Eater's Kitchen— 5 Must-Have Foods That Are Often Overlooked

John La Puma, MD, a board-certified specialist in internal medicine. Dr. La Puma and Michael Roizen, MD, are the first physicians to teach cooking and nutrition in a US medical school. A trained chef with a private nutritional medical practice in Santa Barbara, California, Dr. La Puma is a cofounder of the popular ChefMD video series and author of *Refuel: A 24-Day Eating Plan to Shed Fat, Boost Testosterone, and Pump Up Strength and Stamina.* DrJohnLaPuma.com

---

Take a quick look around your kitchen. If you pride yourself on eating healthfully, chances are you'll find plenty of veggies, fruits, whole grains, fish, lean meat, olive oil and nuts. Pat yourself on the back…then go to the grocery store!

Even the most health-conscious among us are likely to be missing out on the "secret" foods that allow us to turn a nutritious—but sometimes boring—dish into something fantastic. These are the healthful foods that add zing to the basics.

For advice on the items that you need to keep your taste buds popping, we spoke with John La Puma, a medical doctor and a trained chef. *His favorite must-have foods that may be missing from your kitchen…*

• **Beef broth.** This is an ingredient that most chefs would never do without—but that many people never buy or make. Chicken broth—which is much more popular with home cooks—is OK, but beef broth (also called stock) is far more flavorful.

If you're a vegetarian: Try mushroom stock (available in natural-food stores or online).

How to use broth: A rich broth is the secret to good soups—or even a plate of beans. Use it in place of water to cook brown rice…to braise inexpensive cuts of beef, pork or poultry…or to moisten leftovers when reheating them.

To make your own stock: Roast leftover beef bones for 30 minutes in a 400°F oven, and then simmer them for four hours with onions, carrots, celery and herbs (usually thyme, bay leaves and parsley).

But boxed stocks are also good—they're virtually calorie-free and are available in low-sodium, fat-free and organic versions.

Hint: Bouillon cubes or powders work in a pinch, but high-quality, ready-made liquid stocks taste much better.

Tasty shortcut: A demi-glace sauce or stock from MoreThanGourmet.com. Just add water and heat.

●**Dijon mustard.** Usually made with white wine and mustard seeds, Dijon mustard is more flavorful than the classic yellow version and adds a nice "bite" to leftovers.

How to use it: A good-quality Dijon mustard is more than just a sandwich spread. You can mix it with olive oil, vinegar and a little lemon juice to make salad dressings…mix it with a touch of honey and plain yogurt for a tangy vegetable dip… or spread it on chicken to deepen the flavor and brown the skin during roasting.

●**Ground turkey.** Assuming that you eat meat, it's a good idea to keep some antibiotic-free ground meat in the freezer. Ground turkey is an excellent choice. It defrosts in minutes in the microwave, and it cooks quickly on the stove. Compared with ground beef, it's also a little higher in protein.

How to use it: Because ground turkey highlights the flavors of other foods more readily than ground beef, it's great in casseroles, meatloaf and chili. You can add it to just about anything—even canned beans or frozen or canned vegetables.

●**Hot sauces.** These high-octane condiments include old favorites like Tabasco Pepper Sauce (at grocery stores) and newer-to-the-market specialty products such as Acid Rain Hot Sauce or Captain Spongefoot Sriracha Table Sauce, both available at HotSauceWorld.com…and Ghost Pepper Hot Sauce, available at PepperPalace.com.

Capsaicin, the chemical compound that puts the "hot" in hot sauces, is not only a natural flavor-enhancer but also causes the body to burn more calories.

How to use it: Try hot sauce on eggs, meats and otherwise bland-tasting foods, such as cottage cheese and macaroni and cheese. Hot sauce also goes well with cooked carrots or on popcorn.

●**Parmigiano-Reggiano cheese.** I might be biased (I am a third-generation Italian-American), but I think that finely grated Parmigiano-Reggiano gives foods a better flavor than any other cheese and that it's worth its price compared with cheaper, less flavorful versions of Parmesan cheese. Parmigiano-Reggiano is nearly lactose-free, helpful for people who have trouble digesting this sugar found in milk and other dairy products.

How to use it: The slightly nutty taste of Parmigiano-Reggiano goes well with practically all vegetables, fresh salads and even bean dishes. It makes an attractive, delicious garnish—and because it fluffs up when it's grated, one-half cup is only about 121 calories and has just 1 gram (g) of carbohydrates and 8 g of fat.

8 "Forever" Foods Every Healthy Kitchen Needs

Torey Armul, MS, RD, CSSD, a spokesperson for the Academy of Nutrition and Dietetics, counsels clients on sports nutrition, weight management and family/prenatal nutrition through her private practice in Columbus, Ohio.

When are you most likely to order takeout food? If you're like many people, it's when you're low on groceries at home. Keep your cabinets and your freezer stocked with these eight staples, and you'll never be without a fast but healthy meal.

Frozen Shrimp

If you're out of fresh meat, you'll get a convenient protein-rich alternative with frozen shrimp. They're a good source of B vitamins and iron, which can help boost your metabolism and keep you feeling your best. Because of their smaller size, frozen shrimp also can be easier to cook and prepare than frozen beef, pork or chicken.

In fact, you can save yourself a step by buying precooked shrimp. That way you just need to reheat them and season as desired. Thaw the shrimp in a bowl of hot water for three to five minutes and remove the tails. Next, season with olive oil and dried herbs and spices, such as chipotle chili pepper, garlic powder or basil. Reheat for just a few minutes on the stovetop, in the oven or on the grill. Shrimp can be served by itself or added to rice, pasta, tortillas, tacos or salad.

Frozen Broccoli

Vegetables are one of the first foods to spoil in every grocery haul. Don't let that be a reason to skip your veggies! Fruits and vegetables should make up half of what we eat, although few Americans are meeting this recommended daily intake. Once your stash of fresh veggies runs out, frozen makes an excellent substitute. They are packaged at the peak of freshness, which means that they retain their nutritional content. Some frozen veggies taste more like fresh than others—that includes broccoli, which also is especially nutritious. Not a fan of broccoli? Always keep on hand frozen cauliflower, peas, green beans, asparagus, brussels sprouts or a frozen vegetable "medley" that you like.

Easy one-pot dinner: Add your favorite frozen vegetables to a pasta pot a few minutes before the pasta is finished cooking. (Don't worry, the vegetables won't make the pasta too cold.) Then drain the pasta and vegetables together and serve. Easy!

Tuna Packets

Tuna packets are another convenient source of protein, with the addition of heart-healthy omega-3 fats. They're ready in an instant, but unlike cans, they don't require draining (the nutritional content is similar to that of canned tuna, however). Pack-

aged tuna has a long shelf life, making it a pantry prerequisite when your other options are limited.

Branch out from plain tuna with flavored tuna packets, such as lemon pepper, hot buffalo style, sweet and spicy (my favorite!) and sun-dried tomato and basil. They add taste and variety to your meal without adding too much additional sodium or calories. I use flavored tuna packets to spice up my usual sandwiches, salads and pasta dishes.

Canned Soup

Canned soup gets a bad rap for containing too much salt, fat, sugar, preservatives…or all of the above. I still recommend it because it can be a full, balanced meal. The trick is to buy only soups that aren't loaded with unhealthy ingredients. The best soups are broth- or vegetable-based (such as butternut squash, tomato, minestrone or chicken noodle) rather than cream-based. Look for soups labeled "low sodium," which means that they contain 140 mg or less of sodium per serving. "Reduced sodium" indicates only that the soup has less sodium than the original version, so it may not be low in salt after all. While you're comparing labels, choose the soup with less saturated fat (2 grams or less) and more fiber (2 grams or more) per serving.

You also can bulk up a can of soup by adding frozen vegetables, canned beans, leftover rice, packaged tuna or really any healthy food you have around.

Here's another kitchen hack: Canned soup makes a ready-made sauce. Some of my favorite soups to use as sauce are butternut squash, chunky tomato, Italian-style wedding and lentil vegetable. Just add the soup to cooked rice, pasta, quinoa, poultry or fish for a delicious sauce that's ready in seconds. Low-sodium varieties will help to moderate your daily sodium intake.

Canned Chickpeas

Beans are one of the most underrated foods at the store. They are cheap yet remarkably nutritious, loaded with plant-based protein and fiber. Chickpeas, also known as garbanzo beans, are an excellent source of iron, folate, phosphorus and manganese. They are exceptionally convenient and versatile. Eat them plain, with a dash of salt and pepper or mixed into your meal. Enjoy them warm or cold. Mash them to create a creamy hummuslike appetizer or to complement a main dish.

While you're stocking up on chickpeas, grab some canned lentils, black beans and kidney beans, too. They share a similar nutritional profile and can be seamlessly added to soups, salads, rice bowls, tacos and omelets.

Microwavable Rice

There is no faster meal-starter than a packet of microwavable rice. It's ready in just 90 seconds, and the brown and wild rice varieties are major sources of fiber. Rice is a healthy base for a variety of Asian and Mexican dishes, or it can add flavor and nutrition to traditional soups and salads. Should you worry about arsenic levels in rice? Not if you eat a variety of whole grains and practice good portion control.

You do pay for the convenience of microwavable rice, however. I wait for sales to stock up on the microwavable packages.

Whole-Wheat Pasta

Dried pasta will last for a year or more in your pantry, making it a healthy choice when you're out of fresher foods. It's ready in minutes and can be a delicious way to add nutrients to your meal. Most people think of pasta as a carbohydrate-rich indulgence rather than a nutritious meal choice. However, it all comes down to choosing the right kind and watching your portion size.

Buy 100% whole-wheat pasta—meaning that whole wheat is the only ingredient. It typically has a shelf life of one to two years. Whole-wheat pasta is an excellent source of fiber, which keeps your digestive tract healthy and running smoothly. It also contains a moderate amount of protein.

Typical pasta portions are way too large. Limit yourself to a healthy one-cup serving of cooked pasta, and add vegetables and beans to help fill you up.

Frozen Strawberries

Few foods are more perishable than fresh fruit. Luckily, frozen berries are a great alternative. One cup of frozen strawberries is low in calories but delivers 18% of your recommended daily fiber intake and 150% of your daily vitamin C. Like vegetables, fruit is frozen at its peak ripeness, preserving nutritional value.

Nosh on berries straight from the bag for a sweet and satisfying dessert (just give them a few minutes to thaw slightly). Want to sweeten up your breakfast with healthy antioxidants? Sauté frozen fruit in a saucepan for a berry sauce to drizzle over pancakes, yogurt and oatmeal. Strawberries also are great in smoothies and stirred into yogurt.

Save money when buying frozen fruit by waiting for sales, which usually happen when the fruit is in season. Diversify your choices with frozen mango, cherries, peaches and blueberries, all of which make a low-calorie dessert.

Clever Uses for Cooking Spray

TheKrazyCouponLady.com

Coat measuring cups before putting honey or syrup in them—the contents will slide right out. Remove soap scum on glass shower doors—just spray the inside and wipe with an absorbent cloth. Wipe dead bugs off a car grille and bumper—spray the area, and rub gently with a clean cloth. Stop a door from squeaking—spray the hinges. Stop food from sticking to a knife when chopping—spray the knife before using it. Keep candleholders wax-free—spray them before placing the candles inside. Prevent stains on plastic containers—spray them before putting tomato sauce or similar foods in them. Stop ice from forming in a freezer by spraying along walls and shelves. Prevent cheese from sticking to a grater by spraying before use. Remove a stuck ring by spraying your finger. Stop snow from sticking to a shovel by spraying the blade before use.

Get Pesticides Off Apples

Study by researchers at University of Massachusetts and Massachusetts Pesticide Analysis Laboratory, both in Amherst, published in *Journal of Agriculture and Food Chemistry.*

To remove pesticide residue from conventionally grown apples, mix one teaspoon of baking soda in two cups of water, submerge the apples in a bowl with a cover for two minutes, then rinse.

Even better: Buy organic.

Easier Ways to Peel Hard-Boiled Eggs

Prevention.com

Add baking soda to the water in which you boil the eggs—one-half teaspoon per quart of water. This makes the water more alkaline and the shells easier to peel.

Also: Roll the hard-boiled egg back and forth until small cracks appear all over the shell, then start peeling from the larger end of the egg.

Or: Put the cooked egg in a small, strong glass with a little bit of water, cover the top of the glass with your hand and shake vigorously until the eggshell has dozens of cracks—the shell should slip right off.

No More Stinky Milk!

Clarkson University

The "use by" dates on food labels may become obsolete.

Latest development: Researchers have developed "smart labels" that change color when yogurt, milk—even cosmetics—have gone bad.

Better Ways to Freeze Foods

Reader's Digest.

Freeze berries on a baking sheet in a single layer to prevent the formation of large ice crystals that turn berries mushy. Once frozen, store in a plastic freezer bag. Freeze milk at 0°F to keep it good for up to three months. If freezing a full carton, pour out a bit first—milk expands when frozen. To freeze avocados for guacamole, purée them and add one teaspoon of lime or lemon juice to prevent browning. Store in an airtight container for up to five months. Freeze ripe whole tomatoes in a single layer on a tray with parchment paper. Transfer the frozen tomatoes to a plastic freezer bag, and keep them for up to eight months. Thaw by running the tomatoes under warm water—the skin will peel off easily.

Use Your Slow Cooker Like a Pro—Tastier Meals... Easier, Too!

Hope Comerford, recipe developer, blogger, public speaker and author of several slow cooker cookbooks, including *Fix-It and Forget-It Lazy and Slow Cookbook* and *The Gluten-Free Slow Cooker.* Her blog, "A Busy Mom's Slow Cooker Adventures," can be found at SlowCookerAdventures.com.

Many people have slow cookers and love their convenience, but they don't use the cookers anywhere close to their full potential. Hope Comerford, author of the popular *Fix-It and Forget-It* cookbooks, shares her tips and tricks on how you can use your slow cooker to make even more delicious dishes...

•**You can make a large slow cooker smaller.** If you cook a small batch of food in a large cooker, it will cook too quickly and dry out, possibly even burn. If you have a seven-to-eight-quart slow cooker, you still can cook a small batch of food by putting the ingredients into an oven-safe baking dish or baking pan and placing it on a trivet in your slow cooker. Make sure that it's a truly heat-proof trivet, and use the cooking time called for in the recipe.

●**Slow cookers work best when they are two-thirds to three-quarters full.** If you are going to exceed this guideline, it would be wise to reduce the recipe or split it between two slow cookers. Or you may need to increase the cooking time. Conversely, if it is less than two-thirds full, you may need to reduce the cooking time called for in the recipe.

●**Resist the urge to open the lid.** Every time you peek (and let heat escape), you add more required cooking time than you might think! Try to assess how your meal is progressing by looking through the lid. If you simply can't help lifting the lid, remember that it will lengthen your required cooking time depending on how long you leave the lid off.

●**Remove the lid…sometimes.** If you need your dish to thicken, such as for a sauce or a casserole that looks like it has too much liquid, it may be wise to remove the lid for some of the cooking time. Take off the lid for the last half-hour to one hour of cooking time.

●**Do not start your cooking with frozen meat.** The meat typically will not reach the proper internal temperature in the time allotted for the recipe. This is particularly true for thick cuts of meat.

●**Keep your vegetables at the bottom.** This keeps them in more direct contact with the heat, which is best because veggies typically take longer than meat to cook.

●**Beware of your slow cooker's "hot spot."** After using your slow cooker several times, you will notice a spot in which the food is a little more well-done and/or where you tend to have to scrape off burned food. You are most likely to notice this when baking in your slow cooker. To make it so that food doesn't burn in that spot, lay foil over the spot when the cooker is empty, spray the foil with nonstick spray and leave it there throughout the cooking time.

A Healthier Way to Cook Rice

Summary report of data on a study by researchers at the College of Chemical Sciences in Sri Lanka of how cooking methods affect resistant starch in rice, presented at the National Meeting and Exposition of the American Chemical Society in Denver.

Have you heard about the revolutionary new way to cook rice that cuts calories by as much as 60%? It's being touted online as a miracle weight-reducing kitchen trick, and it sounds like a dieter's dream.

Don't believe it. It isn't true.

But there is good science behind a rice-cooking technique that does cut calories—and makes rice less likely to spike your blood sugar levels.

Now that's healthy.

Rice Research

Researchers at the College of Chemical Sciences in Sri Lanka tested eight cooking variations on a variety of rice that's common in their country. One variation resulted in rice that had about 15% more resistant starch, a form of starch that our bodies can't digest, making it act more like fiber.

As a result, the rice cooked this way isn't likely to raise blood sugar as quickly as regular rice—a good thing, because rice, especially white rice, tends to send blood sugar up pretty quickly. Since resistant starch can't be digested, the new rice—at least the variety used in this study—also has about 10% to 15% fewer calories.

The 60% fewer calories claim? That came from the researchers speculating about what they might be able to achieve in future rice-cooking studies using other varieties of rice.

The Formula

The successful technique is pretty simple: Add about one teaspoon of coconut oil to each half cup of dry rice, cook normally—and then refrigerate it for 12 hours.

The best part: You don't have to eat the rice cold. You can enjoy it reheated and get the same benefits.

The oil combines with the starch, and cooling the rice turns that starch into resistant starch. You could also use a different oil such as olive oil, although only coconut oil was used in this study. The cooling technique is well-known to food researchers—potatoes that are boiled then cooled tend to have more resistant starch, for example.

All in all, it's a pretty simple change that could have health benefits. Thinking of rice for tomorrow's dinner? You could cook up a batch tonight—and use it tomorrow. Any healthy recipe for leftover rice is a good place to start.

Cast Iron Is Back!

Linda Gassenheimer is an award-winning author of numerous cookbooks, including *Delicious One-Pot Dishes* and *Quick & Easy Chicken*. Most recently, she created the recipes for *Bottom Line's Beat Diabetes Now!* She writes the syndicated newspaper column "Dinner in Minutes." DinnerInMinutes.com

Cast-iron skillets, pots, griddles and pans are becoming popular again because, when properly "seasoned," they are naturally nonstick without added chemicals...they can be used on stovetops, in the oven and under a broiler...and once heated, they retain their heat beautifully. And high-quality cast-iron cookware costs far less than high-quality stainless steel or enameled cookware ($13 versus $95 for a 10-inch skillet). Seasoning is a process of applying oil and heat that creates a nonstick cooking surface. Some cast iron comes preseasoned.

But there are many myths about cast iron. *Here's what you need to know, plus four delicious recipes to try...*

Myths About Cast Iron

MYTH: **Once seasoned, cast iron won't rust.**

Reality: Cast iron must be dried thoroughly to prevent rust from forming even when well-seasoned. After drying, rub it down with a little vegetable oil or shortening. Cast iron occasionally may need to be reseasoned. This means coating the pan with a thin layer of a vegetable oil, heating it in the oven or on the stove until it starts to smoke, rubbing with a paper towel and letting it cool down. You will know it needs reseasoning when food begins to stick.

MYTH: **Cleaning with soap ruins cast iron.**

Reality: You can wash cast-iron cookware with mild dishwashing liquid. The cookware must be dried immediately and rubbed with a little oil. You even can scrub it with a nylon pad or scraper to remove food residue. One way to remove stubborn stains is to add coarse salt and a little warm water to the surface and scrub with a plastic or silicone brush. If you use steel wool or scouring powders, the cookware will need to be reseasoned as explained earlier.

MYTH: **If rust appears, the pan can no longer be used.**

Reality: If rust appears, scour the rust area with a steel-wool scouring pad. Once the rust is gone, reseason the pan.

MYTH: **Metal utensils cannot be used on cast-iron cookware.**

Reality: Metal can be used. This myth got started because when cast-iron cookware is used often, it can build up a thin layer of carbon. A metal utensil can scrape the carbon, leaving scratches and residue that look like damage. This is not the cast iron and not toxic. But to avoid this, you can use wood or silicone utensils with cast iron.

MYTH: **Cast iron heats evenly.**

Reality: Like all cookware, cast iron can have hot spots. When cooking on the stovetop, preheat cast iron for around 10 minutes, moving it around the burner to make certain that all areas are hot. It is not necessary to continue moving cast iron while cooking.

Great Recipes for Cast-Iron Cooking

My favorite recipes with cast-iron pans are seared steak, fried chicken and frittatas. *Here's a couple newbies to try...*

CHOCOLATE CHIP GIANT COOKIE

This recipe is adapted from *The Lodge Cast Iron Cookbook*.

1 cup brown sugar
½ cup granulated sugar
1 cup butter (2 sticks)
1 teaspoon vanilla

2 large eggs

2½ cups all-purpose flour

1 teaspoon baking soda

1 teaspoon salt

2 cups chocolate chips

Chocolate sprinkles (optional)

Vegetable oil spray

10-inch cast-iron skillet

Preheat the oven to 375°F. Using an electric mixer, beat the two sugars and butter together until smooth. Beat in the vanilla. Add the eggs one at a time, waiting for one to be incorporated before adding the second. Remove the bowl from the mixer, and stir in the flour, baking soda and salt. Stir in the chocolate chips. Spray the skillet with vegetable oil spray. Spoon the dough into the skillet, and pat with a spoon to spread the dough evenly. Spread the chocolate sprinkles on top if using. Bake for 30 minutes. The edges should be golden. Remove the skillet to a rack, and cool for 15 minutes. Cut into wedges. Makes 16 wedges.

SHRIMP AND ARUGULA PIZZA

This recipe uses the cast-iron skillet entirely in the oven. Cast iron gives pizza a crisp crust, evenly golden.

1 package refrigerated, prerolled thin pizza dough (such as Pillsbury)*

3 teaspoons olive oil, divided use

1½ cups pizza sauce

4 ounces shredded mozzarella cheese

2 cups sliced button mushrooms

12 ounces raw, peeled and deveined large shrimp, cut in half

1 Tablespoon chopped fresh oregano leaves or 1 teaspoon dried

2 Tablespoons lemon juice

Salt and freshly ground black pepper

1 cup baby arugula, washed and dried

Olive oil spray

10-inch cast-iron skillet

Preheat the oven to 450°F. Open the pizza dough, and unroll it. Coat the skillet with two teaspoons of the olive oil. Place the dough in the skillet. Spread

*If using other pizza dough, roll it out to make a thin crust.

Trick to Warm a Plate

When you're using the toaster oven, put a plate on top so that it will be warm when your food is ready—you don't want a cold plate cooling off your nice warm food.

Bottom Line Editors

the dough about one-half-inch up the side of the skillet to account for slight shrinkage when it bakes. Cut away the excess dough. Spread the remaining one teaspoon of oil over the dough. Spoon the pizza sauce evenly over the dough, then sprinkle the cheese over the sauce. Spread the mushrooms over the cheese. Place the shrimp evenly over the top, and then sprinkle the oregano over the shrimp. Place the pizza on the middle rack of the oven, and bake for 15 minutes. The crust should be golden. Bake a few minutes more if necessary. Remove the pizza from the oven, and sprinkle the lemon juice and salt and pepper to taste over the top. Place the arugula in the center of the pizza, and spray with olive oil. Serve immediately. Makes two servings.

Take Great Food Photos

Jon Van Gorder, professional food photographer and owner of Van Gorder Studios in Fairfield, Connecticut. His work has won awards from the Advertising Photographers of America and the Connecticut Art Director's Club. His clients include Dannon, WSJ Wines, Spring Valley Foods, Guinness, Dean Foods and Garelick Farms. VanGorderStudios.com

Whether you're shooting a restaurant meal or a homemade creation, you can enhance your food shots with some tricks...

●**Make it look appetizing.** For social postings of restaurant meals, your cell-phone camera is capable of capturing good shots. Your images often are viewed on small screens, so keep compositions simple and tightly cropped. Add a napkin, side dish or a glass to give scale and interest to your food story. *Also...*

• Look for good lighting opportunities. Soft window light and bright artificial lighting work well. In dark interiors, often the brightest lighting is on top of the bar—bring your plate to the bar for the shot. Or you might want to consider lighting when selecting your table.

• Turn off your flash. Newer phones have excellent low-light capability, and ambient light is always more attractive than flash.

• Rotate the plate to find the best composition, and take several shots from different angles.

• Shoot as soon as possible after food arrives so that everything looks fresh.

• Keep hands and faces out—let the meal be your hero.

• Use your phone's crop tool and other editing tools to "finish" your image if you're uploading immediately. Modern smartphones have good resolution, so a onetime minor crop and rotating of an image do little to degrade the image.

• **Show the steps.** If you're shooting home-cooked recipes, consider using a "real" camera such as a DSLR so that the image quality is better. Also, consider shooting your cooking process—people love to see step-by-step shots. Try to keep the background setting, exposure and lighting consistent for your series of food-prep images. Study similar image series from food blogs or magazines for composition ideas—good sites include CookieAndKate.com…ThePioneerWoman.com/cooking…and SeriousEats.com. Unlike in most restaurant shots, it's fine to show hands at work.

Direct or diffused sunlight provides interesting shadows and has a warm quality. You can use white or sheer curtains to soften and diffuse daylight.

To fill in harsh shadows, use white poster board as a reflector. You can cut the board down if it is too large. Place it just outside the camera's view on the side with the deepest shadows. Place it farther out if it adds too much light. Don't overdo it—you want your shots to be three-dimensional, so it's good to have a healthy ratio of shadows and highlights.

If you're shooting at night, home lighting often isn't sufficient. You can purchase a light from photography-equipment stores or at Amazon.com (such as softboxes from Craphy or Neewer).

Summer Cooking Tips… Keep Your Kitchen Cool

Ellie Krieger, host of Healthy Appetite, which runs on the Cooking Channel. She is a registered dietician and winner of the prestigious James Beard Foundation Award for "Best Cooking with a Healthy Focus." Her most recent cookbook is *Comfort Food Fix: Feel-Good Favorites Made Healthy*. EllieKrieger.com

In the heat of summer, cooking can be an unpleasant chore even for those who like to cook. Fortunately, many wonderful meals require little or no cooking—chilled or room-temperature foods are one of summer's great pleasures. And there are ways to minimize kitchen heat when we do cook during the summer, saving ourselves from discomfort and unnecessarily high air-conditioning bills.

To keep cooking from heating up your home this summer…

Countertop Cooking

Countertop cooking appliances generally emit much less heat than ovens and stovetops, and they perform a wide range of cooking chores very well…

• **Toaster ovens can stand in for full-size ovens on most smaller cooking jobs.** And they don't just limit kitchen heat—they also limit serving size, a good way to avoid overeating.

Example: I freeze cookie dough in rolls, then cut off slices to cook four cookies at a time in my toaster oven.

• **Microwaves emit virtually no heat and can do much more than just heat up frozen foods.**

Example: I use my microwave to steam vegetables. Just wash the vegetables, put them in a microwave-safe bowl, add one tablespoon of water, cover the bowl with a plate or a lid, then microwave for the amount of time that you would have steamed the vegetable over boiling water—around five minutes for broccoli or three to four for asparagus.

• **Electric pressure cookers and rice cookers emit much less heat than ovens and stovetops.** And rice cookers can be used for more than just rice—they're good for cooking oatmeal and for slow-cooking soups, beans and stews. Some rice cookers come with steamers to cook vegetables or shrimp and fish fillets.

●**Countertop grills/griddles.** A good example is the George Foreman grill. You can cook a chicken breast in four to six minutes.

Warning: Electric coffeemakers emit more heat than you realize. Turn off your coffeemaker as soon as it's done brewing, and pour the coffee into a thermos to keep it warm. Not only will this keep your kitchen cooler, it will save on electricity and make your coffee taste better because the coffee won't be overcooked.

More Cool Strategies

When you do cook on your stovetop, use pots that are as small as possible, and keep those pots covered (assuming the recipe permits). And of course, backyard barbecue grills remove the heat of cooking from the home entirely. *Also…*

●**Choose lean proteins and thin cuts of meat, which tend to cook quickly.** *Examples:* A pounded cutlet, thin fish fillet or thin-sliced chicken breast is likely to require only minutes of cooking.

●**Replace slow-cooking side dishes** such as potatoes and brown rice with faster-cooking ones such as quinoa and couscous.

●**Prepare cool sauces and soups in your blender** or food processor rather than hot ones on your stovetop.

How to Cook the Perfect Thanksgiving Turkey

Rick Rodgers, a cooking teacher and author of numerous cookbooks, including *Thanksgiving 101: Celebrate America's Favorite Holiday with America's Thanksgiving Expert*. Rick Rodgers.com

---

Every Thanksgiving, most American families cook a turkey. And every Thanksgiving, many of those turkeys disappoint. *Ten steps to the perfect Thanksgiving turkey…*

1. Buy a fresh turkey. Frozen turkeys don't taste as good as fresh ones…they're injected with things that you don't need, such as artificial flavors and sodium…and they require days to defrost safely—24 hours in the fridge for every five pounds of turkey.

Purchase one-and-a-half pounds of turkey per person if you want leftovers. Don't worry about the brand—even a supermarket store-brand turkey can be delicious as long as it's fresh.

2. Remove the giblets. A surprising number of people forget to do this—the giblets usually are tucked away in the body cavity or neck.

Warning: Skip the rinse. Many people think that rinsing poultry in the kitchen sink washes off potentially dangerous bacteria. Actually it just increases the odds that any bacteria on the bird will spread to your sink or kitchen counter. Bacteria will be killed by proper cooking.

3. Rub the bird with a stick of softened butter. Half a stick of butter is sufficient with a bird smaller than 16 pounds.

4. Season the inside and outside of the bird with a light coating of salt and pepper. Don't add any other seasonings—they'll just burn.

5. Stuff the turkey, if stuffing is desired. But stuff loosely—the stuffing will expand as it soaks up the turkey juices.

Warning: Don't make stuffing the day before. Stuffing that spends a night in the fridge can be like a big cold ball inside the turkey when it goes into the oven—and the stuffing might never cook enough.

6. Cover the turkey's open end with foil. This is easier than sewing it up. Crumple the foil a bit so that it stays in place.

7. Cover the turkey's breast with foil. The lean white meat of the breast cooks much faster than the turkey's dark meat. Wrapping the breast in foil deflects some of the oven's heat, slowing cooking in this area. Remove this foil for the final hour or so of cooking to let the skin brown.

8. Pour two cups of chicken or turkey broth into a roasting pan. Then put a metal rack in the pan, and place the turkey on this rack so that it's above the broth. The broth creates steam that helps the turkey cook evenly. This broth also will reduce to a glaze that will improve your gravy.

But: Don't use a disposable aluminum foil roasting pan. The shiny surface reflects the heat away from the pan, and the pan tends to collapse under the turkey's weight.

9. Cook at 325°F for around 15 minutes per pound of turkey. But treat this cook time as just an estimate. The turkey is ready to come out of the oven when it reaches 175°F to 180°F. Insert your meat thermometer into the meatiest part of the turkey's thigh. Don't let this thermometer touch bone—that will throw off its reading. Use an instant-read digital thermometer if possible. Baste the turkey a few times during that last hour to help brown the skin.

10. Let the bird sit, uncarved, for around 30 minutes after it comes out of the oven. This lets the turkey's juices redistribute throughout the meat.

Delicious Asian Cooking Without a Wok

Grace Young, an award-winning food writer and author of *Stir-Frying to the Sky's Edge, The Breath of a Wok* and *The Wisdom of the Chinese Kitchen*. GraceYoung.com

If yours is like most American kitchens, you have a skillet with short, sloped-out sides—aka, a frying pan—but not a big, tall-sided traditional Asian wok. That doesn't mean that sizzling-fresh, authentic and delicious "wok-cooked" Asian recipes are beyond your reach—if you know how to use your skillet. And if you don't have that other staple of Asian kitchens—the bamboo steamer—we've got a work-around for that, too.

There's no question that the wok is a cornerstone of Asian cooking, used for centuries to stir-fry, braise, steam, deep-fry, pan-fry, smoke, boil and poach. In the US, there may be no more passionate advocate for the well-seasoned wok than Grace Young, the "stir-fry guru" and author of award-winning cookbooks. She braves the skeptical eye of Homeland Security to take her well-seasoned wok around the world on her speaking/cooking tours.

Young wants us to know that you can use a skillet for just about any wok recipe with just a few changes. First, don't use a nonstick skillet—most can't handle the high heat that wok recipes require. Cast iron is not ideal—it's heavy, and you have to

remove food as soon as it's done because cast iron retains heat.

Best: A 14-inch stainless steel skillet with a tight-fitting lid and two- or three-inch-high sides. A 12-inch skillet can work, too, though you won't be able to cook as much in it. And use a metal spatula—the thin edge is excellent for getting under meat, rice and noodles.

Stir-Frying in a Skillet

To achieve an authentic Asian result, you'll need to make a few adjustments...

Start with about one or two teaspoons more oil than a recipe calls for. Why? A classic carbon-steel wok develops a natural nonstick surface and has a small cooking "well" so that very little oil is needed.

Don't crowd the skillet with food. When you stir-fry, a hot skillet will give off a constant sizzle sound. Add too much food, and the pan cools so the sizzle disappears.

Guidelines: In a 12- or 14-inch skillet, try no more than one pound of chicken, pork, lamb, shrimp or scallops...or no more than 12 ounces of beef (more than that starts to foam and go gray). When you add vegetables to the skillet, try no more than about four or five cups in a 14-inch skillet or three cups in a 12-inch skillet. When stir-frying rice or leafy greens, the best rule of thumb is to halve the amount in a wok recipe. If you want more, repeat the recipe from the beginning.

Now that you know about the skillet adjustments, all you need to do is follow good stir-frying technique—cut ingredients into the same bite-size pieces so that everything cooks uniformly...prep all your ingredients ahead of time...line up ingredients within arm's reach of the stove in the order in which they will be used.

When stir-frying chicken, beef, pork, lamb, shrimp, scallops or tofu, spread it evenly in one layer and allow it to sear for one minute before stir-frying. Vegetables should be dry—if you add wet vegetables to a hot skillet, you'll get a soggy mess. When a stir-fry is properly cooked, vegetables are lightly seared and crisp-tender to accentuate flavor and texture.

Asian Steaming Without a Bamboo Steamer

If you do not have a traditional bamboo steamer, you can improvise the flat surface needed for Asian steaming in a skillet as well. *Here's how…*

Add water to the skillet to a depth of one-half inch, place a metal cake rack that is one-half-inch high in the skillet, cover the skillet tightly with its lid and bring the water to a boil. Place the food to be steamed on a heatproof dish or shallow bowl that is smaller than the skillet so that there is room to grasp the dish with pot holders when it's very hot.

Helpful: A hot-dish plate lifter (available online for less than $10).

Remove the skillet lid, carefully put the plate containing the food to be steamed on the cake rack, then replace the lid. Monitor the water level in the skillet as you steam, and if necessary, replenish with boiling water from a tea kettle until your food is done.

Now, let's get cooking. These two recipes have been adapted for skillet cooking. One demonstrates stir-frying…the other, steaming. Both are memorable and delicious…

CHINESE TRINIDADIAN CHICKEN WITH MANGO CHUTNEY

Chinese people all over the world have adapted their cooking techniques to local foods, flavors—and cooking vessels. I once met a Chinese-American woman in Mississippi who stir-fried with a frying pan on a woodstove. This is a recipe I learned from a Chinese Trinidadian, and it illustrates well how you can stir-fry without a wok. It serves two to three people as a main dish with rice or four as part of a multicourse meal.

1 pound skinless, boneless chicken thighs or breasts, cut into ¼-inch-thick bite-size slices

2 teaspoons regular soy sauce

¼ teaspoon salt

¼ teaspoon freshly ground pepper

3 Tablespoons mango chutney, large pieces chopped

2 teaspoons dark soy sauce (or regular soy sauce if dark is not available)

¼ to ½ teaspoon (depending on your taste for spicy heat) minced Scotch bonnet peppers, seeds removed (or substitute serrano chili peppers)

2 Tablespoons peanut or vegetable oil

1 teaspoon minced ginger

1 teaspoon minced garlic

1 small onion, cut into ¼-inch-wide wedges

3 Tablespoons chopped cilantro

Combine the chicken, regular soy sauce, salt and pepper in a bowl, tossing the chicken to coat. In a separate small bowl, combine the chutney, dark soy sauce and peppers, stirring well.

Heat a 12- or 14-inch stainless steel skillet over high heat until a bead of water evaporates within one or two seconds of contact. Swirl in one tablespoon of the oil, then add the ginger, garlic and onion wedges.

Stir-fry for 30 seconds or until the onions have just wilted. Push the onion mixture to the sides of the skillet. Pour the remaining tablespoon of oil into the center of the skillet, and swirl to coat the bottom. Add the chicken pieces, and spread them in one layer in the skillet.

Cook for one minute, letting the chicken begin to sear. Then stir-fry for one minute more, incorporating the onion mixture. Add the mango chutney mixture, and stir-fry one to two minutes more, until the chicken is cooked through. Remove from the heat, and stir in the cilantro. Serve immediately.

Recipe adapted with permission from *Stir-Frying to the Sky's Edge* by Grace Young. Copyright © 2010 by Grace Young. Reprinted by permission of Simon & Schuster, Inc.

DANNY CHAN'S STEAMED SALMON WITH LEMON

This is a great illustration of skillet steaming based on a traditional Chinese wok-steaming recipe. It serves two as a main course or four as part of a multicourse meal. *Note*: Before you get started, put the cake rack and heatproof shallow bowl or dish in the skillet, and cover the skillet to make sure everything fits.

1 (one-pound) salmon fillet

1 Tablespoon soy sauce

¼ teaspoon salt

⅛ teaspoon ground white pepper

2 scallions, cut into four-inch pieces

4 quarter-size slices peeled fresh ginger

1 lemon, halved crosswise, with one of the halves cut crosswise into four thin slices so that you get rounds

2 teaspoons sesame oil

Rinse the salmon in cold water, and pat dry. Put it in a nine-inch heatproof, shallow bowl or dish. Drizzle the soy sauce over the salmon, and sprinkle with salt and pepper. Arrange the scallions, ginger and lemon slices evenly on the salmon. Squeeze the remaining lemon half over all.

In a 12- or 14-inch skillet with at least two-inch sides, add water to a depth of three-quarters of an inch. Put a metal cake rack that is about five or six inches in diameter and about one-half-inch high in the skillet. Cover the skillet with a tight-fitting lid, and bring the water to a boil over high heat.

Remove the lid, and carefully place the bowl or dish holding the salmon on the cake rack. Replace the lid. Steam eight to 10 minutes, or until the salmon flakes when poked with a chopstick or fork. (If not done, steam one to two minutes more.) Check the water level occasionally, and replenish if necessary with boiling water from a tea kettle.

Turn off the skillet. Remove the bowl or dish from the skillet using pot holders or a hot-plate lifter. Drizzle the sesame oil over the salmon. Serve immediately.

Recipe adapted with permission from *The Breath of a Wok* by Grace Young and Alan Richardson. Copyright © 2004 by Grace Young and Alan Richardson. Reprinted by permission of Simon & Schuster, Inc.

Broil Like a Pro

Linda Gassenheimer is an award-winning author of numerous cookbooks, most recently, *Delicious One-Pot Dishes…Quick & Easy Chicken…*and *No-Fuss Diabetes Desserts: Fresh, Fast and Diabetes-Friendly Desserts.* She writes the syndicated newspaper column "Dinner in Minutes." DinnerInMinutes.com

Broiling is quicker than roasting, and the direct heat can create a tasty crust on the outside and a juicy flavorful inside. Unfortunately, many cooks aren't broiling effectively. *Here's what you may be doing wrong and what to do instead…*

Common Mistakes

•**Not waiting for the broiler to preheat.** The food won't have a seared crust. It takes five to 10 minutes to preheat a broiler depending on the model.

•**Adding cold food to the broiler.** Food should be at room temperature. Cold food will take longer to cook through, and the outside may burn.

•**Placing the food too far from the heat on the middle or lower oven rack.** The food will bake rather than broil. The food should be about four or five inches from the heat for optimal broiling.

•**Not drying marinated food with a paper towel.** The food will steam and smoke instead of broil.

•**Leaving visible fat on meat.** Trimming the fat prevents flare-ups.

•**Using glass or ceramic dishes under the broiler** (unless specifically made for the broiler). These may crack under the direct heat.

•**Using a fork to turn meat or a knife to cut into it to see if it's ready.** These will prick the meat, and juices will be lost, making the meat dry. Use tongs to turn the meat and an instant-read thermometer, which makes only one small hole, to test for doneness.

•**Broiling different-sized ingredients together.** Some will cook faster than others. So if, say, you're broiling two steaks, make sure they're about the same size—one-and-a-half-inches thick is optimal.

•**Not watching carefully.** Food can go from brown to black in minutes. Set a timer for two minutes to remind you to look at the food. Continue to set the timer until the food is ready.

Broiling trick: Create a bronzed finish to large chicken pieces roasted in the oven by placing them under the broiler for two minutes.

•**Turning delicate food such as fish fillets.** It is better to place a baking tray in the broiler while it preheats. When the broiler is ready, add the fish fillet to the tray. The heat from the pan will help cook the bottom of the fish and will help the whole piece cook more quickly, keeping it moist. You won't have to turn the fillet over during cooking, risking its falling apart.

Delicious: While the fish broils, sauté pine nuts and parsley in a little olive oil. When the fish is cooked, season with salt and pepper and spoon the pine nuts and parsley on top.

Door open or closed?

The general rule is to leave the door open when using an electric broiler and closed with a gas broiler. A gas broiler broils at a higher temperature and can produce more smoke. However, it depends on the broiler—consult your user manual.

A Master Chef's Simple Secret to Sharpening Knives

Michael J. Moran, former head chef instructor at Florida International University School of Hospitality and Tourism Management, North Miami, Florida. One of the many classes he teaches is kitchen management, which includes how to sharpen knives and how to carve. Chef Moran was the official chef to the King and Queen of Jordan.

You might think that a dull knife is less dangerous than a sharp knife. Not so, says Michael J. Moran, former head chef instructor at Florida International University School of Hospitality and Tourism Management. He told our food reporter, Linda Gassenheimer, that a dull knife requires too much pressure to use and can slip rather than cut. *Here, just in time to carve that Thanksgiving turkey, the best way to sharpen knives…*

Sharpening

The simplest way to sharpen a knife that has a smooth, nonserrated blade is to use a sharpening stone, available at Bed Bath & Beyond and other cooking-equipment stores. Average cost ranges from $30 to $125. The easiest way to use the stone is to place a cutting board on a counter and put the stone on the board. (Put a wet dish towel under the stone to keep it from moving.)

Drag the knife along the stone at a 22.5° angle (most new knives have a factory edge with a precise 22.5° angle), starting at the tip of the knife and ending at the handle. Do one side, then the other, for a total of 20 passes.

A knife has a sharp edge when it easily can cut an onion or tomato without pressure. On average,

a knife needs to be sharpened two to three times a year. This, however, depends on how often the knife is used and how it is handled.

Alternative: The Chef's Choice electric sharpener has guides that keep the knife at the proper angle. There are several different models, ranging from about $40 to $290. It is available at most kitchenware stores and online.

To sharpen serrated knives: Sharpening a serrated knife is different from sharpening a straight knife. Each groove must be sharpened separately. There is a special small file for this purpose called a sharpening hone. It looks like a small screwdriver and is available online for $28 to $50. You may just want to replace a serrated knife whenever it seems dull or about every five years (unless your knife is a very good one). Some electric knife sharpeners, including some models of Chef's Choice, sharpen serrated knives.

Keeping It Sharp

Before or after every use, draw the knife across a knife steel. This is a steel rod with a handle. It usually comes with a knife set, or you can buy one separately for about $25. Hold the knife at a 22.5° angle, and draw it against the steel about four to five times on each side. This hones the blade. If you look at a knife with a magnifying glass, you will see hundreds of microscopic teeth. Each time a knife is used, the teeth become crooked and honing the blade straightens them. It keeps the knife sharp and reduces the need to sharpen it.

Storage

Keep edges protected. If the knives are loose in a drawer, they may bump against one another or other utensils, which could dull or damage the knives. Store knives on a magnetic bar attached to a wall. They are readily available so that you can quickly select the one you need. A knife block is another good alternative. Make sure that the knives are dry and clean before placing them in the block—otherwise, bacteria can develop. Wooden drawer inserts made for knives are also good. It is always best to hand-wash knives.

Cutting Board Wisdom

Joan Wilen and Lydia Wilen are folk-remedy experts and home tipsters based in New York City. They have spent decades collecting "cures from the cupboard" and are authors of several books including *Bottom Line's Treasury of Home Remedies & Natural Cures*, *Secret Food Cures* and *Bottom Line's Household Magic*.

A re you stumped when it comes to cutting boards? You wash them and rinse them, but those stains, smells and germs just won't go away. *Here's some help…*

Separate boards: You know to keep raw meat on a separate cutting board from your other food, such as raw salad produce. It also makes life easier to have one cutting board for garlic and onions and a different one for fruit (or anything that you don't want to smell like garlic). We usually use plastic boards for raw meats, garlic and onions…wood for everything else.

Simple smell remover: If there's a smell that's lingering too long on your cutting board—or someone chopped up onions on your "fruit" board—cut a lemon in half and rub it vigorously over the board. Rinse. Sniff. No smell!

Sanitize safely: To sanitize your plastic or wood cutting board, spray with a one-to-one ratio of white vinegar and warm water. Wipe completely with a cloth or sponge. Now give it a spray of hydrogen peroxide (from a separate bottle). Dry thoroughly. Researchers at Virginia Polytechnic Institute found that this system kills germs better than chlorine-based bleach. It's safer, too.

Important: Do not mix vinegar and hydrogen peroxide together—it can create a harsh, chlorine-bleach-like substance.

Cutting boards in your dishwasher? The US Department of Agriculture states that nonporous acrylic, plastic, glass and solid wood boards can be washed and dried with sanitizing high heat in the dishwasher. But it's best to keep a wood board that you want to last (solid or not) out of the dishwasher. Besides splitting and warping, the wood board can pick up water stains that are tough to remove. Laminated wood boards also can crack and split in the dishwasher.

Lemony stain remover and freshener: To remove a food stain from your plastic or wood board, sprinkle kosher salt on it, then rub it with half a lemon. Rinse and dry. The salt draws out the grease and acts as an abrasive, while the lemon juice helps bleach out the stain.

Wood board conditioner: Do the lemon-salt treatment once a month to "freshen" your wood cutting board. Then gently rub with food-grade mineral oil (do not use vegetable oil, which can turn rancid). Your cutting board will love you back!

Cuts run deep: Cuts in your cutting board? It happens. But those grooves and gouges harbor germs. Cuts are impossible to disinfect, so it's best to replace your board, especially if it's plastic. (Damaged plastic cutting boards and containers can release toxins into your food.) If you just can't part with that scratched-up wooden board or butcher's block, lightly buff the cuts away with fine sandpaper…then give it a little oil massage (see above).

Thanks to USDA.gov, CuttingBoards.com, The Kitchn.com and Mandy O'Brien, coauthor of *Homemade Cleaners: Quick-and-Easy, Toxic-Free Recipes* (LivingPeacefullywithChildren.com), for help with these tips.

CHAPTER 13

Lawn Care

The 8 Worst Things You Can Do to Your Lawn

John (Trey) Rogers III, PhD, professor of turfgrass management at Michigan State University, East Lansing. He was a turf consultant and project leader for the 2004 and 2008 Summer Olympic Games and 2008 UEFA World Cup and is author of *Lawn Geek: Tips and Tricks for the Ultimate Turf from the Guru of Grass*. Turf.MSU.edu

Americans spend $40 billion each year on lawns—but money isn't their only contribution. The typical home owner also devotes 73 hours to yard care every year, the equivalent of nearly two full workweeks.

That massive investment of time, effort and money could go to waste if you make any of these eight common lawn mistakes…

1. Skipping a weekly mowing. This seems harmless but can cause lasting damage. Extended gaps between mowings allow lawns to grow tall and shaggy rather than thick and dense. If done repeatedly, fewer blades of grass will grow because tall grass will block out the sun. When that tall grass finally is mowed, the gaps between the blades will be large enough for weeds to take hold.

When grass is allowed to grow tall, there also is a good chance that the subsequent mowing will "scalp" the lawn. Mowing a lawn too low is not the only scalping danger—cutting off more than one-third of the height of grass in any single mowing also is very stressful and damaging to lawns.

If you let your grass grow to about four inches and then mow it down to two, for example, you may open the door to disease or further weed growth—even if two inches is the proper height for the grass.

What to do: Mow at least once a week. Even a 10-day gap between mowings is too long. If a gap of more than a week does occur, adjust your mower's blade height to avoid clipping off more than one-third of the grass height in the next mowing, then mow again a few days later to bring the lawn down to the preferred height.

Tip: Mowing twice a week will yield an even lusher lawn—frequent mowing is the single biggest reason why golf courses and professional baseball diamonds tend to look lusher than yards.

2. Overfertilizing. Excess fertilizer could seriously dehydrate grass, something known as "burning" the lawn. And even if a lawn escapes this fate, the excess fertilizer could make the grass grow faster than normal, potentially leading to scalping of the lawn when it is mowed, as discussed earlier.

What to do: The amount of fertilizer recommended on the packaging is the maximum amount that's safe to use. Spend a little extra for a "time-release," or "slow-release," fertilizer that supplies nutrients to the lawn slowly over a period of weeks, not all at once.

Choose a fertilizer that has about 50% of its total nitrogen as slow-release nitrogen. To determine this, find the overall percentage of "slowly available nitrogen" (indicated in small print on the package) and make sure that it is about half the

207

overall percentage of "total nitrogen" (which is the first of a set of three numbers joined by hyphens on the package).

3. Not knowing what type of grass you have. Grass is not just grass. Many different turfgrasses are grown in US lawns—Kentucky bluegrass, fescue and ryegrass are common in cold climates…Bermuda and St. Augustine grass are found in warmer parts of the country, to name just a few. But the vast majority of home owners do not know what type of grass is growing in their lawns. So they often buy the wrong seed (or seed mixture) to spread over areas of the lawn that have thinned. This results in patches of grass that look and feel noticeably different from the rest of the lawn or that grow at a noticeably different pace.

Not knowing what type of grass you have also means that you can't care for your grass the way that it prefers to be treated. For example, different types of grass thrive at different heights.

What to do: Bring a sample of your grass to your local garden center, home center or hardware store—wherever grass seed is sold—and ask what type of grass you have. You can enter the name of this grass into a search engine to find websites from university extensions and other sources that provide mowing-height recommendations and other care tips for your specific lawn. (Add the word "mow" to this search if the initial search fails to turn up mowing recommendations.)

Examples: Kentucky bluegrass does best when its height is kept between two inches and three inches, while zoysiagrass tends to flourish at one to two inches.

4. Buying off-brand grass seed. Bargain-brand grass seed is inexpensive for a reason—most often it failed to pass an inspection because there was weed seed mixed in with the grass seed. So if you plant bargain seed, there's a good chance that you are introducing weeds to your lawn.

What to do: Pay a bit more for the seed that is at least 99.5% weed-seed free. By law, this statistic should be listed on grass-seed packaging.

5. Overwatering. Overwatering a lawn isn't just wasteful, it also puts your lawn at risk. In fact, more lawns are damaged by overwatering than by underwatering. Overwatering increases the odds of getting lawn diseases…it can wash away fertilizer…

and it can cause a lawn to grow faster than normal, increasing the odds that it will be scalped during a subsequent mowing.

What to do: Purchase a soil moisture meter so that you don't have to guess when your lawn needs water. Simple meters are available in garden and home stores and online for as little as $10. If you are willing to spend much more and you have an irrigation system, opt for the UgMO PH100 (UgMO.com), which uses underground soil sensors to automatically alert the irrigation system when watering is needed.

6. Bagging grass. Grass clippings provide much needed nutrients to your lawn. Contrary to widely held belief, leaving clippings on a lawn does not increase the odds of thatch problems—thatch is a layer of decomposing grass roots, not grass clippings.

What to do: If your current mower has a mulching mode, that's the way to use it. If not, make your next mower a mulching mower. These are specifically designed to finely chop clippings and return them to the lawn. Mulching is easier, faster and better for your lawn than bagging.

7. Ignoring a new home's special lawn needs. When a home is built, the surrounding land often is reshaped to encourage water to run away from the structure. One unintended consequence when the lawn is first planted is that it might be planted in soil that until very recently was subsoil, not topsoil. Subsoil has not had plants growing in it—then dying and decaying in it—so it lacks the nutrients that grass needs to thrive.

What to do: Be a bit more aggressive with the fertilizing schedule when you move into a newly built home—apply fertilizer in both May and June rather than waiting until July for the second application. However, do not increase the amount of fertilizer used per treatment.

8. Mowing with dull blades. Dull mower blades rip grass blades apart rather than making a clean cut. This rough treatment can make grass more susceptible to drought and disease. It also can make the grass appear white.

What to do: Sharpen your mower blades at least once a year—potentially several times a year if your lawn has lots of rocks or roots that often nick your blade.

Get Your Lawn Off Drugs

Paul Tukey, former director of the SafeLawns Foundation and current director of environmental stewardship of Glenstone Museum, a Potomac, Maryland, museum that has maintained its 220-acre grounds without synthetic chemical pesticides or fertilizers since 2010. An HGTV producer, Tukey is author of *The Organic Lawn Care Manual: A Natural, Low-Maintenance System for a Beautiful, Safe Lawn.*

In keeping up with the Joneses—or for your own enjoyment—it's natural to want your lawn to look as good as a golf fairway. But did you know that the average home owner applies as much as 10 times more chemical products per acre of lawn than the average farmer?

"Weed & feed"...fertilizer...insecticides. The chemicals that we use to grow lush, green, uniform lawns are, in many cases, poisons that destroy the underlying soil and harm the surrounding ecosystem while leeching toxins into the ground and exposing them to the water, our families and our pets. On top of that, typical lawn products make your lawn more dependent on additional chemicals, creating a vicious cycle where your lawn is essentially addicted to them!

No matter how lush and green a lawn appears on the surface, it isn't truly healthy unless it's "drug-free." Addicts follow 12-step programs to get healthy. Your lawn, too, can get free of drugs—and still look great—with this 12-step detox program. It's a bit of work, but you'll emerge with a beautiful, healthy and safe organic lawn.

Even better, I have found that organic lawns are less expensive to maintain in the long run. Although more natural fertilizers are more expensive than their mass-produced counterparts, well-cared-for natural lawns are more resistant to drought, which means far less watering over time. About 50% less mowing (because natural lawns grow more slowly) costs you less in time and equipment wear-and-tear. With less watering and mowing, you could easily save hundreds of dollars over time. And because the organic fertilizers become part of the soil, the need to add fertilizer greatly diminishes over time. *Here's what to do...*

STEP 1: Understand that you have a problem. The culture of chemical-based growing has made America's lawns (and gardens) dependent not on nature's own growing mechanisms but on the next application of chemicals. And these are not friendly chemicals.

Example: Check the label on a bag of weed & feed, a common treatment that combines weed killer and fertilizer. You'll most likely see all kinds of warnings about not letting the product run off into storm drains or streams or other water, not letting it come in contact with birds and frogs and other critters (including pets and children), not letting it touch bushes and other plants, not getting it on your skin, etc. It's nasty stuff.

STEP 2: Know the organic lawn concept. If you want a lawn that's self-sustaining and free of toxins, your strategy should be to mimic and enhance nature instead of trying to override it with harmful chemicals.

Cornmeal...fish...alfalfa...compost. These are the types of ingredients in organic fertilizers that nourish not just your lawn but also the earthworms and microorganisms that truly healthy lawns depend on, all of which are killed by many chemical treatments.

STEP 3: Decide what kind of lawn you want. There are three types of organic lawns, each of which requires a different level of commitment. Do you want your yard to look like Fenway Park or Augusta National Golf Club? That control and uniformity are possible without chemicals, but it requires significant time and effort. The second option is a vibrant, healthy lawn made mostly of grass, even if that grass isn't as flawless and consistent as a professionally manicured baseball field. This takes less time than a perfect lawn, although more time than most home owners might want to put in.

The third option requires the least skill and exertion and gets your lawn off drugs right away—being happy to mow anything green that comes up from the ground as long as it's healthy and attractive. This could include significant clover, wild grass and other "unintentional" growth. Don't worry—it doesn't have to include weeds such as dandelions and crabgrass. It feels good under the feet. It's still a lawn. This is the path most novice home owners should start with, and you can always ramp up to the next level if you decide to.

STEP 4: **Listen to the weeds.** Your lawn is trying to talk to you, so listen. Weeds are Mother Nature's messengers. Their presence indicates problems with the soil—your lawn's foundation. When you understand why weeds are growing, you can change the soil to make it more suitable for growing grass.

Dandelions, for example, are telling you that your soil doesn't have enough calcium—add calcium (see Step 6), and you will have fewer dandelions. One of the most common and dominant weeds, plantain, tells you that your soil might need to be loosened through aeration—bingo, less plantain. The presence of clover is your soil's way of asking you to treat it with cottonseed meal, corn gluten, alfalfa meal or some other nitrogen-rich by-product and—you guessed it—if you do, you are likely to see less clover.

STEP 5: **Test your soil.** Before treating your lawn with natural additives as described earlier, confirm what your weeds have told you by getting a soil test. Most state universities maintain soil labs that will conduct an analysis for around $12 to $25. Contact your university system, and ask how to get one. If your state university doesn't provide this service, check with your county's extension office for local sources.

STEP 6: **Treat your soil with high-quality calcium.** Organic lawns grown in most of the country will benefit from an autumn dose of calcium, which will help eliminate the most common and obvious weed—dandelions—as well as many others. Applying lime (which many home owners already do) is one way, but make sure it's the right type. Dolomitic limestone, the most common type, is high in magnesium but fairly low in calcium. Instead use calcitic limestone, which has enough calcium—and use pellets rather than powder to keep potentially harmful dust to a minimum. One brand found in many hardware and garden stores is Soil Doctor.

If the soil test shows that your soil is alkaline—with a pH over 7—use gypsum instead of lime because gypsum won't affect the soil's pH. As with limestone, pellets are better for most lawns.

STEP 7: **Mow high.** The best defense against weeds is tall grass. Many weed seeds need light to germinate, and they don't germinate well with tall grass towering over them. If they do germinate, tall, lush grass will crowd out their sprouts. Set your mower blade height to between three and four inches off the ground.

STEP 8: **Sharpen your blade.** By sharpening your mower blade after every eight hours of mowing, the blade will cut the grass cleanly instead of tearing it. Torn blades of grass are more likely to turn brown, and they're more susceptible to harm from pests and disease. The Home Depot offers a good tutorial on how to safely sharpen mower blades at THD.co/2oGw67u.

STEP 9: **Don't over-rake.** Overzealous leaf-raking can destroy the soil composition and beneficial organisms while spreading weed seeds.

What to do: Drag your rake across the lawn with just enough pressure to pull the leaves away.

STEP 10: **Aerate high-traffic areas.** High-traffic areas—usually patches by the driveway and walkway near the road—are prone to common plantain weeds, which can be identified by their broad, oval leaves surrounding tall, thin flower stalks rising from the center. Plantain weeds thrive in compacted soil. Grass does not. Although the entire lawn can benefit from aeration, it is especially useful for these high-traffic areas. You can rent a "core aerator" (with hollow spikes that remove cores of soil rather than solid spikes that only poke holes) at a hardware store for about $35 to $90 depending on whether you want it for just a few hours or a day. Core aerators require more exertion to operate than lawn mowers—if you'd rather not tackle it, hire a lawn service to core-aerate for you.

STEP 11: **Overseed in the fall.** October is an ideal lawn-care month in most of the country, although it will be a bit earlier in the coldest regions and a bit later in the warmest. This is the time for the calcium treatment mentioned earlier. It's also the perfect time to overseed, especially on thin or patchy areas. Overseeding will rejuvenate your lawn before the frost sets in, and grass seeds will outcompete weed seeds. This is the one time of year when an aggressive raking can help, just prior to overseeding. The raking helps loosen the soil to get better seed-to-soil contact. Be sure to water daily until the seed germinates.

STEP 12: **Top-dress your lawn with compost.** This step can be costly, but top-dressing your lawn with compost in the fall is probably the single best thing you can do. Although it looks like black dirt, compost isn't soil. It is decomposed organic matter that serves several critical functions including adding nutrients.

Order a bulk delivery from a nearby compost manufacturer (search online for "bulk compost delivery" and your zip code) or your municipality.

Natural Weed Kill

David R. Mellor, master groundskeeper at Fenway Park, Boston, and author of *The Lawn Bible* and *Picture Perfect*.

One way to get rid of weeds without toxic chemicals is simply to pull them out. Many lawn tools, such as Grampa's Weeder ($40), can be used for this.

Alternatives: Pour boiling water mixed with white vinegar on the weeds. Or buy a lawn torch, such as Weed Dragon ($70) or Hotspotter ($78), which attaches to a propane tank and can be used to burn weeds—but use it only when the lawn is wet to avoid fire.

To prevent weeds from growing: Use corn gluten in early spring—it is an effective preemergent (a natural nontoxic herbicide) and is available at garden stores.

Best defense against weeds: An active, healthy, growing lawn. It chokes the weeds, which grab hold when a lawn is sparse. To keep your lawn healthy, feed it with Scotts' Natural Lawn Food, and water it with one inch of water (approximately 60 minutes) per week.

Best time to water: Between 2:00 am and 7:00 am.

A Landscaper's Money-Saving Tricks for a Beautiful Yard

Kate Anchordoguy, a licensed landscape contractor and designer in Santa Rosa, California. She has advised consumers as a Master Gardener through University of California Cooperative Extension Service and is author of *Dig This! Landscaping Without a Backhoe or a Big Budget for Northern California and Beyond*.

Improvements in your yard and garden don't have to cost a lot. *Tricks for having the yard you want on a budget…*

Plants

• **Buy plants in the smallest size available.** If the same variety of plant comes in a five-gallon pot and a one-gallon pot, buy the smaller pot. Mature plants are more expensive—you are exchanging money for growing time. Smaller plants look more sparse at the beginning, but they grow faster than large plants.

• **Negotiate a discount.** Once you have determined which plants you want and how many, consider purchasing them all at the same nursery. You probably can negotiate a good price. The nursery also may be willing to hold your purchases for you until you are ready to plant them.

What to say: "Here is a list of the plants that I need. I would like to buy from you, but I also am shopping around for the best price. If I buy all the plants from you, what price would you be able to offer me?"

• **Shop roots, not top.** Ask to see a nursery's "hospital"—the place where plants that have cosmetic problems are kept. Droopy or scorched plants with healthy roots that form a cohesive ball should do fine once they are planted. You can get these ugly ducklings for next to nothing.

Nursery plants look best in spring and progressively worse through summer and fall when you can find bargains.

• **Move low-performing plants.** A shrub or small tree that is getting too much shade or sun may thrive in a different spot. Dig a hole in the new location. Then dig up the plant, getting as much of the roots as possible. After replanting, make sure that the new plant gets plenty of water for the first year or so. In mild winter areas, the winter is the best time to plant. In areas where the ground freezes, fall or spring is better. Summer is never ideal, but if you need to move a plant then, be extra vigilant that it does not dry out.

•**Start lawns from seed, not sod.** A lawn grown from seed doesn't provide the instant gratification of a sod lawn, but the preparation is nearly identical. If you have the patience and are willing to keep dogs and children off the lawn for several months, you can save by using seed (where I live, you can save up to 30 cents a square foot). Your lawn also will be deeper rooted and healthier.

On the other hand, if you already have a lawn and it's not doing well, don't waste time and money tearing it out. Instead, mow the lawn very short. Cover the area with sheets of newspaper, then a layer of topsoil or mulch, and plant on top of it—this works for seed, sod and other plantings.

Supplies

•**Check online.** Scan Craigslist.org for cast-off benches, decorative rocks, ceramics and plants. People sometimes offer these items at no cost just so that they don't have to pay to have them hauled away.

•**Buy local.** You may love the look of Arizona flagstone for a garden path, but if you live on the East Coast, you will pay a premium for it because of transportation costs.

Before setting your heart on a feature that you saw in a magazine or on a TV design show, spend a few hours walking around your local landscape supply store. Get a feel for the range of materials available and how much they cost. Keep an open mind. Rock from a nearby quarry may be just as elegant, and far less expensive, than the current fad.

•**Buy in bulk.** Soil, mulch and gravel are cheaper in bulk from landscape stores than bagged from hardware or big-box stores.

•**Measure carefully.** Ordering more material than you need is a waste of money. Ordering too

little of what you need incurs extra charges to have the additional materials delivered.

Landscape supply yards use cubic yards for bulk orders of mulch, soil and gravel. To calculate cubic yards, multiply the square footage to be covered by the thickness (in inches) of what you need, then divide that number by 324.

Example: You need to cover a 1,000-square-foot area with three inches of mulch. Multiply 1,000 by 3, then divide that amount (3,000) by 324. You will need to order 9.25 cubic yards of mulch.

Learn from the Experts

The more you know, the more you can do yourself. Call on the expertise of Master Gardeners—volunteers who have received intensive training in horticulture from university extension agents. They offer affordable workshops and advice. To find Master Gardeners in your state, visit AHSGardening.org/gardening-resources/master-gardeners.

Also, community colleges and adult-education programs may offer low-cost gardening courses.

Check your newspaper's home-and-garden section for talks and tours. In addition to sharing ideas about gardening, the speakers and attendees at these events often can recommend sources for cheap and sometimes even free materials.

Get Rid of Urine Burn

Christine Bucks, garden book editor, Rodale Inc., Emmaus, Pennsylvania, writing in *Great Garden Fix-Its: Organic Remedies for Everything from Aphids to Weeds.*

To rid your lawn of those yellow spots from dog urine "burns," mix eight ounces of baking soda with one gallon of water. Pour the solution on yellow patches. Baking soda neutralizes urine's acidity so grass can regain its color. Repeat every few days for about three weeks.

Better: Train your dog to relieve himself in a designated gravel patch.

Lawn Rescue! Fixes for Common Problems

Matt Blashaw, a licensed contractor and real estate agent who remodels homes and yards in Orange County, California. He was previously host of the HGTV program *Vacation House for Free* and of HGTV's landscape and lawn-improvement show *Yard Crashers*. HGTV.com

It isn't easy to grow a great lawn, and it's painful when the lawn ends up looking bad despite your best efforts. Here are potential causes of—and solutions for—the things that might be wrong with your lawn...

Bare and Thinning Areas

You might think that the simplest remedy to fill bare and thinning areas in your lawn is to loosen up the soil with a rake and then sprinkle grass seed. The problem with this simple solution is that there's a good chance the new grass will fail as well. These sections of your lawn are struggling for a reason. Before you reseed, it's worth trying to figure out why the problem exists. *Ask yourself...*

•**Is the bare patch in a heavily shaded area, such as under a tree?** If so, one option is to reseed this area using a shade-tolerant grass, such as fine fescue. (Consult a local garden shop for guidance on which shade-tolerant grasses grow best in your part of the country.) But these grasses still generally need at least four hours of sunlight per day to thrive...and even if the grass you choose does thrive, it might look noticeably different from the grass of your surrounding lawn. An alternative is to stop trying to grow grass in the shady area and instead install a mulch bed and/or shade-tolerant plants or ground cover.

Examples: Shade-tolerant shrubs include gray dogwood, laurel and viburnum. Shade-tolerant ground covers include lily of the valley, sweet woodruff and periwinkle.

•**Is the bare patch in an area that is often walked on?** If you reseed this area, use stakes and string to keep pedestrians off it for at least a month to give the young grass a chance to grow. But if you don't want to face the same situation again in future years, rather than growing more grass, construct a path or patio using paving stones, concrete, gravel or other materials so that the grass doesn't have to compete with people's feet.

•**Is something lurking under your lawn?** Probe down a few inches under the bare area. If there's a large rock or the remains of a stump right under the surface, this might be creating a thin soil layer, inhibiting healthy grass growth. Remove the obstruction if possible...fill the hole with soil...cover it with a layer of topsoil, available in garden stores...then reseed.

•**Is there thick thatch where the lawn is failing?** Thatch—the layer of old, dead blades of grass and other organic material immediately above the soil—should not be a problem as long as the thatch layer is no more than one-half-inch thick or so. But if the thatch is much thicker than that, it might be preventing enough rainwater from penetrating into the soil and preventing air from circulating around the bases of grass blades. Clear away thick thatch using a thatch rake and/or a gas-powered core aerator, then reseed. (Core aerators make holes in the soil beneath the lawn, which encourages growth of the microbes that help decompose the thatch layer.)

Helpful: Core aerators are available for rent at many home centers and rental centers, generally for $50 to $100 a day. Aerating helps with other lawn problems as well—see below.

Brown Patches

In the growing season, brown grass is not healthy grass. It might be possible to save the brown sections of lawn, but first you must figure out what is causing the problem...

•**Do you have a dog?** The salts and nitrogen in dog urine can damage or kill grass in the spots where Fido often does his business. The most effective solution is to have the dog urinate elsewhere—ideally in a section of your property that is not covered by lawn or that is out of sight. If that isn't possible, use garden fencing to stop the dog from urinating on the sections of lawn that are brown to give the damaged grass a chance to recover—or better yet, take the dog for a walk.

Meanwhile, water these brown patches heavily (and if the dog still is urinating on other sections of the lawn, water these sections heavily, too, as soon as possible after the dog has peed on them). If the brown grass does not recover, remove a two-inch-thick layer of the topsoil and add new soil before reseeding.

Helpful: Certain grasses, including St. Augustine and Bermuda grass, stand up relatively well to dog urine but are not appropriate for cooler climates.

•**Do you see insects or insect damage?** Take a very close look at the blades in the brown area, as well as the still-green grass immediately adjacent to the brown area. Do you see insects and/or holes suggesting that insects have been eating this grass? Also, carefully peel back the sod—the layer of topsoil containing grass roots—near the edge of one of the brown areas to check for grubs. Grubs are small, soft, whitish larvae, often curled into small "c" shapes, that feed on the roots of your grass. Put a few samples of the damaged grass and/or the pests you find in a sandwich bag, and bring them to a garden shop or home center to ask if these insects might be causing the problem. If so, ask which insecticide is best. (There also are all-in-one insecticides that kill most common lawn-damaging bugs.)

Act quickly, before the infestation spreads any further. Be sure to purchase a "curative" insecticide meant to deal with an existing insect problem, not a "preventive" one designed mainly to avoid future problems. Follow the directions precisely.

•**Have you fertilized the lawn within the past few days?** If so, you might have used too much in the brown areas, causing "fertilizer burn." Water the brown sections heavily and repeatedly during the week immediately following fertilization to dilute the fertilizer, and wash as much of it as possible out of the topsoil and away from the roots of your grass. If this fails to save the damaged grass, continue watering to flush away as much fertilizer as possible from the topsoil down into lower layers of soil below your lawn where it will have much less effect on grass roots. Alternatively, you could replace the topsoil in these areas—then reseed.

Helpful: Fertilizer burn sometimes appears in long brown lines. This occurs when the person ap-

plying the fertilizer with a spreader makes passes that are too close together, resulting in double-fertilized strips.

Swampy Areas

Large, long-lasting puddles in a lawn do not just make it more difficult to enjoy the lawn—that standing water could lead to lawn-killing grass diseases or encourage mosquito growth as well. *Potential causes and solutions…*

•**Do you have a sprinkler system?** If so, keep an eye on the swampy area as the sprinkler operates. Perhaps one of the sprinkler heads has stopped working properly and now is depositing an excessive amount of water in this spot.

•**Is the swampy area very near your house, driveway or road?** The excess moisture might be the result of rainwater running off the roof or off a paved area into this part of the lawn. If so, divert water away from the lawn by improving or extending the home's gutter system and/or adding French drains, buried drainage pipes or drainage ditches along the affected edge of the lawn.

•**Is there highly compacted soil and/or a thick thatch layer in the swampy area?** If the soil is highly compacted, water might not be able to drain down through it properly. And a thatch layer thicker than one-half inch or so can act as a sponge, holding water in the area. Using a core aerator should dramatically improve drainage if either of these is the problem.

•**Is the swampy area in a low spot in the lawn?** Use a shovel to carefully remove the sod, and set it aside. Add topsoil…walk over this soil to compact it somewhat…then add additional topsoil to raise this section of lawn to roughly the level of the rest of the yard…then replace the sod you set aside earlier. (Or if the grass in this area was dead, reseed.)

Additional options: If the do-it-yourself solutions above fail to solve the swampiness problem, you could hire a landscaper to install a drainage system beneath the lawn—but that is a major project that could cost thousands of dollars. If you don't want to spend that much, you could replace the lawn in the swampy area with a mulch bed that is raised perhaps one inch above the level of the lawn so that the swampy area is hidden underneath. Add plants that love wet soil, such as certain river irises…ferns…sedge…hydrangea…or dogwood. This is a beautiful-looking alternative.

Don't Mow Your Grass Too Short and Other Secrets from America's Lawn Geek

John (Trey) Rogers III, PhD, professor of turfgrass management at Michigan State University, East Lansing. He was a turf consultant and project leader for the 2004 and 2008 Summer Olympic Games and 2008 UEFA World Cup, and he is author of *Lawn Geek: Tips and Tricks for the Ultimate Turf From the Guru of Grass.*

Lawns don't come with instruction manuals, and lawn-care folk wisdom often is wrong. *Answers to six lawn-care questions…*

●**It's been a relatively warm, snow-less winter across much of the country. Does that affect the way I should be caring for my lawn?**

Your grass might start growing sooner than usual. If so, it might be wise to tackle spring lawn chores such as overseeding or aerating in April rather than leaving them for May (see below for details).

●**Does it matter how short I cut my grass when I mow?**

It matters a lot. "Scalping" a lawn—mowing off more than one-third of the grass's height—is the number-one lawn-care mistake that home owners make. Doing this sends grass into physiological shock, which leaves the lawn prone to invasion by weeds and less able to cope with drought and other environmental stresses.

The more often you mow—and the less grass you remove with each mowing—the thicker and healthier your lawn is likely to become. If the grass gets so long that you can't get it down to proper length in one mowing, wait a day or two and mow again.

For St. Augustine and bahia grasses and for cool-season grasses, such as Kentucky bluegrass and perennial rye, three to four inches is generally best…for

most Bermuda and zoysia, one to two inches. Various websites, such as American-Lawns.com, can help you identify what type of grass you have.

●**Should I mulch or bag my lawn clippings?**

Definitely mulch. Grass clippings are full of nitrogen and other nutrients. Removing them deprives the lawn of free fertilizer. Modern mulching mowers do an excellent job of grinding up grass into mulch, particularly when you mow off less than one-third of the grass's height, as described previously.

Helpful: Research has shown that mulching grass does not create excessive thatch and thus does not make lawns more susceptible to disease or drought.

●**My lawn feels hard-packed. Should I aerate? And if so, what's the best way to do that?**

It is worth aerating if your soil is hard-packed. It's difficult for grass roots to grow properly when the soil is compacted.

Rent a core aerator (about $40 to $50 for two to four hours), or pay a lawn-care professional to aerate for you. The aerator used should pull plugs of soil from the ground, not just slash the soil, which is far less effective.

Aerate when grass is actively growing. With the cool-season grasses of the northern US, such as bluegrass, fescue and ryegrass, that generally means April or September (and perhaps the months that precede or follow these, depending on temperatures). With the warm-season grasses of the South, such as bahia, Bermuda, buffalo or zoysia, it typically means May through July or August. Aerating once each year for three years usually solves compaction problems.

Warning: If the distance between the holes created by the aerator is greater than three inches, you almost certainly need to make another pass with the aerator.

●**I know that there are dangers to fertilizing too often, but how often is best?**

Excessive fertilizer can "burn" grass, causing severe dehydration that could kill the lawn. Or extra fertilizer might cause grass to grow quickly, making it difficult to keep up with the mowing and increasing the odds that you will scalp the grass, as described at left.

Best strategy: Fertilize on the "holiday plan"—on or around Memorial Day, the Fourth of July, Labor Day and Halloween. Four times a year is all a lawn really needs. Do not exceed the dosages recommended on the fertilizer's packaging.

Warning: Do not fertilize your lawn if it has not rained recently and local water-use restrictions prevent watering. Some home owners faced with this situation think, Well, if I can't water my lawn, I can at least feed it fertilizer. Unfortunately, this makes a bad situation worse—recently fertilized lawns require even more water than those that have not been fertilized.

●**How much should I water my lawn?**

A good rule of thumb is to give your lawn around one inch of water per week, perhaps a bit more during a stretch of very hot days. That guideline includes rainfall. There are new wireless devices on the market that monitor soil moisture and prevent automated irrigation systems from watering when additional water isn't needed. That's not just good for your lawn…it's also good for your water bill.

Example: Toro Precision Soil Sensor ($170, Toro.com).

Water early in the morning so that the grass blades aren't unnecessarily damp come nightfall—lawns are particularly susceptible to disease when they're damp on humid summer nights.

Overwatering is much more common than underwatering except when local drought restrictions ban watering. Signs of an overwatered lawn include the growth of mushrooms or nutsedge (grasslike weeds)…significant runoff from the lawn into the street during watering…or a mushy feeling when walking across the lawn hours after watering. Signs of an underwatered lawn include footprints remaining visible in the grass long after you have walked across it.

●**Burrowing animals are digging holes in my lawn. Is that bad for the grass? What's the best way to get rid of those animals?**

It won't significantly harm your grass. The lawn might get upheaved a bit in places, but you usually can push it back down easily with your foot.

Research suggests that traps are the most reliable way to rid a lawn of burrowing animals. No one has ever shown that burrowing animals are significantly deterred by blocking their holes or by folk-wisdom solutions such as placing chewing gum in their holes.

Fall Is the Time to Fix Your Lawn

Teri Dunn Chace is a garden writer with many titles in publication, including *The Anxious Gardener's Book of Answers*. She lives in central New York. TeriChaceWriter.com

When autumn arrives, it's easy to take a break from your lawn. It's growing more slowly, so it needs less mowing—maybe less watering, too. Time to kick back until spring, right?

Big mistake.

It may sound counterintuitive, but if ever you are going to reseed your lawn, now is the time. The ground in the fall actually is warmer than in spring, so seeds germinate more quickly. Plus, cooler weather slows the growth of weeds, so your baby grass won't have as much competition as it would in spring. Repairing bare patches isn't a lot of work—but it's easy to make mistakes that undermine your efforts. *Here are common pitfalls—and what to do instead…*

MISTAKE: **Procrastinating.** This is especially important if you live in an area with cold winters—your window of opportunity to sow is only a month or two after summer's heat subsides and before the first frost. Do it now, and your baby grass will "get its feet under it," that is, establish a root system and settle in before winter's cold.

What to do: Start by identifying places where your lawn hasn't thrived. These are the places you want to seed.

Tip: If you have bare patches due to foot traffic, maybe it's time to be pragmatic, give up on grass in those locations and put an actual path of stepping stones, gravel or even paving.

MISTAKE: **Picking the wrong type of grass seed.**

What to do: Shop carefully—you'll discover that there are many different kinds, including mixtures. Don't be daunted—narrowing down is easier than you think. "Cool-season" grass seed is right for most of the country, including the Northeast, Mid-Atlantic and much of the Midwest and Plains States. If the area doesn't get much sun, use shade-tolerant blends. Discuss your options with an experienced nursery person.

MISTAKE: **Seeding without preparing an area's soil.** The new grass won't thrive, or it might not grow at all!

What to do: Tug or dig out the disappointing grass—and any weeds—to a depth of at least four inches to be sure that you've removed most or all of the root systems of unwanted or struggling plants. Sprinkle in topsoil and organic matter (compost or dehydrated cow manure) in a 50:50 ratio. Then rake the area level to prepare it for sowing (you don't want little hills or hollows).

MISTAKE: **Waiting to plant too long after you prep.** When you've dug out an area, it's an open invitation for rain and wind—and digging dogs—to take fresh soil away. Plus, weeds can invade.

What to do: If you don't have time to seed right away after you prep an area, cover it with a tarp secured with rocks or bricks until you are ready.

MISTAKE: **Sowing on dry ground.** When you water after planting, you move the seeds around and cause clumping.

What to do: Before you start sowing, sprinkle the area until it is damp but not soggy.

MISTAKE: **Sowing unevenly.** When seeds clump, they still will germinate, but the little grass plants will compete with one another for root space, sun and air. Plus, it doesn't look nice to have uneven grass growth.

What to do: Follow your seed packaging's directions about amount per area, and spread the seed evenly. Hand-broadcasting is easy to do (see below), but if you're sowing a large area, it's easier to use a spreader.

To hand-broadcast seed: Take a small handful of seed and release it as you walk backward. That way, you don't walk on your work!

Tip: Freshly sown grass seed will grow better if you help it get in better contact with the soil. After sowing, you can pat it down with the back of a shovel, rake or garden fork. An old-fashioned lawn roller also does a fine job.

MISTAKE: **Skipping mulch.** Grass seed and baby grass need a several-week commitment.

What to do: Lightly spread mulch on all freshly seeded areas with straw. Just scatter it evenly over the surface but not densely, which would block water and light from reaching germinating seeds. Mulch helps prevent water runoff from washing your seeds away.

Water daily, if it doesn't rain, with a gentle sprinkler. Depending on the type of seed, the grass should sprout (germinate) in a week to several weeks. Cooler weather slows it down—another reason to get started earlier in fall rather than later.

The Sod Option

If you want an alternative to the work of reseeding described above, you can always buy a bit of sod. *Granted, it's more expensive, but there are times when it makes good sense...*

•**You are trying to establish grass on a slope.** Seed sown on a hill tends to wash down—very frustrating. Sod will stay!

•**Weeds have been a constant problem.** Sod is not only weed-free but also thick enough that when laid down, weeds aren't able to break through.

•**You're in a hurry.** Perhaps you aren't willing or able to babysit freshly sown grass seed.

Sod, while convenient, is not a "drop and go" project—as some people have found out the hard way. For best results...

•**Just as with seeding, you must prepare an area.** Dig down to clear out any existing vegetation (weeds, disappointing patchy grass) and rocks, as deep as necessary for the sod to lie flush with a walkway, driveway or adjacent lawn.

•**Water the area before and after setting the sod in place.** Sod doesn't come with a lot of soil attached, and if you neglect to water the ground beforehand, the roots will struggle.

217

•**If rainfall is sparse, water daily for the first few weeks.** If sod dries out, it dies—it cannot be revived as established lawn grass can.

•**Sod doesn't need to be mulched.**

Whether you use seed or sod, as cold weather approaches, the burgeoning young grass patch will slow down and go dormant, just like the rest of your lawn. But its roots now will have a head start, and you will be gratified to see the green results of your efforts when spring returns.

When Spring Seeding Is Better

If you live in a really hot and/or dry part of the country such as Florida, the Gulf Coast, the Southwest or southern California, spring actually is better than fall for reseeding. So save this article! In spring, start with "warm-season" grass such as St. Augustine, Bahiagrass or Bermudagrass so that it has maximum time with warm weather before winter comes.

What you can do now: Apply lawn fertilizer. No need to wait for spring for this.

Tip: Don't use "garden" fertilizer. Instead, buy separate "lawn" fertilizer—it's high in nitrogen, which lawns especially need. Wait until the weather cools down to apply.

Make Your Mower, Blower and Other Outdoor Equipment Last

Danny Lipford, host of *Today's Homeowner with Danny Lipford*, a nationally syndicated TV series. He has more than 30 years of experience as a remodeling contractor based in Mobile, Alabama. TodaysHomeowner.com

Wouldn't it be great if gas-powered lawn and home equipment had dashboard lights, like cars, to warn you of potential maintenance problems? That might help you avoid breakdowns and hundreds of dollars in repair bills for equipment ranging from lawn mowers and snowblowers to leaf blowers, trimmers and chain saws. In the absence of such warning lights, here are some key steps to take to extend the life of your gas-powered equipment and avoid costly problems…

•**Store equipment with a full fuel tank in the off-season.** Some people run all the fuel out of a tank and engine at the start of a period of nonuse because gasoline can degrade in just a few months, resulting in poor engine performance. But allowing fuel tanks and fuel lines to sit empty for an extended period increases the odds that rust will develop on metal engine and fuel-system components.

Better: Leave the tank full of fuel, but add a fuel stabilizer, such as STA-BIL, which can keep fuel fresh for up to 24 months.

•**Use ethanol-free fuel.** Unlike modern cars, which are designed to run effectively on gasoline containing 10% to 15% ethanol, small engines in most gas-powered equipment are likely to run better and last longer if given gas that does not include any biofuel. (The ethanol in gas is made from corn or other starch-based crops.) Pure-Gas.org can help you locate merchants in your area that sell ethanol-free fuel. It's more expensive than ethanol-containing fuel but worth it to extend the life of your equipment.

•**Tackle oil changes at the end of the equipment's usage season.** Old, used oil can damage engine components, and allowing used oil to sit in an engine for months lets any dirt and debris in that oil settle more deeply, which can be bad for the engine as well. When storing equipment for an extended period, make sure that it contains fresh oil.

•**Clean away dirt and grass clippings.** Caked-on dirt and grass can trap moisture and lead to device-destroying rust. Don't just hose away obvious dirt and grass—clean off the undersides of power equipment, too…and remove any covers and clean underneath them if there's a chance that dirt and debris could have worked their way inside. If rust already is forming, use a grinder or sander to remove it, then apply a primer followed by a rust-inhibiting spray paint.

•**Lubricate cables, pulleys and other moving parts.** Apply silicone spray lubricant to all moving metal parts at least once each year, and then work these parts back and forth a few times to spread the silicone.

The Right Way to Rake

Rachel Hazuga, health and fitness consultant, certified Iyengar yoga instructor, La Crosse, Wisconsin.

Rather than suffer those post-rake aches, here are a few tips on how to have a pain-free fall cleanup.

• **To minimize the effort involved, get the right rake for the job.** Don't use a garden rake—its heavy, rectangular head and short, rigid tines are better suited to breaking up hard dirt clods. Instead, you want a yard rake, lawn rake or leaf rake—it typically has a fan-shaped head and long, flexible tines. Opt for a 24-inch-wide head, which requires less pressure to drag the leaves across the lawn than an extra-wide 36-inch head. A padded handle helps prevent blisters and hand fatigue.

• **As a further safeguard against blisters, wear gardening gloves.** Put a Band-Aid on the webbed area between the thumb and first finger of each hand before you start raking.

• **Wet leaves are slippery, so wear shoes with nonslip soles to guard against falls.**

• **Before you start your yard work,** warm up your muscles with a few minutes of light exercise, such as brisk walking.

• **As you rake, avoid over-twisting your spine —this motion can strain your lower back.** It is safer to turn your whole body so that you have easy access to the leaves around you.

• **Don't reach out too far with each stroke.** Instead, use short, quick strokes, extending your arms only as far as you can while keeping the rake nearly perpendicular to the ground at about a 65° to 85° angle. This keeps the work close to your body's center of gravity, allowing for better leverage and minimizing the effort required.

• **It may feel more natural to hold the rake with a particular hand on top,** but to minimize fatigue and muscle soreness, you're better off switching sides every few minutes and spending equal time on each side. With a bit of practice, you'll soon be an ambidextrous raker.

• **When you're done outdoors, do some simple stretches to ward off muscle soreness.** Pay particular attention to your back.

A good back stretch: Stand with feet shoulder-width apart, knees very slightly bent. Bend elbows and position hands as if placing them in the back pockets of your jeans...tilt head to gaze upward, gently arching back...hold for several seconds. Next, straighten arms at sides...slowly bend forward at waist to touch your toes (or shins, depending on your flexibility). Repeat several times.

And the best tip of all: Follow with a nice, warm bubble bath.

Lawn Mower Warning

Wilko Grolman, MD, PhD, professor of otolaryngology, University Medical Center Utrecht, the Netherlands.

Lawn mowers, leaf blowers and loud music can cause temporary hearing loss that lasts up to several hours and may even lead to permanent hearing loss.

New research: When volunteers wore earplugs during a four-hour 100-decibel concert, only 8% had temporary hearing loss, compared with 42% who didn't wear earplugs. And 12% of those who wore earplugs reported developing chronic tinnitus (ringing in the ears) compared with 40% of those who didn't wear them.

Spend Less Time Raking

Christopher J. Brown, co-owner of Teed & Brown, a lawn-care company based in Fairfield County, Connecticut. He has a degree in turf grass science from Penn State University and 20 years of experience in lawn and golf course maintenance. TeedAndBrown.com

Some home owners delay leaf removal until all the leaves are off the trees, but grass needs light and air to survive. Allowing a layer of leaves to sit for most of the season could smother your lawn. Clear leaves every week or two during the fall to keep your lawn healthy.

Mulching Mower

When leaf cover is light, a mulching lawn mower offers an acceptable alternative to leaf removal. Mulching is not appropriate when leaf cover is heavy, however, because too much mulch can smother the lawn. Mow a small section of your lawn with your mulching mower, then view the results. If the mowed area looks mostly green, continue. If you see more chopped leaves than green grass in the mowed area, the leaves must be removed.

Best model: Toro Super Recycler.

Price: $650.* 952-888-8801, Toro.com.

Leaf Blowers

A leaf blower can eliminate the physical strain of raking and dramatically reduce the time required to clear leaves. Home owners who own leaf blowers also tend to have healthier lawns—leaves are cleared more often when the job is quick. *Leaf blower options...*

•**Handheld electric blowers are inexpensive but also underpowered.** They will not save you much time compared with raking and are not recommended.

•**Gas-powered backpack blowers are the best choice for home owners with lawns up to about 8,000 square feet.** *The following model is powerful enough to clear a lawn of leaves, acorns and other debris...*

•Stihl BR500. This 3.0-hp model is a bit less powerful than the Kawasaki but is considerably quieter. It retails for about $540. 757-486-9100, StihlUSA.com.

•**Walk-behind gas-powered blowers are appropriate for lawns 8,000 square feet and bigger that receive significant leaf cover.** They are more powerful than backpack blowers but harder to maneuver in tight areas. *Best model...*

•Fradan model VPB-9HD push blower. This blower has an 9-hp Honda engine that moves more

leaves per minute than the backpack models. *Price:* $1,500. 914-632-3769, FradanPower.com.

Caution: Some municipalities have passed noise ordinances limiting or banning the use of gas-powered lawn equipment, such as leaf blowers. Wear earplugs or noise-blocking earmuffs—and safety goggles—when you operate a leaf blower.

Raking

Raking is appropriate for small lawns and for home owners with more time than money to spend on lawn care. Select the rake with the largest head you can find, preferably two or more feet across. Also, purchase a smaller rake to get into tight spots around flower beds or under shrubs. Plastic and bamboo rake heads are generally better than metal ones, which bend out of shape easily and weigh more.

Before buying a rake, stand with the rake at a 45-degree angle to the floor. The handle should be long enough so that you can rake without hunching and should have a width that is comfortable in your grip—the wider, the better.

Collecting and Disposing

If there are no fences or barriers between your lawn and your neighbors' lawns, start at the edge of your yard and blow leaves toward the middle. If your lawn borders on woods, simply blow leaves in that direction. If you have a fence or a barrier, you can blow the leaves up against it. This should help collect the leaves into a pile.

If you rake your lawn, minimize the distance leaves are raked. Create smaller piles, then use a tarp or wheelbarrow to carry the piles longer distances.

Tarps also can come in handy with leaf blowers. Blow the leaves into a pile, then rake them onto the tarp. If you try to blow them onto a tarp, the tarp is likely to blow away unless it is staked down. Use a heavy-duty tarp, approximately 10 feet by 10 feet.

How you dispose of your leaves depends on your municipality's rules. Some allow residents to put leaves in garbage bags or special paper bags at the curb...others have special leaf pickup days or require residents to arrange for pick up with an independent company.

*All prices are manufacturers' suggested retail and are subject to change.

Gutters

There are many gutter-cleaning gadgets on the market, but none work better than your hands. Wear heavy-duty dishwashing gloves, which, unlike most work gloves, are waterproof.

Caution: To reduce the risks involved with using a ladder, reposition the ladder frequently, rather than reaching or leaning in either direction...and do not postpone this chore until winter, when ice and cold increase the danger.

• **"Gutter shield" systems can make it harder for leaves to cause clogs, but some are better than others.** *Here are your options from best to worst...*

• LeafFilter. This gutter shield system uses a stainless steel filter with holes less than 50 microns across—smaller than a grain of sand—to prevent even small debris from entering. It also has a self-cleaning filtration system, but it is not cheap. Expect to spend perhaps $3,500 to $6,000 or more, installed, depending on the size and complexity of your roof. 800-290-6106, LeafFilter.com.

• Amerimax Hinged Gutter Guard. This much more affordable gutter shield will keep most, though not all, of the leaves out. You still will need to clean your gutters but perhaps only once a year rather than several times. This product's hinges make it easy to clear out the leaves that do get through, an important consideration. Available at The Home Depot in packages of 25 three-foot sections for $384 a pack. 50 guards (2 packs) are needed for an average-size home. You can easily install the sections yourself. 800-347-2586, Amerimax.com.

• Gutter helmet systems (various manufacturers) are the worst option. This type of gutter guard completely covers the top of the gutter. Water clings to its curved surface and flows into the gutter from the side. Unfortunately, some small debris inevitably gets caught up in the rainwater and flows into the gutter. Most helmet systems are permanently fastened in place, so this debris can be nearly impossible to remove. In the long run, these products can do more harm than good.

House and Yard Damaged from the Winter? What to Do...

Danny Lipford, a building contractor based in Mobile, Alabama, with more than 30 years of experience. He is host of the nationally syndicated television program *Today's Homeowner with Danny Lipford* and home-maintenance consultant for the Weather Channel and *The Early Show* on CBS. TodaysHomeowner.com.

Melinda Myers, who has more than 30 years of horticultural experience. She is on the board of directors of the International Society of Arboriculture. She is host of *Melinda's Garden Moments*, which airs on TV and radio stations, and author of numerous books about gardening and yard care in northern climates, including *The Wisconsin Lawn Guide*. MelindaMyers.com

As unpleasant as the ice, snow and frigid temperatures are for many of us, our houses and yards suffer even more during the winter—unlike us, they can't go inside.

Fortunately, most winter home and yard damage isn't hard to repair, particularly when it's dealt with promptly. Significant costs even might qualify as casualty-loss tax deductions—see IRS Publication 547, *Casualties, Disasters, and Thefts,* for details.

What home owners can do now to help their homes and yards recover...

Heal Your Home
DANNY LIPFORD—Today's Homeowner

Winter ice and cold can cause leaks, cracks and other problems for homes. *Seven steps to take now...*

• **Clean and repair gutters.** Remove branches and winter debris from gutters or hire someone to do it. Also, check the condition of the gutters themselves. The spikes that hold gutters in place sometimes pull out from the home during the winter under the weight of ice or because wood surrounding the spike contracted in the cold. Replace any affected gutter spikes with gutter screws, which will stay in place better.

The seams between sections of gutter also can pull apart during winter. Reseal as needed using gutter caulk, such as DAP Butyl-Flex Gutter & Flashing Sealant (800-543-3840, DAP.com).

• **Identify roof leaks and potential future leaks.** Winter cold and ice can cause the sealant securing the metal flashing around chimneys, skylights and other roof openings to fail. Inspect your flashing as closely as possible. If you cannot safely climb onto your roof, use binoculars to look for loose or displaced flashing from the ground. Also, take a bright light up to your attic during a heavy rain, and check for drips and wet spots, particularly around chimneys, vents and skylights. If you find leaks or loose flashing, apply a flashing repair sealant, such as DAP Gutter & Flashing Sealant, or hire a roofing pro.

Ice can cause shingles to buckle or shift, too, most often near the perimeter of the roof. Inspect these shingles up close or use binoculars. Out-of-position shingles often simply can be pushed back into place or renailed. If damage is more significant or you cannot safely reach your roof, hire a professional roofer. Roofers often charge less than $100 for simple service calls.

•**Examine unheated pipes.** Pipes in unheated basements and crawl spaces may have frozen and cracked in the winter cold. Such cracks typically cause obvious flooding, but take a close look for slow leaks and drips, too. Even a slow leak could significantly inflate your water bill and potentially lead to water damage and/or mold.

•**Fix driveway cracks.** Ice and cold can crack concrete and asphalt driveways. These cracks will grow larger if left untreated. Quality sealants include Quikrete Concrete Crack Seal for concrete drives (800-282-5828, Quikrete.com) and Latex-ite Driveway Filler Sealer for asphalt (800-851-5606, Latexite.com).

Warning: Wait for a warm, dry spring day before sealing. Driveway sealants often fail when temperatures dip below 50°F or if it rains before they set.

•**Repair decks and fences.** Nails often rise up slightly from decks, wood fences and other nailed-together home components during the cold of winter, creating the risk that someone will trip or cut himself on an exposed nail head. Use a nail set (a small metal tool that looks like an ice pick) and a hammer to tap these nails back down, or pull out the nails and replace them with coated or stainless steel deck screws.

Apply a lube such as Liquid Wrench White Lithium Grease (866-973-6247, LiquidWrench.com) to outdoor metal latches and hinges to keep them working properly.

•**Clear exterior A/C components.** Tree branches might have fallen on your central air conditioner's condenser unit, or soil might have been pushed up against its base. This debris should be cleared away as soon as possible to encourage airflow and discourage rust.

Warning: Don't use a winter cover for the external components of your central air conditioner. These covers trap moisture inside, accelerating rust.

•**Clean carpets.** Road salt and moisture tracked into your home during the winter could discolor your carpets. Using a carpet shampooer in the spring can limit the damage. Make sure that any cleaning products you use are approved for your specific type of carpet.

Rescue Your Yard
MELINDA MYERS—Melinda's Garden Moments

Your lawn, trees, shrubs and plants might have been bent, beaten, salted and frozen. *Six steps to take now…*

•**Dilute road salt.** Use a hose with a spray nozzle to thoroughly wash sections of lawn near roads, driveways and walkways where salt was spread. Ideally, do this soon after the snow melts and the soil thaws.

Helpful: If sections of your lawn along roads or driveways repeatedly are killed by winter salt, consider replacing this grass with paver stones, gravel or mulch beds.

•**Check for snow mold.** After the snow melts, scan your grass for a gray or pink fuzzy fungus known as snow mold. To reduce snow mold damage, use a light plastic garden rake to gently fluff up the affected areas of the lawn, then wash the rake to remove any fungal spores and fluff the lawn in spots where snow lingered, such as shady areas or where snow was piled. This will help the grass dry out, reducing the risk that fungus will spread. If the grass does die, reseed as described below.

Warning: Don't use a heavy metal rake, which could pull out already stressed grass.

●**Reseed as necessary.** If sections of your lawn died or thinned out over the winter, you probably will want to reseed. If the dead patch is a few feet in diameter or smaller, use a heavy metal rake to loosen up the soil, mix a bucket of topsoil with a handful of grass seed, sprinkle this mixture over the affected area, then water lightly.

Alternative: If the dead patch is large—or there is general thinning throughout the lawn—rent a core aerator and use it to pull small plugs of soil out of the lawn, allowing the grass roots to breathe and allowing better seed-to-soil contact when you reseed.

Warning: If it's possible that road salt killed the grass, hose down the area as described above, then allow it to dry before reseeding.

●**Water your yard thoroughly if it's a dry spring.** Watering is a great way to help lawns and plants recover from a long winter, but many home owners don't water until the heat of summer.

Warning: Do not increase your fertilizer, herbicide or pesticide use. The amounts and application schedules recommended for your region by local garden centers or on product packaging should be adhered to regardless of the severity of the previous winter. Excessive fertilizer use can dry out the soil, resulting in a condition called fertilizer burn, which could kill the grass. Excessive use of pesticides or weed killers could be unhealthy for both your lawn and the people and pets who spend time on it.

●**Prune broken branches.** Do this before the spring growing season begins, if possible, so that damaged trees and plants don't waste energy growing leaves on branches that must be removed. If a multistemmed shrub that develops many new shoots, such as a dogwood or forsythia, has been severely damaged, prune it to near the ground. For other plants, prune just the damaged parts and see if the plant starts recovering by early summer—if not, it may need to be replaced.

The agriculture extensions of many state university systems offer pruning guidance on their websites.

Example: At Udel.edu from University of Delaware, search for "Pruning Woody Plants."

Warning: Do not apply sealant to trees after pruning. It usually does more harm than good except with elms and oaks pruned during growing season.

●**Right toppled plants and small trees as soon as possible.** Use cloth straps, wires and stakes to brace them back into place. They might survive if at least a third of their roots remain intact.

Save Hours on Yard Work

Catriona Tudor Erler, author of many books about gardening and landscaping, including *New Complete Home Landscaping*. CatrionaTudorErler.com

If you don't like yard work and if you would like to avoid or cut down on the expense of hiring a gardener, consider these strategies that give your yard a beautiful look without all the work…

●**Use more mulch.** The more of your property you cover in mulch, the less there is to mow, weed and fertilize. "Islands" of mulch around trees and shrubs look great and eliminate the tricky, time-consuming mowing and edging often required around these areas. Mulch also provides nutrients, reducing the time you must spend fertilizing.

If there are several shrubs or trees in the same general area in your lawn, group them into one large mulch island, rather than creating separate islands for each.

To create a mulch island: Lay about six layers of newspaper on top of existing grass and/or weeds. Then cover with three to four inches of organic mulch, such as shredded bark (different kinds are available at most nurseries). The newspaper helps kill the grass and weeds. Over time, the newspaper will decompose, adding additional nutrients to the soil.

•**Remulch once a year—just put fresh mulch on top of the old.** You don't need to add more newspaper. The fastest way to mulch perennial beds is to do it in early spring, before the plants send up their shoots.

Important: Leave a few inches of open space between mulch and tree trunks to allow airflow. You can safely mulch right up to the base of most other plants.

•**Choose a ground cover other than grass.** Replace all or part of your lawn with an attractive, low-lying ground cover that requires little or no maintenance once established.

Appropriate ground covers vary regionally, so ask a local garden store for advice. (Garden store employees will have more time to talk if you visit on a weekday.)

Options: Sedum, creeping thyme, daylilies, low-growing hostas, Korean grass, pachysandra, certain varieties of clover or moss and more.

Be aware that many ground covers cannot be walked on without damaging the plants. If you like the feel of grass under your feet or have young kids who play on your lawn, maintain a small lawn and use ground cover for the rest of your property.

Or plant Stepables, a line of ground covers designed to survive foot traffic (503-581-8915, Stepables.com).

There also are some grasses that require very little mowing, but these vary by region. Check with the Lawn Institute for more information (800-405-8873, TheLawnInstitute.org).

Place plants where they will get what they need without your help. Ask your garden store what type of soil...how much sun...and how much moisture a particular plant likes before you purchase it.

Position water-loving plants near the wettest sections of your lawn and sun-loving plants in exposed locations. Group plants with similar needs together so that you do not have to tend to each individually.

Also, select native plants. Plants indigenous to your region are likely to thrive in your yard with little attention from you. Your local garden store can suggest appropriate native options.

•**Favor flowering shrubs over other flowers.** Flowering shrubs usually require much less care than other flowers. Popular options include camellia, lilac, abelia and azalea. Ask your garden store to recommend the flowering shrubs most appropriate for your region. Plant a selection of shrubs that flower at different times of year so that your yard is colorful most of the year.

Examples: Encore azaleas bloom in both spring and fall...Glacier azaleas bloom sporadically throughout the summer...witch hazel blooms in winter or early spring.

•**Plant evergreen trees rather than deciduous trees.** If you add trees to your property, avoid unnecessary autumn raking by selecting coniferous trees, such as pine trees, which do not shed needles.

If there already are deciduous trees on your property, create large mulch islands around them. Leaves that fall on this mulch do not need to be raked.

Keep in mind that well-placed deciduous trees can cut your home's energy use by providing cool shade in summer and letting the sun hit the house in winter.

CHAPTER 14

Money Savers

20 Ways to Cut Your Grocery Bills

Judy Walker, retired food editor of *The Times-Picayune*, New Orleans, NOLA.com. She is a member of the Association of Food Journalists, Southern Foodways Alliance and the Arizona Culinary Hall of Fame.

Sticker shock! That's what you face every time you go to the supermarket these days.

So, what's a consumer to do? *Here's how to keep your grocery bills as low as possible...*

Plan Your Trips...

1. Take a shopping list. To keep the list to a minimum, plan your meals for the week and then list the ingredients you need to buy. Stick to your list—but be flexible. Take advantage of store specials you come across.

2. Pay attention to what you have on hand— especially perishables. That way, you won't have to throw away unused food.

3. Learn the layout of your grocery store.

Sneaky secret: Stores put dairy products and meat in the back of the store to force you to walk through aisles of temptation—processed foods sold at higher markups—to get there. If you're making a quick trip for milk, keep this in mind and be resolute—buy only milk.

4. Eat first. This tried-and-true tactic bears repeating. Going to the grocery store hungry is the reason we buy on impulse.

Skip Nonessentials...

5. Drink tap water. Almost all municipal water in America is so good that nobody ever needs to drink water from Italy or France (or Maine, for that matter). Getting the recommended eight glasses a day from bottled water costs as much as $1,400 annually. If you don't like the taste of your local water, buy a faucet filter or filtering pitcher.

6. Don't buy processed foods. They cost more than meals you put together yourself from basic ingredients and generally are not as nutritious.

7. Grate your own. Like processed foods, pregrated carrots, cheese, etc., cost more—and often don't taste as fresh.

8. Skip the precuts. Cut meat and produce yourself, rather than buying individual servings or pieces.

9. Clean your own fish. It's cheaper per pound of edible fish to buy whole fish (the smaller varieties, of course) at the market and then remove the head, tail, etc., at home.

10. Don't buy toiletries at the grocery store. Make a separate list of toiletries and paper products for the discount stores, such as Costco, BJ's and Sam's Club, where they'll cost 20% to 40% less.

Shopping Strategies...

11. Don't be fooled by phony sales.

Sneaky secret: Items displayed on the ends of aisles aren't necessarily on sale. Manufacturers of those items pay for those prime display locations.

Better: Compare prices in the main aisles, where products compete against each other.

12. Know when to buy in bulk. Only buy groceries you know that you'll use before they go bad. Nonperishables are the safest to buy in bulk.

Also: Just because an item is available in a larger size doesn't mean it's cheaper. Take a calculator to the supermarket to check "unit prices" by dividing price by quantity.

13. Buy generic. You can almost always save money by choosing a store label or little-known brand instead of a well-known brand. In some cases, particularly with items such as orange juice and condiments, the savings can be tremendous.

14. Stoop and reach.

Sneaky secret: Food manufacturers pay for prime, eye-level shelf space at grocery stores—and their prices reflect it. So, look high and low, literally, for comparable items on other shelves.

15. Buy "must go" foods. Bypass the more expensive fresh-baked bread and reach for the day-old selection. Keep it in the freezer for toasting. Also, most bakery departments will discount fresh items drastically as the end of the day nears—you may just have to ask.

Stores routinely discount dairy, baked goods, produce and meat as these items approach their "sell-by" dates or become less attractive (think slightly bruised apples or crushed bread). These items are tasty and perfectly safe to eat, even several days after purchase. Ask the staff at your supermarket when they mark items down. Time your shopping accordingly.

16. Shop less often. Shoppers making "quick trips" to the store usually purchase more than they planned. If you go to the store three times a week and spend $10 on impulse buys each trip, that adds up to $120 extra per month. But if you go only once a week and spend the same $10 on impulse buys each time, you'll spend $40 per month on impulse buys. That saves you $80 per month, or $960 per year.

17. Use the buddy system. Save money by sharing costs with someone else.

Examples: Split two-for-one offers…the contents of large, well-priced packages, such as a bag of potatoes…share the price of gas to the supermarket.

Maximize Coupons…

18. Check all sources for coupons. Americans have saved an estimated $30 billion with manufacturers' coupons. Most of the 278 billion coupons redeemed came from Sunday papers. But it can really pay to check manufacturers' websites, as well as specialty Internet coupon sites, such as Deal-Catcher (DealCatcher.com).

Also: Take advantage of store coupons you load onto your supermarket loyalty card. Visit your store's website for details.

Be Checkout Savvy…

You've come to the finish line—don't blow it now…

19. Fight checkout temptation. The candy, gadgets and magazines right around the cash registers are high-profit items for the store—and the least useful to you. Resist!

20. Keep a close eye on the scanner. Americans lose from $1 billion to $3 billion a year on scanning discrepancies. Scanners are not always reset with current sale prices, so your chance of being charged the full price on a sale item is high.

Eat for Less and Enjoy It More

Mark Bittman is author of numerous books, including *Food Matters* and *How to Cook Everything*. He has been writing "The Minimalist" column for *The New York Times* since 1997 and has hosted three public television shows on cooking and food.

I f you're among those spending more time in the kitchen, knowing what to have on hand can make cooking faster, easier and more affordable. *General principles to help you eat better and save money…*

●**Buy in bulk,** whether it's whole grains, pasta or Parmesan cheese (the latter, wrapped well, can keep for a year—you can scrape off mold if necessary). Stock up when these items go on sale, or buy bigger, more economical packages. As long as it is something that won't spoil, you'll be sure to have essential ingredients on hand and save money.

●**Cook in bulk, too.** Doubling or even tripling many recipes is an easy way to make sure that you always have something delicious and healthy around. Grains, beans, soups and stews all can be made in large batches with minimal effort—and leftovers can be frozen. When you have good food ready to eat in the house, you're less likely to order a pizza or run out for a pricey restaurant meal.

•**Think about how much meat you eat.** Since I have started eating less meat, I have saved a lot of money. (I also have lost weight.) Two sausages in a pasta sauce are plenty for four people, and one large roasting chicken, with lots of vegetables, can easily serve 10. Two or three shrimp per person chopped up in a stir-fry offers more than enough flavor.

•**Beware of "convenience" produce.** Those bags of prewashed lettuce or cut carrots save time, but you'll save money buying whole produce and washing and cutting it yourself. Consider adding a salad spinner to your collection of kitchen tools so that you can quickly wash and dry salad greens.

•**Embrace whole grains.** They're good for you and relatively inexpensive—and you can do a thousand different things with them. Keep short-grain rice in the pantry for risotto or paella. Barley drizzled with any pan sauce is delicious. Polenta, quinoa, wild rice, bulgur—add these to your repertoire, and you'll never be at a loss for something wonderful to eat.

If you're in doubt about how to cook any of these, add them to lots of salted water and cook as you would pasta, then drain when tender.

•**Learn to love legumes.** Beans, like grains, are an excellent pantry staple—they're good for you and incredibly inexpensive. They're also very simple to make. Soak overnight and discard the soaking water (discarding the water helps make the beans less gassy). Then simmer in water until tender. Put beans and lentils in soups, stews and salads, or even enjoy a bowl on their own. Skeptical?

Try this: Drizzle a bowl of cooked white beans with olive oil and some freshly chopped rosemary, lemon zest and a generous grating of Parmesan cheese. Or purée some chickpeas with garlic, lemon, cumin and tahini for a delicious homemade hummus.

•**Make use of the whole bird.** Roast chicken for dinner? Use the chicken scraps and bones to make your own stock. Chop half an onion, a carrot and a stalk of celery, and sauté in a little olive oil. Add some whole peppercorns, parsley and a bay leaf along with the bones, cover with water and let cook for about an hour.

The flavor of homemade stock is vastly superior to that of store-bought, and it is better for you by far. Plus, few weeknight dinners are as speedy or satisfying as a bowl of good broth served over angel hair or other noodles with some minced garlic, grated ginger, a few handfuls of sautéed bok choy or other vegetables and a dash of soy sauce.

•**Make the most of your freezer to reduce waste.** You may not even realize how many things you can freeze instead of letting them spoil—fresh mozzarella, aging bananas (for bread or muffins), broth, tomato sauce and bread crumbs. Hearty fresh herbs (parsley, dill, basil) all freeze well. Freshly squeezed lemon and lime juices can go into ice-cube trays and be saved for later. And instead of letting that last quarter cup of wine go down the drain, put it in a zippered plastic bag or ice-cube tray and freeze it to add to pasta sauce or risotto.

•**Do it yourself.** Before you reach for something in a package or a bottle, think about whether you're better off taking the time (and saving the money) to do it yourself. *Examples…*

•Salad dressing. Bottled salad dressing is almost never made from decent oil, usually has preservatives and other unpronounceable junk in it, and is the biggest rip-off imaginable, so why buy it? Combine olive oil with lemon juice or vinegar (in a proportion of about three parts oil to one part vinegar). Add salt and pepper, some Dijon mustard, herbs if you like, and you will have something infinitely better than anything you'll find in a bottle (and lots cheaper).

•Tomato sauce. Instead of paying for a jar of something that will never taste as good as homemade, sauté garlic in a little olive oil, add a large can of tomatoes and cook until it is "saucy"—you'll know when it is ready. Tomato sauce freezes beautifully, so again, making it in larger quantities makes sense.

• Aerosol oil is another rip-off. At about $12 a pint, it's twice as expensive as halfway decent extra-virgin olive oil, and it contains additives. Instead, use a brush or your fingers.

• Bread crumbs. Don't throw out that day-old (or two-day-old) bread. A few pulses in a food processor, and you have a bag of homemade bread crumbs to put into meat loaf or on top of gratins.

A Very Frugal New Englander's Favorite Money Savers

Richard Gray, author of The Frugal Senior: Hundreds of Creative Ways to Stretch a Dollar!

B eing frugal isn't just about scrimping and saving money. It can help you reduce stress over your finances, as well as get more enjoyment out of life.

Here are author Richard Gray's favorite money-saving tricks…

Shopping

• **Make your favorite restaurant foods and beverages yourself.** TopSecretRecipes.com features dozens of free recipes for restaurant dishes you can try at home, including Applebee's Low-Fat Asian Chicken Salad, 7-Eleven's Cherry Slurpee and Starbucks' Hot Chocolate.

• **Make your own greeting cards.** The markup on Hallmark and other greeting cards is outrageous. You spend $1.99 to $5.99 for a piece of paper that often gets discarded moments after it is opened.

Better: Many recent-model personal computers come with software that allows you to make hundreds of different birthday, get-well and holiday cards. You also can find free card-making websites online, such as GreetingsIsland.com and Canva.com.

Your personalized, handmade greeting cards will cost you only pennies and take less time to cre-

ate than traveling to the store. They also will be appreciated far more by the recipients. Be sure to use sturdy paper (24-pound or heavier).

Bonus: Most card-making software includes templates to print personalized monthly calendars. These make very nice gifts.

• **Use the "Rule of Three" when deciding whether to buy something nonessential.** If I can think of three practical uses for an item I am considering buying, it's worthwhile. For example, I bought a new convertible sofa to use as seating for company, a spare bed for overnight guests and a comfortable place to read.

Around the House

• **Extend the life of many household appliances, utensils and other items…**

• Hair dryer. Unclog lint from inside the hair dryer using a cotton swab dipped in alcohol. (Of course, unplug the dryer first.)

• Scissors. Sharpen them by making six to eight cuts in a sheet of fine-grade sandpaper.

• Coffee grinder. Sharpen the blades by placing a cup of uncooked rice into the grinder and whirring it for a few seconds.

• Razors. Store them, blade down, in a cup of vegetable oil so that the oil covers the blades. This keeps them sharper much longer by reducing corrosion. Rinse before using.

• Printer ink cartridges. Refill your own cartridges for less than half the cost of purchasing new ones. While this process used to be messy and potentially harmful to your printer, the technology has improved in the past few years. For more information and answers to common questions, see WebPanache.com/reprint/refillin.htm.

• **Repair household gadgets yourself.** Get advice and instructions for many common household repairs at DoItYourself.com.

Example: The most often used—and troublesome—household fixture is the toilet. Perhaps it won't flush or runs continuously or leaks water onto the floor. You can fix most of these problems your-self without paying a plumber $100 an hour.

Home Products

•**Use low-cost alternatives to store-bought health and beauty products and household cleaners.** Most specialty cleaning and beauty solutions weren't developed until the past few decades. Many of them are expensive and include harsh chemical ingredients. *Until a few generations ago, everyone used more basic mixtures—with excellent results…*

•Glass cleaner. Use windshield washer fluid, often on sale for as little as $1.50/gallon. You also can find cheap washer fluid in large quantities at warehouse clubs.

•Copper polish. Rub ketchup on the copper item. Let stand five minutes. Rinse with hot water.

•Chrome polish. Crumple a piece of aluminum foil, and rub it over the surface you wish to polish. Try this on an inconspicuous spot first, to make sure that the surface doesn't scratch. If the chrome is rusted, try dipping the foil in a carbonated beverage, such as cola, before polishing.

•Plug-in air fresheners. Squeeze a few drops of lemon juice into the bag of your vacuum cleaner each time you run it.

•Car wax. A homemade mixture of one cup of coconut oil (available in health-food stores), one cup of beeswax and one-quarter cup of olive oil. Combine the ingredients and melt over a low flame, stirring occasionally. Pour the mixture into a container. Let cool before using.

•Burn ointment. An aloe plant. Grow one on your kitchen windowsill. Aloe contains dozens of vitamins, amino acids and enzymes that relieve pain and help burned skin heal. Simply tear off a leaf, and squeeze the liquid onto the burn.

•Ice/frozen gel packs. Mix one part rubbing alcohol with two parts water in a plastic freezer bag placed inside a second freezer bag. Put it in the freezer. The alcohol prevents the pack from freezing completely, so you can mold it to any part of your body.

•Skin exfoliants. Plain yogurt—the lactic acid sloughs off dead skin cells. Rinse your face with warm water. Massage in one tablespoon of plain yogurt. Let sit for a few minutes, then rinse with warm water. Olive oil and sugar—wet your face, and massage olive oil into your skin to moisturize. Then scrub your face with a teaspoon of sugar to remove dead skin cells. Rinse with warm water. Wipe off any excess with a warm, wet towel to complete the facial.

•**Download free books.** Curl up in bed or on the couch with your laptop computer to read your favorite novel. You can find thousands of books at Gutenberg.org…Free-ebooks.net…and Digital.library.upenn.edu/books. You also can print them, but you would have to pay for the paper and ink.

Pets

•**Substitute homemade remedies.**

Instead of store-bought flea treatments: Mix a little sage into your cat's or dog's food.

Instead of ear-cleaning treatments: Make your own ear rinse by mixing a solution of one-third rubbing alcohol, one-third white vinegar and one-third water. Squirt a few drops of the liquid into your pet's problem ear…let set a minute…then wipe out the ear with a tissue.

Online Freebies

My favorite sites for free stuff…
BestDealsOnTheWeb.net
TheBalanceEveryday.com/freebies-4161985

Dozens of Senior Discounts Can Save You $$$

Amie Clark, founder of TheSeniorList.com, a website that features ratings, reviews and articles about products and services for older adults. She previously was a social worker specializing in senior housing and care coordination.

Senior discount programs have been disappearing. Earlier this year, Kroger became the latest supermarket chain to discontinue its version. The National Park Service recently raised the price of its popular lifetime pass for seniors from a heavily discounted $10 to the standard $80. Big restaurant chains increasingly are allowing each franchise to decide for itself whether to offer a senior discount—and many are opting to scale back these programs or end them. Some restaurants are offering "senior menus"—with low prices and small portions—rather than bona fide senior discounts.

However, there still are some businesses that offer significant (not just token) senior discounts. These savings usually are available starting at age 60, 62 or 65, but in some cases customers as young as age 50 or 55 can take advantage. Many senior discounts are designated for AARP members, but some of those also are granted to members of other seniors' organizations (see below).

Here are dozens of businesses that still offer attractive senior discounts. Confirm these offers before buying—discount programs can change with little notice…and sometimes not every location in a chain participates.

Supermarkets

Supermarket senior discounts have become rare, but they can be worth seeking out. The typical US household spends about 8% of its budget on groceries, so a 5% or 10% senior discount could be worth a lot of money. Expect certain product categories, including prescriptions, lottery tickets and tobacco, to be excluded. *Two of the largest supermarket chains that still offer senior discounts…*

Fred Meyer: 10% discount for age 55 and up on the first Tuesday of each month.

Harris Teeter: 5% discount for age 60 and up every Thursday.

Restaurants

Within a chain, eligibility and/or other details of senior discounts sometimes vary from location to location. Among the chains that do offer appetizing senior deals and discounts at many or all locations are Arby's…Ben & Jerry's…Burger King…Dairy Queen…Krispy Kreme…Mrs. Fields…Sonic…and White Castle.

The following discounts are available in at least some locations to AARP members…

Bonefish Grill: 10% on select items.

Bubba Gump Shrimp Co.: 10%, which also applies to the meals of up to five other guests accompanying the senior and which also is available at several other chains owned by the Bubba Gump parent company, Landry, including Landry's Seafood House and Rainforest Cafe (though not Rainforest Cafes in Disney theme parks).

Carrabba's Italian Grill: 10%.

Denny's: 15%.

Outback Steakhouse: 10%.

Papa John's: 25% on delivery and take-out orders placed online.

Apparel and Department Stores

Here are four apparel and department stores where seniors can save on clothing, housewares and more. (Typically these discounts cannot be combined with any other percentage discounts, but they often can be used together with coupons and "rewards.")

Bealls: 10% for age 50 and up every Tuesday.

Belk: 15% for age 62 and up on the first Tuesday of the month.

Kohl's: 15% for age 60 and up on Wednesdays.

Travel

Many travel-related businesses offer senior savings—but because these discounts often are applied to the full "rack" rate, they are not always good deals. Better deals might be available either through the company or through third-party travel websites such as Kayak.com or Expedia.com. Still, it's worth investigating—sometimes these discounts truly are money savers. *Among them…*

AARP car-rental deals: Avis and Budget up to 30% off; 5% off Payless Car Rental. The top discount rate is not available at all locations.

Train and bus deals: Amtrak offers 10% off for age 65 and up. Greyhound offers 5% off for age 62 and up.

Hotel savings: Most major hotel chains offer senior discounts, frequently 5% to 20%, though they might not be available at all locations. These savings are available only when the room is booked directly through the hotel, not through a third-party travel app or website.

The good news is that hotel chains are trying to meet or beat the rates offered on these third-party sites on their own websites these days—and at some hotel chains, the senior discount can be applied to the "best available" room rate, not the steep "rack" rate. After finding the best rate you can on a third-party site, visit that chain's website or call its reservation number to check whether you could do better with the senior discount.

Examples: Hotel chains where senior discounts often are available and are applied to the "best available" rate include Best Western (age 55 and up)...Hilton (AARP)...Starwood (AARP)...and Wyndham (age 60 and up).

Airline deals: Several airlines, including American, Southwest and United, say that they offer special fares for travelers age 65 and up. Unfortunately, you typically must call the airline and book directly to obtain these rates—and seniors who do so sometimes report that the senior fares they are offered are no lower than the typical fares. Be sure to shop around before booking one of these senior rates.

Shipping and Office Supplies

If you are age 50 or older, you can join senior associations and qualify for attractive discounts at these businesses...

Office Depot and OfficeMax: These retailers offer a 10% discount on most office products—plus lower rates on copying and printing services—to members of the Association of Mature American Citizens (see below).

UPS: AARP members get 15% off many products and services, plus a 5% discount on shipping.

Movie Theaters

Many movie theaters offer senior discounts that can save you a few dollars or more per ticket.

AMC: Many AMC theater locations offer discounted tickets to patrons age 60 and up, but details vary from theater to theater.

Cinemark: Most offer a "Senior Day" with reduced pricing. Details vary from theater to theater.

Showcase Cinemas: $7.75 admission for age 60 and up on Wednesdays. This applies even to 3-D and IMAX showings that ordinarily cost extra—though not on holidays and for certain special engagements.

Alternatives to AARP

Many senior discounts actually are discounts offered to members of AARP, formerly known as the American Association of Retired Persons, which is open to people age 50 and up and their spouses (AARP.org, $16/year, spousal membership free).

But some seniors disagree with AARP's politics and prefer not to join. Those seniors might consider joining a different group such as the American Seniors Association (AmericanSeniors.org, $15/year, age 50 and up, spousal membership free) or the Association of Mature American Citizens (AMAC.us, $16/year, age 50 and up, spousal membership free). These groups have arranged some member discounts of their own, and businesses that offer AARP discounts sometimes are willing to extend those discounts to members of these senior associations, too, when asked to do so.

Free Food

Clark.com, a money-saving website.

Get free food on your birthday by registering your e-mail with popular restaurants. Some offer food free only on your actual birthday—others give you more flexibility. Consider Applebee's or Chili's for a free dessert...Baskin Robbins for a free scoop...Benihana for a $30 birthday certificate good during your birthday month...Denny's for a free Grand Slam breakfast...Firehouse Subs for a free medium sub...Ruby Tuesday for a free burger, appetizer or Garden Bar entrée...Steak-N-Shake for a free specialty milk shake and free Double 'n Cheese 'n Fries. For a list including other restaurants, go to Clark.com/Deals-Money-Saving-Advice/Free-Birthday-Food.

Caution: Call your local restaurant to be sure that it honors the birthday giveaway. And consider setting up a new e-mail address just for this and other promotions—you will be getting a lot of promotional messages.

Great Streaming Channels That Are Free

Jim Kimble, founder of The Cord Cutting Report, a website about streaming services and related topics. CordCuttingReport.com

There are many great streaming channels that are free (except for the burden of having to watch commercials). *Here are some of the best…*

•**For TV shows from the 1950s, 1960s and 1970s: Shout! Factory TV** offers classic series such as *Car 54, Where Are You?…Route 66…*and *The Saint.* It has films, too, but they're mostly low-budget drive-in-movie fare. Shout! Factory can be streamed on a PC, laptop or through apps on Roku, Android, Apple TV and Amazon Fire TV. ShoutFactory.com

•**For free movies without commercial interruptions: Kanopy** offers more than 30,000 movies with no subscription fees or commercials. It has especially strong classic movies, art house films and documentaries.

Examples: To Catch a Thief…The 400 Blows… Seven Samurai. To use it, you need to have a library card from one of the many libraries that offer Kanopy. Kanopy.com/wayf

Alternative: A rival service called **Hoopla** also offers free digital downloads of movies with no commercial breaks to cardholders of certain libraries. Its selection is less extensive than Kanopy's. HooplaDigital.com

•**For free movies from a pay movie service: Vudu** is best known as one of many services that rents and sells digital downloads of recent films on a per-film basis. But Vudu now also has a few dozen mainstream movies available for free at any given time—click the "Free" tab on its website. These are not the most recent releases, but there's often something worth watching.

Recent examples: Black Mass…Mystic Pizza… City Slickers. Vudu.com

•**For more free movies: Tubi TV** has partnered with movie studios Lionsgate, Paramount and MGM to offer some relatively recent mainstream films.

Recent example: Misconduct (a 2016 Al Pacino/ Anthony Hopkins thriller). Tubi offers TV shows, too, though not many popular shows. TubiTV.com

•**For science fiction: Comet** offers classic sci-fi shows such as *The Outer Limits* and *Stargate SG-1.* It has sci-fi movies, too, but they're mainly drive-in-quality films. CometTV.com

•**For a TV-like flip-through-the-channels experience: Pluto TV** organizes a wide range of streaming content into a 100-plus channel grid that you can navigate as you would a cable provider's onscreen guide. Most of Pluto's content runs on a schedule as it does on conventional TV—but there also is an extensive on-demand menu of movies and a small selection of TV shows you can view if you're using the app. Pluto.TV

•**For national and world news: CBSN** is a 24-hour streaming news network offered by CBS (CBSNews.com/streaming).

Alternative: **Bloomberg Television** is a 24-hour global news channel that's free if you watch through Pluto TV.

•**For local news: NewsON streams** local newscasts from more than 275 stations in more than 165 US markets. Watch live or up to 48 hours after a newscast airs. NewsON.us

Ways to Save This Holiday Season

Real Simple, Time-Life Building, New York City.

Send out holiday postcards—you can save 19 cents a card (a postcard needs only a 40-cent stamp, instead of a 58-cent one). Decorate gifts with yarn instead of ribbon. Ribbon can cost $10 for 20 yards, but you can get about 70 yards of yarn for $2 to $6. Buy wine by the case. Most retailers will give a 10% discount on a case of wine, and some will let you mix and match different brands in the same box. Skip plastic stemware for parties. At restaurant supply stores, you can find inexpensive glassware for about as much as you would spend on plastic glasses—and you can reuse them. Serve a signature punch instead of stocking a full bar. A full bar with liquors, mixers, beers and wine to serve a few dozen people can easily cost hundreds of dollars.

Big Home Upgrades... Small Cost

For less than $100, you can buy paint and rollers and change the look of a room...organize clutter by buying baskets or a low-cost closet system...get plants to change your home's outdoor look or to freshen up the interior...buy low-cost patterned fabrics and use them to make curtain panels or chair cushions...cover an accent wall with reclaimed wood planks, such as old barn siding...upgrade front-door hardware with new locks, knobs and handles...hang a mirror from a consignment store or discount shop over a buffet or dresser...print, frame and hang some of your photos.

WiseBread.com.

Keep the Heat Inside This Winter

Asa Aarons, consumer advocate. His reports have been featured on television, including on NBC's *Today* show. Aarons has won national recognition for reports on consumer strategies to save money on fuel, utilities and taxes.

To reduce your heating costs next winter, take immediate action...

1. Close external leaks. Mail chutes and the spot around the clothes dryer vent are key culprits for heat loss. Ducts running through attics, crawl spaces, garages and basements are another common source of leaks.

What to do: Seal duct joints with mastic paste (reinforced duct sealant), metal-backed tape or an aerosol sealant. Regular duct tape should not be used because it cannot withstand temperature extremes. Ductwork is usually hard to get at, so sealing is best left to a professional.

3. Inspect your house for hidden openings. After dark, with all of the inside lights off, have a friend stand outside and shine a high-powered flashlight around the exterior while you remain inside. Any light coming through walls that you see inside translates to heat leaks that should be sealed.

4. Use incense to help you test for drafts. First, turn off exhaust fans and make sure that windows are closed. Then move about the house holding the incense. If the smoke drifts sideways, it could indicate a leak.

5. Lock windows and sliding doors. This gives the panels their tightest possible seal.

6. Add sealant to the glazing putty in your windows if it is dry and cracked. Also seal any visible cracks around the windows between the sash (the movable part) and the frame with weather stripping or cloth.

7. Close storm windows properly. If you don't have storm windows, put plastic film made for insulating windows on the inside. This acts as an interior storm window.

Cost: About $10 for two three-foot-by-five-foot sheets, available at hardware or building-supply stores.

8. Stop heat loss from under exterior doorways. Place a draft blocker across the bottom of the doorway. For a more permanent solution, attach weather stripping to the bottom of the door.

9. Check the location of your thermostat. A drafty window or an exterior door near your thermostat can turn your heating system on unnecessarily.

Best: Put your thermostat on an inside wall away from a window or door.

10. Cover through-the-wall and window air conditioners for the winter. Close the vents and put an insulated cover, available at hardware or building-supply stores for about $25, on the air conditioners to complete the seal.

11. Buy heating oil in the late summer or early fall. The price of home heating oil is usually lowest in the off season.

12. Add a furnace humidifier. This increases your perception of warmth—68°F with moisture can feel warmer than 72°F without it. A humidifier can be added to any type of heating system.

13. Get a free "energy audit" from your utility company, which evaluates the efficiency of your home's heating and cooling systems in addition to assessing how you can save energy. Get an energy audit by a home energy rater if your utility company doesn't perform this service. A home energy rating will also give you an idea of the energy efficiency of your home and help you make informed choices about which improvements are likely to have the most effect.

You can find a home energy rater at Residential Energy Services Network (RESNet.us). You could also use a Building Performance Institute Inc. (BPI. org) accredited contractor to do an energy audit. Cost for these services is about $250 to $1,000 (depending on your location), but potential savings may make the expense worthwhile.

14. Have your heating system serviced annually. This includes a thorough cleaning of the blower (and nozzle if it uses oil), and making any necessary adjustments. The furnace's combustion efficiency should be tested to calculate how completely the fuel is burned and how much of the heat is transferred into your home.

Cool Your Home for Much, Much Less

Ray Kamada, PhD, energy conservation expert who remodels and retrofits homes in the Pacific Northwest for greater energy efficiency.

Home owners with central air-conditioning typically spend hundreds of dollars on electricity each summer to keep cool. (Those with window air conditioners typically spend half as much.) It's often possible to cut these cooling bills substantially without sacrificing comfort.

One way to save is to replace an old central air-conditioning unit with a new Energy Star model. A new unit could save you 30% to 50% in operating costs compared with one that is 10 years old or more. Modern Energy Star window units offer similar savings. Many local utility companies offer rebates or credits for installing high-efficiency equipment, but a new central-air unit still will cost at least $3,000 installed.

Fortunately, not all savings come at such a steep price. *Among the simple, inexpensive things you can do...*

Sun-Proof Your Home

Your air-conditioning won't have to work as hard if you keep the hot air outside...

●**Insulate your attic.** Install insulation with at least an R-30 value between the attic space and the living space.

Cost: As little as 35 cents per square foot. You even can do the job yourself.

●**Avoid attic fans**—if a fan that is away from your living space burns out and shorts, there's a significant fire hazard.

●**Keep furniture and drapes clear of air-conditioner vents.** Your air conditioner must work harder if vents are blocked.

●**Limit use of major appliances on hot days.** Ovens, ranges, dryers, dishwashers and other appliances add significant heat to your home.

●**Let nature be your air-conditioning on cool nights.** Even when temperatures drop to comfortable levels, some people keep their homes sealed up so as not to "waste" cool air, but it's cheaper to turn off air-conditioning and open windows until morning.

•**Close the drapes on the sunny side of your home before you leave for work.**

Cool Your Home's Surroundings

The surrounding landscape can affect the energy efficiency of your air-conditioning. *Steps to take…*

•**Put mulch on the south side of your house— a layer at least one inch thick.** Mulch retains moisture. When this moisture evaporates in the sun, it lowers the temperature slightly in the surrounding area—including inside your home. (Mulching in the sunniest spot—the south side—produces the greatest benefit.) You can purchase mulch at any garden center.

•**Shade the south side of your home with deciduous trees.** They'll cool your house in summer but won't block the sun in winter, after they have shed their leaves.

Maintain Air-Conditioning Units

Well-maintained equipment will keep you cool for less, whether it's a central air conditioner or a window unit.

•**Clean the coils.** Dirty or dusty coils can reduce efficiency by as much as 20% for central and window air conditioners. Once a year, cut the power at the fuse box to the outdoor section of your central air-conditioning unit and hose off the coils. Then turn off the power to the indoor part of the system, remove the cover plate and wipe down the coils with a moist cloth. The coils on a window air conditioner should be easy to reach—they might not even be covered. Just unplug the unit, and wipe off the coils with a moist cloth.

•**Replace or clean the filter.** For central-air units, replacing the filter every month during cooling season can reduce operating costs by 5% to 15% and improve your home's air quality, according to the US Department of Energy. Replace or clean filters on window units as recommended in the owner's manual.

Other Strategies for Central Air-Conditioning

•**Get your ducts sealed.** As much as 30% of the cool air produced can escape through improperly sealed ducts. Duct tape isn't as effective at solving this problem as a quality sealant, such as mastic (a form of caulk), since duct tape can dry out and lose its grip when subjected to the changing temperatures of ventilation ducts. If you can feel cool air leaking out of the seams in your ducts, purchase mastic at a home center for a few dollars per tube and fill the gaps around your ducts.

If your ducts are difficult to reach, you may need to call in a professional, who might charge a few hundred dollars or more, depending on the accessibility of your duct system.

•**Insulate attic ductwork.** Temperatures in your attic might climb to well over 100 degrees in summer. Adding a layer of fiberglass insulation around ductwork should make a noticeable difference in your system's efficiency.

Cost: Less than $1 per square foot of ductwork if you do it yourself.

•**Shield your outdoor central air-conditioning unit to keep it out of direct sunlight.** A central air-conditioning unit that is left in the sun can use 10% more energy. If you can't easily move it to a shady spot, install an awning over it.

Energy-Smart Renovations

If you're planning some home improvements, keep these energy-saving strategies in mind…

•**When replacing windows, choose ones with fiberglass or vinyl frames.** Aluminum is an excellent conductor of heat, so aluminum window frames bring outside heat into the living space. Fiberglass or high-quality vinyl window frames can cut your cooling bills. (Avoid bargain-basement vinyl—it can become warped in higher temperatures. A quality vinyl window should be reinforced with fiberglass or metal inside the vinyl to help it keep its shape.)

•**For driveways on the sunny sides of homes in warm climates, favor dark asphalt over light-colored cement.** Lighter-colored driveways reflect more sun and heat onto your home. If a driveway doesn't reflect sun onto the home—perhaps because it's on the north side—lean toward a light-colored cement driveway.

● **When replacing your roof, favor light-colored shingles.** A dark roof absorbs tremendous heat on sunny summer days. Studies by the Florida Solar Energy Center and the Florida Power and Lighting Company found that switching from a black roof to a white one can reduce cooling bills by as much as 40%. (Your savings will be lower than 40% if your attic ductwork is well insulated, so it isn't worth replacing your roof until your old one is ready to go. Some towns have ordinances restricting roof-color options, so check the rules before making this change.)

It's true that your home will absorb less heat during cold months if it has a light-colored roof, but the amount of money added to heating costs is significantly less than the amount saved on cooling.

Helpful: Painting your home's exterior a light color also can reduce cooling bills.

Save More Money Every Time You Shop Online

David Pogue, writer and correspondent for *CBS Sunday Morning* and *Nova.* He spent 13 years as the personal technology columnist for *The New York Times* and is author of *Pogue's Basics: Money—Essential Tips and Shortcuts (That No One Bothers to Tell You).* DavidPogue.com

It's no secret that online merchants often offer lower prices than brick-and-mortar stores. But getting the very lowest prices online—and in some cases, at physical stores—takes a little extra ingenuity and some assistance, which you can get from the following helpful websites and strategies…

Discount and Coupon Sites

These sites provide discount coupons…rebates…and/or discount codes—codes that you can use at shopping websites to obtain special deals.

● **RetailMeNot.com,** one of the best-known sites for discounts, is worth checking before you buy almost anything online, ranging from electronics to clothes to pizza. It lists tens of thousands of discount codes at any given time, plus rebates, printable coupons and various other savings opportunities, and it even indicates how likely it is that a certain discount offer will actually work on a given day. Just enter the name of the business you might buy from and/or the product you want to buy in

RetailMeNot's search box to see if any relevant offers are available.

Recent examples: Save up to 50% on thousands of books at BarnesAndNoble.com…25% off at PapaJohns.com.

● **Rakuten.com (formerly EBates.com),** enables consumers to earn cash back when they buy from any of more than 3,500 shopping sites. Rakuten does this by sharing the "referral fees" it gets for sending visitors from its site to the shopping sites. Before buying anything online, check whether Rakuten has a link to the site where you intend to buy. If so, you could earn anywhere from 1% to 40% back on your purchase simply by navigating to that shopping site through the Rakuten link. In addition to retail sites, Rakuten offers cash back for purchases made on many travel sites, including sites for hotel chains, car-rental firms and even some airlines. Every three months, Rakuten will mail you a check or deposit the cash you have earned into your PayPal account—your choice. (The payment will be deferred if you have earned less than $5.01.)

Recent examples of Rakuten cash back from various sites: 10% at 1-800-Flowers…2% at Macy's …3.5% at Red Roof Inns.

● **Coupons.com.** Not only does this site provide discount codes and rebates for online shopping, it also is the best site for obtaining hundreds of coupons to print out and use in physical stores just like coupons clipped from newspapers. You must supply your phone number to use the site, but the number is used only for verification, not for marketing calls. Another coupon website worth trying is SmartSource.com.

Recent examples: Save $2 on Starbucks ground coffee…save $1 on two Airwick products.

Amazon Savings Tricks

More than 300 million customers shop at Amazon. com, including more than 60 million who belong to Amazon Prime, which provides benefits ranging from free two-day shipping to streaming video content and unlimited photo storage. Yet many of those customers are unaware of some of the best ways to save the most at the site...

●**Share a Prime membership.** Amazon's rules allow any two adults to share a single $139 annual membership and get nearly all Prime benefits.

One catch: The two of you also must share access to the same credit/debit cards for use on the site, so share only with someone you trust.

●**Share a digital library.** If you and a friend or family member each has a separate Prime membership, you can link the two accounts and share any Kindle e-books, audiobooks and apps that you have purchased. As with shared Prime membership, you also must share access to credit/debit cards.

●**Complain your way to extra months of Prime membership.** If you are a Prime member and an item that you ordered doesn't reach you by its expected delivery date or the wrong item is shipped or you have any other problem with an Amazon purchase, politely complain about this to an Amazon.com customer service rep. There's a good chance that the rep will extend your Prime membership for an additional month or two to keep you happy. (To reach customer service, call 888-280-4331.)

●**"Clip" Amazon coupons.** Most Amazon users don't realize that there are digital coupons available on the site. These are comparable to those found in newspapers or on Coupons.com, but they can be redeemed at Amazon.com. At Amazon.com, click "Today's Deals," followed by "Coupons." Click the "Clip Coupon" button for any coupons you might want to use. The savings will be applied when you put the appropriate product in your Amazon shopping cart and make your purchase.

Recent examples: $3 off an iHealth No Touch Thermometer...$3 off Pampers diapers.

●**Sign up for the Amazon Prime Rewards Visa Signature credit card or Prime Store Card.** Prime members receive 5% back when they use either of these cards to make Amazon.com purchases. The cards have no annual fee beyond the usual Prime membership fee.

Save on Eyeglasses Without Compromising Service

In a recent analysis, the highest-rated seller of eyeglasses based on quality of frames and lenses, selection, care taken in fitting, employee knowledge, follow-up service and price was Costco Optical, with an average price of $184. Independent shops rated second, but the average price was high—$414 ($230 more than Costco). Third was the chain and web retailer Warby Parker, average price $141...fourth, a private doctor's office, $396...fifth, ZenniOptical.com, $69.

Consumer Reports, ConsumerReports.org.

●**Take advantage of Amazon Warehouse Deals.** When an Amazon customer opens a product but then returns it or when a product's packaging is damaged, Amazon.com sells the item at a big discount through its "warehouse." Savings range from 25% to 75% off the usual price. To reach Amazon's warehouse, click "Today's Deals" on Amazon.com, then select "Warehouse Deals."

Similar: Amazon Outlet offers clearance, overstock and slightly imperfect new items at discounts that range from 20% to 80%. Click "Today's Deals," followed by "Outlet."

●**Use CamelCamelCamel.com to decide when to buy on Amazon.com.** Third-party website CamelCamelCamel lets you view the price history of any item Amazon stocks so that you can make your purchase when the fluctuating price is relatively low. Or choose a target price for an item, and have CamelCamelCamel send you an e-mail if and when the price drops to that level or below.

Additional Online Savings

Two other online money savers...

•**Buy "refurbished" computers through manufacturers' websites.** Most people assume that "refurbished" computers are lemons that have already broken once and are likely to do so again. In reality, many items sold as refurbished on computer manufacturer websites have never been used (or were barely used) and have never experienced any problems. In some cases, an item might have been returned by an earlier buyer because the incorrect item was shipped, for example. In other cases, an item might have arrived with dented packaging.

Even if there was once a problem with a refurbished computer, these computers have been repaired and inspected. They almost always come with warranties when purchased directly from manufacturers, so if there is a problem, you probably can get it corrected at no cost (except perhaps shipping charges). Savings of 15% are common on sites including Apple.com, Dell.com and HP.com, and larger savings are possible. Look for terms such as "refurbished" or "outlet" in these sites' menus.

Recent example: A refurbished $1,200 MacBook Air was available for $929 on Apple.com.

•**Find fine-art photos for free—and have them framed for cheap.** Art photography prints sold in galleries can cost hundreds of dollars or more, and the options are limited. Instead, choose among the hundreds of millions of photos posted on Flickr.com that can be legally printed and used for free. Just enter topics or types of photos of interest—anything from cityscapes to sea horses to rusty tractors—and select "All creative commons" from the "Any license" menu to view those that can be legally used without paying royalties.

When you find a photo that you would like to hang on your wall or give as a gift, click on it, download it to your device using the download button at the lower right of the photo, then upload the file to MPix.com, a site that will print the photo, mat it and put it in an attractive frame for a very reasonable price.

Sneaky Ways Companies Trick You Into Buying Their Stuff

Martin Lindstrom, a consumer advocate and marketing expert based in New York City. His is author of *Brandwashed: Tricks Companies Use to Manipulate Our Minds and Persuade Us to Buy.* MartinLindstrom.com

The tricks and traps marketers use to get us to buy things are more widespread and manipulative than ever before. They range from advertising ploys and clever language to audio and visual cues. *How they do it…*

The Good Old Days

When the economy falters, companies try to sell us memories of happier times. Nearly 35% of brands now are using nostalgia in their ad campaigns.

Examples: Mountain Dew, Doritos and Pepsi often package their products in designs from decades ago.

Psychologists believe our minds paint rosy pictures of the past to help us continue to move forward during hard times—we're more likely to believe today's problems are just temporary if we remember most of our life as being pretty enjoyable. It's why we're likely to buy products with labeling that recalls the past, even if we weren't really in love with that product back then.

People over age 50 are particularly likely to be hit with nostalgic sales pitches—the older we get, the more intense our longing becomes for the past.

What to do: When you find yourself reaching for a product that has a label or slogan designed to evoke past decades, pause and ask yourself, *Do I really need this product…or am I trying to buy a happy memory of the past?* If it is the latter, don't buy the product—you already have that happy memory for free.

A Good "Investment"

Stand in front of a new luxury car, high-end HDTV or pricey piece of jewelry in a showroom these days, and a salesperson is likely to assure you that the item is "a good investment" or "an investment you can enjoy." The salesperson is likely to avoid entirely words such as "purchase, "spend" and "cost."

Fewer shoppers will splurge on pricey products in this economy, but retailers have discovered that shoppers' minds become less resistant to forking over large amounts of cash when the word "investment" is used. Trouble is, consumer products are not investments. Investments are things likely to increase in value—virtually all consumer products decline in value.

What to do: When you hear the word "investment" from a retail salesperson, mentally replace it with the word "purchase."

Hard-to-find Bargains

Department stores now make it intentionally difficult to locate certain products on their shelves. These hard-to-find items might include heavily advertised discounted items or staples that many shoppers need. Hiding these products in unexpected sections of the store forces shoppers to spend

Great Buys at Dollar Stores

Party supplies—they can cost 70% less than at other stores. Gift bags and boxes and wrapping paper—they cost two to three times less. Greeting cards—the fanciest ones may not be available, but selection is wide. Reading glasses—they are as good as the ones found elsewhere at much higher prices. Hair accessories—elastic bands, bobby pins, headbands, combs and brushes are all good buys. Pregnancy tests—these $1 tests are as accurate as ones selling for $10 to $15 in other stores. Vases, bowls, mugs, glasses and dishes—quality is as good as at other stores, and you do not have to buy sets. Also worth considering: Storage containers, picture frames, bagged or boxed candy, socks, washcloths and dish towels.

Roundup of experts on bargain shopping, reported at Daily Finance.com.

more time searching aisles, which increases the odds that they will buy other items, too.

Hiding discounted items also gives the sales staff a chance to lead customers to these deals, which makes those customers feel good and included, increasing their loyalty to the store.

More store-layout and time-management tricks...

•**Various stores, including supermarkets, are installing speed bumps**—textured sections of flooring. They have discovered that shoppers pushing carts slow down and pay more attention when they roll over bumpy flooring, increasing sales of nearby products by up to 6%. Stores often place premium products and things that shoppers don't really need on the shelves near these speed bumps.

Self-defense: When your shopping cart rolls over textured flooring, consider it a reminder that the store is trying to manipulate you into noticing and buying the products placed nearby.

•**Most supermarkets now have their entrance on the right to encourage customers to move counterclockwise through the store.** Research has found that counterclockwise shoppers spend up to 7% more, possibly because most people are right-handed and counterclockwise shopping makes it slightly easier to grab items with the right hand.

Self-defense: If the store entrance is on the right, cut across the store immediately after entering and shop left to right.

•**Muzak is getting slower.** The slower the beat of background music, the longer shoppers stay in the store and the more they spend. Some businesses are even customizing their background music to specific areas within the store to subtly influence shoppers.

Example: Some supermarkets add subtle sound effects that evoke pleasant memories of the products found in that particular aisle—ice clinking in a glass in the beverage section or steak sizzling in the meats section.

Self-defense: Wear headphones and listen to fast-paced music while shopping. If you really want to save money, choose music that you don't like very much—your shopping trips will be faster and less expensive.

Not That Fresh

Many foods in the typical supermarket—ranging from marmalade to fish—are older than we are led to believe. Even produce isn't necessarily as fresh as we think—the typical supermarket apple has been off the tree for 14 months. But supermarkets know that our minds tend to associate freshness with healthfulness and goodness, so they have developed strategies to trick us into believing that their food actually is very fresh...

•**Products closely associated with freshness, such as fresh-cut flowers and fresh fruit, are placed right by the entrance.** Seeing fresh-looking things when we first walk in the door primes our minds to associate the whole store with freshness.

•**Produce prices are displayed on what appear to be chalkboards.** This gives the impression that new produce arrives so often that the prices must be updated frequently. But these "chalkboards" usually are just preprinted signs designed to look as if they were written in chalk.

•**Seafood is displayed on crushed ice**—even though modern refrigerator cases don't need ice to keep seafood at the right temperature. Our minds associate ice with a lack of spoilage.

•**Packaged products are placed near fresh products,** creating a sense of freshness by association in our minds.

Example: A display of high-end salsas or salad dressings might be placed in the fresh-produce section of a supermarket, creating the possibly false impression that these are fresher or healthier than cheaper salsas and salad dressings found elsewhere in the store.

Self-defense: If freshness is something you value, shop at farmers' markets. Do not pay premium prices for freshness at high-end supermarkets such as Whole Foods—you may be paying for the illusion of freshness there, too.

Money Back to You with Easy Rebates

Susan Samtur, aka "The Coupon Queen," author of *Cashing In at the Checkout*.
RefundSweepers.com

Shoppers who dismiss rebate and refund offers as more trouble than they're worth should think again. Each year, I usually receive up to $2,000 in rebate checks for buying products—primarily in supermarkets—that I would have purchased anyway. I have gotten rebates for buying cereal, detergents, dog food, wine, beer and frozen pizza. Many of the rebates are $5 or more. That's a very respectable return on the few minutes required to clip out a few proofs of purchase and complete a short rebate form, even after subtracting the cost of a stamp and an envelope.

Bonus: The IRS considers rebate checks a reduction in purchase price, not income, so this money is tax-free.

Locating Great Rebates

Rebates often are not widely publicized. *To turn rebates into a steady stream of income, you need to know how to find them...*

•**Look for altered product labels.** Specially marked packages sometimes signal rebate offers. Before you put an item in your cart, scan the shelf to see if other boxes, other sizes or competing products feature unfamiliar wording or graphics. Also, keep an eye out for shelf displays featuring small peel-off pads of rebate forms.

Be particularly vigilant when shopping for items in categories with a lot of competition, such as cereal and coffee...household cleaners and detergents...beer...and paper goods. Rebates are particularly common in these categories. These also tend to be products that don't go bad quickly, if at all, making it safe to stock up if multiple items must be purchased to earn the rebate.

Example: Go to 3Mproductivity.com, then click "Special Offers" to find promotions related to Post-It and Scotch products.

•**Sign up for the e-letters of companies that make the products you buy.** This is often the only way to receive coupons from your favorite companies. These newsletters often feature rebate offers as well as other savings. Find a company's website by typing its name into Google, then look for a link on the site labeled "Sign up" or "Special offers."

Recommended: Create a special e-mail account to use for these newsletters so that your main e-mail account is not flooded with product offers and updates.

•**Skim newspaper and magazine ads for rebate offers.** Sunday sales circulars usually are prime sources.

•**Sign up for pharmaceutical chain rebate programs.** CVS (CVS.com), Rite Aid (RiteAid.com) and Walgreens (Walgreens.com) run extensive rebate programs on many kinds of products, including over-the-counter medications, baby food and household cleaners. These programs are now Internet-based, so you don't even have to mail in rebate forms.

•**Examine the packaging of any product marked "new" or "new and improved."** New and updated products are particularly likely to feature rebates because companies know that they must provide special inducements to convince consumers to try something different.

•**Websites of office-supply retailers,** such as Staples (Staples.com) and Office Depot (Office Depot.com). Search for "Rebates." These typically feature a wide range of rebates on everything from paper to computers.

Ritz Camera's website is another good place to find valuable discounts on consumer electronics (RitzCamera.com, then click "Deals").

•**When you shop at Bed, Bath & Beyond,** stop by the customer service department and request the sheet of current manufacturers' rebate offers.

Examples: Recent Bed, Bath & Beyond rebates have included $10 off an Oneida 18-inch nonstick roaster pan and $10 off Cuisinart coffeemakers.

Rebates can be used in conjunction with the widely distributed Bed, Bath & Beyond coupons, which often provide 20% off any single item. If you don't get these coupons already, sign up to receive

Lower the Cost of Pet Care

Lower the cost of pet care. Brush your dog or cat's teeth regularly at home to reduce the need for professional cleaning. Brush fur regularly to lower grooming costs. Search online for ways to make homemade treats to save money on store-bought ones. Buy pet food in bulk. Sign up for a subscription service to have food delivered regularly—many stores offer a discount. Avoid overfeeding—it wastes money and can lead to obesity. Consider pet insurance for veterinary costs, but analyze plans—many have limited coverage or are expensive.

Jon Lal, founder and CEO, BeFrugal.com, writing at Money. USNews.com.

them at BedBathandBeyond.com (click on "Coupons" at the bottom of the page).

•**Before buying oil, antifreeze, air filters and other automotive items that require frequent replacement, check product packaging and shelf displays for rebate offers.** The companies that make these products know that people who work on their own cars tend to be very brand loyal and that a big rebate might be the only way to lure them away from the competition.

Example: Go to Advance Auto Parts site, AdvanceAutoParts.com, then select "Coupons and Deals" under "Special Offers" to check on promotions.

•**Visit the refund discussion boards at websites such as RefundSweepers.com and Hip2Save. com.** It's usually easiest to search "rebates" at these sites to find and read about recent rebate offers.

Ebay.com has sellers offering rebate forms. Just search "rebates" at the site. If anything, you can locate what's available and search online or at your local supermarket rebate center for current offers.

Getting the Most from Rebate Offers

Strategies to maximize rebates…

•**Create a label supply network.** Tell your friends and relatives that you're collecting proofs of purchase and receipts from particular products, or post this on your Facebook page. People who don't

Great Freebies at Libraries…Not Just Books

Great freebies at public libraries. If your library partners with the streaming service Kanopy, you can get access to more than 30,000 commercial-free films from your home. Some libraries offer free access to digital magazines, e-books and audiobooks through apps such as Flipster and OverDrive. Some libraries offer self-improvement seminars and classes. A few provide free passes to local museums and other attractions. Some libraries offer loans of party supplies—such as bakeware, fondue pots, pasta makers and chocolate fountains. Libraries may offer study rooms that can be used instead of renting a desk at a shared workspace…and meeting rooms for nonprofit groups.

Roundup of experts on library offerings, reported at Money TalksNews.com.

bother with rebates might be happy to hand over their labels. Those who do use rebates might be willing to swap with you if you are pursuing different offers.

•**Save promising labels and receipts even if there is no rebate.** Some companies—such as those listed in the box here—offer rebates so frequently that it's worth saving proofs of purchase even when a rebate isn't offered. You might be able to use them if a new rebate offer appears soon. Save your grocery store register receipts, too—many rebates require these.

Helpful: I save proofs of purchase in shoe boxes…refund forms in an envelope…and receipts in another envelope.

•**Seek out free samples.** Receiving a free sample in the mail might not be quite as appealing as receiving a rebate check, but samples have one big advantage over cash-back rebates—you don't have to purchase anything to earn them. You might not even have to use a stamp—many free samples now can be obtained by completing a quick online form.

Example: Free samples of contact lenses abound on the Internet. Acuvue consistently offers a trial pair, with a prescription (Acuvue.com).

More from RefundSweepers.com…

10 Companies for Supermarket Rebates

The following companies regularly offer rebates. It's often easier to Google "Arm & Hammer rebate offer" (for example) than to try to navigate the company's website…

•**Arm & Hammer**

•**Dr. Scholl's**

•**General Mills.**

•**Kellogg's.**

•**Kraft Foods.**

•**Nestlé.**

•**Nabisco.**

Example: Join Nabisco's Facebook page, and qualify for discounts on Nabisco cookies each month.

•**Ragú.**

•**S.C. Johnson.** Brands include Drano, Glade, Off, Pledge, Raid, Shout, Windex and Ziploc. Right AtHome.com

•**3M.** 3mproductivity.com/offers

CHAPTER 15

Personal Care

Simple, All-Natural Personal-Care Products to Make at Home

Dorie Byers, RN, author of *Natural Beauty Basics: Create Your Own Cosmetics and Body Care Products*. She is a registered nurse and herbalist in Bargersville, Indiana.

Why buy high-priced toiletries and over-the-counter medications filled with chemicals and preservatives?

Better: Make your own body-care products and healing remedies, often for pennies. Grow herbs yourself or buy them, along with other ingredients, at health-food stores.

Bad Breath

What You Need...
- 1 cup distilled water.
- 2 tablespoons vodka.
- 2 drops peppermint essential oil.
- 2 drops myrrh essential oil.

Preparation: In a small bowl, mix vodka and oils. Stir in distilled water (which is free of minerals and impurities). With 1 tablespoon of mixture, rinse mouth, then spit out. Repeat daily.

Good to know: Place remaining mixture in a covered, airtight container. Store away from light (to preserve the oils' potency) for up to 6 weeks.

Caution: Do not swallow. These essential oils can be toxic in high amounts if ingested.

Dull Hair Color

What You Need...
- 2 cups distilled water.

For dark hair...
- ¼ cup fresh rosemary leaves

For blonde hair...
- ¼ cup chamomile flower petals.

Preparation: Boil water. Add rosemary or chamomile, cover and simmer 30 minutes. Strain, discarding leaves. Lean head forward and pour infusion over hair, catching run-off in a basin. Repeat twice. Do not rinse off.

Good to know: The herbs help restore natural highlights. For best effect, use after every shampoo.

Foot Odor

What You Need...
- 1 cup apple cider vinegar.
- ½ cup dried sage leaves.

Preparation: Boil vinegar. Add sage, cover and simmer 15 minutes. Strain, discarding leaves. Fill a basin with 1 gallon of warm water, add infusion and soak feet for 15 minutes. Repeat daily.

Good to know: If you prefer a different fragrance, substitute dried thyme or fresh rosemary leaves for the sage.

Itchy, Flaky or Dry Skin

What You Need...

1 cup coarsely ground sea salt

¼ cup olive oil

Preparation: Stir oil into salt. Standing in the shower, massage 2 tablespoons of mixture into skin (reserving remainder for later). Rinse. Repeat weekly.

Good to know: For a pleasing scent, add 6 drops of lavender essential oil to the mixture before using. Store remainder in a glass jar in a cool, dark place.

Pimples

What You Need...

1 cup distilled water.

1 tablespoon dried thyme leaves.

1 tablespoon dried calendula blossoms.

Preparation: Boil all ingredients, covered, for 10 minutes. Strain, discarding leaves and blossoms. Cool infusion. Apply 2 tablespoons to clean skin. Air dry. Repeat twice daily.

Good to know: Also use this preparation to improve an oily, shiny complexion. Store remainder in a glass bottle in a cool, dry place.

Puffy, Tired or Irritated Eyes

What You Need...

2 chamomile tea bags.

1 cup distilled water.

Preparation: Boil distilled water. Add tea bags and steep until water is lukewarm. Remove bags and squeeze out most of the water. Place bags over closed eyes for 15 minutes.

Good to know: If you have ragweed allergies, do not use this preparation.

Sunburn

What You Need...

1 cup distilled water.

¼ cup dried or

½ cup fresh peppermint leaves.

Preparation: Boil water. Add peppermint, cover and simmer 15 minutes. Strain, discarding leaves.

244

Fill bathtub with tepid water and add infusion. Soak 20 minutes. Repeat as needed.

Good to know: Substitute lemon mint, lavender mint or other types of mint leaves for the peppermint to vary the aroma.

Best Ways to Get Rid of a Pimple—Fast!

Ginger Hodulik Downey holds a BS in foods and nutrition, an MS degree in nutrition and a CNS (Certified Nutrition Specialist). She is currently the co-owner and vice president of R&D for DermaMed Solutions. In addition to her work at DermaMed, Ginger devotes time to working with patients in private clinical practice. As a contributor, Ginger hopes to continue to share her passion for holistic health and wellness.

What is the best way to rid your face of an unwanted pimple? In the case of a real emergency like your wedding day or some other special event, a dermatologist can inject the pimple with cortisone. This technique is quite effective, but pricey and time consuming—if you can even get a last-minute appointment.

The good news is that there are many things you can try at home to clear up a pimple...even a painful cystic one. These treatments are not as effective as a cortisone injection, but they will speed up the healing process, typically within two days. *These techniques are most effective when you start at the first sign of a blemish...*

●**Begin with steam.** Heat water to boiling, then transfer to a large bowl. Drape a towel over your head to create a tent and let the steam do its work opening up your pores to clear them out. This is a step that few people know about or, if they do, think they can skip. But the topicals suggested below won't work nearly as well if your pores are constricted. And you really do need the intensity that the steam tent offers—a steamy shower won't do.

●**Then apply spot treatment.** There are many options available. Choose ONE from below and see how it works for you.

Beware: Using all of these at the same time will result in a red, blotchy face, which may make the pimple look better since it will no longer be the focal point but I don't think this is our goal. The options are listed in the order of most-effective to least in my opinion.

• **Using a cotton swab, apply a dab of over-the-counter hydrocortisone cream to the pimple.** The cortisone cream will reduce the inflammation and cause the spot to deflate. OTC hydrocortisone typically contains up to 2% concentration. Stronger is better.

• **Glycolic and salicylic acids are the best choices for spot treatments.** Some people crush an aspirin (which is made from salicylic acid) and make a paste that they apply to the blemish.

• **Tea tree oil.** This is anti-inflammatory and antiseptic, so it reduces the redness and addresses the bacterial overgrowth that caused the pimple. Try a dab of diluted tea tree oil—mix the tea tree oil with a small amount of water and apply to the spot.

The best thing you can do when you have a blemish is to treat it using the techniques above. The steam will help to clear out your pores and allow them to accept the healing topical you apply afterwards. The worst thing you can do is to touch your face excessively, squeeze or pop a pimple. This will lead to more inflammation and a longer healing time.

Better Than Treatment: Prevention

We can't avoid the occasional pimple, but we can take steps to ensure that we get fewer of them. Your diet and habits matter!

• **Many people find that limiting or eliminating dairy and/or refined sugars helps keep their skin clear.**

• **Keeping bacteria away from the face is crucial too.** Be sure to cleanse the face in the morning and especially in the evening before bed.

• **A nightly application of a retinol-based serum will increase cell turnover and prevent future breakouts.**

• **Change pillowcases often—as often as every other day—as they are germier places than you might imagine.**

• **The number one germ catcher is the cell phone!** Use earbuds or your speaker when talking on your phone to keep those germs from touching your cheeks when you speak.

What a Top Naturopath Has in His Own Medicine Cabinet for Common Problems

Mark Stengler, NMD, a naturopathic medical doctor and founder of Stengler Center for Integrative Medicine, Encinitas, California. He has served on a medical advisory committee for the Yale University Complementary Medicine Outcomes Research Project and has been an associate clinical professor at the National College of Naturopathic Medicine in Portland, Oregon. He is coauthor of *The Natural Physician's Healing Therapies* (Bottom Line Books). MarkStengler.com

---

Sometimes you need powerful, fast-acting medications. But prescription and over-the-counter drugs can present serious risks. It's estimated that more than 2 million adverse drug reactions occur in the US every year and are responsible for more than 100,000 deaths annually.

I strongly recommend and use natural remedies. They contain lower doses of chemically active agents. They're less likely than drugs to cause dangerous side effects. And they often work just as well, sometimes better. All are available at health-food stores and online.

Important: Always check with your doctor before taking any new medication or supplement.

Less Joint Pain

Aspirin and related painkillers often irritate the stomach and increase the risk for ulcers. Natural analgesics are much gentler and just as effective.

• **Boswellia,** a tree found in India, Africa and the Middle East, has a milky resin that inhibits the body's production of inflammatory molecules. A study that looked at patients with osteoarthritis of the knee found that boswellia extract relieved pain and stiffness as effectively as the drug *valdecoxib* (Bextra), which has been withdrawn from the market because of side effects. A small percentage of boswellia users experience digestive upset. If that happens, reduce the amount. If you don't start to feel better within 48 hours, stop taking it. If you are taking it for chronic pain, give it two weeks.

Dose: 750 milligrams (mg), two to three times daily during flare-ups.

•**Curcumin** is the active ingredient found in the spice turmeric. In a study, rheumatoid arthritis patients reported that it helped relieve morning pain and stiffness.

Caution: Taking curcumin with blood thinners can increase the risk for bleeding.

Dose: 500 mg, three times daily. You can take it every day to keep pain and inflammation down or just take it during flare-ups.

Less Stress and Anxiety

Chamomile tea is a gentle relaxant that has traditionally been used as a "nerve tonic." Other herbs have similar effects. *One of my favorites…*

•**Passionflower.** Despite the name, passionflower is more relaxing than arousing. It increases brain levels of gamma-aminobutyric acid (GABA), a neurotransmitter that dampens activity in the part of the brain that controls emotions, making you feel more relaxed. In one study, participants drank either passionflower tea or a placebo tea before going to bed. Those who drank passionflower tea slept better and were more likely to wake up feeling refreshed and alert.

How to use it: Steep one teaspoon of dried passionflower in three ounces of just-boiled water. Drink it two to three times daily when you're stressed. Or take passionflower capsules or tinctures, following the label directions.

Migraine Relief

There are many drugs for treating migraines, but they're rife with side effects—and may increase the risk for liver damage or even a heart attack.

•**Butterbur,** a member of the daisy family, is an effective alternative. It contains two potent anti-inflammatory compounds, petasin and isopetasin, which may help blood vessels in the brain dilate and contract more normally.

A study published in *Neurology* found that people who used butterbur had a 48% reduction in the frequency of migraines. You also can use butterbur to reduce migraine intensity.

Dose: For prevention, take 50 mg of Petadolex (a butterbur extract) three times daily, with meals, for one month. Then reduce the dose to twice daily. For treating a migraine, take 50 mg three times daily until the migraine is gone.

Ease Muscle Soreness

For an aching back or sore arms, apply an ice pack or a heating pad…or alternate cold and warmth. *Also helpful…*

•**Arnica is a plant in the daisy family that reduces muscle soreness and swelling.** It also helps bruises heal more quickly.

A new study from the Australian Institute of Sport in Canberra, Australia, published in *European Journal of Sport Science*, found that the topical application of arnica reduced the level of achiness for up to three days after a vigorous workout. The participants included men who ran in five bouts of eight-minute bursts on a treadmill, followed by two minutes of walking on a flat surface. They applied arnica gel or a placebo gel every four hours.

How to use it: Apply a small amount of cream or tincture to the sore areas. Repeat every hour as necessary. Don't apply if the skin is broken.

Helpful: If a large area is sore, you can take arnica orally instead. Take two pellets of a 30C potency three times daily for one to two days.

Reduce Heartburn

I advise patients to start with natural approaches, including sleeping on their left side (sleeping on the right side makes heartburn worse)…avoiding "trigger" foods, such as onions and chocolate…and maintaining a healthy weight (excess weight makes stomach acid more likely to enter the esophagus and cause heartburn). *Also helpful…*

•**Melatonin,** a supplement that is often used for insomnia, also is effective for heartburn. A study published in *Journal of Pharmacology* found that melatonin reduces the amount of acid produced in the stomach without blocking it altogether. This is important because you need stomach acid for good digestion—you just don't want too much of it.

Dose: 3 mg to 6 mg, taken daily at bedtime.

Influenza Fighters

A healthy immune system is the best way to protect against flu. *Starting at the beginning of flu season (typically early October), take…*

•**Influenzinum**, a homeopathic remedy that I've recommended for more than 15 years. The makers of influenzinum reformulate it annually based on the flu viruses that are expected to predominate that year.

Dose: Three pellets (of a 9C potency) dissolved under the tongue, once a week for six weeks.

•**N-acetylcysteine (NAC)**, an antioxidant, reduces both the chance that you will get the flu and the severity of symptoms if you do get sick. An Italian study found that only 25% of older people who were injected with flu virus after taking NAC for six months experienced flu symptoms, versus 79% who took a placebo.

Dose: 1,000 mg daily in tablet form for prevention during the flu months (typically October through April). If you get the flu, increase the dose to 4,000 mg daily until you recover.

Also helpful: 2,000 international units (IU) of vitamin D daily. During the peak flu months, increase the dose to 5,000 IU.

Cold Relief

Don't waste your money on often ineffective over-the-counter cold medicines. *Instead…*

•**Pelargonium sidoides**, a South African plant, has been tested in more than 20 clinical studies. It relieves congestion, sore throat and other cold symptoms. It is available in syrups, lozenges, capsules and tablets. Follow the dosing instructions on the label.

Color Your Hair at Home (No One Will Guess!)

James Corbett, owner and lead colorist at James Corbett Studio in New York City. He also is color director for Clairol and has been featured in magazines including *Allure*, *SELF* and *Cosmopolitan*. JamesCorbettStudio.com

Coloring your own hair, whether you're a man or a woman, can save money ($50 to $150 or more each time). It also can save time and give you great-looking hair—if you do it right. Although modern home hair-coloring kits make it easier than ever to get natural-looking results, mistakes can damage hair and lead to a do-it-yourself look. *Avoid these common errors…*

MISTAKE: Going too dark or light.

Too light: A color that is much lighter than your natural shade can wind up looking brassy.

Reason: Brown hair has underlying red and orange pigments. The chemicals in light-colored dye bring out those red-orange tones.

Too dark: If you go dramatically darker and then change your mind or don't like the effect, the dark color is difficult to correct. Putting a lighter shade over darker dye can damage your hair but won't lighten the color—although it might leave hair darker at the ends than the roots, a telltale sign of a home job.

Better: Choose a shade that matches your current color or that is just one or two shades darker or lighter. If you are lightening your hair, use a cool or ash tone to control brassiness. If you are going darker, consider starting with a semipermanent tint. Because the tint fades gradually over time, you won't have to use harsh chemicals to strip out the color if you don't like it.

MISTAKE: Picking the wrong color for your skin tone. The hair color you love on a friend or celebrity may not flatter you. If your skin has yellow or olive undertones, shades that are cool—such as platinum blond or jet black—will make you look sallow. If your skin has pink undertones, warm hair color can make your skin look reddish or blotchy.

To determine your skin tone: Turn your hand so that the palm faces up, and look at the veins on your wrist. If your veins look greenish—and you look best in peach, orange, gold and tan clothing—you have warm undertones. Choose a warm hair color such as honey, bronze, caramel, amber or gold.

If your veins are blue or purple—and you look better in bluish reds and purples than in yellow or orange—you have pink undertones. Opt for a cooler shade such as ash, smoke or champagne.

MISTAKE: **Not adjusting for gray.** As hair becomes gray, hair texture and skin tone also change. A dark color that used to flatter you may now look harsh against your skin. Also, gray hair does not absorb color as easily. It may pick up more of a dye's underlying blue or pink tones, resulting in a muddy color.

Better: Use a product specifically designed to cover gray. Your hair will absorb the color better, and the undertones will be balanced to look natural.

If you have been dying your hair dark, try lighter shades as you gray.

MISTAKE: **Coloring too often—this makes hair dry and lifeless.**

Better: Color the whole head no more than every six to eight weeks. When roots begin to show after four weeks, either use a root touch-up product or use your usual product and follow the instructions for touching up new growth.

Men: Natural Way to Beat Razor Burn

Janice Cox, natural-beauty expert and coauthor of *Eco-Beauty: Scrubs, Rubs, Masks and Bath Bombs for You and Your Friends.* JaniceCox.com.

Guys, you probably think of "facial masks" as those mysterious items in your lady's half of the bathroom cabinet that might as well be labeled "Don't go there." And when it comes to do-it-yourself skin care—whipping up potions and lotions in your kitchen—maybe you'd rather stick to more manly kitchen endeavors, such as frying bacon.

"Men are often reluctant to try natural skin care—or any skin-care product, for that matter!" said Janice Cox, a natural beauty expert and co-author of *EcoBeauty: Scrubs, Rubs, Masks and Bath Bombs for You and Your Friends.* "After all, most guys limit their 'skin routine' to a bar of soap and a stick of deodorant."

But listen up, dudes: If you suffer from razor burn on your face after shaving—or if you simply have dry, red, bumpy, pimply, itchy, flaky, blotchy or sore facial skin—you might want to get in touch with your feminine side and try using a facial mask. (You heard me!)

Using a facial mask can help men retain moisture in their skin and sooth red, irritated patches, said Cox. She even provided a recipe for a mask that you can make yourself—using ingredients that you likely already have on hand. The best part? You only have to follow this at-home spa routine for 15 minutes, once a week. That ain't so hard—right, boys?

Soothe Your Skin

The right facial mask will contain antibacterial and anti-inflammatory ingredients that will speed healing. There are lots of ready-made facial masks in the drugstore—if you think you'd like to try one, look for soothing ingredients such as aloe and chamomile, as well as ingredients that are natural antibacterial agents, such as lavender and honey, advised Cox. She usually chooses whatever brand in the store has those types of ingredients and has the shortest list of total ingredients.

Or save your money and whip up this easy recipe, created by Cox.

A Homemade Mask For Men

Cox's mask has just three simple ingredients and takes only a few seconds to stir up! *Ingredients for one mask…*

- ¼ cup cornstarch
- 2 Tablespoons honey
- 2 Tablespoons whole milk

Directions: Don't use this mask immediately after shaving because your skin will be sensitive and it may cause irritation. Instead, use it 15 minutes after shaving, a few hours after shaving—and if you're not using it to treat razor burn, you can try using it anywhere from weekly to daily, depending on the severity of your skin condition.

How to do it: Mix ingredients together in a small bowl, then spread onto clean, dry skin including your forehead, nose, cheeks, chin and as far down the neck as your razor burn or beard goes. Avoid your eyes and lips. Leave the mask on for 15 minutes, then rinse it off with warm water and pat your skin dry.

I also asked Cox whether there's anything natural that you can do immediately after shaving, since a lot of razor burn can flare up in the first few minutes after shaving. She said that you should splash cold water on your face and then massage either a few drops of witch hazel or almond or olive oil into your face. (The witch hazel may sting at first—but only for a few seconds.) Try each and see which works best for you.

Note: Discard any leftover mask so the milk doesn't spoil. It's best to make a fresh batch each time.

Get a Closer Shave the Old-Fashioned Way

Lynn Abrams, a longtime straight razor shaver and one of the country's top experts in straight razor honing. He is owner, with Don Addleman, of Straight Razor Designs, a shaving-supply company in Medina, Ohio. He is producer of the instructional DVD *The World of Straight Razor Shaving*.

Over the past decade, more and more men have taken up straight razor shaving. Why? *Because…*

•**It costs less,** over time, than using disposable blades/razors.

•**You get a closer shave.** A man who needs to shave twice a day with a multiblade razor probably will stay just as smooth with one daily shave with a straight razor. And some men with light beards might even get away with shaving every other day.

Some people enjoy the ritual of stropping (swiping the razor on a leather strap) and lathering—it makes shaving a pleasure, not a chore.

What you'll need…

•**The straight razor.** Modern brands include Dovo, Boker and Thiers-Issard, with an average cost at the beginner level of $75 to $125. Also consider…The point. Some straight razors have a rounded end. These are good for beginners—they're less likely than other styles (such as those that have a sharp point) to cause nicks.

•**Width.** Razors between ⅝ and ⅝ of an inch in width are easier to handle and maneuver than wider blades.

•**Grind.** This refers to the thickness and heaviness of the blade. A hollow grind is the thinnest blade…the thickest is known as a wedge.

I advise beginners to use a hollow grind because the thinner steel makes it easier to feel the shave and make adjustments in pressure and angles .

•**The strop.** Swiping the blade back and forth on a leather strop removes microscopic gunk and polishes the edge. The strop can be attached to a mug hook under the sink or you can use a doorknob. You can buy a strop for less than $50. Or use the smooth side of a leather belt .

•**The brush.** Few straight razor shavers use canned shaving creams (although you can)—most whip up their own lather with a shaving brush. Brushes can be made from…Badger hair. These are softer and hold more lather than other brushes. A quality brush starts at around $30.

•**Boar hair.** These cost less than badger brushes but are a bit stiffer and don't hold as much lather. Prices range from $11 to $40.

•**Synthetics.** Synthetic brushes are the least expensive but tend to feel "scratchy" on the face.

Popular brush brands: Progress Vulfix, Kent, Shavemac and Rooney.

•**Creams and soaps.** In general, creams whipped with a brush provide a thick lather with a lot of cushion. High-quality shaving soaps may feel a little bit slicker. The cost is similar, roughly $30 to $50 for a cream or cake of soap, which typically lasts for three to six months and comes in its own container to whip up the lather.

Popular brands: Geo F. Trumper, Taylor of Old Bond Street, Tabac, Truefitt & Hill, D.R. Harris, Mitchell's Wool Fat Soap and Nancy Boy.

•**Technique.** While the whiskers are damp, apply a thick layer of lather. Take at least a minute or two to work it in. Keep the edge of the razor at about a 30° angle (or less) to your skin. Hold it with a light grip—you'll be less likely to cut yourself. (A styptic pencil is still best for nicks.) If you can't see exactly where the entire blade is positioned, shift your position until you can. You're more likely to cut yourself in "blind spots." For more information, go to our website and click on the "Wiki" tab at the top.

How to Erase Years from Your Face: Simple Changes Make You Look Younger

Sanam Hafeez, PsyD, founder and clinical director of Comprehensive Consultation Psychological Services, with offices in New York City, Forest Hills and Uniondale, New York. Her research/clinical interests include neuropsychology, behavior modification and psychopathology. She has a faculty appointment at Columbia University's doctoral program in clinical psychology. ComprehendTheMind.com

Compare the faces of two people in your life. Person One is happy, relaxed and pleased with life. Person Two is overworked, stressed and harried. Guess which face appears younger and more attractive?

Stress can add years to your looks. When you're stressed, your body churns out cortisol, the hormone that primes you for action. Some cortisol is helpful (and motivating), but too much triggers inflammation, which affects every organ in your body, including the skin.

Experts have coined a term for the link between emotions and the skin—psychodermatology. This new field is based on research that shows that chronic stress and other psychological issues can trigger or exacerbate skin changes. But you can re-verse those changes using emotional strategies and other lifestyle changes.

Example: Critically ill children who were given relaxing massages showed improvements in itching, redness and other skin conditions, according to researchers at the Touch Research Institute at University of Miami.

You can spend a fortune on anti-aging products and cosmetic procedures, but unless you manage stress at the same time, you'll still look older than you should.

What Stress Does To Skin

Stress can cause blotches, itching, redness and acne. The cortisol-driven rise in inflammation damages tissues and capillaries that are readily apparent in the mirror. *Stress also causes…*

•**Dryness.** The constant bombardment of cortisol in women with chronic stress can mean a drop in estrogen that's been called mini-menopause. Estrogen is largely responsible for the differences in appearance between young women and older ones. Women who are frequently stressed tend to develop dryness and a loss of skin elasticity.

While women need estrogen more than men and are more impacted on a monthly basis by its regulation, hormonal imbalance also happens in men with the excess secretion of the stress hormone androgen, as well as glucocorticoids. This can cause a loss of estrogen leading to dryness in both men and women and an overproduction of sebum (an oily secretion of the sebaceous glands), which can trigger acne and razor bumps.

•**Wrinkles.** There's a reason that forehead furrows, between-the-eye creases and other wrinkles are known as "frown lines," "worry lines" or even "battle lines." Repeated expressions can etch themselves permanently in your face.

•**Circles under the eyes.** They make you look tired and can age your appearance even more than wrinkles. Some people are genetically prone to under-eye circles. They also can be caused by sun exposure, a lack of sleep or allergic skin conditions, along with stress.

What happens: Stress increases blood flow, and the tiny capillaries under the eyes become engorged. Those dark circles really are blood vessels that are visible through the skin.

•**Under-eye bags.** Like circles under the eyes, these puffy areas are partly due to genetics. But they're also common in people whose stress keeps them up at night. A lack of sleep causes fluids to accumulate under the eyes and makes your face appear puffy and tired.

What to Do

•**Take "mini-vacations."** Almost everyone can benefit from frequent "mini-vacations" that provide a break from stress. These can be as simple as a lunchtime walk…admiring a piece of art…or listening to a favorite song.

•**Eat an estrogen-enhancing diet including fresh fruits and vegetables, salmon and whole grains.** These antioxidant-rich foods fight inflammation. Fruits and vegetables also are naturally rich in phytoestrogens, plant compounds that mimic the effects of estrogen in the body. Estrogen "plumps" the skin and gives women and men a healthy glow.

Avoid excess sugar in all forms, including refined carbohydrates, alcohol and highly processed foods, such as cake and cookies. These cause the body to produce advanced glycation end-products, toxins that trigger inflammation in the skin. The sugars in carbohydrates attach to certain proteins and can break down skin collagen, causing a loss of elasticity and the plumpness we associate with young skin.

•**Drink more water.** People who stay hydrated tend to have plumper, younger-looking skin. Also, water can flush excess salt from the body, which reduces under-eye puffiness. If you don't care for regular water, try coconut water. It is a natural source of electrolytes that help to keep you hydrated.

•**Relax your face.** You're probably not aware of your facial expressions, but you can learn to relax your face. When you're feeling stressed, remind yourself not to squint or frown. Be mindful of your expressions. Eventually, not frowning will become a habit. If you find yourself frowning, make it a habit to smooth your hand over your forehead and think

happy, tranquil thoughts until your face naturally relaxes to a resting state.

•**Get a good night's sleep.** Even if you find that you can't log a full eight hours, at least make sure that the sleep you get is quality sleep. Relax for an hour before going to bed. Turn off the TV and computers. This puts your mind into the "sleep mode" so that it starts to shut down or cool off in preparation for bedtime. Pull the blinds or curtains so that your room is dark. If you can't fall asleep in 15 or 20 minutes, get up and do something relaxing, such as gazing out the window or holding a yoga pose. You want to stay within yourself instead of engaging with electronics or the outside world until you're tired enough to try again. If you find yourself becoming anxious about all the things you have to do, make a list of what needs to be done. You'll feel like you accomplished something and are in control of your tasks. And you won't be worried about forgetting them the next day.

•**Sleep with your head slightly elevated—a thick pillow will do it.** The increased pull of gravity will help fluids drain away from your eyes.

•**Exercise.** Exercise relieves stress. You'll almost instantly see a difference when you attend a yoga class or go for a power walk. Your face will look smoother and younger.

Do-It-Yourself Face-Lift

Shellie Goldstein, LAc, licensed acupuncturist, esthetician and certified Chinese herbologist who maintains a private practice in New York City and Amagansett, New York (Hamptons Acupuncture.com). She is author of *Your Best Face Now: Look Younger in 20 Days with the Do-It-Yourself Acupressure Facelift.*

I f you've got facial wrinkles that you would like to reduce but you don't want to get Botox injections or a surgical face-lift, there's a do-it-yourself option that's far less invasive and far less expensive.

With a technique known as facial acupressure (similar to acupuncture but performed without needles), you can take up to five to 10 years off your appearance—and perhaps even improve your overall health in the process.

Sound far-fetched?

I have treated hundreds of patients who were contemplating face-lifts but found success with acupressure.

Bonus: Unlike Botox or surgery, acupressure won't give you a tight, frozen or pulled-back appearance. The results are softer and more natural.

Why Acupressure?

Acupressure is based on a Chinese healing technique that involves pressing or kneading key points on the body to stimulate energy flow, known as Qi (pronounced chee), through invisible pathways called meridians. It can be used to relax or tone muscles, boost circulation and even improve digestion.

The conventional view: From the Western medical perspective, wrinkles are formed by changes in the skin's composition, thickness and elasticity as well as continuous muscle activity—for example, fore-head wrinkles may appear after years of furrowing your eyebrows or squinting. As a result, the skin covering the muscle creases, eventually creating a wrinkle.

Chinese medicine has a different perspective. For example, specific meridians (that correspond to organ systems, such as those for the "Liver" and "Gallbladder") are believed to affect certain body parts, but they don't always seem to correlate. For instance, a meridian located at the junction between your thumb and index finger corresponds to the head—rubbing that area can reduce headaches and, yes, wrinkles.

Do-It-Yourself Routines

To help reduce wrinkles and puffiness, use the following routines each day until you are satisfied with the results and then as needed…

• **Forehead wrinkles.**

What to do: Begin at the top of your right foot, in the junction between your big and second toes. (This point is called "Liver 3.") Using medium to firm (but not painful) pressure, massage the point in a clockwise circle 10 times. (If you have arthritic fingers, use your knuckle instead.) Repeat on left foot.

Next, move to the back side of your right hand between your right thumb and index finger ("Large Intestine 4"). In a clockwise circular motion, massage this point for 10 rotations. Repeat on the left hand.

Then, move to the back of your neck. Place both thumbs where your spine meets the base of your skull and move them two inches to either side until they each land in an indentation ("Gallbladder 20"). Massage clockwise with firm pressure for 10 rotations.

Lastly, move to your face. Place the pad of each index finger a half inch above the center of each eyebrow ("Gallbladder 14"). Massage with medium pressure in 10 clockwise (right to left) circles.

Repeat the entire sequence three times in a single session each day. For deeper wrinkles, do the sequence several times throughout the day. You should notice a reduction in forehead wrinkles within 20 days.

• **Under-eye puffiness (due to age or allergies).** What to do: Place your index finger two inches above the inside of your right ankle between the bone and muscle ("Spleen 6"). Do 10 clockwise rotations using medium to firm pressure. Repeat on left leg.

Next, move to the back of your right hand ("Large Intestine 4"), as described earlier, and perform 10 clockwise rotations. Repeat on the left hand.

Then, with your arm at your side, bend your left elbow to make a 90° angle. Pinpoint the area located at the outside edge of the elbow crease, between the bend and the bone ("Large Intestine 11"). Use your index finger to massage 10 times in a clockwise rotation using medium to firm pressure. Repeat on your right elbow.

Lastly, move to your face. Place your right index finger just to the side of your right nostril. Move the finger laterally to a spot directly underneath the center of your eye, in your sinus area ("Stomach 3"). Press in and slightly upward, performing 10 clockwise rotations. Repeat on the left side.

Do the entire sequence three times daily. You should notice a reduction in puffiness under your eyes after a few days.

Homemade Help for Dry Hands

Dorie Byers, RN, author of *Natural Beauty Basics: Create Your Own Cosmetics and Body Care Products.* She is a registered nurse and herbalist in Bargersville, Indiana.

Laurie Steelsmith, ND, LAc, is the author of *Natural Choices for Women's Health* and coauthor with Alex Steelsmith of *Great Sex Naturally.* DrSteelsmith.com

D o your hands itch or blotch up after you use a commercial lotion? Your skin is probably reacting to the product. Commercial moisturizers often contain ingredients such as alcohol, which actually can leave skin more parched…mineral oil, which can clog pores…and/or a high water content, which makes the products less emollient and thus less able to penetrate and hydrate the skin.

Fun solution: Make your own pleasantly fragrant salve to soothe your dry hands using only natural ingredients. While the initial cost of the separate ingredients may seem pricier than ready-made moisturizers, ounce for ounce, your mixture will be more economical because you'll wind up with a lot more moisturizer for the money. And because this salve is much more concentrated than many commercially prepared formulations, you'll need less than a pea-sized dab to thoroughly moisturize your hands. (Don't use too much, or you might wind up staining your clothing or bed linens.) You also can use the salve on your feet and elbows, though it is best not to apply it to your face because, if you use the optional essential oils, they can irritate your eyes.

All ingredients are readily available at health-food stores or online. The recipe below makes approximately two ounces of salve, which should last three to four weeks. If desired, you can double, triple or quadruple the recipe, then divide your moisturizer into several two-ounce, wide-mouth glass jars and freeze it indefinitely until you're ready to use it. *Ingredients you'll need…*

1   Tablespoon avocado oil
1   teaspoon beeswax
1   teaspoon jojoba oil
20   drops evening primrose oil
800   IU vitamin E (you can prick two 400 IU vitamin E capsules and squeeze out the oil)

Optional ingredients…
5   drops carrot seed essential oil
3   drops patchouli essential oil
2   drops frankincense essential oil
1   drop rosewood essential oil

To prepare: Put the avocado oil and beeswax in a small heatproof container, such as a Pyrex measuring cup. Fill a saucepan with enough water to surround the bottom two inches of your heatproof container, then place the container in the saucepan "bath" (without letting any water get into the container). Bring the water to a boil on the stovetop and simmer until the beeswax melts. Remove container from the saucepan bath. To the beeswax mixture, add the jojoba, primrose and vitamin E oils and stir. Add the essential oils, if using, and stir until well mixed. Immediately, before the mixture starts to solidify, pour it into a two-ounce, wide-mouth jar. Cover and store at room temperature.

Other Natural Options..

For dry, dehydrated hands: Milk Soak. In a medium-size glass bowl, heat two cups of whole milk in the microwave until pleasantly warm to the touch—do not overheat. Soak your hands in the milk for five to 10 minutes, then rinse hands well. Milk (especially whole milk) contains fats that moisturize and hydrate the skin…plus calcium, vitamin A and vitamin E that nourish the skin cells (nails, too).

For scaly, flaky hands: Oatmeal-Sea Salt Scrub. In a small bowl, sift one cup of instant oats (which are finer than steel-cut or rolled oats) between your fingers, removing any sharp hulls. Mix in one tablespoon of finely ground sea salt. Stir in one to two tablespoons of whole milk, a bit at a time, until the mixture is moist and sticky. Rub the oats mixture all over your hands, massaging it in for several minutes—this acts as an exfoliant to remove dead skin cells. Rinse hands well.

For irritated or itchy hands: Nighttime Nourisher. In a small bowl, combine two tablespoons of olive oil, two drops of calendula extract and two drops of chamomile extract. At bedtime, rub the oil mixture into your hands for several minutes, then put on cotton gloves and leave on overnight. In the morning, remove gloves and wash hands with gentle soap. Olive oil is a natural nonirritating moisturizer…and calendula and chamomile have healing properties that soothe sensitive skin.

For multiple hand woes: All-in-One Honey Treatment. In a bowl, combine one-quarter cup of lard, one egg yolk, one-half tablespoon of honey, one-half tablespoon of ground almonds and a few drops of rosewater for scent. Massage the mixture into your hands, then leave it on until it hardens, about 15 to 30 minutes. Wash off with warm water and a gentle soap. Although this treatment requires more ingredients than the other remedies, its many benefits—moisturizing, nourishing, exfoliating, healing—make it worth the effort when you need extra help.

Hand Care for Men

Barney Kenet, MD, dermatologist specializing in skin cancer, New York City…cofounder, American Melanoma Foundation…and author of *How to Wash Your Face*.

H*and care for men:* Apply sunblock regularly to avoid sun exposure, which causes brown spots, freckles and thinning skin that produces a skeletal look in later years. During the day, apply a rich, unscented lubricating lotion, especially after washing hands and while skin still is damp. Good choices include Neutrogena Norwegian Hand Formula…Kiehl's Ultimate Strength Hand Salve…Curel Fragrance Free Hand Lotion, an especially good product if you wash hands often during the day. All are available in drugstores. Give hands intensive nighttime treatment by soaking for a minute or two in a mixture of half water and half whole milk, then applying Aquaphor ointment and wearing gloves to bed, to keep ointment on hands and off sheets. Aquaphor is too heavy for regular daytime use but is fine at night, especially during winter months.

Alternative nighttime treatment: Apply pure honey to hands and leave it on for five minutes—it is sticky but very soothing and softening.

Save Money: DIY Body Lotion

Aimee Masi, MA, licensed medical aesthetician, department of plastic surgery, Loyola University Medical Center, Maywood, Illinois.

H ere are natural oils to make your skin look and feel better…

•**For dry winter skin.** A nickel-sized amount of evening primrose oil, pressed from the seeds of the evening primrose plant, is great for moisturizing the face in cold weather due to its gamma linoleic acid (a beneficial fatty acid)—and you can use even more if you would like to cover your whole body. According to aesthetician Aimee Masi, it doesn't feel "heavy" like many lotions do, but it still prevents chapping from windburn and becomes invisible when the skin absorbs it. You can apply it in the morning or at night or both times, if needed. Do not use evening primrose oil if you are pregnant because of a possible risk of early uterine contractions. However, data on this is controversial, so consult your doctor.

•**For sunburn and bug bites (including spider bites!).** Any type of olive oil can work very well for relieving the discomfort of sunburns and bug bites because it reduces skin inflammation. That calms the skin, which makes it itch and hurt less and accelerates healing. Use only the amount of oil that you need to lightly cover the affected area, and gently massage it into the skin once a day. If the scent of olive oil reminds you a bit too much of dinner, make your own scented oil.

Masi's favorite: Pour olive oil into a jar containing dried organic chamomile flower buds—use enough to submerge the buds. The buds are available online and in many health-food stores. Then seal the jar and let it sit for a month in a dark, dry place. Before using the oil, strain out the flower buds, and you will be left with a chamomile-scented oil to use on your skin.

•**For rosacea.** To reduce the severity of flare-ups that leave your cheeks and nose glowing red, you can try evening primrose oil (mentioned above) or hazelnut oil. You can't cure rosacea (no one knows how to do that), but due to their astringent properties, both oils cleanse and repair damaged skin, prevent dehydration, reduce inflammation, redness and swelling and stimulate skin regrowth. Put a few drops directly onto the face before bed each night and gently massage them into your skin. If you're wondering if you should mix the two oils, Masi advised not to—instead, alternate the oils each day, she said. (And talk to your doctor before using evening primrose oil if you're pregnant.)

• **To relieve eczema.** Many people with eczema find that they can soothe the redness, itching and soreness with plain avocado oil. For the dry, flaky skin that eczema brings, avocado oil can be mixed with brown sugar and used as a gentle scrub. It not only helps moisturize and calm the irritation, but because brown sugar is coarse (but not too abrasive) and contains a form of natural glycolic acid, it exfoliates, so it also helps eliminate the flaking that is part of this condition. Any oil would moisturize, but avocado oil is particularly helpful for eczema patients because it is unusually thick, so it protects the skin better from dehydration.

To use: Make a mixture by adding just enough avocado oil to granulated brown sugar to create a grainy paste. You can make a batch that will keep in the refrigerator or in a dark, dry, cool place for several months. Apply to the dry portions of your skin using a gentle, circular massage for a few minutes two to three times per week. Then rinse the skin with lukewarm water and pat dry with a towel.

Important: Never scrub over open wounds— avoid those areas until they are completely closed. And if the scrub is too irritating for your skin, then either use less brown sugar, use the scrub less often or less vigorously or stop using the scrub altogether.

• **To reduce fine wrinkles.** Rubbing a nickel-sized amount of evening primrose oil on your face in the morning and/or evening may help because it is high in antioxidants, which help protect and repair damaged cells that lead to wrinkles—so it may smooth out your skin. (Talk to your doctor before using it if pregnant.)

For almost all of these skin conditions, Masi said that the oils will provide immediate relief—except when it comes to smoothing out wrinkles, which could require daily use for a month...so be patient!

Foot Fixes Without Surgery

Johanna S. Youner, DPM, founder and medical director, Park Avenue Podiatry Center in New York City. Dr. Youner is a board-certified foot surgeon and a Fellow of the American College of Foot and Ankle Surgeons. ParkAvenuePodiatryCenter.com

It's easy to ignore your feet, but that's a big mistake. When foot pain eventually happens, you may think that surgery is the only solution. Fortunately, that's not always true. There are several nonsurgical options available.

Here's the catch: Your podiatrist might not suggest these nonsurgical approaches—most doctors who treat foot disorders are used to patients demanding the "quick fix" of surgery (even though there's no guarantee of fast or lasting relief).

But in my experience, nonsurgical therapies such as those described here improve the pain by 60% to 80% in most cases—and completely eliminate it in some people—within six to eight weeks.

If your feet are affected by severe degenerative joint disease, surgery may be required.* But most people are able to avoid the risks associated with foot surgery (such as pain and infection) with one of the innovative and effective options for the conditions listed below...

For Bunions

A bunion is a bony bump that develops over the joint at the base of your big toe. Too-tight shoes are commonly the culprit, but bunions may also be inherited or can occur if you have arthritis.

Besides causing pain, bunions can create tingling from nerve compression. Orthotics and ice can help alleviate pain, and steroid injections can ease joint inflammation. But these treatments won't get rid of the bunion. If you do opt for surgery, a bunionectomy (a small incision is made so that the bunion can be removed and the big toe straightened) can be effective. Most individuals are back on their feet within three days, but full recovery can take up to eight weeks. Swelling may last for six months.

*If you have diabetes or smoke, you may not be a candidate for foot surgery due to poor circulation. Speak to your primary health-care provider for advice.

Healthy Foot Hack

Forgot your flip-flops and worried about the fungus you might pick up walking barefoot on the locker room floor? Use hand sanitizer to clean your feet before putting your shoes back on.

Jeffrey Benabio, MD, FAAD, dermatologist and physician director of Health Care Transformation at Kaiser Permanente, San Diego.

Surprising fix: Before resorting to surgery, start by loosening your shoelaces and/or buying slightly larger shoes. Your bunion may be taking up space in your shoes and compressing the nerves.

To ease pain in the big-toe joint, bunion sufferers should wear rigid shoes that provide extra support to the painful joint. (When shopping for a shoe, try to twist the sole…if you can twist it, put it back.)

Good brands for men: Rockport Dressports, Ecco and Allen Edmonds.

Good brands for women: Munro, Ariat and BeautiFeel. Avoid flip-flops—they provide no support, which worsens bunions.

In addition, consider wearing a night splint (available at drugstores and online), which can help stretch and straighten the joint.

Good product: The PediFix Nighttime Bunion Regulator, about $27.

Exercise will not change the bony overgrowth on the bunion but may help ease the pain.

What to do: While slightly lifting your foot off the ground, point it straight ahead and hold for five seconds. Then curl your toes under for five seconds. Repeat 10 times daily.

For Warts

Plantar warts are noncancerous skin growths on the soles of the feet. The warts are caused by an infection with the human papillomavirus. You can catch the virus if you have a cut or scrape on your foot and walk barefoot in a public shower or gym locker room.

Some people try various over-the-counter products, such as salicylic acid. Others cover the wart with duct tape (with or without Aldara, a genital wart cream), and sometimes it falls off. However, these therapies aren't always successful, so some sufferers opt for surgical removal. Unfortunately, this can cause scarring that may lead to lifelong pain and discomfort.

Surprising fix: An injection of the chemotherapy drug bleomycin sulfate. Multiple studies have shown cure rates of 87% to 96% for plantar warts. Bleomycin sulfate is believed to kill the wart virus by stimulating the immune system to fight off the virus. The FDA has not approved the drug for plantar warts, but it can be used off-label for this purpose. When used in the small dose needed to treat plantar warts, common side effects of chemotherapy (such as hair loss and fatigue) do not occur.

Many insurance companies will cover this technique if it is preauthorized. Ask your podiatrist to inquire on your behalf. Be sure your podiatrist is experienced—permanent pain at the injection site can result if the drug is administered improperly.

Nail Clippers: How to Choose Them… How to Use Them

Janet McCormick, a licensed esthetician and manicurist with more than 30 years of experience. Based in Frostproof, Florida, she operates Spa Techniques, a consulting and training firm for salons, and co-founded Nailcare Academy, which provides nail-care certification programs. She is author of *Spa Manicuring for the Salon and Spa.* Nailcare-Academy.com

The blades of low-quality nail clippers can become dull and jagged after as few as three or four uses. But a high-quality nail clipper never needs to be replaced and can be a pleasure to use. *Here's how to choose and use nail clippers…*

Best Clippers

Buy quality stainless steel nail clippers. They're more expensive than nickel-plated clippers—perhaps $12 to $25—but can last a lifetime.

If possible, test the clippers, especially the push-down bar—the part that the thumb presses down to operate the clippers. It's a good sign if your thumb never feels at risk of slipping off the push-down bar during use…but a bad sign if the spot where your thumb presses down is just one-quarter-inch wide or narrower. *Best brands...*

●**Seki Edge** clippers stand out for their high-quality construction and wonderful ergonomics. They're made in Seki, Japan, a city once famed for producing samurai swords. Their ergonomic design makes them particularly appropriate for those suffering from rheumatoid arthritis or other hand issues.

Example: The Seki Edge Stainless Steel fingernail clipper is $12, and the toenail clipper is $13.50 at SekiEdge.com and often less on Amazon.com.

●**Mehaz** nail clippers now are made in Japan, but the company's roots are in the famed blade-manufacturing town of Solingen, Germany. Its products still do justice to that town's high standards. Mehaz clippers are sold mainly through professional beauty-supply stores, but some retailers also make them available online.

Example: Mehaz's most popular model is its Professional Toenail Clipper, selling for $12 to $32 on Amazon.com.

●**Tweezerman,** a New York company, is famous for its high-quality tweezers, but it also makes good nail clippers. They're not quite as well-made as the clippers mentioned already but are far superior to the clippers typically found in drugstores (Tweezerman.com).

Example: Tweezerman Stainless Steel Toenail Clippers typically sell for $7 to $15 at retailers such as CVS, Target and Bed Bath & Beyond, or on websites such as Amazon.com.

Doing It Right

Do not attempt to trim a nail in a single clip. This flattens the nail out, which can cause horizontal cracking on the sides of the free edges. Instead, use three to seven clips per nail. Start with a small clip from one side of the nail, and work your way toward the middle...repeat the process from the other side of the nail. Then make a final clip across the middle.

Clip no closer than one-eighth to one-quarter inch from the hyponychium (the pink tissue under the nail plate) to avoid nicking it. Use a nail file to smooth the nail edge after clipping.

Nail clippers with straight blades generally are preferable to those with curved blades. People often opt for curved-blade clippers because their nails are curved, but a straight blade works just as well when you use the proper multicut nail-clipping method, and straight blades are safer—the corner of curved nail clipper blades are prone to nicking the hyponychium.

There's no need to buy both fingernail and toenail clippers—one good toenail clipper will work for both.

If you have a toenail that's too thick to cut with nail clippers, see a podiatrist—you might have a fungal infection.

Love Your Toothpaste! Which One Is Best for You...

Natalie Hastings, DMD, division chair of clinical general dentistry in the department of preventive and restorative dentistry at the University of California, San Francisco School of Dentistry. Dr. Hastings is a trained prosthodontist and an associate clinical professor, also serving as the predoctoral director of Fixed Prosthodontics and the Student Dental Implant Program at the university.

Are you a savvy toothpaste shopper? Or do you reach for the same brand that you've always bought...or maybe settle for whatever product is on sale?

With literally dozens of toothpaste varieties on drugstore and supermarket shelves—each one touting different benefits ranging from plaque-fighting to breath-freshening and enamel-protecting—it's tough to know which one is best for you.

You might assume that it's all marketing hype. But the truth is, there are some ingredients that do make a difference—and a few others that you may not need.

Here are answers to the questions that will help you identify the best toothpaste for you...

●**Do I still need fluoride?** You're way past your cavity-prone childhood years, so you really don't need this ingredient, right? Wrong.

Cavities occur at all ages. Your risk depends, in part, on your bacteria levels and diet (sugar provides an ideal breeding ground for bacteria that create decay-promoting acids). Using a fluoride-fortified toothpaste really does help prevent cavities. It strengthens the outer surface of teeth, making the enamel more resistant to tooth decay.

The safety question: In recent years, a growing anti-fluoride movement has asserted that fluoride is a neurotoxin. However, decades of research prove that the amount of fluoride found in toothpaste is not only safe but also necessary to guard against cavities. For general oral health, specific brands don't matter too much—just make sure it contains fluoride.

What you may not know: If your dentist spots a cavity in the outer layer of your tooth's enamel, you can permanently reverse it with the use of fluoride toothpaste and mouthwash.

What to do: Follow the standard advice for anyone—brush twice daily with a soft-bristle toothbrush for a full two minutes (use an electric toothbrush with a timer if necessary), then floss—but also swish with a fluoridated mouth rinse, such as ACT Anticavity Fluoride Mouthwash or Crest Pro-Health Advanced Mouthwash. Your dentist may also apply a topical fluoride varnish after a cleaning and provide a prescription for stronger fluoride toothpaste (such as Clinpro 5000 or PreviDent 5000 toothpaste).

●**What will relieve my dry mouth?** Dry mouth is no fun at all. More than 400 medications, including blood pressure drugs and antidepressants, are known to cause dry mouth. (Be sure to tell your doctor if you take medication and have dry mouth—you may be able to switch to a different drug.) Radiation treatments in or near the mouth can also cause it. With dry mouth, you have less saliva, which is needed to help fight cavities by neutralizing acids from food.

What helps: Sip water frequently throughout the day, and try chewing sugar-free gum or sucking on sugar-free mints made with xylitol (a sugar substitute that reduces risk for cavities) between meals to stimulate saliva production.

If you have dry mouth, also consider asking your dentist to prescribe a prescription fluoride toothpaste, such as Clinpro 5000 toothpaste (mentioned earlier). It contains not only more than four times the fluoride of regular toothpaste but also calcium and phosphate to help remineralize and further strengthen your teeth.

Also helpful: Biotène makes a line of xylitol-containing rinses for dry mouth, including Dry Mouth Oral Rinse.

●**What if my teeth are sensitive?** If you've lost some of your enamel due to grinding, clenching, an acidic diet or receding gums, your teeth may be hypersensitive. If that's the case, a desensitizing toothpaste is likely to help—these products contain compounds (such as potassium nitrate) that help block transmission of pain signals from the tooth's outer surface to the nerve.

What helps: Sensodyne Fresh Mint Toothpaste. You'll need to use a desensitizing toothpaste daily for a few weeks before feeling the benefit—stop using it, and the sensitivity will return.

Important new finding: A 2016 study concluded that arginine, an amino acid naturally found in saliva, is superior to other desensitizing agents.

Good product that contains arginine: Colgate Sensitive Pro-Relief Toothpaste.

If you have acid reflux: Don't brush immediately after eating or during an episode of heartburn—food acids may damage tooth enamel over time.

Instead: Dissolve a few teaspoons of baking soda in a bottle of water, then rinse and spit it out after eating to neutralize any acid in your mouth. Wait at least an hour, then brush with a desensitizing toothpaste.

●**What if I prefer a "natural" toothpaste?** Most "natural" toothpastes (such as Kiss My Face and Jason) are free of sodium lauryl sulfate (SLS), a foaming agent that creates that luxurious lather during brushing.

Some people find that SLS irritates their gums, and a small study found that canker sores may be less likely to develop in people who use SLS-free toothpaste. For these individuals, an SLS-free toothpaste is a good option…just make sure it's a product that contains fluoride, such as Tom's of Maine Clean & Gentle with Fluoride Toothpaste, Peppermint.

Diabetes from Your Mouthwash?

Marvin Fier, DDS, Pomona, New York, about a study titled, "Over-the-counter mouthwash use and risk of pre-diabetes/diabetes," published in *Nitric Oxide*. SmileRockland.com

Using mouthwash twice or more a day may keep your breath "minty fresh," but it also may increase your risk of developing type 2 diabetes.

A recent study observed 945 adults for three years. The people studied, ages 40 to 65, were overweight or obese, so they already were at increased risk for diabetes—but the results may be important even for people who are not overweight.

Findings: Participants who used a mouthwash twice or more a day typically had 55% higher risk for prediabetes or diabetes than those who used mouthwash less frequently or not at all.

This kind of study can't show cause and effect, and it leaves many questions open—especially about the kind of mouthwash people used. But there are reasons to avoid excessive use. Most mouthwashes contain alcohol or other ingredients, either synthetic or essential oils, that kill microbes indiscriminately—including beneficial ones that help the body make nitric oxide. But you need nitric oxide—it's a remarkable compound that is important for everyone's health, protecting against not only obesity and insulin resistance but also high blood pressure.

The truth is, you don't need to use mouthwash at all. It's not particularly effective at improving oral health anyway. For example, brushing and flossing are much better at disrupting plaque, the biofilm that sticks to teeth and causes cavities, gum disease—and, often, bad breath.

Tip: Thin, unwaxed floss is best at physically dislodging plaque. (If you still love the mouthwash habit, choose alcohol-free products to avoid drying the delicate mucous membranes of the mouth.)

Finally, don't ignore persistent bad breath. It could point to a health problem. If you are using mouthwash several times each day to get rid of bad breath or a bad taste, speak with your dentist or other health-care provider.

The 10 Most Toxic Skin-Care Ingredients

Sharima Rasanayagam, PhD, director of science at the Breast Cancer Fund, San Francisco. She was also the founding academic coordinator at the UC Berkeley Institute for the Environment.

Rick Smith, PhD, executive director of the Broadbent Institute, Ottawa, Ontario, and coauthor, with Bruce Lourie, of *Slow Death by Rubber Duck: The Secret Danger of Everyday Things and Toxin Toxout: Getting Harmful Chemicals Out of Our Bodies and Our World.*

By the time a woman steps out of her door in the morning, she's applied an average of nine personal-care products to her face, body and hair—and been exposed to about 126 different chemicals, according to Rick Smith, PhD, coauthor of *Toxin Toxout: Getting Harmful Chemicals Out of Our Bodies and Our World.* Men may use fewer products, but they get exposed to plenty of chemicals, too.

There's no need to panic and toss out everything in your bathroom. Dr. Smith suggests replacing each product as it runs out with a healthier one. Which ones should you toss first? To get more specifics, we asked Sharima Rasanayagam, PhD, director of science at the Breast Cancer Fund, a nonprofit that works to prevent breast cancer by reducing exposure to toxic chemicals and radiation.

1. Parabens. These endocrine disrupters are so common in personal-care products that it's tough to know where to start. A recent Swedish study of mothers found levels of parabens in urine were highest in women who used more makeup, shampoo, hair-styling products, lotion, fragrance, deodorant, massage oil and nail polish.

Shopping tips: Skip any skin-care product that contains the word "paraben" by itself or as part of the another chemical name, such as ethylparaben, propylparaben, butylparaben or benzylparaben.

Or shop for products that specifically claim that they are "parabens free."

2. Triclosan. This antibacterial compound contributes not only to antibiotic-resistant bacteria but is also an endocrine disrupter, says Dr. Smith. "Triclosan is a registered pesticide, and extremely worrisome," he warns. It's found in soft and bar antibacterial soaps, cosmetics, shaving products, deodorants and dry shampoos, according to the Environmental Working Group's Skin Deep Cosmetics Database. The FDA is currently evaluating the ingredient based on animal studies that show that it disrupts hormones and may lead to more antibiotic-resistant bacteria, but it already emphasizes that the soaps and body washes with triclosan provide no extra health benefit to consumers.

Shopping tips: Avoid any product that contains triclosan. In particular, Dr. Smith recommends that if you have Colgate Total toothpaste, toss it immediately even though it is effective against gingivitis. Why? Exposing your gums to triclosan means more may be absorbed than from, for example, washing your hands with liquid soap. When shopping for face- or body-washing products, remember that plain old soap and water is highly effective at removing bacteria—if you wash long enough.

Travel tip: If you want to avoid triclosan-containing antibacterial soaps in, say, public bathrooms, carry a small bottle of alcohol-based hand sanitizer with you.

Editors note: Colgate has recently replaced triclosan with a higher grade of fluoride, but you might have an older tube or store inventories might have older versions of the formula.

3. Polytetrafluoroethylene (PTFE), a suspected carcinogen found in some antiaging creams. According to a recent Breast Cancer Fund study, this compound, originally used to create Teflon, often travels with a related chemical called perfluorooctanoic acid (aka PFOA or C-8).

Shopping tips: The Breast Cancer Fund study names three products to avoid—Garnier Ultra-Lift Transformer Anti-Age Skin Corrector, Garnier Ultra-Lift Anti-Wrinkle Firming Moisturizer and Cover Girl Advanced Radiance with Olay, Age

Defying Pressed Powder. Read labels—in addition to PTFE, other ingredients that may mean PFOA include Polyperfluoromethylisopropyl and DEA-C8-18 Perfluoroalkylethyl. Check for products that specifically state that they are PTFE- and PFOA-free.

4. Resorcinol, found in hair dyes. According to Dr. Rasanayagam, hair dyes often contain "a bunch of nasty chemicals," often derived from coal tar, but resorcinol, a potent endocrine disruptor, is the worst.

Shopping tips: Unfortunately, resorcinol is found in most hair dyes in most colors as well as certain over-the-counter acne products. Says Dr. Rasanayagam, "Hair colorings are particularly difficult to formulate without these chemicals, but some companies are working on better options."

Safer, non–coal-tar dye alternatives include temporary hair colorants and henna, which imbues a reddish tinge and is approved by the FDA as a natural dye. Indigo, which is a dark blue, is another natural nontoxic dye that may also be mixed in with henna. Other botanical-based hair dyes can also be used for lighter colors, including blond. But beware of "black henna," which may contain coal-tar–based hair dyes. The best way to approach the issue? Learn to love your gray.

5. Formaldehyde, dibutyl phthalate (DBP) and toluene, aka the "Toxic Trio," often found in nail polish. Formaldehyede is a carcinogen, DBP is an endocrine disruptor, and toluene is a toxic compound often contaminated with benzene, a carcinogen.

Shopping tips: Read labels, and shop for toxic-trio–free brands such as Honeybee Gardens and Acquarella, suggests Dr. Rasanayagam.

6. Hydroquinone, found in skin lighteners and age-spot removers. Animal studies link topical use of this bleaching compound with cancer, and it can also cause a skin-darkening medical condition in some people. The US National Toxicology Program has proposed removing it from the "safe" list of ingredients—pending more studies. Meanwhile it's banned in Europe in concentrations above 1% but still legal and readily available in the US in concentrations up to 4%.

Shopping tips: Avoid any product with hydroquinone on the label. You may want to try home-remedy concoctions using food-based ingredients such as lemons, honey, oranges and/or milk that help naturally lighten skin without harsh chemicals.

7. Phthalates, commonly found in fragrances and perfumes. These are potent endocrine disrupters, and while exposure in cosmetics is dropping, one big exception is DEP, a phthalate found in fragrances. By law, companies don't have to reveal fragrance ingredients, yet many of those ingredients contain not only phthalates but also parabens and synthetic musk (another endocrine disrupter).

Shopping tips: Avoid any product that just lists "fragrance" or "parfum." Says Dr. Smith, "Because companies aren't legally obligated to disclose the presence of phthalates in their products, look for products that say 'No Phthalates' on the label."

8. Petrolatum, aka petroleum jelly, mineral oil and paraffin oil, found in many moisturizers, ointments and skin creams.

The big exception: Refined petrolatum, also called white petrolatum, has no known health concerns. That's what's in Vaseline, which is safer. But products that simply list "petroleum jelly" may be using less refined products, which may be contaminated with suspected carcinogens including polycyclic aromatic hydrocarbons (PAHs).

Shopping tips: Avoid any product that contains petroleum jelly unless it specifies white petroleum jelly or white petrolatum. Vaseline, as noted, is a safer choice. You may also want to explore moisturizers that contain botanical-based ingredients such as beeswax, coconut oil, olive oil, shea butter and coconut butter instead.

9. Oxybenzone and benzophenone found in sunscreens. How dangerous these are is still a controversy. While the Environmental Working Group warns that these are endocrine disrupters that are absorbed into the skin, the American Academy of Dermatology believes they are safe to use. According to Dr. Rasanayagam , however, you should avoid these chemicals.

Shopping tips: Avoid sunscreens with oxybenzone or benzophenone. Instead, choose cream sunscreens with zinc oxide or titanium dioxide.

10. Formaldehyde, found in hair straighteners or hair-smoothing products such as Brazilian Blowout or keratin treatments. When heated, these products can release formaldehye (a carcinogen) into the air, which can lead to eye problems, headaches, dizziness, breathing problems, nausea and rash.

Shopping tips: Avoid any product that contains formaldehyde—by FDA regulation, it must include a warning on the label. If you go to a salon, ask to look at the product they use to make sure it doesn't contain formaldehyde. However, beware of salon products that claim to be formaldehyde-free but list "methylene glycol" on the ingredient list—that's just formaldehyde by another name.

Some salons use hair-straigthening products that rely primarily on botanicals instead—Aveda makes one, called Smooth Infusion Professional Smoothing Treatment. Also consider going old school with a straight iron.

How to Shop for Healthier Personal-Care Products

Now that you know the ingredients that are most important to avoid, how can you start? *A few tips...*

•**Get familiar with websites.** A site that lets you search for healthy personal-care products is the Environmental Working Group's Skin Deep (EWG. org/skindeep). You can educate yourself about these issues with the Breast Cancer Fund's site, Campaign for Safe Cosmetics (SafeCosmetics.org), as well.

•**Download an app.** The EWG has a Healthy Living app (free), and the Think Dirty app lists thousands of personal-care products. Download one on your smartphone so that you can spot-check products while shopping.

•**Decide what "healthier" means to you.** Safe Cosmetics.org addresses only long-term chronic health issues, but the Skin Deep site discourages not only products with toxic ingredients but also those that cause irritation, trigger allergies, negatively impact the environment or have been tested on animals. But if your body wash, for example, contains a possible irritant and it doesn't irritate you, you may decide to keep it anyway.

•**Don't be fooled by labels** that claim a product is "All Natural" or made with "100% Natural

Ingredients." While the "organic" term is regulated on cosmetics and personal-care products, the term "natural" is not.

Fall in Love with Your Hearing Aids

Barbara E. Weinstein, PhD, professor of audiology and head of the Audiology Program at City University of New York Graduate Center in New York City. She is author of the textbook *Geriatric Audiology*.

Few people relish the idea of getting hearing aids. Some are too embarrassed to wear them, while others are put off by the high cost. Whatever the reason, about three-quarters of the roughly 30 million American adults who could benefit from these remarkable little devices don't get them…and most who do get them postpone the decision for close to 10 years.

So you might assume that the battle is won when a holdout takes the plunge and does get hearing aids. But that's not always true. Nearly 13% of new hearing-aid users wind up tossing the devices in a drawer. And up to 25% of new users wear them for less than two hours a day, depriving themselves of their full benefit.

Why do so many new hearing-aid users falter? One underappreciated trap is that it can take weeks or even months to get accustomed to the sounds (and the feel) of new hearing aids. So it's crucial to not let the initial discomforts put you off.

Proper use of hearing aids can enrich your relationships and social life…possibly guard against accidents that can occur if you don't hear warning signals…and prevent falls that can be precipitated by walking while struggling to understand what someone is saying. Improved hearing may even help protect your brain health because you can better communicate with family and friends and remain engaged.

Hearing and the Brain

People cite a number of reasons for not wearing their hearing aids. Some complain that they hurt their ears. Others notice that the sounds they hear don't seem natural…or that they're bothered by sounds they hadn't noticed before.

While new hearing aids do take some getting used to, they are definitely worth the effort. For one thing, emerging evidence suggests that the part of the brain that processes spoken language (the temporal lobe) may be subject to atrophy and volume declines when not stimulated. This means that people with an impaired hearing mechanism who wait too long to correct their hearing may not benefit as much from hearing interventions.

Even scarier risk: In a study by a group of researchers at Johns Hopkins who tracked 639 adults (ages 36 to 90), mild hearing loss was linked to twice the risk for dementia…and moderate-to-severe hearing loss increased the risk between three- and fivefold.

Adjusting to Change

It's easier to get used to hearing aids in your younger years, so don't wait until you're adjusting the TV volume to wall-shaking levels. The most important part of successful aging is staying socially engaged—and you can't do that when you can't hear or communicate with others. *Secrets to adjusting to your hearing aids…*

SECRET #1: **Wear them all day.** Depending on the degree/duration of your hearing loss, it might have been years since you've heard the sound of your own footsteps…water running in the sink…or the clatter of dishes. The "new" sounds can be distracting—even disturbing—until you get used to them.

My advice: Wear your new hearing aids all day, even when you first get them. We used to advise patients to use them for just a few hours a day at first, but we've found that people often do better with full-on exposure. Just know that it may take days, weeks or even months before background sounds truly fade into the background.

SECRET #2: **When it's too loud, make adjustments.** You'll probably find that most sounds—even the ones you want to hear—are uncomfortably loud at first. Some hearing aids have volume controls, which you can adjust, but it will take your brain time to adjust even to the lower settings. If sounds are too loud, be sure to return to your hearing- aid provider to make the necessary adjustments, as hearing aids have many features that can be adjusted.

My advice: As mentioned above, it's important to wear your hearing aids all day. You might want to make an exception, however, for unusually noisy environments—for example, in the subway, at a concert or at the airport. High-volume venues won't always be an impediment, but they can be a turnoff during the adjustment period.

If the sound of your own voice is disturbing, ask your audiologist if the devices need adjusting. Turning down the volume might not do it. An audiologist can make adjustments—to the sound frequencies, for example, or the shape of the earpiece (known as the mold)—that will often help.

Important: To become comfortable with their hearing aids, most people require one or two additional visits for adjustments, which are typically included in the price of the hearing aids.

SECRET #3: **Cut through the clutter.** People with normal hearing may struggle to hear conversations when there's a lot of background noise, but it is worse for those with hearing loss. Even inexpensive hearing aids typically have a noise-cancellation feature that enhances higher frequencies (typical of speech) while suppressing lower frequencies (from background noise). The setting is often adjustable—learn how to use it.

My advice: If adjusting noise cancellation doesn't help, ask an audiologist to make changes in the "output" and/or "gain." Gain is the power of the signal that affects amplification, and output is the level of "sound pressure" that's produced by the combination of incoming sounds and the gain added by the hearing aid.

SECRET #4: **Master the controls.** Hearing aids keep getting smaller, which means that the controls also are getting smaller—too small, in many cases, for people (especially those with big fingers or limited hand mobility) to easily adjust.

Leave Earwax Alone

Earwax is important for protecting ears—it collects dirt, dust and other matter, preventing these from getting farther into the ear. Trying to clean the ears with cotton swabs, hairpins, toothpicks and the like can push the wax farther into the ear canal and cause hearing loss, dizziness and ringing in the ear. See a doctor if your ears are bothering you.

Seth Schwartz, MD, MPH, chair, guideline update group, American Academy of Otolaryngology—Head and Neck Surgery Foundation.

My advice: Don't buy a hearing aid just because it has a zillion adjustable features. They won't do you any good unless you have the finger dexterity (and the technical savvy) to master them. An audiologist can help you decide which features you absolutely need—and those you can do without.

Helpful: Many hearing aids use Bluetooth wireless technology, which allows them to be adjusted by an app that appears on the screen of your smartphone. This is a great feature if you have one of these phones and you're willing to use it as a remote control. An audiologist talked my 93-year-old cousin into getting this feature…but in order to use it, she had to buy her first smartphone, which she didn't know how to use and actually found annoying.

SECRET #5: **Learn how to fix whistling sounds.** The squealing/whistling sounds that you'll sometimes hear are a type of feedback. It doesn't mean that there's a problem with the electronics. Most hearing aids have "feedback interceptors" that suppress whistles, but they don't eliminate them entirely.

My advice: Ask your audiologist if you need a tighter-fitting ear mold. Squeals and whistles occur when amplified sound from the hearing aid leaks out of the ear…gets picked up by the microphone… and then returns to the ear as a whistling noise.

SECRET #6: Don't put up with ear discomfort. Many people complain that their hearing aids are uncomfortable. They may find themselves constantly pulling/adjusting the ear mold to reduce discomfort, but the frequent back-and-forth adjustments only make the irritation worse.

My advice: You can get a hearing-aid lubricant/cream from an audiologist, online or at pharmacies. Brands include Westone Oto-Ease and Audiologist's Choice anti-itch cream. They're particularly helpful if you happen to have dryness in the ear canal.

Worth a try: If you continue to have problems, your audiologist might need to fashion an ear mold/tip that fits more comfortably. This is one advantage of buying locally. I don't discourage patients from buying hearing aids online, but this type of adjustment can be done only by a local professional.

DIY Honey-and-Lemon Face Mask to Fight Acne and Wrinkles

Sejal Shah, MD, dermatologist in New York City, quoted on TheHealthy.com.

To prevent acne and slow aging, make this simple concoction. Mix one tablespoon organic honey with the juice from one-half lemon. Apply the mask to your face and neck, avoiding your eyes. Leave it on for 20 minutes. Rinse with warm water, then cold. Honey is antibacterial and full of antioxidants, while the vitamin C in lemon juice helps form collagen, the protein that gives skin its elasticity.

CHAPTER 16

Pest Control

Bugged by Bugs?

Richard Fagerlund, a pest-control professional based in Los Ranchos, New Mexico, who has more than 40 years of experience. AskTheBugman.com

Millions of home owners will soon get unwelcome houseguests. The arrival of spring means insect populations are about to boom across much of the US.

Here's how to reduce the odds that ants, flies and crickets will get into your home—and how to deal with them naturally if they do…

Ants

Ants are the nation's most common household pest. There are many different species of ants, but certain ant-control strategies are effective against most of the varieties likely to find their way into American homes.

To keep ants out of your home…

•**Seal or caulk any cracks or gaps** in the foundation or walls of your home, including gaps around pipes.

•**Install door sweeps** at the base of exterior doors to minimize any gaps there.

•**Trim trees back and shrubs** so that they don't come in contact with your home's roof or walls.

•**Examine plants growing close to your home for aphids and scales**—insects that attract ants. If you find these small insects, use a strong jet of water to wash them off affected plants or apply a garlic spray.

To make a garlic spray: Crush two cloves of garlic in a garlic press, and add to one quart of water…or use a blender to blend two cloves and the water. Let it steep for an hour. Strain and spray to deter ants.

If these solutions don't work, ask a local garden shop to recommend additional aphid/scale-control techniques or products.

•**Move stacks of firewood,** lumber and bricks away from the perimeter of your home—some varieties of ant like to nest under these.

•**Sprinkle ground cinnamon around the exterior perimeter of your home and in the crawl space under your home.** Cinnamon repels ants. For an average home, you will need about eight ounces. Walmart sells 18-ounce containers of cinnamon for $9.

Other safe products that repel ants include cedar oil, medicated baby powder, Tide detergent and coffee grounds, but I find cinnamon to be especially effective.

If ants do get into your home…

•**Make ant baits** by combining roughly two tablespoons of peanut butter or jelly with one teaspoon of boric acid powder or borax on small pieces of cardboard. (The laundry detergent 20 Mule Team Borax works well here.) Make several of these baits, and place them in spots where you've seen ants in your home but where pets and kids can't get to them, such as behind kitchen appliances. (This combination shouldn't cause anything worse than a stomachache in a child or pet that consumes a small amount.) NiBan Granular Insect Bait, a commercially sold boric acid bait, also is effective against ants (as well as cockroaches and crickets). Be sure to follow the directions on the label.

Flies

Flies buzzing around a home can be a major annoyance. They even can spread disease.

To keep flies out...

•**Repair holes in window screens**, and seal or caulk other gaps in the home's perimeter.

•**Remove trash containing food debris** from the home as soon as possible.

If flies do get into your home...

Flies generally lose interest in homes if there's nothing for them to eat inside. With houseflies, clean any food residue from sinks, dishes and trash containers. *Also...*

•**Eliminate any other organic debris from inside the home (spilled food, open garbage).** Also, eliminate organic debris around the perimeter of your home, including compost piles, dead leaves and pet feces.

•**If you still need to, make some simple, inexpensive fly baits.** Combine two tablespoons of Karo light corn syrup, honey or sugar water with one teaspoon of boric acid in paper cups. Place these around the house to trap and kill flies.

Helpful: When you attempt to swat a resting housefly, aim the flyswatter one-and-a-half inches behind the fly. Houseflies typically leap upward and backward when they take off from a horizontal surface.

Other types of flies require different solutions...

•**With moth flies**—a small variety of fly often found around drains that has hairy wings that make them look like moths—the best solution usually is to clean the gunk out of bathroom and kitchen drains.

•**With fungus gnats**—a small, mosquito-like variety of fly often found around houseplants—the best solution is to not water the houseplants until

The Best Bug Spray

Greenbug Ready to Use is the most effective safe product for spraying bugs of any sort that you may see from time to time in your home, such as roaches, spiders, ants, flies and others. Its active ingredient is cedar, which is lethal to insects but not harmful to people and pets. ($32.95 for a quart bottle, GreenBugAllNatural.com)

they're virtually wilted. Cover the plants' soil with a layer of aquarium gravel when you finally do water.

•**With fruit flies**—any of several varieties of small fly often found around fresh fruit or vegetables—the best solution is to pour apple cider vinegar into paper cups, then leave these positioned around the kitchen. Fruit flies are attracted to the smell of vinegar, but they can't escape it once they dive in.

Crickets

The chirping of crickets can be peaceful and relaxing when we're outside on a summer night, but it soon becomes irritating when the crickets join us inside our homes.

To keep crickets out...

•**Secure the perimeter of the home** by sealing any gaps and installing door sweeps under exterior doors, as discussed in the section on ants.

•**If you have a crawl space under your home,** dust it with diatomaceous earth, a powdery substance sold in home centers, garden stores and elsewhere. It absorbs the waxy layer on the surface of crickets' skin, causing them to dry out and die. (It's effective against scorpions and certain other pests as well.)

Choose food-grade diatomaceous earth, not the version intended for use in swimming pool filters, which is ineffective against crickets. You will need about five pounds. Wear eye protection while spreading this product.

You may want to hire someone to dust it under the house. Once a year is sufficient for most homes.

If crickets do get into your home...

•**Place pieces of duct tape, sticky side up, near where you believe the crickets are hiding.** The crickets will try to eat the tape—they are attracted to the adhesive—but will get stuck to it instead.

●**Or you can purchase and use NiBan Granular Insect Bait,** the commercially sold boric acid bait suggested above. It is very effective against crickets.

Clever Ways to Get Rid of Garden Pests

Christine Bucks, garden book editor at Rodale Inc., publisher of books and magazines, Emmaus, Pennsylvania. She has edited more than 20 gardening books, including *Great Garden Fix-Its: Organic Remedies for Everything from Aphids to Weeds,* a compendium of garden solutions from dozens of successful gardeners.

N ow that spring is here, it won't be long before critters invade your garden. *Whether it's beetles feasting on your flowers or deer devouring the tomato plants, here's how to get rid of pests without resorting to dangerous poisons...*

Bugs

●**Aphids.** These tiny, green-gray bugs can suck the life from vegetables, flowers and tree leaves. They usually travel in large swarms so, despite their small size, they can devastate a garden.

Aphids are repelled by the scent of citrus rind. Combine one tablespoon of freshly grated citrus rind with one pint of boiling water, steep overnight, strain the mixture through a coffee filter, then pour it into a spray bottle. Add three drops of dishwashing liquid, and spray affected plants and those nearby.

If that doesn't do it, buy an insecticidal soap at a garden store. Test it on one or two plants—insecticidal soaps may do as much damage as aphids. If the sprayed plants show signs of leaf browning, curling or spotting within the next three days, don't use the soap. Otherwise, spray aphid-affected plants every five to seven days as long as the problem persists. Be sure to spray the undersides of leaves as well as the tops.

●**Japanese beetles.** These shiny, half-inch-long copper-colored beetles with green and white markings are a familiar but unwelcome sight to gardeners in the eastern US. Japanese beetles are particularly fond of rosebushes and grape and raspberry plants, but they'll eat virtually any plant.

To fight back, put soapy water in a wide bowl and hold it under the branches of beetle-affected plants. Gently shake the branches. Most of the beetles will drop into the bowl and drown.

A long-term solution is to apply milky spore disease powder—available at garden stores—to your lawn near your garden as directed on the label. In two to five years, the disease will take hold, killing beetle grubs in the soil. The disease is harmless to humans, pets and beneficial insects.

●**Slugs and snails.** These pests eat holes through broad-leaf plants. To limit damage, place a few empty tuna or cat food cans in the soil up to their brims. Then pour beer into them. Slugs and snails are attracted to beer and drown in the cans. Use long-handled tweezers to remove the dead pests, or dump the contents—beer and all—on your compost pile. Then add more beer to the cans. Install beer traps in spring before slugs and snails have a chance to reproduce.

Also put a few boards on the ground in your garden. Slugs and snails love the moist shade underneath. Every day or two, pick up the boards and scrape the collected critters into a pail of soapy water. Remove the boards in autumn so that slugs and snails can't seek shelter there during cold weather.

Helpful: You will substantially reduce your garden's slug and snail population if you water your garden in the morning rather than the afternoon. That way, the soil will be dry by night, when these creatures are active, robbing them of the moisture that they need to survive.

Mint Helps Keep Ants Away

Plant mint around the foundation of your house to make ants less likely to enter.

Wayne Piaskowski, field editor, *The Family Handyman.* FamilyHandyman.com

Animals

•**Deer.** Deer are naturally mistrustful of certain scents. You can hang cheesecloth bags of human hair (hair is available at salons and barber shops) around your garden. Dirty socks or bags of soap also may do the trick.

Organic deer-repellent sprays, such as Deer Away Deer Repellent and Hinder Deer, have odors that are offensive to deer but not to humans. You can expect to spend $25 and up per gallon at a garden store. Odor-based solutions such as these will not stop all deer, but they can cut plant loss in your garden by 30% to 50%.

The only way to stop most deer is with an electric fence. Expect to spend several hundred dollars at a home or garden store for a fence kit large enough to protect a 50-by-50-foot garden. To keep deer from jumping over your fence, smear peanut butter on aluminum foil tabs and attach them to the fence (always turn off the power before touching the fence). Deer that lick the peanut butter will receive a small shock and learn that your garden is best avoided. An electric fence is not an option for households with young children.

You also can switch to plants that deer don't like—or create a living fence of these plants around your yard.

Flowers: Begonias, daffodils, foxglove, globe thistle, iris, lavender, marigolds, meadow saffron, peony, scented geraniums, snapdragons, stars of Persia, sweet alyssum, strawflowers, yarrow, zinnias.

Trees and bushes: American holly, boxwoods, Caucasian daphne, Sawara false cypress, Japanese pieris, northern red oak, pine, red osier dogwood, rugosa rose, spruce.

•**Rabbits.** Rabbits can ravage gardens, consuming everything from vegetables to seedlings. If rabbits are the culprits, you'll find hard, pea-sized dark brown droppings in neat piles.

You can try scaring rabbits away with fake snakes. Cut an old garden hose into serpentlike lengths, and place the pieces throughout your garden.

If that doesn't work, another way to protect your garden is to construct a two- to three-foot-high chicken wire fence around it. The fence must ex-

Natural Slug Repellent

To get rid of slugs in your garden, sprinkle fresh chopped garlic around areas where you see slugs.

Danny Ledoux, pest control expert and consultant, Fort Pierce, Florida, and author of *Pest Control Simplified for Everyone: Kill, Repel, or Mitigate Pests With or Without Pesticides.*

tend at least six inches beneath the ground so rabbits can't burrow under it.

•**Voles.** These tiny rodents can consume close to their body weight in tubers and bulbs each day as they tunnel through your garden.

When you plant bulbs, arrange a handful of sharp crushed gravel around them in the holes to keep voles away. Remove wood chips and mulch from the vicinity of young trees and shrubs in autumn so that voles have less cover during cold weather, when they eat mainly tree roots.

Gardeners with serious vole problems can plant their crops in wooden frames with quarter-inch or smaller wire mesh stapled to the bottom (frames are available at garden stores). The mesh allows roots to grow out but prevents voles from tunneling in. Or grow daffodils, one of the few garden bulbs that voles (and squirrels) won't eat.

A Better Way to Kill Ticks... Before They Bite

Study titled "The heat is on: Killing blacklegged ticks in residential washers and dryers to prevent tickborne diseases" by researchers at Centers for Disease Control and Prevention, Fort Collins, Colorado, University of Vermont College of Medicine, Burlington, University of Massachusetts, Boston, Vermont Agency of Agriculture, Barre, published in *Tick and Tick-borne Diseases.*

When you come indoors after a day in the great outdoors, you toss your clothes into the washing machine—it's a good precaution in case any ticks have hitched a ride into your home. All that hot soapy water will kill any ticks, right?

Maybe not.

Although washing clothes, and then drying them for an hour, has been the official prevention advice of the Centers for Disease Control and Prevention (CDC), it's not the best approach, according to research in the journal *Ticks and Tick-Borne Diseases* by researchers at the CDC, the University of Vermont College of Medicine and the University of Massachusetts.

Ticks, it turns out, love water.

In the study, 94% survived cold-water washes, and 50% survived hot-water washes. Once the clothes were wet, it took 70 minutes to kill the ticks in dryers on low heat, 50 minutes in dryers on high heat.

So while you're probably OK with the standard wash-then-60-minute-dry advice, there's a much more efficient approach—just toss the clothes in the dryer on high heat right away. No washing first.

It kills all the ticks—in six minutes. Most are dead in four minutes.

So when your clothes may have ticks on them, dry them on high for six minutes—then wash if they're dirty.

Plants That Repel Pests

Plants that humans enjoy but bugs really hate...

•**Marigolds** repel mosquitoes, squash bugs and tomato worms—they contain a natural compound used in many insect repellents.

•**Lavender** is attractive to bees but not to other insects.

•**Lemongrass** repels mosquitoes—it contains citronella, used in many repellents.

•**Garlic** repels mosquitoes and other bugs.

•**Rosemary** drives away flies, mosquitoes and cabbage moths.

•**Basil** keeps mosquitoes and flies away.

•**Catnip** attracts cats but repels mosquitoes.

•**Petunias** have a licorice-like scent that repels aphids, tomato hornworms and squash bugs—although some pests, such as slugs and caterpillars, like it.

•**Mint** keeps ants and mice away.

Roundup of experts on plants that repel insects, reported in *USA Today*.

Fight Bugs Naturally

Jamison Starbuck, ND, a naturopathic physician in family practice and a guest lecturer at the University of Montana, both in Missoula.

If you'd rather not use chemicals on your body to help guard against bugs, tweaking your diet during the summer can help reduce the frequency and severity of bites from insects such as mosquitoes, ants and flies.

My advice: Each day, consume minced garlic (one clove) and one-half teaspoon of brewer's yeast (try it in berry smoothies, on popcorn or in a vinaigrette dressing). Though research is mixed, some people find a B-1 (thiamine) supplement (100 mg daily) also helps. Check with your doctor first if you take any medications, since garlic, brewer's yeast and B-1 could interact with them.

If you do get bitten: Insects often carry bacteria that can enter your body via the bite, so clean the insect bite with mild soap and water. Then apply a tincture of calendula, which is an antiseptic, to the bite using a cotton ball. Reapply calendula four times daily until the bite is healed. See a doctor if you have a fever or the bite is red, tender and/or swollen.

Bedbugs Begone

Jerome Goddard, PhD, extension professor, department of biochemistry, molecular biology, entomology and plant pathology,, Mississippi State University, Starkville, and coauthor of a study of bedbugs, published in The Journal of the American Medical Association.

Bedbugs have been found in clothing stores, movie theaters and other public places, and there is no guaranteed way to prevent them from hitching a ride home with you. If you develop itching or bites after being in a public place, all you can do is change your clothes as soon as you get home—in the bathroom, not around upholstered furniture—and then put the clothes in a hot dryer to kill the bugs.

Hotels and other overnight accommodations merit special precautions. In a hotel, put suitcases in the bathroom or on a TV stand or other hard surface upon check-in. Check the bed, box spring and headboard for insects and small black specks. If you find any, ask for a room change and inspect the new room, too.

When you return home, open suitcases outside. Wash and dry clothes on hot settings. Then put empty luggage in the car for a few hours on a very hot or very cold day—extreme heat or cold kills bedbugs.

There Really Is a Better Mousetrap

Michael Bohdan, a licensed pest-control professional for 30 years and owner, The Pest Shop, Plano, Texas. He is author of *What's Buggin' You? Michael Bohdan's Guide to Home Pest Control.* He answers pest-control questions for free through his website, PestShop.com.

Mouse infestations are becoming increasingly common in American homes as rodent predators, including owls, hawks, foxes and snakes, lose their habitats to suburban sprawl. Mouse problems occur in every state and during every season, though new infestations are particularly likely in the fall, when the onset of cold weather encourages rodents to head indoors. Homeowners usually can eliminate all but the most serious mouse infestations without the help of a professional exterminator.

Options for Mouse Control

•**Snap traps.** Old-fashioned but improved spring-loaded mousetraps are among the most effective mouse-control options. The best of these is the Snap-E Mousetrap by Kness Manufacturing (800-247-5062, Kness.com, $15 for six). Its smart design increases the kill rate...makes accidental finger snaps less likely—and allows you to remove dead mice without touching them.

Note: A dab of peanut butter makes an effective mousetrap bait.

Even better: Put a pecan sliver in the peanut butter, then add two drops of vanilla extract. Small

pieces of greasy cooked bacon also work. Cheese is less effective.

Place snap traps wherever you find mouse droppings or mouse holes. (Wear rubber gloves, and use moist paper towels to clean up the droppings.) Mice like to travel along edges, so position the baited ends of snap traps up against walls. Set at least six to 12 traps.

•**Cage traps.** Cage traps capture mice without harming them. They are appropriate for people who prefer not to kill animals, and they can be quite effective. Use the same bait as used in snap traps. Safeguard Multi-Catch Mouse Trap (800-433-1819, SafeGuardProducts.com, usually $10 to $20) and Victor's Tin Cat Live Catch Mouse Trap (855-584-2867, VictorPest.com, $15.99) are among the best. Ask your local animal control office where to dispose of mice.

•**Poisons.** Rodenticides are a commonly used option, but they are not necessarily the best unless you don't want to check traps or you have more than a few dozen mice. Pets or small children might eat the poison...or poisoned mice might die in your walls or attic, infusing your home with their smell.

If you do use poison, those that come in grain form are more effective than the wax-impregnated blocks. Put the poison in tamper-resistant bait stations, and place these wherever you find mouse droppings.

Look for Bell brand stations at pest-control supply stores, and expect to use four to six.

Price: About $14.

•**Glue boards.** A glue board uses adhesive to trap mice. These are no more effective than snap traps or cage traps and are unnecessarily inhumane, because captured mice slowly die of starvation or thirst.

Plug Holes

To keep your home mouse-free, plug holes. Typical points of entry include small gaps where pipes or vents pass through walls...the vents themselves... foundation cracks...and under doors. A mouse can squeeze through a hole the size of a dime.

Easy plug for some holes: A copper mesh product called Stuf-Fit Copper Wool.

Price: About $20 for a 20-foot roll at pest-control supply stores. Keep your garage doors shut as much as possible, and block any gaps around the edges of these doors with rubber strips. Rodents can cause thousands of dollars in damage by gnawing through a car's wiring.

Not Worth the Money

Red fox urine, peppermint oil and other bottled scents sold as rodent deterrents are not very effective. "Sonic" mouse deterrents that claim to drive rodents away with a high-pitched noise also are virtually worthless.

No Bug Repellents! Alternatives…

Joseph M. Conlon, MSc, technical advisor, American Mosquito Control Association, Mount Laurel, New Jersey.

Do you avoid your patio and backyard because of mosquitoes, but hate using chemical bug repellents? *Here are alternative ways to get rid of mosquitoes…*

Since mosquitoes spread diseases, it's important to steer clear of them. Fortunately, there are several nontoxic ways to do that.

•**Use a small electric fan to create a gentle breeze…pleasant for you,** but like a wind tunnel for tiny mosquitoes! Besides making it difficult for them to fly, it disperses the carbon dioxide and human scents that attract them.

•**You can also light your patio with a yellow "bug light" bulb.** It won't attract the little bloodsuckers the way that white lights will.

•**It helps to dress in light-colored, loose-fitting clothing, too,** since mosquitoes are attracted to darker colors, and it's easier for them to bite through tightly fitted clothing.

•**Eliminate all sources of standing water** since mosquitoes need standing water to lay their eggs. Keep the grass cut short and the bushes trimmed so they're less hospitable to mosquitoes.

Get Rid of Mosquitoes

Phil Pellitteri, entomologist, distinguished faculty associate emeritus, College of Agricultural & Life Sciences, University of Wisconsin-Madison.

Treat any water that you can't eliminate. Chlorine kills off mosquito larvae in pools. For ponds, buy inexpensive mosquito-eating fish, such as top-feeding minnows and gambusia.

Alternative: Mosquito Dunks, drop-in tablets that keep mosquitoes from breeding in water for at least 30 days, can be used in both pools and ponds. These are safer than chlorine because they are a naturally occurring bacteria. Check local hardware stores and plant nurseries that sell pesticides. Surround the patio or deck with citronella candles or, for a more organic approach, highly concentrated garlic. Buy one quart of dry minced garlic at a grocery or wholesale food store, and generously sprinkle wherever mosquitoes are bothersome.

Not worth the money: Electric zappers, which can cost up to $250 and typically kill few mosquitoes.

Are You a Mosquito Magnet?

Joseph Conlon, MA, technical advisor, American Mosquito Control Association, Mount Laurel, New Jersey.

Some people are highly attractive to mosquitoes—those who emit a lot of carbon dioxide (tall and/or overweight people, pregnant women and those who exercise heavily) and people whose metabolism results in excess lactic or uric acid or high amounts of cholesterol on the skin. But people with high cholesterol in their blood are not more likely to be bitten. Cholesterol on the skin results not from how much is in the blood but from how quickly it is metabolized.

To protect yourself, the Centers for Disease Control and Prevention recommends repellents that contain one of these ingredients—DEET, picaridin, IR3535 or oil of lemon eucalyptus. You can also spray a product containing permethrin on clothing, which helps keep these pests away.

Keeping Bugs Away with Household Items

Julie Edelman, aka "The Accidental Housewife," is a rich source of everyday tips to maintain your home, family, health and sanity. Based on Florida's Gulf coast, Julie appears regularly on the *Today* show, *Rachael Ray* and *The Doctors*. She is author of *The New York Times* best-seller *The Accidental Housewife: How to Overcome Housekeeping Hysteria One Task at a Time.* JuliesTips.com

---

•**Deter mealybugs with matchbooks.** You can have mealybugs in your pantry and not know it. To keep the bugs from flourishing, take flour, rice and cereal out of their original packaging right after you bring them home and place them in Tupperware-like containers. As an extra precaution, put a matchbook on top of the food before sealing. The sulfur repels mealybugs.

•**Kill fruit flies with red wine.** Fruit flies love the fermented grape! Fill a glass with one-half inch of leftover red wine. Tightly cover the top of the glass with plastic wrap. Poke small holes in the wrap so that the flies find their one-way ticket in.

•**Repel ants, roaches and fleas with citrus rinds.** Bugs hate D-limonene, which is naturally found in the oil in lemon and orange rinds. Place pieces of rind where these pests are likely to enter, such as door and window openings and ledges… cracks between kitchen cabinets…and holes in floors. Replace every few days, as needed.

•**Ward off booklice with silica packets.** Those little packets of silica you find in packaging of elec-tronics, shoes, nutritional supplements, etc., absorb moisture. Booklice live in the damp fungus and mold that thrives in books. Put silica packets behind the books and anywhere you suspect moisture. Packets also are available at Amazon.com.

•**Create flea repellent with apple cider vinegar.** After bathing your dog, spray the animal lightly with a 50/50 solution of vinegar and water. Reapply after every bath.

•**Build a roach trap with apples.** Fill the bottom of an empty, 12-ounce jar with apple peels to lure roaches in with the scent. Then coat the inner rim of the jar with double-sided tape or petroleum jelly, which will prevent the roaches from climbing back out. Place in areas of the kitchen where roaches consistently are present, such as near refrigerators and small appliances such as microwaves, blenders and toasters.

•**Catch garden slugs with old beer cans.** Leave out a beer can with enough beer to drown the slug (about one inch). You also can pour beer in a saucer. Slugs are attracted to beer's yeasty smell.

•**Deter ants with lemons.** Put lemon juice in a spray bottle, and take aim at entryways, windowsills, between kitchen cabinets and other spots where bugs enter. Lemon juice destroys the scent trails that ants follow. This also deters fleas and roaches.

•**Repel spiders with vinegar.** Fill a spray bottle with a 50/50 mix of white vinegar and water. Spray evenly on windowsills, doorjambs and other areas where spiders make their entrance. Do this weekly. Spiders are repelled by the taste of vinegar, and since they taste with their legs, the spray solution will deter them.

CHAPTER 17

Pet Care

Home Remedies and Natural Cures for Dogs and Cats

Robert L. Ridgway, DVM, a veterinarian formerly with the Orange County Animal Services in Orlando, Florida. He previously served in the US Army Veterinary Corps, where he headed the Department of Defense Military Dog Veterinary Service at Lackland Air Force Base. He is author of *How to Treat Your Dogs and Cats with Over-the-Counter Drugs*.

Visits to the veterinarian can cost pet owners a pretty penny, but there are situations when pet owners can safely avoid vet bills by treating their pets themselves or by taking action to prevent dog or cat health problems. *Among them…*

Motion Sickness

Over-the-counter (OTC) allergy medication *diphenhydramine* (Benadryl) is a safe and effective motion sickness treatment for dogs and cats that become nauseated on trips, just as it is for humans. As an added benefit, Benadryl causes drowsiness, calming pets made anxious by travel.

The challenge is getting the dosage right—most pets are significantly smaller than people, and they require lower doses. One milligram of Benadryl per pound of body weight is a reasonable rule of thumb, but start with a much smaller dose—perhaps one-quarter of a milligram per pound—when you give a pet Benadryl for the first time. Though this medication makes most pets and people drowsy, it causes the opposite reaction in a small percentage of users. Discontinue use if the animal becomes hyperactive.

Helpful: To get dogs and cats to take medications, you can put soft cheese, bread or peanut butter around a pill or add liquid medicine to canned pet food or other food that your pet enjoys.

Ear Infections

Signs of ear infections in pets include redness and swelling around the ear, loss of balance, red or yellow discharge from the ear or persistent ear scratching and head shaking. Once a pet develops an ear infection, a trip to the vet is required. But pet owners can help prevent ear infections by cleaning pets' ears when needed. Look for accumulations of black-looking material or other matter.

Lie the dog or cat on its side. Ask a family member to help hold the pet down if it is large or feisty. Fill its ear with mineral oil, massage the area, then fill the ear with warm water to rinse out the oil. Ideally this process should be repeated three times with each ear, letting the pet shake its head to clear out the liquid after each filling of mineral oil or warm water.

Do this ear cleaning in the bathroom or outside. Otherwise the mineral oil and earwax could stain furniture or carpets.

"Prickers" in the Skin

A widespread weed, known as foxtail or grass awns, has aggressive seeds (awns) that stick to pets' fur and burrow into skin, causing infections or abscesses.

273

In some cases, grass awns work their way into an animal's chest or abdominal cavity, causing serious lifelong health problems or even death. Both dogs and cats can be affected, though problems are less common with cats, which often can remove grass awns while grooming. The best solution is prevention—regularly mow lawns where pets spend time and keep pets out of tall, weedy grass.

When a pet does get into tall grass, examine the animal very carefully and remove any seedpods and stickers. A trip to the veterinarian is required once a grass awn gets into the pet's skin.

Canine Kennel Cough

If a dog exhibits a dry and hacking cough that becomes worse when temperatures drop in the evening, the cause probably is kennel cough, which typically lasts two to three weeks. Kennel cough is spread like the common cold, so any contact with an infected dog potentially can transmit the disease. There's little point to bringing a dog with kennel cough to the vet right away—as with the common cold, there is no cure.

To help relieve the cough so that you and the dog can get some sleep, try Robitussin DM, the same OTC medicine that you might use yourself. This won't cure the underlying problem, but it can at least calm the cough for a while so that the pet—and everyone else in the house—can relax and sleep through the night. One teaspoon is a reasonable dose for a large dog...one-half teaspoon for a small dog. If the cough persists, it's probably worth a trip to the vet.

Cat Hair Ball Intestinal Blockages

Cats use their tongues to groom their fur, and some fur inevitably is ingested. While most ingested fur simply passes through the cat, some of it can remain in the stomach, becoming a hair ball.

If you have reason to believe that your cat has developed an intestinal blockage—an empty litter box suggesting constipation, for example, or repeated retching without producing a hair ball—put undiluted Carnation concentrated canned milk in its dish and let it drink. Soon after, the cat will have loose stools, cleaning out the intestines. If symptoms persist, see a veterinarian.

Dogs with Red, Inflamed Lips and Nose

Plastic food and water bowls often are to blame when dogs develop these symptoms—some dogs are allergic to chemicals found in plastics. If so, switching to a stainless steel or ceramic bowl should solve the problem.

See a vet if the dog has not been eating from plastic bowls or if you make the switch and don't see any improvement within two weeks or so. Plastic bowls don't seem to cause these problems for cats.

Natural Arthritis Cures for Dogs and Cats

Jeff Feinman, VMD, CVH, a certified veterinary homeopath and integrated veterinary practitioner with a private practice in Weston, Connecticut. He is president of the nonprofit Academy of Veterinary Homeopathy Foundation. HomeVet.com

Arthritis is no more fun for pets than it is for people. The symptoms (and treatments) are similar, but there's a big difference—your pets can't tell you when they're hurting.

Dogs and cats actually try to hide their pain because animals in the wild know that weakness makes them a target. You have to be a bit of a detective to recognize the signs—a stiff walk...a favorite couch that they no longer use...a groan when they lie down.

About 20% of middle-aged dogs and cats have arthritis in at least one joint, and nearly all will be affected at some time in their lives. The good news is that arthritis often can be prevented—and pets that already have it can get relief without taking drugs. *Steps to take...*

•**Check your pet's weight.** A recent study found that 53% of dogs are overweight or obese. Among cats, the percentage is even higher.

Why it matters: Those extra pounds accelerate degenerative joint disease, the breakdown of cartilage that surrounds the joints. Cartilage damage triggers the release of inflammatory chemicals that cause pain and stiffness.

You don't need a scale to know if your pet is overweight. You have to look and feel. When you look down at your dog or cat, you should see a pronounced waist behind the rib cage. Viewed from the side, the abdomen should be tucked up and not hanging down. You should be able to feel the ribs under a thin layer of fat.

If your pet is overweight, there won't be much of a waist…you'll barely feel the ribs…and the abdomen will be rounded rather than tucked.

Because dogs and cats come in different sizes, you can't count on the portion guides that are listed on food labels.

In general: If your pet is overweight, start by reducing food amounts by about one-fifth. Keep at that amount for a few weeks. If your pet still seems heavy, reduce the portions again.

•**More exercise.** Along with weight loss, exercise is the most effective way to prevent and treat arthritis. Regular exercise increases synovial fluid, the natural lubricant that allows joints to glide rather than grind. Exercise also reduces pressure by strengthening the muscles that surround the joints.

It's usually easy to get dogs to exercise—just snap on a leash and take a walk. Cats need more encouragement—or at least something that engages their interest such as a ball or a moving piece of string. Walk/play with your pet for at least 10 to 15 minutes a few times a day.

Better Than Drugs

The standard arthritis treatments for dogs and cats include nonsteroidal anti-inflammatory drugs prescribed by veterinarians. I recommend drugs only as a last resort. You usually can treat arthritis with natural—and safer—remedies. *Best choices…*

•**Homeopathy.** This is a system of medicine that uses extremely small doses of natural substances to alter the body's energy. I have found it to be quite effective in my practice. It's my first treatment choice because it causes no side effects and can help reduce cartilage damage and inflammation.

Homeopathy is complicated because there are hundreds of potential remedies and doses and be-cause the treatments vary widely from one pet to the next. You can give the remedies at home, but only after they've been chosen by a veterinary homeopath.

Examples: If your pet limps when it first gets up, but the stiffness improves with movement, your veterinarian might recommend Rhus toxicodendron. Arthritis that gets worse in cold/damp weather might respond better to Calcarea carbonica.

To find a veterinary homeopath, go to TheAVH.org/referrals.

•**Physical therapy.** Moving the limbs in certain ways can markedly reduce pain and improve your pet's ability to stand, walk and run. When your pet is lying on its side, for example, you can gently grip the knee and move the leg through its full range of motion. Your veterinarian can recommend exercises for different joints. You might be advised to work with a veterinary physical therapist who might use specialized equipment (such as underwater treadmills) to get your pet moving.

•**Gelatin.** Over-the-counter joint supplements such as glucosamine and chondroitin are effective but expensive. I usually recommend an unflavored gelatin such as Knox, available in any grocery store. Gelatin contains collagen, one of the materials used by the body to manufacture cartilage and bone. Studies have shown that it improves flexibility and can relieve joint pain. Add about one teaspoon of the gelatin powder to your pet's food every day.

•**Bone broth.** This soup has the same bone-building effects as gelatin, and pets love the taste. You can make it yourself by slow-simmering chicken, pork or beef bones until they're soft and fall apart. (It might take up to two days—using a slow cooker is best, as it can stay on safely for that length of time.) Strain the broth carefully so that no bone bits remain. Store the broth in the refrigerator, and give your pet a little taste with each meal.

•**Acupuncture.** Stimulating acupuncture points can increase circulation and boost painkilling chemicals in the body. Use the Internet to find a certified veterinary acupuncturist in your area. A session typically costs between $30 and $50. Your pet may improve after a single session, but you'll probably be advised to schedule two sessions a week for a few weeks, followed by occasional maintenance sessions.

●**Orthopedic beds.** Who doesn't like a cozy bed? Large dogs in particular do better when they sleep on a firm mattress. You can buy orthopedic pet beds in pet stores and online that make it easier to stand up...have memory foam for extra support... and are heated to keep joints limber.

Also: Elevated food and water bowls, which are available at pet stores and online, can help pets with neck or back problems.

How to Stop the #1 Killer of Dogs and Cats

Shawn Messonnier, DVM, a veterinarian and owner of Paws & Claws Animal Hospital in Plano, Texas. He hosted the award-winning radio program "Dr. Shawn: The Natural Vet" and is author of *The Natural Vet's Guide to Preventing and Treating Cancer in Dogs* and *The Natural Health Bible for Dogs & Cats.*

Dogs and cats are more likely to die from cancer than any other single cause. Between 25% and 50% of all elderly pets will develop tumors, either benign or malignant, at some time in their lives. Nearly half of elderly dogs and about one-third of elderly cats will die of cancer.

With conventional treatments, such as surgery and chemotherapy, most pets with cancer survive six to 12 months after diagnosis. When integrative therapies—including supplements and herbal therapies—are included in the treatment plan, the survival time can double.

Best: Pet-care strategies that significantly reduce the risk of the animal ever getting cancer. We know that chronic inflammation causes many cancers in humans. It appears that chronic inflammation is the cause of most cancers in dogs and cats, too. A diet rich in antioxidants, as well as weight control and other measures, can create an internal environment that's inhospitable to cancer development and growth.

Pure-Bred Cancer

All pets are susceptible to cancer, but pure-bred dogs have the highest risk. For example, pugs are especially vulnerable to brain tumors as are boxers and Boston terriers. Dogs with long muzzles, such as German shepherds, tend to get nasal or sinus cancers. Labrador and golden retrievers are more likely than other breeds to get lymphoma.

Mixed-breed dogs and cats (most cats in the US are mixed) benefit from hybrid vigor, a mixing of genetic material that lowers the risk for cancer.

How to prevent cancer in pure and mixed breeds...

Sun Protection

In spite of their fur, skin cancer is common in dogs and cats, particularly those with lighter skin or sparse fur. The main danger is squamous cell carcinoma, a cancer that usually appears as a raw area or a sore that doesn't heal. Pets also can get melanomas, which appear as black tumors—or even small black dots—on the skin. In pets, melanomas can be benign or malignant. Melanomas usually are benign in miniature schnauzers and Doberman pinschers. They're more likely to be malignant in miniature poodles.

Apply sunscreen if your pet spends a lot of time outside. Use a sunscreen made for pets with an SPF of at least 15. Apply it to the nose, tips of the ears, around the eyes and on top of the muzzle.

Protect pets from the sun, particularly in the afternoon when the sun is most intense. Some people keep their pets inside during these hours. For outdoor pets, provide shade with a doghouse, umbrella, lean-to, etc.

Healthy Weight

Obesity is just as dangerous for pets as it as for people. Fat releases inflammatory substances that can damage DNA and lead to various types of cancer. Body fat also produces a dangerous form of estrogen that can increase the risk for uterine and ovarian cancers.

What to look for: Dogs and cats at a healthy weight have a slight narrowing at the waist.

Look at your pet head-on: If the body contour appears totally straight, he/she is probably overweight. Press lightly on the skin—you should be able to feel the backbone and ribs.

Restrict calories. If your dog is overweight, reduce food servings by about one-third. Do this for a few weeks. If the dog doesn't lose any weight, reduce the food by another one-third.

Cats are trickier because losing weight too fast can cause hepatic lipidosis, a serious liver disease. In general, you can safely reduce calories by about 20%. If your cat hasn't lost weight within a few weeks, talk with your veterinarian about other weight-loss strategies, such as switching foods or changing the nutrient balance.

Spaying/Neutering

This is among the most effective cancer-prevention strategies. In females, early spaying will prevent nearly 100% of breast tumors. In males, neutering prevents cancers around the anal area, known as perianal tumors.

When to spay: Females should be spayed before they have their first estrus (heat) cycle. This usually occurs between six and 12 months of age, depending on the breed. Smaller dogs and cats can have their first cycle earlier, often at four or five months of age. But it's never too late to spay a pet.

When to neuter: Timing isn't as critical with males. I advise having it done after puberty, at six to 12 months of age. Neutering limits their exposure to testosterone. This not only helps reduce cancer risk but also can prevent unwanted male behaviors, such as territorial marking and aggression.

Anticancer Diet

There's no scientific evidence that commercial pet foods increase the risk for cancer or that special diets such as Biologically Appropriate Raw Food (BARF) will help prevent it. What is known is that some of the ingredients in commercial foods are less than ideal.

●**Read the label.** I recommend avoiding foods that contain synthetic preservatives, such as *butylated hydroxyanisole* (BHA), *butylated hydroxytoluene* (BHT) or *ethoxyquin*. The word "by-product" also should raise a red flag because it refers to proteins that might not be healthy or readily digestible.

●**Look for antioxidants.** Many pet foods now contain antioxidants, such as vitamin C or tocopherols (vitamin E). These compounds reduce inflammation in the body and can help prevent cell damage that can lead to cancer.

Helpful Supplements

Dogs and cats given certain supplements, particularly those with antioxidants, have stronger immunity, lower levels of inflammatory substances and healthier DNA. I use these supplements routinely in treating pets with cancer because they can enhance the effectiveness and reduce the complications of conventional cancer therapies. Nutritional supplements also can be given to healthy pets to prevent cancers.

The optimal doses of supplements are different for dogs and cats, as well as for pets of various sizes and breeds. Talk to your vet before giving any supplement to your pet.

Some of the best supplements...

●**Fish oil.** It's a potent anti-inflammatory that also improves immunity and inhibits tumor growth. In pets that already have cancer, it may inhibit the formation of new blood vessels that allow tumors to grow and spread.

A study on dogs with lymphoma found that a diet high in omega-3 fatty acids—the main constituents of fish oil—increased survival time, compared with dogs that were treated only with chemotherapy.

●**Vitamins E and C.** Vitamin E promotes apoptosis, the death of cancer cells. It also detoxifies the dangerous free radicals that are produced by chemotherapy.

Because vitamin E is a fat-soluble nutrient that's mainly active in the fatty membranes that surround cells, I advise combining it with vitamin C, which works in the watery component inside and between cells.

●**Probiotics.** These living, beneficial bacteria may reduce carcinogenic bacteria in the intestine, block the adhesion of harmful bacteria to the intestinal wall and possibly prevent intestinal bacteria from converting toxins into carcinogens.

Natural Flea Control for Dogs and Cats

Shawn Messonnier, DVM, veterinarian and owner of Paws & Claws Animal Hospital in Plano, Texas. He hosted the award-winning radio program Dr. Shawn Messonnier, The Natural Vet and is author of *The Natural Health Bible for Dogs & Cats: Your A-Z Guide to Over 200 Conditions, Herbs, Vitamins, and Supplements.*

Chemical flea collars, sprays, topical products and dips can be effective, but the toxic compounds used in these products can linger in your dog's or cat's body and can potentially cause respiratory problems, nausea and other side effects, including convulsions.

Natural forms of flea control can be just as effective with no risk of poisoning. *What to do…*

•**Treat the house before you treat your pet.** Fleas don't spend all their time on your pet. They also are present in the yard, in damp corners, on carpets or under couch cushions. It doesn't help to treat your pet unless you treat the environment as well.

If your home has fleas, steam-clean carpets and upholstery. Then, every day, vacuum and/or mop the areas where your pet spends time. This will eliminate most fleas and their eggs. Also, wash your pet's bedding and clothing in hot water daily.

•**Dust with diatomaceous earth.** This chalk-like form of fossilized algaelike plants kills fleas by penetrating their waxy coating. It is available at pet and garden stores and on the Internet. Follow the directions on the label. Sprinkle it outside on areas where your pet spends time, such as a favorite spot in the garden. In the house, you can sprinkle it in corners or on carpets and area rugs (and later vacuum it up).

•**Treat the yard with nematodes.** If your pet spends time outside, you'll need to treat the entire yard with nematodes in addition to a sprinkling of diatomaceous earth. Nematodes are microscopic worms that feed on fleas in their preadult and larval stages. Nematodes typically come on a small sponge, which contains a million or more microorganisms. They're applied with a lawn sprayer and available at most garden stores. Follow the directions on the label.

•**Give your pet a citrus bath.** Shampoos and sprays that contain the citrus oils D-limonene and linalool kill adult fleas as well as their eggs. They're available at pet-supply stores and on the Internet.

Important: Products that are safe for dogs can be dangerous or even fatal to cats. If you have a cat, read labels carefully to make sure that the product is cat-safe.

You can make your own citrus rinse by putting lemon slices in hot water and letting them steep overnight. Remove the lemon slices from the water, then sponge the liquid on your dog's or cat's skin. It will give your pet a pleasant citrus scent that will help repel fleas.

•**Avoid pyrethrin.** This type of natural pesticide is derived from chrysanthemums. Veterinarians used to recommend it because it is safer than synthetic pesticides. It is safer but not as safe as natural oils.

Safe Ways to Travel with Your Pet

Erin Ballinger, travel expert at BringFido.com, which provides pet-policy information for travel-related businesses. It has a toll-free phone number (877-411-FIDO) that pet owners can use to find pet-friendly businesses.

United Airlines temporarily suspended its pet-travel program in March 2018 following a series of troubling incidents that included the death of a dog stowed in an overhead bin. That incident called attention not only to United's missteps but to a growing travel trend—taking the family pet along on journeys. Despite United's problems, traveling with a pet can be safe, and it can be a money saver, too, when the cost of the pet's travel is less than the cost of a kennel. But traveling with your pet is worth considering only if you plan carefully and make smart travel choices. *Here's what you need to know to successfully and safely travel with your pet…*

Pets on Planes

Whether your pet can travel with you in the cabin of an airplane or must be checked into the cargo compartment depends on the airline's rules and the animal's size. Typically, the pet must fit comfortably into a pet carrier that can fit under the seat in front of you for it to be able to travel in the cabin. Most airlines impose weight limits, too (usually 20 pounds).

For details about a specific airline's pet policies, call the airline or search for "pets" on its website.

Expect added fees whether your pet travels in the cabin or as cargo. These vary by airline but usually are $75 to $125 per direction traveled by the pet for cabin travel…or $100 to $200 per direction in the cargo hold.

Traveling in the cabin tends to be safer for pets than traveling in the cargo hold despite United's overhead-bin fiasco. In the cabin, there's no risk that the airline will misroute your pet…and the cabin and terminal are almost always climate-controlled. The cargo area often is not climate-controlled until the plane is in the air, so pets headed for cargo might wait in the heat or cold of the tarmac before loading.

But even the cargo hold is not tremendously dangerous—on most airlines. In 2017, US-based airlines transported animals more than half a million times, and the total number of deaths, lost animals and reported injuries came to just 40. But dig a little deeper into the animal air-travel data and you'll discover that pets faced more than twice the usual danger on one airline—United. (Delta has a poor record, too, but it has largely discontinued its pet-transport program.)

Better: When possible, fly on Alaska Airlines or American Airlines if your pet will be traveling as cargo. These two airlines have done a significantly better-than-average job keeping animal passengers safe.

Six pet air-travel details worth knowing about…

• **Airlines that generally do not accept pets as cargo include Delta, Frontier, JetBlue, Southwest and Spirit.** Pets small enough to travel in the cabin usually can travel on these airlines, however.

Also: Pets might not be permitted to travel in the cargo areas of other airlines, either, if the flight is longer than 12 hours or is to or from a location that is expected to have very hot or very cold temperatures.

• **Airlines generally require a "health certificate" signed by a veterinarian.** This form confirms that the pet's vaccines are up to date and that it is healthy. The vet might have to sign this certificate no more than 10 days before departure date.

• **If your pet travels in the cabin, it is likely to count as your carry-on item.** You will need an FAA-approved pet carrier that does not exceed the airline's (or the flight's) size limits.

Recommended: The Snoozer Roll Around Travel Dog Carrier Backpack 4-in-1 ($119.95 to $129.95 depending on size, SnoozerPetProducts.com) has wheels so you can tow your pet through the airport, and it can convert into a backpack, dog bed and car seat.

• **Pets need reservations.** Airlines restrict the number of pets they accept per flight both in the cabin and in cargo. If you arrive at the airport with a pet that does not have a reservation and the flight's animal quota is full, you might have to take your pet back home—and potentially miss your flight.

• **Airlines do not necessarily transport pets of every species, breed or age.** Many accept only dogs and cats…and most will not accept snub-nosed dogs or cats in the cargo hold because of increased risk for potentially fatal respiratory problems. Animals that are younger than eight to 12 weeks might not be accepted either.

• **Do not give your pet antinausea or antianxiety medication before a flight unless your vet recommends doing so.** Some pets have adverse reactions to these medicines.

Pets in Trains and Rental Cars

Dogs and cats weighing up to 20 pounds now can travel on most Amtrak routes. The fee is $26, a bargain compared with the airlines. The pet must remain in a pet carrier no larger than 19" x 14" x 10.5" while onboard. (For details online, go to Amtrak.com/onboard/carry-on-pets.html.)

Most car-rental companies allow pets to ride in their cars with no official added pet fee. But these companies are notorious for tacking on steep cleaning fees when they find pet hair on car seats after cars are returned—potentially $100 or more.

Helpful: Pack an old sheet and put this over the backseat of the rental car if your pet will be traveling outside its carrier. Carefully inspect the car for hair and other pet-related issues before returning the vehicle.

Pets in Hotels

Four hotel chains that are particularly pet-friendly...

•**La Quinta Inns & Suites** allows guests to bring up to two dogs and/or cats with no additional fees or deposits at most of its 900-plus locations. (See LQ.com/en/landing/pet-policy for details.)

•**Red Roof Inn** allows guests to bring one pet weighing up to 80 pounds at most of its 670-plus locations. Not only are there no additional pet fees or deposits, guests also can get 10% off if they bring a pet and book directly through Red Roof Inn's website. Pets cannot be left unattended in rooms, however. (See RedRoof.com/guestfaq.)

•**Aloft Hotels,** part of the Starwood chain, not only allows dogs that are up to 40 pounds in size at most of its 210 locations with no fees or deposits, it also offers amenities such as dog beds and bowls at no charge. (Contact the specific Aloft property where you wish to stay to confirm that the location is dog-friendly...and/or to request permission to bring a dog larger than 40 pounds or a different species of pet.)

•**Kimpton Hotels** allows guests to bring any pet with no additional charges or deposits at most of its 60-plus locations. There are no official limits regarding pet species, quantity or size...except that the pet must fit through the hotel's doors. Pet beds, bowls and mats are available at no cost, and pets are welcome at Kimpton's nightly wine receptions.

Helpful: Rover.com can help you locate a doggie day care facility in the area you are visiting if your pet won't be joining you for all your vacation activities.

Taking a Pet to a Foreign Country

Traveling abroad with an animal adds to the complications—you'll have to navigate the foreign country's animal-entry rules in addition to airline and hotel rules. These rules are becoming less oner-

ous in most places—quarantines are no longer common—but expect plenty of paperwork, fees and other hassles. Don't leave this to the last minute because it can take weeks to sort it all out. *Five international animal travel tips worth knowing...*

•**Consult the US Department of Agriculture's website** to learn the rules for bringing a pet to a particular foreign country...and for bringing your pet back to the US (www.APHIS.USDA.gov/aphis/pet-travel).

Example: A dog might need to be inspected for screwworm by a vet before you can return to the US from a country where that parasite is a problem. Affected countries are mainly in South and Central America, Asia and Africa. BringFido.com offers country-by-country guidance as well (BringFido.com/travel/international).

Vaccinations often must be administered well in advance of travel.

Example: Some countries will not allow an animal to enter unless it received its rabies vaccination at least 21 or 30 days prior to entry, depending on the country.

•**The European Union has a consolidated "EU pet passport"** system that allows animals to enter and travel through the region with relative ease. But there's a catch—these passports are issued only in the EU. If your pet doesn't yet have one, it will need an "EU Health Certificate" to enter the region. To obtain this, the animal will have to be examined by a "USDA-accredited" veterinarian, typically no more than 10 days prior to the trip. The certificate this vet issues then must be endorsed by a Department of Agriculture office. (Visit www.APHIS.USDA.gov/aphis/pet-travel and click "USDA Endorsement Offices" for help finding a vet who can do this in your area.) The fees for the exam, certificate and endorsement can easily top $200. (If you expect to bring your pet to the EU multiple times, it is worth obtaining a passport for it to make future trips simpler.)

•**Taking a pet from the US to Canada is comparatively straightforward.** You generally need only a certificate signed by a vet confirming that the animal has been vaccinated against rabies within the past three years. (Visit the US Department of Agriculture website for details.)

There's a chance that your pet might be denied entry despite your best efforts. Occasionally, travelers spend weeks getting a pet all the paperwork and shots it needs…only to be told by a customs official at an airport in the foreign country that they've made some mistake. This can put travelers in a bind—they might have to leave their pet in quarantine, paying steep fees for the privilege…or get right back on a flight out of the country with their pet.

Bottom line: Follow the pet rules of the countries you visit to the letter.

Make Car Rides Pleasant for Pets

Michael W. Fox, DSc, PhD, BVet Med, a veterinarian based in the Minneapolis area and former vice president of The Humane Society of the United States. He writes the syndicated newspaper column "The Animal Doctor" and is author of several books about animals including *Dog Body, Dog Mind* and *Cat Body, Cat Mind.* DrFoxVet.net

Do you dread car rides with your pet? Does the animal pant or get physically ill in the car? Some dogs and cats suffer from anxiety or motion sickness in cars. *To make car rides more enjoyable…*

Overcoming Anxiety

•**Desensitize your pet to your car.** Play with the pet inside the vehicle with the engine turned off. Provide treats. Do this several times until the pet seems calm, then repeat the process with the engine on but the car stationary. Then take the pet on short drives, providing treats along the way, before attempting longer trips.

•**Try lavender oil.** Lavender has long been known to have a calming effect on humans. Studies have shown that it has a similar effect on nervous dogs. Anecdotal evidence suggests that it works for cats, too. Mix 10 drops of lavender oil into one ounce of water in a spray bottle, then spray the inside of your vehicle approximately one hour before taking the pet on a ride. Bring this spray bottle along on long drives, and give an additional spritz in the air if the animal shows signs of anxiety, such as excessive movement or barking. Or you could put drops of lavender oil on cloth strips and hang these in the car…or put a few drops on a bandanna, then tie this around the pet's neck.

Warning: Don't spray lavender oil onto a cat's fur. Licking up lavender oil can cause stomach discomfort for cats. This does not seem to be an issue for dogs.

•**Buy a pet harness or transport crate, and use this to secure the animal in the car.** Some cats and dogs do not like crates and harnesses at first, but these items generally do help pets feel more secure once they get used to them. (Crates and harnesses significantly decrease the odds that the pet will be injured in a car accident, too.) And a pet in a harness or crate cannot run around the vehicle making you anxious as you drive—your pet can sense your anxiety, and it will make the pet more anxious. Avoiding sudden starts and stops and listening to soothing music can help both driver and pet stay calm in the car.

If all else fails, ask your vet if he/she can prescribe an anxiety medication such as Xanax or Valium for your pet before long trips.

Combating Motion Sickness

Place a small amount of ginger—crystalline ginger or fresh chopped gingerroot—into a small ball of a food the dog loves, such as cream cheese or peanut butter, and feed it to the pet around 30 minutes prior to a car trip. A fingertip-size piece of ginger is sufficient for a 30-pound dog. For cats, you can try shredding a tiny bit of ginger into food, but cats are notoriously finicky.

If the ginger does not do the trick, give your pet Dramamine 30 to 60 minutes before car trips. The typical dosage is 12.5 milligrams for a cat…or two to four milligrams per pound for a dog.

Road Trip with Your Pet

Jeff Feinman, VMD, CVH, a certified veterinary homeopath in Weston, Connecticut, HomeVet.com.

Think about how you'll travel with your pet in your vehicle before you depart, planning ahead for safety and convenience. *Ideas…*

• **Keep the pet on a harness attached to the seat belt or in a carrying case.** An animal that jumps around can be a distraction and could also be hurt in an accident or if you have to stop suddenly.

• **Feed animals three or four hours before departing** so that they won't start agitating for food too soon into the trip.

• **Bring plenty of water.** The excitement and stress of a trip can make your pet thirsty.

• **Bring along a litter box for a cat.**

• **Never leave your pet in the car unattended**—you may be away from the vehicle longer than you expect or your pet could even be stolen. It's also dangerous to leave any animal in a poorly ventilated vehicle.

Don't Forget Your Pets…

Your Dog. TuftsYourDog.com

Take steps now to ensure your pet is taken care of if you are in an accident: Choose a caregiver—someone your dog or cat is familiar with who can get into your house and knows how to take care of the animal. Keep the caregiver's contact information in your wallet so that you can give it to emergency personnel if you are involved in an accident. Draft instructions for the caregiver. Provide information that includes your pet's feeding and walking schedule, your vet's phone number and the location of the animal's medical records, food, leash and other items. Approve treatment in advance. Sign a statement for your vet that allows him/her to treat your pet if needed. Post a rescue alert sticker on your window—this tells firefighters and other emergency personnel that a dog or cat is in the house.

Best Way to Bring Home a Second Pet

Roundup of experts in pet care, reported in *Health*.

Introduce two dogs in neutral territory, such as a park—with both dogs on leashes—so that the first dog does not see the second as an intruder and competitor. Bring a new cat home in a carrier, and keep it for a few days in its own room with its own food and litter box. Spend extra time with your older pet when the new one arrives—use play and affection, not treats, which can make pets gain weight. Walk dogs one at a time, or ask a friend to come with you on walks so that each dog has its own human walking companion. If you have two dogs, feed them in different places in the house or across the room from each other until they adjust fully. If you have a cat and a dog, separate meals carefully—it is best to feed cats in areas dogs cannot reach, since cat food is too high in protein for dogs.

Dental Disease in Dogs Is on the Rise—And It Can Kill Your Pet

Jean Joo, DVM, dental and oral surgeon at Sage Veterinary Centers, Redwood City, California. She was previously at Tufts Veterinary Emergency Treatment and Specialties clinic in Walpole, Massachusetts, and an assistant clinical professor in the department of clinical sciences at Tufts University Cummings School of Veterinary Medicine, West Grafton, Massachusetts.

Dental disease is the most common disease in dogs. It affects 59 out of every 100 dogs seen by vets, according to researchers at Banfield Pet Hospital in Portland, Oregon. And it's on the rise—since 2006, it has increased by more than 12%. The reason for the increase isn't known.

Dogs with dental disease may have difficulty chewing. They can lose their teeth. But the biggest danger is that they face a higher risk for other diseases because the bacteria that are responsible for dental disease can enter the bloodstream and infect the heart, kidneys and/or other organs.

Here's how to protect your dog from dental disease...

It Starts in the Gums

The most common form of dental disease in dogs is periodontal disease. Periodontal disease in dogs is similar to periodontal disease in humans. It is an ongoing inflammation of the gums that can cause bleeding and tenderness.

Dogs with gingivitis—the earliest stage of periodontal disease—usually will have tooth discoloration near the gums. The gums will be red and swollen. Without treatment, gingivitis can progress to periodontitis, a more severe form of inflammation that can damage the underlying bone and lead to tooth loss, as well as more dangerous conditions.

Example: A Perdue University study, published in *Journal of the American Veterinary Medical Association*, found that dogs with periodontal disease had a higher risk for congestive heart failure, as well as endocarditis, an inflammation of the heart valves.

Which Dogs are Most at Risk?

Any dog can develop dental disease. Some breeds are more prone to it, however. The breeds most likely to develop dental problems are toy poodles, Yorkshire terriers, Maltese, Pomeranians and Shetland sheepdogs. These breeds tend to have more severe problems because they have large teeth relative to the size of the jaw. This causes tooth-crowding that traps food and hair, along with plaque, the sticky substance that leads to gum disease.

Also at increased risk: Bulldogs, pugs, boxers and other brachycephalic breeds with "pushed-in" faces. Because of the shape and size of their jaws, the teeth are crowded.

Danger Signs

If your dog has a few discolored teeth, it may indicate dental disease. If all the teeth are uniformly discolored, it's probably just normal staining. If just one or a few teeth are discolored, your dog needs to get checked.

In addition, any change in your dog's breath—particularly if it is accompanied by gum redness or apparent mouth discomfort—should be checked by a veterinarian. Veterinarians routinely do mouth-and-gum examinations when you bring your dog in for a checkup. You should take your dog to the veterinarian at least once a year, although dogs that already have dental disease may need to be checked every six months.

Doggie Dental Care

Important steps to protect your dog...

• **Brush your dog's teeth at least every other day.** Daily brushing is ideal. Dogs need to have their teeth brushed for the same reasons that people do—it removes bacteria-laden plaque before it has a chance to harden and turn into tartar.

• **Use a toothbrush your dog likes.** There are toothbrushes made for dogs, including finger brushes, which go on the end of your index finger. But a child's toothbrush can work...and some dogs will accept electric toothbrushes.

• **Never use human toothpastes for your pet.** These contain ingredients such as xylitol that are not safe for dogs. Pet stores sell a variety of toothpastes in dog-friendly flavors, such as liver or poultry.

• **Feed dogs dry food.** Wet foods leave a sticky coating on the teeth that makes it easier for plaque to accumulate. Dry foods don't leave as much of this film. Also, the crunching that's required to eat dry food can help clean the teeth.

• **Some foods promote dental cleaning.** These include Hill's Prescription Diet t/d and Purina's DH Dental Health foods. They have larger-sized kibbles that help clean the teeth.

Also helpful: Dry dog foods from Iams/Eukanuba. They're coated with substances that prevent minerals in saliva from accumulating and hardening on the teeth.

• **Provide tooth-friendly toys.** A variety of chew toys are promoted for dental benefits. There's no real evidence that these work better than other chews, but they might help.

I like sturdy rubber toys because they have a little "give"—dogs can chew them without the risk of breaking a tooth. A company called Kong makes good ones. Special rawhides, such as Tartar Shield Soft Rawhide Chews, also are a good choice for many dogs.

Important: Look for the foods and treats that have been awarded the Veterinary Oral Health Council (VOHC) seal. It's displayed on products that have been proved to help control plaque and tartar.

•**Spike their water.** You can add liquid products to your dog's water that reduce the concentration of oral bacteria and inhibit the formation of plaque. Products such as Dog Essential HealthyMouth, made by HealthyMouth, can reduce plaque by more than two-thirds.

Professional Cleaning

If you have a dog that has never or rarely had its teeth cleaned, you may want to schedule a professional cleaning. This is particularly important if tarter is already present, since it can't be removed by brushing alone.

What's involved: The procedure is done under general anesthesia. The teeth are "scaled," or scraped, to remove tartar. The veterinarian also will clean under the gums where infections and periodontal disease originate.

Cost: Generally between $100 and $500.

Reduce the Cost of Pet Care

MoneyTalksNews.com

Here are some smart ways to lower the cost of pet care...

•**Check animal-welfare groups,** shelters and rescue organizations for low-cost vaccinations and spay/neuter services. A clinic may charge just $50, versus at least $200 to $300 at a vet.

•**Look into veterinary schools**—procedures are done by students but supervised by a vet. Shop around—veterinarians' prices vary.

•**Ask your vet for a discount** or at least a payment plan if your pet needs expensive treatment and you are a steady client.

•**If you still cannot afford the cost,** visit the website of the Humane Society of the United States (HumaneSociety.org), and search for organizations that may help with some veterinary costs.

•**For prescriptions,** try warehouse-store pharmacies—Costco and Sam's Club…or websites such as PetCareRx or Drs. Foster and Smith.

Safely Carry a Dog or Cat

Joseph H. Kinnarney, DVM, past president of the American Veterinary Medical Association. He is a practicing vet at the Reidsville Veterinary Hospital in Reidsville, North Carolina. ReidsvilleVet.com

Pet owners often lift their dogs and cats in ways that are uncomfortable or unsafe—for the pet and/or the owner. *What to do instead…*

•**Lifting and carrying a small dog.** Kneel or stoop facing one side of the dog. Reach over the dog with the arm that is toward the dog's back end, and then arrange that hand and forearm so that they are parallel to the dog's body, on the opposite side of the dog from your body. Position that hand under the dog's chest between its front legs. The rear legs of the dog should still be between your arm and your body. While holding the dog's chest, gently move your elbow toward your body, scooping up and supporting the dog's rear legs on your arm. Position your other hand along the side of the dog that's away from your body to prevent it from falling or scrambling away and/or to provide additional support to the animal's front end if necessary. If you ever played football, picture how your coach taught you to carry the ball.

Important: Periodically confirm that the dog's rear legs still are supported by your arm, not dangling, which is bad for the dog's spine. (It's fine if the front legs dangle.)

•**Lifting and carrying a larger dog.** If your dog is too big to be comfortably supported on one forearm, instead position the dog on a dog bed, blanket or stretcher and have several people carry this. (Or put the dog in a wagon that you can pull.)

When you have no choice but to lift a large dog by yourself, kneel facing one side of the dog. Wrap one arm behind the dog's rear legs, and place that hand against the far side of the dog. Wrap your other arm around the dog's chest—right in front of the top of its front legs, not up by the throat. Scoop in and up so that the arm around the front end of the dog supports the chest as much as possible without forcing the front legs backward and the arm around the back end supports both the upper rear legs and hips. Some people instead lift the rear end of a large dog by placing one arm under the abdomen, in front of the rear legs. That's acceptable for quick lifts, but it's not preferred for extended carrying—it leaves the rear legs dangling, which places stress on the dog's spine.

•**Lifting and carrying a cat.** The small-dog directions are appropriate for cats as well. But when carrying a cat that's prone to scratching, also secure one of its front legs between the thumb and forefinger of your carrying hand and the other front leg between the forefinger and middle finger of your other hand so that the cat can't scratch you.

5 Steps for Adorable Pet Photos

Jeff Wignall, a photographer and writer who has written more than 20 books about photography. He is a contributing editor with Pro Photo Daily and Motion Arts Pro Daily and a former "Camera" columnist for *The New York Times*. JeffWignall.com

What do you give the person who has everything? How about an adorable photo of his/her pet? *Here's how to take winning shots that make great gifts…*

•**Use the camera you're most comfortable with,** even a cell-phone camera, because you'll be able to concentrate on your subjects and not worry about learning camera settings. But a camera with a lens that has a large zoom range (12x or greater) will let you grab great shots from more positions, including from a distance. My favorite lens for photographing my two cats is a 70-300mm telephoto zoom because it lets me shoot close-ups from across the room. That said, the "stretched out" look created by a very wide-angle lens (equivalent to 24mm or wider on a traditional 35mm camera) is a fun way to exaggerate your kitty's morning stretch or your pooch's gaping yawn.

•**Use familiar places and routines.** With dogs especially, the more familiar the locale, the less distracted they'll be. If you're going to shoot around the house, keep the camera with you rather than breaking the spell of quiet moments by getting up to find it.

•**Try playful action shots.** If your pet is in a lively mood, bring out a favorite toy and try to capture action shots. Put your camera in the shutter-priority exposure mode (in this mode, the camera lets you set the shutter speed that you want and will automatically choose the corresponding aperture setting) and choose the highest shutter speed available for the existing light (1/250 second or faster is good) to freeze motion. For the best chance of grabbing a winning shot, use your camera's "burst" mode for firing multiple shots in rapid succession.

•**For formal portraits, get their attention.** For posed portraits, pets look best when they are engaged with you and have their eyes wide-open. Dogs respond well to a favorite squeaky toy and cats to a dangling string, and you can get them to look into the camera or over your shoulder by holding the object up where you want them to look. You may need an assistant to help with this. Pooch Selfie (PoochSelfie.com, $9.99) is a neat little accessory that lets you attach a squeaky tennis ball to your cell phone to get your dog's attention—just squeak the ball and shoot.

•**Shoot at your pet's eye level.** For more natural poses, kneel or lay down and shoot at eye level or slightly up at your pet rather than aiming the camera down. You also can try placing your camera on a tripod (low down) and firing it with a remote shutter release (or have a helper press the shutter button) so that you can primp the pose and then lean out of the frame and shoot.

Reduce Your Dog's Fear of the Vacuum Cleaner

Pat Miller, dog trainer and behavior consultant, writing in *Your Dog*. TuftsYourDog.com

Put a nonrunning vacuum at a distance where the dog can see the vacuum and not be fearful. Give your pet a treat. Bring the vacuum nearer and nearer over time, giving a treat each time, until the dog is happy being right next to the machine. Then return the vacuum to the first distance and push it back and forth—without turning it on—again giving a treat when the dog shows no fear. Bring the vacuum closer and closer, moving it back and forth each time, until the dog is comfortable having it moving nearby. Then return the vacuum to the first distance and have someone else turn it on briefly. Give the dog a treat as soon as it comes on, then turn it off and stop the treats. Gradually increase the time the vacuum is on. Slowly move the dog and the vacuum closer together until the dog is comfortable being near the vacuum while it is running.

No More "Bad Dog": How to Break Your Pet's Bad Habits

Victoria Schade, author of *Bonding with Your Dog: A Trainer's Secrets for Building a Better Relationship* and *Secrets of a Dog Trainer: Positive Problem Solving for a Well-Behaved Dog*. Based in Bucks County, Pennsylvania, she was the featured trainer on the Animal Planet TV show *Faithful Friends*. VictoriaSchade.com

Does your dog ignore you when you call its name? Does it jump on you when you walk in the door? Does it pull at its leash when you go for a walk?

Before you blame your dog, consider that the way you train and interact with your dog could be at the heart of the problem. Many widely used, seemingly sensible dog-training strategies are not very effective—some actually are counterproductive.

Here, nine dog-training mistakes...

MISTAKE: **Calling your dog to you by yelling its name.** Dog owners say their dogs' names so of-ten and for so many different reasons that dogs can become uncertain what to do when they hear their names. Some dogs start ignoring their names entirely.

Better: Select a word like "Here" or "Come" that you will call to your dog only when you want it to return to you. Call out this word in a friendly tone, not a stern command as many dog owners do. A stern voice could make your dog think you're angry, discouraging it from rushing to your side. Reward the dog with a treat when it responds properly to your recall word. (You can phase out these treats once your dog responds reliably, but don't do so too quickly. Coming when called takes time to cement.)

Do not use this recall word only to call your dog for things that it doesn't like, such as going back inside when playtime ends. Your dog is much more likely to come when called if it often receives something nice when it does, such as praise or food.

MISTAKE: **Pulling back when your dog pulls at its leash...or letting yourself get pulled along.** This teaches the dog that straining at a taut leash is normal and acceptable.

Better: When you walk your dog, carry dog treats and a "clicker"—a small device available in pet stores that makes a clicking sound. Immediately sound this clicker whenever the dog walks next to you with a slack leash as it is supposed to, even if it's just for a few steps, then quickly reward with a treat. The clicking sound marks the good behavior in the dog's mind, and the treat is a powerful reward for a job well-done.

When your dog pulls at its leash, stop and don't budge until the dog either turns around to see what's wrong or just stops in its tracks. Continue this process until your dog is reliably walking by your side, and then slowly wean down from the frequent click and treating. Because the great outdoors is filled with distractions, you'll probably have to use the clicker and treats for several weeks before you can begin weaning.

MISTAKE: **Chasing a dog that grabbed something it shouldn't have.** If you chase your dog when it picks up something that it isn't supposed to have in its mouth, you increase the odds that the dog will engage in this misbehavior again. Dogs love to play chase with their owners.

Better: Get a dog treat, squat down to the dog's level, and call the dog to you. When the dog approaches for the treat, place it in front of your dog's nose and say, *"Drop it."* Reward the dog with the treat when it does drop it.

Similar: If your dog gets loose, don't chase after it—your dog can probably outrun you and likely will enjoy the chase. Instead, get the dog's attention, then run away from it. This might cause the dog to change its game from running away from you to chasing after you, making it easier to calmly take hold of your dog when it catches up to you.

MISTAKE: **Giving a jumping dog attention.** Dogs that jump up and put their front paws on people crave attention. They will continue jumping as long as their owners give them attention—even if the attention they're receiving is just hearing their owners tell them, *"Get down."*

Better: Walk away from the jumping dog without making eye contact or saying a word to it.

Later, when the dog is calm, start to teach it to sit when you cross your arms across your chest. Many dogs tune out verbal commands when they get excited, but most still notice body language.

To teach your dog to respond to a crossed-arm sit command, start by combining the verbal sit command with crossed arms. Provide treats when the dog responds. Then eliminate the verbal command and use the crossed-arm signal alone, still rewarding with treats.

Once your dog masters the crossed-arm sit command, instruct house guests to use it, too. Otherwise they might accidentally give the dog attention when it jumps up, undermining the training.

MISTAKE: **Letting your dog use old household items as chew toys.** If you let your dog chew on an old flip-flop or towel, don't blame the dog when it chews up your new flip-flops or towels, too. Dogs generally can't figure out the difference.

Better: Never let your dog chew on anything that could be mistaken for something you don't want it to chew on. Limit your dog to products made for dogs, including toys and bones.

MISTAKE: **Failing to notice that a puppy is about to go to the bathroom inside.**

Better: If you can hustle the puppy outside before it relieves itself, this will help the puppy figure out that outdoors is the proper place to do its business.

What to do: When your puppy becomes distracted and wanders away from people, dog toys and/or other dogs, quickly take it outside—there's a good chance that the puppy is about to heed nature's call.

When the puppy must go to the bathroom inside—when you're away all day at work, for example—provide grass-textured pet potties, not smooth-surfaced potty pads. The feeling of the artificial grass underfoot can help the puppy learn that it is supposed to use the yard to relieve itself.

MISTAKE: **Yelling at a barking dog to get it to quiet down.** Making noise is not an effective way to convince a dog to stop making noise. Your dog might think that you're joining in on the fun.

Better: Look for the reason behind the barking and address it. *Examples...*

•**If your dog barks to defend its territory** against animals and people that it sees nearby, block its view. You could do this with curtains, fencing, landscaping or opaque window privacy film, available in home centers, that temporarily adheres to windows. You don't have to cover the entire window, just the lower section that is in the dog's sight line. You can gradually lower the privacy film until you don't need it at all.

•**If your dog barks to get your attention,** ignore the dog until the barking stops, wait a few beats and only then see what it wants. Eventually the dog will figure out that barking will not get it attention, though you might have to put up with considerable barking until this message gets through. Stay strong—many dogs try barking louder just before they finally give up on barking. You also can teach your dog the "hush" command. Say, *"Hush,"* and when the dog stops barking, give it a treat.

MISTAKE: **Waiting for misbehavior to become entrenched before acting to correct it.** The longer you tolerate a dog's misbehavior, the harder it will become to alter.

Better: Correct misbehavior when you notice the dog doing it a second time. Once could be a fluke…twice suggests that this is a habit.

MISTAKE: Using pain to train. Choke chains and other training tools that hurt dogs might suppress misbehavior, but they don't change the way the dog thinks. If your dog lunges at other dogs, for example, a correction from a choke collar might convince it not to, but your dog still might feel antagonism toward other dogs and react when you're not around.

Better: Provide treats when the dog behaves properly, rather than pain when it does not.

Easy Pet Teeth Cleaning

Roundup of experts on pets' dental health, reported in *Better Homes & Gardens*.

Rub dogs' and cats' teeth daily with gauze if you cannot clean them with a toothbrush. It is important to clean pets' teeth—they have plaque buildup just as people's teeth do. Rubbing the teeth with a gauze pad on which you place a small dab of pet toothpaste can help loosen and remove plaque. Or you can try Maxi/Guard Oral Cleansing Wipes or Excel Medicated Dental Wipes, which are textured to create friction to remove plaque more efficiently.

Also helpful: For cats, Purina Pro Plan Dental Crunch Cat Snacks…for dogs, C.E.T. VeggieDent Chews.

Do Not Let Dogs Play with Tennis Balls

Consensus of veterinarians, reported at Lifehacker.com.

Tennis balls are not sturdy enough for sustained chewing—and if a dog swallows pieces of a ten-

nis ball, it can cause an intestinal blockage. Chemicals used in making tennis balls also are dangerous to dogs. And excessively chewing tennis balls can damage the enamel of dogs' teeth. Safe chew toys should give a little to avoid hurting the dog's teeth but not be so soft that they can be ripped or torn apart. Avoid any flavors or coatings that might upset the dog's stomach. The size of the toy should be based on the dog's mouth and head—not too small or too large. Ideally, all toys should also be washable.

How to Train Your Cat

Jackson Galaxy, a cat behaviorist and host of the Animal Planet show *My Cat From Hell*. He is coauthor of *Catification: Designing a Happy and Stylish Home for Your Cat (and You!)*. JacksonGalaxy.com

Sarah Ellis, PhD, feline behavior specialist at International Cat Care. She is coauthor of *The Trainable Cat: A Practical Guide to Making Life Happier for You and Your Cat*. ICatCare.org

Does your cat scratch the furniture? Jump up on the kitchen counter when you're cooking or when guests are over? Urinate on the carpet?

That can be changed! Despite the misconception, cats of any age can be taught to alter problematic behavior. But to accomplish this, the cat owner must work out why the cat is engaging in a particular behavior, then help it learn an alternative behavior that is acceptable to both person and cat. *Common problems and solutions…*

PROBLEM: Furniture scratching. For a cat, scratching can be a form of exercise and a way to remove dead outer nail sheaths from the claw. But mainly it's a way to claim ownership of territory via the scratch marks—and the accompanying scent left behind by scent glands in the cat's paws. It's the cat equivalent of scrawling "Kilroy was here" on a wall.

Cats are particularly likely to scratch couches, easy chairs and beds because these are places where the scent of the humans of the household is strongest. To a cat, a strong human scent on a piece of furniture is like that human saying, "I own this." When a cat scratches it, the cat is saying, "No, you

Natural Odor Reduction

Cheap, odor-free cat litter. Buy the least expensive scoopable cat litter, and combine it with an eight-ounce box of baking soda. The baking soda costs less than 60 cents. When combined with cat litter, it eliminates odors for a fraction of the cost of the brand-name litters.

Bankrate.com.

don't—it's mine." Or a cat might scratch curtains or windowsills to let the people or animals it sees outside the house know that the space inside the home is the cat's.

What to do: Put double-sided sticky tape on the furniture that you want to stop the cat from scratching—cats don't like the feel of it. Use enough tape to cover the area your cat likes to scratch. Also, place an acceptable scratching option, such as a scratching post, right next to each piece of furniture that the cat likes to scratch. Position each as close to the scratched spot as possible. This new scratching option will be in the same "scent zone" as the furniture, so scratching it will satisfy the cat's need to smell its own scent in this area. You can remove the tape when the cat has consistently abandoned the furniture for the scratching post.

PROBLEM: **Urinating/Defecating Outside the Litter Box.** Cats do this to mark their territory when they feel this territory is threatened. Start by considering where the cat is urinating/defecating. Common patterns…

Urinating/defecating near windows and exterior doors. There's a good chance that the cat sees or smells something outside the house that it considers a threat—possibly another cat.

What to do: Place a litter box near each door or window where this occurs. If this means litter boxes are in locations that you consider unacceptable, such as by the front door, you can very slowly slide these boxes toward more acceptable spots. But don't start to do this until the cat has used the litter box consistently (no peeing outside the litter box) for at least a few weeks. Cats generally accept repositioning the box as long as the litter box is not moved more than one foot each day.

Urinating/defecating on or near the possessions of a new member of the household…or urinating/defecating in a spot outside the litter box shortly after someone new has joined the household.

What to do: Encourage the cat to form positive associations with this new person. (For information on how to introduce your cat to a new animal in the house, go to my website JacksonGalaxy.com, click on "Care & Blog," then search "New Animal in the House.") Have this person feed the cat…play with the cat…and give the cat new cat toys. Move the cat's food dish to a spot where this person's scent is strong. If the cat's peeing issues started when a new baby joined the family—a common trigger for this problem—feed the cat right next to the baby's crib.

Exception: Urinating or defecating outside the litter box may stem from a health problem such as a urinary tract infection. Take the cat to see a vet if it makes pained noises when peeing/defecating…if there is blood in its urine or feces…or if the cat has a history of urinary or bowel-related health issues.

PROBLEM: **Interfering with Food Prep or Mealtime.** Some cats like to be close to the action when their owners are preparing or consuming food.

What to do: Cover the tops of place mats with double-sided sticky tape. Position these place mats where the cat tends to jump up on countertops and tables.

Also purchase a "clicker"—a handheld training device sold in pet stores. Teach the cat to associate its clicking sound with receiving its favorite treat. Click the clicker and very quickly provide a treat. Do this again and again for as long as the activity holds your cat's interest. Repeat this every day until you can tell that the cat anticipates a treat when it hears the clicking sound. (This might take a few days or several weeks of practice, depending on the cat.)

Next, teach your cat to sit. While the cat is standing, move a treat slowly back over its head. Sometimes the cat has to lean so far back to watch the treat that its backside will hit the ground, leaving the cat seated. Immediately click the clicker, and give the cat the treat when this occurs.

Important: If there's a delay of more than two seconds between the cat's action and receiving its treat, it is unlikely that the two things will become linked in the cat's mind and the training will be ineffective. Repeat this until your cat reliably sits down when it sees that you're holding a cat treat.

Finally, teach the cat to sit in a specific, elevated spot in the kitchen where it can see what you're doing but is not in your way or overly close to your food. This might be a cat tree positioned in the corner of the room or on a stool. Use a treat to tempt the cat to this location, and sound the clicker and provide a treat as soon as it sits there. When the cat reliably sits in this location when in the kitchen, you can slowly phase out the clicker and remove the taped place mats.

Helpful: Attempt treat-based cat training only before mealtimes when the cat is hungry. Use extremely small treats during training so that your cat doesn't fill up too quickly. Choose soft treats, not crunchy ones, which take longer for cats to eat.

PROBLEM: Getting Your Cat into the Carrier. Cats typically aren't fond of carriers because they don't like feeling trapped. And many times carriers are associated with negative experiences such as harrowing visits to the vet or a boarding facility. But you can change your cat's response to the carrier to a much more positive one, reducing stress for the cat and for you when you need to use the carrier.

•**Choosing a carrier.** When buying a carrier, make sure that the entry door allows your cat to walk in rather than be lifted in and that the door can be completely removed in the initial training. The lid should be removable, too, so that in the initial training stages the carrier appears less enclosed. (A removable lid also may allow a veterinarian to examine your cat while the animal remains "safe" in the base of the carrier.)

•**Do not hide the carrier.** Most pet owners make the mistake of keeping their carriers tucked away in closets when not in use, but that's a mistake. Your carrier should be left out at all times so that your cat is familiar with it.

•**Familiarize your cat with the carrier well before you have to use it.** Start by removing the lid and the door of the carrier so that you have just the base. If your cat seems very wary of the carrier, begin carrier training by rewarding your cat when he stays in the same room as the base of the carrier. You can take the "relaxation blanket" and slowly move it closer and closer to the carrier, rewarding your cat each time he relaxes on the blanket. Eventually, place the blanket in the carrier. This should be enough to get the cat into the carrier.

Once your cat is comfortable in the base of the carrier—he has slept in it or lays down to groom in it—you can gradually slide the door into place. Start by sliding the door in partway, and reward your cat for staying relaxed. Continue to use the marker word "good" to condition your cat to know a food reward is coming—and continue to reward anytime he does not attempt to leave the carrier. Use the same steps when putting the lid back on.

•**Keep the carrier stable.** Cats find being carried in the air unsettling. Always use two hands to keep the carrier steady, and begin to train your cat to be comfortable in a moving carrier by holding the carrier off the floor for only a few seconds. Progress to walking a few steps at a time, and then farther, always continuing to reward your cat.

Cats Love to Hunt

Sarah Ellis, PhD, feline behavior specialist, quoted online at ICatCare.org, the website of International Cat Care, Tisbury, UK.

Cats should work for their food. In the wild, they would need to catch around 10 small mammals a day to get the energy they need. Feeding cats from a bowl undermines basic cat-hunting instincts, reducing problem-solving behavior and physical exercise.

What to do: Try a puzzle feeder—a device that the cat must manipulate in some way to get the food. It stimulates the cat mentally while encouraging it to eat small amounts frequently as it would in a hunting existence in the wild.

CHAPTER 18

Problem Solvers

Robot Vacuum Cleaners and Other Great Gadgets…That Make Your Life Easier

Katherine Belknap, former project director of AbleData, an organization funded by the US Department of Education to provide objective information on assistive technology, Falls Church, Virginia.

M ost people are unaware of the huge array of products—both high-tech and low-tech—that are designed to help those who have trouble with their eyesight, hearing, memory, physical strength and many related problems.

Known as "assistive technology," these devices aren't always expensive yet they can allow many seniors to engage in activities that would otherwise be out of bounds. In many cases, they help seniors live independently.

Making Life Easier

Among today's innovative assistive-technology products…

• **LCD Monitor Magnifier.** If your computer can't display screen images large enough for your eyesight, consider an attachable magnifier that can increase images by more than 100%.

Typical retail price: $164 for a 17-inch screen magnifier.

Information: Kantek, 800-536-3212, Kantek.com.

• **iRobot vacuum cleaner.** These battery-operated vacuum cleaners scoot all around the house by themselves, picking up dirt, dust and other debris.

Example: The Roomba 694, which measures a compact 18.7 x 16.5 x 5.5 inches, and recharges itself when needed.

Price: $274.99.

Information: iRobot Corp., 800-727-9077, Store. iRobot.com.

• **Oversized TV remote.** For people without perfect vision, SMPL Large-button TV remote control, 5.5 x 2.5 inches that's hard to lose and easy to use. The buttons are larger than those on regular remotes, and they light up.

Typical retail price: $39.99.

Information: Health Products for You, 866-316-0162, HealthProductsforYou.com.

• **Active Hands gripping aid.** As we grow older, we often lose our grip in a very real sense of the term, often from a physical injury or stroke. One solution is wearing a glove with a wraparound Velcro strap to hold your hand firmly to tools, kitchen equipment, golf club or whatever needs a firm grip.

Price: $95.

Information: Access to Recreation, Inc., 800-634-4351, Accesstr.com.

• **Easy-to-use medication reminder.** Regardless of your age, it's often easy to forget medication. The TimeCap Multi-Alarm is a battery-operated electronic pill-bottle cap that can be programmed to beep when it's time to take your medicine. The "last-opened" time stamp indicates the last day and time that your medications were taken.

Price: $44.95.

Information: Epill.com, 800-549-0095.

•**Electric-powered jar opener.** No matter how strong you are, some jars are difficult to open. The Lids Off Jar Opener Ultra does the job in nearly all cases.

Typical retail price: $144.

Information: Black & Decker, 800-544-6986 and 410-716-3900. Purchase on Amazon.com.

•**Mailbox alerts.** For people who use a walker or have difficulty getting around, it can be risky to go outside to check on the mail several times a day, especially in bad weather. Mail Chime is a battery-operated device that you attach to an outside mailbox. When the mail arrives, a small indoor receiver beeps and flashes a red light.

Price: $58.95.

Information: Hannah Products, 309-788-1982, MailChime.com.

•**Flashing smoke detector.** If you're hard of hearing, you might miss the important sound of a smoke detector. One solution is a detector for both smoke and carbon monoxide that emits a piercing 85-decibel alarm and flashes a strobe light.

Price: $189.95.

Information: Hear-More, 800-881-4327 voice and 800-281-3555 TTY, HearMore.com.

For More Help

Unfortunately, the need for assistive technology often increases so slowly that many seniors fail to recognize it. Moreover, it's easy to overlook new assistive technology because much of it is marketed to people with disabilities, not to older people in general. If you suffer from macular degeneration, for example, your doctor may recommend a computer screen that magnifies images. A physician is less likely to recommend the device

to a person whose eyesight is gradually worsening due to a more benign condition.

Problem: A spouse, relative or friend refuses to acknowledge the need for assistive technology.

There's not always a solution if the person is adamantly opposed to the idea. But you can often be persuasive by avoiding the words "assistive" and "disabled." Instead, talk about taking advantage of the "great new technology that makes life easier."

If possible, get the person to try one of the devices. If it helps, the person will probably be reluctant to part with it.

Where to find out about assistive technology...

•**The assistive-technology program in your state.** Agencies differ from state to state, but all provide information, and some hold events where assistive devices are demonstrated.

To locate a program: Go to the AT3 Center website at AT3center.net/stateprogram. This site provides a one-stop connection for State Assistive Technology Programs, the Assistive Technology Act and general assistive technology.

•**Your physician.** Be aware that some doctors are more knowledgeable than others about assistive technology.

•**An occupational therapist (OT).** If you believe that you might need assistive technology, ask your primary care physician to refer you to an OT. An OT will examine you and suggest the products that he/she believes will be the most helpful.

The American Occupational Therapy Association (301-652-6611, AOTA.org) has a "Buyer's Guide" on its website where you can search for manufacturers of assistive technology.

Important: Before using assistive technology that affects the way you physically exert yourself, tell your doctor and/or OT to make sure that the device is appropriate for your specific needs.

Five Cleaning Tools That Make Housekeeping Easier

Linda Cobb, author of *Talking Dirty with the Queen of Clean*. Based in Phoenix, she previously owned one of the largest cleaning companies in Michigan and is founder of the website QueenOfClean.com.

Sometimes mops, brooms and vacuums just can't get the job done. *These effective, affordable products can make your cleaning easier and keep your home sparkling…*

•**Clean baseboards without bending.** Baseboard Buddy lets you clean baseboards from a standing position. Baseboards are a common cleaning trouble spot because their ridges collect dirt and dust. Baseboard Buddy's flexible microfiber pad works its way into baseboard ridges to grab grime, and its handle extends to four feet, so you can clean baseboards by simply walking this tool around the room's perimeter—no kneeling needed. $24.99 for Baseboard Buddy and three reusable cleaning pads. A 10-pack of replacement pads costs $14.99. Available at Amazon.com

•**Vacuum where vacuum hoses can't reach.** VaccUFlex is a simple, effective kit that uses a narrow plastic hose to convert your vacuum cleaner or wet/dry vac into a tool capable of reaching into and cleaning out small, hard-to-access spots such as the tracks of sliding windows…inside car seats…and dryer vents. When attached to a wet/dry vac, VaccUFlex even can suck clogs out of drains. $26.95. VaccUFlex.com

•**Scrub tough-to-reach tile.** OXO Good Grips Extendable Tub & Tile Scrubber is a scrubbing pad on the end of an extending pole, so you can clean bathtubs, shower stalls and tile floors from a comfortable standing position. This OXO scrubber is particularly helpful for cleaning behind toilets. $15.99. Replacement scrubber heads cost $6.99. OXO.com

•**Pull pet hair out of carpets.** Evriholder FURemover Pet Hair Removal Broom with Squeegee & Telescoping Handle has rubber bristles that extract pet hair from carpets far better than vacuums. Flip it over, and the squeegee feature can clear liquids off floors and windows. $12.44. Available at Chewy.com

•**Clean floors without chemicals.** Bona microfiber mops have reusable pads featuring millions of extremely tiny fibers. These little fibers generate a modest static electric charge that attracts dirt, pet hair and even microbes. Microfiber can clean without the help of chemical cleaning products, so there's no buildup of shine-deadening residue on floors or in the grout between tiles. $19.99 for mop; $10.88 for an additional three microfiber pads. US.Bona.com

Alternative: Norwex microfiber mops are even more effective than Bona but more expensive. $115.99 including one wet and one dry pad. Norwex.biz

Unexpected Uses for Everyday Items

Heloise, columnist and contributing editor for *Good Housekeeping* magazine. Based in San Antonio, she is author of numerous books on household hints and organization, including *All-New Hints from Heloise*. Her legendary mother, the first Heloise, began writing her column, "Hints from Heloise," in 1959. Heloise.com

WiseBread.com

Famed household hints guru Heloise has discovered hundreds of alternative uses for everyday products. *We asked her to tell us about some of her favorites…*

Mouse Pads

Companies sometimes give away free foam mouse pads as advertisements.

•**Jar opener.** Use the grippy underside to open stubborn jar lids.

•**Kneeling pad for gardening or home-improvement projects.**

•**Pedicure spot.** Place a mouse pad under your foot when you give yourself a pedicure to catch any drips.

Plastic Gallon Jugs

Water, milk and orange juice often come in plastic gallon jugs. *When empty, these jugs have many uses…*

●**Scooper.** Slice a capped jug in half on the diagonal to scoop ice-melting granules or dirt for the garden.

●**Funnel.** Turn the jug upside down, cut it in half horizontally and use as a funnel for liquids or dry material, such as dog food or bird seed.

●**Fishing buoy.** Use a capped jug to mark where you've placed a fishing line.

Mayonnaise

Be sure to use real mayonnaise, not diet mayonnaise or salad dressing.

●**White mark remover for wood furniture.** If you see a cloudy white mark on a wood table where a coffee mug or some other hot item recently stood, put a dab of mayonnaise on your finger and rub the stained area in the direction of the wood grain until your finger feels a bit warm and the oil from the mayo gets absorbed into the wood. Let the mayo sit overnight, then wipe it off and buff the surface. A little mayo also can hide light scratches on dark wood.

●**Leaf shiner.** Apply a light coat of mayonnaise to plant leaves, and buff gently with a paper towel. Use mayo only on the tops of leaves—it might interfere with plants' ability to breathe if applied to the underside, too.

●**Hair conditioner.** Rub one to two tablespoons of mayonnaise into the bottom inch or two of your hair. Pin the hair up (if it is long enough to do so), put on a plastic shower cap, then wrap your head in a bath towel and leave the towel on for at least 30 minutes, preferably an hour. Be sure to rinse thoroughly afterward.

Fingernail Polish

●**Organizer helper.** Use nail polish of different colors to differentiate similar items.

Example: I put a dot of pink nail polish on the end of my tools so that my husband will not think they are his and move them to his toolbox.

●**Contact lens case marker.** Place a dot of red nail polish on the right side of your contact lens case. This will make it easy to tell which lens is stored on which side of the case, even when you

do not have your contacts in. Remember that both "right" and "red" start with the letter R.

●**Childproof medication bottles.** Use a brightly colored nail polish to mark both the bottle and bottle cap of any childproof medication bottles where the top must be properly lined up to open. These bright marks will be easy to see and align (of course, do this only if you don't have young children in the house).

Helpful: If you take several medications, also use nail polish to write the first letter or two of each medication on its bottle in large print so that you do not have to squint at labels to figure out which is which.

●**Rust preventer.** Use colorless nail polish to provide invisible protection.

Example: If there is rust on the screws holding your toilet seat or lid in place, remove the screws, soak them in vinegar to clear off the rust, dry them, put the screws back, and then apply a coat of clear nail polish to ward off future rust.

●**Button saver.** Apply a layer of clear nail polish to the threads on top of dress-shirt buttons. The nail polish will help the threads endure the heat of laundering, keeping the buttons on the shirt longer.

Hair Spray

●**Panty hose run stopper.** Spray a small amount of hair spray on minor snags in panty hose to prevent them from becoming longer runs. (Clear nail polish also works.)

●**Needle threader.** Spray the end of a piece of thread if you are having trouble threading a needle. Let the hair spray dry for 10 seconds, then try threading the needle again. The spray will stiffen the end of the thread and make it easier to thread the needle.

Panty Hose

There might be more uses for old, clean panty hose than any other household product...

●**Item finder.** When you drop a small object on the floor and can't find it, stretch a piece of old panty hose over the end of your vacuum hose, secure with a rubber band, then vacuum the area. The vacuum will suck up the lost item, but the panty hose filter will prevent it from being sucked past the nozzle. Shut off the vacuum to release the item.

●**Plant ties.** Use strips of panty hose to tie garden plants in place. Unlike rope or plastic ties, panty hose will not cut into the plants, and its natural color will blend unobtrusively into your garden. You also can put a piece of panty hose across the bottom of the inside of a pot to keep soil from falling out through the drainage holes.

●**Shoe bags.** Slide a pair of shoes into the snipped-off leg of old panty hose before packing the shoes in a suitcase. It keeps the pair together and prevents the shoes from coming in contact with other clothes.

●**Onion and potato storage.** Keep potatoes and onions fresh longer by snipping the legs off panty hose and storing these vegetables in the legs. Put in one onion (or potato), tie a knot, followed by another onion and another knot for the length of the leg, then hang the leg inside a pantry door. Onions and potatoes will last longer because they will have better air circulation than they would have had in a bag. When you need an onion, just take a pair of scissors and clip off the bottom section, leaving the rest of the panty-hose leg in place.

Used Tea Bags

●**Help for tired eyes.** Used tea bags can be placed on tired eyes to reduce swelling. Rinse gently with cold water before using.

●**Window cleaner.** Rub mirrors and windows and dry completely.

●**Odor absorber.** Just put them in a mug, and leave the mug on a shelf.

Hair Clips

●**Cord and cable organizer.** Use clips that coordinate with wire colors.

●**Bag sealer.** Keep large bags of chips, popcorn or cookies closed.

●**Sock keeper.** Use hair clips to keep pairs of socks together—strong, water-resistant ones also can be used to keep socks together in the washing machine.

Trick to Protect Your Passwords

When signing up for a website, don't answer security questions honestly—such as your mother's maiden name or your birthplace. You'll actually better protect your account and identity if you always use the same wrong answers.

Keith Bradford, author of *Life Hacks.*

Attack Stubborn Odors—Naturally

Heloise, internationally syndicated newspaper columnist and contributing editor to *Good Housekeeping* magazine. Based in San Antonio, she is author of the syndicated "Hints from Heloise" column that runs in more than 500 newspapers around the world. She has written more than 15 books about household cleaning and organization, including *Handy Household Hints from Heloise.* Heloise.com

Musty spare rooms...lingering cooking smells...dogs overdue for baths. Even well-maintained homes develop unpleasant odors from time to time. Living in a foul-smelling home could leave you in foul mood—what people smell affects how they feel far more than they tend to realize.

Here are natural ways to solve 11 common home odor problems...

Kitchen Smells

●**Stinky dishwasher.** Mold or mildew usually is the culprit when dishwashers develop unpleasant odors. Pour several cups of standard household vinegar into the bottom of the dishwasher, and let it sit for an hour. Then run the dishwasher through a full cycle. You don't need to add soap. The vinegar should kill any mold and mildew.

Alternative: If you know your dishwasher is going to sit unused for a few days or longer—when you go on vacation, for example—sprinkle a few tablespoons of baking soda inside. This reduces the odds that it will smell musty when it is next used.

●**Malodorous microwave.** Unpleasant smells can linger in a microwave. Cut up two or three oranges (or another citrus fruit), and put the pieces in one to two cups of water in a large microwave-safe bowl. Microwave this fruit/water combo until the water boils, then stop the microwave but leave the microwave door shut with the steaming mixture inside for at least another 15 minutes. When you do eventually remove the bowl, leave the microwave door open for a few minutes.

Tip: Select a bowl that has a wide opening for this—the greater the surface area of water, the more effective this odor-removal strategy will be.

●**Smelly kitchen sink drain/garbage disposal.** Pour one-half cup of baking soda down the drain, followed by one cup of vinegar that you've warmed up slightly in the microwave (warming the vinegar makes it more effective)—foam might rise up out of the drain. Wait 15 to 20 minutes, then put the stopper in the drain and fill the sink with cold water. When the sink is nearly full, remove the stopper. (Do not let the sink get so full that it overflows when you reach in.) The rush of water down the drain will flush away both the baking soda residue and any bits of food that were rotting in the drain.

If you have a double kitchen sink, it works best if you do this in both sinks at the same time.

If it's a bathroom sink drain that's smelly, pour one-half cup of hydrogen peroxide down the drain. Use the highest concentration hydrogen peroxide you can find—it's available at grocery stores and drugstores (it won't damage pipes). Hydrogen peroxide is especially effective at clearing away the hair- and skin-oil–based residue often responsible for unpleasant bathroom drain smells.

If you want, before pouring in the peroxide, you can lift out the stopper and remove any hair and gunk that may have gotten caught on the underside of the stopper.

●**Foul-smelling trash cans.** Anytime you throw out something that's especially smelly, put a few drops of lemon essential oil or vanilla extract on a paper towel or paper napkin and place this in the trash on top of the smelly garbage.

Also: Sprinkle a little baking soda into the bottom of the can each time you change trash bags. Occasionally wash out trash cans with hot, soapy water.

●**Lingering cooking odors/smoking odors.** Dampen a dish towel or hand towel with vinegar, then wring it out over a sink until it is no longer dripping. Walk around the affected rooms waiving this towel around like a flag for a few minutes. This will not remove all of the odor, but it often can reduce it by more than half.

Act fast—the longer you wait, the more odor-causing molecules will settle onto surfaces and into carpets and fabrics where more extensive cleaning might be required to remove them.

●**Rank refrigerator.** Save the squeezed-out remains of a lemon, lime, orange or grapefruit after you use the juice in a recipe or drink. Place these fruit remnants in a small bowl, pour a few tablespoons of salt on top of them, then put the bowl in the fridge. The bad odor soon should be replaced by a fresh citrus smell.

Alternative: People often place a box of baking soda in the fridge to absorb odors, and baking soda can indeed be effective here. But if you choose this solution, pour the baking soda into a bowl (or some other container with a wide opening) rather than leave it in the box. The more baking soda surface area exposed to the air, the greater its odor-absorbing capacity.

Outside the Kitchen

●**Bedrooms.** Place a few drops of lavender essential oil on your pillows, then put the pillows in the dryer for five to 10 minutes on the fluff or low-heat setting. This will leave the pillows smelling clean and fresh, and most people find the scent of lavender very relaxing—that's why baby oils often are lavender scented.

●**Musty closets and spare rooms.** Fill a shallow bowl with fresh ground coffee, and place it in this underused space. Coffee grounds not only have a pleasing aroma, they do a wonderful job of absorbing musty smells in confined spaces.

●**Sick rooms/hospital rooms.** Each day, place two to three drops of orange (or lemon) essential oil on a tissue. Wave the tissue around in the air of the sick room or hospital room for a few minutes, then discard it in a trash can in the room.

People tend to associate orange and lemon scents with cleanliness and health, so this actually can help sick people feel a bit better. It certainly supplies a more uplifting odor than the typical medicinal hospital room smell.

Example: When I did this in a friend's nursing home room, everyone who came in commented on the wonderful smell. The doctors even stayed longer than usual.

Simple Way to Make Your Whole Home Smell Fresh

Place a few drops of lemon extract or lemon essential oil on the filter of the home's forced-air heating/cooling system. Each time the heat or air-conditioning comes on, it will circulate the clean, pleasant smell of lemon throughout the home. A single application typically lasts for a few days, though this varies depending on how often the system runs. Do not apply more than a few drops of essential oil or extract, or the smell could be overbearing.

Nail Polish Remover Does More Than Remove Nail Polish

Reader's Digest. RD.com

It eliminates ink stains from skin…takes paint off windows…removes stains from china…removes melted plastic from heating appliances…and dissolves Super Glue.

Hard Water on Drinking Glasses

Good Housekeeping. GoodHousekeeping.com

To remove hard-water deposits on drinking glasses, microwave two cups of white vinegar for about two minutes and pour the vinegar into a plastic basin. Place two glasses on their sides in the vinegar for about three minutes. Turn the glasses to make sure that the vinegar covers all sides. Remove the glasses, rinse them in clear water and dry them with a lint-free towel. If spots remain, moisten the glass with water and sprinkle some baking soda on it. Then, using your fingertips, polish it inside and outside, rinse and dry.

Quick Fix for Scratches on a Glass Table

"Ask Heloise" column published in *Good Housekeeping.*

To remove scratches from a glass tabletop, sprinkle with baking soda, add a little white toothpaste and rub with your finger in circles. Wipe with a towel dampened with water, then dry. If this starts to help, repeat.

For deeper scratches: Buy a windshield-scratch-repair kit at an auto store. The kit contains resin that will fill the cracks.

9 Little-Known Uses for Baby Oil

MoneyTalksNews.com

Baby oil comes in handy for a variety of tasks. *See below…*

●**Drip a little onto a swollen finger to make ring removal easier.**

- **If a jewelry chain is knotted**, rub a drop of oil onto the tangle and then pick it apart with a straight pin.

- **Use to shine stainless steel or chrome**, and put a small amount on a cloth before dusting wood—the dust will stick to the cloth.

- **Lubricate a squeaky hinge with a drop or two.** Saturate a bandage and wait a bit—after absorption, the adhesive should lift off easily.

- **Baby oil lifts off price-sticker residue and can fix a stuck zipper**—use sparingly to avoid staining the garment.

- **Use on legs before shaving**, instead of gel or soap.

- **Dab some on a temporary tattoo to take it off.**

- **Saturate cuticle edges with baby oil before polishing nails**—afterward, use a cotton ball or tissue to remove the oil and any excess polish.

- **Use baby oil instead of massage oil or cream.**

---

8 Things to Do with Dental Floss (Besides Floss)

Joan Wilen and Lydia Wilen are folk-remedy experts and home tipsters, authors of *Household Magic* and *Treasury of Home Remedies & Natural Cures.*

While good oral health is the reason dental floss was invented, you can use unflavored floss in many more ways…

- **Fix eyeglasses.** Ever lose one of those tiny screws that attaches the earpiece to the front of the frame? As a quick fix, thread a piece of dental floss through the holes that the screw goes through. Then knot the floss, and cut off the excess. The floss will allow you to wear your glasses until you can replace the screw.

- **Sew a button.** Children's clothes and some types of work clothes often test the endurance of cotton thread. Sew buttons on with dental floss, and they will pass the test with flying colors.

If you have buttons floating around in a drawer, use dental floss to string all the same-color buttons together. Next time you need a button, you'll be glad they're organized that way.

Floss also can be used to repair any kind of fine netting, such as some fishing nets and mosquito netting.

- **Relieve the dripping sound.** Dental floss will not stop a faucet from leaking, but it will stop the sound of the drip-drip-drip until the plumber arrives. Cut a piece of floss long enough to tie around the spout of the faucet, and let it hang down into the drain. You may have to use tape to position the floss so that the drip is touching the floss, enabling each drop to slide down the length of the floss into the drain, eliminating the annoying noise it makes when it falls from the faucet to the sink.

- **Cut cake and more.** Dental floss will cut a cheesecake better than most knives. Take a piece of floss that's a few inches longer than the diameter of the cake. Hold an end in each hand, making the floss taut. Then maneuver the floss through the cheesecake to cut it in half. Slide the floss out from the bottom of the cake. Now that there are two halves, you can cut slices—one at a time—using the same taut-floss method.

You also can use this floss method to cut soft cheese, some kinds of bread, hard-boiled eggs and canned cranberry jelly.

- **Remove cookies.** Having a hard time taking freshly baked cookies off the cookie sheet? Holding a piece of floss tautly, gently slide it under each cookie, coaxing the cookie off the pan.

- **Clean furniture.** If you have furniture with hard-to-get-at crevices, take about 12 inches of floss, tie or wind the ends on your index fingers (loose enough to keep the circulation going, of course) and clean out the furniture's wedged-in dirt. Floss also may be used to clean between cracks or crevices around the stove, sink, counter and wherever else dirt gets imbedded.

- **Tie it up.** When a shoelace tears and you have no string around, use floss to keep your shoe tied until you replace the lace.

If you lose your luggage lock while traveling, keep the luggage zipper closed by tying it with floss.

•**String a roast.** Some recipes for roasts call for the meat to be tied with cotton butcher string to make it more uniformly shaped, preserve moisture, keep any stuffing in place and ensure even cooking. If you have the meat but no string, use unwaxed dental floss. Rest assured, it won't burn or melt!

It is recommended that poultry (chicken, turkey, duck) also be tied (trussed) before roasting. Once again, unwaxed dental floss can be used as a string substitute.

3 Club Soda Tricks

Reader's Digest. RD.com

Three reasons you should always have club soda on hand…

•**Pour club soda into a spray bottle,** and keep it in your car—a quick spritz dissolves bird droppings quickly so they're easy to wipe away.

•**Drizzle it over a screw that's rusted stuck,** and wait about five minutes—the rust will dissolve so that the screw is easy to turn.

•**Pour a bit into a glass,** and soak jewelry with gemstones overnight—by morning, they'll be sparkling again.

Your Old Family Photos Are Fading Away

Jeff Wignall is a photographer and writer who has written more than 20 books about photography. He is a contributing editor with *Pro Photo Daily* and *Motion Arts Pro Daily* and a former "Camera" columnist for *The New York Times.*

The family photo album filled with old printed photos still is among our most valuable possessions because it is an irreplaceable history of our family and our ancestors and their times. Even if we create digital copies of these photos (a smart thing to do, see below), the original prints themselves always will resonate with us as precious objects, literally cre-

ated and treasured by our ancestors, in a way that pixels on a screen never could. But time is not kind to print photos, and when they're gone, they're gone.

Problem: Many people keep these photos in albums that actually accelerate their deterioration. *Happily, there are simple steps you can take to preserve your cherished photos for generations to come…*

•**Move prints to archival storage.** The pages and glues in many photo albums contain acids and other chemicals that accelerate deterioration of photos. And popular "magnetic" albums, which let you easily move photos around, often have clear sheets that cover each page—but over time these sheets stick to photos, ruining them.

Solution: Store your valued photographs in "archival," acid-free albums or boxes. Look for labels that show the product has passed the Photographic Activity Test (PAT). Reliable online sources include Light Impressions (LightImpressionsDirect. com) and Gaylord Archival (Gaylord.com).

Archival albums and boxes are more expensive than nonarchival types but are well worth the price. You can buy self-adhesive archival "corners" to mount on the pages to secure the images.

If the photos in your old family albums were placed there by the people who took the photos, be sure to maintain the order of the original photos on each page. Odds are your relatives knew the family time line and relationships and arranged photos accordingly—and even if they didn't, the way they displayed their photo treasures adds to the collection's authenticity.

Tip: Use your smartphone to take snapshots of the original album pages before you transfer the photos to an archival album, then use these snapshots as a placement guide.

•**Scan originals to create digital files.** Since digital files don't fade, the only truly permanent solution to saving the images in your photos is to scan them and digitize them. It's easy to do on a flatbed scanner. The scanner on a basic all-in-one home printer usually does a very good job. No scanner? Your local library likely has one for free use. Local photo labs or photo studios may provide scanning services for a fee.

The correct scanner setting for photos is 300 pixels per inch (ppi)—it's a simple menu option.

Tip: If you want to make a print that's larger than the original, simply increase the scanner setting.

Example: If you double the resolution to 600 ppi during a scan and then reduce it back to 300 ppi when you go to print it from your computer, you can double the print size on the printing/editing software with no loss in quality. You even can triple the resolution to 900 ppi in a scan and then bring it down to 300 ppi in printing to triple the size of a printed photo.

If scanning your photos isn't appealing, use your phone. The quality won't be as good, but it's very convenient, and at least you'll have saved the images.

Useful app: Photomyne for Android and iOS (free for up to three albums, unlimited use for $19.99/year with a free trial). It is geared specifically to turning print photos and albums into digital photo albums.

Important: Back up your new digital files onto DVDs or thumb drives, and store one copy at home and another in a safe-deposit box.

Alternative: Back up digital files to the cloud.

•**Restore damaged prints.** Almost any amount of damage to an old paper photo can be magically repaired in digital editing. When the new digital image is printed, it will look like the old one—without the blemishes. You can master the basic skills (such as cropping and adjusting brightness and contrast) using a basic editing program—one great free one is GIMP (Gimp.org), but you'll want to turn to a pro for restoration to, say, hide a water stain or fix a torn photo (especially a tear through a face). I've seen photos that I thought were a total loss brought back almost as good as new. You'll still have the original for authenticity, but the new digitally enhanced print will be closer to how the original looked when it was taken.

Cost for pro restoration of old prints: $25 up to several hundreds of dollars, depending on the restorer and what's involved in the restoration.

•**Store your new archival albums safely.** The National Archives suggests storing print photos in

a dark place (away from direct sunlight even in an album), at room temperature (60°F to 75°F) and with a relative humidity less than 65%, which means not in an attic or a basement.

No More Dusty Clothes

Reader's Digest. RD.com

Easy way to prevent dusty clothes in your closet. Cut a hole in the center of a cloth napkin, and place it over the clothing on the hanger.

Better Way to Hang a Picture

Woman's Day.

Use two small D-rings on each picture—screwed directly into the sides of the back frame rails. Hang the D-rings on two hooks mounted on the wall. Use hooks that attach with two or three nails—they are stronger than ones using a single nail. Do not use wire—it makes pictures wobbly, and they easily can be knocked off the wall.

If you have multiple pictures to hang: Consider hiring someone recommended by a local gallery or frame shop. It typically costs $40 to $75 to have a professional hang five or six small frames.

Use Books for Soundproofing

Woman's Day. WomansDay.com

Arranging books against a wall on shelves from floor to ceiling can help reduce the sound coming through a thin wall. If you do not have enough books of your own, you can find them for very low prices at garage sales or at libraries that are getting rid of little-used volumes.

Better Ways to Care for Silver

Bruce and Jeanne Lubin, authors of the money-saving tips book series *Who Knew?* writing at QuickAndDirtyTips.com.

If the silver develops spots, add a little salt to lemon juice and rub the mixture onto the silver with a soft cloth, then rinse and buff with chamois. For easier polishing, use an old sock—slip it over your hand, and use one side to apply polish and the other to buff it out. To polish old heirloom silver, add four tablespoons of lemon juice to one quart of whole milk and let your items soak overnight—then rinse them off and dry them. Store silver in airtight containers or wrap it in tarnish-proof cloths. Do not use plastic food wrap—it can cause tarnishing.

Help for Household Blunders

Marjory Abrams, chief content officer, Bottom Line Inc., 3 Landmark Square, Suite 201, Stamford, Connecticut.

Prompted by a conversation with a coworker after he used dish soap in the dishwasher (bad idea—bubble city!), I asked friends and coworkers about their more memorable household blunders. *Here are some of the situations they got into and their solutions...*

•**Shrunken sweater.** Soak for at least five minutes in a mixture of hair conditioner (use one to two tablespoons) and lukewarm water. Do not rinse. Roll the sweater up in a towel to remove excess water. Then lay it on a dry towel, and gently pull the sweater to reshape.

Oddball alternative: Wear the damp sweater—preferably over an extra layer—until it is dry.

•**Stinky wet clothes.** If you have left washed clothes in the washing machine too long, send them through the rinse cycle again and add one cup of white vinegar.

•**Overflowing toilet.** One new home owner had a plumber reconnect the basement sink and toilet, which the previous owners had disconnected. During the next storm, water gushed out of the toilet and flooded the basement.

Solution: The plumber added a check valve—an inexpensive device that prevents backflow.

•**Objects dropped down a drain.** Cover the nozzle of the hose on a wet/dry vacuum—not a regular vacuum cleaner—with the leg from a pair of panty hose. Stick the nozzle into the drain opening, and turn on the vacuum. After the object has been retrieved, run water into the drain to refill the trap.

•**Bleach spots on furniture.** A friend's husband cleaned a living room fan with bleach. When he turned on the fan, bleach sprayed all over the room. The navy blue sofa now has permanent bleach spots. My friend covered them with a decorative throw blanket, but fabric paints, available online and at craft stores, could also make the spots less conspicuous.

•**Bleach spots on clothing.** If it's a garment you really love, try using color remover—usually found near the clothing-dye supplies in department and grocery stores—on the entire garment, and then re-dye.

Alternative: One friend ended up with an artsy T-shirt by carefully spattering more bleach on the garment.

•**Scratched hardwood floors.** A coworker colors in scratches with matching permanent marker.

•**Stuck candle wax.** Freeze wax-covered candle holders, and then carefully chip off the wax.

Tablecloth: Place a paper towel over the hardened wax and under the tablecloth, and then iron the top towel. The iron should be at a medium, not hot, temperature.

•**Crayon on walls.** Apply WD-40, then rub the crayon mark using a damp sponge. After the crayon is removed, clean the area with soap and water, and dry with a paper towel. WD-40 is a multipurpose item. Some people have used it to remove nail polish from hardwood floors…camouflage scratches and remove Rollerblade marks on linoleum or ceramic tile floors…and get gunk off piano keys.

How to Properly Dispose of Household Items

WiseBread.com

Small appliances: Use the website Search.Earth 911.com to find local recycling centers for your old coffeemakers and microwave ovens.

Worn-out linens: Donate old sheets to animal shelters to be used as bedding. Alternatively, you can give them to the Salvation Army or other local charities. They work with partners to recycle the used linens into rags or fiber for furniture or insulation.

Hangers: While Goodwill does not accept plastic hangers, other thrift or secondhand clothing stores are more than happy to take them. Wire hangers can be returned to the dry cleaner.

Worn-out athletic shoes: Nike Stores have a shoe-recycling program, called Reuse-a-Shoe, which will accept worn-out athletic shoes from all brands and recycle the components to create athletic and playground surfaces.

Expired medication: You may be tempted to flush your old medication down the toilet, but this can contaminate the water system. Instead, find an independent pharmacy authorized to take back your outdated medication using the website DisposeMyMeds.org.

Outdated cell phones: Best Buy accepts defunct cell phones for recycling, but if you have a working device, donate it to Cell Phones for Soldiers (CellPhonesForSoldiers.com).

Whodathunk Household Tricks That Save You Money

Julie Edelman, aka "The Accidental Housewife." Based on Florida's Gulf Coast, she is author of *The New York Times* best-seller *The Accidental Housewife: How to Overcome Housekeeping Hysteria One Task at a Time.* JuliesTips.com

You can save hundreds and potentially thousands of dollars a year with these money-saving household tips and tricks…

Clever Fix-Its

• **Hide wood furniture scratches with coffee grinds.** Rub a cotton swab in steeped grounds, and dab on scratches to make them less noticeable. Test this first in a hard-to-see area to make sure the coffee works with the color of your wood furniture.

• **Avoid overwatering potted plants by using packing peanuts.** Place a one-inch layer of Styrofoam peanuts at the bottom of gardening pots before adding soil. Styrofoam peanuts won't decompose or absorb the water, and they prevent water buildup, bacteria, fungus and root rot.

• **Unstick zippers with pencils.** Place the item on a newspaper or paper towel to catch the lead debris. Rub a pencil on both sides of the teeth of the zipper where it is stuck. Repeat until you can move it up and down. The graphite in the pencil acts as a dry lubricant. Wipe away any excess graphite with a slightly damp cloth or paper towel. You could also try candle wax.

• **Prevent dogs from destroying furniture with cayenne pepper.** Use a 1:10 ratio of cayenne pepper to water in a spray bottle. Shake well. Apply to wood legs or the wood base of furniture. (Test on an inconspicuous area to make sure that it doesn't damage your furniture.) Dogs will be put off by the burning taste. You also can spray your pet's favorite potty spots in the house to deter the pet from peeing and marking the area as its territory.

• **Save water-stained suede with stale bread.** Gently rub the dried stain with a piece of stale bread or unseasoned bread crumbs. When using bread crumbs, use a toothbrush to work the crumbs into the stain and lift the fibers. An emery board will also do the trick.

Making Things Last Longer

•**Get more servings from near-empty condiments with vinegar.** Vinegar is a common ingredient in many of our most common condiments, including ketchup, mustard and barbecue sauce. Add two teaspoons of white vinegar to your near-empty bottles, and shake.

•**Squeeze more out of tube products.** When you feel you can't squeeze any more out of the tube, snip the other end and you'll have a few more applications. Seal with a binder clip.

•**Remove sweater pills with a pumice stone.** Gently rub the stone in one direction until the pills are removed.

•**Prevent mold on cheese with oil.** Apply a light film of vegetable oil or soft butter with a pastry brush or paper towel (or use cooking spray) to the outside of the cheese, and store in an airtight container in the fridge. This prevents airflow to the cheese. If mold begins to grow on the film, simply wipe off with a paper towel.

•**Keep flowers fresh with vodka and sugar.** Add a few drops of vodka and a teaspoon of sugar to the vase water. Both agents help reduce bacteria growth, keeping flowers fresher longer.

•**Fix DVD scratches with bananas.** Gently rub a freshly cut banana in a circular motion to coat and fill in scratches. Use the inside of the peel to clean and polish. Wipe with a clean, soft cloth.

Stain Removers

If you don't have stain stick or stain spray handy, try these remedies…

•**Use aspirin to remove sweat stains.** Crush and dissolve four to six aspirins in warm water. Submerge the stained areas into the solution. Let soak for two to three hours, then launder.

•**Remove ink and lipstick stains with rubbing alcohol.** Place a clean cloth or a paper towel under the stained area to prevent bleeding. Gently dab the stain with a cotton ball that has been dampened with rubbing alcohol. Repeat until the stain is gone. Let dry, and launder as usual.

•**Get out grass stains with vodka.** Gently rub the stain with a clean cloth saturated with vodka. Rinse with cool water and launder.

Dryer Lint Can Be Used to Keep the Home Fires Burning

Good Housekeeping. GoodHousekeeping.com

It burns longer than newspaper because of the cotton fibers often trapped within it.

What to do: Stuff the lint into a cardboard egg carton or empty toilet paper tube before lighting.

8 Tips and Tricks to Make Your Holidays Easier

Julie Edelman, aka "The Accidental Housewife." Based on Florida's Gulf Coast, she is author of *The New York Times* best-seller *The Accidental Housewife: How to Overcome Housekeeping Hysteria One Task at a Time.* JuliesTips.com

Here are tried-and-true tips and tricks to make your holidays a bit easier…

Cleaning Tricks

•**Fallen pine needles.** If you don't want to lug out the vacuum, wrap a piece of duct tape around your hand and pat to pick up pine needles.

•**Dried candle drips.** Set your blow- dryer with a nozzle on a high setting. Direct the heat over drippings, and hold for 20 seconds or until the wax melts. Wipe immediately with a paper towel.

For Hanukkah candle holders: Remove the melted wax with Q-tips.

•**Cranberry sauce stains.** Remove any remains with a butter knife. Rinse with cold water. Place a clean paper towel or cloth under the stain to prevent "bleeding." Douse with aerosol hair spray to loosen the stain. Blot with a clean cloth or paper towel. Launder per care instructions.

•**Carpet indents.** Place a damp cloth on the indent, and hold a steam iron at least four inches above it for 30 seconds. The steam helps the carpet fibers return to their original upright position. Next, use the edge of a coin to work out the dent by rubbing it back and forth until the carpet is fluffy again.

Holiday Help

•**Fill glass vases with candy, pinecones, ornaments or fruit.** Rather than buy floral centerpieces that can cost $40 (or more) each, fill cylinder vases you've collected from flower deliveries (or you can buy them cheaply at a dollar store) with candy canes, peppermint swirls ($5 for about three pounds) or red and green Hershey Kisses. Or use pinecones, ornamental balls or fruits such as oranges, lemons, limes or apples.

•**Use decorative cupcake liners for individual snacks.** Fill with items such as mixed nuts, small pretzels or trail mix so that guests can chomp and toss.

•**Dab incandescent lightbulbs with peppermint oil.** The scent will be "activated" when the lights are turned on, warming the oil and adding a fresh holiday scent. Make sure that the bulbs are off and cold before adding the oil.

•**Make a ribbon dispenser out of a shoebox.** Cut a hole at each end of the shoebox wide enough to put a paper towel tube through it. Trim the tube to fit. Place spools of ribbon on the tube, and insert it into the holes. On the long side of the shoebox, cut half-inch slits to thread ribbon from each spool. Pull each ribbon through its slit. Do not seal the ends where the tube is inserted so that you can restock the spool.

CHAPTER 19

Renovation and Maintenance

Wow! This Is My House? Simple Renovations That Can Transform Any Home

Jonathan and Drew Scott, hosts of *Property Brothers*, an HGTV program about renovating fixer-uppers. Jonathan is a licensed contractor…his twin brother, Drew, a real estate agent. Together they own Scott Real Estate Inc., which has offices in Las Vegas and Vancouver and Calgary, Canada. HGTV.com

You might be surprised at how much you can change the character of your home—and make it much more attractive to potential buyers—without going broke doing it.

If you make changes that are popular with today's buyers, your renovation won't just provide you with a nicer home to live in—it will make the home easier to sell.

Here are eight renovations and modifications that you can enjoy now and that can help you sell your home in what remains very much a buyer's market…

•**Add a full glass wall.** Glass exterior walls provide three benefits that today's buyers love—they bring in massive amounts of natural light…make the home feel more connected to the outdoors…and make a small room feel bigger.

Replacing a 12-to-14-foot wall with floor-to-ceiling windows that slide open will cost around $15,000. Adding nice curtains or blinds sufficient to cover this window wall could add several hundred or more to the price, depending on the materials selected. Yes, that's a lot of money, but it really will turn the room into a distinctive selling point for the home.

Consider adding a patio and deck furniture right outside the sliding glass wall to create some outdoor living space. That's like adding a room to your home without the relatively high costs of an addition.

•**Remove interior walls in the main living space.** Today's home buyers like open floor plans with good sight lines. Ripping out some of the walls that separate the kitchen, dining area and living room could make an old, cramped home seem significantly more modern and spacious.

Costs will vary greatly depending mainly on whether the walls removed are load-bearing walls. Pulling down nonload-bearing walls and patching and repainting the resulting gaps in the drywall, ceiling and floor could cost as little as $500 to $1,000.

Removing a load-bearing wall could cost well into the thousands—perhaps as much as $10,000—depending on the size of the wall and the amount of structural work required.

Warning: Consult a contractor or residential structural engineer before removing any walls unless you have access to the blueprints and are absolutely certain that the wall is not load-bearing.

•**Combine two bedrooms of modest size into a master bedroom suite.** An impressive master bedroom suite featuring a big bedroom, spacious closets and a roomy master bath helps sell a home these days—more so than a large number of bedrooms. Perhaps that's because couples are marrying later and having fewer children.

It typically costs just a few thousand dollars to convert two small adjacent bedrooms into one big one. However, prices could climb into the low five figures if the project includes adding a new bathroom or completely remodeling an existing bathroom and/or if a load-bearing wall is removed.

•**Turn a dining room into an office.** Today's home buyers don't see much value in having multiple eating areas. If a home's kitchen is large enough for a full-sized table, consider alternative uses for the dining room.

It could become part of an open floor plan, as discussed earlier, but another option is to convert the dining room into an office. This might be as simple as framing a door into an open dining room entryway, which should cost well under $1,000.

Warning: Some people turn their dining room into an extra bedroom, but having a bedroom right next to the kitchen usually is an awkward configuration. An office is more appropriate in this location. Buyers with big families still can use the office as a bedroom if they like.

•**Add built-in storage.** Americans don't like stowing their stuff in dank basements or hard-to-access attics. That's one reason why many home buyers consider extensive built-in storage a big plus.

Woodworkers might charge tens of thousands of dollars to build custom cabinets, but there are more cost-effective options.

For example, Ikea's wardrobe systems are well-designed, stylish and affordable. On the Ikea website (Ikea.com), select "Go Shopping," then "Rooms," then "Bedroom," then "Storage and Organization" to see the styles that are available. For a few thousand dollars, you can line an entire wall with these, then hire a drywall contractor for about $500 to add wallboard above and at the ends of the wardrobes so that they appear to be built-in components.

•**Add windows, skylights or solar light tubes to bring more natural light into dark rooms.** Older homes often have less sunlight than today's buyers like. Adding windows or skylights could be an option, depending on the layout of the home, but each one that you add could cost upward of $1,000, between the cost of the unit itself and the cost of professional installation.

Solar light tubes are a more affordable and versatile option. These use a small rooftop dome and reflective tube to pull a surprising amount of sunlight down into the house—even into interior rooms where adding windows and skylights is not feasible. From inside the room, these just look like overhead lights on the ceiling.

One light tube should be enough for a small room, though two or more might be needed in a large space. They can make a dark room sunny and bright for perhaps $500 or $600 apiece installed. Solatube is the nation's leading provider (888-765-2882, Solatube.com).

•**Replace your kitchen countertop.** Countertops are the single kitchen element most likely to influence a buyer's opinion of the room. Granite and quartz countertops convey a sense of high-end quality—even though they have come down significantly in price in recent years.

Shop carefully, and you now can find these for as little as $3,500, including installation, assuming that your kitchen is of average size.

Adding impressive new countertops above old, worn kitchen cabinets won't fool anyone, however. If your cabinets are showing some age but they still are in reasonable shape, you could paint them white and add attractive new hardware—big-box stores such as Walmart, Lowe's and The Home Depot sometimes sell bags of attractive brushed nickel cabinet hardware for as little as $1 per piece.

If your kitchen cabinets are beyond basic rehab, new prefab cabinets of reasonable quality can be found at big-box stores for as little as $3,000 to $4,000 for a complete kitchen update.

•**Replace old bathroom vanities.** The single most cost-effective way to make a bathroom seem more upscale is to install a vanity that has a granite or quartz top and dark-wood cabinets.

I've come across these for as little as $800 at Costco (Costco.com). Grab one if you see such a deal and the item seems right for your bathroom—that's less than you would normally pay for the granite top alone, and these vanities tend to sell out fast.

Make Your Home Look More Upscale: For Hundreds, Not Thousands

Hilary Farr, cohost of *Love It or List It*, which airs on HGTV. She is president of Toronto-based interior design company Hilary Farr Design. HilaryFarr.com

The trouble with upscale home upgrades to your home is that they tend to come with up-market price tags. But there are home projects that can bring a sense of class and distinction to a home for $1,000 or less—sometimes much less. These upgrades won't just impress your guests and make your house a more appealing place to live— they also could help attract buyers when you sell. We asked Hilary Farr, cohost of the popular HGTV show *Love It or List It*, for inexpensive ways to make a home appear more upscale inside. *Here are six of her favorite ways to get an expensive look for less…*

•**Install crown molding, a decorative strip traditionally made from plaster or wood that runs along the tops of interior walls.** This molding creates a visual transition between wall and ceiling and adds design detail, making a home feel more upscale. (It also hides drywall imperfections where walls and ceilings meet.)

Hiring a skilled plasterer to install a traditional plaster crown molding would be very costly… as would hiring a carpenter to put in an elaborate wood molding. There are less expensive, pre-formed moldings made from fiberboard, but those are very heavy and difficult to install well. Fortunately, there's a fourth option—install polystyrene foam moldings, which can be glued in place. Unlike wood moldings, polystyrene moldings do not expand and contract with changes in temperature, so

cracks and gaps will not develop over time, and unlike fiberboard moldings, they are not very difficult to install. They are quite sturdy and can be lightly sanded and painted.

Select a crown molding that is at least five inches in height—anything smaller won't make enough of an impression to be worth the trouble.

Cost estimate: Expect to pay about $2 per linear foot—that's less than $200 for a 20-foot-by-20-foot room. If you opt for professional installation, it might add up to $200 more per room to your bottom line, depending on the amount of molding and local labor rates.

Related project: Beef up your baseboards. Replace the insubstantial-looking molding found along the bottoms of most walls with baseboards that are five-and-a-half to six inches tall. These should match the room's crown molding in color and style, but they should be made of wood, which can take the beating that baseboards can get over time.

•**Expand the trim around interior window frames to make windows seem grander.** Windows are the single most important feature in the typical room—our eyes are drawn to them. The easiest, least expensive way to make windows appear more upscale and impressive from the inside is to expand the trim around them. Just add a "backband"—a three-quarter- to one-and-a-quarter-inch strip of wood that is nailed in place around the outer perimeter of the existing interior window trim and painted to match.

If you're willing to tackle a larger project, you could remove the existing window trim and replace it with something more substantial. This will look even better and save the effort of searching for a backband that will work with the existing trim. If you want to improve your home's curb appeal, upgrading the trim around the exterior of windows is worth considering, too.

Cost estimate: Backband molding made of paint-grade wood such as poplar for interior use or pine for exterior use typically costs just $1 to $2 per linear foot, so even factoring in the price of paint and finish nails, this project should cost no more than $30 to $50 per window.

Related project: Expand your window dressing. Purchase curtain rods that extend six to 18 inches beyond the edges of your windows on each side. Install these rods at least four inches above the tops of the windows and ideally all the way up near the ceiling or crown molding. Purchase curtains that extend all the way from this rod to the floor—they should just touch the floor, not stop a few inches above it. This also makes windows of modest size seem grand.

●**Install subway tile in your bathrooms and/or kitchen.** Home owners who want tile that seems upscale and special have three choices. They can pay up for expensive tile …they can choose unusual colors or patterns that stand out but that might later go out of style or alienate future home buyers…or they can install subway tile.

Subway tile is rectangular—typically three inches by six inches—so it is more eye-catching than ordinary square household tile. It has been in use for well over 100 years but is timeless and has never gone out of style. White subway tile with black grout or black subway tile with white grout produces a particularly upscale result. A staggered "brick" tile pattern creates a traditional look…a straight-line tile-on-top-of-tile "stack" pattern creates a more modern look…while chevron and herringbone patterns, created by laying the tiles on a diagonal, are distinctive.

Cost estimate: Three-by-six-inch ceramic subway tile often costs just $2 to $3 per square foot. A typical kitchen backsplash of 15-to-20 square feet could be done for less than $200 per backsplash if you do it yourself. Professional installation can add $5 to $10 per square foot.

●**Upgrade interior doors.** High-end homes do not just look more upscale than other homes, they also feel more upscale. Their components are solid and substantial to the touch. One simple way to make a conventional home feel more solid and substantial is to replace its hollow-core wood interior doors with solid-core wood doors. This works because doors are among the parts of the home that are handled most frequently by home owners and guests.

When doors open with some weightiness and close with a subtle thunk, the whole house feels more upscale. Also, solid-core doors keep out noise better than hollow-core doors.

Cost estimate: Solid-core wood interior doors can be found for around $200 apiece. One way to control the cost of this project is to upgrade just the doors that you and your guests use most often, such as guest bathroom doors and/or master bedroom doors.

Related project: Upgrade doorknobs. Select new knobs based on their solid feel, not just their appealing looks. You can get a good-quality doorknob for $20 to $30.

●**Transform entryways from clutter receptacles into visual greetings.** In many homes, entryways are ad-hoc storage areas. Shoes and umbrellas are lined up near the front door…keys, mail and other clutter rest on any available flat surface. Clutter is inelegant, especially as a first impression. Your home instantly will seem more upscale if you remove all clutter that can be seen from its entryway. If necessary, purchase closet organizing products to make it easier to stow entryway clutter in the hall closet…and/or an elegant, understated cabinet or a small table for the entryway featuring drawers to hide small clutter including keys and mail. Use the surface of this cabinet or table to place a beautiful element of welcome such as a vase containing one fresh flower.

●**Install laminate kitchen countertops that look like quartz, marble or granite.** Quartz, marble and granite countertops make homes look upscale because they are upscale—they typically cost $75 to $100 or more per square foot, installed. But these days, there are laminate countertops that do an excellent job of mimicking the look of those desirable, high-end materials for less than half the cost.

Examples: Wilsonart HD laminates (Wilsonart.com)…and Formica 180fx laminates (Formica.com).

Take a close look at the edge of laminate countertops in showrooms before buying. Some do a wonderful job mimicking high-end materials when you look only at the top but ruin the illusion by looking like laminates along the edge

Cost estimate: $30 per square foot, installed, for laminate countertop.

---

8 Common Mistakes Home Owners Make

The late David E. MacLellan, a home builder in the California Bay area for 25 years and a 2011 inductee into the California Homebuilding Foundation Hall of Fame. He was chairman emeritus of Pacific InterWest Building Consultants, Inc., which inspects homes during the construction process. He was a licensed general contractor and one of the coauthors of *The Home Book: A Complete Guide to Homeowner and Homebuilder Responsibilities.* HouseFixIt.com

---

Some seemingly simple do-it-yourself projects can do substantial damage to a home. And placing certain possessions in the wrong spot in a house can lead to expensive problems, too. *Eight common and potentially costly home owner mistakes…*

●**Overloading upper kitchen cabinets.** The upper cabinets in a kitchen are hung from the walls by a relatively modest number of screws—or sometimes only by nails in older homes. If you fill every shelf of one of these cabinets with stacks of heavy dinnerware or cookware, the cabinet could sag or even come crashing down from the wall.

Better: If you have lots of heavy kitchen items, store some or all of them in lower cabinets, which are supported by the floor. Or at least divide heavy kitchen items among several different upper cabinets. Each cabinet might contain some heavy dinnerware and some light glassware, for example. Peek behind upper kitchen cabinets every few years to see if they have begun to pull away from the wall behind. If so, reduce the load they're carrying immediately, then add more or longer screws for greater support. Make sure that these screws enter wood framing, not just drywall.

●**Hanging a ceiling fan from a light mounting box.** When home owners replace an overhead light with a ceiling fan, they often just attach the new fan to the existing mounting box. But ceiling fans typi-

cally need more support than can be provided by a mounting box designed for a light. Fans not only weigh more than the average light fixture, they also vibrate when in use, adding greatly to the strain on the mounting. A mounting box that isn't up to the challenge could rip free from the ceiling.

Better: If you're not certain that the existing mounting box is designed to support a ceiling fan, buy and install a new mounting box that is. Make sure that it's rated to handle your fan's weight. Mounting boxes generally cost about $10 at hardware stores or home centers. Professional installation of a fan box could range from $40 to $150, depending on your area of the country.

●**Improperly attaching a trellis or similar structure.** Some home owners bolt or nail these structures to their home's siding. But siding often isn't strong enough to support the added weight, so the structure comes crashing down, damaging the siding and anyone or anything that is under it when it falls. Some home owners also fail to adequately prevent rainwater from getting into the bolt or nail holes.

Better: When attaching anything heavy to your home's exterior, bolt holes should be drilled into the home's framing, not just into the siding. To keep out rainwater, after you drill bolt holes, fill them with caulk before inserting the bolts. If you attach something made of wood to the exterior of your home, such as a trellis, insert metal flashing between the house and this wood to prevent termites from using it as a path into the house. Check whether local building codes require you to obtain a permit before attaching a trellis or other structure to the outside of your home.

●**Overloading upper floors.** Heavy items such as pool tables, waterbeds, large aquariums, pianos and weight-lifting equipment can overload floor systems—even when those floor systems are built to code. That's especially true when these heavy items are on a home's second floor. Even when there's a basement underneath, a home's first floor tends to be much better supported than upper floors, particularly near first-floor walls.

Better: If you have something very heavy in your home, keep it downstairs, ideally next to a wall. Watch for signs of excessive floor deflection, or movement, such as cracking in nearby walls.

•**Tinting the inside of multipane windows.** Home owners in the southern and western US often attach adhesive tinted films to their windows to limit the amount of sunlight and UV rays that get through. This can reduce both air-conditioning bills and sun damage to furniture and carpeting. But if you tint the inside of a multiple-pane window—most modern windows incorporate more than one pane of glass—the tinting will reflect the sun's rays back into the area between the panes, raising the temperature of the air or other gases sealed inside until the window's seals rupture. Ruptured seals greatly diminish a window's insulating value. Window warranties typically do not cover multipane windows that have been tinted on their interior.

Better: Apply tinting film on the outside of multipane windows, not the inside. Use a high-quality product, such as 3M's Sun Control Window Films. A low-quality tinting film won't last long exposed to the elements on a window's exterior. This generally does not void window warranties—but read your windows' warranty literature to confirm this before proceeding. Alternately, you could purchase and install pretinted windows.

•**Connecting fences to the exterior of a home.** Nailing or screwing the final post of a fence to the side of your home could cause rainwater to become trapped between the post and the wall, leading to rot or mold. It also could create a path for termites to enter the home.

Better: Leave a gap of perhaps one inch between the final fence post and the home.

•**Installing a patio or sidewalk that blocks the slope of the land near a home.** The ground immediately surrounding most homes is sloped away from the structure to discourage water from pooling against the foundation. But when home owners put in patios or sidewalks adjacent to their homes, the concrete often juts up above the "finished grade," creating a barrier that prevents water from flowing away. Over time, the resulting pool of water can lead to curled slabs, foundation cracks or moisture or mold problems in basements or crawl spaces.

Better: Dig a few inches down into the ground before putting in a sidewalk or patio near your home. The top surface should not extend above the original soil level.

•**Walking on tile roofs.** Roofing tiles made of concrete, clay, slate or another relatively brittle material can crack under the weight of a single person and should be walked on only by a professional roofer. (Composition asphalt shingles can be walked on, but it is not recommended, since walking will loosen the protective mineral granules.) Cracked tiles are likely to shift out of place, allowing water to enter the home where it can cause damage or encourage mold. Damage to a roof caused by walking on it usually is not covered by roof warranties. Walking on roofs also is quite dangerous for home owners.

Better: If you have a tile roof, use a ladder and telescoping pole to clear any debris from it, rather than walk on the tiles.

Never Do This to Your Home! Renovations That Will Reduce Its Value

Scott McGillivray, host of the HGTV series *Income Property*. He is a real estate investor and contractor in Toronto, Ontario, Canada, and Fort Myers, Florida, and author of *How to Add Value to Your Home*. ScottMcGillivray.com

Home-renovation projects rarely pay for themselves when the home is sold. Sometimes the financial hit is considerable. For example, if you add a sunroom…put in a swimming pool in a cold-weather state…or remodel a home office, you would be lucky to recoup half your costs when you sell. But some specific home projects are even worse financially—not only do they not pay for themselves, they actually will make your home sell for less than it would have if you hadn't done them at all.

Things not to do to your home…

•**DO NOT expand your master bedroom if that means eliminating another bedroom.** Small master bedrooms are a common complaint, particularly in older homes. But in many cases, the only realistic way to expand a master bedroom is to sacrifice one of the home's other bedrooms, which is likely to be a costly mistake.

Fewer bedrooms means fewer potential buyers—most buyers have a specific number of bedrooms in mind and never even look at homes that fall short of this number. The buyers who remain will expect your home to be priced in line with the mostly smaller homes that share its now-lower bedroom count.

The financial hit is greatest when a home starts with three or fewer bedrooms. Dropping from three to two or two to one will greatly reduce both the potential number of interested buyers and the eventual selling price—it could cost you tens of thousands of dollars.

Exceptions: Removing a bedroom might not detract from your home's value if the home currently has six or more bedrooms...or if the home is in an area where a large percentage of buyers are retirees—bedroom quantity is not a major concern for many empty nesters.

•**DO NOT convert a garage into living space.** Finishing a garage can seem like a cost-effective way to enlarge a home—it is significantly less expensive than having an addition built from scratch. Trouble is, many buyers will not even look at properties that do not have garages. As a result, converting your garage into part of your home could reduce the value of the home by $10,000 or more—particularly if you convert the garage into a family room or an office rather than an extra bedroom that would at least increase the home's appeal for some larger families. Finishing part of the basement is almost always a better financial move in the long run, assuming that the ceiling is at least eight feet high.

•**DO NOT add artistic flourishes or personal touches to the home itself.** The smart way to add art and/or personality to a home is to hang art on its walls, not to alter the home in ways that can't be easily undone when it is time to sell.

Examples: Do not have a mural painted on a wall or ceiling—or if you do, paint over it before you put the home on the market. It would be relatively easy for buyers to paint over it themselves, but

most buyers prefer homes that already are the way they want them, not homes that require even modest amounts of work. Do not have a large masonry fountain built in your yard. Do not incorporate a mosaic artwork into the tile of your kitchen or bathroom.

It's perfectly fine for a home to have style, but that should be a mainstream style that fits in with the neighborhood and the overall architecture of the home—a home in a rural area could have a farmhouse style, for example. If a home's style is out of character for the neighborhood...dramatically out-of-step with the size and value of the property...or reflects only your personal tastes, your home's value is likely to take a hit—even if the flourishes you added truly do look nice. Buyers want a home to be a blank slate for them to fill, not a reflection of a prior owner's tastes.

•**DO NOT paint interior walls dark colors.** Dark interior walls were a trend at one time—decorators will tell you that they can make rooms feel cozy and elegant. But many home buyers do not think "cozy and elegant" when they walk into a dark-walled room—they think "small and unwelcoming." Light-colored walls might not be trendy, but they make spaces feel larger and friendlier, which buyers value more than stylishness.

If you do paint walls dark colors, repaint them before putting the property on the market. You might have to apply primer before repainting to cover the dark color with a light one.

Similar: Avoid garish and unusual wall colors. Neon pink or lime green, for example, will be off-putting for many potential buyers.

•**DO NOT attempt do-it-yourself home repairs if the result will look like do-it-yourself repairs.** Home owners who have the skills to do basic home repairs can save themselves thousands of dollars over the years. But when home buyers (or the home inspectors they hire) see evidence of do-it-yourself work, they often start to worry about what else the home owner might have done on his/her own that isn't so evident—such as electrical and plumbing work or foundation work—and whether this work was done properly. Potential buyers feel much more confident when it appears that a home has been professionally maintained.

Before you tackle a do-it-yourself project, consider not just whether you can do it, but whether you can make the finished job look like professional work. It might be worth paying a paint or drywall pro to expertly close up the wall or ceiling you had to open up, for example.

When you are about to sell, point out your do-it-yourself projects to your real estate agent and ask whether there is anything that should be done to make the work look more professional.

•**DO NOT texture interior walls and ceilings.** Drywall compound can add texture to interior walls and ceilings, resulting in a stucco look. This textured look goes in and out of style and might not be in vogue when you sell.

•**DO NOT install a chain-link fence in your front yard.** These look low-end and unwelcoming, giving potential buyers a negative first impression of your home. If you must have a fence, it's worth paying extra for wood (or if you don't want to deal with the ongoing upkeep that wood requires, perhaps a composite or vinyl fence designed to look like wood). These can cost twice as much as chain link, but they will not reduce the value of the home—a nice wood picket fence could even increase the value.

Exceptions: A chain-link fence is unlikely to detract from the value of your home if most of the homes in your neighborhood have one…if it is in the backyard and not easily seen from the road…or if it is hidden by tall, attractive hedges.

Less Expensive Way to Enlarge Your Home

Money, Time-Life Bldg., Rockefeller Center, New York City. Money.com

Build a bump-out instead of an addition. A bump-out is extra space that hangs off the side of a house. It usually can be up to three feet from the existing exterior wall and can run almost the whole length of your home. It does not require a founda-

tion, as a full addition would, so it costs much less to build—usually about $6,000 to $12,000. This could be enough space to allow an eating area or large closet, for example.

6 Home-Remodeling Projects That Pay for Themselves (and 4 That Don't)

Clayton DeKorne, chief editor of the JLC Group, which publishes *Remodeling Magazine's* annual Cost vs. Value Report. He previously was a renovation contractor and carpenter in Burlington, Vermont. Remodeling.HW.net

How much will that remodeling project cost? The size of the check you write to a contractor might not be the best possible measure. Assuming that you eventually sell your home, the number that matters most might be the price of the remodeling project minus the amount that the project boosts the home's selling price. On average, home owners receive around two-thirds of their remodeling costs back when they sell, according to *Remodeling Magazine's* 2019 Cost vs. Value Report—but some projects tend to provide a much higher return on investment than others.

Here are six projects that return 70% to 100% of the amount they cost, on average, and four projects that return a whole lot less…

Remodeling Projects That Nearly Pay for Themselves

Real estate agents often stress that a home's "curb appeal"—how nice it looks from the street—can have a significant impact on its sales price. The remodeling report suggests that they're right—projects that improve the exterior appearance of a home dominate the top of the list, and one interior project continues to provide an appealing return…

•**New garage door.** *Average cost recouped:* 97.5%. The garage door often is the easiest, most cost-effective way to upgrade a home's exterior appearance. Garage doors are large enough that they're a significant percentage of the front façade of many homes. Existing garage doors often are badly degraded from the weather, and many are dented as well, but a replacement is relatively affordable. An attractive steel door with foam insulation and windows costs around $3,600 on average.*

●**Manufactured stone veneer.** *Average cost recouped:* 94.9%. Replace the lower third of your home's siding on the street-facing façade with a stone veneer—an outer layer that creates the impression of a stone foundation—and you're likely to recoup almost all of your expense when you sell, assuming that the veneer is in keeping with the style of the home. (A real stone veneer also is an option, but prices tend to be higher and the appearance is similar.)

This type of upgrade gives a home a sense of weight and solidity, and most people like the mix of textures and colors it creates with the siding above. Stone veneers first became popular in the Midwest but now are catching on in other parts of the country as well.

Warning: If a stone veneer is not installed properly, it can create moisture problems for the home. Confirm that the contractor you hire will either apply an added layer of housewrap beneath the stone (most homes have just a single layer under the siding)…or better yet, install a drainable matrix, such as Masonry Technology Inc.'s Sure Cavity Rainscreen Drainage Plane. (A metal trim called a "weep screed" also should be installed at the base of the veneer to let moisture escape.)

Average price: Around $9,000 for approximately 300 square feet.

●**Minor kitchen remodel.** *Average cost recouped:* 80.5%. This is one interior project that offers a very solid return on investment. But take care—not every kitchen remodel will produce such an impressive return when the home is sold. You'll want to control the scope and scale of the project, particularly if you expect to sell the home soon.

*Project costs provided in this article are national averages. Home owners' actual costs could vary significantly based on the quality of the products and contractors selected…the part of the country…and other details about the home and project. The costs include both parts and labor.

While a "minor" kitchen remodel—average cost $22,500—can return around 80% of the money spent, an "upscale major kitchen remodel" averaging more than $100,000 typically returns only 59.7%. Major remodels should be done only when you plan to stay in the home for many years so that you can enjoy the remodel.

A minor face-lift often is sufficient to dramatically improve the look of an older kitchen. Cost-effective improvements include replacing old appliances, countertops, flooring, sinks/faucets and cabinet door and drawer fronts, plus repainting walls, trim and ceiling. Farmhouse-esque shaker-style cabinet doors and drawer fronts are a good choice—they're timeless and popular with home buyers.

If your goal is to recoup as much as possible of your remodeling costs when you sell, do not change the layout of the kitchen, replace cabinets entirely or purchase luxury-brand appliances or expensive countertops.

●**Wood deck addition.** *Average cost recouped:* 75.6%. Home buyers tend to like decks—they imagine spending pleasant afternoons outside enjoying sunny summer days. Note that it's pressure-treated wood decks, not composite decks, that are listed here. Composite decks last longer and require less maintenance, so they can be a great choice if you intend to remain in the home for many years to come…but if you expect to sell in the not-too-distant future, the higher cost of composite decks leads to a somewhat lower return on the investment—just 69.1%. Prices vary, but based on nationwide averages a 16-foot-by-20-foot composite deck might cost $19,200, versus $13,300 for a wood deck of the same size.

●**New siding.** *Average cost recouped:* 75.6%. These days there are durable, affordable vinyl- and fiber-cement-siding options that hold up well to the weather and very effectively mimic the look of wood. The average cost of siding replacement is around $16,000 for 1,250 square feet, and as noted above, the average payback is a relatively strong 75.6%. But payback of this project can vary significantly—much depends on how badly the current siding needs to be replaced.

●**New entry door.** *Average cost recouped:* 74.9%. A new front door—like a new garage door—is an inexpensive way to help a home make a great first impression. An insulated 20-gauge steel door that is factory finished with paint is an attractive but cost-effective option. The total price of the project averages only around $1,800, even when the jambs and threshold are replaced in addition to the door itself. Wood doors might look even nicer, but they are difficult to maintain and cost more.

Similar: For a more substantial front-door upgrade, have a prefabricated "grand entryway" installed. These typically feature a fiberglass door stained to look like wood and include "sidelights"—tall vertical windows on each side of the door, as well as a transom window above the door. Replace the door hardware including the lockset, too. Cost is around $9,000, but home owners typically recoup 71.9% of that when they sell.

Projects with Lower Payback

Home owners tend to recoup a low percentage of the cost of remodeling projects when they pay big bucks for upscale work. Future home buyers inevitably appreciate the upscale aspects of the home—they just don't want to pay the premium to cover the high costs of the work.

Four projects where home sellers tend to recoup less than 60% of the cost of the project when they sell...

•**Upscale master bedroom suite addition.** *Average cost recouped:* 50.4%. Upscale master bedroom suites might include fireplaces, walk-in dressing areas with natural light, spacious bathrooms with walk-in showers and soaker tubs—but the costs often climb upward of $200,000, and there's a good chance that you'll lose nearly half that money when you sell. Even a more modest "midrange" master suite addition has a relatively modest payback of 59.4%.

•**Backyard patio.** *Average cost recouped:* 55.2%. Why do patios offer a poor return while wood decks do much better? The reason isn't that home buyers don't value patios...it's that they don't value them enough to make up for the fact that professionally installed stone patios tend to be much pricier than decks. The average bill for a 20-foot-by-20-foot patio is nearly $57,000.

•**Upscale bathroom addition.** *Average cost recouped:* 58.1%. Adding a luxurious, high-end bathroom to a home will boost its eventual selling price —just not nearly enough to cover the steep cost of these projects, which average $87,700. The payback for a more modest midrange bathroom addition is only slightly better in percentage terms—60.6%.

•**Upscale major kitchen remodel.** *Average cost recouped:* 59.7%. As mentioned earlier, dropping six figures on the kitchen of your dreams isn't likely to pay off when you sell. Potential buyers who value high-end kitchens typically prefer to make their own appliance and styling choices, which might differ from your choices.

Home Renovations to Age in Place

Roundup of experts on home design, reported at US News.com.

These home renovations look good and help you age in place. Some changes can be made at any time—they will benefit people of any age while allowing seniors to remain more easily in their own homes.

•**Lighting improvements include redesign for more natural light, more lamps, recessed lighting and task lighting in the kitchen.**

•**Bathroom grab bars now look like towel bars and other accent pieces.**

•**Kitchen drawers and pull-out shelves are better than cabinets for access to items.**

•**Easier-to-use appliances range from a raised dishwasher or wall oven to appliances with larger, easier-to-see controls.**

•**Adding a bench in the shower provides a place to sit.**

•**Wider doorways can make a home look more open.**

•**Replacing doorknobs with levers**—they are easier to use and make it possible to open doors with knees or elbows if you're carrying packages.

Update Your Home to Stay Out of a Nursing Home

Charles B. Inlander, consumer advocate and health-care consultant based in Fogelsville, Pennsylvania. He was the founding president of the nonprofit People's Medical Society, a consumer advocacy organization credited with key improvements in the quality of US health care in the 1980s and 1990s, and is the author or coauthor of more than 20 consumer-health books.

Most people I know are adamant that they want to stay in their homes as long as possible as they grow older. The good news is that there are now many affordable—and sometimes surprising—alternatives to nursing homes. *Best approaches...*

●**Use new technology to stay at home.** Innovative technological solutions now allow many people to remain independent. For example, you can now buy home medication-dispensing devices that store all your pills, unlock when it's time to take them and alert you with a signal at pill time. These devices are even wired to a remote command center that will call you or a relative if you miss just one dose! In addition, home-care agencies can set up devices (with sensors worn by the patient) for daily monitoring of blood pressure and body temperature.

Recent development: Medicare has just agreed to cover many such home services for people who otherwise would be placed in a more costly nursing home.

●**Consider "campus" living.** It may not be quite as much fun as a college campus, but assisted-living facilities do offer their own activities (such as bridge, yoga classes and book clubs) and can be ideal for people who can't stay in a traditional home or live with relatives. With assisted living, you have your own apartment and receive three meals a day, medical monitoring and medication assistance (by a nurse or an aide).

Cost: $1,000 to $5,000 per person per month.

Recent development: Growing numbers of so-called continuing-care communities. They offer independent (often freestanding homes) and assisted-living programs in addition to skilled nursing home services all on the same campus. These communities can be expensive, often requiring a front-end, onetime payment of $100,000 or more, plus monthly fees for meals and other services.

Good to know: Many continuing-care communities offer varied levels of care to fit individual needs and affordability. Go to SeniorHomes.com to learn what's available in your area.

10 Low-Cost Ways to Make Your Home Easier and Safer to Live In

Tom Kraeutler, a former professional home inspector and contractor in New York City. He is host of *The Money Pit*, a nationally syndicated radio show on home improvement broadcast to more than three million listeners. He is also the home improvement editor for AOL. Moneypit.com

Remodeling a house to make it safer and more user-friendly can run tens of thousands of dollars. *But there are clever ways to improve and update your home without spending much...*

Throughout the Home

●**Replace round doorknobs, which are difficult to grasp and turn, with lever-style handles that you push down to open.** Most of the time, the lever handles can be attached to the existing latch mechanism already on the door. You can do the job yourself with just a screwdriver. Also, consider replacing cabinet door and drawer knobs with easy-to-grasp C- or D-shaped handles.

Cost: About $30/lever and $10/handle. Available at home-improvement centers.

●**Switch to rocker light switches.** They are on/off switches that rock back and forth when pressed. They are larger and easier to operate, and many people find them more attractive than the standard, small flip switches used in most homes. Rocker switches let you turn on a light with your elbow or fist if you're entering a room when your hands are full, and they're easier to find in the dark.

Cost: About $5 per light switch. Available at home-improvement centers.

• **Raise the position of some electrical outlets.** Wall outlets that are close to the floor can be hard to reach and inconvenient for plugging in appliances that you use intermittently, such as vacuums, heating pads and chargers for phones and laptops. Use those low outlets for lamps and other devices that you rarely unplug. Hire an electrician to raise other outlets at least 27 inches off the floor. They'll still be inconspicuous but much more accessible.

Cost: Typically $250 and up to move about half a dozen outlets.

• **Use remote controls for more than TVs.** They can operate window coverings, such as drapes and blinds, so you avoid stretching and straining, and let you control interior and exterior lights from your car or from within the home to prevent you from tripping in the dark.

My favorite: Lutron Caseta (844-588-7661, Lutron.com).

Cost: The Caseta Wireless Deluxe Smart Dimmer starter kit goes for $140. Online retailers, such as Amazon.com, offer it.

• **Create "wider" doorways.** Residential building codes and home builders don't consider the needs of older people who may need more than the standard 32-inch doorway, especially if they use a wheelchair or walker. Actually widening a doorway can be expensive and impractical, especially if it's along a weight-bearing wall.

Instead: Replace your standard door hinges with expandable "offset" hinges. These special hinges allow the door to close normally. But upon opening, they swing the door clear of the door frame by an extra two inches. This lets you use the entire width of the doorway when you enter or exit.

Cost: About $20 for a set of two door hinges. Available at home-improvement stores. A handy person can install these hinges because they fit in the existing holes in your door frame. Otherwise, a carpenter may charge about $100/hour.

• **Add a second handrail to staircases.** It's easier and safer to climb and descend when you can use both hands. Adding an extra handrail is an inexpensive and easy way to increase safety. Make sure both handrails are at the same height and between 30 and 34 inches above the front edge of the step. Also, for maximum safety, handrails should extend about six inches beyond the top and bottom steps if possible.

Cost: About $60 to $400 for each new handrail plus carpenter installation. Available at home-improvement stores.

Kitchen

• **Lower your microwave.** Many home builders, contractors and home owners like to save space by mounting microwave ovens above the stove or high on a wall. This position is hazardous because it requires you to reach above your head to get hot foods or forces you to balance on a stool.

Better: If your existing microwave is on the wall, build a shelf under it where you can rest hot foods after they finish cooking. Or choose a new model with a tray feature that slides out and is easier to reach.

Example: The Sharp Microwave Drawer Oven installs just beneath your countertop. The entire oven slides open, drawer-style, giving you access to the cooking compartment from above.

Cost: About $1,300 for the microwave and $150 and up for carpenter installation.

• **Install a pullout kitchen faucet.** Lugging heavy pots of water to the stove can be difficult and even dangerous. Many plumbing manufacturers now offer kitchen faucets featuring high-arc, pullout spouts. You can remove the spout and use it as a sprayer hose to fill pots within three to five feet of the stove.

Cost: Starts at about $150 plus plumber installation. Available at home-improvement stores.

• **Install a pull-down shelving system inside your kitchen wall cabinets.** Top shelves in cabinets are difficult to reach. This simple device rests in your upper cabinet until you grab a handle on the shelf frame. A set of three or four shelves swings out of the cabinet and down toward you. The shelves lock in place so you can get the item you need.

Afterward, the whole unit swings back into place.

My favorite: Rev-A-Shelf's chrome pull-down shelving system for 24- and 36-inch cabinets. You can do the installation yourself.

Cost: $892 to $939 (800-626-1126, Rev-a-shelf. com).

Bathroom

•**Add upscale grab bars near toilets and tubs.** Some people have avoided installing grab bars in their bathrooms because they look too institutional. Now, there are much more attractive versions. Brushed nickel or oil-rubbed bronze grab bars by Moen are designed to match other Moen bath accessories and faucets for a coordinated look. The grab bars meet all federal government guidelines. They have a stainless steel core and are 1¼ inches in diameter, making them easy to hold.

Cost: About $25 to $70 for the bar. Available at home-improvement stores. You can install them yourself, but it requires drilling holes in the wall.

6 Common Home-Maintenance Goofs...and How to Avoid Them

Danny Lipford, who has been a remodeling contractor for 37 years. He is based in Mobile, Alabama, and is host of *Today's Homeowner with Danny Lipford,* a nationally syndicated TV program. TodaysHomeowner.com

Replacing an air conditioner filter...lubricating a lock...cleaning dust off a refrigerator coil—what could possibly go wrong? More than you would expect! Make a mistake with seemingly simple home-maintenance tasks, and you could create a big home repair bill. Here's what home owners need to know before tackling six common—and commonly mismanaged—maintenance chores...

MISTAKE: **Backward furnace and air conditioner filters.** Most home owners know that furnaces and air conditioners have filters that should be replaced every few months when they are in use. (Certain filters can be cleaned rather than replaced.) But some home owners do not realize that these filters are designed to work in only one direction, and even home owners who do realize this often get the direction wrong. Install them backward, and not only will they do a poor job filtering airborne particulates—they will inhibit airflow, making the system less energy-efficient and potentially burning out components.

Look for the arrow on the side of the replacement filter. This arrow should point in the direction of airflow—which almost always means it should point toward the furnace or air conditioner, not away from it, because air going through the filter should be flowing into the unit, not out of it.

Most home owners also neglect to vacuum out the filter compartment when they replace these air filters. This is an important step that is easy to do with a vacuum or shop-vac wand.

Similar: Even home owners who change their furnace and air conditioner filters usually ignore the air filters in their oven range hoods. These should be popped out and cleaned at least a few times a year. Most can simply be washed in the dishwasher. Failing to do so can reduce a range hood exhaust fan's ability to remove smoke and cooking smells from the kitchen by as much as 50%.

MISTAKE: **Cleaning central-air drain lines without checking for clogs.** You might already know that in order to inhibit mold and mildew growth, once or twice a year it's smart to pour one cup of bleach down an air conditioner system's condensate drain line—the plastic pipe through which condensation produced by the evaporator coil drips off. But if you're like most home owners, you probably don't bother to check this line for clogs. Clogs caused by mold, algae or insect nests could cause water to back up in the line, potentially leading to musty odors in the home and even water damage, particularly if the air conditioner evaporator is located in the attic.

Before pouring bleach into the condensate drain line (there typically is an access opening in the drain line near the internal component of the A/C system), ask someone to watch the other end of the line where water from the line drips outside the home or down a basement drain. If you're not certain where to find the end of your condensate drain line, fol-

Home Repairs You Should Not Put Off Even If Money Is Tight

Annual heating and air-conditioning inspection costs around $200 to $300, but it could save you thousands by providing maintenance before you need to replace major components. Chimney inspection costs about $65 to $150 and could prevent a fire—or show that you need minor repairs to stop water leaks that can cause mold. Termite inspection costs $75 to $200 or more—termites can cause far more than $200 of damage. Power washing and sealing of a wood deck cost $100 to $300 for a 200-square-foot deck and get rid of algae and mold that can make the deck dangerously slippery.

What else to do: Have dryer vents cleaned every year to avoid lint buildup…clean carpets at least once a year to reduce pollen, bacteria and dirt in your home.

Bankrate.com

low the PVC tubing leading away from the A/C unit inside your house. If you pour water in and your helper does not see water flow out, you'll need to clear away clogs before treating the line with bleach. The easiest way to clear clogs is to use duct tape to create a seal between the end of a shop-vac hose and the external end of the condensate line (or purchase a shop-vac hose adaptor), then turn on the shop vac to suck out the obstruction. You'll save $150 or more by avoiding a maintenance call. (The bleach method does not apply to systems that pump condensation upward. Check with the pump maker if you suspect a clog.)

MISTAKE: **Wrong lock lubricant.** Home owners typically spray lubricant into keyholes when door locks start sticking. Unfortunately, they usually use the wrong lubricant—the most common household lubricant in the US is the multipurpose WD-40, which is poorly suited to this job. A multipurpose lube might provide some short-term improvement in a lock's function, but soon it will

start gumming up the intricate mechanism, leaving the lock worse than ever.

Graphite is a far better lubricant for sticking locks. Graphite lubricants are available in home centers and hardware stores, but you don't even need to buy these. Just rub a #2 pencil liberally all over the surfaces of the key that will enter the sticking lock, then insert this key into the lock several times, turning it each time. (Wipe any remaining graphite off the key afterward so that it doesn't make your purse or pocket messy.)

Similar: Home owners tend to use a multipurpose lube on garage door hinges, wheels and chains—if they bother to lubricate their garage doors at all. This is the wrong lube here, too, because it tends to drip all over the garage and cars below. Lithium grease lubricant, available at home centers and hardware stores, is a better choice because it is more likely to cling without dripping.

MISTAKE: **Damaging floors when cleaning refrigerator coils.** Most home owners know that they're supposed to remove dust and pet hair from their refrigerator condenser coils a few times a year. Doing this helps refrigerators work efficiently, reducing energy bills and extending the life of fridge motors. But cleaning these coils has become more difficult. Traditionally, a refrigerator's coils could easily be accessed by removing a kick plate on the front of the fridge. But the coils of refrigerators made in the past decade or two often can be accessed only from behind the fridge—and home owners sometimes damage their kitchen floors when they try to slide the fridge away from the wall to access the coils. To avoid this, slip a thick piece of cardboard or a carpet remnant under the fridge before sliding it.

MISTAKE: **Using chemicals to clear clogged sink, tub, toilet and shower drains.** Not only are drain-cleaning chemicals often ineffective, they sometimes damage pipes and septic systems. The best way to clear drain clogs is almost always with a plunger.

Buy a small plunger—this will be easier to fit over sink drains. When plunging a bathroom sink, cover the overflow drain hole with your hand so that the plunger can create suction. Try moving the plunger up and down in a series of small, quick movements—that's a good way to form a seal and dislodge drain debris.

Similar: To avoid garbage disposal clogs, run cold water when you use the disposal, not hot. Hot water tends to soften food debris, increasing the odds that it will stick. Cold water tends to solidify food debris, making it easier for the disposal to chop it up and send it down the drain.

MISTAKE: **Cleaning out gutters but neglecting to clear the roof.** Removing dead leaves and other debris from gutters is an essential autumn home-maintenance chore. Fail to do this, and leaves might clog your gutters and downspouts in the winter, leading to ice dams and, potentially, water damage. But while most home owners do clear leaves from their gutters (or hire someone to do this for them) once tree branches are bare each year, some neglect to also clear leaves and debris off their roofs. This roof debris eventually gets swept into their gutters by rain or wind and ends up causing the clogs they worked so hard to avoid. When you clean your gutters, clear off your roof, too.

Little Problems You Must Fix Now and Those You Can Let Slide

Danny Lipford, who has worked as a contractor for more than 30 years. Based in Mobile, Alabama, he hosts the nationally syndicated TV program *Today's Homeowner with Danny Lipford*, airing on more than 200 stations nationwide. TodaysHomeowner.com

Houses sometimes develop problems in bunches, and there isn't always enough money or time to tackle all the needed repairs at once. *Here's how to decide which projects must take priority…*

PRIORITY #1: **Leaky roof.** If water is dripping into your home, it must be stopped immediately. Delay would almost certainly lead to mold, mildew, rotted wood and/or water-damaged ceilings. A small roof leak might drip into an attic for months before it shows through the ceiling of the living space below. Take a bright flashlight into your attic during heavy rainstorms a few times each year to scan for leaks. Pay special attention to the areas around chimneys and roof vents.

Related: Dripping pipes and plumbing fixtures also should be treated as a top priority if the water is dripping into the home, not into a drain. If you can't stop the drip, turn off the water main—or at least position a bucket to catch the drip—and call a plumber immediately.

PRIORITY #2: **Electrical issues.** If your circuit breakers often trip…or turning on power-hungry electrical devices causes your lights to dim… or some of your home's switches or outlets work sporadically or become hot to the touch, call an electrician to evaluate your system very soon. Your home might have serious electrical issues that could cause a fire. The $100 to $300 or so that an electrician will charge to evaluate your home and perhaps replace a breaker or an outlet is worth it for the peace of mind alone. If the electrician finds serious shortcomings in your electrical system, it might cost $2,000 to $3,000 to upgrade your electrical service or $4,000 to $8,000 or more to rewire the home.

PRIORITY #3: **Slip-and-fall risks.** A slippery step might seem like a mild annoyance—until someone has a serious fall. Do not wait until that happens. Eliminating household slip-and-fall risks usually is an inexpensive do-it-yourself project. *Common danger spots…*

●**Slick concrete porches.** Paint these with a textured antislip paint to reduce the risk. Expect to pay around $30 per gallon, which covers 300 square feet.

●**Slick or steep stairs.** Apply antiskid tape to the steps, especially near the front edge of each step.

Example: A two-inch-by-five-yard roll of 3M Safety Walk Indoor/Outdoor Tread costs less than $15. Or install carpeting.

●**Loose or weak handrails.** A handrail that isn't strong enough to support someone leaning on it is a fall waiting to happen. If the loose rail is attached to wood, remove the screws and reattach the rail using wood screws that are at least one inch longer than the existing screws. Screw these into studs or floor joists, not just drywall or flooring. If the handrail is attached to concrete, sink lead anchors into the concrete, then screw stainless or coated steel bolts into these. If the concrete is cracked or crumbling where the handrail attaches, use a concrete repair product, such as concrete repair epoxy, to hold the lead anchor in place.

PRIORITY #4: Foundation cracks. The longer a foundation crack is left unrepaired, the larger that crack is likely to grow—and the more expensive it will likely be to correct. Meanwhile, this foundation crack will serve as a path for water and insects to enter the home, and it could cause shifting, settling and cracking in the house. Helpful: Hairline cracks usually are not big problems, but horizontal cracks and wide cracks often are.

For $150 or so, a structural engineer or home inspector should be able to take a quick look and tell you how serious the problem is. You might be able to patch a minor crack yourself with a tube of mortar repair caulk, available for less than $10. This caulk should at least stop more water from entering, preventing the problem from becoming worse. If major foundation repairs are needed, they could cost anywhere from $1,500 to $10,000 or more.

PRIORITY #5: Loose or damaged shingles or roof flashing...or tree limbs that rub against the roof during storms. These problems might not be causing water leaks through your roof yet, but they eventually will if allowed to linger. Use binoculars to scan for shingle or flashing problems if you're not comfortable climbing onto your roof. A roofer should be able to fix minor shingle or flashing issues for $200 to $400. Hiring a professional tree trimmer to cut back branches rubbing against the roof could cost $250 to $500 or more.

PRIORITY #6: Peeling exterior paint. This isn't just an aesthetic issue. It lets water penetrate your wood siding or trim, leading to rot. If your paint is peeling in only a few spots that are accessible, you could sand, prime and paint these areas yourself. This won't look perfect, but it should prevent further water damage to the siding. If the peeling is widespread, a new paint job is needed relative-

ly soon. A quality job is likely to cost $8,000 to $12,000.

PRIORITY #7: Aged heating and air-conditioning components. If your furnace or boiler, air conditioner and water heater still are working, you can safely put off replacing them. Still, updating old heating, ventilation and air-conditioning (HVAC) systems and water-heating components should be somewhere on your to-do list—today's high energy costs make it expensive to operate inefficient equipment. Once these heating and cooling components pass their twelfth birthday, it is wise to replace them rather than repair them when they break down.

Showerhead That Saves Money

Consumer Reports Money Adviser. ConsumerReports.org

Save $75 a year in wasted hot water by installing a ShowerStart tsv3 adapter available at ShowerStart.com and Amazon.com for about $30. The adapter slows water to a trickle as soon as it is warm, so if you tend to wait a long time before you get into the shower, you'll stop wasting hot water. Pull a chain to return water to full flow when you are ready to shower.

No More Clogged Drains!

Jon Jesse, former vice president for industry development at the International Housewares Association (IHA), Rosemont, Illinois. He is a former senior vice president of Kohl's and, prior to that, was a housewares buyer for Marshall Field's in Chicago. Housewares.org

Stop clogged shower drains with the Shower-Shroom. This clever gadget keeps hair from ever clogging your drain. The small, cylindrical silicone device fits inside standard stall-shower drain openings (you place it underneath the drain cover) and catches hair with minimal disruption to the flow of water. Pop it out every few weeks, swipe the hair off with a paper towel and put it back. There's also a TubShroom and SinkShroom for bathtubs and sinks, respectively. About $13. TubShroom.com

Shorten Your Daily Shower

Woman's Day, 1633 Broadway, New York City.

Shortening your daily shower by five minutes can save at least 9,000 gallons of water each year.

House Noises You Should Never Ignore

Danny Lipford, who has been a remodeling contractor for more than 30 years. He is based in Mobile, Alabama, and is host of the nationally syndicated TV program *Today's Home-owner with Danny Lipford*. TodaysHomeowner.com

Young children are not the only ones frightened by things that go bump in the night. Fully grown home owners often become terrified when they hear bumps, bangs or other noises emanating from their houses—that's because these unfamiliar noises might mean steep home-repair bills. Although some house noises do indeed mean that it's time to call in a pro, others point to simple problems that home owners can fix on their own…and certain sounds can be ignored entirely. *Here's what home owners need to know about 11 worry-inducing types of house sounds…*

Heating and AC Noises

Heating and air-conditioning can make any number of noises…

•**Pings and dings from ducts and radiators are perfectly normal and can be safely ignored—**they're just metal expanding and contracting due to temperature changes.

•**High-pitched squeals or a grinding noise from a furnace or an air conditioner could mean that a moving part is not moving the way it should**

and requires quick action. Immediately shut off the system, then wait a few moments and turn it back on. (If the troubling sound is a whine, replace the unit's filter before turning it back on—the restricted air flow caused by a dirty filter could be the cause.) If the sound returns, shut down the system again and leave it off until a heating, ventilation and air-conditioning (HVAC) professional can take a look unless temperatures are so extreme that you have no choice but to use it. The problem could be something simple such as a worn bearing or belt that an HVAC pro can replace for just $100 to $150.* But the longer you allow the unit to make the sound, the greater the odds that the small problem will cause a larger one as parts strain or overheat, and then a motor or pump may have to be replaced.

•**Frequent clicking sounds from a furnace or air conditioner often mean an electrical relay is malfunctioning.** This, too, requires a call to an HVAC pro, but the repair bill shouldn't be much greater than the basic service call rate, usually less than $100.

Electrical Humming

•**Humming or buzzing sounds from an outlet or switch usually mean that a wire has come loose.** (Dimmer switches can hum for other reasons—see below.) If so, the switch or outlet might be warm to the touch as well—although not necessarily. A loose wire is a fire hazard, so call an electrician right away to check out the humming or buzzing. If it is just a loose wire, fixing it should cost no more than the basic service call rate, typically less than $100.

•**Humming or buzzing noises from a lighting fixture could point to a loose wire as well—**but with lights, there's a good chance that something else is to blame. If the humming light is on a dimmer switch (or the dimmer switch itself is humming), replace the bulb with a different type of bulb or one made by a different company. Some bulbs mention on their packaging that they are designed to work well with dimmers. If that doesn't end the sound, replace the dimmer. If a fluorescent bulb is making the noise, the fixture's "ballast" might need to be replaced (the ballast is the part of the fixture that controls voltage to the bulb).

Wall or Attic Sounds

•**Scratching or scurrying from within a wall or ceiling.** You can probably guess what this means—a rodent (or some other small animal) has gotten into your house. Get it out as soon as possible. The longer this uninvited houseguest lingers, the greater the odds that it will chew through wiring...die in your walls, causing an unpleasant lingering odor...or give birth to babies.

A pest-control professional should be able to solve the problem for between $100 and $300 (potentially more with major infestations or in expensive areas). Or purchase and set traps—avoid poisons, which could be consumed by your pets or result in the pests dying and rotting inside your walls.

•**Do not just evict the pest**—also search for and seal the opening that it used to get into your home so that other animals can't get in. Expanding spray sealants are a simple and effective way to fill small gaps.

One spot to check: If you have a crawl space under your house, look under tubs and showers—builders often fail to properly seal off the openings beneath drain assemblies.

•**Dripping.** A water leak inside a wall can destroy wallboard and insulation and lead to mold or mildew problems. Fortunately, not every water sound signals a problem—sometimes the water is safely inside pipes.

First, check your basement or crawl space below the spot where you hear the water sound. If there is a water leak, that water likely would find its way down there. If you see water or water damage, call a plumber immediately (or a roofer if the water dripping sounds occur only when it is raining and/or when there is ice or snow on the roof). If you do not find water beneath the location of the dripping sound but the troubling water sound persists, conduct a water-loss test. Stop all water use in your home for 30 minutes—instruct family members to refrain from flushing the toilet and using the sink, tub, shower, dishwasher and washing machine during this time...and turn off the ice maker, sprinkler system and any other systems in the home that use water on their own.

Note the exact reading on your water meter at the beginning and end of this half hour. If this reading has not changed, it's unlikely that you have a leaky pipe. If it has changed even slightly, shut off the water to your toilets and redo the test—leaky toilets are the most common source of phantom water use. If this second test still shows water use, consider replacing the toilet's flapper valve or call a plumber.

Alternative: If you have a heating system that uses hot water or steam, the leak could be from there. Monitor the boiler's pressure gauge—if the system is leaking, this is likely to show a loss of pressure over time.

If you have a well: You won't have a water meter to check, so instead, stop all water use and then stand near your water pump for 30 minutes. If you hear clicking sounds from the pump, that could mean you have a water leak.

Banging or Thumping Pipes

This is called "water hammer" and is caused by water changing direction or being brought to a sudden halt in pipes. Water hammer almost never causes any problems for the home, but the noise can be annoying. If you want it to stop, install "water heater arrestors" in the waterline near appliances and fixtures that tend to trigger the noise. These cost just $10 to $15 at home centers and provide a cushion of air that absorbs the force of the water, greatly reducing the noise. If you call in a plumber, it should not cost much more than $100 (you can save $85 by doing it yourself).

Water-Heater Noise

Water heaters fueled by natural gas or oil make a subtle "poof" noise when the gas ignites at the start of a heating cycle. Other than that, water heaters should operate almost silently. If you hear gurgling or popping noises coming from your water heater, that means it's struggling to operate and might soon fail, most likely because sediment has built up around its coils. You might be able to save the water heater by draining it to flush away this sediment. Check your heater's manual for specific instructions, but typically the procedure involves shutting off the water and electricity to the water heater, attaching a hose to its drain spigot near the base, running the other end of the hose to a drain, then opening the drain valve. After the water heater has drained, close the drain valve and turn on the electricity and water to the tank. Do this every year.

Well Pump Clicks

Occasional clicks from a well pump are normal—it just means that the pump is working. Frequent clicks when no water is being used in the house suggest that either an electrical relay in the pump is faulty or that there is a water leak in the house. Use the leak-check procedure described in the water-dripping section on page 322. If that does not turn up a problem, call in a well professional to see if there's a faulty relay switch. Replacing the switch shouldn't cost more than $100. Don't let this problem linger—until it is fixed, your well pump is under unnecessary strain, which could shorten its life.

Fireplace Dripping Sounds

If you hear dripping from your fireplace when it rains, it could mean that rain is finding its way down your chimney. You need to put a stop to this or the metal firebox inside your fireplace could rust, creating a fire risk. The source of the problem could be as simple as loose flashing or a dislodged chimney cap. If so, a roofer probably can correct it for less than $100. You even might be able to solve this yourself, perhaps using caulk to seal gaps between the flashing and the chimney if you are comfortable walking on your roof. If bricks are coming loose, you might need a brick mason, which could cost hundreds or thousands of dollars depending on what's needed.

6 Kitchen Renovation Mistakes to Avoid

Carolina Fernandez, a financial adviser based in Stamford, Connecticut, who previously worked in interior design. She recently renovated her own kitchen and is author of *Country French Kitchens*.

A down-to-the-studs kitchen renovation can run well into five figures, so it's important to keep costs down and get your money's worth.

Here, a financial adviser, who formerly worked in interior design and has renovated eight homes, tells how to get the most bang for your buck by avoiding these common mistakes…

MISTAKE 1: **Shopping before budgeting.** People who start exploring kitchen renovation ideas without first nailing down how much they can spend often wind up with a dream kitchen—at a price they can't afford.

Better: Decide on your budget before going into a showroom. Then, for each kitchen component—countertop…appliances…lighting fixtures…flooring…cabinets—select a "top choice" and a corresponding "I could live with that" alternative. Ask yourself which one truly justifies the cost.

Examples: Are the imported tiles really $3,000 nicer? Will you use the extra burners on that eight-burner "professional" cooktop enough to justify the added expense?

MISTAKE 2: **Making everything built-in.** We forfeit a portion of the money we invest in renovation each time we move. Buyers will pay extra for a home with a renovated kitchen, but usually not enough extra to fully compensate for the money we put in.

Better: Spend as much of your renovation budget as possible on components that you could later take with you to a new home…

• Rather than install a kitchen island, purchase an attractive table that can serve the same purpose and move to a new home when you do.

• Rather than invest thousands in high-end custom cabinetry to hold your dishes and cookware, invest in top-quality cookware and beautiful dishes that you will have for the rest of your life. Then incorporate these into your kitchen design.

Examples: Display copper cookware by hanging it from hooks in the kitchen…store dishes on inexpensive exposed shelves/racks on the wall so that the dishes themselves are a focal point.

• Rather than install expensive decorative flourishes into your kitchen walls, ask your contractor to mount them in a manner that makes them easy to move.

Example: I spent a small fortune on 300-year-old antique French tiles for my kitchen. Rather than permanently mount them on the wall, I had the tiles mounted on a board, then attached the board to the wall. If I move, I can easily take the whole unit with me.

MISTAKE 3: Attempting a full renovation on a limited budget. If a tight budget means that you cannot have the new kitchen you want, it often is best not to attempt a complete renovation at all. If you're not satisfied with the result, you'll just want to renovate again in a few years, and the money you spend on the initial renovation will be wasted.

Better: If your budget is limited, invest your money in one or two new kitchen components that you truly love rather than a completely new kitchen that's only marginally better than what you currently have. Install new lighting...update the appliances...or refinish existing cabinets and add new knobs and drawer pulls. Make sure the new components have a place in your dream kitchen so that the investment isn't wasted if you decide to do a more complex renovation later on.

MISTAKE 4: Thinking wonderful kitchen design items come only from high-end sources.

Better: Discounters, including TJ Maxx (TJ Maxx.com), HomeGoods (HomeGoods.com) and Marshalls (Marshalls.com), are excellent sources of simple-but-beautiful decorative items.

Example: I purchased glass apothecary jars for less than $30 at TJ Maxx. Filled with grain and displayed on the kitchen countertop, they're as visually appealing as expensive antiques.

MISTAKE 5: Installing an island sink. It has become common to install a small sink in a new kitchen island as a supplement to the room's main sink.

Better: Don't bother. Plumbing in an extra sink is likely to add $1,000 or more to your renovation bill and detract from the counter space of the island. One sink is enough for the average home kitchen.

MISTAKE 6: Thinking a "dream" kitchen must be a flawless kitchen. Kitchen renovations take so much time and money that it is only natural to want the result to be perfect. Unfortunately, it rarely works out this way, and correcting small

imperfections late in the renovation process can be expensive.

Better: Minor imperfections often are not worth worrying about.

Example: When the expensive imported countertop that my husband and I ordered was not perfectly aligned, our cabinetmaker simply added a strip of wood that hid the flaw.

Kitchens are functional rooms—even if your renovation is perfect, stains, scratches and dents will soon appear.

How to Buy Appliances That Will Last Much Longer

Chris Zeisler, technical services supervisor with Repair Clinic.com, a Canton, Michigan–based website that sells appliance parts and offers free appliance-repair videos and advice. Zeisler has more than 30 years of experience in appliance repair.

Your major appliances don't have long to live. While today's cars last longer than ever, the phrase, "They don't make 'em like they used to," is nearly 100% accurate when it comes to refrigerators, dishwashers, clothes washers and dryers—even as these major appliances creep upward in price.

Why? Appliance makers are continuing to cut production costs by replacing durable metal parts with cheaper plastic ones. They're also stuffing their appliances with more and more electronics and advanced features. Those latest, greatest features attract shoppers in showrooms—but packing more features into an appliance means there are more systems that can fail...and many of those electronic components are absurdly expensive to replace, so you end up replacing the entire appliance instead.

Here's how consumers can identify the appliances that are likely to last as long as possible—and avoid those likely to fail fastest...

Three General Strategies

●**Pick appliances that have only the features you truly value.** New features might seem neat, but as noted above, each extra system or feature is one more thing that could fail. That doesn't mean we must buy stripped-down, nothing-but-the-basics appliances, but it does mean that it's prudent to choose appliances that have only the features that really matter to us.

Example: Some refrigerators include two ice makers—one in the freezer and another in the fridge. One ice maker is great…but how badly do we really need the second one?

•**Favor brands that have easily available and relatively inexpensive replacement parts.** These include Amana, Jenn-Air, KitchenAid, Maytag and Whirlpool (all made by Whirlpool Corp.) and Electrolux and Frigidaire (both owned by Electrolux of Sweden). Having readily available, affordable parts makes it more likely you will keep an appliance longer.

Example: If the part you need for your eight-year-old washing machine will cost $50 and arrive in two days, it makes sense to fix it…but if it will cost $150 and arrive in three weeks, you might reasonably decide it's time for a new washer.

•**Whatever appliances you buy, buy surge protectors, too.** Most people are savvy enough to plug their computers or televisions into surge protectors…but very few think to do the same with their appliances. That's unfortunate because most of today's appliances are loaded with electronic components that are just as vulnerable to power surges as consumer electronics.

Helpful: Many electric dryers and some other appliances have special plugs that do not plug into standard outlets—or standard surge protectors. Either obtain a surge protector designed for this outlet from an appliance store or protect this and all of your other appliances and electronics by paying an electrician $500 to $1,000, depending on your area, to install a whole-home surge-protection system.

Appliance-Specific Tips

•**Refrigerators.** For a longer life, avoid fridges that have multiple separate compartments, each with its own access and temperature settings, such as fridge drawers that can be opened without opening the main doors. These can be convenient, but each separate compartment might have its own fan and fan motor, among other parts, greatly increasing the number of parts that could fail.

Also consider the positioning of a refrigerator's condenser coils before buying. You probably already know that regularly clearing dust and pet hair off a refrigerator's coils can reduce the strain on its motor and compressor, extending the refrigerator's life (and reducing its electricity consumption). Home owners are much more likely to do this if they can get to the coils relatively easily. If getting to the back of a fridge would mean pulling the heavy appliance away from the wall, lean toward one that has coils on the bottom (with a removable "toe kick plate or grill" at the base of the front for access). If your kitchen layout allows relatively easy access to the back of the fridge, coils located there might be easier to get to.

Note: Refrigerator buyers often wonder which fridge configuration lasts longest—top freezer…bottom freezer…or side by side. It turns out that none of these configurations has a notably longer life span than the others. Buy whichever you prefer.

Brands: Whirlpool and its higher-end sister brand KitchenAid tend to make more reliable refrigerators.

•**Dishwashers.** For a longer life, avoid units that boast of multiple moving spray arms and "wash zones." The added complexity and extra moving parts increase the odds of problems—and many dishwashers without these features do a fine job washing dishes.

Also, check how well a dishwasher's warranty covers its dish racks before buying—you want at least five years of coverage. Dish racks might seem like a very simple part not worth worrying about, but dish-rack failure often is the problem that dooms a dishwasher. When the vinyl coating on a dish rack wears through, the metal beneath soon rusts and breaks apart. Replacement racks tend to be so expensive—often $200 to $300—that it can make more sense to replace the entire dishwasher. (Continuing to use a rusty dish rack is unlikely to be a long-term solution, either—bits of rusty metal are likely to damage the inner workings.) If the dishwasher comes with at least five years of dish-rack coverage, that's a sign that the manufacturer has confidence its racks will last.

If dishwasher noise doesn't bother you, perhaps because you usually run your dishwasher when no one is in the kitchen, consider skipping units that trumpet their exceptionally quiet operation. Quiet dishwashers are no more likely to fail than other units, but when they do break down, their added sound insulation can make it time-consuming to access and replace failed parts, increasing repair cost and the odds that it will make sense to replace rather than repair the machine.

Brand: KitchenAid is the most reliable dish-washer brand (and its warranties typically include five years of dish-rack coverage).

•**Clothes washers and dryers.** For a longer life, avoid washers and dryers that have especially elaborate digital display screens and control panels with large numbers of buttons, lights and LED readouts. Electronic control systems tend to be expensive and failure-prone. The more elaborate these are, the more cost-prohibitive it tends to be to replace them—some cost more than $300 for the screen alone.

Front-load washers tend to last slightly longer than top loaders, on average. Why? Front loaders use less water on average—although there are some low-water-use top loaders on the market, too—reducing the stress on their pumps. They also have sturdy metal bearings holding their tubs in place,

How to See That Tiny Serial Number

When you need an appliance model number or a serial number for a repair or part, especially when the placard is hard to see, use your smart-phone to take a photo of the number. It will be easier to read on your phone, and you can enlarge it if necessary. Also, you can easily e-mail it to anyone who needs it.

RepairClinic.com

whereas many, though not all, manufacturers use less durable plastic bearings in top loaders.

Brands: Whirlpool and its sister brand Maytag tend to be dependable choices. These brands offer an extremely wide range of washers and dryers, they have a record of reliability at reasonable price points, and parts for them are readily available. It's not clear that spending more for a prestige-brand washer/dryer will result in longer product life.

When Not to Clean Your Oven

Vernon Schmidt, who has more than 35 years of experience in appliance repair. He is author of *The Appliance Handbook for Women: Simple Enough Even Men Can Understand,* available through Amazon.com.

How long your appliances last isn't just a matter of how well they're built. How you treat them matters, too. *Here are some simple tricks to keep your major appliances running as long as possible and avoid expensive repairs…*

•**Dishwashers and clothes washers.** Use less detergent. People tend to fill dishwasher soap cups to the brim and use the amount of clothes detergent recommended on the bottle or box. That's way too much. Modern dishwashers and washing machines use less water than those of decades past, so less detergent is needed. Also, more powerful and concentrated detergents are available today. Using excessive amounts of detergent creates a soapy residue inside the machine that results in a buildup of mold and mildew, which smells and eats away at the rubber parts, shortening the appliance's life.

In a dishwasher, try using just one-half to one full teaspoon of liquid or powder detergent. If that doesn't clean your dishes—perhaps because you have hard water—gradually increase the amount up to one tablespoon.

If you have used too much detergent in the past, also use a dishwasher cleaner, available in most supermarkets, to remove soap residue. Leading brands include Glisten and Finish.

Alternative: Use solid tablets that include pre-measured amounts of detergent. If you have soft water, split the tablets in half. Don't use liquid gel packs, because they contain too much detergent and are too sudsy.

In a clothes washer, use just two tablespoons of regular detergent, or one tablespoon of concentrated detergent if you have soft water and your washer is a modern front-load or high-efficiency top-load machine.

If you have hard water and/or your clothes washer is not a modern front-load or high-efficiency top-load machine, use one-quarter of the amount of detergent recommended on the detergent label.

Only if you are washing extremely dirty clothes should you use the amount of detergent recommended on the label.

•**Clothes dryers.** Clean out your dryer's exhaust line at least once each year. If the plastic or flexible-metal ductwork that your electric dryer uses to vent hot air is clogged with lint, the dryer's heating element will overheat and might fail. Clogged lines can cause serious mechanical problems for gas dryers, too. And with either electric or gas, a clogged vent can double or triple the amount of energy required to dry a load of clothing. On a gas dryer, the lint that builds up also can cause carbon monoxide to vent into the home and possibly start a fire.

If your dryer's exhaust line is too long to clear out by hand, purchase a dryer-vent cleaning kit with a flexible extension rod long enough to reach the full length of your dryer's exhaust line. These are available at home-improvement stores for less than $50. Remember to clean both the portion of the exhaust line that leads from the dryer to the wall and the part inside the wall.

•**Refrigerators.** If your older refrigerator's rubber-door seal gaskets are becoming brittle, apply a layer of Vaseline to keep them supple. Reapply whenever the gasket feels dry to the touch.

It's probably time to replace the gasket if it has cracked or split. Replacing door gaskets on older machines with screw-on gaskets is a labor-intensive job that usually costs $200 to $300 per door.

Also: On most refrigerators, you need to clean the coil—the metal piping typically located behind a removable panel at the base of or behind the refrigerator—at least once a year. Clean it at least twice a year if a dog or cat that sheds lives in the home. A refrigerator's compressor is forced to work much harder when the coil is coated with dust or pet hair. That can cause overheating and compressor failure. Having a new compressor installed is likely to cost more than $400 in parts and labor.

Your refrigerator's manual should include directions for cleaning the coil. Even if the owner's manual says that the coil is self-cleaning, it still needs to be cleaned at least once a year. I have never seen a clean "self-clean" coil on a refrigerator after two years of use.

•**Ovens.** There isn't much you can do to extend the life of an oven, but there is something you can do to reduce the odds that it will fail at a particularly inconvenient moment.

Best: Wait until after the November/December holidays to run the self-cleaning cycle.

People tend to run oven self-cleaning cycles immediately before big cooking days, such as Christmas, Thanksgiving and important dinner parties. Unfortunately, ovens are most likely to fail during or soon after these self-cleaning cycles because of the very high temperatures involved. It isn't easy to get a broken oven fixed around the holidays, either—appliance repair shops and parts distributors often are closed.

Never Put These Items in Your Dishwasher

Roundup of experts on proper cleaning of household items, reported at Today.com.

Items that should never go in the dishwasher. Cast-iron skillets, which require special care and seasoning...wooden cutting boards, which can warp and crack because of heat and water...Brass, bronze and pewter, which can become discolored...high-quality knives, including ones with wood handles or carbon-steel blades, which easily can be damaged…fancy china, which can discolor or fade…aluminum bakeware that does not specify that it is dishwasher-safe…crystal barware, which can shatter…gold-plated cutlery, whose coating can wear off…anything repaired with glue, since heat may loosen the glue…items with printed words or measurements that can become illegible…nonstick pans, whose coatings can wear off or become damaged.

Never Put These Foods in Your Disposal

Angi.com

Fibrous or stringy foods, including celery, artichokes, asparagus, corn husks, onion skins, carrots and potato peels, can wrap around blades. Grease, fats and oils cause a film on blades, making them less effective, and when grease starts to decay, it causes an unpleasant odor. Egg shells contain stringy membranes that can wrap around a disposal's shredder ring, and the shell itself is ground to a sandlike consistency that may clog pipes. Pasta, rice, potatoes and beans can swell when wet to form a pastelike substance that can cause clogs.

Don't Waste Your Living Room and Dining Room

Sarah Susanka, an architect based in Raleigh, North Carolina, who was named one of the 30 most notable innovators in the housing industry of the past 30 years by *Builder* magazine. She is author of numerous books on home design, including *Not So Big Remodeling…More Not So Big Solutions for Your Home…*and *The Not So Big House*. Susanka.com

Formal living rooms and dining rooms are underused in most homes. They often are uninviting, uncomfortable spaces designed for a way of life that few families live.

What a waste! Here's how to affordably transform an underused living room and dining room into comfortable, functional spaces where people want to be…

Your Living Room

Four strategies to make an unused living room more inviting…

• **Connect your living room to a heavily used room.** The simple fact is, people become much more likely to spend time in their living rooms when they can see them from a space where they spend lots of time—a visual reminder that the living room exists is all it takes to increase usage. To achieve this, call in a professional to take down all or part of a wall between your living room and your family room or kitchen (or any other oft-used room that is next to your living room). This typically is not as expensive as you might think.

Bonus: Besides making your living room more connected, it will make it feel larger.

• **Or do the opposite.** Close your living room off to create a single-purpose space. Add a set of French doors (or take other steps necessary to give the living room privacy from the rest of the home) and make it your "away room"—an escape from household noise and activity. When segmented from the rest of the home like this, a living room can make a wonderfully spacious painting studio, home office, yoga or meditation room, music room or library.

• **Update living-room furniture for your real lifestyle.** Old-fashioned, formal, uncomfortable furniture is among the biggest reasons many living rooms are uninviting spaces. Home owners often feel that this is the kind of furniture they're supposed to have in a living room or that they can't replace this furniture because it's been passed down through generations. Replace it anyway—your ancestors (or you) bought it for a life very different from the life you are living.

• **Add a window seat and/or vary living-room ceiling height.** In most living rooms, the ceiling is a uniform height throughout, making the room a boring box. Though it may sound counterintuitive, lowering ceiling height by as little as six inches along one side of the room or over an alcove can create visual interest and, surprisingly, make the room feel larger and more inviting.

Example: Lower the ceiling height above a living-room seating alcove that contains one or two chairs—it will make this area feel cozier and make the entire room seem more engaging.

You can do this even if your living room's ceiling is only eight feet high—dropping the ceiling by just six inches over an alcove or along the length of a wall fools the eye into believing that the eight-foot section is taller than it actually is. It's the contrast between the two ceiling heights that makes the space as a whole seem bigger.

Adding a built-in living-room window seat is another good way to add interest and coziness to the room. It usually is a good idea to lower the ceiling above this window-seat area—then the combination of built-up, built-in seating with the lowered ceiling above results in a space that feels "safe" and appealing and connected to both the interior of the home and the world outside. Place a comfortable cushion across the width of the seat, and you'll have a wonderful space for curling up with a book.

Your Dining Room

Some dining rooms go unused...while others are used principally for purposes unrelated to dining—where bills are paid or where kids do their homework. *To make your dining room more inviting and useful...*

• **Have the wall between your kitchen and dining room partly or totally removed.** The kitchen is the social center of most homes these days. If it were possible for people sitting in your dining room to make eye contact and conversation with people in your kitchen, the use of that dining area would skyrocket. If the layout of the home makes it impractical to completely remove the wall between the kitchen and dining room, even partially removing it or creating a pass-through opening between the rooms could be sufficient—the key is that eye contact and comfortable conversation are possible.

Example: Perhaps a section of wall above the kitchen counters could be removed, leaving the lower wall (and counters) in place.

• **Add a set of bookshelves along a dining-room wall.** A wall of bookshelves displaying the books, photos and artwork of your choice can dramatically reduce the formality of your dining room, making the space cozier and more inviting. Built-in, floor-to-ceiling shelving can look especially nice, but freestanding bookshelves are a viable and often less expensive alternative.

Alternative: Have attractive bookshelves installed along the upper section of one wall...with drawers and cabinets below. In homes where the dining-room table is the place to pay bills or do other paperwork, these papers must be repeatedly carted off to a different part of the house when the space is used as an actual dining room. Having appropriate drawers or cabinets in the room makes it easier to stow papers and other projects, reducing clutter and saving time. This storage area could be designed to look like a sideboard or buffet table.

• **Troubleshoot your table.** If you have a dining-room table that's so small your guests often have to squeeze in next to one another (or sit at a card table)...or a table so large that it dominates the room and yet it's almost never used to capacity—you have the wrong-sized table, and this greatly limits enjoyment of your dining room. Replace your table with one that can be expanded by adding leaves or sliding out extensions. Then your table will always be the right size for whatever you want it for at the time.

• **Purchase a protective pad for your dining-room table.** If someone in your house (maybe you!) shouts, "Don't scratch the table," whenever someone uses your dining table for a project or chore, the single best way to improve your enjoyment of your dining room (or, at least, to reduce your stress) is to buy a cover that will protect its surface. The best of these are pads with a hard top surface and a soft underside that won't scratch the table beneath. Some are decent-looking, too, though keeping an attractive tablecloth on top of most table pads looks better.

Fix Your Home's Weak Wi-Fi

Eric Geier, owner of Wi-Fi Surveyors, a Wi-Fi consulting firm, and On Spot Techs, an on-site computer services company. Based in Dayton, Ohio, he is a certified wireless network administrator and author of nine books on computer technology, including *Geeks on Call: Wireless Networking: 5-Minute Fixes*. EGeier.com

D o Netflix movies keep stopping and starting when you stream them to a laptop or TV over your wireless Internet (Wi-Fi)? Does e-mail take forever to download on your iPad in certain rooms? The problem is likely your wireless router. The radio wave signals that your router emits may be too weak when they reach your devices. *Some smart solutions to get a stronger, steadier signal…*

•**Make sure that the router signals aren't impaired by physical barriers that cause interference and signal degradation.** These may include concrete and brick walls, heavy furniture and metal objects such as tall filing cabinets.

•**Move the router to a more central location in relation to where you use your wireless devices most.**

Resource: Use the free Android smartphone app Wi-Fi Analyzer to locate the areas of your home where the router signals are strongest and weakest, and then place the router in the best possible spot that still is close enough to an available Internet cable or phone jack.

Helpful: It's usually best to place the router in a high position, such as on a high shelf or on top of a bookcase, to avoid barriers such as furniture.

•**Pay your Internet service provider for more speed.** No matter what kind of router you have or where it is positioned, it can transmit data only as fast as the connection you have from your cable or telephone company. Internet speed is measured in megabits-per-second (mbps) and can vary at different times of day based on what else you are doing at that time on your home network.

To stream HD movies, for instance, at least 10 megabits per second (mbps) is recommended to avoid having the picture freeze up. Keep in mind that having multiple users in your home requires higher speeds. A dial-up modem transmits at up to 56 kilobits per second (1,024 kilobits is a megabit)…

DSL service, typically up to 6 mbps…standard Internet cable service, typically 10 mbps or faster for an extra charge. *More elaborate fixes are possible…*

•**Consider a mesh network.** For homes with more than two stories and/or multiple dead zones, a mesh network replaces your router and extender with a set of small devices that include powerful internal antennas. You hook up one to your modem and place the others around your home. Unlike multiple extenders, whose Wi-Fi signals weaken as you add more, each mesh network device boosts the signal, so you get the same signal strength and speed everywhere. They do a great job of giving your home optimal coverage for your Wi-Fi signal. Popular brands are Netgear Orbi, AmpliFi, Eero, Google Wi-Fi and Linksys Velop. They come in packs of three for larger homes of more than 1,500 square feet.

•**Switch your router's channel.** Wi-Fi routers send radio waves on different frequencies or channels. During setup, some routers automatically detect the least crowded channel as the default setting. But if you live in a neighborhood or apartment building with lots of new wireless connections, those routers may be using the same channel and weakening your signal.

What to do: Start by downloading to your computer the inSSIDer diagnostic tool, which will analyze what channel your router is using and which one can offer you the best signal strength (free, Metageek. com). Then refer to your router owner's manual for instructions on how to change the router channels.

Better Appliance Shopping

WiseBread.com

C onsider a refurbished major appliance if it is one or two years old, includes a full warranty and comes at significant savings compared with a new one. But before buying, look for low prices on new appliances through a site such as PriceGrabber. Then compare total costs, including delivery and installation charges. Buy refurbished appliances only at stores you know and trust.

8 Ways to Warm Up a Cold Spot in Your Home

Richard Trethewey, heating, ventilation and air-conditioning (HVAC) expert for the PBS-TV series *This Old House* since 1979. He is founder and owner of RST Thermal, which provides energy-efficient solutions for home heating and cooling to home owners and businesses in New England. He is based in Westwood, Massachusetts. ThisOldHouse.com

Is one room or area in your home much colder than others? There are various ways to solve the problem, some of them simple and inexpensive... others involving greater effort and expense.

We asked heating expert Richard Trethewey how you can figure out what's wrong and what to do about it...

Simple Solutions

Home owners often think that they have to live with temperature inconsistencies in different parts of their homes because they are reluctant to spend tens of thousands of dollars to upgrade their heating systems and insulation. *But in many cases, the solutions are so simple and inexpensive that people may overlook them...*

●**Check the arrangement of the furniture and drapes to make sure that heating vents or radiators are not blocked.**

●**Shut the damper in the fireplace firmly when you aren't using it.**

●**Feel for drafts along windows by holding a lit candle along the gap between the window and the trim.** Watch if the flame bends or flickers, indicating a leak, and then caulk or weather-strip to close the gap. If a window still feels drafty, pry off the interior wall trim around the window and spray foam sealant between the wall and window frame. Then press the trim back into place.

●**If you need to heat only a specific part of a room such as the desk area in a home office or a couch near a TV, get an energy-efficient, 1,500-watt portable electric space heater.**

Bigger Problems

Here, cold-spot problems and cost-effective solutions...

PROBLEM: **Major heat loss through exterior walls.** Does one wall or part of a wall feel cold all the time in the winter? Traditional fiberglass insulation in the wall may be inadequate because it has broken down over time or has left gaps around electrical boxes or light fixtures, creating drafts.

Solution: Blow Icynene into the walls. Icynene is a new type of expanding foam insulation that is injected into wall cavities through small holes. It's much denser than fiberglass and reduces air infiltration with double the effectiveness of fiberglass. Icynene can be sprayed in without removing the fiberglass and directly onto electrical and plumbing work. (If you need to access pipes and wires for repair in the future, the Icynene foam can be cut away). For more information and to find a licensed Icynene contractor, go to Icynene.com.

Cost: About $4 per square foot for the material and installation.

PROBLEM: **Heat from your furnace is not making it to the room that is cold.** If you have a forced-air heating system and the airflow out of a room's vent feels weak, you may be losing heat to tiny cracks and gaps in the ductwork in your walls. In older homes, as much as 20% of the heat never makes it to rooms, especially those farthest from the furnace. Trying to seal ductwork yourself with mastic tape often is ineffective because leaks can be hard to identify and much of the ductwork in a house is not accessible.

Solution: Use Aeroseal duct sealant, a nontoxic polymer spray that contractors pump into both rigid and flexible ducts, sealing gaps from the inside of the ducts. This product received a Best New Product award from *This Old House* magazine. It has proved so effective at improving heat flow (and saving on heating costs) that it's worth doing in your entire home. Go to Aeroseal.com to locate a dealer near you.

Cost: About $1,000 to treat the ductwork of a 2,000-square-foot home.

PROBLEM: **Your thermostat is poorly positioned.** If your thermostat is in a sunny room that cools slowly, there will be a delay before the heat kicks in. If the room warms quickly, it shuts off the furnace too early.

Solution: Add a wireless thermostat in the chilly room. You can easily replace your old wall thermostat with a wireless receiver and place a wireless thermostat, which contains the temperature sensor, anywhere in the house. These units transmit up to 500 feet through walls, ceilings and floors.

Recommended: ZoneFirst Wireless Thermostat and Receiver (ZoneFirst.com).

Cost: About $200 plus a one-hour service call from an electrician.

Note: If moving your traditional thermostat wiring to a chilly room is easy to do, consider installing the Nest thermostat (Nest.com) instead. It's not wireless, but it can be linked to your computer and/or smartphone so that you can control it remotely, adjusting the temperature up or down on short notice even when you are not at home. The Nest also can learn your daily patterns, so it can turn down the temperature when you leave the house.

Cost: $250 plus a one-hour service call from an electrician.

PROBLEM: **Heat from a warmer room is not dispersing into an adjoining colder room.** Rooms with an additional heating source (for example, a stove or a fireplace), as well as rooms on the south side of a house that get a lot of sun, tend to be warmer than the rest of the house.

Solution: Install a room-to-room ventilator. These ultraquiet fan systems are positioned between rooms right in the wall. One side of the ventilator draws heat from the warm room…the other side disperses it into the cold room. Ventilators run off of a manual wall switch or an automatic thermostat.

Cost: About $100, depending on the size of the ventilator, plus two to three hours for an electrician to open up your wall and install the ventilator.

PROBLEM: **You just want to add extra heat to an entire room without having to turn up the thermostat for the whole house.**

Solutions: Put in a ceiling fan that includes a space heater. The Reiker Room Conditioner with remote control installs and functions just like a regular ceiling fan. But in the winter, with the heater engaged, the fan blades circulate heat quickly through the room.

Cost: $350 plus a two-hour installation service call from an electrician.

Install radiant-floor heating, especially for rooms with cold, ceramic tile floors such as bathrooms, mudrooms and kitchens. Radiant-floor heating consists of ultrathin heating cables in mesh mats—not unlike the wires in an electric blanket—that are installed underneath your flooring.

Drawback: Because the heating system must be installed under the tile, this option is best reserved for when you are planning to redo your floors anyway.

Cost: About $6 per square foot for materials and installation.

If these solutions don't work, your problems may be more complex and you may need a professional energy audit.

How to Choose the Right Garage Door

Don Vandervort, founder of HomeTips.com. Based in Glendale, California, he is author of more than 30 books on home improvement and served as a segment host on the HGTV program *The Fix*.

Garage doors are underappreciated. They spend decades exposed to the elements. They are the largest moving part of the typical house. They are so large, in fact, that a deteriorating or unattractive garage door can make the entire home look shabby, particularly if the door is on the front of the home.

But it's easy to go wrong when the time comes to replace a garage door. There is an increasing number of door options. Price, appearance, durability and maintenance all need to be considered. The good news is that there's no need to spend a fortune—you can get a well-made, durable, attractive two-car garage door* starting at around $700 installed. A one-car door typically costs about two-thirds as much as a two-car door. Including an automatic opener will add perhaps $200 to $300 to your bill.

Money saver: Installing a garage door yourself could save you $250 to $450, but it's a challenging job appropriate only for skilled do-it-yourselfers. Advice on how to do it is available at Hometips. com/diy-how-to/garage-door-installation.html.

Explore options at home-supply centers...on websites of leading door manufacturers—C.H.I. Overhead Doors (CHIohd.com), Clopay (Clopay Door.com), Raynor (Raynor.com) and Wayne Dalton (Wayne-Dalton.com)...and in your area's garage door showrooms.

To choose a garage door...

Door Materials

Most garage doors are made of either steel or wood, but there are other options worth considering...

•**Steel garage doors are economical, durable, secure and require little maintenance.** They have overtaken wood in popularity. Quality steel doors come with long warranties—often 10 years or more—an indication of their durability. Today's steel doors can be attractive, too. Great strides have been made in recent years in crafting steel garage doors. They come in a wide palette of colors, and some are designed to look like stained wood. It is possible to paint steel garage doors, but special paints or primers might be required depending on the door's finish or cladding.

On the downside, steel doors can dent and low-end steel doors might rust or simply look unattractive.

What to look for: The thickness of the steel can provide a clue about the door's overall quality. Top-quality steel doors tend to be made from 24-gauge steel, moderate-quality doors from 25- or 26-gauge steel, and low-quality doors from 27- or

*Prices in this article are typical costs for 16-foot-by-7-foot, two-car garage doors of reasonable quality, including hardware and installation, except as noted.

28-gauge. (The higher the number, the thinner the steel.) Thin steel is more prone to dents.

Doors made from galvanized steel that has a baked-on polyester finish are especially rust-resistant. (Vinyl-clad steel doors are very rust-resistant, too, but might look "plastic-y.")

Opt for an insulated steel door if keeping the garage warm or controlling noise between the garage and outdoors is a priority. This might be the case if you use the garage as a workshop or spare room... or if a room immediately above or adjacent to the garage is cold. Polyurethane garage door insulation is superior to polystyrene.

Price: Expect to pay $750 to $1,200 installed for a two-car steel door of reasonable quality.

•**Wood garage doors offer a warm, homey appearance.** Composite-wood doors are affordable and are meant to be painted—a reasonable choice if price is your primary concern or if you want the color of your garage door to match the siding of your house. Appearance-grade wood doors are meant to be stained for an attractive natural-wood look. Custom wood garage doors are made by skilled craftsmen and can be extremely attractive, distinctive—and pricey. Wood is a better insulator against cold and noise than steel alone, but not as good as an insulated steel door.

However, wood garage doors require significant upkeep, including periodic painting or staining. (Steel doors might occasionally require painting, but not nearly as frequently.) Wood doors age quickly, especially when frequently subjected to precipitation or direct sunlight. They tend to have short warranties that reflect their often short lives—one-year warranties are standard. Wood doors are heavy, too. Still, a wood door might be appropriate if used in a location that doesn't get much direct sunlight and is sheltered from precipitation by an overhang.

What to look for: Choose a roll-up wood garage door rather than a tilt-up model. The latter might save you a few dollars, but it will be heavy and inconvenient to operate. (A tilt-up door might be appropriate if the goal is to cover the garage door with the same siding that's on the rest of the house—it's difficult to put siding on a roll-up.) It's particularly important to stick with doors made by the leading manufacturers when choosing a composite-wood door. Obscure-brand, low-priced composite garage doors often are very poorly made.

Price: Perhaps $700 to $1,000 installed for a two-car composite-wood door, or $1,500 to $2,000 for an appearance-grade two-car door—possibly more, depending on the wood. Custom-made wood doors can cost anywhere from $2,000 to $9,000.

•**Glass and aluminum garage doors feature perhaps eight to 16 frosted-glass or fiberglass panels supported by an aluminum frame.** These doors have a distinctive, contemporary look. The panels typically are translucent but not transparent, so they allow plenty of light into the garage without letting people see in—a nice option for someone who uses a garage as a workshop or active storage area.

The aluminum frames on these doors are very durable, but the glass or fiberglass panels can crack or break—fiberglass is especially brittle in cold weather. Fiberglass also can yellow with age. Warranties vary widely—one to five years is typical—but they usually don't cover cracked panels. Glass and fiberglass panels don't provide much insulation or security.

What to look for: Choose glass rather than fiberglass panels—they weigh a bit more but won't fade or yellow over time, and burglars might be leery of breaking in by shattering a glass panel because of the noise.

Price: $1,500 to $2,000 or more installed for a two-car door.

Warning: All-aluminum garage doors also are available but are best avoided. While aluminum garage-door frames can be quite strong, sheet aluminum can dent very easily.

•**Vinyl garage doors are another option.** They are lightweight, affordable, maintenance-free (you don't ever need to paint them) and extremely durable—they won't rust or rot. Compared with steel or aluminum, vinyl is extremely dent-resistant. That dent-resistance is particularly useful for home owners with kids who play sports in the driveway.

Vinyl also stands up well to salt air, making these doors a good option in coastal communities. Vinyl-

door warranties often last 20 years, a sign that they are built to last. Insulated vinyl doors are available if garage sound or temperature is a concern.

What to look for: Choose a vinyl door that's light in color—darker colors are more likely to fade. Never choose a vinyl door from a catalog photo. View an example in person to confirm that it doesn't look too "plastic-y"—they really don't look like wood. Their lack of visual appeal might make them the wrong choice if your garage door is on the front of your house.

Price: Around $800 to $1,300 for a two-car door.

Quality Hardware—A Must

The quality of a garage door's springs, rollers and hinges can have a major effect on its durability and operation...

•**The rollers should contain ball bearings**—the more the better. Nylon rollers are quieter than metal but generally don't last as long.

•**Hinges should feel solid and substantial.**

•**Springs should have a warranty of at least three years.** It isn't easy to judge the quality of a spring by looking at it, but a lengthy warranty can be a clue.

Warning: The warranty length cited for a garage door generally refers only to the door itself. Different warranty lengths apply to the door's hardware.

•**Tracks that are "powder-coated"**—a painting process that yields a more long-lasting finish than conventional painting—actually don't do a lot to improve garage door performance, but they can be a sign that the manufacturer has spent a little extra to provide higher-end hardware.

Insider tip: Ask if a hardware upgrade is available with the door you select. It may be possible to get higher-end hardware for $50 to $100 more, and higher-end hardware may have an extended warranty.

The Smartest Things You Can Do to Protect Your Home from Winter

Richard Trethewey, an expert adviser on the popular home-improvement show *This Old House* since it debuted in 1979. Based in Boston, he is president of RST (Thermal) Inc., a manufacturer's representative company that provides training to the skilled trades, and also is on the editorial board of *This Old House* magazine. ThisOldHouse.com

In much of the country, winter is a home owner's worst enemy. Extreme cold and the cycle of thawing and freezing attack your home's critical systems and sap expensive heat and energy. Sure, turning down your thermostat helps, but only so much—and who wants to shiver? Truly preparing your house for winter can protect vital systems, greatly reduce energy bills and make you more comfortable. But what if time or money doesn't allow you to make every winter preparation? No problem. *Here's what to do for the best result and to get the most bang for your buck…*

●**Prioritize.** Every house is an ongoing progression of problems. When one problem is fixed, another eventually will appear—and usually there are multiple problems at once. In the weeks and months before winter, however, you should focus your attention on fortifying your home to keep warm air in…and to keep cold air and water out. Since heat rises and water and cold air fall, you must concentrate your finite time and resources on shoring up the roof and insulating the attic—in that order.

●**Invest in a roof inspection.** Hire a roofer to conduct an inspection before you spend a single dollar anywhere else. The reason? If you have even a trickle of water coming in through the roof, it can turn into a huge headache.

The tiniest leak may not be a big deal in the fall. But when that thin stream of water freezes and expands as ice in winter, your tiny leak will become a big leak, which will then freeze and expand even more. Water rots your home's wood frame, saturates and ruins insulation, creates a breeding ground for dangerous mold and generally causes havoc inside the home.

Keeping water out in winter should be your number-one priority—and water is most likely to enter through the roof, where even the most observant home owner might not be able to spot a small leak. Faulty roofs also enable the formation of ice dams, which are ridges of ice that prevent water and melting snow from properly draining off the roof. Ice dams, which form when uneven roof temperatures cause snow to melt and then refreeze in concentrated areas, can cause catastrophic damage to ceilings, walls, insulation and the roof itself.

The national average cost for a roof inspection is $217, according to HomeAdvisor.com, although it could be as low as $75 or as high as $700. If you have it, spend it. Hopefully, your inspector will tell you that your roof is in great shape, get in his/her truck and leave. If that's the case, it's time to move on to insulation. However, if the inspector finds some problems that need fixing, expect to spend $770 for the average roof repair, according to HomeAdvisor.com. (The typical range is $331 to $1,223.) You won't enjoy writing that check, but keep in mind that replacing damaged portions of the roof and dealing with water damage inside in the spring would come with a much less forgiving price tag.

●**Insulate your attic—big time.** Unless you have the means to cloak your home in a thermal barrier by hiring a crew to insulate your walls, garage, basement and rafters, you should plug the heat leaks in order of priority. The attic is your priority—that's where rising warm air tries to escape from inside and sinking cold air tries to enter from outside. If you wouldn't go outside in a blizzard without a warm hat, don't let winter arrive without a well-insulated attic.

Many attics are already insulated…poorly. Either insulation is where it should be but there's not enough of it…or some parts are insulated but others aren't. And some attics, even in cold regions, aren't insulated at all, sometimes because insulation was removed to perform work on the underlying structure and simply never replaced. Insulation should cover the attic floor, fill the gaps between joists, protect any open penetrations around piping and fill knee walls, which are walls with attic space immediately behind them.

The average cost to have a professional insulate an attic ranges from $1,357 for blown-in cellulose insulation to $1,574 for roll or batt fiberglass insulation—that's the familiar fluffy pink stuff—to

$2,170 for spray-foam insulation. (Some builders find that the denser and more rigid rockwool, also called mineral wool, batt insulation performs better than fiberglass rolls, even if it can be more difficult to work with. Rockwool batts add about 25% to 50% to the cost of fiberglass, installed.)

Attic insulation can pay for itself fairly quickly through lower energy costs. The Department of Energy website Energy.gov/energysaver/types-insu lation can help you sort out the pros and cons of different types, including how well they lend themselves to do-it-yourself (DIY) projects. Because it's dusty work in a cramped environment, installing attic insulation generally is not considered a DIY project, but it can be done. It must, however, be done right. Even small gaps left behind can dramatically reduce R-value, which is a measurement of heat retention by which all insulation is classified. *This Old House* offers a primer on insulating your own attic, which is a good place to start. Go to ThisOldHouse. com and search "insulate attic."

•**Consider a home-energy audit.** Poorly insulated attics bleed more energy than any other part of the home, but your entire structure has vulnerabilities that are likely invisible to you. This is where a home-energy audit comes in. Home-energy auditors examine houses from top to bottom with equipment such as thermal imagers, special fans and prods to find leaks, drafts, weak spots, shoddy insulation, exposed pipes, inefficient appliances and other chinks in your home's energy armor.

Energy.gov and the federal Energy Star program (EnergyStar.gov) will help you learn what to expect from an audit. Contact your utility company, and ask whether it offers free or discounted home-energy audits, which many utilities do. If not, the average cost to hire a professional is about $394. While that's a hefty price tag for many people, it will be money well-spent if the audit unmasks your home's neediest points.

Things You Can Do for Less...or for Free.

•**Clean your gutters, or have them cleaned, before freezing weather comes.** Clogged gutters encourage the formation of ice—which can push or pull your gutters loose, lead to destructive ice dams and even result in injuries from massive falling icicles.

•**Upgrading older, energy-inefficient windows is a worthwhile but expensive improvement.** If that's not possible, consider buying transparent insulating film that adheres to the glass portion of your existing windows. It doesn't obstruct your view—in fact, you can leave it on year-round if you choose—but it can significantly reduce window-based energy bleed in both winter and summer.

Example: The Gila LEG361 Heat Control Residential Window Film, which says it cuts cooling costs by up to 30%, sells for about $32 and includes a roll that measures 36 inches by 15 feet.

•**If you're confident that you can safely do so, flush your water heater through its drain valve to clear out sediment and sludge,** which can improve efficiency and reduce costs in the high-demand winter months. If this isn't something you want to do yourself, pay a plumber to do it (about $100)—it should take less than an hour and is worth it.

•**Heat escapes and cold air enters through gaps under exterior doors.** A $10 draft guard can prevent most of that waste. Virtually all homes will benefit from weather-stripping tape applied to doors and windows. Each roll costs about $5 and can service two or three doors. If you have forced-air heating, replacing the filters for about $10 each can take enormous pressure off your heating system, reducing the cost of running it.

•**Finally, walk around the exterior of your house, and examine the siding for holes and gaps.** When you find a gap, fill it with regular household caulk, which costs $5 to $10 per tube and can be applied with a $15 caulk gun.

The Best Home Sauna for You

David Brown, editor of *Sauna Talk*, a website based in Melville, New York, that reviews sauna brands and offers sauna-related advice. He has been installing and writing about saunas for more than 20 years. Sauna-Talk.com

I f you have access to a gym with a dry sauna and you can get there four or more times a week, wonderful. But it's a lot easier to take 20 minutes of the sauna experience if it's inside your own home or in your backyard. Here are the best home saunas for different budgets—for each model, larger versions are available at additional cost.

Outdoor Finnish-Style Sauna

The best, most pleasurable saunas in Finland are heated by wood—there's something that feels "soft" about wood heat, and the sound of crackling logs doesn't hurt, either. High-end electric or gas-fired saunas do come close to that experience—and are easier to use and maintain. A wood-fired heater may make sense for you if you want a freestanding sauna on your property, assuming zoning laws in your area allow it.

Recommended: Saunacore Country Living barrel sauna, a freestanding, outdoor, cedar, wood-fired sauna, arrives in a kit that's relatively easy to assemble. Delivery generally is included, and many dealers will assemble it for around $1,000.

Cost: About $9,500 for a 6' x 6' x 8' sauna. Sauna core.com

Indoor Finnish-Style Sauna

For an inside-the-house sauna, consider a model with an electric heater, which does not require a chimney or air-intake system. It heats up quickly and is easy to control. Indoor saunas often are situated in or near a bathroom (it's nice to shower off immediately after a sauna) or in a basement.

Recommended: Saunacore Infra-Core Dual is a prebuilt unit, like a walk-in closet, made from wood and glass. The smallest model (4' x 4' x 6'2" high) can be plugged into a standard outlet and costs around $9,500. Many sellers include shipping. Larger units require a dedicated, higher-powered outlet wired in by an electrician.

Indoor Infrared Saunas

Infrared saunas don't elevate air temperature dramatically—instead, the infrared light directly heats the body. Sauna purists complain that they don't deliver a true sauna experience because they don't heat the air. But infrared saunas tend to cost far less than wood-fired or electric-heated models.

Less research has been done on the health benefits of infrared saunas than on conventional saunas—though the research that has been conducted is encouraging.

●**Bargain-priced.** There are many home infrared saunas available online for less than $2,000, but most are of poor quality. But two companies—Dynamic and JNH Lifestyles—outpace the competition at this price point by offering reasonable build quality and effective infrared heaters.

Recommended: Santiago 2-Person Low EMF FAR infrared sauna (3'8" x 3' x 6'3" high, recently $2,100, DynamicSaunasDirect.com) and JNH Lifestyles Joyous 2-Person infrared sauna (3'11" x 3'3" x 6'2" high, about $2,200, JNHLifestyles.com).

●**Premium.** These models are a big step up in quality—and price. They have the highest-quality woods, heaters, components and quality of workmanship. Many also have built-in high-quality sound systems and higher-end digital control systems.

Recommended: Sunlighten Signature (3'3" x 3'2" x 6'5" high, $4,597 delivered, dedicated circuit required, Sunlighten.com) and the Clearlight Premier IS-2 basswood sauna (3'9" x 3'4" x 5'9" high, $4,100 delivered, plugs into a standard outlet, InfraRedSauna.com, sold under the Jacuzzi brand name). These are walk-in wood-and-glass cabinets made with real craftsmanship and attractive woods. Each requires some assembly—generally just an hour or two.

No More Leaky Skylights!

Danny Lipford, host of the nationally syndicated *Today's Homeowner with Danny Lipford* television and radio programs. He has been a licensed contractor based in Alabama for more than 36 years. TodaysHomeowner.com

A skylight can transform a dark room into a bright and welcoming space. Trouble is, some skylights let in drops of water along with the rays of sunlight—water that can cause unsightly damage or even mold issues if the water finds its way into ceilings or walls.

Here's what you need to know before you have a skylight installed...

Selecting a Skylight

It typically costs $1,000 to $2,000 to purchase a two-foot-by-four-foot skylight and have it professionally installed—more if it's an especially complex installation or you choose a skylight with high-end options. Don't try to save money by buying a low-end skylight or installing a skylight yourself (unless you have extensive experience)—the risk for leaks is just too high. If your budget is tight, there are smarter ways to save—more on that below.

What to look for in a skylight…

• **The Velux brand name.** In my experience, no other manufacturer can match Velux's reliability and overall quality. (I have no financial interest in Velux.) Velux skylights are sold at Lowe's and The Home Depot among many other locations (Velux USA.com).

• **Multiple panes of glass with argon gas in between.** These are more energy-efficient than single-pane skylights and much less likely to allow water drips due to condensation—home owners who think their skylights leak sometimes actually are experiencing condensation.

Helpful: Spraying foam insulation between the outer edge of the skylight frame and the wood framing of the roof during installation can help prevent condensation, too.

• **Never install any skylight made from translucent plastic rather than glass.** These invariably are low-quality.

• **Built-in blinds.** There likely will be times when the sunshine coming in through your skylight causes problems. The light might shine in your eyes when you try to take a nap on a couch or shine on the TV screen, making it hard to see. It also could overheat the room on a hot day. For an extra $100 to $200, you typically can get a quality skylight that includes blinds. It can be very difficult to add blinds after a skylight has been installed—the aftermarket skylight-blind kits tend not to work well—so it's worth spending this extra money up-front. If the skylight is not easily reached, select remote-control blinds.

Helpful: Some remote-control blinds are solar-powered. This eliminates the cost of running electrical wires up to the skylight. If the blinds are installed by the end of 2022, they might be eligible for a 26% tax credit (22% for systems installed in 2023). Solar tax credits decrease in subsequent years. Your contractor should be able to provide a bill that breaks out the cost of the blinds from that of the skylight itself. The manufacturer's website will provide details if its solar blinds are eligible.

Two Money-Saving Strategies

There are ways to cut skylight costs without ending up with a low-quality, leak-prone product…

• **Skylights that don't open.** A "fixed skylight"—one in which the glass is fixed and cannot be opened—can cost hundreds of dollars less than a "venting" skylight of the same quality. They're a smart way to save money because most home owners do not open venting skylights very often anyway.

Exception: It might be worth paying extra for a venting skylight in rooms that get extremely hot in the summer…and/or in bathrooms that have moisture or mildew issues. If you do opt for a venting skylight, a remote-control venting system is the best choice if the skylight is difficult to reach—those long poles used to crank open manually operated venting skylights are awkward and frustrating. A remote-controlled venting system powered by small solar panels can eliminate electrician's bills and make the entire skylight eligible for the 30% federal tax credit mentioned above. (*Sample savings:* An average of $850.) Solar-powered blinds often are an option on a solar-powered venting skylight.

• **The tubular alternative.** Tubular skylights, also called light tubes, don't provide a window to the sky like a traditional skylight. Instead, they feature a rooftop dome that collects sunlight…a "diffuser" on the interior ceiling that distributes sunlight throughout the room below…and a reflective sheet-metal tube connecting these two components. This brings a surprising amount of natural light into a room for a reasonable price—often for $500 to $800 installed. Solatube is the leading brand and a good choice…Velux makes high-quality tubular skylights, too.

Tip: Have the metal tube of the tubular skylight wrapped in R-15 or R-19 fiberglass insulation. This reduces energy loss and the risk for condensation.

Tubular skylights make sense if…

• **The ceiling of the room you wish to brighten is many feet below the roofline.** With a traditional skylight, this would require the construction of a long shaft—which would increase installation costs and decrease the area lit.

• **Structural elements in the roof make it impossible to position a traditional skylight where you would like.** A tubular skylight's tube can be routed around trusses and other impediments.

• **The room contains expensive rugs or furniture.** Tubular skylights are unlikely to cause UV damage.

• **The room is a long hallway.** For the same price as one traditional skylight, you could add two or three tubular skylights, which will do a better job illuminating a long, narrow space.

Having a Skylight Installed

Installing skylights is a specialized job. You want someone who has installed the particular brand of skylight many times before. Ask stores that sell the brand of skylight you choose to recommend someone to do the installation. The skylight manufacturer's website also might provide installer recommendations.

If your goal is to bring the maximum possible amount of sunlight into your home, the south or southwest side of your roof generally is best—assuming it is not obstructed by tall trees or buildings. The north side of a roof gets the least direct sunlight in the Northern Hemisphere, so a skylight placed there generally will not let in as much light.

It may be possible to reduce costs and increase the light that a skylight lets in by positioning it just above an exterior wall rather than higher up on the roof. The distance between a home's exterior

roof and the ceilings of the rooms below tends to be shortest near where the roof meets the home's exterior walls and greatest near the middle of the home, where attic headroom is most substantial. The shorter this distance, the shorter the shaft that must be constructed for the skylight, reducing labor costs and increasing the amount of light in the room. This is not an issue if the home has a flat roof or a cathedral ceiling.

An experienced skylight installer can safely cut through rafters—the beams directly beneath the exterior roof—by reinforcing neighboring rafters. But if your roof is supported by trusses—that is, there are angled wood "webs" in the attic providing additional support to the rafters—these should not be cut. Doing so could cause major structural problems. It might be necessary to adjust the position of the skylight to fit between trusses. Trusses typically are positioned 24 inches apart, so a 22.5-inch-wide skylight should fit.

How to Fix a Leaky Skylight

If you can safely climb up onto your roof, there's a good chance you can fix a leaking skylight. Leaks typically develop when small cracks or gaps form between the skylight and the roof.

First, clear away any debris that has accumulated against the top edge of the skylight. It could be causing water damming.

Next, carefully scan along the edge of the skylight's frame for any cracks or gaps between the frame and the flashing (the strips of metal that provide protection where the skylight joins the roof). Remove old caulking or roofing cement you find between the flashing and the skylight frame if it seems to be cracking or crumbling, then reseal using polyurethane-based sealant. This costs a bit more than roofing cement, but it's less likely to crack.

If the leaks continue, install a rain diverter. This is a long L-shaped piece of metal positioned on the roof slightly above the skylight to steer rainwater away. (See TodaysHomeowner.com/Installing-A-Rain-Diverter for details.)

If this fails, it is to time call in a roofing pro or skylight repair specialist.

How to…Buy a Workbench That Works

Danny Lipford, who has worked as a remodeling contractor for more than 30 years and hosts the nationally syndicated TV program *Today's Homeowner with Danny Lipford,* airing on more than 200 stations nationwide. He is based in Mobile, Alabama. TodaysHomeowner.com

If your fix-it tasks are performed on a kitchen table or on an old wooden door held up by two sawhorses, it may be time to spring for a workbench. There are plenty of reasonably priced ones that can make home-improvement projects safer, easier and more productive—and more fun. Not all workbenches are worth their prices, though.

To find the best workbench for you…

•**Think about how you'll use the bench.** If you need a temporary workspace to do small repairs in several areas around the house or you simply have no space for a permanent workbench, a folding portable one that's relatively lightweight or has wheels may serve you better. They are inexpensive and require little or no assembly.

Disadvantage: The top typically is two feet by three feet, not enough for most woodworking projects but useful for mixing paint, cutting small pieces of lumber and repairing small items.

Top portable models…

•Kreg Mobile Project Center has a heavy-gauge steel frame and a two-piece top that doubles as a clamping station. 27 inches by 31 inches. *Cost:* $170. KregTool.com

•Rockwell Jawhorse Sheetmaster Portable Work Support Station RK9002 has a three-legged design that makes it easier to balance on uneven surfaces and a powerful vise operated by a foot pedal, which is great for clamping and sawing heavier objects. It weighs 43 pounds. 4.5 inches by 3 feet one inch. *Cost:* $300. Available at Amazon.com and RockwellTools.com.

•**Opt for a stationary bench if you want to do more extensive home repairs and projects.** *Top stationary models include…*

•Gladiator Modular Workbench, with a hardwood top, is 5 feet 6.5 inches by 20 inches. Its adjustable legs compensate for uneven floors, and there is room underneath to add rolling storage cabinets. *Cost:* $299.99. Gladiator offers benches of various lengths with maple tops ranging from $260 to $500. GladiatorGarageWorks.com

•Diversified Woodcrafts Maple Woodworking Workbench comes in a model that is 5 feet by 24 inches ($993). It has a solid maple hardwood top and a sturdy bottom shelf. Other sizes and configurations available. WorthingtonDirect.com

•**Important accessories.** *These are crucial add-ons…*

•Steel pegboard. Attach it to the wall behind the workbench to hang and organize your tools. Lower-end workbenches sometimes come with quarter-inch high-density fiberboard pegboards, but they are not rugged enough to store heavy items. *Cost*: Less than $60.

•Protection. Add a few coats of wipe-on varnish to the top surface to minimize scratches and dings. Also, buy sheets of Homasote to lay over your workbench when you're staining, gluing or painting. Homasote is thick fiberboard made from compressed recycled paper that's easy to cut to size and more effective than newspaper. *Cost:* $32 for a 4-by-8-foot board at Lowe's.

•Lighting. The simplest, most cost-effective lighting is a four-foot-long fluorescent fixture with two 32-watt bulbs that you can hang from chains on the ceiling over the workbench. *Cost:* About $30.

Renovating? Tricks to Contain the Dust

Jeffery C. May, principal scientist with May Indoor Air Investigations LLC, an air-quality assessment company in Tyngsborough, Massachusetts. He is author of *Jeff May's Healthy Home Tips: A Workbook for Detecting, Diagnosing, and Eliminating Pesky Pests, Stinky Stenches, Musty Mold, and Other Aggravating Home Problems.* MayIndoorAir.com

Home fix-ups can release renovation dust into a home's air. The dust can spread throughout your home, making cleanup difficult. And the dust even can cause respiratory distress. *What to do to protect your home and family…*

•**Isolate the work area.** Hang fire-resistant, clear six-mil-thick polyethylene sheeting to separate the area under renovation from the rest of the home, or ask contractors to do so. Expect to pay about $100 for a 20-foot-by-100-foot roll at a home center.

"Zipper tape"—a zipper designed to adhere to plastic sheeting—is an effective way to seal the entrance to the work area. It typically costs $10 to $20 in home centers.

Helpful: The extending pole system ZipPole allows plastic sheeting to be hung without stapling or taping to walls and ceilings (800-718-2255, Zip Wall.com, $160 for a four-pole system on Amazon. com).

Use plastic sheeting to create an enclosed walkway from the work area to the nearest exit, too. If that's impractical, at least place an adhesive doormat by the work-area exit to collect dust from shoes. Products include Pro Tect Tacky Mats (800-545-0826, Pro-Tect.com, $46 for two 30-sheet mats) and Americover Sticky Mats (one tray, one 30-sheet mat $130 at Americover.com).

•**Create negative air pressure.** Place an exhaust fan in a work-area window. Aim it outward so that it pulls air from the work area to the outdoors. This prevents airflow from circulating work-area dust to the rest of the home—the airflow will move in the other direction.

•**Cover carpets.** If there's carpeting in the renovation area, cover it with Pro Tect's Carpet Protection Film (800-545-0826, Pro-Tect.com, $65 for a 2.5-foot-by-200-foot roll). Otherwise, dust from the renovation will settle in the carpet, where it becomes a long-term problem. All vacuuming during renovation and cleanup should be done with a high-efficiency particulate air (HEPA) vacuum.

Warning: Basic plastic sheeting does not adequately protect carpets during renovations—workers' feet are likely to pull it out of place.

•**Protect your home's heating, ventilation and air-conditioning (HVAC) system.** Do not operate your home's duct system during a renovation unless the registers and grilles—the openings where air is released from or returned to the duct system—in the work area have been completely covered by plastic sheeting or aluminum foil that is securely taped in place with removable tape. Otherwise, dust from the renovation will get into the ducts, where it could cause long-term air-quality issues. Renovation dust such as sawdust could encourage the growth of mold inside the HVAC system.

Also, radiators and baseboard convectors in the work area should be covered with plastic during renovations. After renovations, vacuum the radiators (use a crevice tool if needed) and the baseboard convectors. For dusty "fin" tubing in the baseboards, use compressed air or a steam vapor machine to clear away any dust that got past the sheeting.

Helpful: If heating or cooling is needed in the work area, rent portable heaters or a window air-conditioning unit.

Avoid Mistakes Finishing an Attic

Danny Lipford, host of *Today's Homeowner with Danny Lipford*, a nationally syndicated TV program. He is based in Mobile, Alabama. TodaysHomeowner.com

A finished attic can provide a very welcome addition to living space, but it's not appropriate for every home—in fact, it can be a very bad decision. *Here are the key things to consider when deciding whether to finish your attic, either on your own or with a contractor...*

Height and Space

These are factors that many home owners don't fully anticipate and that could ruin the whole project...

•**Ceiling height.** Building codes typically require a ceiling height of at least seven feet in all or some specified part of a finished attic. What many home owners don't realize is that a seven-foot ceiling—especially one that slopes down to the floor—will make the space feel much more cramped.

Best: Don't finish your attic unless a large part of the unfinished ceiling is at least eight feet high.

•**Staircase space.** If your attic currently is accessed via a ladder and there's no obvious spot for a staircase, installing stairs might be so expensive and require so much space in the attic and the floor below that the project isn't worth it. Ask an experienced remodeling contractor for an evaluation and estimate—attic access issues might mean that it's actually less expensive to have an addition put on your house instead.

Warning: Spiral staircases take little space, but home owners are rarely happy with them. For one thing, you cannot move most medium- or large-sized furniture up and down.

Cooling, Floors and Windows

These are challenges that can almost always be overcome, but many people plunge into finishing projects without fully accounting for them…

•**Cooling is probably a must.** Many attics get stiflingly hot in the spring and summer, and your existing cooling system may not be adequate.

Recommendation: A "ductless split system" such as the Toshiba/Carrier Residential Series Ductless is an energy-efficient way to cool and heat a finished attic. It typically costs $2,000 to $5,000 installed.

•**You might have to reinforce the floor.** Unfinished attics often have joists sufficient only to hold up the ceiling below, not to support much additional weight above. Consult an experienced remodeling contractor or structural engineer about this even if you finish your attic yourself. Expect to pay about $500 for this consulting help.

•**You'll probably have to add windows.** Windows not only provide natural light and air—some also qualify as emergency exits, and building codes typically require at least two exits from a finished attic. Dormer windows, which protrude upward from sloping roofs, increase ceiling height, too, and therefore make the finished space feel less constricting. Expect to pay $3,000 to $5,000 per newly installed dormer…more for long dormers containing multiple windows.

Simple Way to Strip Paint from Decorative Hardware

The Family Handyman

There's an easy way to strip paint from decorative hardware, such as hinges, cabinet pulls, etc. Fill an old slow cooker with water—no chemicals are required—and set the dial to high. Leave the parts in the cooker overnight. Heat and moisture soften the paint, which often falls off. This works on oil, latex and spray paints—it may not work on some clear finishes.

Caution: The process may cause rust spots on steel, and it can stain or contaminate the slow cooker, so only use one that is no longer needed for food—or buy an inexpensive one for less than $20 and keep it in your workshop.

Best Easy-Care Decks and Patios

Danny Lipford, host of the nationally syndicated program *Today's Homeowner* and a regular contributor to CBS's *The Early Show*. He has worked as a remodeling contractor for more than 26 years in Mobile, Alabama, and has renovated more than 3,000 homes. TodaysHomeowner.com

Patios and wood decks can deteriorate into eyesores or even safety risks if they're not properly maintained. For home owners who would rather spend their time lounging on their decks and patios than working on them, there are lower-maintenance options…

•**Plastic-resin composite decks.** Man-made composite planks, typically a mixture of polyethylene and fine sawdust, don't require staining or sealing, just an occasional wash. Early composite decks tended to fade in the sun. Today's products fare better. The best composites, which also are used for railings, do an excellent job of mimicking the look of natural wood. Reliable brand names include ChoiceDek, Envision, EverGrain, Geodeck, TimberTech, Trex and Veranda. Select a product that has a warranty of at least 10 years.

Cost: $3 to $7 per square foot for composite deck boards. That's about $15 per square foot including installation, which is comparable to redwood and slightly higher than cedar or fir.

I don't recommend decking that is made entirely of plastic. It stands up to the elements better than composites, but it doesn't look like wood.

•**Concrete patios.** Today's concrete patios are pleasing to the eye. They last for decades and require very little maintenance—just a wash or a sweep every now and then. You can minimize the effect that hairline cracks have on the appearance of your patio by cutting quarter-inch-deep "control joints" into the concrete—at least one every eight feet—using a circular saw with an abrasive blade. Cracks will tend to form only along these thinner joints, where they'll be mostly hidden. Make additional cuts in a square or diamond pattern, and you can spice up the look by making the concrete appear to be large tiles. This is cheaper and more convenient than buying and installing large concrete tiles.

Cost: $2 to $3 per square foot for materials, or $4 to $8 including installation. Add an additional $2 to $3 per square foot to have a decorative pattern cut into the surface. (These labor estimates assume that your yard is flat.)

Helpful: About a month after the slab is poured, it can be stained or acid-washed to add color. This job is best left to a professional. It will add $4 to $5 per square foot to the project's cost.

•**Paver patios.** Pavers are durable and classic-looking, and they don't require much maintenance. They have been on the market about 20 years. They're similar to traditional bricks but available in a wider range of colors and sizes and often are made from concrete. Paver patios also are a great do-it-yourself project. Just clear a flat piece of land and dig it out two to three inches deep. Then remove all plant material…spread crushed stone…add an inch of masonry sand…firmly set the bricks…and sweep masonry sand into the gaps between them. Home stores sell plastic or aluminum forms that hold the outermost bricks in place. For details, search "paver" on my website, TodaysHomeowner.com.

Cost: $7 to $10 per square foot for materials. Add $6 to $8 per square foot for professional installation.

6 Thrifty Tricks to Spruce Up Your Deck

Lawrence Winterburn, president of GardenStructure.com, which builds decks and other outdoor structures in 17 metro regions in the US and Canada. The company sells plans for decks and related structures to do-it-yourselfers. He has nearly 30 years of experience as a master carpenter.

The typical residential deck is an uninspired, unattractive rectangle of rapidly weathering wood. Very few home decks are truly engaging spots from which to enjoy the outdoors. But having an elaborate new deck constructed is likely to trigger a five-figure bill. *Fortunately, there are some relatively simple and affordable ways to make an older or uninspired deck look much better…*

•**Emphasize the surrounding landscape.** Paint or stain the deck a dark brown, then surround it with brightly colored plants. Your local garden center can suggest plants appropriate for your climate and budget. This is a remarkably effective way to trick the eye into barely noticing a deck's shortcomings.

•**Install a vine-covered privacy trellis.** Do you feel that you're on display to the neighbors when you are on your deck? Adding a trellis—a framework of lightweight rails—on one or more sides of the deck can provide a sense of privacy without completely blocking off your sunlight and/or view.

Home centers sell a variety of lattice panels and premade trellises. Four-by-eight-foot sections cost as little as $20 to $30. Replace your deck's handrail posts with posts tall enough to support the trellis. Growing vines over the trellis will soften the look of the deck and make it feel more connected to the landscape.

•**Put on a skirt.** Deck skirting is solid or lattice paneling that extends from the deck down to near the ground. It's an affordable way to hide the unsightly area under a deck. Appropriate paneling made from wood or a wood textured composite is available in home centers for as little as $20 to $30 per four-by-eight-foot section.

If your deck is a single step up from the ground, this skirting can be nailed to the deck's outermost joists (joists are the horizontal structural elements directly beneath the decking). If your deck is significantly higher than this, nail the skirting to the deck's support posts or to other vertical posts added below the perimeter of the deck for this purpose. Skirting typically is painted to match the home's siding but also could be stained a natural color or painted white.

Leave at least two inches of space between the bottom of the skirting and the ground. That way, a winter frost that raises the ground level won't damage or dislodge the skirting or the deck itself.

Helpful: If your deck is more than three steps above ground level, you could cut a door into the skirting, creating a storage area for lawn and garden items under the deck. Use hinges and latches to hold this door in place, and screw in plastic or fiberglass corrugated roofing to the underside of the deck joists above to keep this storage area relatively dry. Position plastic or fiberglass at an angle so that water drains off.

●**Replace your deck's steps.** Rickety, rotting steps can make an entire deck look and feel flimsy. If you have some basic woodworking skills, you can construct sturdier steps that will instead convey a sense of solidity and quality. This generally doesn't cost more than $100 or so in lumber, assuming that your deck is no more than a few feet above ground level. If your deck is much higher than this, it might be safer to leave the staircase building to the pros (this can cost a few hundred to a few thousand dollars).

Tip: Each step in your staircase should be the same height. Unequal heights signal amateurish construction.

Ideally you should position the deck steps where people won't have to squeeze past a table or other deck furniture to get from inside your home down into your yard. Poor "flow" also subtly detracts from the impression created by a deck.

●**Add attractive caps to handrail posts.** Decorative wood or copper post caps are an easy and a potentially inexpensive way to dress up a deck. Post caps are available for as little as $10 apiece in home

centers, though higher-quality caps made by local craftsmen can cost significantly more. Or you can design your own post caps if you have basic woodworking skills.

Solar-powered post caps that light up at night are available in home centers, too, often for just $10 to $20 apiece. Purchase 50% to 100% more of these fixtures than you need so that you have replacements when some of the fixtures inevitably fail. You might not be able to find the same style of light fixture in stores in future years.

●**Use long-lasting wood protector.** The product One Time costs more than most deck stains and sealers—$85 per gallon (one gallon covers around 250 square feet of older wood). But One Time needs to be applied about once every seven years, instead of every two years for traditional sealers. Thus, over seven years, you'll spend $85 on One Time versus about $200 on a traditional sealer—a savings of $115. OneTimeWood.com

Questions to Ask a Contractor

Danny Lipford, host of the nationally syndicated program *Today's Homeowner* and a regular contributor to CBS's *The Early Show.* He has worked as a remodeling contractor for more than 26 years in Mobile, Alabama, and has renovated more than 3,000 homes. TodaysHomeowner.com

When a home construction or renovation project goes wrong, it's often because the home owner chose the wrong contractor. *Asking these questions can help you find the right one…*

What are your favorite types of projects to take on? You want a contractor who focuses on and enjoys the sort of work you want done. For example, if you are doing a renovation, you want someone who loves to remodel versus someone who builds only new houses and hates the remodeling process. Ask before you tell the contractor what type of project you have in mind. Do not accept the answer "I like all projects."

How is your business structured? Do you have a lot of full-time employees? Who are your key subcontractors? You want a contractor who has worked with the same core group of trusted subcontractors and workmen for years. This core group does not necessarily have to include full-timers—certain subcontractors such as plumbers and electricians are rarely on staff—but if they're independent, the contractor should note that he has been hiring these subcontractors time and again for many years. What you don't want to hear is something vague such as, "I find people when I need them."

When you get to the end of a job, how do you handle closing things out? The contractor's response should include that you will have an opportunity to list things that you believe still need to be done before the crew packs up and leaves. Example: "When we feel the job is substantially complete, we will invite you to provide a list of anything you see that needs attention. We'll tackle your list immediately."

Follow up by asking what you can do if you spot a problem a month after the project is complete. Get a written warranty or guarantee confirming that the contractor stands behind his work and the materials he uses. The warranty should be a minimum of one year on all labor and materials the contractor furnishes.

Are you licensed and bonded? Is everyone who is going to be on my property covered by workman's compensation? Don't work with a contractor who answers no or gives a vague response. If the answer is yes, follow up with, "Can your insurance provider send me confirmation of your general-liability coverage?" Do not work with a contractor who acts as if this request is inappropriate—it's not. A contractor who implies that it is inappropriate is either trying to hide that he does not actually have coverage, which could put you at financial risk…and/or he's a pain to work with. Contractors who have coverage generally are happy to prove that they have it—doing that makes them feel that they are getting their money's worth out of their insurance policies.

How will I communicate with your company once the project starts? You want to hear that you will have one specific person whom you can call or text—either the contractor himself or a project foreman—and that this person will either pick up or get back to you promptly. "Just call the office and leave a message" is not acceptable.

What will be the normal working hours for the crew on this project? It's a great sign if after you are told a daily schedule, you are asked, "Does that work for you?" This suggests that the contractor prioritizes the client's needs.

Will you use a standard contract? The answer you don't want to hear is, "I don't bother with contracts." It's fine if the contractor has had his own contracts drawn up, but confirm that this contract will lay out in detail what the contractor will be providing…what he will not be providing…what the payment schedule will be…and what the total payment amount will be.

How long have you been a contractor? What did you do before that? Three years of experience might be sufficient for a small renovation, though five or more is better. For a large project, look for someone with at least 10 years of experience. It's a good sign if the contractor previously worked as a supervisor or project manager for a builder… or as a framing contractor. It's a bad sign if he did something unrelated to building—whenever the economy booms and construction surges, people with limited background in the field try to become contractors, often with poor results. (Prior profession is less important if the contractor has been a contractor for a decade or longer.)

Have you always operated under your current business name? Changing business names can be a red flag—the contractor might have closed an earlier business to escape lawsuits from dissatisfied clients and unpaid vendors or other problems. If the contractor says that he never has changed company names, enter that contractor's first and last name and the word "contractor" into a search engine to see whether you can find any evidence that he actually has. You also could ask building inspectors in nearby towns whether they know anything about the contractor's background and for an off-the-record opinion of the contractor…or, especially if you are planning a large project, ask a lawyer to do a quick search for lawsuits naming this contractor as defendant.

Home and Appliance Warranties Are Bad Deals

Kevin Brasler, executive editor at *Consumers' Checkbook*, a publication from the Center for the Study of Services, Washington, DC, an independent, nonprofit consumer organization. Checkbook.org

Home-warranty ads claim that obtaining this type of coverage shields home owners against the high cost of home and appliance repairs. But when parts of your home break, having one of these policies—which typically costs $600 to $1,000 per year—is more likely to cause you frustration. *Three big problems…*

●**Big-ticket repairs tend to be covered poorly, if at all.** Exclusions and caps hidden in the fine print mean that many home repairs are not covered—and the pricier the repair, the less likely it is to be covered.

Examples: Roof leaks and basement moisture problems, issues that can cost many thousands of dollars to fix, often are excluded. Heating and air-conditioning repairs frequently are capped at just $1,500 per year.

●**There are hefty co-pays.** Home owners must shell out a co-pay of at least $75 to $125 every time the warranty provider sends a repair person or contractor, even if the repair service claims that the work isn't covered by the warranty after all—which happens regularly because of the many exclusions.

●**Home owners can't pick their own repair pros.** The warranty provider typically decides who does the work—which often results in shoddy work, judging by the volume of complaints. And because these repair people answer to the warranty provider, not the home owner, they are more likely to declare that repairs are not covered by the warranty.

What's more, home warranties usually contain language absolving the warranty provider from any liability if the repair person it picks accidentally damages the home or bungles the repair.

Example: One home owner reported that the repair person sent by her warranty provider to unclog a pipe instead got his snake stuck inside the pipe—then simply cut off the stuck snake line and left. When she asked him to return and remove it, he said it would cost her $750.

What to do: Don't buy a home warranty —they don't make financial sense. Policy holders receive only around 50 cents in services for every dollar they pay in premiums, based on the financial filings of publicly traded companies in the sector.

Exception: There's no need to avoid home warranties offered by home builders on new homes at no additional cost.

CHAPTER 20

Safety and Security

Disaster-Proof Your Home

Tim Reinhold, PhD, retired chief engineer and senior vice president of research for Insurance Institute for Business & Home Safety, a nonprofit research and advocacy organization supported by the property insurance industry, based in Richburg, South Carolina. DisasterSafety.org

CNBC.com

Natural disasters cost the US $91 billion in 2018 due to 14 natural disasters, ranging from wildfires to winter storms. According to the National Oceanic and Atmospheric Administration, 2018 had the fourth-highest total costs from natural disasters since the NOAA started tracking data in 1980.

There's no way to make a house completely disaster-proof, but there are home-improvement projects that can significantly limit damage and/or improve the odds that a home will survive. Not all of these projects make financial sense for every home owner, but many provide considerable protection at a reasonable price.

Helpful: Insurers sometimes offer discounts to home owners who invest in home-protection upgrades.

Wildfires

Wildfires are most common in hot, dry areas but can strike any homes built near wild lands. Managing vegetation within 100 feet of your house, especially the closest 30 feet, helps keep away flames and intense heat. Keep this area clear of leaves and other dead-plant debris, and choose fire-resistant vegetation (search for "Fire-Safe Landscaping" at USFA. fema.gov). *Additional wildfire-protection steps…*

•**Have a Class-A fire-rated roof installed when you next replace your roof.** The roof is the most vulnerable part of your home in a wildfire. If it is not sufficiently fire-resistant, a single ember from a fire a mile or more away could drift on the wind, land on your roof and burn down your home.

Class-A roofs typically feature asphalt shingles (though not all asphalt shingles achieve a Class-A rating), clay or concrete tiles or steel roofing products. Roof coverings that don't qualify as Class A on their own still can qualify as Class A as part of a roof design that includes fire-resistant underlayment materials, such as fiberglass.

If leaves collect where roofing intersects with siding—along the side of dormers or where the lower section of a split-level roof meets the higher part of the home, for example—ask your roofer to install metal flashing (thin continuous pieces of sheet metal) along these intersections. Otherwise, if those leaves catch fire, the fire could spread to the siding and then into the home.

Also: Cover roof vent openings with ⅛-inch metal mesh. This costs very little and reduces the size of embers that can get into the attic through vents.

•**Add metal flashing between your wood deck and your home.** If your deck catches fire, this flashing will significantly reduce the odds that the fire will spread to the rest of the home. The flashing ideally should extend 18 inches or more above the deck surface. A contractor typically can do this for a few hundred dollars.

●**If you are replacing your deck and you are in an area that is prone to wildfires, consider having the new deck made from a composite material that includes fire-retardant chemicals or from wood that has been treated with an exterior fire retardant.** This is likely to increase the cost of materials by at least 50%, and potentially much more.

●**Replace wood fencing within a few feet of the home with fencing made from a nonflammable material, such as metal or brick.** Otherwise, the wood fence could act as a wick, leading a wildfire right to your home. Even replacing just the portions of the wood fence that are directly adjacent to the home with a noncombustible material will reduce the odds that a fence fire will spread to the home.

●**Select double- or triple-paned windows with a fully tempered outer pane the next time you replace your windows.** These are less likely to shatter in the heat of a wildfire. Shattered windows give wildfires a way to enter the home. Double- and triple-paned windows are expensive, but their energy efficiency can help recoup those costs.

Floods

Projects that can help protect homes located in flood zones...

●**Have components of the heating-ventilation-and-air-conditioning (HVAC) and electrical system raised as high as possible**—ideally to 12 inches or more above the base flood elevation (available at FEMA's online Map Service Center, MSC.fema.gov, search for "Flood Maps") or above the high-water mark reached in previous floods, whichever is higher. Electricians and HVAC contractors might charge anywhere from a few hundred to many thousands of dollars to do this, depending on the extent of rewiring and ductwork alterations required, but this could prevent destruction of those systems.

●**Have a sump pump installed in your basement to remove any water that gets in.** Select one

that has battery backup that will last up to 24 hours or more so that it doesn't stop working if flooding knocks out your power. Expect to pay perhaps $500 to $1,000, installed.

Earthquakes

Destructive earthquakes are possible in parts of the US located far from the famously quake-prone Pacific coast. *Among home owners' options...*

●**Have flexible connections spliced into gas and water lines.** The odds of a gas or water line snapping in an earthquake can be significantly reduced by replacing sections of rigid pipe with flexible piping near where these lines connect to appliances and equipment. A plumber should be able to do this for a few hundred dollars.

●**Strengthen cripple walls.** Cripple walls are short, wood-framed walls found above the foundation in basements or crawl spaces. They're often vulnerable to collapse in earthquakes. Contractors can affix plywood or cross-bracing to strengthen cripple walls, greatly reducing the risk for collapse, typically for just a few thousand dollars.

●**Add strapping or bolts to strengthen the connection between the home and its foundation.** A contractor should be able to do this for a few thousand dollars.

Also: Have your water heater strapped to a wall so it is less likely to break away.

Hurricanes

Screwing plywood over windows isn't the only way to protect a home from hurricane damage...

●**Strengthen the connection between roof decking and framing when you next have your roof reshingled or replaced.** Driving additional nails through the decking (the structural skin of a roof) and into the framing below it significantly decreases the odds that the roof will be ripped off in a hurricane—the single greatest hurricane damage risk. Ask to have 2⅜-inch (eight-penny) or longer ring-shank nails used to do this, not the six-penny nails or staples that most roofing contractors use. Installing these extra nails should add only a few hundred dollars.

When the roof is replaced, have the roofer install a secondary moisture barrier that's more robust than the usual layer of felt paper. This protects against moisture damage and also, in the winter, prevents ice dams from forming from melting snow. This could be a synthetic underlayment, two or more layers of underlayment cemented together or a self-adhering waterproof membrane called a polymer-modified bitumen sheet. For specific guidance, check DisasterSafety.org (put "Roofing the Right Way" in the search box). This could add from a few hundred to $1,000 or more to the cost.

Warning: Your roof-strengthening options are less appealing if you are not reshingling. There are foam adhesives that improve the connection between decking and framing when sprayed onto the underside of roof decking along all the joints with the roof framing, but these provide minimal benefit. Contractors sometimes recommend adding hurricane strapping to tie the roof to the walls of a home, but this often just causes the top of the walls to be ripped away, along with the roof, in a hurricane. To be effective, strapping must connect the roof all the way down to the foundation—a cost-effective project only during initial home construction.

•**Strengthen doors and windows.** Once hurricane winds have found a way into the home, the odds that the roof will be blown off increase dramatically.

Inexpensive Lifesavers

Baking soda can put out small fires, especially grease fires. A car hammer is specially designed to break window glass if your car is ever submerged in water. A personal water filter can remove potentially harmful organisms from lake or river water in case you run out of water while hiking or camping. An emergency blanket can protect against sun, wind and water during a hiking or camping trip, can be turned into a makeshift shelter and can be hung as a distress flag. Each of these items can be bought for $15 or less.

Roundup of experts on inexpensive lifesaving items, reported at MoneyTalksNews.com

Plywood window and door coverings are a cost-effective solution. If hurricanes are very common in your area, consider getting commercially produced shutters that have permanently installed anchor systems and are easier to install when a storm threatens. Hurricane shutters range from $10 to $50 per square foot installed. Impact-resistant windows can be a viable alternative, though expensive.

Tricks to Keep Burglars Away from Your Home— Former Jewel Thief Reveals His Secrets

Walter T. Shaw, one of the most notorious jewel thieves of the past half-century. Based in Fort Lauderdale, Florida, he is author of *A License to Steal*, an account of his career as a jewel thief and his father's career as a telecommunications inventor.

A man's home might be his castle, but few homes have moats and battlements. If a burglar wants to break in, he probably can—and in these tough economic times, a burglar is more likely to do so.

Fortunately, most burglars are lazy and fearful. They target the homes that look like they will be the easiest to rob with the lowest risk of capture. Your home does not need to be impregnable—it simply needs to be less appealing to burglars than others in your neighborhood.

How to reduce the odds that your home will be targeted—or send the would-be burglar running if it is…

•**Keep your garage door closed as much as possible.** Leaving the garage door open when you go out tells all who pass that there's no car inside and it is likely that no one is at home.

Open garages also provide convenient cover for burglars. They can simply walk or drive into the garage, shut the door behind them, then force open the door connecting the garage to the home without worry that they will be seen.

Regularly leaving your garage door open when you are home and there is a car parked in the garage is a bad idea, too. A burglar might figure out that your garage door tends to be closed only when no one is home.

Of course, if you have expensive bikes or yard equipment in your open garage, you're inviting burglars to walk right in and take them.

●**Stay out of the obits.** The newspaper obituary page offers burglars a handy guide to which homes are going to be vacant when. Burglars simply wait until the time and date listed for a funeral or memorial service, then break into the homes of the local residents mentioned among the relatives of the deceased.

If you provide an obituary for a family member to a local paper, either do not list survivors or do not mention when the memorial service will be held. Instead, provide a contact phone number for those who wish to attend.

●**Post a "Beware of Dog" sign.** Dogs bark and bite, which makes them effective burglar deterrents. Even if you do not own a dog, a sign warning that you do could encourage a burglar to target a different home. You also could attach a dog's chain to a stake in your yard to add to the illusion.

If you buy a dog to scare off burglars, favor a small, "yippy" dog over a big one. Most little dogs bark incessantly when strangers approach their homes. Big dogs might bark a few times, but unless they are trained as guard dogs, they're less likely to keep it up.

●**Leave a sandbox, tricycle or other outdoor toys in your yard even if you don't have young kids.** Most burglars prefer to stay away from homes that have young children. These homes are less likely to be vacant than others—a stay-at-home parent might be inside during working hours, and families with young kids are less likely to go out at night.

Find a cheap used tricycle or sandbox at a garage sale so that you can leave it outside without worrying that it will be stolen. Leave toys on your lawn even when you go on vacation. Most families take children's toys inside before heading out of town, so leaving them out creates the impression that the home is not vacant.

●**Post a "video surveillance" or "you are being videotaped" sign on the front gate or elsewhere around your home.** Burglars fear being photographed even more than they fear alarm systems. They have time to flee if an alarm sounds, but there might not be much they can do once their image is caught on tape.

Putting up inexpensive, fake video cameras in conspicuous locations around your home improves the illusion. Fake cameras are available in home stores or on websites, such as Amazon.com, for $10 to $20 apiece, sometimes less.

●**Remove thick hedges and privacy fences.** Burglars love to break into homes with doors or windows that are not visible from the road and from neighboring homes. They can take their time breaking into these homes without fear that they will be seen.

If a high hedge or fence around your home provides potential cover for burglars, replace the hedge with plants no taller than knee-height…and replace the fence with a lower fence, a chain-link fence or a wood fence that has spaces between the slats.

●**Don't let mail or newspapers pile up when you are on vacation.** This makes it easy for burglars to see that the home is vacant. Unfortunately, stopping delivery informs newspaper deliverymen and other strangers that you will be away. It is better to ask a trusted neighbor to collect your mail and newspapers for you.

Also, be sure to have someone mow your lawn in the summer or shovel your walk if it snows in the winter.

●**Use lights and radios to make it seem that someone is home.** Homes that are completely dark before bedtime are obvious targets for burglars. Timers, available for a few dollars at home stores and hardware stores, are a reasonably effective solution.

Also, leave a radio on and tuned to a talk station when you're away so that anyone who approaches the home will think someone is inside.

●**Install motion-activated floodlights on every side of your home, not just over the driveway and front door.** Bright lights scare away most burglars.

Where to Hide Your Valuables

The master bedroom is the first place that all burglars search. Valuables stored there are likely to be found even if they are well-hidden. The main living area of the home also is likely to be well-searched.

Least likely to be searched are young children's rooms…garages…unfinished basements …and the space above hung ceiling panels.

I would not recommend installing a safe. Home safes consolidate the family's valuables in one place, which makes them easier to steal. If the burglar lacks the know-how to crack your safe, he might take the whole safe with him…or wait for you to return and force you to open the safe, turning a bad situation into a dangerous one.

One potentially effective strategy is to set up your home so that it convinces the burglar that he has found your valuables before he actually has. Hide your most precious possessions in a room unlikely to be targeted, but leave a few less important "valuables" in a location a burglar is likely to search, such as a drawer in the master bedroom. These "valuables" might include a stack of small bills with a $20 bill on top…a few credit cards that are expired or cancelled…a broken but impressive-looking camera…or some costume jewelry that looks more precious than it is.

For maximum security, rent a bank security deposit box. Banks always are more secure than any location in the home.

Home Security System Scams

Steven Weisman, an attorney based in Waltham, Massachusetts, and founder of the scam-information website Scamicide.com. He is a professor at Bentley University and author of numerous books, including *The Truth About Avoiding Scams*.

A home security system monitored by a security company is supposed to increase your safety and protect your property—but scammers and burglars have worked up some ways to turn these systems to their advantage and victimize home owners who have them.

Make Your Home Look Lived-In While You're Away

To reduce the chance of burglary, you'll want to make your home looked lived-in while you're away. *What to do…*

- **Ask a neighbor to park a car in your driveway.**
- **In addition to having the post office hold all mail and packages for you,** have a neighbor check in case FedEx, UPS or another delivery service drops anything off.
- **Have a trusted neighbor take your trash and recycling bins** out on collection days and bring them back afterward.
- **If it could snow while you are gone,** hire someone to shovel your walk.
- **Consider buying gadgets that can turn lamps in your house on and off**—BeOn bulbs can learn your lighting habits and replicate them when you're away.
- **Consider FakeTV.com,** which sells a programmable device that looks, from outside your home, like a TV being watched but uses much less energy than actually leaving a TV on.

BobVila.com

The scam works like this—you receive a call from what you think is your security company saying that there's a problem with your system that must be fixed…or that your system is due for a free upgrade. Soon a technician appears at your door.

This technician might have a shirt or an ID tag that identifies him/her as an employee of the security company. (In some versions, there is no initial phone call—a technician simply arrives unexpectedly. A legitimate home security company will not do this.)

But this technician actually is a criminal who learned which security company you use from the sign posted on your lawn or in your window. If you give him access to your security system, he might case your home to see if it is worth burglarizing and then disable your security system (or get you to divulge your security code) so that he can safely break in later. He also might say that he needs to schedule a follow-up visit, then try to get you to say when you will be unavailable so that he knows when it is safe to break in.

Variation: Rather than burglarize your home, the fake security technician might ask you to sign some paperwork that he says is routine but that actually locks you into an expensive, long-term contract with a different and untrustworthy provider.

What to do: If someone calls or shows up at your home claiming to represent your security system company, call the company using a phone number that you know to be authentic to confirm this person's identity before letting him in. If you're told this person is not with the company, refuse him entry and, if possible, jot down his license plate number and give this to the police.

If possible, swap lawn signs with a friend who uses a different security company—that way, if a scammer tries to pull this on you by phone or with a surprise visit, he will claim to work for the wrong company, immediately exposing his ruse.

Surprising Things Your Homeowner's Insurance Covers

Laura Adams, former senior insurance analyst at InsuranceQuotes.com. She also is host of the free "Money Girl" podcast, which has been downloaded more than 40 million times. LauraDAdams.com

Your homeowner's insurance covers more than just your home. These policies also provide protection for things that few policyholders would expect them to—in some cases, even things that occur thousands of miles away from home.

There is a catch—making a claim may lead to increased premiums for the next five to seven years. As a result, it generally is not worth making claims that result in payouts of less than $500 to $1,000 after accounting for the policy's deductible. (See page 354 for additional details about the risk of filing a claim.) But there are good ways to use your policy that you probably never thought of. (Of course, check your policy for specific coverage.)

Here, nine unexpected things covered by most homeowner's policies...

Don't Let Home Wi-Fi Spy on You

The potential for personalized attacks in your own home are unnerving. What if a cyberthief opened your Wi-Fi–enabled door locks or garage door, disabled your security system or turned off your home heat? Relying on antivirus software on your computer won't necessarily protect you because your router and devices don't depend on the computer to connect to the Internet.

Steps that you need to take...

•**Change the default password set by the factory on your home router and all of your Wi-Fi–connected devices.** Each device should be given its own unique password, at least eight characters that mix numbers, upper- and lower-case letters, and symbols. To change passwords, see the instructions in the software or app that you used to install your devices, or search for instructions on the manufacturers' websites.

•**Set your router and other devices to automatically update their internal software.** Manufacturers commonly issue software patches to improve product performance, add new features or address security weakness. But you won't get these patches unless you elected to receive them when you set up your devices. You typically can re-select this option at the same time that you change your password.

Robert Siciliano, CEO of the consulting firm Safr.me, Boston, and author of *99 Things You Wish You Knew Before… Your Identity Was Stolen.* Safr.me

Common Coverage

•**Lawsuits against you stemming from incidents that did not occur on your property.** The liability section of your homeowner's insurance does not just provide coverage if a guest slips and falls in your kitchen or your dog bites a deliveryman in your front yard. It generally will pay settlements and judgments against you and provide legal representation even if someone sues you over an incident that occurs elsewhere.

Examples: You break someone's nose playing pickup basketball...your dog bites someone at the park. Personal liability coverage included with homeowner's insurance usually has a cap that is low by today's standards—perhaps $100,000—but it is there if you need it.

Exceptions: Homeowner's insurance usually will not cover you if a suit against you involves a motor vehicle or watercraft…business activities… intentionally causing injury or property damage… and in certain other situations. Read the "Liability Coverage" section of your policy for details.

●**Sheds and gazebos.** Most policies cover outbuildings on a property up to either 10% or 20% of the amount of coverage provided for the primary structure. That generally is more than enough to replace a shed or gazebo. This component of your coverage also might cover any freestanding guesthouses, barns, retaining walls, swimming pools and other things built on the property aside from the main house, so if you have pricey outbuildings, a wall and/or a pool, check the "Other Structures" section of your policy to confirm that you have sufficient coverage. If you don't, find out how much it would cost to increase this coverage.

●**Possessions stolen from storage units, hotel rooms, cars, luggage or kids' dorm rooms.** Your homeowner's insurance provides coverage for your stuff even when that stuff is not in your home. In fact, it protects your possessions even overseas.

This away-from-home coverage typically is capped at 10% of the maximum amount that the policy would pay to replace the contents of the home. Losses due to theft or disasters such as fires typically are covered (though usually not losses due to floods or earthquakes, which typically are specifically excluded from homeowner's insurance). Note that possessions in dorm rooms, or stolen from children who live in dorm rooms, are covered, but possessions in off-campus apartments, or stolen from students who live in off-campus apartments, are not. A student living off campus would need his/her own renter's policy to have coverage. Look for the section of your policy labeled "Off-Premises Coverage" for details.

Helpful: Items stolen from people when they are not at home sometimes are items those people have only just purchased. If so, contact the issuer of the credit card used to make the purchase before con-

tacting your insurance company. Many cards offer coverage for the theft of recently purchased items.

●**Spoiled food.** Your policy probably provides coverage if a prolonged power failure ruins your frozen and/or refrigerated food. Some policies even offer a lower deductible or no deductible at all. The coverage typically is capped at $500 or less.

Exception: Food ruined by a power failure caused by an event specifically excluded from coverage in your policy, such as a flood or earthquake, likely will not be covered. Details about this coverage might be in the "Property Coverage" section of your policy or in a "Special Endorsements" section. Insurers generally do not raise a policyholder's rates because of spoiled food claims, but there are no rules prohibiting them from doing so, and proof generally is not required.

●**Home upgrades required by new laws and ordinances.** If your home is more than a few years old, new building codes and ordinances might have taken effect since it was constructed. If you try to have the home repaired or rebuilt following a disaster, you might be required to comply with those new rules, potentially increasing your costs. Most homeowner's policies will pay some or all of these additional costs, though details and limits vary. Look for a section of your policy labeled "Ordinance or Law" or a similar phrase for details.

Wintertime Car-Safety Kit

Be sure to include the following in your car during winter…

Pack a car cell-phone charger because areas with weak reception can kill a battery quickly…a first-aid kit…a warning light, hazard triangle or road flares…water…foods with a long shelf life, such as protein bars…a tire jack and lug wrench, tire sealant and a portable compressor…a flashlight and extra set of batteries…tubes of sand to spread around tires if you get stuck and need extra traction…jumper cables or a portable battery booster…a blanket…winter boots and socks.

Consumer Reports, CR.org.

A small percentage of policies will pay a portion of the cost of upgrading the home to meet current codes and ordinances even when the upgrade is unrelated to a disaster that's covered by the policy.

•**Landscaping.** Your trees, shrubs, flowers and other landscaping probably are covered by your insurance. This coverage usually is capped at 5% of the home's coverage limit. And the coverage might provide protection only if landscaping is damaged by specific causes listed in the policy—and wind, a common cause of landscaping damage, sometimes is not listed. Typically only trees and plants you purchased for the property will be covered, not plants that grew on the property on their own. Look for a section of your policy labeled "Trees, Shrubs and Other Plants"…"Landscaping"…or something similar for details. Take photos of your landscaping so that you have evidence of the damage and/or save receipts and invoices from landscapers, nurseries and home centers.

Less Common Coverage

These are included in some, but not most, policies. Be sure to check yours so you'll know…

•**ID theft and counterfeit money.** Some homeowner's insurance policies include a limited amount of coverage for losses related to ID theft and/or accidentally accepting counterfeit currency. This coverage often is capped at around $500, however, and usually covers only very specific types of ID-theft losses. A cynic might say that it's more a marketing gimmick than real insurance. Look for a section of the policy with a label featuring terms such as "ID Theft," "Credit Cards" or "Counterfeit Money" to see how much, if any, coverage you have. If you want more extensive coverage, you're likely better off buying specialized ID-theft coverage from a company that offers it.

•**Fire department service charges.** Your homeowner's insurance might pay some or all of the bill if a fire department charges you after it responds to a call to protect your property. If you have this coverage, there should be a section of your policy labeled "Fire Department Service Charge" or words to that effect. When offered, it typically has a lower deductible than the policy's standard deductible, if it has any deductible.

•**Grave markers.** Your homeowner's insurance might cover the cost of repairing or replacing a loved one's grave marker or mausoleum—even if the grave is not located on your property. Look for a section of your policy labeled "Grave Markers" or similar for details. Cemeteries typically are responsible for repairs to grave sites but not grave markers unless cemetery equipment caused the damage.

The Risk of Filing a Claim

When a home owner files a single claim, his/her homeowner's insurance premiums increase by an average of 9% for the next five to seven years, according to a study. *But this is just an average. Some*

Protection for Windows

Are there any guaranteed ways to protect windows against hurricane winds and debris?

New impact-resistant windows are designed like car windshields, with polyester film or plastic between layers of impact-resistant glass. They will withstand most debris and very strong wind. These windows are required in new construction in some coastal regions and hurricane-prone areas, such as southern Florida.

Changing all the windows in a house to the new type could cost $10,000 or more, assuming 10 to 15 windows.

Hurricane shutters are a less costly option. They give good protection but are less aesthetically pleasing.

Alternative: Hire a contractor to custom-make window guards out of three-quarter-inch plywood. Cost: $50 to $100 per window. Stack the guards in your garage. When a storm threatens, use screws—not nails—to put them up. You can fill in the holes with caulk after the storm passes.

In an extreme hurricane, there is no way to protect windows—such winds can destroy entire buildings.

Caution: Beware of anyone selling products designed to modify ordinary windows to make them resistant to high winds and flying debris. Those claims are scams.

Bill Keith, remodeling expert, St. John, Indiana, and host of *Quick Tips* on Chicago-area PBS stations.

policyholders have discovered that their rate increases are significantly higher or lower, often because of...

●**Where they live.** Rate hikes for filing one claim were 17.5% or more on average in Wyoming, Connecticut, Arizona, New Mexico, California, Utah, Illinois and Maryland. They were 5% or less in New York, Massachusetts, Florida and Vermont.

Warning: Filing multiple claims within a five-to-seven-year period will lead to substantial rate increases everywhere.

●**What type of claim they filed.** A claim related to liability, fire, theft, vandalism or water damage typically results in an increase of 12% or more. But a claim related to weather damage to the home (especially weather damage unrelated to hail or wind) or a medical bill stemming from an injury suffered by a guest on the property usually results in an increase of just a few percentage points.

---

7 Surprising Things That Could Get Your Homeowner's Insurance Canceled

Laura Adams, former senior insurance analyst at Insurance Quotes.com. She is host of the free weekly *Money Girl* podcast. QuickandDirtyTips.com/money-girl. LauraDAdams.com

You might not be surprised if your homeowner's insurance premium is increased after you file a costly claim. But did you know that the insurer might go a step further and cancel your coverage or refuse to renew it? And it isn't just claims that can torpedo a policy. Insurers sometimes terminate a policy or raise premiums to prohibitively high levels for much more surprising reasons—ranging from a drop in your credit score to your purchase of a trampoline to a broken gutter.

Having a policy terminated can be more than a minor inconvenience. When you seek to replace your policy elsewhere, other insurers might quote very steep premiums or decline to offer coverage at all. That's because when an insurer terminates a policy, the insurer typically notes that it has done

so in a database that other insurers check before approving applicants. That policy termination can scare off other issuers.

Here, seven surprising reasons your homeowner's insurance could be terminated or your premiums pushed up...

Things Seemingly Unrelated to Your Home (or to You)

●**Credit score.** A drop in your credit score could result in nonrenewal of your policy or a dramatic increase in your premiums. How dramatic? In 37 states, people with poor credit pay more than twice as much as people with excellent credit, on average, according to a recent study. Only two states—Maryland and Hawaii—prohibit homeowner's insurance issuers from considering credit scores. (Credit scores also seem to have little effect on homeowner's insurance in Florida.) Insurers have determined that people who are responsible with credit also tend to be responsible with home maintenance and make fewer claims.

If your insurer tells you that your credit score is among the reasons your policy is not being renewed or your rates are rising, examine your credit report for any inaccurate information that might be unfairly pulling down your score. (You can obtain a free copy of your report each year at the website Annual CreditReport.com.) If you find inaccuracies, inform your insurer of this and ask whether it would reconsider its decision if you get the problem sorted out. If not, resolve the credit problem as quickly as possible and then ask to be "re-rated" by the insurer.

Helpful: If there is no easy way to improve your score, apply for homeowner's coverage through small and midsize regional homeowner's insurance issuers, which are less likely to check scores. An insurance-shopping website, insurance broker or your state department of insurance could help you locate these smaller issuers.

●**Driving infractions.** Believe it or not, speeding tickets can affect your homeowner's insurance. Insurers have concluded that irresponsible drivers tend to be irresponsible home owners, too.

There are no hard-and-fast rules here, but if you get more than two moving violations that put points on your driving record in a year—or even one serious citation such as for a DUI—you could have trouble maintaining your homeowner's insurance at a reasonable rate. It's worth investigating whether your state offers any way to quickly remove some of the bad-driving "points" that will appear on your record, such as by taking a driver-safety course. It's these points—not the violations themselves—that can catch the notice of homeowner's insurance providers.

●**Insurance claims by your home's previous owners.** If the home's previous owners filed multiple claims, that could increase the risk that your policy will not be renewed if you make even one or two claims. This is particularly likely if the claims are similar and point to a serious underlying problem with the home, such as wiring issues that have led to multiple fires.

What to do: If you have owned your home for less than seven years, request the property's Comprehensive Loss Underwriting Exchange (CLUE) report. You can obtain this report for free as often as once per year at PersonalReports.LexisNexis.com (click on "FACT Act"). If you discover multiple claims by the prior owners, you should consider that an additional reason to pay for covered repairs of modest size out of pocket rather than file claims. (By law, CLUE reports can include claims only up to seven years old—less in some states—so if you have owned your home longer than that, there's no reason to check for former owners' claims.)

Helpful: Before purchasing a home, insist that the seller provide you with the property's CLUE report. This report could point to underlying problems.

Things that Might Seem Inconsequential

●**Small claims.** It isn't just big claims that scare off home insurers. Repeated small claims can lead to termination, too. Insurers sometimes consider policyholders who file repeated small claims to be nuisances who are not worth the trouble.

What to do: Increase your deductible to at least $1,000 and preferably $2,000 or $2,500 to remove the temptation to make small claims. Use the money this saves you in premiums to pay for minor home repairs.

●**Asking questions.** Call your insurer to discuss the possibility that making a claim could lead to an entry in your CLUE report. Having a number of CLUE entries that your insurer deems excessive can cause nonrenewal.

Do not contact your insurer to discuss a potential claim unless it is extremely likely that you actually will make a claim. If you feel you must call your insurer to discuss the possibility of making a claim, speak in hypothetical terms and make it very clear that you are not currently making a claim. Example: "I'm not filing a claim, but in theory, if someone had the following happen, would it be covered?" There is anecdotal evidence that phrasing things this way reduces the odds that the call will be logged into your CLUE file, though it still is possible.

●**Home-maintenance issues visible from the road.** Your insurer might be watching you. Insurers sometimes conduct unannounced drive-by inspections of properties. If your property is deemed to have maintenance issues, you might receive a letter threatening cancellation or nonrenewal if repairs are not made within 60 or 90 days.

Inspectors often focus on things such as missing shingles or broken gutters that can lead to greater home damage and insurance claims, but even basic upkeep issues such as an unmowed lawn could trigger unwanted insurer attention. To insurers, such things can be signs that the home is not being well-maintained in other, more important ways.

Warning: It is especially important for landlords to keep the portion of property that is visible from the road well-maintained—drive-by inspections of rental properties are particularly common.

●**Trampolines, tree houses, swimming pools and dog breeds that are considered dangerous.** Many home owners do not realize that their policies require them to inform the insurer if they obtain one of these potential liability risks. Some policies prohibit these things altogether or have detailed rules that must be followed if they are obtained—perhaps a fence is required around a pool, for example. Read your homeowner's policy carefully before obtaining any of these things.

Similar: Many homeowner's policies restrict or prohibit renting out the home, such as through Airbnb. Violating this rule could result in policy cancellation or nonrenewal.

What to Do If Your Policy Is Terminated

Homeowner's insurance policies can be terminated through either cancellation or nonrenewal. Cancellation means that the policy is ended during a contract period. Nonrenewal means that the insurer declines to continue covering the property when the policy term expires.

Issuers generally must provide at least 30 or 60 days' notice. Start shopping for a new policy as soon as you learn that your current one is ending—other issuers might be wary once the termination is on your record, so it might not be easy for you to find coverage at an appealing rate.

If all the quotes you receive are significantly higher than what you previously paid, also contact your state's insurance department to see if it has a high-risk insurance pool for home owners. (To find it, go to NAIC.org, then select your state under "Insurance Departments.")

This coverage could be expensive and/or limited, but it might be your best option if private issuers do not want your business.

Create a Visual Home Inventory

Jeff Wignall, a professional photographer who has photographed home, municipal and estate collections for home owners, municipalities and insurance companies. He is author of more than 15 books, including *The Photographer's Master Guide to Color*. He is a contributing editor to *Popular Photography* magazine. JeffWignall.com

As your insurance company will tell you, having a comprehensive visual record of your home's contents in the event of a fire, natural disaster or someone burglarizing your home is one of the best ways to prove that those things were in your home. A visual inventory will speed payment on your insurance claims and likely result in higher payment because you have a more detailed and comprehensive tally.

You can use any still camera or video camera, including your cell phone camera, shooting a mix of video and stills. It is a good weekend project, working a few hours per day.

●**Shoot exterior views,** either still or video, to demonstrate the "before" condition of your home and your landscaping. First take an "establishing" shot that shows the home and surroundings. Then take individual shots of expensive items such as barbecue grills, lawn furniture and exterior lighting fixtures. Then head into your garage or shed to shoot yard tools and equipment such as mowers, snowblowers and generators. Anything you can move to the driveway, such as your car or bicycles, can be shot there.

●**Shoot an overall shot of each room on video,** and then create a record of items with still photos.

●**Document individual items.** Expensive items such as electronics, jewelry and collectibles/antiques should be photographed individually and from various angles. With electronics, be sure to show brand and model. Open drawers (your silverware drawer, for instance) and jewelry boxes to show the contents. If you collect books, shoot wide views of each bookshelf, then take individual shots of rare volumes. Stamp and coin collections can be scanned on a flatbed scanner—the same one that you use to scan documents for your computer (a simple flatbed scanner sells for between $50 and $100, but many all-in-one printers have a scanning function built in).

●**Create a simple studio.** To speed the shooting of small items, make a simple studio space using a sheet of white poster board as a background. I simply tape the poster board to a wall and curve it down to the surface of a card table to make a seamless background. Use light from a nearby window or simple desk lights or your camera's built-in flash.

●**Don't forget closets.** Take wide views but also include individual shots of designer items (and labels). To get a good shot, hang an item on the back of a closet door or lay it on a bed.

•**Make copies.** Once your record is complete, download all of the videos and photos to your computer and then burn multiple DVD copies (and/or save to the cloud) and store your discs off premises.

Don't Let a Water Disaster Ruin Your Antiques and Collectibles

Terry Kovel, author of more than 100 books about collecting, including *Kovels' Antiques & Collectibles Price Guide 2018*, the book's 50th anniversary edition. Her nationally syndicated newspaper column appears in more than 150 newspapers. Kovels.com

---

The exhibits at the Dalí Museum in St. Petersburg, Florida, escaped damage when Hurricane Irma struck—the museum has 18-inch-thick storm-proof walls. But the typical home doesn't offer much protection to antiques and collectibles when hurricanes hit, floodwaters rise, pipes burst, roofs leak or sewer lines back up—and unless your valuables are all made of, say, solid gold, even brief exposure to water could turn your treasured possessions into soggy garbage.

Here's how to protect your antiques and collectibles from water damage…

Prepare for Flooding

If a hurricane or flood warning is issued, time permitting, move antiques and collectibles to higher ground if possible—for example, to the second floor if you live in a two-story home. If your home is one-story high, store what you can on upper shelves.

Exception: Store glass and ceramic items at floor level—these are at greater risk from falls than from floodwaters.

Larger antiques that cannot easily be relocated can at least be raised up on concrete blocks. Remove drawers from wood furniture that is too big to relocate, and move those drawers to a higher spot if possible. This prevents the drawers from getting stuck in place if water causes the wood to swell. (If there

are multiple drawers of similar size, label each as you remove it.)

Last-minute tip: Stash valuable small items in your dishwasher and/or washing machine, ideally after sealing them in plastic bags. These appliances are designed to keep water in, but in an emergency, they can seal floodwaters out. They don't keep out floodwater 100% of the time, however, so do this only if there's no way to get items to safety.

After a Flood…Limit the Damage

When it is safe to reenter your home, go room to room taking photos or video, documenting the damage for an insurance claim. Next, move any valuables that appear undamaged to safer, drier locations in your home if possible.

Tip: Contact your insurance provider as soon as possible to say that you expect to make a claim, but if you have valuable antique wood furniture, don't be in a rush to have the insurance adjuster visit—wood often does not show the full extent of water damage until it dries and potentially cracks a week or more later.

Even after a flood, you might be able to limit the water damage to your antiques and collectibles—if you act fast…

•**Wood furniture.** If wood furniture is standing on a water-saturated carpet, put it up on concrete blocks or put plastic bags under its legs as soon as possible to prevent additional moisture from wicking up into the wood. If you have an antique that has wood veneer on its top—a very thin, decorative wood layer—cover this with waxed paper and gently place weights on it. This reduces the odds that the veneer will warp as it dries.

Use fans, dehumidifiers and/or air conditioners to circulate and dry air and slowly dry out the wood. If your electricity is out, consider renting a generator to power the equipment…or relocating valuable waterlogged antiques to a friend's home that has power or to a climate-controlled storage facility.

Warning: Do not place water-damaged wood antiques in the sun to dry or use hair dryers or other heat sources to dry them. Heat dries wet wood too quickly, increasing the odds that it will warp or crack. Do not even turn on your home's heating system unless necessary.

If a white film or white spots appear on the wood, soak a cloth in a solution of 50% ammonia and 50% water, rub this gently on the affected area, wipe the area dry, then polish with wax.

If the film or spots persist and the antique is worth thousands of dollars or more, the prudent option is to contact a professional antiques furniture restorer. A local museum or antiques seller should be able to point you to a skilled restorer.

Exception: Upholstered furniture usually cannot be salvaged after a flood. One option is to save the wood frame and have the piece reupholstered.

● **Silver, ceramics and glass.** If ceramics, glass or silver pieces that got wet are used for dining, wash these at least twice using a phosphate-free detergent before serving food on them again—floodwaters can be contaminated by sewage.

Warning: If glass or ceramics were exposed to muddy water, use water and a soft cloth to gently clear away any visible mud residue before attempting a more thorough cleaning. If clean running water is available, put them under that. Aggressive cleaning while there still is dirt on the surface could cause scratches or embed dirt particles in the surface.

If your silver has hollow spaces, such as hollow-handled flatware, shake it and listen for a subtle swishing sound. If you hear this, water is inside and you need to bring these pieces to a professional restorer.

If ceramic items were packed in newspaper that is now wet, remove the paper. The ink from wet newspaper can stain ceramics. (It's always better to wrap items in unprinted, plain packing paper than in newspaper.)

● **Paper collectibles.** Baseball cards, paper money, prints and books that have sustained water damage often are a total loss. You could take them to a professional restorer, but even a pro is unlikely to be able to return a water-damaged paper item to anything close to mint condition, so this generally makes financial sense only with very rare items that are worth thousands of dollars even in less-than-pristine condition. Still, there are steps you can take

that will improve the odds that water-damaged paper items will remain in presentable, if not collectible, condition.

Sprinkle cornstarch on wet paper items as soon as possible. Blow off this powder after the paper has dried, and any mold spores that are present often will blow away along with it.

Then to make sure that the paper is completely dry, place the paper between sheets of dry white paper, and place all three under something flat and heavy, such as a baking pan or cookie sheet with weights on top. This reduces the odds that the paper will curl as it continues to dry.

Wet books are difficult to rescue. One strategy is to place dry sheets of absorbent white paper, such as paper towels, between as many pages as possible—ideally between every page. Replace these periodically with new sheets of absorbent paper until this paper feels almost dry as you remove it. Then place sheets of absorbent paper between the pages one more time, lay the book flat and place something heavy on top of it.

Tip: If you do not have time to deal with water-damaged paper items immediately, wrap them in plastic and put them in your freezer. The wet paper won't deteriorate any further as long as it is frozen.

Do You Have the Right Insurance for Antiques and Collectibles?

Your homeowner's insurance policy probably provides antiques and collectibles coverage—but this coverage likely is capped at just a few thousand dollars, and it usually does not cover damage from flooding or backed-up sewer lines. (It generally does cover water damage from broken pipes and falling rainwater, however.) *Additional coverage options...*

● **You can add a rider to your homeowner's insurance policy to cover backed-up sewer lines.** These riders usually are inexpensive—often less than $50 a year—but their antiques and collectibles coverage typically is capped at just a few thousand dollars.

● **You can obtain flood insurance through the National Flood Insurance Program.** This could be very expensive if your home is in a flood zone, however, and the antiques and collectibles coverage provided by these policies is capped at just $2,500. What's more, antiques are covered only for their functional value.

Example: If a flood ruins your antique chair, this insurance will pay only the amount it would cost to buy a brand-new chair.

•**You can purchase a specialty antiques and collectibles insurance policy.** These tend to be fairly inexpensive—perhaps $100 a year for $20,000 in coverage—and are worth having when homeowner's insurance and/or flood insurance is insufficient. Be sure to confirm that the policy selected includes flood protection!

Whatever insurance you purchase, use a digital camera to photograph your valuables, create a file of the photos and keep a copy of this file somewhere other than in your house—and e-mail a copy to at least one friend or relative for safekeeping. These photos will help tremendously should you ever have to file a claim for destroyed items.

Are Electric Blankets Safe?

David O. Carpenter, MD, director of the Institute for Health and the Environment, University at Albany, New York.

Do you enjoy staying warm and cozy under an electric blanket on cold days and nights? Is this a safe practice?

You can stay safe under your electric blanket if you follow a few important guidelines. Electric blankets emit an extremely low frequency (ELF) level of radiation that has been linked to increased risk for certain types of cancer and Alzheimer's disease, although this link is still being debated. To be on the safe side, warm the bed before you get in and then turn the blanket off…or choose one with a timer that will automatically shut it off. And select a blanket with a UL logo on the label (this indicates it has met safety standards set by Underwriters Laboratories). Inspect it every month or so to make sure no wires are sticking out or the cord

hasn't frayed, especially if your pet snuggles with you. A cat's or dog's paws can damage the wiring.

If you have diabetes or neuropathy, do not use an electric blanket. You may not sense when the blanket has become too hot and may end up with a burn.

Beware These Costly Deductibles

Michael Barry is a senior vice president at the Insurance Information Institute, New York City. III.org

For damages related to a hurricane, deductibles in 19 states may range from 1% to 5% or more of the home's insured value. That typically would mean a deductible much higher than the flat $500 or $1,000 that is common for damages related to most other causes. (For a full list of states and rules, go to III.org and search for "hurricane deductibles.")

What to do: Ask your insurer whether you have the option of paying a higher premium in exchange for a lower hurricane deductible.

How to Be Financially Prepared for Any Disaster…

Nigel B. Taylor, CFP, Santa Monica, California. His wealth-management firm, Taylor Associates, serves individuals, families and businesses. He is former president of Los Angeles Society of the Institute of Certified Financial Planners. Protect Assets.com

If you had 10 minutes to evacuate your home during a natural disaster, what would you take with you? Where would you get cash if ATM and credit card networks were down? Would your insurance be adequate to rebuild your home?

Obviously, the safety of you and your family is your first concern—but ensuring your financial security is second. *As a certified financial planner based in disaster-prone Southern California, here's what I tell my clients…*

•**Keep enough cash in the house for a weekend away.** It can take that long after a disaster for merchants to be able to accept credit or bank cards.

Also keep $300 in one-dollar bills on hand.

Reason: Stores may not be able to make change. After the last earthquake in this area, some people had to hand over $20 bills to pay for a carton of milk or a bottle of water.

•**Keep important items in a secure, fire-safe box near the front door—perhaps in a coat closet.** (Keep original documents in a safe-deposit box or a fireproof safe.) The box should be lightweight so that you can carry it to your vehicle in an emergency. *It should contain...*

•Legal papers. Copies of titles to your home and vehicles, marriage and birth certificates, passports, insurance policies, military and medical records, Social Security cards, driver's license numbers, wills and powers of attorney.

•Extra supplies of medications if your doctor will prescribe them. Rotate them monthly so that the newest medication always is available. Also keep lists of medications, doctors' phone numbers, etc. People with extreme allergies should include Epi-Pen injectors.

•Financial records. Copies of credit card and employee benefit statements, household budget, tax returns for the last three years, contact and account numbers for financial accounts.

•Key to your safe-deposit box, if you have a box.

•Extra checks.

•Inventory of household possessions, including professional appraisals for valuables, such as jewelry and antiques, and receipts for the cost of major home improvements, such as kitchen remodeling or a new deck.

Helpful: Use a digital camera or camcorder to record your home's contents for insurance purposes. Go room by room, giving an audio or written description of the approximate cost, condition and age of each piece of furniture, appliance and decorative element—even towels and clothing. Send a copy on DVD or CD to your insurance agent, as well as copies of receipts for big-ticket items, to expedite future claims.

While many documents may also be stored in a bank safe-deposit box, keep in mind that your local bank could be closed for several days or weeks after a disaster.

Backup plan: Scan documents into a single electronic file, and save it on your computer hard drive. Regularly back up the file to a removable flash storage device that you can take with you in the event of a disaster. These portable devices are the size of a cigarette lighter and plug into your computer's USB port. They are available for as little as $8 in electronics or office-supply stores.

You can buy a scanner for as little as $69, or have your documents scanned at an office-supply/photocopying store.

•**Maintain an emergency fund.** Keep three months' to a year's worth of basic living expenses—rent/mortgage, food, insurance, etc.—in safe, liquid investments, such as short-term CDs and short-term municipal bonds. This will protect you from a disaster as well as a loss of income—if your place of work is damaged, you may be without a paycheck for some time.

Also: Recent laws have forced all financial institutions to implement disaster-continuity plans. Obtain copies of the plans from your bank and brokerage house to learn how to access your money after a disaster.

•**If you live in a disaster-prone region, look into retrofitting your home with the help of government grants.** Consult a home inspector about what steps to take. The Federal Emergency Management Agency (FEMA) offer grants that cover up to 75% of the project's expenses, which can include upgrades such as reinforcing roofs, installing flame-retardant shingles and elevating a building.

Such upgrades can substantially reduce insurance premiums. Generally, local communities sponsor applications on behalf of homeowners and apply to the state. Because funds are limited, only projects that meet local and state priorities are forwarded to FEMA. Homeowners cannot apply directly for hazard mitigation funding, but they can petition local government. Visit FEMA.gov/grants/mitigation.

•**Make sure your homeowner's insurance includes appropriate disaster coverage.** Depending on where you live, you might need flood insurance through the government's National Flood Insurance Program (annual premiums vary per state, averaging around $800) and riders for hurricanes and/or earthquakes ($2,500 a year and up for a $200,000 home with a $10,000 deductible). Such riders are expensive, but losing everything because you're not covered is more expensive.

Smart: Increase your hurricane deductible to as high as 5% (higher in some regions) of the insured structure value of your home and adjust your emergency fund to cover that amount. Premiums drop when deductibles are increased, making riders more affordable. For more information, contact the Insurance Information Institute at iii.org.

Make sure you have "replacement value" coverage that pays you the amount necessary to replace articles with ones of similar quality at current prices. Check that you will be reimbursed for living expenses if your home is damaged and uninhabitable.

Cost: Less than $100 in annual premiums for $10,000 of coverage.

If you have a home office, you will need a commercial policy to cover damage to business-related equipment. (Homeowners' policies do not cover home-based businesses.) Many homeowners' policies limit replacement of computer equipment to $2,500. You can double this coverage for $20 to $30 per year.

Helpful resources: Visit Ready.gov and Disaster Safety.org. FEMA also offers *Are You Ready?*—a free guide to disaster preparation.

Index